Civil War Talks

A NATION DIVIDED:
STUDIES IN THE CIVIL WAR ERA

Aaron Sheehan-Dean, Editor

Civil War Talks

FURTHER REMINISCENCES
OF GEORGE S. BERNARD
& HIS FELLOW VETERANS

EDITED BY
Hampton Newsome, John Horn,
and John G. Selby

University of Virginia Press
Charlottesville and London

To Edwin C. Bearss and William D. Henderson

University of Virginia Press
© 2012 by the Rector and Visitors of the University of Virginia
All rights reserved
Printed in the United States of America on acid-free paper

First published 2012

9 8 7 6 5 4 3 2 1

LIBRARY OF CONGRESS CATALOGING-IN-PUBLICATION DATA
Bernard, George S., 1837–1912.
  Civil War talks : further reminiscences of George S. Bernard and his fellow veterans /
edited by Hampton Newsome, John Horn, and John G. Selby.
    p.   cm. — (A nation divided—studies in the Civil War era)
  Includes bibliographical references and index.
    ISBN 978-0-8139-3175-3 (cloth : alk. paper) — ISBN 978-0-8139-3183-8 (e-book)
    1. United States—History—Civil War, 1861–1865—Personal narratives, Confederate.
2. United States—History—Civil War, 1861–1865—Campaigns. I. Newsome, Hampton.
II. Horn, John, 1951–   III. Selby, John Gregory, 1955–   IV. Title.
  E484.B49 2012
  973.7′82092—dc23
  [B]

2011025261

Title page illustration: George S. Bernard, from *War Talks of Confederate Veterans* (1892).

The present generation, our children, are too tired of our war talks and not far enough removed from the events of 1861–5. . . . They are neglecting to secure and preserve many things that would be of inestimable value to future generations. But after them will come our grandchildren who will ransack garret and closet for old books and papers bearing on those heroic days. They will appreciate the work done by the Geo. S. Bernard's of the South in saving some of the material for future history.

—Joseph W. Eggleston, 1895

Contents

Maps

Preface

IN THE SUMMER OF 2004, a collector in Roanoke, Virginia, purchased a box stuffed with an odd collection of faded documents. The container held ticket stubs, a college transcript, hand-drawn maps, newspaper clippings, papers pecked out by an ancient typewriter, and a stack of letters and stories scrawled by nineteenth-century hands. When the buyer examined his new find closely, the materials revealed themselves to be the papers of George S. Bernard, a Petersburg lawyer and member of the 12th Regiment Virginia Infantry during the Civil War. Packed into the box were many reminiscences of the Civil War prepared by Bernard and other veterans. Several months after the discovery, the Historical Society of Western Virginia purchased the collection. This find in Roanoke coincided with an independent effort to collect and publish the Civil War diaries and narratives of George Bernard.

Over the course of his life, Bernard wrote extensively about his wartime experiences, and also collected accounts from other veterans. In 1892 he published the acclaimed work, *War Talks of Confederate Veterans,* a rich collection of firsthand accounts focusing on the battles and campaigns of the 12th Virginia. The book is still in print today. Bernard prepared a "War Talks, Volume II" but was never able to publish it. His notes indicate that he considered a few different titles for this second volume ("War Talks of Confederate Veterans: Volume Two" and "Musket and Cartridge Box") and, at one point, he may have planned to publish two separate works. In the end, however, he was never able to follow *War Talks* with another book. Nevertheless, a small number of chapters from the unpublished material made their way into the Southern Historical Society Papers. For the most part, though, much of the book remained with Bernard or trickled into newspapers and elsewhere between 1893 and 1908, becoming virtually lost.

Sometime after his death in 1912, Bernard's papers became scattered. Descendents placed some of his war diaries and other materials at the University of Virginia, where Bernard had studied law before the war. Another set of his papers, including fragments of a "war narrative" describing events in 1863 and 1864, was found in an abandoned farmhouse in 1970. These materials now rest at the Southern Historical Collection at the University of North Carolina. Still more of Bernard's papers, including a notebook of his war experiences, are now at the Duke University library. These various university materials, coupled with a large number of war reminiscences published by Bernard in obscure old newspapers, led to the assembly of a manuscript containing much of what was to have been "War Talks, Volume II," the book Bernard sought to publish in the 1890s. The Roanoke discovery in 2004 provided the last piece of the puzzle. Those papers, now housed at the Historical Society of Western Virginia, contain a number of previously unknown speeches and letters, along with drafts of Bernard's table of contents for the book he planned to publish.

With the assembly of the present volume, nearly all of the pieces of Bernard's lost book have now been reunited. The resulting work is a detailed, extensive collection of firsthand accounts covering the major military campaigns in Virginia, Maryland, and Pennsylvania. Most of these reminiscences have remained obscure and, until now, have been largely unknown. They appear in the form of speeches and letters covering many battles and campaigns, including Seven Pines, Malvern Hill, the Maryland campaign, the Gettysburg campaign, the Overland campaign, the Petersburg campaign, and the Appomattox campaign. Bernard, a political ally of and personal lawyer for William Mahone, solicited several battle accounts from the former Confederate general, including descriptions of Seven Pines, Malvern Hill, Weldon Railroad, Burgess Mill, and the Appomattox Campaigns. The book also features descriptions of civilian life in Dinwiddie County during the Petersburg Campaign, and the recollections of a boy who participated in the defense of Petersburg and joined Lee's army on its march to Appomattox. We have excluded several items, as noted below, including some that made their way into the *Southern Historical Society Papers* (52 vols., Richmond: Virginia Historical Society, 1876–1959) and other sources, and thus have enjoyed wide circulation over the years.

For the general reader, we hope this collection will offer an array of riveting eyewitness accounts of important campaigns. The material does not dwell on general descriptions of the conflict, but instead focuses on the individual experiences of the men who fought through those difficult years. In addition to its appeal to the general public, this book should provide serious scholars with convenient access to many accounts that have not been widely available or have been simply unknown. Although some of the talks and articles have been available to researchers in university collections, published papers, and obscure newspapers, this is the first time that they have been pulled together, as Bernard intended to do.

The speeches and letters published here offer a wide spectrum of accounts of combat and soldier life during the war. The stories prepared and solicited by George Bernard contain highly personal stories of the war's battles and campaigns, largely devoid of any discussion of slavery and the other political and social issues undergirding the conflict as a whole. Some of the accounts incorporate diary entries and other writings prepared at the time of the events described. Many of the stories, however, were put to paper during the 1890s, nearly three decades after the conflict had passed into history. The reader should understand these latter accounts for what they are: war stories viewed through the lens of distant memory. Such accounts can fall victim to a host of distorting factors. Much had occurred between the events depicted and the creation of the speeches and letters. The Union victory, the crushing Southern defeat, the abolition of slavery, the impacts of Reconstruction, the reconciliation of Union and Confederate veterans, and the personal and political squabbles between individuals and factions—all weighed on the reminiscences of veterans. The reader should remain mindful of these considerations when examining the enclosed accounts.

In selecting the material for this book, we excluded several articles that were prepared for Bernard by others and eventually published in the *Southern Historical Society Papers* (*SHSP*) or other widely available sources, or that otherwise have little connection to Bernard's war experiences. These accounts include:

"The Beginning and the Ending: Reminiscences of the First and Last Days of the War," by George J. Hundley. This account describes Hundley's experiences during the First Manassas and Appomattox Campaign. First published in the *Richmond (Va.) Times* in two parts on January 26 and February 2, 1896, it subsequently appeared in the *SHSP* (23:294). A letter from Hundley to Bernard describing cavalry combat at Spotsylvania is included in chapter 6 of *Confederate Cavalry at Spotsylvania*, by George J. Hundley.

"War Recollections: Story of the Evacuation of Petersburg by an Eye-Witness," by Charles F. Collier. This article appeared in the *Richmond Dispatch* on June 12, 1894, and was subsequently published in the *SHSP* (22:69).

"Beauregard at Drewry's Bluff and Petersburg," by Johnson Hagood. This speech appeared in the *SHSP* (28:318).

"The Fight of the Citizen Soldiers of Petersburg, Va. under R. E. Colston and Col. F. H. Archer on the 9th of June, 1864," by Raleigh E. Colston. A very similar account appears in Robert Underwood Johnson and Clarence Clough Buel, eds., *Battles and Leaders of the Civil War* (New York: Century Co., 1884), 4:535.

"Recollections of the Fight on the 9th of June, 1864," by John F. Glenn. This appeared in an article titled "Brave Defense of the Cockade City" in the *SHSP* (35:1).

"Gordon's Assault on Fort Stedman on the 25th of March, 1865," by General James A. Walker. See the *Petersburg Daily Index-Appeal* for May 17, 1903; and the *New Orleans Picayune* for October 25, 1903 (with no attribution to Bernard save for the article's footnote bearing Bernard's initials: "G.S.B."). The account then made its way into the *SHSP* (331:31).

"Recollections of a Federal Cavalry Officer—Service in the Valley of Virginia on the Fall of 1864, and Experiences as a Prisoner of War," by Capt. Geo. N. Bliss (see George N. Bliss, *Cavalry Service with General Sheridan, and Life in Libby Prison* (Providence, R.I.: The [Soldier and Sailors Historical] Society, 1884), 103.

"Father and Son Meet in Battle on Opposite Sides: An Incident of the Recapture of Galveston," by Major J. N. Stubbs (Bernard Collection, Historical Society of Western Virginia).

It is possible that Bernard prepared or solicited additional articles that are still undiscovered. For instance, his papers at the University of North Carolina contain fragments of an article on the battle of Fort Stedman. Similarly, much of the material Bernard gathered from others was first presented in the form of lectures, or "war talks," before the Confederate veterans group in Petersburg, Virginia. Most of the chapters in *War Talks of Confederate Veterans* (1892) consisted of transcripts from such lectures. The same is true for many of the chapters in this book. In our research, we identified references to several such war talks delivered before the A. P. Hill Camp for which no transcript or published account has been found. Perhaps these accounts are tucked away in a dusty attic somewhere. They include:

"The Last Days of the Confederacy," by John B. Gordon, a talk delivered on June 22, 1894. (This talk is mentioned in the *Petersburg Daily Index-Appeal* for June 23, 1894; see Edwin D. Shurter, *Oratory of the South* [New York: Neale Publishing, 1908], 39.)

"Recollections of Battle at Cold Harbor in May 1864," by John T. Parham;

"Incident at Castle Thunder in Dec. 1864," by Geo. Bernard; "Battle of Five Forks," by Freeman W. Jones; and "Daring Exploits of the Cavalry of the Army of No. Va.," by General Stith Bolling. (These talks are mentioned in the *Petersburg Daily Index-Appeal* for January 20, 1895.)

"Battle of Hampton Roads," by Mr. C. H. Hasker, boatswain of the *Virginia*. (This talk is mentioned in the *Petersburg Daily Index-Appeal* of February 23, 1897.)

"Reminiscences of Service with Martin's Battery," by Samuel H. Pulliam. (This article appears in Bernard's draft table of contents for "War Talks, Volume II," but no copy of Pulliam's account has been located.)

In presenting the material included in this book, we have tried to avoid altering the text of the articles and letters written by Bernard and his colleagues. In some cases, we have excised from the articles material that is published elsewhere (e.g., lengthy quotations from the *Official Records of the War of the Rebellion*). We have also corrected minor typographical and punctuation errors in the text, and occasionally broken long date or address lines for readability. Some of the original material is hand-written and extremely difficult to decipher. Where words or phrases are missing or illegible in the original material, we have indicated that in the text. Where words in the sources are partially legible, we have provided our interpretation of the unknown words in brackets. In a few cases, we have inserted words in brackets, where it appears a word or phrase was omitted from the original. Many of the footnotes in the chapters contain material found in the original articles or letters, in the form of editorial or explanatory notes added by Bernard or his correspondents. Such footnotes, prepared by Bernard, are preceded by the designation GSB. Footnotes that we, the editors, have prepared for the reader carry no such identification. Text prepared by the editors to provide background or supplementary information appears at the beginning of chapters and, occasionally, set in brackets within chapters or following Bernard's notes.

We would like to thank several people and institutions for their help in guiding us on our way in preparing this book. Without their patience and kindness, it would not have been possible to gather the enclosed material: Lynn Kristianson of the Arlington Public Library, who graciously and effectively fielded an endless string of interlibrary loan requests for obscure material; Janie C. Morris at Duke's Perkins Library; John E. White at the University of North Carolina's Southern Historical Collection; the staff at the University of Virginia's Alderman Library; Anne M. Horn, who researched the lives of numerous individuals mentioned by Bernard and his correspondents; and Gregg Ashe, who enthusiastically shared knowledge of his native Norfolk. William Zielinski, a distant relative of Captain Joseph Richard Manson, helped transcribe Bernard's diary entries. He deserves our special thanks for deciphering most of Bernard's War Diaries 3, 4, and 5, which were written in pencil and later traced-over by Bernard in ink, rendering them nearly illegible in many parts. We are also grateful to Ruth Steinberg for her hard work and patience in editing a long, complicated manuscript. Likewise, Linda Miller, the archivist for Roanoke College, deserves our thanks and praise for preparing an index covering the hundreds of names, places, and events that flood this book. Finally, we owe an unpayable debt to the Historical Society of Western Virginia. George Kegley, David Robbins, and Kent Chrisman prodded the society to purchase the Bernard papers, which provided the basis of much of this book. The steadfast support of the society has made this a truly collaborative effort.

Introduction

*My little boy, George, now between nine and ten years
of age, never tires of hearing about the war. A few nights
ago I was telling him some personal experiences on the
march from Gettysburg. Said he "Papa you ought to
write that out" and this I think I shall do.*

—George S. Bernard, March 23, 1891

GEORGE SMITH BERNARD, lawyer and Confederate veteran, lived most of his years in Petersburg, Virginia. Like many other young men from his hometown, he marched off in 1861 to fight for the Confederate cause. As a lawyer and legislator after the war, the reform-minded Bernard served his community on the Petersburg School Board, as a state delegate in Richmond, and as the Commonwealth Attorney in Petersburg. As a former soldier, Bernard was active in his local veteran's group. He collected war stories from his aging comrades, organized reunions with Union veteran groups, and participated in other activities that helped foster "blue-and-gray" reconciliation at the turn of the century.

Before the war came to Virginia, Bernard was a struggling lawyer in Petersburg. After completing his law studies at the University of Virginia in the 1850s, he had hoped to find gainful employment in his hometown. But he found little success. To make ends meet, he borrowed money from his father, and even considered moving to Texas. But sectional conflict soon brought an end to such plans.[1]

---

1. Bernard's father, David Meade Bernard, was the clerk of courts in Petersburg for almost twenty-five years. His mother, Elizabeth Mildred Ashby, died shortly after Bernard's birth in 1837 (*Petersburg Daily Index-Appeal,* February 21, 1912). Bernard wrote of his sagging career: "I can not well shake off the idea that I am yet nothing but a boy, and whether one or not that I am regarded as one. When in company with the older members of my profession I can not help thinking that they look upon me as a sort of upstart, who had better be at some other business more adapted to my capacity than presume to take rank among them" (Diary entries for January 20, 1860 ["I can not well shake off . . ."] and April 5, 1861 [moving to Texas], George S. Bernard Papers, Albert H.

Bernard and many of his peers welcomed secession. His diaries and letters demonstrate a clear support for the separation. In his mind, the North had treated the South unfairly. To him, the Republicans were the "real aggressors" in the dispute and would reap the blame for the destruction of "our once proud and noble Union should no settlement be made." Though he acknowledged that Southerners may have "erred a little," he was proud that Virginia had set the example for the slaveholding states by "arming to the teeth for self protection." By March 1861, he would report to his Unionist-leaning father that, in Petersburg, "secession fever is almost universal—certainly among the more enlightened part of the Community."[2]

After Sumter fell and Virginia left the Union, Bernard abandoned his law practice to serve in the Petersburg Riflemen, a company in the city's militia battalion. While waiting with his unit to board a train to Norfolk on April 20, 1861, he wrote his father, saying: "It may be that I do not fully realize the horror of war but I feel the greatest anxiety to commence the conflict now that it is about to be on us, and this anxiety I believe pervades our whole force."[3] Hours later, Bernard was off to war. As a soldier in the 12th Virginia Regiment of William Mahone's Brigade, he participated in every major campaign fought by the Army of Northern Virginia, except for Fredericksburg and Appomattox. He detailed his experiences during the conflict in contemporaneous diary entries and later narratives.

When the conflict drew to a close in 1865, Bernard returned to Petersburg and cast around for work. With military occupation and the closure of the courts in Virginia, his prospects for success as an attorney were as dim as ever. He eventually landed a position as an editor for the local *Petersburg Express.* He also taught at a Petersburg school to earn additional money. By December 1865, however, he had begun practicing law again, and continued to do so for the rest of his life.

In 1870 Bernard married Fannie Rutherford, the niece of former Virginia governor John Rutherford. During their courtship, Bernard observed the formality of the day, writing to Miss Rutherford's father to seek permission to wed Fannie. At first, the senior Rutherford offered a discouraging reply. Without more information about Bernard's means and future plans, Rutherford was reluctant to deliver his daughter into the hands of the stranger.

---

and Shirley Small Special Collections Library, University of Virginia, Charlottesville, Va. [hereafter cited as Bernard Papers, UVA]).

2. Diary entries for January 14, 1861 and December 21, 1859, Bernard Papers, UVA; George S. Bernard to David Meade Bernard, March 9, 1861, ibid.

3. George S. Bernard to David Meade Bernard, April 20, 1861, Bernard Papers, UVA.

Apparently, Miss Rutherford had not advertised her relationship with Bernard widely. Eventually, her father's doubts faded and Bernard took Fannie's hand. Bernard and his wife enjoyed a long partnership, having five children together—Fanny R., Kate E., Janet M., Ella A., and George S.[4]

Over the next several decades, Bernard led a full and active life as a citizen of Petersburg. During the 1870s, he served several terms on the city's school board. In 1878, he successfully ran for one of Petersburg's two seats in Virginia's House of Delegates. During his term in Richmond, he was a member of the Committees on Courts of Justice and Internal Navigation. He was also the patron of a bill requiring insurance companies to disclose restrictive conditions in clear and conspicuous print in their policies.[5]

Bernard's tenure in the legislature coincided with a political transformation in Virginia that, for a time, would set the state apart from the rest of the South. Following the end of Reconstruction in the 1870s, Virginia suffered from a severe economic depression that saddled the state with tremendous debt. This crisis hampered efforts to fund the state's public schools and other social services. Conservatives—as the Virginia Democrats called themselves at the time—and their Republican opponents, sought ways to alleviate the debt problem. In the late 1870s a new political faction, the Readjusters, emerged, advocating the repudiation of part of the state's debt. This movement, led by Bernard's former commander, William Mahone, gained the support of some Conservatives and Republicans.

Those who opposed repudiation of the debt came to be known as the Funders. Their opposition was a matter of honor. To them, it was preferable to neglect the public schools than to disgrace the state by ignoring its financial responsibilities. While other states solved their debt problems through repudiation, Virginia's Conservative Party, heavily populated by Funders, slashed resources for institutions such as public schools, penitentiaries, and mental hospitals during the 1870s. The resulting decline in the state's education system touched off a political disaster from which the ruling Conservatives did not recover for years.[6]

4. John Rutherford to George Bernard, 1869, Bernard Papers, UVA; *Petersburg Daily Index-Appeal,* February 21, 1912. See also R. A. Brock, *Virginia and Virginians* (Richmond: H. H. Hardesty, 1888), 636–37.

5. Brock, *Virginia and Virginians,* 636–37.

6. According to a modern student of the Funders, the typical Funder was a "middle-aged lawyer with a good family background, a University of Virginia education, and a distinguished war record as a Confederate officer" (James Tice Moore, *Two Paths to the New South: The Virginia Debt Controversy, 1870–1883* [Lexington: University Press of Kentucky, 1974], 27–28; see also Jane Dailey, *Before Jim Crow: The Politics of*

Bernard at first aligned himself with the Funders, publicly defending that group's positions. After his term in Richmond ended in 1879, he came back to Petersburg and resumed his law practice, taking a position as an attorney for the Norfolk & Western Railroad Company. In 1882, he returned to politics, seeking office as the Commonwealth's Attorney of Petersburg in that year's election. By that time, Bernard had joined Mahone and the Readjuster coalition, running as the candidate for the "Readjuster-Fusionist" Republican ticket.[7]

By 1882, the Readjusters had become a driving force in Virginia politics, girded by a successful political alliance of blacks and whites unparalleled in the post-Reconstruction South.[8] The Readjusters, led by the fiery Mahone, split with the Conservatives and eventually aligned with the Republican Party, gaining surprising success in elections during the late 1870s and early 1880s. As the historian Jane Dailey argues in her recent work on the Readjusters: "To a degree previously unseen in Virginia and unmatched elsewhere in the nineteenth-century South, the Readjusters became an institutional force for the protection and advancement of black rights and interests." During its short hold on power, the movement controlled the state legislature, elected a governor (William E. Cameron, one of Bernard's comrades in the 12th Virginia Regiment), and sent two senators and many congressmen to Washington.[9]

Mahone and his followers earned wide support by reducing the state's enormous debt. In addition, they expanded social services, increased funding for schools, and abolished the poll tax and the whipping post. In 1881, Mahone proclaimed that the party was dedicated to "the complete liberation of the people, the preservation and improvement of the public schools, the final readjustment of the public debt and restoration of the public credit, the overthrow of race prejudice, the removal of unnecessary causes for sectional contention, the liberalization and equalization of the laws."[10] Whether an op-

---

Race in Postemancipation Virginia [Chapel Hill: University of North Carolina Press, 2000], 29).

7. In March 1879, Bernard publicly defended Funder positions in a debate with Mahone in Petersburg (William Henderson, *Gilded Age City: Politics, Life and Labor in Petersburg, Virginia, 1874–1889* [New York: University Press of America, 1980], 71, 112). Unfortunately, Bernard never explained in his diaries nor any public writings the reason for his change of position.

8. Carl N. Degler, "Black and White Together: Bi-Racial Politics in the South," *Virginia Quarterly Review* 47, no. 3 (1971): 421–44.

9. Dailey, *Before Jim Crow*, 1–3 (quotation on p. 1).

10. Ibid., 81.

portunistic politician or an enlightened reformer, Mahone openly supported positions at odds with many of his former Confederate comrades, who sought to repress black political rights. In 1882, Mahone wrote, "I have thought it wise to live for the future, and not the dead past . . . while cherishing honorable memories of its glories."[11]

During the 1880s, Bernard publicly supported Mahone, and advocated Readjuster and Republican positions at both the state and local levels. He also began to write extensively on civil service reform, emerging as a vocal advocate of a merit-based system for the placement of individuals in government posts. He prepared a series of articles on the subject and arranged to have them published in the *Petersburg Daily Index-Appeal* under the pen name "Zero." In 1885, these articles were consolidated and published in a book titled *Civil Service Reform versus the Spoils System*. He succinctly described his cause as follows:

> "Civil service reform," as understood in England and the United
> States, has for its object the improvement of the civil service of the
> government by adopting a plan under which its officers and employ-
> ees are selected and kept in position solely upon their merits, and
> will cease to hold their places as the reward of service in political
> campaigns, or by the favoritism of some influential politician. The
> move means war to the death upon what has afflicted this country
> for a half century, and is known as the "spoils system."[12]

Bernard's views aligned him with what was known as the Civil Service Reform Movement, a coalition of professionals across the country united against the spoils system.[13]

Bernard believed that candidates for civil service spots should be considered without regard to race or party. His views were out of step with many conservative Southern whites, particularly former Confederates. At the same time, he openly acknowledged a political angle to his reform proposals. He expressed a concern that, given the realities of race relations in the South, the continuation of the spoils system would eventually doom the Republicans in

---

11. Quoted in Carl N. Degler, *The Other South: Southern Dissenters in the Nineteenth Century* (New York: Harper and Row, 1972), 275; see pp. 269–310 for a short history of Mahone, the Readjusters, and the Republicans in Virginia in the 1880s and 1890s.

12. George S. Bernard, *Civil Service Reform versus the Spoils System: The Merit Plan for the Filling of Public Offices Advocated in a Series of Articles Originally Published in a Virginia Journal* (New York: John B. Alden, 1885), 11.

13. Ari Hoogenboom, *Outlawing the Spoils: A History of the Civil Service Reform Movement, 1865–1883* (Champaign: University of Illinois Press, 1961).

that part of country. Under a merit-based system, the Southern Republican would "no longer have to answer the damaging charge that the success of his party means, or may lead to, negro supremacy in sections where the colored race is found in large numbers." Likewise, Bernard argued that under the merit-based system the "colored man will rejoice to feel that under the new order of things he may enter into competition for official position with the assurance that, 'merit and competency' being the sole test of fitness to hold public office, neither the color of his skin nor the character of his 'political belief' will turn the scales against him."[14] Like many other white Readjusters, Bernard's approach combined support for black political rights with a sensitivity to the concern that extensive black political control could lead to a backlash among moderate and conservative whites.

Bernard urged his colleagues in the Virginia Republican Party to adopt his views on civil service reform. His was an uphill battle though, for the patronage system was a key instrument of political power in the Commonwealth and had served as a fulcrum for Mahone's ascent.[15] Nevertheless, on July 5, 1885, Bernard met with W. C. Elam, the editor of the Readjuster-leaning *Richmond Whig,* and William Mahone. During the evening, the men discussed Bernard's views on civil service reform and the Republican Party. Bernard wrote:

> Whilst Elam and myself were discussing this question Gen M. taking a piece of paper & pencil, wrote out a few lines in substance, as follows: "Whilst the party in power may select those in sympathy with it preferentially, the fittest and best qualified should be selected to fill the public offices." After writing this, he handed it to me and said: "Here is a civil service platform for you." Reading it, I said: "General I am glad to see that it is at least a step in the right direction."[16]

In July 1885, the Virginia Republican convention featured its share of drama as Mahone characteristically stamped his will on the proceedings. With little fanfare, however, the delegates approved platform language supporting "civil service in which character and capability shall be regarded as paramount tests for public employment." Bernard's efforts had yielded modest success. In 1886, he raised his reform views as an issue in his reelection campaign for Commonwealth Attorney. In a card he drafted and submitted

14. Bernard, *Civil Service Reform versus the Spoils System,* 90–93; Hoogenboom, *Outlawing the Spoils,* 240–47.

15. See Dailey, *Before Jim Crow,* 48–76.

16. Diary entry for July 5, 1885, Bernard Papers, UVA.

to Petersburg's Republican Party and its nominating convention, Bernard appealed for the use of the merit system in the Petersburg government. He went so far as to condition his nomination on the adoption of his views. Bernard pointed to pledges made by the national and state Republican Party in support of the merit system, including the resolution passed by the convention the previous summer.[17] On election day, he won, but not by much. At the time, he attributed the lukewarm support to confusion created by his views on civil service reform. He noted in his diary that his positions had caused him "some injury, not being endorsed by many republicans, and being cordially disapproved by many leading democrats."[18]

After the 1886 election, he also acknowledged a gradual loss of interest in political office. Although involvement in political life was rewarding for him, Bernard harbored private concerns about financial problems. Money issues continued to weigh heavily on his mind, and by 1888 he had chosen to abandon political office altogether. The financial worries that had plagued him had overtaken his desire to continue public service. In addition, he felt that his activities as a Republican had restricted his ability to generate work as an attorney. Commenting on his decision, the *Richmond Whig* wrote, "Mr. Bernard has discharged the duties of the office in an able, dignified, and conscientious manner." In his diary, Bernard resolved to "break off connection with all matters political."[19] He soon directed his energy to other projects. In the late 1880s, he wrote extensively to close and distant relatives seeking information on his family history. He continued this correspondence for years and amassed a large collection of detailed genealogical information.[20]

After leaving political office, Bernard also became active in the newly chartered A. P. Hill Camp of Confederate Veterans in Petersburg. The camp was organized in December 1887 with the intent of preserving and maintaining "that sentiment of fraternity, born of the hardships and dangers, shared in the march, the bivouac and the battlefield—avoiding everything which partakes of partisanship in religion and politics." The veterans in the A. P. Hill Camp held regular meetings on the first Thursday of the every month at the camp's hall on West Tabb Street. Every year, the former rebels held a banquet on Robert E. Lee's birthday in January, and also regularly participated in the

17. *New York Times,* July 17, 1885; *Petersburg Daily Index-Appeal,* May 8, 1886. By this time, however, some of the air had gone out of the issue, as President Arthur had signed the Pendleton Act in 1883, creating competitive examinations for some federal jobs.

18. Diary entry for June 20, 1886, Bernard Papers, UVA.

19. Diary entry for May 6, 1888, Bernard Papers, UVA; *Richmond Dispatch,* undated clipping in Bernard's diary entry for May 6, 1888, ibid.

20. These letters can be found in Bernard's papers at the University of Virginia.

city's memorial observance on June 9, the day on which Petersburg's militia had repelled attacks by Union cavalry in 1864. The camp also organized a relief committee to provide support for sick veterans and to pay for burial services. Its members gathered written materials about the war for the camp's own library, a project with which Bernard was closely involved.[21]

The camp quickly became one of the most active in the state, in a city long known for its memorialization of Confederate veterans. From its first Memorial Day, on June 9, 1866, and continuing through the next fifty years, the Petersburg Ladies Memorial Association organized and ran the ceremonies. The association also supervised the reinterment of 30,000 Confederate soldiers in Blandford Cemetery, which thus became the largest Confederate cemetery in the State of Virginia. When George Bernard spoke at the unveiling of a tablet at Blandford Church in 1911 honoring Confederate soldiers who had died during the Battle of the Crater, he was speaking at one of the epicenters of Confederate memorials in the South.[22]

What drove Bernard to become so active in veterans' affairs is a mystery. Neither his diary nor his correspondence refer in any detail to his nearly twenty-five-year participation and leadership in the A. P. Hill Camp. At best, we can make some educated speculations, based on his actions and words.

To begin with, Bernard and the members of his camp were part of a vast movement among veterans, North and South, to tell their stories to each other and anyone else who would listen. The Grand Army of the Republic (GAR) reached its peak membership in the 1890s, and the United Confederate Veterans (UCV) reached its height of membership in the following decade. According to the historian Gaines Foster, the official magazine of the UCV, the *Confederate Veteran* (established in 1893), "featured . . . illustrated pieces of human interest material, often on the experience of the war by its troops and leaders." The *National Tribune* served the same purpose for the GAR, carrying a column entitled "Fighting Them Over," in which veterans were encouraged to send in "first person accounts of battles and camp life."[23]

As these veterans sat and listened to monthly talks on the war, marched in

21. *Petersburg Daily Index-Appeal,* January 19, 1896; *Roster and Historical Sketch of A. P. Hill Camp C. V. No. 6, Va.* (Petersburg, Va., 1915).

22. Caroline E. Janney, *Burying the Dead but Not the Past: Ladies' Memorial Associations and the Lost Cause* (Chapel Hill: University of North Carolina Press, 2008), 58–60, 201; *Petersburg Daily Index-Appeal,* August 1, 1911.

23. David W. Blight, *Race and Reunion: The Civil War in American Memory* (Cambridge, Mass.: Harvard University Press, 2001), 181; Gaines M. Foster, *Ghosts of the Confederacy: Defeat, the Lost Cause, and the Emergence of the New South, 1865 to 1913* (New York: Oxford University Press, 1987), 106–7.

parades honoring Memorial Day or Decoration Day, traveled to other cities to visit veterans and walk old battlefields, attended dedication ceremonies for monuments, and avidly read their magazine and newspaper articles on the war and its memorialization, they became, in David Blight's words, "America's first Civil War buffs." They had a particular passion for getting names, dates, positions, statistics, and dialogue right, perhaps in an effort to bring some order to the chaos of war, or to place on record their role in the war in a manner that could *never* be questioned for its veracity. Or such activity may have become, as Blight says, "an end in itself, a pastime of enduring psychological value."[24]

Whatever his reasons for joining the A. P. Hill Camp, Bernard was quite active in the organization from its inception. He was a popular speaker and was regularly called upon to share his knowledge of the war at camp functions. During more than two decades of involvement, Bernard gave dozens of informal and formal talks before the camp. In 1889, he delivered a speech on the Battle of the Crater, an engagement that was especially important to the veterans of Petersburg because of the key role the 12th Virginia played in stopping the Union attack. That same year, Bernard gave a talk before the camp on his experiences during the Maryland campaign, including his wounding and capture at Crampton's Gap. Over the next few years, he began to gather transcripts of the war talks given by his comrades before the camp. In 1892, he arranged for these stories to appear in the *Rural Messenger,* a weekly Petersburg newspaper. The publication of the battle stories spawned additional recollections from other veterans. Bernard compiled the initial accounts and the additional correspondence into a book titled *War Talks of Confederate Veterans,* which was released near the end of 1892 by the Petersburg publisher Fenn and Owen. The rich collection of stories in *War Talks* stands as an important source of firsthand accounts of military operations in the Eastern Theater of the war, especially the Petersburg Campaign. Bernard's chapter on the Crater, which includes his address coupled with more than a dozen additional letters, provides perhaps the most detailed set of Confederate accounts of that engagement available anywhere. The accounts written, collected, and edited by Bernard were largely absent of the overt partisan rhetoric so common in postwar publications. The book received wide acclaim in reviews in newspapers throughout the country for its detail and impartiality. In praising the book, the *Philadelphia North American* wrote:

> Another charm of the book is the absence of theories by the author as to the probable cause of the results which happened; he leaves

24. Blight, *Race and Reunion,* 182, 186.

the reader to judge for himself from the succinct statement of the facts, and we think he may safely do so. The author appears to have approached his subject in a fair-minded spirit and with a desire to relate the unvarnished facts. It is evident from his account of the brutality of some of the Confederate troops to the Negro soldiers of the Federal army, and from other incidents related, not creditable to the Confederate side, that he is faithful in depicting the facts, whether creditable or otherwise, and is judicial in his desire to do only justice.[25]

There was also a pecuniary side to the telling of the veterans' stories. Bernard, for instance, obtained subscriptions in advance for *War Talks,* and he was in the process of doing the same for "War Talks, Volume II." Whether he earned a profit on the sale of *War Talks* is unknown, but for a person as obsessed with debt as Bernard, he surely would have been well aware of the potential market for a book on Civil War reminiscences.[26]

Following the publication of *War Talks,* Bernard continued to give presentations about the war based on his diaries and information gathered from fellow veterans. During the 1890s, he delivered speeches and gathered accounts of several battles and operations, including First Manassas, Seven Pines, Malvern Hill, the Gettysburg Campaign, the Weldon Railroad battles, Burgess Mill, Fort Stedman, the fall of Petersburg, and Appomattox. From this material, Bernard planned to publish "War Talks, Volume II." Some of the speeches and correspondence found their way into local newspapers, and these were also published in the *Southern Historical Society Papers.* Bernard gathered accounts from other veterans, including accounts by William Mahone describing the general's recollections of Seven Pines, Malvern Hill, Burgess Mill, the Weldon Railroad, and the Appomattox Campaign. By 1896, it appears that most of the chapters for "War Talks, Volume II" were complete, but, for some reason, Bernard never released the planned sequel to *War Talks.* Bernard's papers found in

---

25. "War Talks of Confederate Veterans: Opinions" (an undated pamphlet containing review excerpts of the book, apparently distributed with some copies of the book; in possession of the editors).

26. See Bernard Collection, Historical Society of Western Virginia, Miscellaneous folder. To be fair to Bernard, his camp passed a resolution in 1892 that approved his planned volume ("War Talks, Volume II") and agreed to Bernard's stipulation to "share equally with the camp all profits that come to him from proposed publication, *provided* the camp will apply the money to the purchase and collection of books and other literature relating to the late war, for the use of the camp" (Preface to *War Talks of Confederate Veterans,* comp. and ed. by George S. Bernard [Petersburg, Va.: Fenn and Owen, 1892], iii).

Roanoke contain two versions of the table of contents for this second book. It appears that by 1900 Bernard was considering creating two separate books: one covering his own, contemporary war diaries as well as a post-war "narrative" and a second volume containing the reminiscences provided to him by other veterans. The collection of Bernard's papers at the University of North Carolina contains a draft preface for "Musket and Cartridge Box," apparently the name of the volume he planned for his own war writings. Like the unpublished "War Talks, Volume II," "Musket and Cartridge Box" never saw the light of day. Many of the component parts of these projects, however, would trickle into Petersburg and Richmond newspapers, particularly the *Petersburg Daily Index-Appeal,* over the next several years.

"War Talks, Volume II" would have had some marked differences from the original volume. The first, published, volume had many more "statements" (many no longer than a page) from participants, but far fewer battles. Published in 1892, the first book served *political* as well as *historical* purposes. For more than twenty years, William Mahone had been involved in a historical feud with other Confederate veterans, and the publication of *War Talks* allowed both sides to bring some of their grievances to a wider audience. Mahone had angered a number of Confederate veterans—Jubal Early, Cadmus Wilcox, and James Lane, to name a few—by calling into question their competence, if not their bravery. He had also accepted and lionized his own role at the Battle of the Crater in 1864, for which he had earned a promotion to major general and a popular nickname, "The Hero of the Crater." Almost half of the material in the original *War Talks* focused on just three events: the Battle of the Wilderness, the defense of Petersburg, and the Battle of the Crater.[27] Although Bernard (and many of the men in his old unit, the 12th Virginia) supported Mahone politically and defended his role as a leader at the Crater and other battles, Bernard also included a number of Mahone detractors in *War Talks.* What exactly happened at the Crater may never be known. As one recent student of the battle, Kevin Levin, concludes, "No doubt the confused nature of the fighting in and around the Crater made it possible to draw numerous conclusions surrounding central questions related to the battle.... Neither side was interested in forging a mutually agreeable account of what happened at the Crater because they were content simply to make political use of their disparate memories."[28]

27. A total of 154 pages out of 335 pages in *War Talks* (Morningside reprint edition, 1981) are devoted to the three events.

28. Kevin M. Levin, "William Mahone, the Lost Cause, and Civil War History," *Virginia Magazine of History and Biography* 113, no. 4 (2005): 405.

The planned "War Talks, Volume II" would have been a completely different volume. More than half of the text would have consisted of either Bernard's diary entries, or the diary entries turned into a narrative with statements and stories from a variety of veterans, ranging from privates to generals. Bernard planned for this volume to contain accounts of most of the major battles and campaigns in the East during the war, as well as some "human interest" stories that would not focus on the battles. In short, Bernard had intended to widen his scope, perhaps hoping to attract a broader audience, while also depoliticizing his planned book by excluding competing versions of battles. Still, he would not have broken completely from his filial devotion to Mahone: there were to be included four statements from the general, as well as another controversial letter from him on the last days of the Army of Northern Virginia.

It is not known whether this planned second volume was different by design, or simply because of the nature of the new material Bernard had accumulated since the publication of the original *War Talks*. It is also not known whether Bernard may have thought that his own experience of the war, as a private and sergeant in the ranks for four years, might not have been more appealing to an audience satiated with the accounts of generals and grand tactics. Surely Bernard was aware of the success of Carlton McCarthy's *Detailed Minutiae of Soldier Life in the Army of Northern Virginia, 1861–1865* (published in 1882), and he may have felt that his own day-to-day experiences at specific battles over four years would also be of interest to fellow veterans (McCarthy, after all, had only served in the army in the last year of the war).[29]

The critic Thomas Leonard has characterized stories such as Bernard's wartime experiences and the recollections of the veterans as being "above the battle."[30] The soldiers' actions usually swing between the heroic and humorous. In these accounts, most Confederate soldiers are portrayed as brave men fighting for their cause and their home. And their Union foes are seen as fellow countrymen, tough in battle but tender in distress. Politics is largely ignored.

In revisiting his wartime history, Bernard may have been motivated by personal concerns. In the space of a single year, he had lost both his beloved brother, David "Meade," and his sister Elizabeth "Lizzie" Newman. Both died suddenly and unexpectedly—Meade of "apoplexy," and Lizzie from complications after childbirth. Meade, a respected jurist and fellow veteran of

---

29. Carlton McCarthy, *Detailed Minutiae of Soldier Life in the Army of Northern Virginia, 1861–1865* (1882; reprint, Lincoln: University of Nebraska Press, 1993).

30. Leonard quote is in Blight, *Race and Reunion*, 185.

the 12th Virginia, was particularly close to his brother, and had contributed several "statements" to *War Talks*. With their deaths in 1894 and 1895, respectively, Bernard, at age fifty-seven, surely felt his own mortality, and may have felt compelled to get out his story, and those of the other veterans, while he still could.[31]

Whatever his reasons for gathering stories and retyping his own, the archives are silent on the key question: why did Bernard fail to publish his work (or works)? His rare diary entries in the late 1890s do not address this question, though they never fail to mention his financial exigencies.[32] Nor are there any letters extant that discuss this situation.

Even as his manuscript languished, Bernard continued to speak at reunion banquets and monument dedications. In 1895, he delivered a public lecture about the war using photographs and a stereopticon, one of several talks that raised money for the A. P. Hill Camp's library fund. In 1897, he praised the deceased William Mahone at the presentation of a large portrait of the general to the camp. In May 1909, he spoke at the dedication of a tablet honoring those Confederate soldiers and Petersburg residents who had repelled an assault by Union cavalry on the city's defenses on June 9, 1864. At the ceremony, Bernard provided "a brief but comprehensive and interesting account of the battle and the movements of both forces." And, as noted earlier, in 1911 he was the principal speaker at the unveiling of a tablet at Blandford Church to the memory of the Confederate soldiers who died at the Battle of the Crater. In addition, he often spoke at the annual celebrations of Lee's birthday and at other official camp functions.[33]

In the 1890s, as reunions between veterans of the blue and the gray grew more frequent, Petersburg became the destination for various Northern delegations. In the autumn of 1894, a group of former soldiers visited that city to dedicate a monument to the First Maine Heavy Artillery. Bernard took part

31. Diary entries for August 5, 1894 (death of Meade Bernard) and April 21, 1895 (death of Lizzie Newman), Bernard Papers, UVA.

32. For example, see the diary entry for August 26, 1897: "Tomorrow, if alive, I will be sixty years of age, and overwhelmed, almost to the point of exhaustion, with debts that I am utterly unable to pay" (Bernard Papers, UVA).

33. See the *Petersburg Daily Index-Appeal* for the following dates: May 29, 1895; December 8, 1897 ("Mr. Bernard declared that General Mahone was as great a man in the camp as on the battlefield"); May 16, 1909; August 1, 1891; January 20, 1892; January 20, 1893; January 20, 1895 (Bernard "told of how he got in and out of Castle Thunder, one day in Christmas week, 1864"); January 20, 1897; January 21, 1908; January 20, 1910 (Bernard, the Commander of the A. P. Hill Camp, served as master of ceremonies); and January 20, 1911 (Bernard "told interestingly of the various battle-fields where he had seen General Lee").

in the ceremonies, speaking of the sacrifice made by Maine's soldiers at the initial assaults on the city in June 1864, and of the Southerners lost in the attack on Fort Stedman in March 1865. In recalling the men lost in those fights, Bernard explained that no stone was required to perpetuate their deeds of bravery and honor, because the "pen of the historian has done that." A newspaper reporter at the ceremony recalled Bernard's remarks in this way:

> Mr. Bernard said the war was settled against the south, but he believed that an all ruling Providence knew what was best for us. We have not only the respect of our adversaries, but the respect of mankind for the manner in which this contest was waged. He believed if a peace had been patched up at Hampton Roads there would have been long ere this another civil war. It was for the best that the contest should have been, as it was, fought to a finish. Mr. Bernard was of the opinion that, if the people and soldiers of the south had the war to fight over again with the same lights before them they would do just as they then did, but now, after the lapse of nearly thirty years he for one would venture to say that ninety nine out of ever[y] hundred southern soldiers were glad that the war ended as it did, and he was glad to be present on this occasion [to] say so to friends.[34]

As the spirit of blue and gray reconciliation crested in the 1910s, the A. P. Hill Camp contributed to the sectional healing. In 1910, Bernard led a contingent of Petersburg veterans to Springfield, Massachusetts, in what was perhaps the most prominent blue–gray reunion for the A. P. Hill Camp. The Petersburg veterans were well acquainted with these men from Springfield. As early as 1900, delegations from the two camps had visited their counterparts on numerous occasions.[35] These exchanges appear to have been masterminded by James Anderson, a Union veteran who spent much time in postwar Petersburg and who had become a member of both the A. P. Hill and Wilcox posts. The visits between the two veteran groups featured large banquets, speeches full of good feeling, and battlefield tours.

To reach Springfield, Bernard and his companions boarded the steamer *Jefferson* at Norfolk, bound for New York City. As the ship approached New York Harbor, Bernard received a curious transmission from James Anderson bearing the message "Read Luke fourteenth chapter, last clause, seventeenth verse." Bernard pulled out his pocket Bible and read, "Come, for all is ready." After the group arrived in New York, a procession of automobiles carried

34. *Petersburg Daily Index-Appeal,* September 15, 1894.
35. See *Petersburg Daily Index-Appeal,* April 6, 1900.

them to Grand Central Station for the final leg of their journey to Spring-field. Decked out in their uniforms and campaign hats, the veterans made quite an impression on the large crowd of New Yorkers heading out of town for the holiday. Anticipating a pleasant visit in Springfield, Bernard told the *New York Times:*

> We expect to capitulate body and soul on or about 7 o'clock tonight and when it is all over we are going to make the boys in blue come down to Virginia and let us capture them in the same delightful fashion that we know they will receive us. I hope this is the begin-ning of many such reunions of the Blue and Gray, and I am certain that nothing could be more effective in wiping out the last shred of bitterness if any exists between the two sections of our country.[36]

Once in Springfield, the aged rebels had the run of the city. Restaurants and movie theaters opened their doors at no charge. The week was filled with banquets and speeches. As usual, Bernard contributed thoughtful remarks to the proceedings. At the gala banquet, he observed that, forty years earlier, he never would have imagined that men "who had done all that they could to break up the Union" would receive the greeting afforded to the members of the A. P. Hill Camp that week. The rebel veterans acquitted themselves well during the July 4th parade. A reporter from the *Springfield Republican* even admitted that the Confederates "changed their line formation on Main Street with greater alacrity and military precision than did the Union veterans who preceded them." When Bernard and his comrades returned to Petersburg, loud cheers greeted them as they marched from the railroad station to their hall on West Tabb Street. According to accounts, the veterans had nothing but praise for the reception they had received in Springfield.[37]

In 1911, the A. P. Hill Camp returned the favor and welcomed the Massa-chusetts veterans to the unveiling of a monument to the Northern state's sol-diers on the Petersburg battlefield. Led by James Anderson, a Massachusetts commission erected a memorial to the soldiers of the Army of the Potomac near the Crater. The *Petersburg Daily Index-Appeal* cheerfully announced that the "Yankees again invaded Petersburg last night coming 150 strong." The A. P. Hill Camp threw an official welcome party for their friends at the camp's meeting hall. Bernard delivered the introductory address, describing the war's horrors and acknowledging that "the sons of each state reddened the soil with their blood." In the spirit of the event, Bernard concluded: "Happily, all of this is in the past. The wounds have healed." The popular event culminated

36. *New York Times,* July 3, 1910.
37. *Petersburg Daily Index-Appeal,* July 7 and 8, 1910.

in dedication ceremonies on the battlefield, where flowery speeches from the governors of Virginia and Massachusetts highlighted the proceedings.[38]

Bernard's speeches at the 1911 reunion event and elsewhere exuded the reconciliation spirit that pervaded these gatherings across the country at the turn of the century. In the twilight of their lives, veterans of the blue and the gray sought to erase the bitterness of the war and Reconstruction. Many Southern veterans and political leaders repeatedly argued that the Confederate states had fought primarily for their constitutional rights and independence. In this view, slavery was only incidental to the fundamental legal principles for which Southerners had fought and died. Proponents of this "Lost Cause" interpretation of the war tended to deify the Confederacy's military leaders, and insisted that the rebel's losses on the battlefield resulted only from the overwhelming resources arrayed against the Southern states. These beliefs, broadcast with such volume and conviction, became a widely accepted interpretation of the war in popular culture throughout the twentieth century.[39]

For his part, Bernard did not fill his many public speeches with claims of Southern infallibility and shrill appeals to Southern honor. Generally avoiding specifics, he acknowledged error on the part of the South, and, on more than one occasion, that the war's final result was best for all concerned. At the same time, he did not hesitate to praise his wartime comrades and commanders. He made no effort to distance himself from other rebel veterans, nor did he openly repudiate the decision of the Southern states to secede. When he spoke of the war's causes, he acknowledged the central role played by slavery in the dispute. In 1906, Bernard delivered an extraordinarily long speech to the camp on the history of slavery, titled "Slavery Agitation Leading Cause of Secession." During the marathon talk, divided over two meetings, he meticulously chronicled the country's struggle with the slavery issue in the years leading up to the war. Echoing sentiments he had shared at the unveiling of the Maine monument, he described the assertion of the rights of the states as the "principle" involved in the war, but acknowledged there was no doubt that that "slavery was the paramount or leading cause of difference between the people of the two sections of the Union that culminated in the clash of arms during that period of four years."[40]

38. *Petersburg Daily Index-Appeal,* November 11 and 12, 1911.

39. For recent discussions of the impact of reconciliation and the Lost Cause interpretation of the Civil War, see Blight, *Race and Reunion,* especially chaps. 5, 6, and 8; and Gary W. Gallagher and Alan T. Nolan, eds., *The Myth of the Lost Cause and Civil War History* (Bloomington: Indiana University Press, 2000).

40. *Petersburg Daily Index-Appeal,* December 9 and 11, 1906, and March 24 and 26 (quotation), 1907.

By positioning slavery at the center of secession, Bernard placed himself in the minority among white Southerners speaking about the issues of the Civil War in the early twentieth century. As David Blight explains in *Race and Reunion,* "The stock Confederate Memorial Day speech contained four obligatory tributes: to soldiers' valor, women's bravery, slave fidelity, and Southern innocence regarding slavery." Blight is hard-pressed to find white Southerners who owned up to the role of slavery in the coming of the Civil War, finally turning to the memoirs of the Southern warhorse of reconciliation, John B. Gordon. Gordon acknowledged that slavery was the "immediate fomenting cause" of the conflict, but "responsibility" could not be "laid at her [the South's] door."[41]

Unfortunately, no record exists of the reaction of Bernard's audience to his controversial stance on the causes of the Civil War. Indeed, it might be argued that more leeway for heterodoxy existed than is currently assumed, for in 1909 Bernard was elected commander of his camp, an office he held for a year. During that time, he also kept busy with his legal work for the Norfolk & Western Railroad Company, and for Dinwiddie and Nansemond Counties.[42]

On a Monday evening in February, 1912, a small note on the front page of the *Petersburg Daily Progress* informed readers that Bernard, "one of the leading members of the Petersburg bar and one of our most honored and beloved citizens," was suffering from pneumonia at his home on North Adams Street. Bernard's illness caused the postponement of hearings in a bank-related litigation for which he was serving as lead counsel. The following day at 2 o'clock in the afternoon, he died. Former comrades and fellow citizens paid their respects in the Petersburg papers. When news of Bernard's death reached Springfield, Massachusetts, James Anderson paid tribute to his Southern comrade in the local paper. The Petersburg Bar Association issued a resolution praising Bernard which stated: "Stern and inflexible in his devotion to the truth and right and rigorous of his personal conduct, he was yet kind and considerate in his judgment of others, exemplifying the Christian virtue of character which is the bond of perfectness." The editors of the *Petersburg Daily Index-Appeal* also described the community's loss:

> No citizen of Petersburg was better known than George S. Bernard. None was better beloved. None was more deserving of the respect

41. Blight, *Race and Reunion,* 282–83 (John B. Gordon is quoted on p. 283).

42. *Roster and Historical Sketch of A. P. Hill Camp C. V. No. 6, Va.* (Petersburg, Virginia, 1915), 24; Lyon G. Tyler, *Men of Mark in Virginia* (Richmond: Men of Mark Publishing Co., 1907), 3:31.

and the affection of his fellow citizens. . . . His high conception of duty; his devotion to the truth as he saw it; his kindly consideration of the feelings and the comfort of others; his old-fashioned and never-failing courtesy, made of George S. Bernard a man and a citizen of a character all too rare. The burden of his long life laid aside, he rests from his labors, and his works do follow him. Peace to his ashes.[43]

43. *Petersburg Daily Progress,* February 19, 1912; *Petersburg Daily Index-Appeal,* February 21 (quotation) and 23, 1912.

Civil War Talks

1

Norfolk, 1861–1862

PETERSBURG'S SONS GO TO WAR

JUST DAYS AFTER Fort Sumter's fall in April 1861, Virginia succumbed to the fever of secession and dispatched its militia to wrest the state's strategic locations from Federal control. Virginia forces quickly seized the armory at Harper's Ferry and converged on the Gosport Navy Yard near Norfolk, a vital shipbuilding facility. To bring about Norfolk's capture, secessionist leaders drew from militia forces throughout Virginia and the South. Petersburg supplied some of the first of these units.

On April 20, 1861, George S. Bernard and many of his neighbors and friends, all members of the Petersburg Riflemen, boarded a train bound for Norfolk. The Riflemen comprised a company of a larger force known as the Petersburg (or 4th) Battalion of the Virginia Militia, a unit that would eventually become the nucleus of the 12th Virginia Infantry Regiment. "The Fourth Battalion as it left Petersburg on the 20th of April, 1861, was made up of the flower of the manhood of the Cockade City [Petersburg]," wrote John Herbert Claiborne, a doctor and former legislator in the Petersburg Riflemen. In Claiborne's estimation, the battalion was the City's "crack company."[1] Private Westwood A. Todd, a Norfolk lawyer who would eventually join the

---

1. John Herbert Claiborne is quoted in James G. Scott and Edward A. Wyatt, *Petersburg's Story* (Petersburg: Titmus Optical Company, 1960), 126. Petersburg was known as "the Cockade City of the Union" as the result of the exploits of a company of its soldiers who wore cockades in their hats in the War of 1812. John Herbert Claiborne, a physician and politician from Petersburg, supervised all the military hospitals in that city from February 1862 through the end of the war. Afterwards, he continued his practice of medicine and wrote articles for medical journals. He also penned a volume of reminiscences titled *Seventy-five Years in Old Virginia*. He died in Petersburg in 1905.

unit, wrote: "This company was composed of the best blood of Petersburg. Indeed, I have never seen a finer body of men. They were intelligent, refined, well-educated, and proved themselves on many fields to be brave and constant soldiers. They ranked with the highest type of the Confederate Soldier. Their personal gallantry on the field was splendid, and I recall with the greatest pleasure and pride many instances of individual valor."[2] Eighteen of the command's forty-one soldiers had attended college. Twenty-four members would count themselves among the 12th Virginia's officers during the war.[3]

Before Bernard and the rest of the Petersburg battalion arrived in Norfolk, the Federal commander at the navy yard ordered his men to destroy any guns and ships that could not be removed. As Bernard and his new comrades watched from Norfolk on the evening of April 20th, the Gosport Yard burned and Union forces fled by ship to Hampton Roads. Early the next morning, the Virginians found the damage to the facility was less than feared. Notably, the fire had spared the hull of a large Federal ship, the *Merrimack*. In an endeavor that would help revolutionize naval warfare, the Confederates would eventually convert the *Merrimack* into the ironclad *Virginia*.

As Bernard and his fellow soldiers settled into their new surroundings, the Confederates maintained a tenuous hold on Norfolk and the nearby naval facilities. Weakly tethered to the balance of the South by two railroads, Norfolk was vulnerable to attack from several directions. To the north, the Federal ships in Hampton Roads sealed off the Elizabeth River and Norfolk from the sea and threatened the city's safety. Across the Roads, Union troops stationed on the peninsula near Fort Monroe posed an amphibious threat to Norfolk. To the south, the Dismal Swamp canal led to eastern North Carolina and provided yet another avenue for Federal forces. To protect Norfolk, Portsmouth, and Gosport from naval attack, Virginia troops constructed batteries at Sewell's Point, Craney Island, Lambert Point, and other positions along the Elizabeth River. To augment these fixed installations, Confederate infantry units, including Bernard and the Petersburg Riflemen, stood ready to protect Norfolk from Federal attack.

Bernard prepared an account of his experiences at Norfolk in a handwritten document titled "Narrative," now located in his papers at Duke Uni-

2. Westwood A. Todd Reminiscences, Southern Historical Collection, University of North Carolina.

3. William D. Henderson, *12th Virginia Infantry* (Lynchburg, Va.: H. E. Howard, 1984), 116–17. Sources for the brief biographical sketches throughout this volume include Henderson's book, the Historical Data Systems' American Civil War Research Database (at civilwardata.com), and Ezra Warner, *Generals in Gray* (Baton Rouge: Louisiana State University Press, 1959).

versity. In 1901, he published the first portions of this narrative, along with additional material, as part of a series of articles in the *Petersburg Daily Index-Appeal.* Those articles and the remaining parts of the "Narrative" make up the substance of this chapter.

>—0—‹•—I—‹·····›—I—•›—0—‹

"Reminiscences of Norfolk, May–June 1861," by George S. Bernard

The Petersburg Troops Leave for Norfolk — The Burning of the Navy Yard[4]

In April 1861, when the civil war began, the writer was a resident of the city of Petersburg, Va., and a member of the Petersburg Riflemen, a military company organized in December 1859, under the excitement of the John Brown raid, and perhaps one of the finest organizations of the kind in the South.[5] Almost all of its members were young men of education, intelligence and good social standing, residents of Petersburg. A few days before hostilities began he commenced to keep a diary, or journal, in which he wrote, not every day, but frequently. From this and other little books of like character kept during the war extracts will be freely made in this and subsequent chapters of this volume; as also from a note book, wherein immediately after the close of the war, when its four years' experiences were vividly fresh in memory, he wrote much not entered in these diaries. By such contemporaneous, or nearly contemporaneous, records of impressions of things mentioned the reader can be best made to see and understand that which is narrated.

The 4th battalion of Virginia volunteers, commanded by Maj. David A. Weisiger, and composed of the five Petersburg volunteer companies, on Friday, the 19th of April, 1861, were ordered to hold themselves in readiness for service.[6]

4. See the *Petersburg Daily Index-Appeal* for April 28, May 5, and May 19, 1901. The heading of the articles included the following: "From MSS. of Geo. S. Bernard's 'Musket and Cartridge Box.'" With a few noted exceptions, the material written by Bernard here matches passages in his "Notebook" housed in Bernard's papers at Duke University.

5. The Petersburg Riflemen were originally a part of Virginia's state army. By law the state army became part of the Confederate army in June 1861, and the Petersburg Riflemen became Company E of the 12th Virginia Infantry. For ease and uniformity of comparison, the enlistment dates for the soldiers use the Confederate army unit designations.

6. David A. Weisiger, a commission merchant in Petersburg, helped raise the regiment he led for three years as colonel, the 12th Virginia. In 1864, he was appointed

The record in the diary under this date is as follows:

Today a day of intense excitement in Petersburg, the military making their preparations for immediate service.

The next day the order came for the battalion to go to Norfolk, for service in the capture of the navy yard near that place, and on the afternoon of that day the command was aboard the cars of the Norfolk and Petersburg railroad en route for Norfolk.

The following entry in the diary narrates the experiences of this and the next day:

> Norfolk Barracks of the Petersburg Battalion
> 6:30 o'clock, Sunday morning, April 21, 1861

Seated upon my knapsack & waiting for Sergeant Patterson[7] to march to breakfast his squad, of which I am one, I take the opportunity of recording some of the events of the past twenty four hours.

The Petersburg Battalion, consisting of the Petersburg Riflemen, the Lafayette Guards, the City Guards, the Petersburg Artillery and companies A & B Greys, numbering in all about three hundred and seventy-five men, under the command of Major Weisiger, left home on yesterday afternoon about 2:30 o'clock. The departure I shall never forget. Hundreds of persons were assembled at the depot to bid farewell, perhaps for the last time, to those who were leaving. Many a sturdy man could be seen with his eyes suffused with tears. I could but be struck with an affecting incident I witnessed as we passed along down Sycamore Street. A lady with several others, as we approached, commenced, apparently with a joyous heart, to wave her handkerchief. She could not stand it. Her feelings overcame her and she burst into tears. But no more upon this sad subject. As the train moved off—

---

brigadier general, and led William Mahone's former brigade until the conflict's end. After the war, he worked in banking and business.

7. John Rice Patterson, a native of Lunenburg County, was a grocery and commission merchant in Petersburg before the war. Enlisting as a sergeant in Company E of the 12th Virginia in April 1861, he was promoted to 2nd lieutenant in March 1862. Wounded at Crampton's Gap in 1862, he recovered after a year and returned to his unit, where he held a variety of posts, including brigade commissary officer and head of Mahone's provost guard. After the war, he lived in Petersburg, where he was postmaster general in the 1880s during the Cleveland administration. For several decades, he was a merchandise broker.

Sunday afternoon
April 21, 1861 —

After some interruption I now resume. I was about to say that, as our train moved off, there was much cheering, both on the part of the crowd we left behind and on the part of our men. Arriving within a mile or two of the depot in Norfolk, our commandant had the train stopped and our men were ordered to get out, fix on their accoutrements, load their guns and prepare for action, should an attack be made upon us as we neared the depot.[8]

8. GSB: The *Petersburg Express,* in its issue of Monday, April 22, 1861, gave the following graphic account of the memorable twentieth of April, 1861, a day of intense excitement not only in Petersburg, but all over the country:

"Saturday will hereafter add another to the list of times and dates made memorable in history. Were one to attempt now to collect the materials for some future historian, how much would he find against this day! No proud record of battle triumph, no pompous account of warrior's deeds—but a tender apostrophe of woman's worth, and a merited compliment to man's devotion to his unhappy country. The day was set apart for a general muster, but it was destined to witness many varied and interesting scenes.

"At an early hour, the streets were thronged, volunteers were hurrying to their rendezvous, and the sun lent a bright radiance to the 'burnished armor and glittering steel.' The crowd increased, the roll of drums was heard, and then the sound of trumpet announced the approach of cavalry. It was a glorious scene to witness, and but for the look of deep gravity, which every countenance wore, one might have fancied the gay carnival had been incorporated among our city pageants. In front of the courthouse, an anxious throng was assembled, drawn thither to see the troops formed into line, by the news, which passed with the rapidity of an electric current through our city of their having received order to depart. What a thrill, indeed, was caused by these little words 'ordered away'! 'Tis no holiday scene now, for all feel that there are hearts to school—tender feelings to master—and but a brief period to give affection's gently ministerings. A few moments for home, and then away, for duty calls, and our noble women would have every man at his post.

"We have never witnessed a spectacle which addressed the feeling in such a solemn manner as that which presented itself to our view on Saturday, on the departure of the volunteers for Norfolk. As we said above, every member of the different companies was dressed in uniform and calmly awaited his orders to march. As soon as the dispatch from Richmond was received, the citizen soldiers commenced congregating, and by half past 12 o'clock the line was formed and the gallant companies marched down Sycamore and Bollingbrook streets to Norfolk depot, escorted by Captain Fisher's splendid troop of cavalry, and making a most imposing display. Flags were flying from every prominent building on the line of march, and every window, every balcony, every available spot, was crowded by ladies who, with weeping eyes and bursting hearts, had come to take a last fond look at those whom they might possibly never behold again. Many were the recognitions on both sides. After the troops had passed by, a great number of ladies

There was apprehension of a possible broadside from one of the war vessels in the harbor, as the train passed within range of their guns. But we reached the depot in perfect safety and quietly and in perfect order disembarked. The companies being soon formed, we proceeded up Main Street to our quarters. As the battalion marched along with solemn and decided step,

––––––––

followed them to the depot to witness their departure, and happily to obtain one more lingering glance at those who were so fondly loved.

"Around the depot a dense mass of thousands of human beings was assembled; male and female, old and young; mothers bidding farewell to their sons, wives to their husbands; sisters to their brothers, and all imploring a benediction on their heads. There was scarcely a dry eye in all that vast assemblage. Many incidents of a most touching nature occurred, and, altogether, it was the most affecting—indeed the most heart-rending scene we ever witnessed.

"What made it all the more affecting, was the fact that a very large proportion of the volunteers are under twenty years of age, and only a small number over twenty-four.

"At length, when the train was ready to start, the Rev. Wm. H. Platt, in obedience to the unanimous desire of every one present, delivered a brief and impressive address to the companies substantially as follows

'Soldiers of Liberty! Go forth upon your mission of defense, strong and sustained in the mighty conviction of right. In these thrice are you armed. The history of our flag is yet to be written, and you are a portion of the brave men who are to achieve its victories and establish its glory. Be prayerful to God, and with your souls washed in the precious blood of His Son, be firm to the duty required by your country.

'Drive back the invaders from our soil, and the deepest and most earnest prayers of your mothers, sisters and wives will hourly ascend to the God of battles for your safety and success.

'In the name of this vast multitude and of the whole community, I bid you an affectionate farewell and may God the Father, God the Son, and God the Holy Ghost, bless, preserve, and protect you. Amen.'

"After the conclusion of this most solemn and affecting address, the soldiers were marched in single file to their seats in the cars, entering them from one and marching through the entire number, filling up the seventh and last car first. As near as we could judge there were about 400 volunteers composing the following companies:

> Grays, A and B—Capts. Lyon and Bond
> City Guards—Capt. May
> Petersburg Riflemen—Capt. Dodson
> Petersburg Artillery—Capt. Nichols
> Lafayette Guards—Capt. Jarvis

As the train moved off, cheer after cheer from thousands of voices rent the air.

"If woman's tears and woman's prayers avail anything—and we are among those who believe they avail much, very much—then our gallant volunteers in this hour of Virginia's need, be protected by a divine panoply, and neither the gates of hell nor the myrmidons of Northern aggression, shall prevail against them."

scores of ladies waved their handkerchiefs to us and cheer after cheer was given by the men and boys along the street.

Upon reaching our quarters, we soon addressed ourselves with assiduity to the contents of our haversacks, immediately after which most of our men fixed themselves for the night. For an hour or two, there was no such thing as sleep for most of us. A few humorous fellows by their talk made it quite impossible. About 10:30 o'clock, quite a stir was made, in our apartment at least, by the announcement of an order to hold ourselves in readiness to move at a moment's warning.

Some, thinking we were about to be off, even went so far as to buckle on their accoutrements. Soon, however, quiet prevailed, and continued until it was announced that the Navy Yard was on fire. Many immediately rushed[9] to the upper story of the building in which we were quartered to see the fire. From some mistake I had made in my bearings, I concluded as soon as I saw the fire that it was not at the Navy Yard, but somewhere in the direction of the naval hospital. Several others being persuaded by me that the fire was not at the navy yard, most of us returned to our room, and quiet being restored, we soon fell asleep, and did not rise until about six o'clock next morning. Going up to the upper story again to look at the fire, I was now convinced that it was the navy yard that I saw burning. Several present declared they could see ships on fire. I could distinguish none. Several were, however, burnt — among them the *Pennsylvania*. The Federal officers seemed determined to leave nothing that would be useful. We heard last night that on yesterday they spiked all the guns in the Navy Yard and threw overboard large quantities of small arms.[10]

9. Bernard's original note book says "walked up" here.

10. GSB: Mr. John W. H. Porter, of Portsmouth, VA, in his "History of Norfolk County, Va., 1861–5," in the chapter entitled "First year of the war in Portsmouth," gives a full and very interesting account of the destruction of the navy yard and vessels lying there, from which the following paragraphs are taken:

"There were at the navy yard at that time, the sloop-of-war *Cumberland,* 22 guns, in commission, with a full complement of officers and men on board; the sloops-of-war *Plymouth,* 22 guns, and *Germantown,* 22 guns, and the brig *Dolphin,* 6 guns, almost ready for sea; the steam frigate *Merrimac,* 40 guns, almost ready for sea and undergoing repairs; the line of battle ship *Pennsylvania,* 120 guns, in commission as a receiving ship, with a considerable crew on board, and the 74-gun ships *Delaware* and *Columbus,* and the frigates *Raritan, Columbia* and *United States,* dismantled and in ordinary. The force of sailors and marines on the various vessels and at the navy yard was probably about 600, well armed and abundantly supplied with ammunition. . . .

"The work of destruction began a little before noon on the 20th, and the frigate *Merrimac* was the first object of the destroyers. Carpenters and machinists were at work on her at the time. The carpenter of the *Cumberland,* with a small squad of sailors to

About seven o'clock this morning our company (the Riflemen) began to march off to breakfast in squads of ten. I was fortunate enough to be in squad

---

assist him, opened her bilge cock and she filled with water and settled quietly until she rested on the bottom. Owing to her great draft of water she did not settle far.

"After the 12 o'clock bell was rung for the workmen to knock off for dinner, the gates of the navy yard were closed, and no one was permitted to enter without the approval of the Commodore. The work of destruction then proceeded very rapidly. . . .

"During the afternoon it became generally known in Portsmouth that the vessels and stores in the navy yard were being destroyed and a rumor became prevalent that it was the intention of Commodore [Charles] McCauley to set the building on fire. This, it was feared would cause serious damage to the city, as it was separated from the yard only by the width of Lincoln street, which was but sixty feet wide, and a meeting of the citizens was held, at which Messrs. Samuel Watts, James Murdaugh and William H. Peters were appointed a committee to wait upon Commodore McCauley and endeavor to persuade him to reconsider that purpose, if he really entertained it, but the Commodore refused to see them and they were denied admission into the yard.

"About dusk the sloop-of-war *Pawnee,* under Captain [Hiram] Paulding, steamed up to the navy yard, and her crew were added to the wrecking force. It is said the torch was applied by the order of Captain Paulding. . . .

"The fire from the ship houses communicated to the *Merrimac, Plymouth, Germantown* and *Dolphin,* and all of them that was above the water was consumed. The *Pennsylvania, Raritan* and *Columbia,* which were anchored out in the stream, shared the fate of the ship houses. They were set on fire and burned almost down to their keels. Several buildings, containing stores of various kinds, were fired and, together with their valuable contents, totally destroyed.

"An effort was made to destroy the usefulness of the heavy cannon, hundreds of which were in the yard, by breaking off their trunions with mauls, but this was successful in only a few instances. There was a large quantity of liquor in the spirit room in the naval store house, and the sailors, getting possession of this liquor, filled themselves so full of it that they were unable to keep up the work of destruction. They spiked a number of the cannon with nails, but these were easily gotten out subsequently by the Confederates."

Having in the next three paragraphs narrated how the dry dock was saved from destruction by the friendly act of a Federal seaman, Mr. Porter concludes his interesting account of this important act in the drama of the civil war as follows:

"But, to return to the navy yard and its destruction. The old frigate *United States,* around which clustered so many, memories of brave deeds and gallant victories, was the only vessel which was spared in the general devastation, and that night of the 20th of April was a night of anxiety in Portsmouth. The immense ship houses with their millions of feet of timber, were seething volcanoes of flames, and the huge ship *Pennsylvania* was a pyramid of fire, while the burning *Merrimac, Dolphin, Germantown, Plymouth, Raritan,* and *Columbia* and the large store houses added to the conflagration and lighted up the heavens with a lurid glare that was seen for thirty miles. To add to the

No. 1. Our sergeant (J. Willcox Brown[11]) took us to the Atlantic Hotel, where we had a most sumptuous breakfast. Breakfast over, we employed ourselves variously. In the meantime, arrangements were made for those of us who wished to do so to attend church. Sergeants were to take us to the different churches in squads. But soon this programme was interfered with by an order to "fall in," dressed "in fighting trim," which order created no little excitement, though no discernible alarm. In obedience to this order, we immediately hurried to our rooms, pulled off our dress coats and put on our blue uniform shirts and our overcoats, with our accoutrements, leaving knapsacks, haversacks &c., at our quarters. Where we were about to go no one knew. Our men, however, seemed anxious for the fight, if there was to be one. The line formed, somewhat to our surprise, we were marched back to our rooms and directed to put on all of our baggage, when it is quite evident to us that we were merely going to take up quarters at some other place, which turned out to be the case.

Getting in motion, we marched out to the Fair Grounds, about one and

---

dangers of the night the dwelling houses on the north side of Lincoln street in Portsmouth caught fire and the whole city was threatened with destruction, which was only averted by a change of the direction of the wind. Occasionally one of the guns of the *Pennsylvania* which had been left loaded by her crew would be discharged as it became hot enough from the fire to ignite the powder, but, fortunately no one was hurt by them and amid all of this crackling of flames, booming of guns and deluge of falling sparks, the cry arose that the *Pawnee* was about to bombard the city.

"A correspondence had taken place between General [William B.] Taliaferro (who by authority of General Letcher was in command of the Virginia forces at Norfolk. Lieutenants Robert R. Pegram and Catesby Ap. R. Jones being by the same authority made captains in the Virginia navy with orders to take command of the naval station and organize naval defenses) and Commodores McCauley in which the General proposed to the Commodore that if he put a stop to the work of destruction the *Pawnee* and *Cumberland* would be permitted to leave the navy yard and the port in safety. He had no means to prevent them from leaving, and in fact was very anxious to have them go, but Commodore McCauley was not aware of that and accepted the proposal. Accordingly, about midnight the *Pawnee* left the yard with the *Cumberland* in tow. Captain Paulding returned an answer to General Taliaferro threatening severe retaliation in case they were molested. This was construed to mean the bombardment of the two cities and probably gave rise to the rumor which was prevalent in Portsmouth."

11. John Willcox Brown, a well-educated (he held a master's degree from the University of Virginia) grandson of a prosperous Petersburg merchant, enlisted as a 2nd lieutenant in Company E of the 12th Virginia in April 1861. Elected 1st lieutenant in October 1861, he declined reelection to that rank in 1862, instead serving as a private until receiving a medical discharge in 1863. He then served in the Virginia State Reserves, the Ordnance Department, and, finally, in the artillery, as a lieutenant colonel.

a half miles from the old establishment near Main Street in which we spent last night. The two companies of Greys and the Riflemen were assigned comfortable quarters in what seems to be an old *ten-pin* alley very near the Fair Grounds. Soon we were relieved of our heavy knapsacks, which had quite broken us down, and a few minutes thereafter we might have been seen lolling about in the pleasant grove which surrounds our quarters.

Nothing of much interest transpired during the day. About sunset, however, the Riflemen were detailed as a scouting party, to give warning of any effort to surprise the camp tonight, as it is thought that a force may be landed from boats a few miles below Norfolk and be marched to the powder magazine, not far from our camp. The Company was divided into two squads, of which Lieutenant Banks[12] has command of one. This squad embraces the platoon in which I am, and I now write from our quarters, the humble cottage of an old negro named Edmund Ferby, about a mile distant from our encampment. The other squad left us at the forks of the road near the encampment, to keep a look out in another direction.

Arrived at this place, Lieutenant Banks detailed his first squad of four men to march down the road in the direction of the river. This or the next squad hailed one or two men, who proved to be scouts sent out from one of the companies of this county.[13] It is thought that if troops are landed tonight it will be about one or two o'clock, about which time the moon will go down. Our Lieutenant has now divided his command into three squads for scouting. The first of which has just gone out. I must now bring this imperfect record to a close but not before mentioning the elegant coffee served out to us by old Edmund and his lady, which has made us all feel like different men.[14]

12. "Lieutenant Banks" was Robert R. Banks of Petersburg. A commission merchant in Petersburg before the war, he enlisted as a lieutenant in Company E of the 12th Virginia in April 1861 and rose to the rank of captain. Severely wounded at Chancellorsville, he resigned his commission in 1864. He died in 1871 from the aftereffects of his wound.

13. At this point in the article, Bernard did not include the following text, from his original Notebook: ". . . and who were on their way back to our encampment to give information that the *Cumberland* had passed beyond the obstructions in the river and was on her way out. The *Pawnee* had also passed out. This vessel however went into the harbor last night passing over the obstructions."

14. GSB: In Volume 4, series 1, of Naval Records, pages 287 to 309, are full and interesting reports of Commodore McCauley, Captain Paulding, Captain Charles Wilkes (who commanded the *Pawnee*) and Commander James Alden of the U.S. navy and of Major-General William B. Taliaferro and other officers, all made in April, 1861, giving the details of this historic act at the opening of the civil war:

Service about Norfolk in the Months of April and May, 1861—The
Federal Vessels Attack the Battery at Sewell's Point—A March
to Sewell's Point

The experiences of the next two weeks as recorded in the note book, entries
in this book being a transcript from the diary with a few verbal changes, are
as follows:

Quarters near Fair Grounds
Wednesday April 24 1861

My last record left us—at least my section of the Riflemen—on picket
Sunday night at and about the house of old Edmund Ferby. The squad with
which I myself was on duty were out from 1:30 o'clock until 3:30, during
which time nothing of interest transpired, no Federal troops making their
appearance, though we strained our eyes watching for them in the direction
of the river. The other detachment of our command under Captain Dodson
& Lieutenant Stevens,[15] from accounts, had a more eventful expedition, if
not a more pleasant one than had we. Soon after our detachments separated
at the forks of the road near our encampment, the party under these officers
descried down the road upon which they were then marching a body of men,
soon discovered to be cavalry and infantry, who by a sudden maneuver threw

---

"At 1:45 a. m.," says Captain Wilkes, in his report to Flag Officer Paulding, "it was
reported to me by Commander Rodgers, Alden and Sands that all of the men that
could be spared should be sent on board immediately, retaining only those necessary
to ignite the material, and that the signal would be a rocket from the *Pawnee,* to be ordered by yourself. The troops and marines were rapidly embarked, when it was reported
to you by the youngest son of Commodore McCauley, tears streaming down his cheeks,
that his father refused to vacate his post, and declined all inducement to do so. Commodore Alden was selected by you to make the endeavor to induce him to yield, and
to state that it was your intention speedily to fire the building and his life must be lost.
This last effort succeeded, and he was induced with great reluctance to remove to the
Cumberland . . . the *Pawnee* had left the wharf at 2:25 a.m. winded, and hausers were
passed from the *Cumberland* for the purpose of towing her out. At 4 o'clock, after a
detention of nearly two hours, the *Cumberland* slipped her moorings, and both vessels
stood out and down the harbor. At 4:20 the signal was made the torch applied and in
a few minutes the whole area of the yard was one sheet of flame—the two ship houses
and the whole line of stores, as well as the *Merrimac.*"

15. Daniel Dodson began the war in April 1861 as the captain of Company E of the
12th Virginia, but resigned in September 1861; Samuel Stevens, a prewar merchant of
glassware, enlisted in the 12th Virginia as a 1st lieutenant. He was promoted to captain
and regimental quartermaster in September 1861. After the war, he served one year as
city sergeant of Petersburg.

the former in front, who immediately charged at full speed in the direction of the little band of Riflemen. Fixing their bayonets in the twinkling of an eye, they at once stationed themselves in readiness to receive what they confidently believed, at least for a time, were the enemy. Not a man flinched, each standing his ground with the firmness of a veteran. Most of the party, however, confess to some alarm.

Next day we began our preparations for establishing a regular encampment. The work commenced, but a few minutes sufficed for the utter demolition of several hundred yards of good fencing, enclosing the premises upon which we are stationed. A few minutes more and the various "messes" were erecting their "kitchens," as they called them. A few bricks put together upon three sides of a square, protected by a plank shed six feet high and about the same in length and breadth, was the model after which the principal of these establishments were constructed. Various inventive geniuses improved upon, or fell short of this model. While these culinary establishments were going up, tents were being pitched and shelters of other sorts erected. The party in which I was very soon metamorphosed an old sail and a few sapling poles into a canvas house of very respectable dimensions, sufficiently large to accommodate the three messes of Sergeants Brown, Patterson & Keiley,[16] twenty, odd in number.

These establishments erected, the sun had scarcely set when numbers of camp fires were springing into existence, soon to illuminate the whole encampment with their cheerful light. Around these fires were to be seen various cooks, preparing supper for their messmates. Happening to be one of those engaged in my own mess, I fancied that the supper which I assisted in preparing would have done honor to a cook from Paris. It is almost needless to mention that this meal was enjoyed—the first we had prepared by ourselves since

---

16. Sergeant Anthony M. Keiley, a Petersburg lawyer, enlisted as a sergeant in Company E of the 12th Virginia in April 1861. Son of an Irish immigrant, Keiley was co-publisher of the the *South Side Democrat* before the war. Elected 1st lieutenant in May 1862, he was wounded in the foot at Malvern Hill but returned to the ranks. After his wounded foot "gave out" during the Gettysburg Campaign, he resigned from the army and became editor of the *Petersburg Express*. He was captured while serving in the militia during the battle of June 9, 1864, at Petersburg. Imprisoned at Point Lookout, Elmira, and later Castle Thunder, Keiley wrote about his POW experiences in his 1866 book, *In Vinculis; or, The Prisoner of War* (New York: Blelock and Co., 1866). After the war, he was mayor of Richmond, a member of the Virginia House of Delegates, and later president of the International Court. In 1905, he was killed in Paris by "runaway horses."

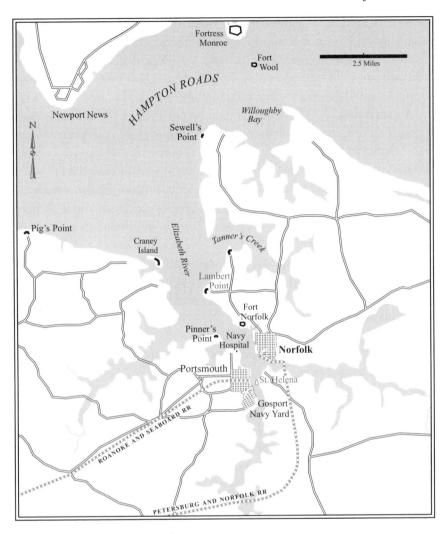

NORFOLK AND VICINITY, 1861

leaving home. I thought I could never desire better coffee than that appeared which I drank on this occasion, sipped from a tin cup, minus milk or cream, & sweetened with sugar dropped in from my neighbor's fingers.

Marine Hospital Ferry Point
Near Norfolk Va.
May 2, 1861

Until Saturday last, nothing of much interest transpired at the old camp ground. Rumor after rumor we heard, but very few were ever confirmed.

General Beauregard[17] with a large body of troops arrived in Portsmouth several times. One man certainly saw him there. Then there was a report which created some sensation, to the effect that Fort Pickens had been captured with a loss of 2,800 men to the Confederates. But I will not undertake to enumerate all the rumors that had currency.

About the middle of last week, our Surgeon, Dr. J. H. Claiborne, advised a change of our quarters, on account of the scarcity and bad quality of the water about camp. Accordingly at dress parade on Friday afternoon, an order was read directing us to be in readiness to move at an early hour the following morning, the object of the move, as we learned, being the change of quarters advised by our surgeon. At this we were all highly delighted and with light hearts set to work packing our knapsacks. Later in the afternoon we received orders to hold ourselves in readiness to move at a moment's warning, and as the military expression has it, "we slept on our arms" during the night, that is, with them near at hand. There was no occasion, however, to arouse us and we slept accordingly until the "reveille" summoned us at 4:30 o'clock next morning to roll call.

By 6:30 o'clock the battalion was formed and in motion for Norfolk, the line of march being through the principal streets, upon which we fancied we presented a very imposing appearance. After a fatiguing tramp of nearly three hours' length we reached this place.

The Riflemen were assigned two spacious rooms, a wide passage and a long corridor on the first floor of the Marine Hospital for their quarters. The City Guards were given the rooms above us, whilst the other companies of the battalion—the Artillery excepted, who were now on detached duty—occupied neighboring houses. We have here an abundant supply of good water, and enjoy a magnificent view of Norfolk Harbor.

We are now fully into the merits of camp life. Its novelty has worn off and its hardships are borne with less pleasure.

Monday, May 6, 1861

"Slept on our arms" last night. What the occasion, have not heard. This the fourth time we have "slept on our arms." Troops continue to arrive at this place. Number about Norfolk at this time estimated at between 2,000 and 3,000. It seems very difficult for us privates and subordinates to hear anything

---

17. Pierre Gustave Toutant Beauregard entered Confederate service as a brigadier general and quickly earned promotion to full general. Fort Pickens was a brick fortification on Santa Rosa Island near Pensacola, Florida. It remained under Union control throughout the war.

authentic. Went to Norfolk this afternoon to see Ned Mann,[18] who is sick in that city. Went also to see _____,[19] to bid her good bye. She leaves for Orange tomorrow, with my Brother Meade.[20] Met with an old college mate, R. S. Thomas, whom I visited at his law office. Overstaid my two hours permit one hour. No questions, however, were asked on my return. Restrictions of camp discipline very irksome. Very annoying to be required to ask permission of our officers to do this or that little thing. I have resolved, however, to submit in patience. Not so many persons come down from Petersburg each day to visit us now as did a short time since. Boxes of good things, however, continue to arrive.

The following are the entries in the diary made during the next three weeks of the month of May:

Wednesday, May 8, 1861

Our morning's drill was concluded earlier than usual by an order given us to prepare to assist in doing some work at St. Helena.[21] Upon reaching our quarters—we had been drilling at a beautiful place opposite the Navy Yard—we were ordered to get our dinners as soon as possible which we did, though it was only 11 o'clock; but soon the order was countermanded, when we were informed that we would be needed to-morrow morning at 7 o'clock. I am one of the twenty drafted from our company for the purpose. What we are to do I don't know, although I have heard we are to throw up a breastwork at that place.

From indications a bloody war is almost inevitable. It is said that Federal troops took possession of Alexandria today and that Letcher[22] will tomorrow issue a proclamation calling out 75,000 volunteers. If this is true, it is such an aggression as will at once precipitate a fight.

18. Edward Murray Mann of Petersburg enlisted in Company E of the 12th Virginia as a private in April 1861. He rose to the rank of sergeant before being discharged in 1863 to serve as clerk pro tem of the Petersburg circuit court.

19. In his unpublished Notebook, Bernard wrote here "Annie Bell Bernard." In the published version, he left a blank in the space.

20. David Meade Bernard Jr. was George Bernard's half brother. He enlisted as a private in Company E of the 12th Virginia and served with that unit and two cavalry regiments during the war. After the war, he moved steadily up the ladder in the field of law, from lawyer to Commonwealth attorney to judge.

21. St. Helena was a small island on the east bank of the Elizabeth River adjacent the Gosport Navy Yard.

22. John Letcher was governor of Virginia from 1860 to 1864.

Friday, May 10, 1861

Reports about the occupation of Alexandria by Federal troops proved to be untrue. We had quite a hard time of it yesterday, "clearing up" at St. Helena. There were twenty men from each of the five companies detailed for the duty. Those detailed today will probably commence throwing up breastworks. The object of this fortification is to guard against an attack upon the Navy Yard from a southeasterly direction. Troops continue to arrive here almost every day. Eleven hundred from Alabama reached here night before last. Stationed over here at the Marine Hospital, we see very little of the soldiers who reach here. In a few days the public property about this place will be out of all danger of recapture, if such is not already the case. The batteries at Sewell's Point, Craney Island, the Naval Hospital and Fort Norfolk are a very good safeguard against any attack by water. Every evening a little steamer is sent out probably as far as Craney Island to give the alarm, should any thing suspicious be done by the vessels in the Roads.[23] Our sentinels now are every night directed to watch out for "rockets" in that direction.

Saturday, May 11, 1861

Was on duty yesterday and last night "post" guard. From 12 o'clock until 4 I had quite a good nap upon the paved walk-way that runs near the guard house, using my blanket as a bed and cartridge box as a pillow. This morning for the first time, I visited the Naval Hospital and Fort Norfolk, and was pleased with my visits.

There are seventeen guns mounted at the Hospital battery and about the same number at the Fort Norfolk battery.[24]

Sunday, May 19, 1861

We had quite a stir at this place on Thursday night last. Two of the City Guards happening to be in the yard about 9:30 o'clock observed an unusual light in the direction of Craney Island and at the same time heard the cry "Attack! Attack!" Supposing it to be an alarm, they at once informed Colonel

---

23. Craney Island sits just west of the mouth of the Elizabeth River, about four miles from the city of Chesapeake. The CSS *Virginia* was scuttled here when the Confederates evacuated Norfolk in May 1862. The "Roads" referred to here were the Hampton Roads, an area of water at the mouths of the James, Nansemond, and Elizabeth Rivers which is bordered by the cities of Hampton, Newport News, and Norfolk.

24. Bernard's entry for this date in his unpublished Notebook reads: "After an account of an ordinary *tour* of guard duty around the quarters, we find the following:— 'did last night what I never did before, viz. slept out in the open air. From 10 o'clock until 4. I had quite a good nap (If our memory serves us it was quite *otherwise*) upon the paved walkway near the guard house, using my blanket as a bed & cartridge box as a pillow.'"

Weisiger of it and rushed up to their quarters to give the alarm to the men. From the manner in which these men ran up the steps to their quarters on the second floor of the building and from the stir thus occasioned, I was satisfied that something unusual had happened. Being in the act of lying down for the night, as was the case with all or nearly all in our room, I instantly sprang up, when I heard two orders "Get Ready Riflemen." "Get ready immediately" rapidly repeated. Hardly had we begun to dress ourselves when our drummer began to beat his drum most rapidly. Before, I thought the enemy were coming, but this terrific rattle of the drum, in the porch of the building a few feet from us, coupled with the increased activity of the men in dressing, putting on their accoutrements, getting up their guns &c., made me fancy that the whole host was upon us. I don't know whether the frame of mind in which I was might be termed fright or mere agitation, but certain it is, I discovered my heart to be beating with much more than its ordinary activity, and I felt by no means comfortable.

In two minutes time we were all in the yard and the line formed. All excitement—at least with us—had now subsided and each man seemed cool. After standing in line for a few minutes, we were dismissed & told to return to our quarters, the alarm proving to be false.

Today we have had some little excitement, occasioned by an Order received soon after breakfast to hold ourselves in readiness for a march. It is said our destination is a farm about nine miles down the river at which point we are to guard the main road leading to Norfolk from that direction.

We dislike leaving this place very much, being now quite comfortably fixed. Indeed, I know of no place at which I would prefer being stationed. Our move now in contemplation must in a measure be due to some apprehension growing out of the events of yesterday. Yesterday morning some officers from the Federal fleet—some say Commodore Pendergrast[25] himself—came up in a boat under a flag of truce, ostensibly for the purpose of asking the privilege of removing from the City the commodore's wife, but really, it is supposed, for the purpose of viewing our fortifications. Thoughtlessly, the officer sent out from Craney Island to meet the flag of truce party and to learn their mission, permitted the boat to pass up to Norfolk, for which it is said Genl. Lee gave the officer a reprimand.[26] Later in the day an engagement took place at Sewell's Point, resulting it is said in the complete demolition of the battery

25. Garrett J. Pendergrast commanded the USS *Cumberland* in 1861 and seized many Confederate ships off Fort Monroe in the early days of the war. In 1862, he received command of the Philadelphia Navy Yard.

26. "Genl. Lee" is General Robert E. Lee.

at that point, although "nobody was hurt." The firing was seen from Craney Island and very distinctly heard here.

It is thought the Federal troops will make the effort to re-possess the Government property at this point at an early day—certainly before next Thursday the 23d upon which day the vote upon the secession ordinance will be cast. The fanatics think the State is really opposed to Secession, and that an invasion of the state will give the Union men courage to vote down the ordinance.[27]

Sunday May 26 1861

The past week has been a very eventful one. The report of the complete demolition of the battery at Sewell's Point proved untrue, the only damage done being the driving away of several negroes engaged preparing the breastworks. We heard the firing distinctly at this place. It continued the whole afternoon, the guns being fired at intervals of about fifteen minutes. We had no guns mounted at the battery; the firing was all from the vessels, the *Monticello* and one or two other vessels that came up to assist her. The next evening there was an actual engagement. Saturday night secretly the Virginians began to mount guns and by 4 o'clock Sunday afternoon three were in position, when they were discovered by those on board of the *Monticello,* then lying a short distance below. Coming up within range, this vessel soon opened upon the battery, which immediately returned the fire. The engagement lasted about an hour, with no damage to the battery, but with so much to the *Monticello* as to force her to retire, apparently in a disabled condition. Two small rifled cannon, which were brought to the assistance of the three heavy guns, it is said were quite efficient.[28]

No one was hurt on our side. Six men according to one account—four

27. On May 23, 1861, Virginia voters ratified the ordinance of secession, which had been drafted the month before, with 128,884 voting in favor and 32,134 voting against.

28. The USS *Monticello* was a 655-ton screw steam gunboat built in 1859 for peaceful purposes but converted into a man-of-war in 1861 by the U.S. Navy. Sewell's Point was one of several Confederates positions fortified to protect the approaches to Norfolk. On May 18 and 19, 1861, the Union navy attacked the battery before it was completed. In addition to the USS *Monticello* (as described by Bernard), the steamer USS *Thomas Freeborn* also took part in the bombardment. The garrison at Sewell's Point, which was commanded by Captain Peyton H. Colquitt of Georgia, consisted of the City Light Guards of Columbus, Georgia, Wood's Rifles of Norfolk, a portion of the Norfolk Juniors, and a detachment of Light Artillery Blues. The exchange of fire at Sewell's Point, described by Bernard, was one of the war's earliest combat episodes in Virginia (see John S. Salmon, *The Virginia Civil War Battlefield Guide* [Mechanicsburg: Stackpole Books, 2001], 67–69).

according to another, were killed on the *Monticello.* Another statement still is that only one person was killed and that one a boy. Although the engagement lasted probably an hour or so, no one at this place, that I know of, heard any firing at all. However, two or three of us who had walked out to St. Helena after supper were told by a member of the Norfolk company stationed at that place that he had heard firing that evening and his captain said there certainly had been fighting somewhere down the river. Returning to our quarters, we heard this statement confirmed and at tattoo[29] we received orders to get ready to march.

I will not now attempt a report of the march we took, but refer to an account given by a correspondent of the *Petersburg Express* published in that paper on the 24th instant. Suffice it to say, we went to Sewell's Point, found [no] enemy[30] there and after resting an hour or two marched back to our quarters at this place, marching in all a distance of twenty miles in less than thirteen hours, marching the whole distance going out in the night time and most of the way through the rain, and returning almost completely used up, but standing the trip in manner surprising to every one, most of us resting ourselves and recovering from our sore feet in the next forty-eight hours.[31]

On yesterday we received news of the occupation of Alexandria by 5,000 Federal troops and of the killing of Colonel Ellsworth of the Zouaves by the heroic Jackson, who died defending the flag of his country, which for several days he had kept floating in sight of the enemy from his hotel. This news has created some sensation. What was meant by General Lee in allowing the act we do not know—many think there is some strategical design in the thing.[32]

29. "Tattoo" is a drum roll or bugle call directing soldiers to their quarters for the night.

30. Bernard's published version says "the enemy" here. His unpublished narrative says "no enemy." The latter appears to be correct.

31. Bernard's unpublished Notebook says here: "About midday on Monday we were back at the Marine Hospital, completely used up by the tramp."

32. Colonel Elmer Ellsworth, a personal friend of President Lincoln, led Union troops into Alexandria, Virginia, on May 25, 1861. Ellsworth entered the Marshall House Inn to remove a Confederate flag that had been hoisted over the establishment. The Inn's enraged owner, James W. Jackson, shot the colonel in the chest. Ellsworth's men immediately killed Jackson. This incident, so early in the war, sparked heated rhetoric on both sides. Many Southerners, as exhibited here by Bernard, believed Jackson acted well within his rights. Northerners, however, viewed the incident as murder, some using the term "assassination" (see Russell Beattie, *Army of the Potomac, Birth of Command* [New York: Basic Books, 2002], 157–58).

Rumor says there was a battle at Hampton this morning. A gentleman just arrived from Craney Island says that at that place this morning from about 5:30 o'clock until about 8 o'clock a continuous musketry fire was heard in the direction of Hampton, the firing being very rapid from 6:30 o'clock to 8:30, whole companies seeming to discharge their pieces together, with the precision of soldiers firing a salute. Nothing however could be seen, even with the aid of glasses.

Service about Norfolk in the Months of April and May, 1861 — The Federal Vessels Attack the Battery at Sewell Point — A March to Sewell's Point[33]

The letter of the correspondent of the Petersburg Express giving an account of the march to Sewell's Point, having the same authorship with the diary, may be properly here reproduced, and was as follows:

> Marine Hospital
> Near Norfolk, Va.
> May 22, 1861

Dear Express: — You have already been advised of the proceedings at Sewell's Point, on Saturday and Sunday, and of the march of troops from this place and about Norfolk to that point on Sunday night, in anticipation of another attack in that quarter. Your readers may wish to know how the Weisiger command and the other gallant fellows who went out with us stood the novelty of a long march, how they found things at the Point, &c. Early Sunday morning we received orders to get ourselves in readiness for a march, and accordingly in a few minutes the whole camp was astir; the packing of knapsacks, trunks, &c., and the cleaning and brushing up of arms and accoutrements being quite different from the usual quiet of a Sabbath morning. Where we were to go no one seemed to know with certainty, although the general opinion was that our destination was Garrison's farm in Princess Anne, a few miles from Norfolk.[34] No orders to march, however, were received until "tattoo." Providing ourselves with two days' rations, and taking along with us our knapsacks, the five companies stationed at this place were soon on their march — to what point going we were still in ignorance, although we rightly believed we were to be carried to Sewell's Point, where

---

33. This article appeared in the *Petersburg Daily Index-Appeal,* May 19, 1901.

34. This should probably say "Harrison's farm," not "Garrison's." Princess Anne was a Virginia county located east of Norfolk along the Atlantic coast in what is now Virginia Beach. In the mid-twentieth century the county merged into neighboring localities, as the result of annexations by the city of Norfolk.

we had heard there had been an engagement that afternoon. Stopping at the National Hotel as we passed through Norfolk, the Richmond Grays, now a part of Colonel Weisiger's regiment, joined the expedition.

Through a drizzling rain, which continued a good portion of the way, and through dismal passages along the road, where it was so dark one could not see his hands before him, briskly and steadily we pushed ahead mile after mile, until the light of day broke upon us as we halted, the rain now rapidly falling, at a point which, if we were not already satisfied of its warlike appearance, with a number of field pieces and horses standing about, was certainly sufficient to convince us was Sewell's Point, the scene of the recent fight. In a few minutes we broke ranks and repaired to the grove that skirts the shore. Here was to be witnessed a spectacle which from its sternness and its ludicrousness I almost despair of describing.

Think of two or three hundred men, like so many sheep, wrapped up head and ears in their blankets, stretched out fast asleep upon the wet ground, under the bushes and against the trees, and at every possible place where could be had scanty shelter from the chilling rain and wind that was driving in from the water. Think of hundreds of others groping about in the woods, looking for something wherewith to start fires, and you have some idea of the appearance of Sewell's Point at daybreak Monday morning, when reached by the boys from Richmond and Petersburg. Bleak, cold and inhospitable, it seemed the dreariest place in the world to us, now fatigued with a forced march of not less than twelve miles. Soon starting several fires, in the hour or two that we remained at the place, most of us warmed and dried ourselves, and visited the breastworks, which were a short distance above the point at which we halted. Here, we saw the evidence of the recent fight, in the broken limbs of trees lying about the breastworks. The battery itself, though struck by both shot and shell, was unhurt.

The coolness and bravery of a young Georgian, about seventeen years of age, a member of the Columbus Light Guards, ought not to be passed over in silence. Something needing attention at the muzzle of one of the guns, then in position pointing through the embrasures, the little fellow, with the coolness and deliberation of a veteran, in the face of the shot and shell which were being poured upon the battery, walked out upon the gun, put in order what was wrong, and returned as coolly and deliberately as he went out. I regret being unable to record the name of one so brave.

Having seen the sights, the order was now given to "fall in," and no little was the difficulty of getting the men together straggling about or asleep as most of them were, and no little, too, was the grumbling—there will be grumbling in the best of causes. Some grumbled because we had to march back, some grumbled because they thought there was a possibility of our not marching back, anything being preferable to remaining there; others, if not all, grumbled because the march itself seemed utterly aimless—nothing more than a wild goose chase. Finally, however, we made the start preceded by a large company of Louisianians. Imagine a body of some seven or eight hundred men, all the companies as it were, blended into one, the men marching at the route step. The column stretching along the road for a mile or more, and you have some idea of the Weisiger regiment, and the Louisianians as they appeared on the march from Sewell's Point. When the line was formed near Norfolk, hardly more than half were to be found—the remainder had tarried behind, or had gone on in advance. It is needless to say that we were tired. A journey of some twenty-four or twenty-five miles had quite broken us down. Some complained of this thing, some of that, but almost all of their feet, which the long walk had blistered. Some suffered so much as to be under the necessity of discarding their shoes and walking home barefooted. But all stood the march remarkably well, and I believe almost all would now be able to go through the same again. Those who suffered from sore feet have generally entirely recovered. It is well, however, to remark that our preference consulted, we will remain here sooner than take the march again.

An attack there to-night is thought not improbable.

Another engagement took place yesterday morning. Only a few shots were exchanged, with what effect we have not heard.

Peter S. Burg.

The following is the next entry in the diary:

Friday May 31, 1861

The report that a battle was fought at Hampton last Sunday morning proved untrue, but the report itself has proved a most remarkable one. On Sunday evening some of the particulars of the fight were given by a person or persons reported to have come over from the scene of operations, and so confidently believed was the rumor that the newspapers of Richmond and Petersburg on Monday morning gave information of it through their telegraphic heads. The *Richmond Dispatch* a day or two afterwards, excusing itself for the error into which it had been led, mentioned the fact that besides the dispatch it had received there had also been received private letters giving details of the battle.

On Monday morning another report reached us of some apparent credibility being brought by a regular bearer of dispatches as he was supposed to be. The report was that 1,500 Federal troops had landed in Currituck N.C.[35] This report has also proved untrue. But it would be idle for me to attempt to enumerate all of the various stories which Madam Rumor is continually putting afloat.

Every day develops new indications of the intention of the North acting through the Federal Government to subdue us if possible. The occupation of Alexandria on Friday last by 5,000 men and its further reinforcement by 7,000 more and the landing of 2,500 at Newport's News on the 27th last are acts quite unequivocal—they are positive invasions of the soil of Virginia, now one of the Confederate States. Maryland & Missouri are already in the hands of the Federal Government—it seems in almost hopeless subjection.

The presence of several thousand hostile troops keeps and will keep for some time thousands of Southern men in those states from asserting their rights, and it is to be feared that the same thing will be true of poor Kentucky, which yet lingers in the old Union. Had not Virginia, at the time she did, as the *Richmond Examiner* says, upon being insulted by Lincoln's proclamation of the 15th of April, after she had spent weeks in efforts to reconcile her erring sisters indignantly walked out of the Union like an old queen, she too might have ere this shared the fate of Maryland and Missouri. Even now portions of her territory are subjected to the rule of the Northern dynasty. At this moment freedom of speech is not allowed a citizen of Virginia in the City of Alexandria. A secessionist who would proclaim his opinions would soon find himself hurried before the Lincoln authorities to be tried—no doubt nominally only—as a traitor.

But this war will prove a bootless one to the North. As for conquering the South it is something simply impossible. Beside the advantage of fighting on our own soil, our population, not so much inferior to theirs in point of numbers, furnishes a material for war conceded on all sides to be *much* superior to theirs. Then too this war knits together and builds us up, whilst it ruins them. It is true that they will have on their side the prestige of the old Government, its flag, its army, its navy. Whilst in the latter they have an arm of strength which has already given us trouble and is likely to give us more, the army is but nothing scarcely, the great strength of the United States as a military power having always rested in her volunteers—and the flag is mere moonshine.

35. Currituck is located on North Carolina's coast on the Currituck Sound near the Virginia border.

George S. Bernard War Narrative: June 14, 1861 – May 8, 1862

[The following entries are part of Bernard's unpublished manuscript titled "Narrative" and recount the remainder of Bernard's experiences in Norfolk up to the beginning of the Richmond Campaign in 1862.[36]]

Friday June 14, 1861

... It cannot be long before our military authorities will make a decided movement against the enemy. To judge from the large number of troops that have been daily poured into Virginia for several weeks, there cannot be less than 125,000 at present in the State. It is said that two or three days ago there were only two or three companies in Richmond. The large number of troops which have been collecting there have been sent off—a large proportion to Manassas Gap Junction, where it is said there are now 80,000 men. Much secrecy has been wisely observed as to the number & destination of our forces, the newspapers prudently refraining from publishing anything which would give the enemy a clue to our operations. Spies in our midst keep them well enough informed.

PICKET DUTY AT THE HARDY HOUSE

Rumor says another engagement has taken place at Philippi in which our forces were victorious.[37] Gov—I should have said *General*—Wise[38] will soon be over in that part of the State with his guerilla *legion,* and will do no little to strike terror into the enemy. His brigade is fast filling up. The men arm themselves with what weapons they please—rifles, double barrel shotguns, pistols, bowie knives &c &c. This band is likely to prove as effective as any in the service and Gov Wise is just the man to command it.

Our encampment at this point is fast breaking up. The B Greys, Capt. Bond,[39] left this morning for the entrenched camp at Harrison's farm.[40] Two

36. Written in Bernard's hand, the documents are housed in the George S. Bernard Papers, Perkins Library, Duke University.

37. On June 3, 1861, Union forces under Brigadier General Thomas A. Morris converged at Phillipi, Virginia (now West Virginia), and soundly defeated a smaller Confederate force there led by Colonel George A. Porterfield. The thorough rout became known as the "Philippi Races."

38. Brigadier General Henry Alexander Wise had previously been governor of Virginia.

39. Thomas H. Bond, a railroad station agent before the war, enlisted as captain of Company C of the 12th Virginia in April 1861. He resigned his commission in August 1862, and later mustered into the Virginia State Reserves (Hood's Battalion) in 1864. After the war, he was commissioner of revenue in Petersburg.

40. Harrison's Farm was near Tanner's Creek, north of Norfolk.

other companies are already there, the A Greys, Capt. Lyon,[41] and the Lafayette Guards, Capt. Jarvis,[42] having gone down several days ago. We who
remain, the City Guards & the Riflemen, expect to leave about next Monday.
We will leave with regret our pleasant quarters and the many kind people who
live around the place, and who on Friday last gave most substantial evidence
of this kindness in a sumptuous dinner which they prepared for those of our
regiment then on the *point,* which dinner we enjoyed no little. We have thus
far omitted to mention the devoted kindness of the "Hardy" family who re-
side in an elegant brick establishment near the draw bridge spanning the river
to Norfolk, at which point we have had a *picket* post for several weeks. Since
the first establishment of the post at that point Mr. Hardy has regularly every
day furnished the guard of eight or ten men with their meals and a bed in his
house upon which to sleep when not on duty at night. The proprietor of the
"Hardy" mansion is a brother of H. C. Hardy, formerly of Petersburg.

Sunday, June 16, 1861

... The Riflemen & City Guards have orders to leave for the entrenched
camp tomorrow. One of our company, C. Holmes Clarke,[43] formerly of
Clarke Co. Va., on yesterday afternoon attempted suicide by taking lauda-
num. When he drank the deadly drug he was on board the little foot boat
which plies between Norfolk and Ferry Point under the escort of a corporal
and one man who had been sent to bring him from Norfolk where he had
overstaid his permit several hours. It is said he has been unfortunate, having
married a woman much beneath him, an actress, from whom he separated,
and it is also said his father disinherited him on account of the marriage. A
party of us prevented him from falling asleep last night by keeping him constantly walking, slapping him, pinching him and otherwise worrying him.

Entrenched Camp Wednesday
June 19, 1861

Bidding farewell to our pleasant quarters at the Marine Hospital and to
our friends on the Point on Monday afternoon about 1 o'clock we started for

---

41. John Lyon, a Petersburg lawyer, joined the 12th Virginia in April 1861 as captain
of Company B. He served in various capacities throughout the war, including judge
advocate and mustering officer. After the war, he continued his law practice and worked
in Petersburg, Richmond, and Washington.

42. William H. Jarvis, proprietor of a Petersburg grocery store before the war, enlisted as the captain of Company D in the 12th Virginia in April 1861. He received a
furlough several months later. During the last two years of the war, he served in the
Virginia State Reserves. He was captured as Petersburg fell in April 1865.

43. Charles H. Clarke, a civil engineer, enlisted as a private in Company E of the
12th Virginia in April 1861. He transferred to the cavalry in 1862.

this place, at which we arrived after an hour's march very wet and miry from the morning's rain. The portion of the cornfield assigned our company as its camp limits seemed particularly uninviting to men who had just vacated the spacious & comfortable rooms, passage & corridor of the Marine Hospital. But we soon set to work and before night had pitched the sixteen tents allowed the company, which with the pieces of timber we picked up about the encampment we rendered quite respectable resting places for the night. Very much fatigued by the march and the evening's work we enjoyed the hot coffee prepared us by our cook and upon retiring to our tents found no difficulty in soon surrendering ourselves to old Morpheus.

On yesterday we had a busy day. In accordance with orders our tents were to be pulled down, the grounds laid off and leveled, ditches dug &c. So at 8 o'clock in the morning we began work and not until quite "tattoo" had we finished the *street* between the rows of tents and repitched our tents. Again today we will be as busily engaged as on yesterday, having not yet laid the floors of our tents. These tents, each occupied by five or six men, I have no doubt we will soon prefer to quarters of any other kind—certainly until winter sets in. In our tent there are at present six—Julian Beckwith, Emmet Butts, Miles Branch, Robertdeau Holderby, Jim Wilson and myself.[44] Thus far we have been much pleased at finding this place (Harrison's Farm) better in so many respects than we had anticipated from the various accounts we had of it.

The papers of yesterday & the day before bring the surprising news of the

44. In the brief biographies of these tentmates of Bernard's is covered much of the history of the war. All of the men were initially members of Company E of the 12th Virginia. A clerk in Petersburg, Julian R. Beckwith enlisted as a private in April 1861; he was killed in action at Seven Pines in 1862. Robert Emmet Butts was a student from Petersburg who enlisted in May 1861. He was sick for much of his time in the service, returning to duty in March 1864, only to be killed in action at the Battle of the Crater. Miles B. Branch, of Petersburg, worked for grocery and commission merchants before the war, and joined the service in April 1861 at the age of twenty-eight. Discharged in 1862, he then purchased a substitute, and later served in the Virginia State Reserves from 1864 to 1865. He survived the war. Andrew Robert ("Robertdeau") Holderby was a graduate of Hampden-Sydney College and working as a teacher in Petersburg when the war began. He enlisted as a private in April 1861, but soon thereafter received a medical discharge (August 1861). He helped in hospitals for much of the war, and served in the Virginia State Reserves in 1864 during the Battle of Petersburg. After the war, he earned a Doctor of Divinity degree and became a well-known Presbyterian minister. James R. Wilson, of Scotland, was working as a bookkeeper in Petersburg when the war began. He enlisted in April 1861. He was discharged the following year, and not required to serve, as he was a "citizen of a foreign nation."

evacuation of Harper's Ferry by our troops on Friday last. It is believed to be a mere strategic move.

Sunday, June 23, 1861

... Harper's Ferry is again in our possession. The Federal troops did not occupy it when evacuated by Gen. Johnston.

POLITICAL NEWS

Wednesday, June 26, 1861

Events of interest continue to transpire with a rapidity which makes it quite difficult to keep up with them. At Wheeling during the past week a bogus State convention has repudiated the action of the Convention at Richmond, declaring its acts null & void and that the offices of the present Governor and Lieutenant Governor were rendered vacant by their revolutionary & treasonable acts. To these offices the "Tory" Convention has appointed Frank P. [H.] Pierpont and ... John S. Carlisle it has appointed to the Federal Congress.[45] All of this is due to the 20,000 votes cast against the Ordinance of Secession at the late election. In Tennessee a similar Convention has been in session, but appears to have gone not quite so far as the Wheeling Convention, not declaring any offices vacant.

The Richmond Convention has chosen delegates to the Confederate Congress which meets in Richmond on the 24th of July. The following selections were made: 1st District R. M. T. Hunter, 2nd Jno. Tyler, 3rd Wm. H. MacFarland, 4th Roger A. Pryor, 5th Thos. A. Bocock, 6th Wm. C. Rives, 7th Ro. E. Scott, 8th Jas. M. Mason, 9th Jno. W. Brockenborough, 10th Chas. W. Russell, 11th Ro. Johnston, 12th Walter R. Staples, 13th Walter Preston, At Large Jas. A. Seddon for Eastern Va., Wm. Ballard Preston for Western Va.[46]

This delegation comprises men [not] originally *secessionists* and men who were for submission until driven by the Federal administration to take the step of secession.... It is thought by many that this war will be brought to an early termination. They think that the *peace* resolutions recently passed by one or two Northern Legislatures indicate such a revolution of public senti-

45. A convention of leaders from western Virginia counties, as well as Fairfax and Alexandria, met in Wheeling from June 11 to 25, 1861. The convention chose Francis H. Pierpoint as the governor of the "Reorganized" Government of Virginia. In July, the new legislature elected John S. Carlisle and Waitman T. Willey to the U.S. Senate. The activities of these leaders led to the eventual creation of the state of West Virginia in 1863.

46. A history of the work of this convention and biographies of delegates noted by Bernard can be found in Ezra Warner and W. Buck Yearns, *Biographical Register of the Confederate Congress* (Baton Rouge: Louisiana State University Press, 1975).

ment at the North as will stop the war. I can but hold a different opinion. It would be surprising should there be no opposition to so iniquitous a war as this. It is indeed surprising there has been so little. When the Federal Congress meets, which will be on the 4th of July next, the fanatics of that body will doubtless unhesitatingly pass the necessary laws appropriating money for the prosecution of the war, which they regard a war to suppress a rebellion. The limited resources of the North will be an obstacle to the prosecution of the war. But there is but little doubt that the people of that section having now fully entered into the *enterprise* will resort to every device to carry it through. A National Bank is even talked of.

HOW THE RIFLEMEN SPEND THE 4TH OF JULY 1861

July 4, 1861

... We heard the National Salute fired at Fortress Monroe today. The Riflemen have spent the day putting up *awnings* to their tents. These awnings are a present from Lt. J. Willcox Brown.

A VISIT TO CRANEY ISLAND

Wednesday July 10, 1861

Visited Craney Island yesterday morning in company with Everard Meade. Taking the "through way" to Norfolk as it is termed, we enjoyed no little the delightful fragrance inhaled in the early morning from green trees & wild flowers in the woods as we passed along the beautifully shaded paths, so invigorating was it and so vividly did it call up other places & other circumstances. Reaching the little steamer, it was not long before we were under way and were passing the batteries at the Naval Hospital and Fort Norfolk, were viewing with our open glasses those at Penner's & Lambert's Points and were straining our eyes to discern those at Boush's Bluff and Sewell's Point, both of which are quite concealed by trees &c. Arrived at Craney Island we were soon up in the parapets, looking towards Fortress Monroe & Newport News, at both of which places we could plainly see a number of old Abe's craft, the huge man of war, the *Cumberland,* looming up like a great leviathan before the walls of Fortress Monroe. The view was quite interesting. No tents of the enemy were to be seen at Newport News, as could have been seen a few days since, lining the shore for a mile or more. At Craney Island, we were shown a battle ground of the war of 1812, where our forces engaged the British. The enemy had first attempted to pass their ships up the river, being foiled in which by the fire of our battery on the Island, they disembarked and attempted to carry the place by a land attack, fording the shallow water, which separates the island from the main land. The circular earthwork in the Northern part of the island still remains, as do the foundations of the old Round Tower, to which our men were forced to retire when driven from the breastworks, and from which they delivered a raking fire upon the advancing British. We were so fortunate as to meet with an old negro drummer who was present on the occasion of the fight, the veritable old negro who was the subject of an incident related in the *Petersburg Express* a few weeks ago. From his own lips we heard his story. The day he left the Island in 1813 he buried his pipe, after which he thought of it no more until returning to the Island with his master a few months ago, when the old pipe was brought to mind, upon which he told his friends he had buried it at a certain place in 1813 and that he intended to go & look for it. Though ridiculed for even the idea of finding it, the old fellow persisted in making the search, and upon digging for the old relict and to the surprise of all found the identical pipe buried 48 years ago.[47]

A VISIT TO THE NAVY YARD

Upon our return to Norfolk, we went immediately over to the Navy Yard where we were much pleased to see the progress made by those in charge. The old *United States*—an old hulk—has been made a floating battery, and the guns pointing from her port holes look fierce enough. The *Germantown,* another old hulk, which was sunk by the Federals, has been raised, as also the *Plymouth* a three masted vessel. The *Merrimac,* which was burnt to the water's edge, has also been raised and is now in the drydock. To judge from what now remains of her, she was a monster steamer.

The Navy Yard is undoubtedly well protected on the landside. The long brick wall pierced with holes for small arms and six or eight thirty two pounders ranging along at intervals will furnish no small protection. To pass along through the various spacious buildings in which are stored away vast quantities of seasoned timber, and through the many workshops of different sorts, and to consider at the same time what immense quantities of arms and other material of war have already been removed from this place, one is almost overpowered with an appreciation of good fortune in getting so much that is valuable at the hands of the enemy. It is estimated that property good & recoverable to the amount of $40,000,000 at least was left in our hands by the abandonment of the Navy Yard.

47. Fortress Monroe (also known as "Fort Monroe"), located at Old Point Comfort on the James River peninsula, commanded the main shipping channel into Hampton Roads and Norfolk.

MARCHING ORDERS

Tuesday, July 23, 1861

A furlough of six days commencing July 23 & a trip to Petersburg during which nothing of especial interest occurred, beyond the general excitement & glorification of the people everywhere over the victory at Manassas.

Monday, August 12, 1861

On Saturday last the long expected paymaster reached this place and performed the agreeable operation of paying us off. This personage has so frequently been expected and as frequently disappointed expectations, he had come to be regarded as perhaps a mythical character. His *spare change* however is very acceptable to the men, with most of whom the *wherewithall* had become scarce to a very troublesome degree.

Tuesday, August 27, 1861

The monotony of camp life at this place was on yesterday broken by a dispatch from Headquarters directing Col. Weisiger to get his regiment in readiness to move out at a moment's notice, supplied with two days' rations. The order was received last evening just after dress parade, when we were all at supper, and was the occasion of considerable cheering. But a few minutes sufficed to put the camp in a general *stir*. The spectacle of five hundred men hurrying to & fro providing ammunition, packing their knapsacks, &c &c. and the whole camp brightly illuminated by the various fires of the cooks preparing our rations, was from its novelty quite interesting. By tattoo all were in readiness to move and anxious for the order, but none came. Yet our orders were to sleep with our accoutrements where we could easily "put our hands upon them."

Up to the present time—dress parade—no order to move has reached us. It is generally supposed our destination is Willoughby's Point, where it is said our authorities propose erecting batteries to annoy the enemy's shipping near Fortress Monroe.

The above is the last entry we find in my journal bearing date at Harrison's farm. The following furnishes the explanation.

SICKNESS

Monday, Dec. 23, 1861, Orange Co. Va.

Since it was last my pleasure to write in this little book many have been the changes and much have I undergone. A severe attack of sickness—intermittent bilious fever—as the doctors called it, has transformed me once more into a *civilian*. The disease I think is to be attributed to imprudently *bathing* in one of the creeks near our encampment, going into the water as I did so late in the season as September, and at an unfavorable time of the day, about 11 o'clock in the morning. Feeling unwell for two or three days afterwards, two hours' guard duty an exceedingly sultry morning—I think the morning of Wednesday, Sept 4th—made me quite sick, upon which going to my tent, I took my bed and continued to grow worse until the following Monday when at my request to be removed from my tent, I was transferred to very good quarters in one of the regimental hospital tents and Everard Meade detailed as my nurse. For seven weeks I was confined to my bed a helpless invalid, a portion of the time so sick as to excite some fears as to my recovery. After seven weeks' confinement in the hospital tent, it was my good fortune to be carried to the house of Mr. Ths. G. Broughton Jr. in Norfolk City, where the kind attentions of himself & Mrs. Broughton soon "brought me out," though it was more than a week before I could leave my bed & another still before I ventured to leave my room.[48]

The extract from his journal above given furnishes some account of a severe spell of fever in the fall of '61, which resulted in the discharge of the writer from the army, who went to his father's in Orange Co. as soon as his condition permitted the fatigue of the trip, arrived at which place he rapidly recovered his health, to an extent sufficient to enable him to undertake a school in Greensville Co. Va. in January. "Fair View Academy," immediately on the Weldon R Road and about 2 miles from Jarratt's Depot, was the place, whereat "for a brief space" he experienced some of the "trials & tribulations" of pedagoging. Let the journal speak for itself:

TEACHING SCHOOL

Greensville Co. Va.

Feb. 5, 1862

Reached this county Thursday Jan. 23rd, the opening of my school being deferred by the trustees until Jan. 27th. Had a pleasant time at Ned Wyatt's until Saturday afternoon, when I came to this place (Mr. R. Goggin Gregg's), where I am boarding. Opened school the following Monday with ten scholars. Four more came in during the week—Andw. F. Creath, Saml. Creath, Geo. Seaborn and Jas. D. Brown. The number increased this week by the entering of Wm. St. Clair Bailey, Jno. Watkins, Wm. F. Hobbs, Wm. Dilliard

---

48. Without further description, it is hard to tell whether Bernard contracted malaria or typhoid fever, though the former seems more likely. Henry Everard Meade, his hospital assistant and a private in Company E of the 12th Virginia Infantry (enlisted in June 1861), would die of typhoid fever in July 1862.

and Wm. Watkins. Upon the arrival of Kidder Friend, who has been engaged, the school will number twenty.

The business no less disagreeable than was apprehended, it proves a severe tax upon my powers of endurance. I fear that considerations of health will necessitate my giving up the school very soon. I have certainly improved none since leaving Orange, but believe I have lost both flesh & strength. As regards my new home, I am pleasantly situated, except to one particular. I have no less than four boys as *roommates!* And they are not the best boys in the world. I mean to request a *change.*

Greensville Co.,
Monday, Feb. 10, 1862

Went up to see Cousin Ned Wyatt[49] last Friday afternoon. As usual spent a very pleasant time. Attended church yesterday morning, where we had a very good sermon from Mr. Galusha. After church Cousin N & I went home with Cousin Geo. Field & returned to Cousin N's after dinner. Reached schoolhouse this morning nearly an hour after my usual time, which was due to "Peter's" failing to receive Cousin N's message directing an early breakfast. My boys I am sure did not object to my late arrival. Two new scholars this morning, Kidder Friend and Jno. A. H. Whitehorne, the latter quite a little fellow. A scholar refused admission this morning by one of the trustees on the ground of the school being full. Teaching continues exceedingly irksome to me. A combination of circumstances alone forces me to it for the present—a combination which I pray may never re-occur.

STIRRING NEWS

The papers of today & yesterday bring news of Confederate reverses on the Tennessee River & at Roanoke Island, reverses which seem to be rather serious. Our loss at Roanoke Island is nearly 3000 men, killed, wounded & prisoners. There was hard fighting there on Friday & Saturday last and the island is now in the possession of the Yankees. The news from the west is that Fort Henry on the Tennessee River has been taken and the Memphis & Ohio Railroad bridge destroyed. A dispatch from Memphis, dated Feb. 8th, says the Yankees have gone up the river as far as Florence & Tuscumbia, which places are in Alabama. This looks rather serious, and the intelligence of these movements is creating some sensation.[50]

49. Bernard may have exerted some peer pressure on "Cousin Ned" to join the service: Edward Wyatt enlisted in Company F of the 12th Virginia in March 1862, and transferred to Company C the following year.

50. Bernard refers here to the fall of Forts Henry and Donelson to Ulysses S. Grant in February 1862 and the capture of Roanoke Island by Union forces under Ambrose

JOINING THE MEHERRIN GRAYS[51]

Greensville Co.,
Saturday, Feb. 15, 1862

Unexpectedly went to Petersburg Thursday afternoon. Returned last evening & am teaching today to make up time lost. Think of returning to the service. This indeed partly the object of my trip to Petersburg. The recent disasters to our arms are arousing everyone. Large numbers of twelve months' volunteers are reenlisting and new companies are forming. I still think the war is to last at least twelve months longer. Many however think differently. I was laughed at in Petersburg a few weeks ago for not thinking it would end as early as next May. We are bound to succeed ultimately, but the Yankees think differently. Their confidence of success will serve to keep up the war for some time. We have relied too much upon foreign aid, such as England & France would render by breaking the blockade, should they recognize the Confederacy. The blockade is of great service to us. Its sudden removal would materially injure us by frustrating our infant manufactures.

We find in our little book no further entries for several months. The times were stirring and eventful, and we trusted to memory to retain what transpired. On the 22nd of February we enlisted at Belfield in Greensville Co. as a member of a company gotten up by Dick Jones[52] & Dick Manson[53] of Greensville and Dr. Nicholson[54] of Brunswick, composed mainly of men

---

Burnside on February 8, 1862. After the fall of Fort Henry, Union gunboats churned up the Tennessee River and destroyed the Memphis & Ohio Railroad bridge there.

51. The Meherrin Grays formed in Greensville County in February 1862 and soon became incorporated into the 12th Virginia as Company I.

52. Richard Watson Jones, son of a wealthy Greensville County landowner, enlisted as a captain of Company I of the 12th Virginia in February 1862. He rose to the rank of major, and commanded the regiment when it surrendered at Appomattox. After the war he served as a professor of chemistry and administrator at a number of Southern colleges.

53. Joseph Richard Manson was a Brunswick County planter, Methodist lay minister, and Petersburg wholesale commission merchant. Married to Charlotte Ashby, Manson was distantly related to Bernard, whose mother was Elizabeth Ashby. Both men were related to Brigadier General Turner Ashby. Manson helped Jones organize Company I of the 12th Virginia, then served faithfully for three years, including a time as a prisoner-of-war. After the war, he resumed his duties as a planter.

54. Samuel Nicholson enlisted as a 2nd lieutenant in Company I in February 1862, and would remain at that rank despite being court-martialed in February 1863 for being absent without leave (he received a private reprimand from the regimental commander). He resigned the next month, reenlisted as a private, then received a discharge by furnishing a substitute.

from those two counties, & which organized at Belfield on the 22nd of Feby, by electing as its officers Dick Jones Captain, Dick Manson 1st Lieutenant, Dr. Nicholson 2nd Lieutenant and Smith Green[55] as 3rd Lieutenant. The company being organized, Capt. Jones dismissed it with orders to report at Belfield on Wednesday the 13th of March in readiness to take the train for Petersburg, where we were to be mustered into service. Having joined this company, I succeeded in getting the trustees of the school to accept my friend, Weller Meade, as my substitute, and having equipped myself for service reported, as ordered, at Belfield on Wednesday afternoon, the 13th of March.

THE PETERSBURG MILITIA AT POPLAR LAWN

The heterogeneous collection of rough country men I found at the depot and the constantly arriving squads of the same gave me no pleasant anticipation of social enjoyment among my new comrades. Yet there were a few, whom I at once found were congenial spirits. The next morning, *the line* being formed—a *long,* but not a very well *dressed* line it was—Capt. Jones read out his appointments of noncommissioned officers, among which he had placed myself with the rank of 3rd sergeant.

Embarked on the train, after a rough ride in the freight boxes we reached Petersburg about one o'clock in the afternoon, and at Jarratt's Hotel were regularly mustered into service by a Major Bradford, which ceremony being over, the company was at once marched to Indiana, in the western suburbs of the city where we were assigned the dwelling house as our quarters. Here for several days we spent quite a pleasant time, having no duty to perform beyond drilling, feasting on the profuse quantities of good eatables the men had brought from home with them, and enjoying the *novelty* of the life. But we were soon broken up by an order removing us to the Poplar Lawn, our company being called upon by Col. Wm. Pannill, the Provost Marshall of the city, to assist in doing duty in & around the city. Just here, we may mention that all the militia of the city had been called out and were quartered at the Lawn. The object of the call was mainly for *police* purposes, but it occasioned no little stir & excitement among the *"milish"* & the people generally. We have often been amused when recalling the scenes & incidents of those days—the public highways leading into the city picketed as heavily as if the enemy were at any time expected to make his appearance thereon. Every man, woman & child who passed halted & passports demanded, the militia officers

---

55. Stephen "Smith" Green enlisted as a 2nd lieutenant with Company I in February 1862, but was dismissed in June 1862 for deserting his command during the Battle of Seven Pines.

of the day, with flaming red sashes, dashing about town seemingly bent on the most urgent business, officers of the guard just from the outposts coming in with countenances which fully indicated their thorough appreciation of the responsibility of their trusts & reporting that "all was quiet," and lastly our friend Jimmy McCulloch,[56] acting "adjutant of the post."

Whilst our company was quartered at the Lawn I succeeded in getting a furlough of ten days to visit my father's family in Orange.

REJOINING THE 12TH REGT.

Our company had but recently been organized when arrangements were made to incorporate it into the 12th Va. Regiment of Infantry, then stationed at Norfolk on Harrison's farm. Accordingly in obedience to orders bidding adieu to our militia friends & their provost duties, and to our drills & dress parades on Poplar Lawn,[57] on the morning of Saturday, the 19th of April, we took the cars for Norfolk, arrived at which place the company was at once marched to the encampment of the 12th Regt. at Harrison's farm, where we found a sufficiency of quarters—A tents—in readiness for us, our company grounds having been previously laid off and our tents pitched.

It is almost needless to say that the veterans of the 12th seemed to regard us newcomers with considerable interest, and evidently felt a small amount of pride in contrasting their discipline & experience with the awkward greenness of "The Herrings," as they styled *the Meherrin Grays.* Col. Weisiger could not be horrified by the sight of such recruits at his brilliant *dress parades,* and accordingly we were spared that annoyance. We were in need of drillmasters too, so privates from the other companies were detailed to drill "the Herrings" in squads, and so deficient were we thought to be, on the *Sunday* before we left Norfolk, the "Herrings" were drilled by special order, no other companies being drilled on Sunday.

THE 12TH VA. REGT. AT HARRISON'S FARM

At Harrison's farm we found the other companies of the regiment most comfortably quartered in neatly constructed houses, living almost *in luxury.* As to eatables, they were faring sumptuously. Rations were still abundant and the Norfolk market afforded the extras. The rooms in the quarters were provided

56. "Jimmy McCulloch" may be Patrick D. McCulloch, son of a wealthy Petersburg tobacconist. McCulloch enlisted in Company C of the 12th Virginia in April 1861. Promoted to corporal later that year, he was killed in action at Seven Pines.

57. Poplar Lawn Park, an open space in Petersburg approximately 200 yards square, is bordered by Sycamore and South Jefferson Streets.

with "bunks" and all the messes generally indulged in the luxury of cooks & dining room servants. The men seemed really to enjoy the life they were leading. Let us mention here that there prevailed throughout the regiment a great laxity of discipline compared with that which had previously ruled both officers & men almost to the letter of the army regulations. The reason was to be found in the *elections* which were soon to be held at the reorganizations of the companies of the regiment.

My tentmates now were Tommy Pritchard, O. H. Hammonds, Abner Steed, Ned Jolly, and John Jones. Fred Lanier & Sandy Mallory were normally with us, but were absent sick. Of these young men a word at this time may not be out of place. The first, Tommy Pritchard, quite a youth, scarcely 18 years of age, was with us but a short time. Disease contracted but a few days after the battle of Seven Pines, when with the company at that horrid old "mud camp" on the Charles City Road, necessitated his being sent first the field hospital & then to Chimborazo in Richmond, where he died much regretted by all of us comrades.

Young Hammonds, after serving with the company, through several campaigns, received in the battle of Brandy Station, Culpeper Co., Saturday afternoon Aug. 1, 1863 a severe wound through the leg, of which he died a few weeks afterwards at his home in Brunswick.

In the same action, John Jones received a severe wound through the arm & chest, I think, from which he never sufficiently recovered to be fit for active service. Ned Jolly was severely wounded through the leg in the battle of Second Manassas, August 31st 1862, and was never afterwards fit for service. Abner Steed, after passing through almost a dozen engagements untouched, being one of the brigade sharpshooters, in the little engagement of Bradshaw's Farm, Spotsylvania Co., Sunday afternoon, May 8, 1864, was severely wounded through the arm & both hands, and was never afterwards fit for service. Fred Lanier[58] I think was never wounded and Sandy Mallory furnished a substitute soon after the Richmond Campaign in '62 and I think never afterwards joined the army.

EVACUATION OF NORFOLK

Our stay at Harrison's Farm was short. The movements of McClellan on the Peninsula[59] rendering Norfolk untenable, early in May preparations were

58. Lanier was captured at the Battle of Burgess Mill on October 27, 1864. Bernard's brief account of each man can be verified and supplemented in Henderson, *12th Virginia Infantry*, 106–67.

59. Bernard refers to the Peninsula Campaign begun by Major General George Brinton McClellan.

made to evacuate this portion of Virginia. On Wednesday afternoon, May 7th orders reached our regimental headquarters to get in readiness for a march. One battalion of the regiment in which was Capt. Jones's company, now called "Co. I," were before sunset marching through the streets of Norfolk, *en route* for the Petersburg Depot. It was indeed a sad evening to us. The streets were filled with ladies, most of whom seemed the picture of despair. By 10 o'clock next morning our train had reached Petersburg and we were marching to the Poplar Lawn where we pitched our tents & quietly awaited the arrival of the remainder of the regiment, which reached the city the following Sunday afternoon.

2

The Richmond
Campaign of 1862

IN EARLY 1862, the U.S. War Department set its sights on the Confederate capital. In late March, the Army of the Potomac, under the command of General George B. McClellan, disembarked at Fort Monroe and headed west toward Richmond. By May, McClellan had forced the Confederates, led by General Joseph Johnston, to abandon positions at Yorktown. The Union advance along the peninsula formed by the James and York Rivers effectively isolated Norfolk and forced the Confederates to abandon the city and port there. Bernard and the 12th Virginia joined the withdrawal west toward Petersburg and Richmond.

As Johnston's army established defensive positions outside Richmond in mid-May, Mahone's Virginia brigade (including the 12th Virginia) received orders to help protect Drewry's Bluff, a strong position south of Richmond where artillery emplacements overlooked the James River. Shortly before eight in the morning on May 15, a Federal naval squadron led by the ironclad *Monitor* appeared downriver. A sharp engagement followed as the Confederate batteries on the high bluff hurled shells down on the *Monitor,* the *Galena,* and other attacking vessels. After more than three hours of combat, the Union vessels withdrew — some of them seriously damaged by the plunging fire from rebel batteries. The action at Drewry's Bluff effectively ended Union hopes of taking Richmond by ascending the James. The success of the Confederate guns freed the 12th Virginia and other infantry units to fight with the rest of Johnston's army against McClellan's army east of the capital.

An engineer by training, McClellan believed that siege operations and heavy artillery would bring about Richmond's fall. His plan yielded a deliberate, cautious approach. But by late May, the Union army found itself astride the swampy Chickahominy River, in a dangerously exposed position as it inched westward. Sensing opportunity, Johnston ordered a major Confederate attack on Union forces isolated south of the Chickahominy. Johnston's action precipitated the Battle of Seven Pines. On the first day of the fight, confusing or misunderstood orders tangled rebel attacking columns into a massive traffic jam and delayed the assault. The disjointed affair yielded thousands of casualties but no decisive result. A wound received by General Johnston late in the afternoon, however, triggered one of the war's most significant command changes when, on the following day, President Jefferson Davis directed General Robert E. Lee to command the Confederate army defending Richmond.

Bernard's unit did not participate until the battle's second day. On that morning, the regiment advanced into its first significant combat of the war. It was a violent, bewildering experience. As recounted by Bernard and his correspondents, the resulting casualties were high and there was little advantage gained by either side that day.

Several weeks of relative inaction followed Seven Pines. On June 25, though, McClellan launched a limited attack at Oak Grove (or "French's Farm" as referred to by Bernard). On that day, the 12th Virginia marched from its positions and into combat. However, the Union probe achieved nothing, and the next day Lee unleashed his own offensive. Once in charge of Confederate forces around Richmond, Robert E. Lee had strengthened his lines while looking for an opportunity to seize the initiative. Wed to the unwavering view that aggressive offensive operations held the key to Confederate victory, he sought to drive McClellan back to Washington. With Jackson's army arriving in secret from the Shenandoah Valley, Lee concentrated most of his force for a decisive blow against the Union Fifth Corps isolated on the north side of the Chickahominy. He left a meager force, including the 12th Virginia, to the south, standing between the bulk of the Union army and Richmond. During two days of fierce combat, Lee's men lurched forward and finally drove the Fifth Corps south over the river at the Battle of Gaines Mill.

In response to these initial rebel victories north of the Chickahominy, McClellan abandoned his supply line and ordered a full-scale retreat south to the James River and the protection of Union gunboats. Lee sought to annihilate the enemy. At Savage Station, Glendale (or Frayser's Farm), and finally Malvern Hill, the Confederates threw themselves at the retreating column. Lee's inexperienced army, however, could not land a decisive blow. Nevertheless, this series of battles yielded final Confederate victory in this campaign (often referred to as the "Seven Days"). The 12th Virginia's part of Benjamin

Huger's division took part in the fighting at Frayser's Farm (spelled "Frazier's" by Bernard) and lost heavily during the assault at Malvern Hill.

Three decades later, on the evening of March 1, 1894, Bernard delivered a long address before the A. P. Hill Camp, titled "From Drewry's Bluff to Seven Pines." A transcript of this speech along with additional notes appeared in a series of articles published in the *Petersburg Daily Index-Appeal* in 1903.[1]

This series also included an account of Bernard's experiences during the Seven Days' battles, titled "From Seven Pines to Malvern Hill." Earlier in 1880s, Bernard also wrote an article on the Battle of Malvern Hill which appeared in the *Index-Appeal* (and was subsequently published in the *Southern Historical Society Papers*). We have included an excerpt from that article here. In the 1890s, Bernard prepared additional information on this battle, including a letter from General William Mahone sent to Bernard shortly before the general's death. A handwritten version of Mahone's letter and other notes gathered by Bernard, titled "Addenda," is found in Bernard's papers at the University of North Carolina, and has been reproduced in this chapter.[2]

>━○━◄▶┤◄┄┄┄▷┤◀▶━○━◄

"War Recollections: From Drewry's Bluff to Seven Pines," by George S. Bernard

The Engagement with the Federal Gunboats May 15, 1862, and the Battle of June 1, 1862 [3]

Comrades: Having been requested by the commander of our camp to read before you a paper giving some account of experiences in the Confederate army during the campaign, in the months of May and June, 1862, around Richmond, I have collated from a note book in which I wrote out in the latter

---

1. See the *Petersburg Daily Index-Appeal* for June 14, 21, and 28, and July 6 and 12, 1903. The heading in each article states "from MSS. of Geo. S. Bernard's 'War Talks of Confederate Veterans, Vol. II.'"

2. See the Bernard Malvern Hill article in the *Petersburg Daily Index-Appeal* for September 26, 1887; and the *Southern Historical Society Papers* (52 vols., Richmond: Virginia Historical Society, 1876–1959) [hereafter *SHSP*], 18:57–71.

3. This article appeared in the *Petersburg Daily Index-Appeal* on Sunday, June 14, 1903. The heading also states, "An Address Delivered Before A. P. Hill Camp of Confederate Veterans, of Petersburg, VA, by George S. Bernard, on the Evening of Thursday, the 1st of March, 1894."

part of 1865, or in the early part of 1866, my recollections of this period of service in the Confederate army, and from other sources what will be read to you tonight, much of it being still fresh in my memory although after a lapse of more than thirty-one years.

At the time of my service in this campaign I was a member, not of the Petersburg Riflemen, but of the Meherrin Grays, Co. I, 12th Va. Regiment, Mahones's brigade. Without further preliminary remarks I will now draw from the note book its account of the movements of our regiment, commencing with its departure from Dunn's Hill, immediately north of Petersburg, and will let this book, helped out by extracts from one or two letters written during the campaign and by the statements of several ex-Confederates recently sent me, furnish in the main the narrative of the two and a fraction eventful weeks, beginning with our departure from Dunn's Hill and terminating with the battle of Seven Pines on Sunday, June 1st, 1862, in which our regiment received its baptism of fire.

My recollections of these stirring weeks are recorded in the note book referred to as follows:

On Monday the 12th of May the whole regiment was transferred to Dunn's Hill[4] in Chesterfield, where we pitched our tents and remained until the following Wednesday evening, when we took the Richmond train for Drewry's Bluff, our movement being occasioned by the reported advance of gun-boats up the James. Disembarking at the Half-Way House,[5] we marched up the turnpike to within a mile or two of the Bluff, & stacking arms in the road halted for the night. An order given us as the train was moving along not to sing or make any noise caused us to reflect that our campaigning was about to assume a serious phase. It was something new to be so near the enemy and to be under the necessity of preserving silence. Thursday morning, May 15th, when we aroused ourselves from the unsatisfactory naps we had taken on the damp ground, everything seemed perfectly quiet, until about 8 o'clock, when we hear two or three reports as of heavy guns, to which we paid but little attention until a huge thirty-two pound shell came whistling over the tops of the trees towards us and ended its career by snapping off the top of a large tree within a hundred yards of the left of our regiment. This was our first introduction to the missiles of the enemy. As soon as the shell had fallen the men cheered. But in a few minutes we were called to attention and were marching towards the scene of action. It is almost needless to mention that it was anything but pleasant to

4. Dunn's Hill was north of the Appomattox River overlooking Petersburg.

5. The "Half Way House" stood along the main road between Richmond and Petersburg, about three miles due south of Drewry's Bluff.

hear the ponderous shells hurled from the gun-boats crashing among the trees to our left as we filed along the edge of the woods. Being carried within sight of the fort at Drewry's Bluff & placed under the cover of a hill, we thus remained during the whole action between the fort and the gun-boats, our regiment and the 3rd Alabama being thus posted to guard against any land force the enemy might disembark to operate against the fort. The action, as seen by us, was quite interesting, though the gun-boats on each side were hid from view, the fort being shut off by intervening trees and the gunboats by a hill. Yet their respective positions were marked by the smoke from the guns and each shot or shell was traced by the ear. Frequently did we hear the loud crash of a shot or shell as it struck the enemy's boats. Here we saw the first stragglers from an engagement. Two men came to our regiment during the fighting and reported that our battery had been utterly demolished and that the enemy's boats were then passing up the river. A cessation of the firing a few minutes afterwards and a glimpse which we got of the masts and smoke stacks of the retreating vessels as they passed a bend in the river told the result of the action.[6]

6. GSB: Commander Wm. Smith, commanding U.S. Steamer *Wachusett,* in his official report of this engagement made May 19th 1862 says:

"On the 15th inst. the *Galena, Monitor, Naugatuck, Port Royal,* and *Aroostook* ascended this river to within about 8 miles of Richmond, when they met with obstructions in the river which prevented their farther advance. The obstructions consisted of a row of piles driven across the channel, and three rows of vessels sunk also across the channel, among them the *Yorktown* and *Jamestown.* Just below these obstructions on the south or west side of the river were very formidable batteries, mounting fourteen guns, among them 11-inch shell, 100-pounder rifles, and nothing less than 8-inch shell guns. The river there is very narrow—the bank some 200 feet high, and the guns so situated that they can be pointed directly down on the decks of the vessels. The sharpshooters can come on the banks and pick off the men on the vessels' decks. The gunboats were engaged about four hours with the batteries and then retired, having expended their ammunition.

"Our loss was 12 killed and 13 wounded; the vessels not much injured except the *Galena,* which had eighteen shots through her sides and deck." —War Records, Vol. XI, pt. I, p. 636.

"Companies A and I of the 41st Va. Regiment, armed with Mississippi rifles," says Capt. Geo. J. Rogers, of Petersburg, who was adjutant of the regiment, in a statement made in August 1894, "were posted on the edge of the bluff overlooking the river and within range of the gunboats below the fort and did some good service in picking off officers and men who exposed themselves on the vessels."

General Cullen A. Battle, of Petersburg, Va., who was at the time of this acting lieut. colonel of the 3rd Alabama regiment, in a statement made in November, 1896, says:

"On the 15th of May, 1862, when the Federal gun-boats made their attack upon the Confederate fort at Drewry's Bluff. I was in command of a battalion of the 3rd Alabama

After the affair with the gunboats our regiment went into bivouack in a body of woods about a mile in the rear of the fort at Drewry's Bluff, where we remained about a week and then moved to an open field immediately upon the Richmond & Petersburg Turnpike, where we went regularly into camp. We were now about a mile and a quarter from the Bluff. Our diversions at this camp were the usual drills, dress parades and inspections, varied by an occasional stroll into the country around.

On the night of Wednesday, the 28th of May 1862, an order reached us to proceed at once to Richmond, in obedience to which we at once struck our tents and by 10 o'clock p.m. were groping our way in the darkness of the night en route for the Half Way House on the R. & P. R. Road [Richmond and Petersburg Railroad], where our whole brigade,[7] consisting of the 12th Va. Infantry, 6th Va. Infantry, 16th Va. Infantry, 41st Va. Infantry. and the 3rd Ala. Infantry, under the command of Gen. Wm. Mahone,[8] took the cars for Richmond, arrived at which place the whole command was marched through the streets and created much sensation, the neat appearance of the men, just up from Norfolk, contrasting so strongly with that of the veterans from other portions of the Confederacy whom the people of Richmond had been accustomed to seeing. After spending several hours on the Capitol Square, late in the evening we were marched to a point on the Williamsburg Road about two miles east of the City, where we halted and remained for the night.

The next day (Friday) we were again in motion and marched northwardly some two or three miles, crossing the York River Rail Road and halting on a hillside known as "Randolph's Hill," where we at once set to work to protect ourselves against a storm which was threatening soon to come up and which did soon come up and gave us no inconsiderable drenching, having no shelter

---

regiment, deployed as skirmishers along the south bank of the river near the vessels. Two of the companies of the battalion, one of which was commanded by Lieut. E. S. Randolph, concentrated their fire on the *Galena,* and at that time effectually silenced her guns for several minutes. The skirmishers would fire directly into the portholes of the vessel, and thus impeded the management of her guns. I remember that Lieut. Randolph came to me and called my attention to this during the progress of the action."

See Naval Records, Vol. VII, first series, pages 356 and 371, for full reports of this engagement, Federal and Confederate.

7. GSB: I was in error in this statement as I have since learned. The 6th Va. was at Chaffin's Bluff and the 16th Va. in the county of Orange.

8. Brigadier General William Mahone was formerly colonel of the 6th Virginia Infantry and president of the Norfolk & Petersburg Railroad. The soldiers of Mahone's brigade styled themselves "the Kid Glove Boys" (Alexander Whitworth "York" Archer to George S. Bernard, November 29, 1893, George S. Bernard Papers, Southern Historical Collection).

from the driving rain but that which some small cedar brakes upon the hill-side afforded.

[Confederate General Joseph Johnston had conjured an elaborate plan for a May 31 attack which called for six divisions and multiple routes to the battle-field. His orders directed the several columns to converge at Seven Pines east of Richmond. The scheme unraveled, however, and by the end of the battle's first day, only two divisions reached Seven Pines and engaged the Federals.]

STATEMENT OF ALEXANDER W. ARCHER

In a letter dated November 29th, 1893, Comrade Alex'r W. Archer,[9] of Richmond, Va., ex-commander of R. E. Lee Camp No. 1 of Confederate Veterans, responding to a request for an account of his experiences on this day and in the engagement on the following Sunday, says:

After the regiment left Richmond, on its way to Seven Pines, it halted for the night, I think, near Gillie's Creek.[10] Our guns were stacked and all tried to find a comfortable place to sleep. In the hunt Littlebury Stainback[11] of Co. E and myself (I being a member of Co. B) cast lots together under a small fly tent and were soon in the land of dreams, but, alas, ere morning, our dreams were dispelled by a deluge of rain, and almost before we could think, Berry said to me, "G____d____it, Aleck, there is a river running down my back." We were on the slope of a hill and the water ran down in streams. Of course we arose and there was no more sleep for us that night. I never saw it rain harder in my life, and as for the thunder and lightning, it was terrible. It seemed as though the powers of heaven and hell were turned loose. We built fires and dried ourselves as best we could, and ate our breakfast and once more moved forward.

9. Alexander Whitworth "York" Archer, a store clerk in Petersburg, enlisted as a private in Company B of the 12th Virginia in July 1861. He was wounded at Seven Pines and, after serving in a hospital in Petersburg, received a medical discharge in November 1863 because of partial paralysis of his right side. He was nicknamed "York" because he resided in New York City when the war broke out (Alexander Whitworth Archer, "Recollections of a Private Soldier—1861," Papers of R. E. Lee Camp, United Confederate Veterans, Virginia Historical Society).

10. Gillie's Creek begins several miles east of Richmond and runs westward toward the city, emptying into the James River near downtown.

11. Littleberry E. Stainback, a clerk in prewar Petersburg, enlisted as a private in Company E of the 12th Virginia in April 1861. Captured at Crampton's Gap, he was exchanged in October 1862 and discharged from the 12th Virginia in November 1862. He was then commissioned major and quartermaster on the staff of General John Pegram's brigade.

STATEMENT OF JOHN E. CROW

Mr. Jno. E. Crow,[12] of Wilmington, N.C., a member of the Petersburg Riflemen, in a letter dated December 15, 1893, narrates the following incident of this night about Julian R. Beckwith,[13] a splendid young man, of high promise, a brother of Comrades Thos. S. and Edmund R. Beckwith of this camp, who realizing his gloomy forebodings, lost his life, not on the next day, but on the Sunday morning following, on the field of Seven Pines in the fore-front of battle: "When we reached this place," says Mr. Crow, referring to the place on Randolph's Hill where we halted for the night, "it was nearly dark, and one of the most gloomy and dismal evenings I ever remember. The sky was overcast with low, overhanging leaden-looking clouds, which sent down a fine chilling rain that sifted in under the brim of one's cap, found its way into his shirt collar, down one's back, causing a longing desire for the fireside at home and a cup of hot coffee. We were worn out and weary with marching and I do not remember that we made any preparations for a meal, or even kindled a fire, but I think went immediately to work spreading down our oilcloths and blankets to get what rest we could. Julian Beckwith slept with me that night, and after we had gotten under our blankets, and our heads covered up, he reached into his pocket, and taking out a small meersham [meerschaum] pipe, said to me, 'John, I want you to take this pipe and keep it as a memento of our friendship and the happy times we have had together on Tanner's Creek when we were stationed at the Entrenched Camp at Harrison's Farm, for I feel sure that tomorrow I shall be killed.' 'Julian,' said I, 'I will not take the pipe. I gave it to you and I want you to keep it, and I would not humor such dismal thoughts by acceding to your wishes. Besides, is it possible that you, who have served in the old navy and traveled so much, with such cosmopolitan ideas, will allow yourself to be demoralized by such a presentiment? There is nothing in it: 'tis weather and surroundings, and tomorrow you will laugh at yourself for being so down in the mouth.' 'John,' he replied, 'I know I am to be killed tomorrow.' The tone of his voice expressed such painful earnestness and hopeless despair it sent a chill to my heart. We said nothing more to each other and finally went to sleep."

12. John E. Crow was working as a clerk for a hardware dealer in Petersburg when he joined Company E of the 12th Virginia as a private in May 1861. He was detailed to the provost guard in 1863, and promoted to corporal that same year. He surrendered at Appomattox in 1865.

13. Julian Beckwith is discussed in note 44, chapter 1.

····

Let us now resume the narrative of the next two days, May 31, and June 1, 1862, as we find it in the note book:

The next day, Saturday, May 31st, we receive orders to hold ourselves in readiness to march. The orders reach us early in the morning, but we do not move until about 2 o'clock in the afternoon. In the meantime, however, we hear constant artillery, seemingly three or four miles to our front. Getting in motion, we retrace our steps to the Williamsburg Road, arriving at which we move in the direction of the firing. On the way we meet wounded men coming from the battle which we know is raging ahead of us, the small arms as well as the artillery being distinctly audible. Instead of continuing down the Williamsburg Road, which leads off to our left and in the direction of the battle, our command—at least our brigade—move down the Charles City Road, and forming a line of battle perpendicular to the direction of the road, about sunset bivouac in a piece of woods. We are directed to make as little noise as possible and to build no fires, although the evening is damp and chilly. As we rest in this position, the fierce rattle of musketry, some two or three miles distant, was anything but pleasant to our ears. We begin to realize that we too would soon be called to face the foe.

[As General Johnston directed troops on May 31 near Seven Pines, he received a serious shoulder wound. His incapacity created a leadership vacuum on the immediate battlefield, which was poorly filled by Major General Gustavus W. Smith. The next day, Smith ordered James Longstreet to march his command along the Williamsburg Road and drive north toward the York River Railroad. Longstreet brought four of his own brigades, and two from Benjamin Huger's division, including Mahone's brigade and the 12th Virginia regiment.

When Mahone reached the battlefield on the morning of June 1, a perturbed D. H. Hill, whose division had fought hard the day before, ordered the newcomers into woods north of the Williamsburg Road. The Confederates blundered into a solid federal battle line, the rifles of Israel Richardson's division. The 41st Virginia and 3rd Alabama led the way and, in the crowded trees and swampy ground, blundered into two Union brigades. Lewis Armistead's Confederate brigade advanced on Mahone's right.

After the initial advance failed, the 12th Virginia received orders to enter the woods, where it met a devastating Union volley at close range. The regiment withdrew from the woods and took a position along the Williamsburg Road. It was here that D. H. Hill uttered disparaging remarks in front of the Virginians. Hill's comments form a focal point in the following accounts. For the most part, the role played by Bernard's regiment at Seven Pines ended there. Further combat occurred on the Confederate right, but the fight soon ended. Bernard included a diagram with the noted positions marked by letters; for ease of reference, this information has been incorporated into the map of Seven Pines.]

Pieces of white linen are given us to tie around our hats or caps to distinguish us in battle from the enemy. At light next morning, June 1, we are put in motion for the scene of the conflict of the evening before. All is now quiet—we hear no sounds of battle ahead of us. Soon we get into the Williamsburg Road and are moving down it. The road-way is in terrible condition—full of mud and water. On the road sides we pass large numbers of troops who we suppose were engaged in the battle of last evening. We also meet hundreds of stragglers and other persons coming from the battle field, many of whom were bringing away spoils. I will remember one fellow perched up on a piece of captured artillery which a detachment of artillerymen were removing from the field. Munching a piece of orange, or sucking a lemon, with a face that bespoke the utmost enjoyment of the luxury, he cried out to us as we passed him, "Hurry up boys, there are lots of oranges and lemons, sugar and coffee, and every sort of good thing ahead of you." A straggler whom we meet returning from the field, with a countenance expressive of no less satisfaction holds up for exhibition to the passing troops his gun, the stock of which had been perforated by a bullet and in loud voice cries out, "Nobody needn't say the Yankees don't know how to shoot. See here (pointing to the bullet hole), what they did for me." This fellow, in my own mind, I voted at once a hero. We had not then the experience of after years to whisper the damaging suspicion that such as he had never—but perhaps I do injustice. Let us pursue our story. We are trudging along the muddiest of roads towards what was known afterwards as the battle field of Seven Pines. On the roadside we get our first glimpse of a man who had fallen in battle. How strange our feelings as we look at this corpse! Soon we emerge into an open field where there are houses and breastworks. Here was evidently the hottest of the fight of last evening. The ground is very much trampled and several bodies of men and horses are to be seen lying just as they fell.

Our regiment files off to the right and forms a line of battle facing to the southeast, but we scarcely get into position and come to an "order of arms" before we are startled by a heavy volley of musketry about three hundred yards to our left and in a piece of woods north east of us, (*B–B* in diagram [see the map of Seven Pines]), the position of our regiment at the time of the volley being *A*. A stray ball finds its way into the regiment and wounds one of our men. We look in the direction of the houses and the firing and see dozens of men, probably picking up plunder, running away towards us and also in the

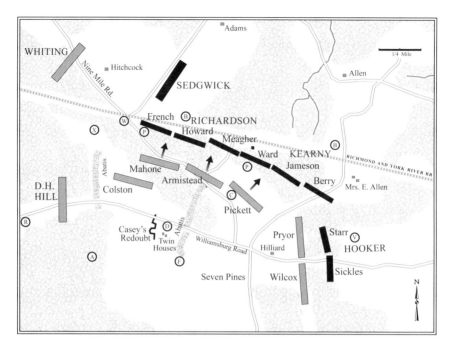

SEVEN PINES, JUNE 1, 1862

direction of Richmond (*R*). We are immediately put in motion and double quick in the direction of the firing to a point near the Yankee camp *C,* where we were formed into line of battle facing the firing, which continues in the woods in front of us about *B–B*. Our line is formed but a minute or two before the word "forward" is given and we are moving in the direction of the firing, obliquing slightly to the left. A hundred yards brings us to the edge of the pines *P–P,* when the enemy's balls begin to whistle over our heads.

Fifty yards further into the swamp and we are hotly engaged with the Yankees, who fire upon us from behind trees and small bushes some fifty or sixty yards distant. The firing continues for ten or fifteen minutes, when it ceases in our immediate front and our regiment is withdrawn, and, reforming about the point [*C*][14] from which it moved into action, returns towards the houses and takes position behind the embankment of the road at *D*. Soon after which the enemy advance a small piece of artillery [to the point *W*], only two or three hundred yards distant and shell us for a few minutes, being driven off by a small force advancing upon them from the direction of [*X*].

14. Bernard's unpublished Notebook contains several references to his map that did not appear in his published article. These references have been inserted in the text in brackets.

Whilst we lie behind the embankment [at *D*] receiving the fire of the little piece of artillery one of its round shot, barely missing our little embankment as it whizzes over us, strikes the body of a dead Yankee lying near one of the tents a few feet behind us and hurls it several feet into the air. A profane fellow in the regiment remarks, "That Yankee went nearer Heaven just now than he will ever go again." Whilst about this place Gen. D. H. Hill,[15] as a North Carolina regiment filed by us, going into battle, rather towards the pines [*P–P*] where we had been fighting, for they did not themselves get into action, foolishly remarked, "Hurry up my brave North Carolinians. Let the Virginians see that you know how to fight," or words to that effect, reflecting strongly upon our regiment which had just returned from the [woods][16] much scattered. The imputation was promptly resented by the brave and gallant Lt. Col. F. L. Taylor[17] of our regiment, who excitedly told him that he, Col. Taylor, considered himself a brave man, and he knew that his regiment did not leave the woods until he left, and furthermore until they were ordered. A man in our ranks, as Hill made the remark, with considerable boldness pronounced it "a lie." Hill, in extenuation, said he only intended what he had said as an encouragement to the regiment just going into battle, but the offense he had given always made him an object of execration with the 12th Va. Regiment.

A few moments after the shelling, our regiment is carried off to the Yankee camp distant about half a mile. Here we find abundant spoils in the tents and lying about on the ground, and numbers of dead bodies and a few wounded Yankees lying in the tents.

The ground is swampy. As soon as we reach the camp, a line of battle is formed and two companies of the regiment, the Richmond Grays and Petersburg Riflemen, are sent forward as skirmishers and soon engage the enemy, the bullets of whom whiz over us as we lie in rear in the line of battle. Very soon the skirmishers are withdrawn and again take their place in the regiment. In a few minutes we hear a heavy volley of musketry in our rear [about *V*],

15. Major General Daniel Harvey Hill, a West Point graduate, was superintendent of the North Carolina Military Institute before the war. During the Peninsula Campaign, he served as a major general in Lee's army. However, disagreements with Lee and other members of the high command left him without an active role in the last years of the war. Afterward, he was a magazine editor and university president (Ezra Warner, *Generals In Gray* [Baton Rouge: Louisiana State University Press, 1959], 13).

16. The *Index-Appeal* article mistakenly says "works" here. Bernard's original notebook say "woods."

17. Fielding Lewis Taylor entered service in April 1861 as a lieutenant colonel of Virginia Militia and by June 1861 had been assigned to the 12th Virginia. Wounded at Crampton's Gap, he died several weeks later.

about a hundred or two yards distant, the combatants hid from view by an in-tervening hill. What can it mean? We feel uneasy. In a minute or two a piece of artillery near the scene of conflict opens vigorously. We cannot see it, but we know it is ours. At each discharge, we hear so distinctly the rattle of the grape and canister hurled at the foe. It is the first time our artillery has been to the rescue. What a feeling of security it gave us! We shall always remember the relief we felt at each discharge reverberating among the hills so near us.

Soon after thus being relieved from the move of the enemy upon our right flank and rear we were withdrawn and carried to the position [F] near the houses, where we remain the balance of the day, the men spending their time discussing the events of the morning, roaming about the battlefield, [picking up plunder,][18] helping the wounded, &c &c. During the afternoon we expect no fighting. Indeed we cease to regard the enemy as near us.

They still however hold the position held when we encountered them. Perhaps they were so worsted by the conflict as not to desire to renew it. When night came on, we began to think they may attack us the next morn-ing. But what a miserable place to fight them! Nothing but woods on all sides—woods filled with swamps. If we drive the enemy, it will be into a swamp. If they drive us, we must retreat into a swamp. View the place where we were in any light, it was anything but agreeable. Dead bodies of men and horses lay near us on all sides, some of them in or near the very ditches from which we were compelled to get water. But much wearied by the exercise and excitement of the day, we find no difficulty in yielding to sleep in which we forget we are soldiers. About 1 o'clock in the morning, we are waked up and cautioned to be as silent as possible. What does it mean? In the darkness, we indistinctly see a column of troops passing within a few yards of us moving towards Richmond. We soon understand that we are evacuating the position. But how slowly those ahead of us seem to move! Day will dawn and catch us not yet out of sight. Seeing us retreating, the enemy would rush upon our column so embarrassed by the woods and the swamps as to be unable to resist them successfully. The suspense is very trying to soldiers who the day before had seen the enemy for the first time. But we get well on the road to Rich-mond before it is light, at which we feel no little relief, glad to leave behind us the famous field of Seven Pines. By eleven o'clock we are quietly bivouacked on the Charles City Road, on the very ground upon which we had spent the previous Saturday night, and enjoy a day or two of refreshing rest.

18. Bernard's notebook says "picking up plunder" here. He omitted the term from the published version in the *Index-Appeal.*

....

The following extract from a private letter I wrote from the camp of Mahone's brigade the morning after the battle may properly be introduced here:

A grape shot (I think) whacked off a little sapling just in front of me. Soon we retired from this place, a perfect trap for us. It is a great wonder that more of our men were not killed. We were led along through the woods right down into a swamp, wading through water over our ankles. We went through the woods more like a drove of mules than a regiment marching in battle order. We did, however, quite as well as the trying circumstances would allow. Of course the enemy had the advantage of us. Fifty men in that swamp, acting on the defensive, could have kept us back had they tried. However, we soon retraced our steps and crossed back to the side of a ditch along the road running parallel to the woods.

In a subsequent paragraph of this letter is the following statement:

Last night we rested on the field fully expecting to go at the dreadful work this morning at dawn. We were mistaken, and I am glad we were for that swamp is no place for men to fight. A battle can not be decisive there. We had as well attempt to whip out the lizards and the snakes that infest it as the Yankees if they chose to remain there. The same would be true if they wished to get us out and we wished to stay. We have now fallen back to a place where we will have fair play at them.

A few days later, June 15, 1862, I wrote my father from the camp of our regiment on the Charles City Road as follows:

If you have seen the recent papers, you have a better idea of the fight in which our regiment was engaged than any I can give you. We fought under the most disadvantageous circumstances, having to charge an unseen enemy through a marshy thicket, and under a very brisk fire. It was this time that so many of our men fell killed and wounded. Only one man in our company was hurt, and he not dangerously. Three others—among the number myself—received slight scratches. I am not fully satisfied that my wound was not from the explosion of a cap from the gun of some who were firing immediately on my left. Major General Hill, of North Carolina, has seen fit to speak very disparagingly of the conduct of the 12th Regiment on this occasion, but it is believed very unjustly. His bad generalship threw us into a difficulty and this he wishes to conceal by throwing as much of the blame as possible upon our regiment. It is true that we all retreated from our position down in the thicket, but it was only after being ordered to do so, which order was not given until it was apparent that the right wing of our regiment overlapped the left of the 3rd Alabama, and we were thus, in part, firing into our friends. When we did retreat we did so slowly and in good order, and immediately reformed outside of the woods. Some few from every company,[19] as might be expected, took to their heels at the first opportunity to do so upon entering the woods, running clear out of the way, and, in some cases, did not return to their companies for two or three days. But this was by no means true of the body of the regiment. Officers and men alike behaved very gallantly. Weisiger, I understand, intends to demand a court of enquiry.

As I subsequently learned, the 3rd Alabama was on our left and not on our right, and the overlapping was therefore by the left and not the right wing of our regiment. Whilst making this correction in my letter, I should further state that in the many engagements after the battle of Seven Pines in which the 12th Virginia regiment participated, some of them being among the severest of the war, neither the regiment as a whole, nor any part of it, so far an my observation went or information goes, ever acted in such manner as to merit adverse criticism, and the suggestion made in my letter, with only the experience of that one badly managed battle, that a few from every company might be expected in each engagement to take to their heels and remove themselves from the scene of danger, I am glad to find, was unjust imputation.

STATEMENT OF GEORGE J. ROGERS

Adjutant Geo. J. Rogers,[20] of the 41st Virginia regiment, in a letter written in November, 1893, gives me a full and valuable account of the battle from which I take the following paragraphs:

The rain was over in the morning and the men were early trying to get something to eat. Our division, Gen. Huger's[21] composed of the brigades

19. The published version omitted the following words, from the unpublished notebook: "the woods. Some few from every company."

20. George J. Rogers, a resident of Sussex Court House, Virginia, enlisted as a sergeant in Company A of the 41st Virginia in May 1861. Wounded at Malvern Hill, he became a quartermaster the next year. Steadily promoted to major, he left the Quartermaster Department in April 1865 to join Kirkland's brigade in General Johnston's army. He surrendered at Durham, North Carolina. After the war, he sold real estate in the Richmond area.

21. Major-General Benjamin Huger, a native of South Carolina and an 1825 graduate of West Point, commanded a division during the Peninsula Campaign of 1862. Following his lackluster performance there, he was assigned to lesser roles as an artillery inspector and ordnance chief. After the war, he farmed in Fauquier County, Virginia.

of Mahone, [Lewis] Armistead[22] and [Albert G.] Blanchard,[23] was to move out on the Charles City Road, which left the Williamsburg Road, just after Gillie's Creek was crossed. Moving out on the Williamsburg Road, before 9 o'clock we reached this creek, which was so much swollen by the heavy rain that it was not easily fordable. A foot bridge was made across it by hauling a wagon mid-stream to serve as a trestle, on which planks were laid from each side over which the men passed in almost single file, which, of course made crossing very slow. While we were here Gen. Longstreet[24] came up with his division, and, after a long conference with Gen. Huger, claimed to rank him and took the right of way, crossing over his division first, while ours waited, though Gen. L's troops did not proceed after crossing, as I distinctly remember that our brigade marched between the lines of his men near the creek after we had crossed, as we went forward about one o'clock or a little earlier, to go out on the Charles City Road to relieve the brigade of Gen'l Rodes,[25] so that he might join Gen. D. H. Hill's division (to which it belonged) on the Williamsburg Road. We heard firing before reaching our position some distance to our left front, we supposed on the Williamsburg Road.

This firing was quite heavy from half past two or three o'clock until after dark, though not all the time continuous. We put out a strong picket line and the regiments bivouacked in line of battle across the Charles City Road. We were not disturbed by any enemy during the night, and the men were in good spirits, chatting and eating around their camp fires, though some with foreboding of the morrow.

Before daylight on Sunday morning, June 1st, 1862, the brigade was on the march, going north from the Charles City to the Williamsburg Road, along

22. West Point graduate and old Army regular Lewis Armistead began the war as the colonel of the 57th Virginia Infantry. Promoted to brigadier general in April 1862, he led his brigade until the Battle of Gettysburg, where he was mortally wounded during Pickett's Charge.

23. Albert Gallatin Blanchard was also a graduate of West Point, and a veteran of the Mexican War. He entered the Confederacy as colonel of the 1st Louisiana Volunteer Infantry. Promoted to brigadier general in September 1861, he never held field command after the Peninsula Campaign.

24. General James Longstreet led a division of six brigades during the Peninsula Campaign and would be one of General Lee's top subordinates for the remainder of the war.

25. Robert E. Rodes, a native of Lynchburg, Virginia, and a graduate of the Virginia Military Institute, commanded a brigade during the Peninsula Campaign of 1862. In early 1863 he was promoted to division command, and led with distinction at Gettysburg and throughout the Overland Campaign of 1864. He received a mortal wound in fighting at Winchester during the Valley Campaign.

a by-road but little used and where the mud was very deep. So bad was it that Gen. Mahone directed Col. Chambliss[26] — whose regiment was marching in front, as we moved off as the regiments were in line of battle, left in front — to have his ordinance wagon sent back up the Charles City Road and across by a better road in our rear. This was just after we started, and he asked me to ride back and give the same order to Col. Lomax[27] of the 3rd Alabama regiment marching immediately in our rear, which I did. Riding along a short distance with that officer after delivering the order of Gen. Mahone, I found him much depressed and full of forebodings, and he said as I left him that he felt that something terrible would befall him during the day. How truly this was fulfilled! In a few hours he was shot down while at the front of his gallant regiment, bravely urging them against the enemy in the thick woods which had fired on them before they were seen.[28]

We entered the Williamsburg Road a short distance west of the battle-

26. John R. Chambliss, a West Point graduate, commanded the 41st Virginia during the Seven Days' Campaign. Later he led a cavalry brigade consisting of Virginia regiments for much of the war. He was killed on August 16, 1864, along the Charles City Road during the Second Deep Bottom Campaign. While searching his body, Federals recovered a detailed map of the Confederate defenses ringing Richmond (see Noah Andre Trudeau, *The Last Citadel, Petersburg, Virginia, June 1864–April 1865* [Boston: Little Brown and Company, 1991], 155).

27. Tennet Lomax enlisted as a lieutenant colonel of the 3rd Alabama Infantry Regiment in April 1861. Promoted to colonel in July 1861, he was killed at the Battle of Seven Pines.

28. GSB: Comrade J. Smith Egerton, of our camp, narrates another instance of premonition of death before going into this engagement. Capt. Jno. C. Camp, before going into the fight, told his men, who had requested him to take charge of their money just received from the paymaster, that he expected to be shot and for this reason he would not take charge of their money. His watch and chain he gave to Lieutenant Mingea of his company to be sent home. Getting under fire he soon received a mortal wound. Men from his company (Co. C, 41st Va.) went into the woods where he was shot to bring him out, but were fired upon by the enemy and were driven off. Soon after the seven days' battles, when the enemy had evacuated the territory around Richmond occupied by them in June, 1862, his father went to the battle-field to find his body, if possible, but there was no trace of it or his grave. For many years, however, his mother clung to the hope that he would some day return alive. A few days ago upon examining the volume of the War Records relating this battle, I found and brought to the attention of his brother, Comrade W. H. Camp, a paragraph in the official report of Col. Jno. C. Pinkney of the 61st N.Y. Vols. in which he says: "Among the killed was Captain Camp, Forty-first Va. Regiment. I carried this body to be buried at nightfall on the left side of the road entering the woods." This young man I knew well, and like Julian Beckwith he was of high promise.

field of the previous day on that road, and found it almost impassable, the mud being knee deep and broken wagons and caissons left in the mud in many places.

We reach the "redoubt" and the line of works in the opening around Barker's House, captured from Gen. Casey[29] by Gen. D. H. Hill's division the evening before, and came by left into line in front of those works, facing east, the left of the 41st Va. Regiment being near the Williamsburg Road, our line extending south and at nearly a right angle to that road. My recollection is that the 12th Va. Regiment was not extended on the right of the 3rd Alabama, but was a little in rear of us in an abatis the enemy had felled in front of the works we occupied.

We must have arrived about 6 o'clock a.m. The men were allowed to rest while Gen. Mahone reported to Gen. D. H. Hill, whose quarters were near and to the east of us, and gladly and eagerly possessed themselves of some of the captured stores in a house near the "redoubt," such as boxes of crackers, coffee, ground and sweetened, &c. I remember that I secured a quantity of Gen. Casey's head-quarters stationery, which I distributed among the different officers of our regiment. There was only an occasional rifle shot heard, but no enemy was in sight. In a short while Gen. Hill rode up and said, "Gen. Mahone, take your brigade in there" (pointing to a thick woods some three or four hundred yards north of the Williamsburg Road), "and take position in line of battle in those woods, parallel to that road" (pointing to the Williamsburg Road).

As we rode off, Gen. Mahone and staff, a few steps in advance of Col. Chambliss and myself, Gen. Mahone called to Gen. Hill and said, "Gen'l is there any enemy in those woods? Shall I throw out skirmishers?" Gen. Hill replied, "There is no enemy there. I've had it examined this morning." As our regiment reached the edge of the woods, Col. Chambliss said to me, "Although there are no orders to put out skirmishers, I am going to put out some in front of my regiment. Order Capt. Brinkley[30] to deploy his company in our front and direct him to keep 40 or 50 yards in advance of us."

This direction I carried out and Capt. Brinkley's company, being on the extreme left, was deployed to the right as we advanced. The woods and swampy undergrowth here were very thick, and the line being ordered to

29. Major General Silas Casey spent his whole life in the army and served as commander of the Third Division of the Fourth Corps of the Army of the Potomac at the Battle of Seven Pines. He assembled and edited one of the most influential manuals of the war, *Infantry Tactics,* published in 1862.

30. Robert B. Brinkley, a prewar merchant, enlisted as captain of Company I of the 41st Virginia in June 1861. He died in fighting at the North Anna River in May 1864.

march by the flank to keep aligned by the right,[31] ours being the regiment to the left, we twice uncovered our front, and I rode forward and ordered Capt. Brinkley to march to the right in order to keep us covered, but it proved that he did not march far enough, as we were fired on by a line of the enemy lying down not over forty or fifty feet from us, just as we had crossed an abatis. We formed line at once immediately in rear of this felled timber and commenced firing. Capt. Brinkley's company, deployed as skirmishers, was to our left and rear when we struck the enemy's line, and was not in this part of the fight.

In a few minutes part of Gen. Armistead's brigade came rushing through the woods to our left front upon the left wing of our regiment, in great disorder, everybody talking and wanting to know if we were "friends" or "enemies." I noticed among these men of Gen. Armistead's brigade a number of the 53rd Va. Regiment.

STATEMENT OF E. LESLIE SPENCE

Capt. E. Leslie Spence,[32] Richmond, Va., now captain of Co. E., of the 1st Virginia regiment of infantry and commander of R. E. Lee Camp, of that city, in a letter dated December 1st, 1893, says:

My recollection is, that the regiment, when at the point "A" in your diagram, was at an "order arms," and the first sergeant of each company was calling the roll, when we were fired on, and the 3rd Alabama regiment with the gallant Col. Lomax riding at its head went into the woods on our left, and

---

31. GSB: Some idea of the extraordinary disorder and confusion to which Adjutant Rogers here refers may be gathered from the following extract from the official report of Col. H. B. Tomlin, who commanded the 53rd Virginia regiment of Armistead's brigade:

"Discovering troops coming towards our right wing with white bands on their hats, (I) ordered mine not to fire; that they were friends; but the fire continuing(ed) down the whole line, yet too high to do much injury. Some one, without authority, on the right wing gave the command to retreat, which was passed down the line by the captains, and the men fell back in great disorder in to the field on which they had just emerged, reformed, and, with every company in proper position, double-quicked back into the woods, and shortly after crossing the road came up with Forty-first Virginia Regiment, marching directly towards us. From this direction we received a constant fire, which we returned until some of our officers, recognizing some of the officers of the Forty-first Regiment (Maj. G. M. Waddill, who was upon the left wing, while I was upon the right), commanded them to march in retreat." War Rec. Vol. XI, pt. 1, p. 985.

32. E. Leslie Spence enlisted as a private in Company G of the 12th Virginia in April 1861. Wounded at Crampton's Gap, he convalesced in a hospital for seven months, then was released as unfit for field service. He later served as a messenger and in the quartermaster department. He was quite active in veterans' affairs after the war, even serving one term as commander of R. E. Lee Camp No. 1, United Confederate Veterans.

that our regiment immediately changed front and went into the woods where the Yankees were, on the flank of the 3rd Alabama. Col. Lomax was soon killed and his horse came running through our lines, and very nearly ran over me. It was in these woods that Hardgrove[33] and Grattan[34] of the Richmond Greys, (Co. G 12th Va. Regiment, of which you know I was a member), were killed.

I well remember the incident of Gen. D. H. Hill's disparaging remark. Whilst we were lying behind the ditch where we had reformed our lines, after being ordered out of the woods by Gen. Mahone, a North Carolina regiment or brigade marched by our left flank, and as they passed along Gen. D. H. Hill said, "Go in North Carolinians and show Virginians that you can fight. Here is a whole brigade that ran." Our men, stung to the quick at this base slander, at once cried out, "Are they Hatteras and Roanoke Island heroes?"[35] Our lieutenant colonel, Col. F. L. Taylor, called down the lines for Gen. Mahone, and, when the general rode up, said to him, "Your men are being slandered on the field of battle," and then reported to him what Gen. Hill had said. Gen. Mahone rode right to Gen. Hill, and said, "You are a G—d d——d liar, and I will hold you personally responsible for this hereafter. I ordered my men out of the woods, and if I had known it was by your order I would not have carried them in there." Just at this time a courier, or staff officer, rode up to Gen. Hill and said, "Gen. Pickett says his right flank is exposed and asks for reinforcements." Hill, referring to our command, remarked, "I have no troops but these, you can have them." Gen. Mahone asked him (Hill) where to go, and, on being informed, gave the command "Attention" and the brigade would have charged a ten-gun battery alone, if ordered, as they were all so mad that such a stigma had been put on them on their first battlefield. Their record on a score or more battlefields in after years provide how foundationless was Gen. Hill's imputation.

We then moved over to the right and formed our line, when the Richmond Grays and Petersburg Riflemen were ordered to the front as skirmishers, and I do not hesitate to affirm that the two companies deployed and advanced firing with the same precision and exactness with which they had so often executed this movement on the drill grounds at Harrison's farm. I have

33. John S. Hardgrove enlisted as a private in Company G of the 12th Virginia Infantry in April 1861. He was killed at Seven Pines.

34. George G. Grattan enlisted as a private in Company G of the 12th Virginia in April 1862. He was killed at Seven Pines.

35. The question refers to the Confederate defeats earlier in 1862 at the hands of General Ambrose Burnside during his successful coastal occupation of eastern North Carolina.

hundreds of times since the war spoken of their conduct on this occasion, and there is no company today in the First Virginia regiment that can go through the skirmish drill as well as the Greys and the Riflemen did that day under fire.

I will write Gen. Mahone and get his recollection of the Hill incident, and will forward you his letter.

STATEMENT OF WILLIAM MAHONE

Captain Spence, having written to Gen. Mahone, received from him the following letter in reply, written from Washington under date of December 9, 1893:

Dear Mr. Spence: I have read your note of the 5th inst. covering your letter of the 1st last, to Mr. Bernard.

On our arrival at "Seven Pines" the three regiments of the brigade then with it, the 41st, the 12th Va. and the 3rd Alabama, were massed just in front of the little redoubt (Casey's). I had ridden with Gen. Stuart to Gen. D. H. Hill's tent. At that moment up rode in great haste a person who excitedly reported to Gen. Hill that the enemy was right there in the point of woods projecting out in the field near Gen. Hill's tent. Gen. Hill said to me, "Take your brigade in there," referring to this point of woods.[36] Promptly I put the brigade in motion, column by companies, left in front, and, as I brought it into line facing the woods, the 41st on the left, the 3rd Alabama in the center, I discovered that the 12th, which should have come into line on the right, had [been] without my knowledge diverted by Gen. Hill and sent off to another part of the field. I sent Maj. Smith of my staff to bring the 12th back and put it in on the right. Meanwhile, the 41st and 3rd Alabama had rushed in. Col. Lomax was in front of the right of his regiment on foot, and, as it moved off, he turned to the regiment and waving his sword exclaimed, "Do your duty Alabamians," and right into the woods they rushed running quickly into a Federal camp and on to the front. The 41st came in on the left. Then there appeared a regiment of another brigade on the ridge over which to the right, the 3rd Alabama had passed. Here this regiment of another brigade met a fierce fire of the enemy and fell back. About this time Smith had brought up

36. Note that Mahone's recollection of his initial discussion with D. H. Hill does not match that of George Rogers, who recalled that D. H. Hill assured Mahone the woods in front had been examined and no enemy was there. Mahone, however, recalled that both generals learned of the enemy's presence from "a person who excitedly reported to Gen. Hill." Mahone's account here is consistent with his earlier letter to Gustavus W. Smith on December 14, 1885 (see Gustavus W. Smith, *The Battle of Seven Pines* [1891; reprint, Dayton: Morningside Press, 1974], 119).

the 12th Va. I caused it to dress on the colors and fix bayonets preparatory to a charge I intended to make. The enemy's fire was coming nearer and was getting more, vigorous, but at this moment, and when my horse had been shot, some unknown person on the right of the line gave the order to fall back, and the regiment, somewhat pell-mell, commenced to fall back, I thought it was useless to attempt to halt them and reform under the enemy's fire. Later on this could have been easily done, but now they were green troops. The regiment was halted on the line of the road. Then it was, as you relate, that Gen. Hill accused the brigade of cowardice and Lieut. Col. Taylor called for me and related what Gen. Hill had said. Gen. Hill was sitting on his horse near by, surrounded by some mounted persons. I asked him if he had made the insulting remarks reported by Col. Taylor. He replied evasively, when I denounced the statement as a mendacious slander and the author as an infamous liar and coward.

I do not think that Lomax was killed on horseback. My recollection is quite distinct, and that he went in on foot, and my information gathered from his regiment at the time that he was killed in front of his regiment when it had reached its farthest point inside the enemy's lines. I made every effort to recover his body, but in vain. I sent his widow a very handsome sword taken from the body of a Federal officer of rank who fell in front of the 3rd Alabama's charge.

STATEMENT OF THOMAS P. POLLARD

Capt. Thos. P. Pollard,[37] of Richmond, Va., late captain of Company B, 12th Va., Regiment, and ex-commander of R. E. Lee Camp, of that city, in a letter written in December, 1893, says:

Though I did not hear Col. F. L. Taylor's response to Gen. Hill, I heard it from others in the regiment who did hear it and who told me of it at the time. I did, however, hear Maj. Forsyth,[38] of the 3rd Alabama, tell Gen. Hill that, if he or any other man said that Mahone's brigade ran or acted cowardly, he lied, and that he (Forsyth) was personally responsible for what he said.

37. Thomas Poindexter Pollard, a clerk in prewar Petersburg, enlisted as a 2nd lieutenant in Company B of the 12th Virginia in April 1861. Wounded at Antietam in 1862, he returned to service with light duty as a conscript officer, but when he recovered fully, he became the 1st lieutenant of Company B, and later a captain in the same company. Hospitalized for dysentery for five months, he returned to the 12th Virginia in 1864 and remained with the unit through surrender at Appomattox.

38. Charles Forsythe of Mobile, Alabama, became lieutenant colonel of the 3rd Alabama in May 1862 and then colonel of the same regiment in August 1863.

····

Mr. Jno. E Crow, in his letter of Dec. 15, 1893, already referred to, says:

Gen. D. H. Hill, on horseback at the head of his command, said: "Come on, my brave North Carolinians, and take the place of these Virginians, who have run."

"That's a lie," went up from many a voice, and many hallooed out that we were ready to go anywhere we were ordered.

The deeds of Mahone's brigade have passed into history, and its reputation for courage and dash was won on too many a battle field to need any further commendation from me. . . .

After receiving the fire from the masked battery, to which I have referred, we were ordered to our right into a piece of pine woods, and immediately engaged the enemy who were protected by the woods. We could only occasionally get a glimpse of them. Meade Bernard was a little to my right, and getting a sight of a "blue coat" who appeared on the road in these woods, fired at him. One of our boys near Meade, but further to the right, having a better view of the road, hallooed out: "Meade, that was a double shot! You killed two 'blue coats' at that fire!" We continued firing for some considerable time, and were finally withdrawn and taken to the same position we had occupied before going into action, in front of Casey's works. Here we remained all night getting what sleep we could. As for myself I remember getting three fence rails and sticking the ends in the breastworks across the ditch, which, as I have before stated, was filled with water. Lying on these rails, I slept until early dawn, when we were ordered to fall in line very quietly and to fall back with as little notice as possible. Upon looking around I saw two men lying near me on each side, and, taking them to be some of our boys asleep, I put my hand first on one and the on the other, and was horrified to find that they were the dead bodies of some of our brave boys who had been killed in the charge the evening before, with their feet in the very ditch of the enemy.

We started off as noiselessly as possible, the morning star was shining with great brilliancy, and was, for a long time, taken by some of the boys to be some signal light of the enemy giving notice of our movements and we expected every minute to be fired into from the rear.

STATEMENT OF WILLIAM E. CAMERON

Ex-Gov. William E. Cameron,[39] formerly of this city, now of Chicago, who was adjutant of the 12th Va. Regiment and subsequently assistant adjutant-

---

39. William Evelyn Cameron, a future governor of Virginia, was born, raised, and educated in Petersburg. He began college studies at Washington College in St. Louis,

general of Mahone's brigade, sends the following letter narrating his recollections of "Seven Pines":

Chicago, Ill.
January 26, 1894

Geo. S. Bernard, Esq.,
Petersburg, Va.

My Dear Comrade: After a lapse of more than thirty years it seems rather presumptuous to write you about "Seven Pines" entirely from memory, and yet that is all that I have to guide me, and if it should play me tricks you must get some such encyclopedic authority as Jim Phillips[40] to furnish the correction.

From the camp near Drewry's Bluff we moved on the night of Wednesday, May 28, 1862, arriving in Richmond about midday on the day following. An incident of our march through the city was a review by the governor (Letcher), who stood on a granite carriage block (still remaining in front of the executive mansion), flanked, rather backed by our good old friend, Bassett French,[41] then colonel and military secretary to his excellency. The brigade, composed entirely of Virginians, one regiment excepted, numbered nearly four thousand muskets, was—thanks to our one year of garrison duty at Norfolk—thoroughly uniformed and equipped, and in fine drill and discipline, and created a sensation.

---

but quit and found work as a clerk on a Mississippi steamboat in 1860. He was scheduled to attend West Point, but did not because of the war. In May 1861, he was captured by Federal troops at Camp Jackson in St. Louis, Missouri. In a little over a month, however, he was free and back in Virginia. In July, he joined the 12th Virginia and was elected 2nd lieutenant of Company D. He was wounded at Second Manassas in August 1862. Later in the war, he served as General William Mahone's assistant adjutant general. Following the conflict, he was a newspaper editor. From 1876 to 1882, he was mayor of Petersburg. Elected governor of Virginia in 1882, he served one term of four years. He left the state for several years, but returned by the end of the nineteenth century and was elected to the Virginia Constitution Convention of 1901. From 1908 to 1919, he edited the *Norfolk Virginian*. Cameron's reminiscences of the Gettysburg Campaign appear in chapter 4. Chapter 10 contains his account of a scouting expedition in 1864.

40. James Eldred Phillips, a master tinner in Richmond, enlisted as a private in Company G of the 12th Virginia in April 1861. He rose steadily through the ranks to 1st lieutenant by November 1863. He commanded his company from March 1864 until the surrender at Appomattox. His papers, including a diary and memoir, are at the Virginia Historical Society.

41. Samuel Bassett French, a native of Norfolk, was an attorney, judge, editor, and a soldier in the Confederate army during the war. He prepared biographical information on thousands of men for his unpublished work "Annals of Prominent Virginians of the XIX Century."

The itinerary for the few days next preceding our arrival on the battle field you have already [heard] from other sources. The rain and thunder storm at Randolph's Hill was an event, however, that made a great impression on men as yet unused to exposure. I was then a very light hearted youth and was entertaining Col. Weisiger, Capt. Owens[42] and others with some giddy reflections on the utility of a metallic coffin as part of an officer's outfit—as a camp-chest, a water proof bed, and a handy thing to have about in case of accidents—when a flash of lightning forked down upon the muskets stacked in a long line to our front and ran with diabolical friskiness along the bayonet points, lighting up the scene with a ghostly glare of yellow and blue, while a crash of an earthquake followed and the smell of brimstone pervaded the atmosphere. There may be members of the camp who still remember how abruptly my fun-making closed.

We marched through mud and [water][43] and in the morning of the second days fighting arrived by a cross road in the field fronting the fort at Seven Pines which had been taken from the Federals the previous day. We halted in the abatis, on the border of a deep ditch, or drain, facing eastward, and stood there from some time. I recall the figure of a dead North Carolinian on the outer slope of the fort, who had been killed while mounting the embankment, and remained as if cut in stone—one foot embedded in soft clay, resting on the other knee, the gun advanced in the right hand, and the face bent eagerly forward. The figure would have been the fortune of any sculptor as a model.

One man of Capt. Bond's company (C) was wounded by a stray shot while we remained in this position. Probably about ten[44] o'clock orders came to move. The regiment counter-marched and moving across the Williamsburg Road formed line of battle facing nearly north, there being an interval, an open field, of probably one hundred yards between the road and the heavy forest of pines and oaks. While going into position through mud ankle deep and of the consistency of custard we passed the unsightly corpse of a Federal officer, utterly encased in mud. The late Richard H. Christian,[45] then a

---

42. Thomas F. Owens, owner of a dry goods store in Norfolk, enlisted as 1st lieutenant in Company H of the 12th Virginia in April 1861. Elected captain in May 1862, he was wounded at Second Manassas. After eight months of convalescence, he returned to service, only to be captured at Chancellorsville. Exchanged during the summer of 1863, he returned to his unit to serve as acting regimental quartermaster until the end of the war. After the war, he founded a Masonic lodge in Norfolk.

43. The article states "watch" here. The intended word is likely "water."

44. GSB: It was much earlier in the morning.

45. Richard H. Christian enlisted in April 1861 at age fourteen as a private in Company A of the 12th Virginia. In August, he was appointed a Confederate state military cadet and assigned to the color guard of the 12th Virginia. He was temporary commander of Company A at Crampton's Gap, where he suffered a severe wound to the foot.

youngster of fourteen and a cadet of the Confederacy attached to the 12th regiment was without a suitable sword. His quick eye discerned the fact that a handsome one was covered by the body of the fallen foe, and undismayed by the repulsiveness of the corpse or the newness of such a sight, he turned the corpse over and cooly unbuckled the coveted prize. Afterwards such an incident would have been nothing: but at that time and under all the circumstances, it struck me as an exhibition of sang froid worthy of note.

Troops entered the woods in advance of our movement. Firing began to our left and front. We marched in without skirmishers, and had gone about two hundred and fifty yards when I saw a man from our line sink into the bed of a brook which crossed our line of advance. Meantime I had heard the zip-zip of bullets, but had not realized what they were in the slightest degree. My impression was that the man was skulking, and I approached him with up-lifted sword and an imprecation; I shall never forget the remorse I felt when the poor fellow turned his face up to me for answer and I saw the blood pouring from a ghastly wound under the left eye.

About this time we encountered the heaviest fire of the enemy—it was never such as we met afterwards in regular engagements. I remember seeing Lt. Col. Taylor, mounted on his old black mare, riding slowly to the front, parting the overhanging boughs with his disengaged hand, and his usually saturnine face aglow with excitement. A little later I heard him rivaling the army in Flanders with strange and muscular expletives. He told me afterwards that he did not remember to have used a word inconsistent with usual pious habit. Col. Weisiger's evidence was required to support mine to make the old gentleman believe it: but he did swear most mightily.

Another picture which recurs to my mind's eye as vividly as though in actual presence is that of Dr. Jim Claiborne,[46] the surgeon of our regiment, riding forward on his comely sorrel steed, his movements as deliberate and his expression as imperturbable as if going to make a professional call. Col. Weisiger went into action on the big raw-boned bay, which bore him through all the campaigns to the last scene at Appomattox. His horse was lightly wounded unless my memory is entirely at fault shortly after encountering the enemy's fire, and we all dismounted after reaching the furthest point of advance. The undergrowth in spots was dense, and while moving forward I only

---

Praised by commanding officers, he was recommended to transfer to the artillery, where he was commissioned a 2nd lieutenant in Reese's Battery, F. H. Carter Battalion, in 1864.

46. James W. Claiborne, M.D., enlisted as a private in Company E of the 12th Virginia in April 1861. Commissioned assistant surgeon of the regiment in May 1861, he held that rank until commissioned surgeon the next year. He served with his unit until the surrender at Appomattox.

caught a glimpse of one or two of the enemy, seemingly skirmishers firing in retreat and did not at any time during the period of the day see any body of men in our front of sufficient force to be designated as a line a battle.

How long were we in the woods? Is there any evidence on this point? I should say half an hour at the outside, but this is only an impression. I think we obliqued to the left during the advance, as our right flank was uncovered and troops under fire instinctively and unconsciously gain ground toward their supports. Certainly when the order came to retreat two of our companies on the left flank had gotten on the other side of a wagon road which entered the forest perpendicularly to the Williamsburg pike. The order was communicated from the right of the line, and was accompanied by the retiring of the companies on that flank, but with steadiness and no hurry. I was with the color guard where an exciting scene, sad in its consequences, else where related, had just occurred,[47] when Col. Taylor gave me instructions to go to the left and communicate the order for retirement. The rest of the regiment was moving back already when I got to those two companies. I think they were E and G but possibly C instead of E. That one of them was the Richmond Grays (G) I am positive: for I came out with some of the men of that company, Sgt. Kelly[48] and Private Graeme[49] among the number, and

47. GSB: The sad scene to which Gov. Cameron here refers was the taking of the colors from Color Sergeant Williamson by Col. Taylor, of which he writes as follows in his contribution to the history of the Maryland campaign in Vol. I of "War Talks of Confederate Veterans" (Appendix p. 299.)

"Another fact, closely connected with the history of our regiment during the campaigns of 1862, should be mentioned: James D. Williamson, whose name occurs among the killed at Second Manassas, was the color-bearer in our 'baptism of blood' at Seven Pines. His hesitation, under a conflict of orders, was, mistaken for want of courage by one of his superiors, and, without opportunity for defense, he was deprived of the colors on the field and degraded from his position. For months he bore bravely the undeserved stigma, but went about his duty like one weary of life: and though the harsh and cruel edict was never withdrawn by the officer who issued it, the victim had the sympathy and respect of his comrades throughout the ordeal, and at Manassas he fell in the fore-front of the fight, and found his vindication in a hero's death. His unjust judge did not long survive him, and his faults may be remembered with greater charity, in that he too met a soldier's end, and met it bravely."

48. Oscar R. Kelly of Richmond enlisted as a private in Company G of the 12th Virginia in April 1861. Severely wounded at Seven Pines, he returned to service after nine months in a hospital. He was promoted to corporal in May 1863, and sergeant in June 1864. He was wounded again on the retreat to Appomattox, and finished the war in a hospital in Danville.

49. William Grame enlisted as a private in Company G of the 12th Virginia in April 1861. Wounded at Second Manassas, he was hospitalized for nine months. He was then

the regiment was already forming a new line near the main road when we joined it.

The enemy came rapidly down the byroad, having doubtless ascertained the retirement of the right of the line. This road was of white sand and straight enough to afford a view to the front (now rear) for a couple of hundred of yards. On gaining it, I was proceeding leisurely toward the turnpike, when a half dozen shots passing near, and some striking the ground hard by, gave notice of danger. Looking over my shoulder, I saw a group of blue-coated gentry trotting in the fringe of the woods on either side of the track-way, firing as they came. Though the situation was new, I appreciated its meaning at a glance. Some thirty yards in the direction of Seven Pines two huge trees stood together, and the road opened wide on either side. I broke at a run for this place of temporary shelter, reached it in safety, but out of wind, and as I drew a breath of satisfaction, heard a voice say dryly, "I'm glad to see you taking things so cooly, adjutant." The speaker was young Graeme of the Richmond Grays, above referred to who was capping his gun as he spoke, and immediately afterwards leaned around the tree and fired into the nearest group of Federals with the effect of forcing them to cover. The gallant fellow was subsequently killed in battle after a brave career.[50] I can still see the gleam of his blue eyes as he indulged his quiet humor at the expense of his superior officer. By the way, I had on my belt that day the pistol, which, with an immense bowie-knife made at Uriah Wells foundry, had constituted a part of the outfit with which an infantry private repaired in Norfolk twelve months before. While behind the tree, I sought to improve the first opportunity ever presented of "shooting a Yankee," but every chamber snapped fire, and I never carried it into action again. (At Chancellorsville I came into possession of a repeating carbine which served as a trusty companion and did good service until I lost it during a scouting expedition within the enemy's lines in the fall of 1864, while swimming a ford in Blackwater then swollen by rains. At some future time I will write you the eventful history of that "scout.")[51]

I have said that the regiment was forming a new line when we joined it. The right of this line rested on the Williamsburg Road, and at this point

---

assigned special duty as a clerk to a provost marshall. Captured at Burgess Mill in 1864, he was released from Point Lookout military prison in May 1865.

50. Cameron appears to be mistaken about Graeme's fate, for, as explained above, William Graeme of Company G (the Richmond Grays) was a prisoner at Point Lookout at the war's end.

51. William Cameron's account of his scouting mission appears in chapter 10 in an article titled "The Confederate Scout"; see *Petersburg Daily Index-Appeal*, March 27, 1895.

faced eastward, and thence bent around semi-circularly until the left wing faced the woods to the northward.

While lying here I was in the rear of the Petersburg Riflemen, just by the side of Lieut. (afterwards) Captain John R. Patterson. The enemy got our range with a small piece of artillery which I have since heard was a rifled howitzer mounted on a car on the York River Railroad. The little balls, not more than an inch and a half in diameter, enfiladed the position exactly and whizzed just above our heads with most disagreeable frequency. In those days I was the leanest of the lean kind, and Capt. Patterson was rather inclined to corpulency, especially about the stomach. We were hugging the ground with affectionate closeness when Patterson turned and said, "I wish I were as thin as you are; you look as flat as a pancake." The emphatic sincerity of the utterance made it doubly funny.

It was just when our line joined the road that Gen. D. H. Hill had located himself; and here occurred the altercation of which Gen. Mahone, Capt. Spence and others have written you. Attracted by the gathering of mounted officers I rose and drew near to them, and heard the remarks of Gen. Hill, Col. Taylor, and the men in the ranks substantially as reported. I do not remember at this time to have seen Gen. Mahone but it is probably that he was not present when Gen. Hill made his remark, but came up afterwards, and asked him about it, &c. My recollection is that a general officer (either Pickett or Pryor) rode up and asked Hill for reinforcements. The latter replied, "I have no troops but those Virginians and they have just run out of action." The other officer replied, "I will be perfectly satisfied with Gen. Mahone's brigade," or words to that effect. And then Col. Taylor opened his vigorous battery upon Gen. Hill, with an accompanying chorus of protests from the officers and men in hearing.

In connection with this incident the Camp will be interested to know that in Gen. Hill's official report of the battle of Malvern Hill, in referring to the troops who made the attack on Magruder's front and who held the advanced position that night, he pays the most exalted compliment to the valor and steadfastness of Mahone's brigade. I hope you will look up the report in the proper volume of the Official Records (I have not the book by me) and read it to our comrades, as a proof that at least it was not from prejudice that the sturdy old Carolinian misjudged them in their first engagement.[52]

---

52. See U.S. War Department, *The War of the Rebellion: A Compilation of the Official Records of the Union and Confederate Armies,* 70 vols. (Washington, D.C.: Government Printing Office, 1880–1901) [hereafter cited as *O.R.*], 11: pt. 1, 943. All references are to Series I unless otherwise noted.

Well, we moved down the Williamsburg Road about half a mile and again facing the north moved into the woods and occupied a crest among the tents which Casey's men had abandoned after their rout. Here we exchanged shots with the enemy briskly but with no result of movement. In fact the battle was over. Here we confronted the regiment (the 81st New York) of the late Col. Jno. B. Raulston[53] then adjutant of his command, as I was of the 12th: and we got a portion of the new silver instruments just purchased by him for the regimental band, and they were afterwards utilized to the playing of Confederate music under the leadership of the never-to-be-forgotten Haggerdorn.[54]

While lying at this place an amusing episode came under my eye. Two men of Company A took possession in partnership of an immense iron pot which was part of the furnishing of Casey's cooking camp. This they put to the novel use of a fortification, a very efficient one, as no artillery was in action, and the iron furnished a complete protection against balls from the rifles then in service. The men would take it by turns to cover head and shoulders while loading and would emerge and fire. This was kept up for some time until at last one of them attempted to monopolize this bomb-proof. A dispute followed, in the midst of which Ben May[55] walked to the spot and with a vigorous kick sent the object of discussion rolling down the hill, to the discomfiture of the disputants and the great amusement of all who witnessed the incident.

Just here, too, our lamented friend James Dunlop[56] gave me a hearty laugh. He, like John Patterson, was pretty corpulent. He was prone upon the very crest of the ridge, looking for an opportunity to shoot something. The enemy were sending a brisk, but not heavy fire, best described as annoying. I noticed Jim moving uneasily from time to time, and at last I called out, "What is the matter? Are you hurt?" His answer was to burst out laughing, while he held up in one hand his canteen. "No," said he, "but I thought I was lying on a mountain all this time; and it was nothing but this confounded canteen."

53. John B. Raulston enlisted as captain of Company H of the New York 81st Infantry in April 1861. Eventually promoted to colonel, he mustered out in January 1865.

54. Henry Hagadorn, a private in Company I, enlisted as a substitute for E. Wyatt in January 1863. Appointed musician two months later, Hagadorn was captured in April 1865 on the retreat from Petersburg.

55. Benjamin Harrison May enlisted as a private in Company A of the 12th Virginia in April 1861. Son of a wealthy Petersburg lawyer, May became ensign of the color guard in 1864. He was wounded at Spotsylvania and died in a field hospital there.

56. James Dunlop enlisted as a private in Company B of the 12th Virginia in April 1861. Absent for over a year because of chronic diarrhea, Dunlop returned to his unit and surrendered at Appomattox. Cameron might also be referring to John Dunlop, a private in Company C of the 12th Virginia.

I recall nothing else worthy of remark except the long, yet, dreary night, during the hours of which the command retired. Capt. John Lyon was left with two companies on picket with orders to withdraw at daylight, and I was left at the junction of the Williamsburg Road with that by which we had come in that morning to conduct the picket back to the regiment. The enemy made no attempt to follow.

We entered Seven Pines very strong, eleven or twelve hundred muskets. It was our baptism of fire. In the next day's bivouac we had about eight hundred men for duty. Our apparent loss had been over three hundred, whilst our actual loss was not one fifth of this number.

The difference was in the chaff which thus at that outset became separated from the wheat. Most of the missing, from one cause or another, remained so to the end of the war. Most of those who stood this first test endured to the end or fell upon the field of battle.

This weeding out of the bad material from our regiment was the only good result of the affair at Seven Pines, which, so far as our particular command was concerned, was in no sense a battle—but merely a purposeless, ill-ordered, inconsequential collision with the enemy. We gained neither experience nor confidence from its blind confusion of movements. Our own officers were not to blame, for they only obeyed orders, but later they would not have obeyed such orders without seeing for themselves that the ordinary precautions of our advance had been taken and discovering the position of the enemy by an attack with skirmishers instead of blundering and stumbling upon it in line of battle. The day lies in my memory like a bad, but blurred dream, of which the only distinct features are the noble fellows whose dead faces haunt it. In all the after years of blood I never again felt so grievously the shock of sudden death as when looking upon the corpse of my kinsman and dear friend Pat McCulloch[57] of the field of Seven Pines.

The next morning, when, with the picket, I rejoined the regiment in bivouac, the late Maj. Daniel Lyon[58] had already arrived there in a jersey wagon, among the furnishing of which was an extremely plethoric demi-john of whiskey, chemically pure and of venerable age, which was intended for the sole consumption of the sick and wounded. I have no idea that John Lyon, or Tom Pollard, have yet forgotten how very sick we all were until relieved by a dose of that medicine.

57. Patrick D. McCulloch is described in note 56, chapter 1.

58. Daniel Lyon Jr. was a prewar tobacco seller in Petersburg who joined the 12th Virginia in March 1862. He served as hospital steward until discharged in July 1863, when he became clerk in the Medical Director's Office in Richmond.

The major was rejoiced and surprised to find any of us alive, as on his journey he had encountered many of the early fugitives who had reported themselves as the only survivors of a disastrous engagement, and even furnished circumstantial accounts of the "taking off" of some of those who now claimed his welcome and craved his medical treatment. The most fleet of foot of these volunteer couriers had already borne their tales of woe to the horror-stricken ears of our relatives in Petersburg, who had not yet learned to take cum grano salis the extravagant reports of "the last survivor" of a destroyed command; and wide-spread was the mourning there until authentic accounts arrived, bringing tidings of a fearful import to a few, but joyful relief to the minds of many. One Falstaff reached the house in Richmond of some connection of my own, before dinner was served, and relating all the details of my heroic end, including an eloquent dying apostrophe to the flag under which I had fallen, the rascal destroyed the appetites of the family, and thereby gained a larger range of freedom for his own sharpened by his long and speedy flight. Poor fellow, he never came back to duty, but his seven league boots did not avail him much in the race with death, for he fell a victim to disease before the year was out, only one of many illustrations that fate is not to be escaped.

Yours,

William E. Cameron

[Bernard concludes:]

With the help of the foregoing and extracts from other letters kindly sent me by friends who took part in the battle of Seven Pines, I have given you, Comrades, I hope, some insight into this, to Mahone's brigade, unsatisfactory engagement, to which its members never looked back except with feelings of regret. As suggested by Gov. Cameron, this action separated the chaff from the wheat, and what was left constituted the material which contributed its part towards enabling the brigade in its subsequent career, when it took part in all of the great battles in which the Army of Northern Virginia won its splendid fame, to achieve a most enviable reputation. I might tell you more of what was done on that memorable Sunday in June, but the length of this address forbids.

ADDENDA: STATEMENT OF J. WILLCOX BROWN

After the foregoing address was delivered the following letter from Col. J. Willcox Brown, of Baltimore, Md., who as a member of the Petersburg Rifleman took part in the battle of Seven Pines, was received and is an interesting contribution to the history of the engagement:

Baltimore, March 12th, 1894

George S. Bernard, Esq., Petersburg, Va.,

Dear George: I am deeply indebted to you for the opportunity of reading "From Drewry's Bluff to Seven Pines." Your address with accompanying communications, presents a very complete and accurate account of that period in the history of the 12th Va., and, while highly appreciating your kind invitation to me to give you my recollections, I find very little to write which would not be in the way of mere repetition.

Although the 12th at Seven Pines was put in badly at first, suffered heavily and was grossly insulted by the general who was responsible for its losing some noble men without accomplishing any results, I can never regret that I was present as a private in Co. E. I was proud on the field of the way in which the regiment behaved under very trying circumstances, and I have ever since been proud of my comrades who came out of their first fight with such untarnished honour.

I will give a little account of my personal experiences between the time the regiment halted under fire and the time when it was reformed a short distance to the rear, which may throw some light on the questions of lapse of time, &c.

When we halted just on the edge of a camp and were subjected to a fire of what I learned subsequently were Berdan's Sharpshooters,[59] I began to immediately use my rifle. Very much to my disgust and surprise the cap snapped, and so did another one, and I was forced to resort to my pricker. The third time the gun went off, but I only fired two shots in all. By this time the Petersburg Riflemen found that the colors had gone back, and the rest of the regiment, so far as we could ascertain, and we were near the centre. We had not however heard any order given to retire and refused to leave our ground until the matter was finally settled by our saying to our gallant captain, R. R. Banks, that we would do so if he would go back and report to us that proper order had been given to that effect. He soon returned and informed us that it was all right and we started to rejoin the regiment. I was detained for a very few moments, first by my going to see whether or not Serg't. Theo. Meade,[60] who had been shot near the right of the company, was really dead as I had been informed, and next by stopping to pour some brandy (from a flask I had)

59. "Berdan's Sharpshooters" was a Federal unit commanded by Colonel Hiram Berdan.

60. Theophilus Meade enlisted in April 1861, rose to the rank of sergeant by May 1862, and was killed in action at Seven Pines.

down the throat of Lem Peebles[61] who had been shot through the body just at my left and was then being taken from the field in a fainting condition. Poor fellow! He died a very few days after and Theo. Meade's heart, when I reached him, had ceased to beat. I lost no time after this in getting to the regiment which even after this brief lapse of time I found fully formed and all I had to do was just to take my place in the ranks of Co. E.

Soon after this we were subjected to some shelling. The sensation was novel and not altogether agreeable, I remember to have looked with some admiration on the insensibility to it of an officer who rode along our rear from left to right, but my feelings underwent a decided change when as he got in rear of where I was, I heard him say, "Ah, boys, you ran away and let poor Pickett be cut to pieces." I also heard the rejoinder from Col. Fielding Taylor, "It is a lie, sir!" Many years have passed since then, but it would not be possible for me to be persuaded that I did not hear these very words. It would not be possible to exaggerate the horror and disgust with which our regiment, officers and men, received this rebuke, which they so little deserved, for, no matter who was to blame, they were not and knew they were not, and at the moment were ready for any service.

I will recall that so far as two companies were concerned, the Petersburg Riflemen (Co. E.) and Richmond Grays (Co. G.) their spirits were wonderfully revived when a short time afterward, we were sent forward as skirmishers and did some good work very well indeed and without loss. I certainly never saw our men cooler and more cheerful than they were then. They felt that they were accomplishing something.

I will mention an incident which occurred at this time, especially because it tends to confirm me in my recollection that I did hear General Hill use General Pickett's name and that I at the time even located the latter's command. It so happened that I was occupying quite an advanced position ahead of the skirmish line with Bill Davis[62] and Henry Cowles[63] of the Riflemen, when an officer came riding from our right to left along a road and within

61. Lemuel J. Peebles Jr. of Petersburg, son of a wealthy commission merchant, enlisted as a private in Company E of the 12th Virginia in April 1861. He was killed at Seven Pines.

62. William H. Davis was the son of William T. Davis, president of Petersburg Female College. He enlisted as a private in Company E of the 12th Virginia in April 1861 and rose to the rank of sergeant. He died in a hospital in Charlottesville in May 1863.

63. Henry Brown Cowles, son of a wealthy Methodist minister in Petersburg, enlisted as a private in Company E of the 12th Virginia in July 1861. He died of typhoid fever in the Virginia Hospital in Petersburg in August 1863.

very easy gunshot. My comrades were just about to fire and the result would have been certain death, for they were both crack shots, when I under the impression that this officer must be coming from Pickett's command which I in my mind had located as in advance of our right, begged them not to fire. I have always regretted that they yielded to my wishes. I was near-sighted and I don't think they had any doubt as to the facts of the case. I have often thought of these two gallant young men and have deemed it quite an example of the "irony of fact" that they should both have died in hospital, while of them it is told that in the dreadful charge at Malvern Hill they were heard to ask each other: "Isn't this glorious?"

My recollection of the later events of that day (June 1st), and of the night and the morning after, coincides entirely with the account given by you and your correspondents.

Many, many incidents come back to me which will always be cherished memories and to my latest day there will ever be present to my mind the most pleasing remembrances of the men who in one capacity or another, constituted the 12th Virginia regiment of infantry.

Your friend sincerely,

J. Willcox Brown.

STATEMENT OF CULLEN A. BATTLE

The following from Gen. Cullen A. Battle,[64] of Greensboro, N.C., giving some interesting details from the stand point of the 3rd Alabama regiment, of which he was lieutenant-colonel at the time of the engagement:

Petersburg, Va., April 11, 1895.

Geo. S. Bernard, Esq., Petersburg, Va.

My Dear Sir: You have kindly urged me to write out my recollections of "Seven Pines," and especially the part acted by the 3rd Alabama regiment, Mahone's brigade, on the "ill-starred field."

I shall write entirely from memory, with the understanding that your are at liberty to exclude anything from publication that you do not approve.

The battle of Seven Pines, while it was the theater of brilliant exploit, was a series of military blunders. The battle of the 31st of May was fought by two divisions, indeed, almost entirely by one while five divisions were in easy reach of the battlefield.

It had been said that the wrangle of Longstreet and Huger over the ques-

---

64. Major-General Cullen Andrews Battle was born in Georgia and grew up in Alabama. He led the 3rd Alabama early in the war, and rose to brigade command in 1863. He was severely wounded at Cedar Creek in October 1864.

tion of rank occasioned the absence of Huger's division from the field, but, in truth, Huger ought to have been in line of battle long before Longstreet came to him while crossing Gillie's creek. Johnston's order to Huger was to move early in the morning, but he delayed until the afternoon, and then set about crossing the creek, one man at a time, on two fence rails. It was while this was going on that Longstreet arrived on the field in time to take part in the engagement, while Huger "snuffed the battle from afar." A month after Seven Pines Gillie's creek would have been an insignificant obstacle in the way of a division advancing to battle.

But, it is with the engagement of the first of June that we are most concerned. On the memorable morning of that eventful day, Mahone's brigade was marching in column when it was suddenly fired upon. Instantly forming in line of battle, the brigade rushed upon the enemy. I was at my post as lieutenant-colonel, on the right of the 3rd Alabama. So dense was the thicket into which we had plunged that it was impossible for me to see to all my own battalion. Indeed, not more than two companies were visible at a time, and even these were imperfectly seen. Never was there a hotter fight. When the fire slackened I passed down my line and was surprised to find that I had but four companies. What had become of the rest I had no idea. Returning to my position on the right, Captain Sands of Company A, Mobile Cadets, said to me, "We are being fired on from the rear." And just then several balls, from the rear, struck the tree by which we were standing. I at once dispatched an officer, who soon returned and stated that the shots came from the 12th Virginia, and that the 3rd Alabama was far ahead of the other troops. At first I greatly censured the 12th Virginia, but soon accepted the blame my self on the supposition that I had, unconsciously, obliqued too much to the right. Just after this the enemy advanced again, and was driven back by my four companies. The firing then entirely ceased in my front, and I cautiously withdrew my men in perfect order. When I reached the open I saw a body of Confederates a considerable distance to my left and soon found that it was the left and center of the 3rd Alabama under Major Forsythe. Then I learned for the first time, that Colonel Lomax and Adjutant Johnston were killed early in the engagement. Hence it was that no one was sent to inform of the situation. I received no order to retreat, and held my ground until the firing had ceased.

At this late day I cannot tell what was the loss of the 3rd Alabama at Seven Pines. The regiment went into action about 1,100 strong and lost more than upon any other field of the war, although it participated with distinction in all the great battles of the Army of Northern Virginia.

It is to the discredit of General D. H. Hill that he reflected on the conduct of Mahone's brigade at the battle of Seven Pines, and it is to the honor of the brigade that he virtually admitted his error when in general orders he directed that "Seven Pines" be inscribed on the regimental battle-flags of Mahone's brigade.

General Longstreet in his report of the battle of Seven Pines says:

> Our loss in valuable officers and men has been severe, Colonel Giles[65] (Fifth South Carolina), Jones[66] (Twelfth Alabama), and Lomax (Third Alabama) fell at the head of their commands, gallantly leading them to victory.

Regretting my inability to do full justice to the 3rd Alabama and Mahone's brigade at the battle of Seven Pines.

I am yours, most truly.

Cullen A. Battle

[At the end of his article, Bernard included General Pickett's official report on Seven Pines. It has been omitted here, but can be found in the *Official Records* (O.R., Series I, vol. 11, pt. 1, 982).

Throughout the Peninsula Campaign, McClellan sought to bring his siege guns within range of Richmond. On June 25, several weeks after the fighting at Seven Pines, he launched an attack with the hope of seizing the high ground in the vicinity of Old Tavern along the Nine Mile Road. From there, he hoped to commence his final approach to Richmond. The ensuing fight at French's Farm, just west of the Seven Pines battlefield, yielded little and marked an end to McClellan's progress against the rebel capital. The following account from Bernard appeared in the *Petersburg Daily Index-Appeal* on July 26, 1903.]

"From Seven Pines to Malvern Hill—Battles of French's Farm, June 25, 1862, and Frazier's Farm, June 30, 1862," by George S. Bernard

About Wednesday, June 4, 1862, we are again moving—leave at daylight and march eastwardly down the Charles City Road for more than a mile—form a line of battle across the road—a battery of artillery placed near us to rake

---

65. John R. R. Giles enlisted as a captain in the 5th South Carolina and was promoted to colonel.

66. Robert T. Jones enlisted as a captain in the 12th Alabama.

the road—their near presence give us a feeling of security—a detachment of eight or ten men are sent forward to burn a house standing a hundred or two yards from our line, in an open field immediately in our front—it is feared it may serve as a protection to the enemy's sharpshooters. Soon after we halted and took position across the road, not having heard up to that time that the enemy were reported advancing, some of us fall to sleep. The writer was awakened by sounds somewhat unusual, as of a person addressing a crowd. He got up at once. Something surely was at hand. Col. Lewellen[67]—then Capt. commanding Co. K—was addressing his men urging them to do their duty in the coming conflict. We then heard the report of the enemy advancing and saw the artillery in position. But no enemy came. Col. Lewellen's speech was all for naught.

We go into camp just where we stood in line of battle. It is useless now to give details. This miserable camp—the "Mud Camp on the Charles City Road" as it was afterwards known—we occupy for several weeks, until we move to take part in the battles of French's Farm, Frazier's [Frayser's] Farm and Malvern Hill. I never think of it with pleasure. As for comforts, we had none then. The water was deficient and miserable, making large numbers of the men sick. Our rations were cooked for us, far back in the rear and brought to us. Can we ever forget those barrels of cooked peas hauled to us in the commissary wagons, soured before they reached us? Or the clammy cakes of tough flour bread, made up with the sole ingredients of flour, salt & water, and thrown together in the barrels whilst yet hot?

In the letter written to my father from this camp under the date of June 17th, 1862, from which a paragraph has already been taken, the following extract relating experiences at this camp may properly be here given:

Our regiment is still down here on the Charles City Road, in the advance. We are now entrenching ourselves. The enemy are not more than two and a half miles distant. Our pickets encounter them every day. When the great battle will come off no one, of course, can tell—possibly it may never come off. For the past three or four days everything has been very quiet along our lines—which has been kept up every day until three or four days ago. We are having rather a better time now than we had a short time since. We now have some of our tents, and the weather is much better. Before we got the tents it would rain almost every night, and several times I have waked up soaking wet.

---

67. John Richard Lewellen, a Mexican War veteran and prewar newspaper editor, enlisted in Company K of the 12th Virginia in May 1861. Promoted to captain in July 1861, he was wounded at Crampton's Gap. Steadily promoted up the ranks to colonel, he survived the war to return to newspaper editing.

Our fare continues very bad on account of the scarcity of provision—we live on half rations. It is impossible for this state of things to hold out long.

Let us again draw from the notebook:

Can we ever forget the frequent "alarms"—how we were suddenly gotten under arms at different hours of the night & tramped off a half a mile or so in the direction of the enemy, to lurk about in the thickets, watching their approach!

Here may be mentioned an interesting incident that I have often recalled:

One night, a few days after we occupied this position, a detachment of Co. I. under the command of Lt. J. R. Manson, was sent forward to do picket duty a short distance in front of our camp, and was posted along the edge of a field skirted by a body of woods. The whole detachment, or at least the part of it with which I was (in the capacity as sergeant), stationed immediately on the right of the Charles City Road, by which the enemy was expected to advance. Everything was perfectly quiet during the whole night until about daybreak, when there rang out in the damp morning air the sharp, startling crack of a rifle. Immediately every one was on the *qui vive*. Who fired the shot? What was the occasion? I walked down the line from the position I occupied at the time and enquiring of the men who fired the shot soon found it was Private Jno. J. Jones,[68] of our company. I asked what he fired at.

"A man on a horse," he said.

"Where?"

"Just down in the woods there!" he replied, pointing to a place in front of him.

I asked the man who occupied the adjoining post a few feet away whether he had seen a mounted man in his front or had seen or heard anything unusual in that direction. He said he had not. Nor was there anyone along the line besides John Jones who had heard or seen anything unusual in our front. Jones, however, who was in all respects a reliable man, insisted that he could not be mistaken—he certainly saw a man on horseback, and shot at him, he said. In a little while it was broad daylight, and with a view to ascertaining what it was that he fired at, I went to the spot indicated by him as the place

68. John James Jones enlisted as a private in Company I of the 12th Virginia in February 1862. Promoted to corporal in February 1863, he was then court-martialed and sentenced to hard labor for 30 days for being AWOL. He returned to his unit in time for the Battle of Brandy Station, where he was wounded. After five months in a hospital, he returned to service, but received a medical discharge in November 1864. He survived the war.

where the horse and its rider stood, but found no dead or wounded horse or man, and no track or sign of any kind that showed that either horse or man had been there. This was reported back to Lt. Manson and Private Jones but the latter insisted that he was not mistaken.

For many years after the war I occasionally met Comrade Jones on the court green at Greensville C.H., Va., on court days, and would refer to the incident, but he was always unshaken in his belief and contention that it was a mounted man of flesh and blood at whom he fired his gun that June morning, and would not for a moment entertain the suggestion that he was wearied with long watching, and was, perhaps dreaming, as I indeed found myself one night whilst on picket duty near Atlee's Station, during the campaign of 1864. The regiment was doing duty on a skirmish line on the night of May 31st, 1864, and, when we took our positions in the rifle-pits, the officers and men were informed that it was expected that the enemy would make an advance on our right. In this event the men were ordered to retire, not by falling back to the rear, but to left, going out by the flank along the line of the rifle-pits. Constant service since the opening of the campaign at the Wilderness had nearly broken us down, and that night it fell to my lot to go out on a vidette post some fifty yards in front of the line of the rifle-pits to do a tour of duty there, and whilst on this post, although I realized the responsibility of the position, I was able, with the greatest difficulty, to keep my eyes open, and once or twice almost fell asleep. Although not more than two hundred yards in our front I could see what I took to be the picket post of the enemy, its position being indicated by a small fire. Having served my tour of vidette duty I returned to the rifle-pits where I took my position with one or more of our company, all of us under instruction to keep awake. Suddenly I heard, as I believed, the reports of several guns fired on the picket line to our right, and, as I thought, saw the men from the pits on our right retiring along our line just in rear of our particular pit in strict accordance with our orders, and were retiring along the line of the pits. I immediately seized my blanket-roll and haversack, which were lying by me, and began hurriedly to put them on, and was about taking my rifle when a comrade, Thomas C. Branch,[69] of Brunswick county, Va., who was in the pit with me, seeing my actions and not understanding what they meant, caught hold of me and asked what I was doing, remarking at the time: "You're asleep!" I asked him if he had not heard all

69. Thomas C. Branch, a clerk for a Petersburg dry goods firm, enlisted as a private in Company C of the 12th Virginia in June 1861. He transferred to Company E in May 1862. Absent for nearly a year because of dysentery, he rejoined his unit in 1864 and was captured at High Bridge in April 1865.

that firing on our right. His reply was the he had not, but had heard one gun fired somewhere down the line, I was soon convinced that I had been dreaming, but a more vivid or realistic dream I never had. Nothing short of reality could have been more distinct than the numerous shots I believed I heard and located a hundred or two yards to our right and the men from the pits on our right I believed I saw moving to our left singly and in small squads in the pines immediately behind our line of pits.

[Seeking to advance his siege guns to an area of high ground in his front, General McClellan launched an attack at French's Farm (or Oak Grove) on June 25 with Hooker's division of the Federal Third Corps. The ragged Federal advance made modest gains but was eventually driven back by a Confederate counterattack (which included the 12th Virginia).]

Let us again draw from the note book:

But no more of this. The 25th of June (Wednesday) came. About ten o'clock in the morning we heard unusually heavy musketry about a mile to our front and left. Within a few moments we are under arms and moving in that direction, the firing in the meantime ceasing. We will not now recount the events of this day. In the afternoon—near sunset—the little affair known as "French's Farm" is fought. Fifteen or twenty of the 12th are killed & wounded.[70] Old Billy Smith,[71] who commanded the 49th Va. Infantry com-

70. GSB: Among those who fell was a gallant young North Carolinian, Color-Sergeant Robert E. Jones, of Co. B of the 12th Va., a brother of Hon. Wm. M. Jones, the present (1903) mayor of Petersburg, Va. Young Jones was a member of the color-guard, and, when Lt. Col. Taylor took the colors from Color-bearer Williamson in the battle of Seven Pines, claimed that it was his privilege to carry them, and the colors were placed in his hands. A few days after the battle, being taken sick, he applied for and obtained a furlough, which reached him just before the regiment received its marching orders on the morning of the 25th of June. His father, who was in camp to take him home, urged that he return with him instead of going to the front with the regiment. To this appeal he replied with a smile: "I am a North Carolinian in a Virginia regiment, and, if I don't go into this fight, some one will say I am a coward. These colors are mine, and as long as I live no one else shall carry them. When this battle is over I will go home." Thus treating the entreaty of his father and the advice of his comrades, he insisted on going forward with the regiment, although a sick man, and whilst bearing the colors at the post of honor received a mortal wound, of which he died a few days later in the town of Manchester.

71. GSB: Ex-Governor Wm. Smith, one of Virginia's truest and most distinguished sons, who knew nothing and cared nothing about military tactics, but was one of the most gallant officers in the Confederate army. He was twice Governor of Virginia.

pliments the manner in which the 12th move into action. At nine o'clock at night we are back at our quarters at the "Mud Camp." The next morning at light we move again for the same place, and spend the day in the edge of the woods skirting the open field around French's house in which the battle was fought. The enemy make no advance. Their dead lie unburied where they fell. At night we again return to our quarters. Long after we get there, we hear the rapid sounds of artillery, far to our left. They come from the battlefield of Mechanicsville, where on Thursday evening (June 26th, 1862) a terrible conflict raged. The next day (Friday), we repair to the same position at the edge of the woods, to watch the enemy—but still no advance from them. We now hear the most extravagant rumors from the battles which have been fought on our left.

[On June 26, Lee launched a large-scale offensive against McClellan's right flank north of the Chickahominy, beginning with a limited attack at Mechanicsville that afternoon. The next day, a series of poorly coordinated Confederate assaults eventually overran the Union Fifth Corps at Gaines Mill, pushing McClellan's right off the north bank of the Chickahominy. In just two days, Lee had cut McClellan's supply line (the Richmond & York River Railroad) and wrecked the Federal commander's plans for Richmond.]

Everything has gone for the Confederates, McClellan captured, thousands of prisoners & the remainder of the enemy retreating—in time, the war about to be closed in short order. Such reports as these come from the scene of action. But again (Saturday) we are carried back to the same position at the edge of the woods, to remain all day and return again at night to camp as before.

Sunday morning (June 29) everything seems quiet. I believe we had an inspection. But about 11 o'clock A.M. we are ordered under arms, and are soon moving down a country road leading eastwardly from our camp and in the direction of the enemy. We leave without our baggage—not even taking our blankets.

Where are we going, and upon what errand? We move cautiously along, our route being through the swampy woods where we had scouted and had encountered Yankees. But none of the latter were now to be seen, but we see where their pickets had stood—pick up and read scraps of newspapers, letters &c, left by them. We had marched perhaps a distance of five miles, when we came to a halt. A shot or two is fired just ahead of us. Every man is ready to fire. The enemy are near at hand. No—those in front of us are our friends! Word is passed along down the line to that effect. The supposed enemy prove

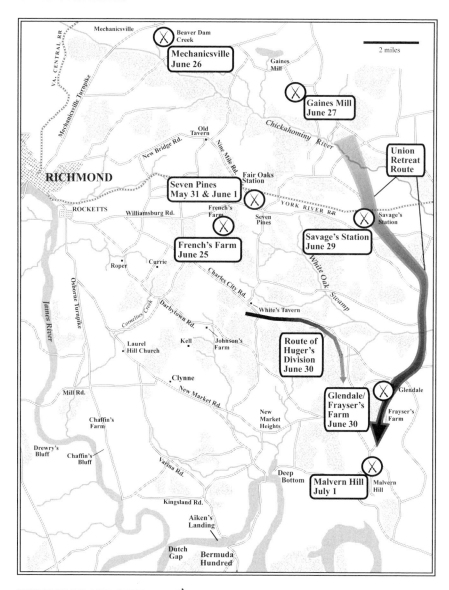

SEVEN PINES AND SEVEN DAYS' BATTLES

to be old Billy Smith's regiment, the 49th Va. of our brigade who were moving down the Charles City Road, and had taken us just emerging from the woods, to be Yankees. This little affair over, our regiment now files into the Charles City Road and the column continues its eastward movement down that road, but marches only a mile or two before we meet a regiment of cavalry coming from the direction of the enemy. "Where are the Yankees, boys?"

we ask. "Not very far—you will see them presently," they reply; immediately after which we are thrown into line of battle perpendicularly across the road and ordered to be in readiness to receive the approaching enemy said to be cavalry.

In this position we remain for an hour or two, but no enemy appear— somewhat to our disappointment as we had a good position and fancied we could easily have driven them back. Being called to attention, we again move down the Charles City Road, but advanced not more than two or three hundred yards before we are again thrown into line of battle, perpendicularly across tshe road as before, and portions of our line to the left of Co. I immediately began to exchange shots with the enemy who were but a short distance—only a hundred or so yards—in front of us in the dense pines. Just now, the 16th Va. Regt of our brigade, disgracefully breaks,[72] and leaves our left flank exposed. But the enemy in their front as also in ours, also retreat, not, however, without firing a few shots over our heads. In this position we remain all night—resting upon our arms.

[After Lee's attacks at Beaver Dam Creek on the 26th, and Gaines Mill the next day, McClellan abandoned his designs on Richmond and sought the safety of the James River to the south. On the 29th, Confederates under Major General John Magruder attacked Edwin Sumner's Second Corps at Savage's Station, west of Seven Pines. Though Southern forces gained no resounding victory, they continued to hound McClellan. On the 30th, Lee sought to tear apart the long retreating column with three columns of his own. One of these, Benjamin Huger's division containing the 12th Virginia, received directions to push down the Charles City Road to intercept the Union line of march. But along the thickly wooded road Union pioneers constructed multiple barricades and successfully delayed Huger throughout the day. Another column, containing forces under Stonewall Jackson, failed to advance along the White Oak Road. As a result, only one prong of Lee's command made contact with the enemy. Confederate troops attacked the enemy at Frayser's Farm, where Federal commanders there cobbled together a battle line. After several hours of brutal fighting, the Union line held. The battle at Frayser's Farm (or Glen-

---

72. GSB: After inquiry I am satisfied that it was only a small part of this regiment that gave way on the occasion here referred to, and that the statement that the regiment "disgracefully" broke was not justified by the facts as I now know them. Of the five regiments of Mahone's brigade that gave it fame, not one had a better record than the 16th Va.

dale) produced great loss but no decisive result. That evening, the retreat to the James continued.[73]]

Next morning (Monday June 30) everything seems quiet and about 11 o'clock we begin to move forward, occasionally halting and taking position in line of battle. About three o'clock in the afternoon the column halts in the road and the pioneers are sent forward with their tools. In a few minutes we are again in motion, and soon discover that the pioneers were sent to the front to cut up and remove two or three large trees which the enemy had felled, throwing them across the road to impede our progress. But we are now near our journey's end—for the day at least. Whilst we stand at a halt in the road, we hear the report of a piece of artillery a short distance—a half a mile—ahead of us. A solid shot whistles over us, striking among the old dead pines to our left. A second, a third and other reports of artillery and shot or shell coming from the same direction, and crashing among the limbs of the trees near us, tell unmistakably of the intention of the enemy to dispute our further advance. Our line is ordered out of the road, and artillery under the gallant Col. De Lagniel[74] is hurried past us to the front and soon engages the Yankee battery. The shots of the enemy enfilade our line, but pass mostly to our front—sometimes raking the road we had just left. In a few minutes the firing ceases and we change position, taking a new line, perpendicular to the line of the road. Very soon the enemy's artillery again opens and from the manner in which the shot & shell were hurled near us it really seemed as if our present position was known to their gunners, although a body of woods intervened. Some of our regiment were struck by fragments of shell.

About sunset the artillery fire in our front has somewhat slackened, and at dark had ceased entirely. What a gloomy evening that seemed! War—how horrible! Nothing so demoralizing as a prolonged artillery fire upon unresisting infantry. That afternoon after being subjected to a heavy fire for nearly an hour from guns we could not see, we were called to attention and began to move forward, we supposed for the purpose of charging the artillery which had long been harassing us. Strange as it may seem, it was really a relief to believe that such was our object. Anything that would put an end to the terrible

73. See Stephen Sears, *To the Gates of Richmond: The Peninsula Campaign* (New York: Ticknor and Fields, 1992), 277–307; and Brian K. Burton, *Extraordinary Circumstances: The Seven Days Battles* (Bloomington: Indiana University Press, 2001), 264–305.

74. Lieutenant Colonel Julius Adolph de Lagnel began the war as a lieutenant colonel, fought at Rich Mountain, and was captured. When exchanged, he declined his commission to brigadier general, preferring to serve in the ordnance bureau in Richmond.

ordeal to which we were subjected, we felt willing to do. But we did not go forward to the charge. We had gone forward scarcely a hundred yards before the fire of the enemy's batteries slackened and then entirely ceased. We rest for the night in the pines, uncertain of the real condition of things. My dreams, I remember, as I dozed on the damp earth, were of terrible battles. Solid shot and shell must have figured prominently in them.

To the foregoing account of experiences on the evening of the 30th of June, I will add one of a personal character that I have often recalled: As we lay in the woods flat on our faces, receiving the severe shelling to which we were being subject, I noticed a small sapling, scarcely three inches in diameter, which stood some five or six feet to my front and left. As small as it was, I looked wistfully at it with a strong inclination, and a half-formed purpose, to change my position, and locate myself with my head behind it. A guardian angel, however, came to my rescue, with a suggestion that the safest place was my proper place, which (I being then third and acting as second sergeant) was on the left of the company line, where I was then lying and I accordingly there remained. The wisdom of this course appeared a few minutes later when a hissing shell came with terrific force through the woods in our front, and landed (without exploding) at or about the very spot where I had contemplated placing my head for safety, the missile violently tearing up the earth enough to fill a wheel-barrow, and scattering it over a number of the men lying near, myself among them. With what I fear was a touch of superstition the lesson [of] that shell, reminding me that the safest place for a soldier is generally his proper place, whatever the appearances may be, often had its influence in regulating my conduct on subsequent occasions.

STATEMENT OF E. LESLIE SPENCE

Capt. Spence, in his letter from which extracts have been taken, says:

The coolest thing I saw during the war occurred the afternoon of the day before the Malvern Hill fight. While we were lying down in those woods and that artillery duel was going on at White Oak Swamp between the Lynchburg Beauregard's and Phil. Kearny's artillery, Gen. Mahone was on his horse directly in front of me, and several field officers were standing around him talking while the shells were bursting all round us. Soon a shell burst in front of Gen. Mahone and the general with the utmost calmness, and I might say 'sang froid,' said to one of the officers, "Colonel, please see if my horse is hurt." No wonder that such nerve and coolness as that inspired our brigade with such entire confidence in our brigade-commander, that we ever afterwards were willing to follow where he led.

....

Let this chapter be concluded with following from the note-book descriptive of our march from the battle-field of Frazier's Farm to Malvern Hill:

About nine o'clock the next morning, July 1, 1862 (Tuesday), we are again in motion. The enemy had retreated, and the roads are filled with columns of troops pushing ahead. Soon we see evidences of last evening's conflict — among them dead men along the road. At one place piles of knapsacks, over-coats, oil cloths, blankets &c. point out the position held by a Yankee line of battle. Our men appropriate the abandoned plunder. The march grows inter-esting. On all sides we see evidences of the recent possession of the country by the Yankees, the ground in some places appearing quite blue with the vast quantities of old and cast away clothing.

After making several halts by the wayside, allowing other troops to pass ahead of us, we finally leave the Charles City Road, taking a right hand road leading off southeastwardly. As we march along this new road, we see more dead men lying in or near the ditches of the road. We pass also a section of wooded growth through which a fire had swept, apparently the evening or night previous. Next we came to an open field where much to our surprise we see traces of what must have been a very hotly contested battle. The ground is much trampled and dead men and horses lie scattered over the field, with here and there a wounded Yankee. This infantry contest we had heard nothing of, though waged at a distance of only three or four miles from our position of the previous afternoon. The engagement was afterwards known as that of "Frazier's farm," and the artillery which had shelled us so seriously we presume belonged to the same body of Yankees which had engaged our infantry on the same battlefield.

Stopping at this place but a few moments we push on. Matters seem com-ing to a crisis. We pass long lines of troops halted in the road and we hear artillery ahead of us. We debouch into an open field, along the distant edge of which we see several pieces of artillery, apparently in position.

Next after this there follow in the notebook a description of the battle of Mal-vern Hill. In the year of 1887 I prepared and published in the *Petersburg* (Va.) *Index-Appeal* an account of this engagement, embodying my personal recol-lections of it. This account, to which are added some notes, is reproduced in the next [article].

[By July 1, McClellan's retreat to the James had come to an end. He arrayed his army on a wide plateau named Malvern Hill, a position of great natural strength. Undaunted, Lee attacked. Formidable Union artillery fire blasted back Confederate attempts to take the ground. Bernard and the 12th Virginia participated in the fruitless attacks on the Union left flank that day. In 1887, Bernard prepared an account of the 12th Virginia's role at the Battle of Malvern Hill. The article appeared in the *Petersburg Daily Index-Appeal* on September 26, 1887, and was later published in the *Southern Historical Society Papers* in 1890 (18:57–71). Much of his article contains passages from reports readily available in the *Official Records.* We have omitted those portions here. The following excerpts from the article comprise Bernard's own recollections of the battle.]

"Malvern Hill: Graphic Pen Pictures of This Historic Battle," by George S. Bernard

A Day of Dire Disaster—Recollections of the Fight By One Who Was There—Sketches of Thrilling Incidents—Extracts from Official Federal and Confederate Records—A Story of Valor and Sacrifice

To the Editor of the *Index-Appeal:*

As a confederate soldier, a member of one of the regiments of Gen. Wm. Mahone's brigade of Virginians, I was present with a musket in the my hand in nearly a score of the principal engagements between the army of northern Virginia and its opponent, the army of the Potomac, but of all these I remember no engagement which in its dramatic incidents came up to my preconceived idea of a battle as did that of Malvern Hill. Fought in an open field, with desperate valor on both sides, the combatants in full view of each other, except when the smoke of battle or the darkness of night enshrouded them, the struggle of the contending forces, the one attacking, the other repelling, presented a scene never to be forgotten by those who were present. To give some account of this memorable conflict, recalling its well remembered features to many ex-soldiers, is the object of this article. From the official reports of prominent federal and confederate officers not readily accessible to the general reader striking passages descriptive of the battle,—and these reports singularly abound in such passages—will be taken, and the writer will give his own personal recollections of the engagement as he now, after a lapse of a quarter of a century, vividly remembers it almost distinctly as if it were an occurrence of yesterday.[75] In view of the fact that this twenty-fifth anniversary has but recently passed a sketch of the battle so prepared, it is believed, will interest the readers of your journal.

On the afternoon of July 1, 1862, the federal army under Gen. Geo. B. Mc-Clellan occupied the hill and plateau upon which stood some dwellings, and other buildings erected upon a part of the land belonging to the old Virginia country-seat situated in the county of Henrico some fourteen miles below Richmond known during and since colonial time as "Malvern Hill." The confederate army under Gen. Robt. E. Lee, flushed with a succession of victories during the preceding six days, was pushing forward, and the federal army strongly posted, had determined to make a stand. . . .

About four in the afternoon our brigade (Mahone's), which had been slowly marching along the Quaker, or Willis Church, road in the direction of Malvern Hill, is halted. A few paces ahead of us is a dashing looking general officer, mounted and splendidly uniformed, with a large retinue of staff officers and couriers. Gen. Mahone rides up to this officer to receive orders. Just at this time a solid shot fired from a gun of a federal battery near Crew's house, now concealed from our view by an intervening body of woods, comes skipping along, nearly spent, narrowly missing the group of officers and couriers and passing through our ranks opened from the purpose as we saw it bounding slowly towards us—a reminder that the enemy were near at hand. All around the open field through which this shot came bounding towards us were pieces of artillery. In the road in which we halted were long lines of troops, and the dashing looking officer was not other than Gen. Magruder.[76] His orders to Gen. Mahone to charge the enemy's batteries along with Gen. Wright[77] were then given. The men in the ranks understood this order to be to charge the battery that fired the shot, which, like a gauntlet thrown down, seemed to challenge our assault.

In a few moments we are in motion, forming a line of battle with our faces in the direction of the federal artillery, whose fire seems now to increase. Between us and the enemy intervenes the body of woods referred to, and we see nothing of them as we move forward. A hundred or two yards of for-

75. GSB: See, "The War of the Rebellion," published pursuant to act of congress approved June 16, 1880, series I, vol. XI part II, for the several reports have referred to.

76. Major General John Bankhead Magruder was commander of Magruder's Command, Department of Northern Virginia, during this battle, and transferred out West in late 1862.

77. Brigadier General Ambrose Ransom Wright, commander of the Georgia Brigade in this battle, was later promoted to major general after fighting in some of the major Eastern battles.

ward movement brings us into these woods, a body of large chestnuts and oak. Through the tops of these tall trees, far above our heads, the shot and shell of the now vigorously used federal artillery howl and crash, putting us in constant danger of injury from falling fragments of huge limbs of trees. But on we go, until we reach a ravine, or gully, along the bottom of which ran a small branch. Here we halt. In the ravine is a brigade of troops, all sitting with their backs to the wall of the gully next to the enemy, seemingly secure from danger, ensconced, as they were, in what appeared to be comparatively a bombproof, and looking far more comfortable than we felt under an order to charge a battery and on our way to execute this order. The occasion of our temporary halt just here was an examination as to the route by which it would be best to go forward. In the dilemma one of the couriers attached to our regiment suggested to our colonel that we might go through a little gate in sight a short distance to our right. The courier's suggestion is taken and we move to our right and file through this gate, meeting, as we pass, a poor fellow with a bullet hole through his neck and the pallor of death on his face, his friends as they bear him past us saying, "Look out for sharp-shooters"—another reminder, and not an agreeable one either, of the presence of our armed adversaries.

We are now very close to the enemy. We are at the foot of the hill upon the table-ground of which stands the Crew house and other buildings and McClellan's army awaiting our assault, so close that we feel the vibrations of the earth at each discharge of the federal guns. Not three hundred yards intervene between us and these guns, the slope of the hill, however, perfectly protecting us, we being now opposite to the extreme left of the federal line of battle. To our right in a beautiful field, the meadow mentioned by Gen. Wright, with its yellow shocks of recently harvested wheat, are stationed the federal sharp-shooters against whom we have been warned. Posted behind the shocks of wheat, they see us, but we cannot see them whilst they pick off our men as they come up to take position in line of battle at the foot of the hill preparatory to the intended charge. As each man files up he is ordered to lie down, an order most cheerfully obeyed, the recumbent position affording much protection from the fire of these sharp-shooters whose bullets are constantly hissing past us.

As I marched along to this position, I looked over towards the woods on Turkey Creek skirting the meadow. The prospect was beautiful, and as my eye took in the landscape, everything in that direction so tranquil that clear summer afternoon and in such striking contrast with the harsh notes of war every second reaching the ear from the hill in the front and to the left of us, I was reminded of a certain meadow in a neighboring county, which with its

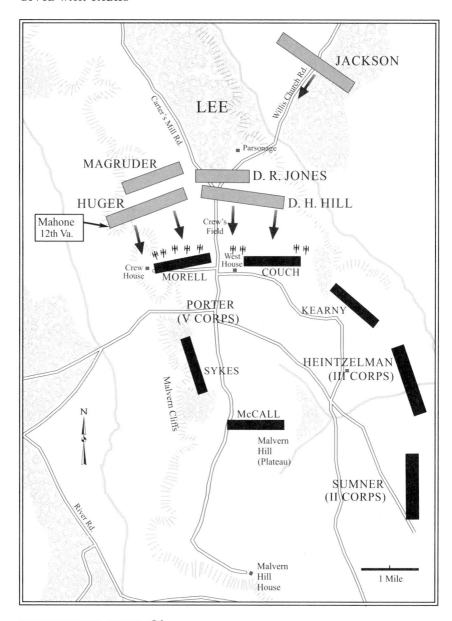

MALVERN HILL, JULY 1, 1862

low grounds and its fringe of dense woods, were delightfully familiar to me in the holiday seasons of my then recent boyhood. The wheat shocks, the low grounds, the woods in the distance, now before me, seemed to duplicate in every particular those elsewhere located and now vividly recalled, over which with gun and dog I had so often hunted, and with which I associated nothing but happiness, and a crowd of memories rushed upon me. This would not be a truthful record, if I did not here state that I would have gladly then and there ended the war, changed the situation of affairs and transferred myself to the scene of these memories, far away from the angry roar of the cannon.

The crisis is now at hand. Gen. Mahone, seizing the colors of one of our regiments, commands us to move forward. We rush up the slope of the hill towards the enemy, yelling at the top of our voices. Just as we near the brow of the hill, when my eye, on a level with them, takes in the field with its houses, I catch a glimpse of four artillery horses hitched to a gun, or to a caisson, dashing away at the full speed. At the sight of this, my heart leaped with joy. The enemy are flying! Their artillery and infantry are routed! We are victors, without firing a gun! These were my thoughts. But I was terribly mistaken. My eye saw only those four horses in flight. No men, no other horses drawing pieces of artillery, no infantry, are flying. It was imagination, the wish being father to the thought, which, magnifying for the instant what was actually seen, had drawn the picture of the whole force of the enemy in full retreat.

Our line of battle was allowed to get well upon the hill, when the enemy's infantry stationed not more than one hundred and fifty, or two hundred yards in front of us, and their artillery in the rear of the infantry, suddenly opened upon us with terrific fury. Our men are driven back with terrible loss, but only to gain the protection of the brow of the hill, there to rally and return to the charge. The enemy's infantry line meanwhile is seemingly immovable. It stood as if at a dress parade. I could scarcely believe my own eyes as I looked upon it. Soon, however, dense volumes of smoke considerably obscured their line, but there were the red flashes of the guns and the crimson looking federal colors floating over the dark line of men plainly visible.

The company of which I was a member being next to the right company of the 12th Virginia regiment and this regiment being the right regiment of Mahone's brigade, and Mahone's brigade being on the extreme right of the confederate line of battle, just where I was the fire from the enemy was not so severe as it appeared to be on our left, and this gave me an opportunity to watch the troops to our left as they repeatedly moved forward in the line of battle to charge the enemy. What I now saw impressed me very much. Every few minutes, a column, a regiment or two, would move steadily forward in line of battle towards the enemy, cheering as they advanced. Then there would be the deafening roll of musketry and in few moments all would be hidden from view by smoke. On the occasion of one charge my eyes were upon the advancing line when it received the fire of the enemy. The poor fellows reeled and fell, it seemed by the dozens. The line, broken, is forced back to seek shelter under the brow of a hill. In a few minutes the men are rallied, and returning to the charge meet the same fate. This was a fair sample of the many charges made during the afternoon. . . .

About sunset an advance is ordered and we move forward to the next hill some seventy-five yards, in our front, Col. David A. Weisiger, the colonel of our regiment, gallantly leading it in the charge; and from this new position we open fire upon the enemy. At this point occurred, a little incident that I have often recalled. A colonel of some regiment—who he was, or what his regiment I never knew—an elderly man, hair and beard very gray, was squatting among the men under the brow of the hill where were a large number of our regiment, all of us mixed up together, the enemy being very close at hand just over the hill, the men rising to fire and resuming their squatting positions whilst loading. Being within a few feet of the old fellow, I heard him earnestly urging those near him to fire fast upon the enemy. "Fire fast, men." "Fire fast." "Give it to 'em." "Give it to 'em boys," he would say. Just then some one cried out, "Boys, we are firing into our friends!" Brandishing his sword with considerable energy at the man who volunteered the information, he exclaimed, "Firing into your friends! They are damned Yankees. If you say we are firing on our friends, God damn you, I will cut you in two with my sword." Turning to the men around him, he continued to urge them to "fire fast." "Give it to 'em boys," he repeated. "Give it to 'em boys," he repeated. "Give it to 'em. Fire fast. They are nothing but damned Yankees." Lieutenant John R. Patterson of our regiment, enthused with admiration at the old officer's conduct, exclaimed, "Go it, colonel! I'll stand at your back," or words to that effect. Hearing Lieut. Patterson's hearty but rather familiar endorsement, and struck, as he had been, with the conduct and words of the old gentleman, turning to Lieut. Patterson, I said, "Who is that old officer you are speaking to so familiarly?" "Don't know," energetically replied Patterson, still enthused, "I just know he is a colonel."

Night coming on, some of our men actually got in among the enemy before discovering their position, so close were the contending forces on the extreme right of our line. A member of our regiment, private Henry B. Cowles, thus came very near being captured, but before being discovered made his way back to our line. . . .

The firing is kept up until nine o'clock at night, when both parties, wearied with the fight, seemed to cease firing by consent. Soon after the firing ceased, numbers of the enemy could be seen in our immediate front, moving about with lantern in their hands, looking after their dead and wounded. The crest of the hill where we now are is held by a thin line of battle consisting mainly of the remains of the depleted brigades of Mahone and Wright. . . .

Stretched as we were on the naked ground on the slope of the hill now occupied by those forming the thin line of battle which held the position, with a slight rain occasionally falling, with no blankets to protect us (our baggage had been left in the rear), and with the pitiful cries of wounded men audible all around us, although very much wearied, we found the place where we lay on the gravelly soil anything but comfortable. Yet there we slept. Although the noises heard from the direction of the enemy unmistakably indicated their retreat, yet in the early morning they are still in position in our front and exchange a few shots with the pickets posted at points of our line. That there was a retreat and no assault by any considerable force [by] our enemy[78] at this time was, indeed, a God-send to us. . . .

When it became light enough to see and I looked over that part of the field within the range of our vision, it presented a horrible sight. In all directions could be seen the corpses of the slain. The slaughter of the confederates had been terrific. . . .

As soon as the enemy retired, what remained of our brigade was marched back to the body of the woods through which we had moved the line of battle the afternoon before, and there went into bivouac. Soon after we were dismissed, several of us returned to the field of battle and strolled over it, and I thus had a better opportunity of forming a correct idea of the great slaughter on both sides. The enemy as well as ourselves had suffered no little. The position of their line of battle of where it confronted our right was distinctly marked by a long line of thickly strewn corpses of federal soldiers.

After walking about the field for an hour or more, I returned to our bivouac, thoroughly impressed with the severity of the conflict of the preceding day, as must have been all who participated in it or had a like opportunity of going over the bloody field so recently after the combatants ceased their fierce struggle. In this sketch of the engagement, I have endeavored with the help of the official reports to furnish a simple narrative of its leading and most striking features, giving at the same time an account of it as viewed from the stand-point of one of the several thousand soldiers who took part in this exceptionally tragic action with muskets in their hands, without attempting to account, or to fix upon any officer or officers in command or troops engaged the responsibility, for the failure of the confederate forces to accomplish more after such frightful loss of life. If what I have written has interested the reader and has given him a clearer conception of this closing scene of the seven days' battles around Richmond, the sketch will have served its purpose.

Geo. S. Bernard

Petersburg, Va., Sept. 23, 1887.

78. Bernard's published account says "no assault by any considerable force upon our enemy." It should probably read "by our enemy" instead.

ADDENDA: WILLIAM MAHONE'S ACCOUNT OF MALVERN HILL[79]

In a letter, dated July 20, 1895, Gen. Mahone says:

Responding to your request to furnish you an account of the incident of my taking the colors of a Virginia regiment (not of my brigade) and being seized by a member of this regiment for so doing, and to give you some other incidents of the Battle of Malvern Hill, I will state that the flag incident occurred after the Virginia (Mahone's) brigade had taken position along the crest of the hill, on the extreme right of the Confederate line of battle. A regiment moving to the front, which by its flag I recognized as a Virginia regiment, came into the little gulch to our left and rear. Malvern Hill, it must be understood, was a huge plateau, a plain gently sloping from the position occupied by the enemy's line of battle a half mile or more to the woods where we first entered the field, with low grounds on the right (our right), the plateau descending by a steep hill to these low grounds, but indented at several points by gulches, or ravines, that ran up from the low grounds into the high table land. The Virginia brigade was occupying the crest of the hill on the enemy's side of one of these gulches, in the position it took when it encountered the musketry of the enemy as described in your account of the battle. The Virginia regiment above referred to was preparing to go to the crest on the left of the Virginia brigade. With the purpose of encouraging the regiment, I seized its colors and started to lead it up to the crest. Quickly some one from behind me seized my coat collar and commenced shaking me and making a to do about my having the flag of his regiment. I could not see the man, but from his accent and broken English knew he was a Dutchman. At this juncture several members of the 12th Va. Regiment of the Virginia brigade rushed up and were about to bayonet the fellow. I raised my hand, signifying to them to desist, and they did. My little Dutch captor, who had been so greatly disturbed at my taking the colors of his regiment, now discovered who I was, and, begging a thousand pardons, asked the privilege of doing my will. I told him that if he would go to the crest and shoot, all would be well. Quickly he was in the line of the Virginia brigade and energetically did his duty. It was not long before, having exhausted his supply of cartridges, he came to me for a fresh supply. He was [successful] and I do not remember to have seen the brave little fellow again.

79. The following letters appear in the form of notes found in the Bernard Papers at the University of North Carolina. The first few lines of Mahone's letter are typewritten. The rest of the letter appears to be in Bernard's hand—perhaps Bernard's transcription so that the original letter could be returned to Mahone.

I will tell you some other incidents of this unhappily organized and ill-directed attack on the enemy's well-chosen position at Malvern Hill.

The Virginia brigade was to support Wright's Georgia brigade, and both brigades were directed to go in on the slope of Malvern Hill on the right, whilst a like number of brigades were to attack on the front and a like number on the left—all simultaneously.

When the Virginia brigade got into position as directed, the Georgia brigade ahead, it was discovered that the head of our column was perpendicular to the enemy's formidable line of battle. An awkward change of front was necessary. It was effected, however, and brought the Virginia brigade on the crest of a hill on the enemy's side of one of the gulches, or ravines, already described. This was the nearest position to the Federal line reached by Confederates during the action, except as will be directly mentioned. From this front the men, fairly covered by the crest of the hill, poured an oblique fire into the enemy's lines to their left. About sunset, as mentioned in your account, an advance was made, led by Col. D. A. Weisiger of the 12th, and a position secured still nearer the enemy's lines. Previously to this there were several unorganized, ineffectual, efforts to advance made, one of them under the lead of Col. J. H. Ham[80] of the 16th reg't, at the instance of the brigade commander. Col. Ham advanced gallantly, with flag in hand, but was compelled to return, the staff of the flag he bore shot to pieces, the scabbard of his sword bent and indented in several paces by the enemy's lead. When this fighting ceased, the men of the Virginia brigade were very close to the enemy. The next morning I saw the body of a young member of the 6th Va. regiment whom I knew personally lying within a few places of the position occupied by one of the federal guns.

The battle being over, the crest of the hill from which they had fought was occupied by what remained of the Georgia and Virginia brigades. Every man was placed in his proper position along this crest, man by man to hold the position, and the line thus reformed was, indeed, a short one. At this juncture, there appeared, marching across the field in our front from left to right, a dark line of men moving in line of battle, aiming apparently to reach the extreme right of our line, which was very near the enemy's left. Col. Ham was sent out to meet this moving line of men and instructed to fire his pistol if he should discover them to be Federals, but if Confederates to bring them in. He soon

---

80. Joseph Hutchinson Ham enlisted as captain in Company F of the 16th Virginia Infantry in August 1861. He served for four years, receiving wounds at Second Manassas, Spotsylvania, and Petersburg. After the war, he was a teacher, businessman, and court clerk.

ascertained that these troops were Confederates and were a North Carolina regiment that had come from the left of the field and were going, they knew not where. Col. Ham brought them in and I took command of the regiment and carefully posted it as a skirmish line in front of our line occupying the crest, as far out as could be reached.

At this time, and now sometime after dark, we could distinctly hear the commands given within the Federal line, among them "Right shoulder shift arms! Right step, march!" From these and other instructions it was evident that the enemy were moving off.

Later on the colonel of the North Carolina regiment commanding the skirmish line reported to me that the enemy were advancing and that they had lanterns. I told him that Shakespeare in one of his plays makes mention of an advance of that kind, and if the enemy were coming with lanterns, we would have an easy time. I then went with him to the skirmish line and soon satisfied him that the advancing enemy were nothing more than an ambulance corps looking after the wounded, as in fact they were.

The next morning, I found that the line of the crest was comprised entirely of the Virginia brigade and mainly the 12th regiment, and that there were not more than two hundred men on it, and further more that these and the North Carolina regiment on the skirmish line were all the troops on the field visible. At this time a squadron of Federal cavalry appeared on the Federal line. It did nothing. Just then Gen. Ewell[81] rode up to our position. Referring to the Federal cavalry he remarked "They are harmless." I recall thinking, as I looked at them, that, if they did not charge, we might let them ride upon us and break their necks down the precipitous slope in to the gulch in our immediate rear.

The cavalry soon disappeared and not long thereafter we were withdrawn from the field.

STATEMENT BY PHILIP F. BROWN

Mr. Philip F. Brown,[82] of Blue Ridge Springs, Va., a member of the Petersburg "B" Greys (Co. C, 12th Va.), in a letter dated March 22, 1895, narrating the incidents of the battle, says:

As I lay upon that historic hill, I could hear the delirious screams of the

81. Major General Richard S. Ewell, division commander in the Army of Northern Virginia during this battle, was later promoted to lieutenant general and commander of a corps, and finally commander of the Department of Richmond. He was captured at Sailor's Creek (also called "Sayler's Creek") in April 1865.

82. Philip F. Brown was a clerk at the Bollingbrook Hotel in Petersburg before the war. He enlisted as a private in Company C of the 12th Virginia in April 1861. He was

wounded and dying men, some calling for loved ones in then distant homes, others the names of their regiments. "Third Alabama!" as uttered by one poor fellow still rings in my ears and tells me that the men of this famous regiment were among those who fell on that blood stained field.

Although it was nine o'clock at night, or later, the enemy were still throwing shell far away to our rear, the blazing fuses illuminating the battle-field and giving a ghastly scene to the frightful night. The sorrowful [*illegible word*] soundings impressed me greatly, and I could understand how "Achilles restored the body of Hector when Priam wept."

Whilst thus subdued by the solemnity of the occasion, a comrade approached, accompanied by two others and asked if I would accompany them. They were going out to the front, they said, to recover a member of our own color-guard, young William Brown[83] of [Greensville] county of company F, who had been shot in the thigh and was lying about fifty feet over the brow of the hill. I assented and we had not difficulty in passing through our lines and soon found our wounded comrade, placed him in our oil-cloth and started back towards our lines with him. But this was attended with such pain that he screamed out loudly, "Put me down! Put me down!" This drew the attention of the enemy and a volley of bullets swept by as, although there were many of the enemy, not fifty feet distant from us, engaged with lanterns searching for their own dead and wounded. The men on our line, not aware of the cause, returned the fire, and for some minutes there was an exchange of shots and a serious night-engagement seemed imminent. When the firing ceased, we ventured from our positions and cautiously crawled into our lines, whispering as we approached "12th Virginia!" "12th Virginia!" The "three guardsmen" of Alexander Dumas, accompanied by Dartagnan, were never in a more dangerous position. A deep sigh of relief and a prayer to a merciful Providence was in our hearts and on our tongues when we safely got among our men. The sad echoes of groans from wounded men all around us was a melancholy accompaniment to the slumbers that fatigue forced upon us.

Young Brown, I was informed, a few days subsequently died of his wounds at Manchester, Va.

---

wounded and captured at Crampton's Gap in September 1862. Exchanged in October 1862, he received a medical discharge in 1863. After the war, he wrote *Reminiscences of the War of 1861–1865* (Richmond: Whittet and Shepperson, 1917). See also Philip F. Brown, "Vivid Memories of the War In Virginia," *Confederate Veteran* 18 (1910): 64.

83. William O. Brown enlisted as a sergeant in Company F of the 12th Virginia in June 1861. Wounded at Malvern Hill, he died in a Richmond hospital in August 1862.

....

My own impressions of this famous engagement were given in the following brief letter to my father written the next day, before I knew the name of the place at which we fought or had an opportunity to learn further details than those that came within my personal knowledge:

James River Road 17 miles
Richmond, Wednesday, July 2, 62

My Dear Father

I have a small scrap of paper & drop you a line to relieve all uneasiness about myself. A kind providence has spared me through the perils of another engagement. Yesterday afternoon we encountered the enemy at this place, when one of the most terrific battles of the war took place. Our loss was tremendous. The field was strewn with our dead & wounded. The fight commenced about 2 in the afternoon with artillery. About four our brigade was ordered to charge the enemy's battery, which we did with tremendous cheering. The battery fell back and as we rose upon the summit of the hill from which it had been firing both parties opened with musketry which continued until after dark. Hardly had the enemy's artillery left its first position than it opened again on us & played incessantly upon us *unreplied to* by our own. We slept on the battle field surrounded by the dead & wounded. Our regiment behaved most gallantly. Every brigade & regiment wavered but the 12th—I wish I had time to write more. I have heard nothing from Dick.[84] Brother[85] still at camp. Our regiment suffered severely—two of our company (I) killed outright, several missing. Love to all I trust we may not meet the enemy again.

Yr Aff Son
G S Bernard

[The following passage is designated "Note 9" on an unnumbered page of Bernard's War Narrative.[86]]

... Whilst I sat squatting on the slope of the hill watching these charges Thos J. Harwell,[87] of Greensville County, Va., the 2nd sergeant of my com-

84. "Dick" was Private Richard S. Bernard, George Bernard's brother.

85. "Brother" was Bernard's half-brother, Private David Meade Bernard Jr. (described in note 20, chapter 1).

86. See War Narrative, George S. Bernard Papers, Southern Historical Collection. Bernard's Malvern Hill "Addenda" notes also contain a lengthy quotation about Malvern Hill from William Swinton's *Army of the Potomac* (C. B. Richardson, 1866). That has been omitted here.

87. Thomas J. Harwell, a farmer from Greensville County, did not have a long time in service before he was wounded. He enlisted in March 1862 as a sergeant in Company I

pany—he was 2nd and acting 1st sergt., and I was acting 2nd sgt. of our company—was about the crest engaged [I am satisfied] loading and firing at the enemy. Seeing me and probably others not engaged, my musket, a little while before that had become heated from firing, and bending using the buck and ball cartridge I remember that I had some difficulty in loading, and he remarked excitedly, "Why are you all not shooting at the enemy?" He was a plain farmer, at least thirty five years of age and ordinarily a man of quiet, calm demeanor. As he stood on the crest of the hill and made the enquiry, his very nature seemed transformed. He was all aglow with the excitement of battle. His face was alight with enthusiasm. I felt rebuked, that I had been colder for a moment. Said I, "Where are the enemy?" "Don't you see them?" said he, pointing to the front where there was to be seen only heavy volumes of smoke and the red flashes of rifles. Determined that he should not think that I was afraid to go wherever he would go, I went with him over the crest and down the slope of the hill towards the enemy, he still in this excited state, which seemed to have made him forget all sense of danger, pointing towards the smoke and fire a little to the left of our immediate front and saying to me, "Don't you see 'em there? Don't you see 'em?" A little near-sighted, I did not see them with the distinctness that I am satisfied he saw them, but did see some individual men in our immediate front. He fired his gun. I think I also fired mine. Immediately afterwards he fell to the ground. I helped him to his feet and found he had received a wound to his arm. I assisted him back to the crest of the hill, from which he made his way to the rear. The surgeons amputated his arm, and he never returned to service again. In after years I often met him until he died, but never without recalling as I looked at his empty sleeve his splendid conduct at Malvern Hill.

---

of the 12th Virginia, and was wounded at Malvern Hill—according to Bernard. Official records note his wound came at Seven Pines on June 1, 1862. He received a medical discharge in November 1862.

3

The Maryland
Campaign, 1862

AFTER THWARTING MCCLELLAN'S designs on Richmond during
the Seven Days' battles, Lee redeployed his forces to meet a new threat,
in the form of General John Pope's army in northern Virginia. Following a
series of maneuvers that included a stunning fifty-mile flank march by Jackson's corps, Lee defeated Pope's force on the Manassas battlefield in late August. Sensing an opportunity to take the war onto Northern soil and promote
foreign recognition of the Confederacy, Lee led his army into Maryland in
early September. The Army of the Potomac, once again commanded by Mc-
Clellan, emerged from the Washington defenses to meet the rebels. McClellan's advance eventually resulted in the bloody stalemate of Antietam. With
the rebel offensive stopped in its tracks, Lee and his army limped back across
the Potomac to winter in Virginia.

Bernard's regiment, the 12th Virginia Infantry, was in the thick of the
action during these operations. On September 14, 1862, the Confederates
sought to delay the advance of the Union Sixth Corps at Crampton's Gap
with a portion of Mahone's brigade, a brigade under Brigadier General
Howell Cobb, a small cavalry force, and an artillery battery. Though the
Union troops managed to drive the Confederates from their position, the
action bought precious hours for Lee to draw together his scattered forces.
During the brief combat, Bernard received a serious leg wound and fell into
enemy hands. Bernard described his experience of the campaign in detail during a lengthy address to the A. P. Hill Camp on the evening of May 2, 1889,
which was published in Bernard's *War Talks of Confederate Veterans,* under
the chapter title "The Maryland Campaign of 1862."

In 1894, John T. Parham, a veteran of the 32nd Virginia Infantry regiment, addressed the camp and described his experiences during the Maryland Campaign. A transcription of Parham's address was found in the batch of papers discovered in Roanoke, Virginia, in 2004, and has been reproduced here. Parham was born in Prince George County, Virginia, in 1843. Before the war, he was a merchandiser in Williamsburg. He enlisted with the Williamsburg Junior Guards in April 1861, a company which eventually became part of the 32nd Virginia regiment commanded by Colonel E. B. Montague. Parham held various posts in the regiment and received wounds at Sharpsburg, during the Overland Campaign, and at Fort Harrison outside Richmond in the fall of 1864. After the war, he held a variety of jobs while living in Petersburg, then Norfolk, and also Memphis for a period of time. In 1887, he returned to Petersburg, where he served as Deputy City Sergeant.[1]

><0><>+<····>+<>0><

"Reminiscences of the Maryland Campaign of 1862,"
by John T. Parham

An Address Delivered before A. P. Hill Camp of Confederate Veterans of Petersburg Va. by John T. Parham on the Evening of Thursday, Sept. 6, 1894

Comrades:

I have selected as the subject of my address this evening the Maryland Campaign of 1862, in which I participated as a member of Co. C of the 32nd regiment of infantry, Semmes' brigade McLaws' division, doing service on the regimental color guard.

Our command did not confront the enemy until we reached Maryland

---

1. On September 7, 1894, a short description of a recent A. P. Hill Camp meeting in the *Petersburg Daily Index-Appeal* mentioned that John T. Parham had delivered a war talk titled "Reminiscences of the First Maryland Campaign, including the Battle of Sharpsburg." A transcript of his talk, titled "Reminiscences of the Maryland Campaign of 1862," is reproduced here. This transcript, in Bernard's hand, is housed in the Bernard Collection at the Historical Society of Western Virginia. Parham wrote another article about the Battle of Antietam, titled "Thirty-Second at Sharpsburg: Graphic Story of Work Done on One of the Bloodiest Fields," that appeared in *SHSP,* 34:250; the same letter reappeared the next year, in *SHSP,* 35:348. A short, undated biography prepared by Parham for Bernard resides in the Bernard Papers, Southern Historical Collection, University of North Carolina.

but I will give you a hasty sketch of its movements before we were face to face with the foe.

After the battle of Malvern Hill, in which we participated, McLaws' division camped for several weeks near James River in the vicinity of Chaffins' farm and did picket duty from this river to Bottom's Bridge on the Chickahominy, our regiment frequently marching from the James and the Chickahominy whilst thus watching the enemy, with an occasional slight picket firing or skirmish.

Whilst we were thus engaged between [June and the middle of August], the main body of our army moved to Northern Virginia, leaving our division below Richmond to [*three illegible words*] watch the enemy.

About ten days before the battle of Second Manassas was fought, the division was ordered to Richmond and boarded a freight train at the depot of Va. Central Railroad (now the Chesapeake & Ohio). [It] . . . was carried to Hanover Junction, arrival at which place we disembarked and went into bivouac for a day or two, after which we began our march northward through the counties of Louisa, Orange, Culpeper, and Fauquier, until we reached Warrenton Springs in the last mentioned county; the march up to this point being uneventful.

Reaching just south of Warrenton Springs, a stream we had difficulty in getting across it, the enemy having recently burnt the bridge and the water being too deep to ford. We felled trees, however, and crossed over them. It was nightfall when we got across, and we halted for the night at the Springs, where we enjoyed the fine sulphur water as well as a good night's rest. The next morning we were early put in motion and hurried on toward Manassas, where our army had the day before fought the great battle of Saturday, August the 30th. Late in the afternoon we reached the outskirts of the battlefield upon which we saw numerous dead men, Confederates as well as Federals, from nearly all of the latter of which, their clothing had been stripped, some of whom were almost nude, even their underclothes being taken. There were some notable exceptions and these were the dead Zouaves for whose scarlet pants our boys had no use and for this reason, doubtless, left them [*four illegible words*].[2] There [were] also numbers of wounded men, Confederates as well as Federals, lying about on the field [who] were still unattended to;

2. The scarlet clad dead and wounded under feet were most likely members of the 5th New York Infantry, a unit that had seen hard combat in the Peninsula Campaign. Dressed in the popular Zouave uniform of red fezzes, blue jackets, and baggy red pants, the 5th New York was one of the few regiments guarding the Union flank on August 30. That afternoon, Longstreet launched a devastating assault into Pope's exposed left. The isolated Zouaves lay in the path of this Confederate tide. Out of 500 men present for

between these then were numbers of dead and wounded horses. The public high way through the battle field appeared to be very much encumbered and obstructed with this debris of the battle, broken down wagons, and disabled pieces of artillery, to say nothing of dead men and horses being scattered along the road, and this condition of things probably accounted for our march across the battle field.

It was growing dark as we were marching across the blood stained ground, the outlines of the stiff corpses still meeting our eyes and I greatly feared that we would be halted and made to spend the night on this field, among the dead and wounded, the thought of which was horrible, fortunately we were marching until we cleared the battlefield, and crossing Bull Run went into bivouac [*illegible word*] on the north bank of the stream.

Halted here we were very tired from day's march, and very hungry. Our rations scant; nothing but fresh beef, with no salt and no bread. We got some hickory ashes and used these as a substitute for salt. We had no substitute for the bread.

Early next morning we started for Leesburg; our regiment commissary provided rations when we reached that town. On the road side were some orchards, and the boys having had no bread for twenty four hours, made fine with the apples. About dark, we reached Leesburg and, instead of bringing the rations the commissary had promised, we were informed that the wagons bringing them would not be up until late in the night and that each man must go into some neighboring corn field and get enough roasting ears for our meal (supper) and report to his company sergeant how many he got in order that that the owner of the corn might be properly paid. Although I was nearly fagged out by the hard march, I went into a field near by and gathered ten ears for my supper—and pretty good ears they were too—and succeeding in supplementing the meal [with] a piece of shoat given me by my commissary sergeant, and cooking these, had a square meal, minus salt or bread. Being very tired I quickly unrolled my blanket and was soon asleep. Before morning however, I began to pay the penalty of my imprudent eating, as I was about the sickest boy you ever saw with a genuine case of cholera morbus, which I did not get over entirely for under ten days. Luckily for me, we rested at this point all of the next day and night. Feeling better in the afternoon, I went to a neighboring orchard and got some very nice peaches, which I enjoyed very much.

Refreshed by our rest of two nights and a day, early on this morning of

---

duty, the regiment lost almost 300 killed and wounded in only ten minutes time (see John Hennessey, *Return to Bull Run: The Campaign and Battle of Second Manassas* [New York: Simon and Schuster, 1993], 366–73).

Wednesday, Sept. 3rd we were again in motion and passing through Lees-burg, pressed our forces towards the Potomac and by sunset had forded it and halted for the night on the soil of Maryland for the night on the north bank of the river.

I should mention just here that before reaching Leesburg, Capt. Octavius Coke,[3] who commanded my company, informed us that the colonel of our regiment, Colonel E. B. Montague,[4] had sent to him for a corporal to go on the color guard, and that he knew of no better man than myself. I did not like this dangerous promotion, but said nothing and took my place by the side of the color sergeant, Sergeant Robert Forrest.[5]

I must mention here an amusing incident I witnessed as we were fording the Potomac. A dressy captain of a company in the 10th Georgia regiment, of our brigade did not wish to take off his pants as others were doing to avoid getting wet but mounted one of the horses of the colonel of this regiment [behind] a colored servant who had charge of the horse and so proceeded to cross the river. When about midway the stream, the horse stumbled and fell, throwing both riders into the Potomac and giving the captain a good dunking and playing havoc with his fine uniform, coat as well as pants. The boys who were wading nearby enjoyed a hearty laugh at this captain's expense.

Having enjoyed our first night's rest on the territory of Maryland, we started bright and early the next morning and after a moderate march reached the rail road bridge about the Monocacy Junction and went into bivouac in [*two illeg-ible words*]. Here we quietly rested for several days, details from our command being engaged a part of the time in the work of destroying the bridge.

[Lee's army crossed into Maryland in early September and marched to the town of Frederick. Concerned that the Federal garrison at Harper's Ferry

---

3. Octavius Coke, a lawyer before the war, enlisted as a 1st sergeant in Company C of the 32nd Virginia in April 1861. Elected captain in May 1862, he was wounded at Antietam and later at Five Forks. He was recovering in a hospital in Danville when the war ended. After the war, he moved to North Carolina, where he worked as an attorney and became active in state politics.

4. Another lawyer, Edgar Burwell Montague, raised his own battalion in 1861, then served as the lieutenant colonel of the 53rd Virginia until elected colonel of the 32nd Virginia in May 1862. He led the 32nd Virginia until its surrender in 1865. After the war, he returned to the practice of law.

5. Robert James Forrest, a sailor before the war, enlisted as a private in Company F of the 32nd Virginia in June 1861. He rose steadily through the ranks, from private to corporal to color sergeant, and 4th sergeant by December 1862. He then deserted in July 1863, was captured by Union forces, took the oath of allegiance, and was discharged from military service.

would threaten his line of communications, Lee divided his force into four parts. He sent three sections under Stonewall Jackson's control to Harper's Ferry and directed the balance of his troops north to Boonsboro. Lee demonstrated little concern for the Union army. He assumed the Federals were still recovering from the fight at Second Manassas. He was mistaken. In fact, the Army of the Potomac was on the move, with George McClellan once again in command. And, to make matters worse, a copy of Lee's orders revealing his plans to spread his forces all over western Maryland fell into Union hands. McClellan reveled in his good fortune and hastened to engage the scattered Confederates in detail. To accomplish this, Union forces pressed toward the gaps of South Mountain, a ridge shielding Lee's troops. Once across, McClellan could interpose his heavy columns between the fragments of Lee's command at Harper's Ferry and Boonsboro. On September 14, several Union corps lurched westward toward three openings in the South Mountain range. Their most direct route ran through Crampton's Gap, and this is where Parham and his comrades rushed following news of McClellan's approach.]

Our next move was to march to and through Frederick City a few miles north of Monocacy Junction and there westwardly toward South Mountain. As we marched through the city we were jeered by the female portion of the inhabitants. If there were any southern sympathizers, they were very scarce when our command passed along I certainly saw none. We were called "ragged rebels," and were told that we were "lost" and would "soon be coming back" faster than we went. Many other taunting remarks were made to us from the sidewalks, porches, doors and windows as we marched through the streets. We took all of this in good part, disturbing and insulting no one.

When night came on we were marching westwardly with Frederick City several miles behind us, we thought we would go into bivouac, but no such good luck was in store for us. We kept on marching all through the night, with short rests of ten minutes, the boys catching cat-naps at each rest. A short distance east of Burkittsville, a little village at the foot of South Mountain, in the early morning, after daylight, we halted for an about an hour, and then, resuming our march, went in to Burkittsville and crossed the mountain near the village at the gap next below (south of) Crampton's Gap and getting into Pleasant Valley went down it towards Harper's Ferry, as far as Brownsville, a little hamlet, and there went into bivouac. This was Saturday, September 13, 1862.

We had no sooner stacked arms than I prepared to get myself a square meal and then have a quick rest. I accordingly went in a neighboring orchard and gathered a lot of nice apples, and soon had a [pan] full on the fire baking.

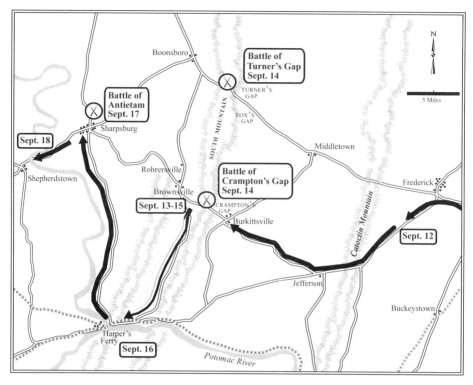

ANTIETAM CAMPAIGN (PARHAM'S ROUTE)

But before the apples were half cooked, the long roll beat and we had to fall in and move off, whither bound we did not know. We soon learned, however, that our destination was the gap in the mountain through which we had that morning entered Pleasant Valley, and that we were to do picket duty there, as the enemy were reported as rapidly following us from the direction of Frederick City and were in fact so doing. Having an eye to my apples, I made arrangements with one of the cooks to finish cooking them and bring them up to me on the mountain that night with the rest of the rations.

About nightfall we reached the position on the mountain where we were to do duty and at once pickets were posted down on the eastern slope of the mountain, the reserve force with which the color guard were being kept about the highest point or [right] of the gap. Not having had the rest we expected to get when down in the valley, those of us in the reserve at once began to look about for some smooth place to sleep, and in so doing, in the darkness, did no little stumbling about trying to find such a place, which it was difficult to do, for it seemed as if every square foot of ground on the ridge was covered with sharp rocks, large and small. At last I discovered a rock about four feet high, with a surface of about an ordinary [*illegible word*] lounge, with a cavity under it. I spread my oil cloth and blanket on this rock and awaited my expected apples, which my friend the cook, brought along with the other rations in due season. Before lying down to sleep a comrade, Dick Spraggins,[6] sought the cavity under my rock couch as a place in which to make his bed and spend the night. I warned him against the danger of rattle snakes. He did not however, heed my warning remarking that he could stand it if the snakes could. Thus fixed for the night, I on top of the rock, and Spraggins in the cavity under me, we slept with considerable comfort until broad day the next morning.

The next afternoon (Sunday the 14th), the enemy appeared in sight on the farm fields, east of Burkittsville, advancing in large number, from our elevated position we could see them for several miles wending their way towards us. Although they were but a small portion of the Federal forces, they looked as if they might be the whole of McClellan's army. We watched them until they reached the vicinity of the village (Burkittsville) and formed their lines of battle about the place. It was, indeed, a beautiful sight. As soon as they came within range of our artillery, four or five pieces of which were at the gap with us, they were opened upon. The five of these guns seeming to be too much for them, they obliqued toward their right in a north westerly direction and attacked the Confederate force at Crampton's Gap, where a portion of Mahone's brigade, the 6th, 12th, and 16th Va. regiments, under Col. Wm. Allen Parham[7] of the 41st regiment were stationed, and kept them back until about sunset, a portion of our division (Cobb's legion and [*illegible word*] other troops) coming in fresh as the Virginians, overwhelmed, retreated up the mountainside after one of the most gallant fights of the war.

6. Richard M. Spraggins was a farmer from James City County before the war. He enlisted as a private in Company C of the 32nd Virginia in April 1861 and by 1862 had been detailed to the Quartermaster Department. He was present for all rolls except for one when he was sick. Captured on the South Side Railroad in April 1865, he was released from Hart's Island POW camp in June 1865.

7. William Allen Parham, a prewar planter, enlisted as 1st lieutenant of Company A of the 41st Virginia Infantry in May 1861. He rose steadily through the ranks, finally reaching colonel by September 1862. He commanded the 41st Virginia from July 1862 until September 1862, when he assumed temporary command of Mahone's brigade until November 1862. He was absent because of illness for most of the next two years, and relieved of his command in November 1864 because of illness. He was transferred to the Army Invalid Corps in 1865. There does not appear to be a relation between this Colonel Parham and the author of this article, John T. Parham, or his brother, William Henry Parham (see note 12, this chapter).

Just before night a courier rode up to Gen. Semmes[8] with an order, and immediately we were marching by the left flank along the ridge of the mountain in the direction of Crampton's Gap at which point we heard the firing still in progress. Getting within a hundred or two yards of the combatants, we were halted, and finding that our forces at the Crampton's Gap were in retreat we were about-faced and double-quicked back to the place from which we had been moved, and then descended the mountain into Pleasant Valley and formed a line of battle across the valley, facing northward. In this position we spent the night expecting the enemy to appear at any moment. I am satisfied that the other portions of our division, together with the troops of Mahone's brigade, formed this line of battle across the valley.

Having slept on our arms in line of battle about daybreak Monday morning we received whispered orders to fall back a few hundred yards to take position in line of battle near and immediately south of the village of Brownsville. As we were moving along quickly one of my old company, who did not understand the full purpose of our orders exclaimed "Skadaddling, by thunder!" This remark caused considerable merriment among the boys, which, however, was promptly checked by our officers as our orders were to make the move as quickly as possible to prevent the enemy from knowing what was going on.

After passing the village we formed the new line of battle and awaited the approach of the enemy. At this point I saw several boys belonging to the 12th Virginia regiment who had been wounded in the engagement the evening before—Sergeant W. W. Tayleur[9] of the Petersburg Riflemen. While we were in line of battle, expecting an attack any moment, I noticed an old white haired gentleman, clad in white, riding along the mountain side near its foot, and near the left of our line of battle and apparently in front of it. I saw him ride several times some distance forward and return. He seemed to be watching the enemy's movements and reporting them to our commanding officer,

8. Paul Jones Semmes was captain of a militia company in Columbus, Georgia, when war broke out. Elected colonel of the 2nd Georgia Infantry Regiment in 1861, Semmes brought his unit to Virginia. Promoted to brigadier general in the spring of 1862, he soon commanded a brigade in Lafayette McLaws's division. He fought at Williamsburg, Seven Pines, Crampton's Gap, Antietam, Fredericksburg, and Chancellorsville. He received a mortal wound on the second day of fighting at Gettysburg and is buried in Columbus, Georgia.

9. William W. Tayleur (sometimes spelled "Tayleure") was a bookkeeper and hardware merchant from Petersburg. He enlisted as a corporal in Company E of the 12th Virginia in April 1861. Promoted to sergeant in October 1861, he was wounded at Crampton's Gap in 1862. He survived that wound, only to be wounded again at Cumberland Church on the retreat from Petersburg in April 1865. He remained with the regiment and was paroled at Appomattox.

and this we heard at the time he was in fact doing, acting as a scout. I heard that his name was Boteler. The boys dubbed him "Old White Coat."

About noon we heard that Harper's Ferry, which was only about five miles south west of us down the Valley, had been surrendered to our forces, with about eleven thousand prisoners and a large quantity of commissary stores, arms and other munitions or war.[10] I think we remained about Brownsville all of Monday afternoon and night.

The next day we went down the Valley to the Potomac, crossed the river on a pontoon brigade and entered Harper's Ferry, and saw the results of the capture of the preceding day, large numbers of prisoners, and large quantities of provisions and arms. I well remember the abundance of mess-pork, hard tack, cakes of maple sugar, and coffee, which to our hungry eyes looked delicious. The men in the ranks helped themselves as they marched along with their supplies, and enjoyed no little [*illegible word*] what they thus got.

We marched a mile or so beyond the town, went into bivouac, drew ten days full rations, sugar and coffee included, and were happy. We were in fine spirits at the thought of getting on the south side of the Potomac again. I for one was sufficiently amazed with my experience in "Maryland, My Maryland." My delight, however, was doomed to be of short duration for during the offering of rations I received a painful cut in my arm from a knife carelessly handled by a comrade. I went at once to our regimental assistant surgeon to have the flow of blood stopped and the wound dressed. "You got wounded early!" was the sneering remark with which this officer greeted me and which stung me to the quick. I replied, "If you mean by that to say that I got hurt intentionally to escape duty you tell an untruth, and wounded as I am I will stand up as long as you or any other man. If you do not want to dress my wound, I will go over to the surgeon of the 15th regiment and ask him to do it." I was pretty hot when I said this. The assistant surgeon made no reply. He put a piece of new cotton on the wound, bound it and put my arm in a sling. I will not mention the name of this officer, as I think he is now dead but it is [enough] to say that, on the next day, the 17th on the field of Sharpsburg he was cashiered for cowardice because he would not come to the field hospital to give attention to the wounded men—this at least was the information I had and believed to be true.[11]

10. "Stonewall" Jackson seized Harper's Ferry on September 15, 1862.

11. Parham may be referring to Powhatan Bledsoe, assistant surgeon of the regiment, who was assigned to the unit in June 1862 and present until Antietam. He was dropped by order of the secretary of war in November 1862 (see Les Jensen, *32nd Virginia Infantry* [Lynchburg, Va.: H. E. Howard, 1990], 175).

Just before night, on the evening of Tuesday the 16th, our division was ordered to fall in and started off whither to go we knew not. It was a great disappointment to us to have to move at all. After the great events of the day before we fancied that the Maryland campaign was at end, we being then on the south side of the Potomac. As we marched along we thought we were going towards Richmond, at least I so thought. About midnight, however, I found to my sorrow that we were on our way to Maryland, again. About 10 o'clock we filed off the road into an open field, as we thought for the purpose of halting for the night. A good many of the boys immediately started on forage expeditions to neighboring farm houses hoping to get milk, apple butter and other good things, as was then custom whenever anything that looked like an opportunity for success in this line offered. With the assistance of a comrade, I unrolled my blanket and oil cloth spread them on the ground, stretched myself upon them for a good night's rest and was soon fast asleep. In about four hours I was awakened by the beating of the long roll and the colonel of our regiment, Col. E. B. Montague, riding out among the men who had been lying around, as I had been, asleep on the ground and were then getting on their feet, the colonel hurrying them up and saying that everything depended upon them being at the ford at the Potomac by daylight. It then flashed across my mind that we were not on our way back to Virginia as I had up to that point supposed, but were going to cross the Potomac into Maryland again! As you may imagine, before this discovery, I was in very bad plight mentally as well as physically. My arm had gotten quite sore and painful, and but for the help of a comrade, I could not have rolled up my blanket and oil cloth and gotten in readiness to march. I took my stand, however, on the left of the color-bearer and was ready to start, but feeling almost as if I had as soon be dead as alive. Just as we were about moving off, the foraging party above referred to returned. They had but two hours' rest but reported having enjoyed a good supper at a farmer's house. Whilst we were standing in line ready to march Leonard Taylor exclaimed, "Boys! We are going to catch the devil today! I have been dreaming that we were in a terrible battle, and I believe we are going to catch it sure!" Alas! The dream came true, for before the sun had set we had been upon the bloody field of Sharpsburg and lost a large number of our command in killed and wounded.

Getting in motion we started towards Shepherdstown, marching rapidly, as our orders were to cross the Potomac at daylight. I was very thirsty when we reached Shepherdstown just before daybreak. So I left ranks and marched along on the side walk to look out for some well on the wayside. Whilst looking out over a fence for a well I reached a break in the side walk and not looking I fell forward several four or five feet. It is a good [*illegible word*] that I did not break my neck or fracture some limb. I escaped, however, unhurt, a few scratches and a severe [*two illegible words*], picking myself up the best I could, I concluded I would look out for no more wells but would return as I then did to my place on line and there remained.

Soon reaching the river, I ran to it, and wading in, I took my tin cup and filling it with the warm Potomac water drank to my heart's content.

Whilst we were waiting at the riverbank before fording (we reached the river before daybreak), the assistant surgeon previously mentioned came up to me and asked about my arm. I told him it was very sore and painful. He told me I had better not go over the river with the regiment, as there would be hard work to do over there and I was in no condition to do duty. He said he would excuse me and put me on the disabled list. I told him that, after what had passed the evening before, I did not desire to be excused, and would go with my regiment if I never returned. I further told him that I would see him through that day.

About sunrise we forded the river and reaching the northern bank marched up the river until about 8 o'clock when we left the road, filed into a neighboring field and then halted and had details for each company sent with the canteens of the men to fill them with water, something which to the mind of an old soldier generally means that a fight is ahead. Whilst we were standing at this place, we could hear the firing of artillery, and small arms, in the battle there being fought about Sharpsburg.

[After the battles along South Mountain, Lee sought to concentrate his army at Sharpsburg, behind Antietam Creek. McClellan followed, and on the morning of the 17th he initiated a large-scale attack on the Confederate left flank there. Confederates referred to the Battle as Sharpsburg; Federals called it Antietam.]

After a short rest—of hardly thirty minutes—we started for the scene [of] action, to reinforce Gen. Early who was being sorely pressed by the Federal forces on our extreme left. On our way I met my brother Wm. H. Parham,[12] then a member of Shumaker's battery, which has been, as I was informed, engaged the afternoon before. I stopped and had a few words with

---

12. William Henry Parham enlisted as a private in Company C of the Virginia Danville Light Artillery in August 1861. He was promoted to sergeant in December 1861, and 2nd lieutenant in September 1864. During the Battle of Antietam his battery was one of five batteries under the command of Major L. M. Shumaker in General Thomas Jackson's division.

my brother, the first time I had seen him in about four years. We soon parted, he saying, as he bade my good-bye. "Boy, if I never see you again, do your duty!" I promised that I would and, hastening, soon overtook my regiment and took my position on the left of the colors.

When we got within a half mile of the field of battle, Gen. Stonewall Jackson,[13] who was within a few yards of our regiment, had the command halted, and by his order we got in light fighting trim, unloading our luggage (haversacks and canteens excepted). We then moved forward at a double-quick, marching by the right flank across fields, creeks, woods, stone-walls, and often fences. Gen. Jackson riding along with us and [seeming] by his manner impatient for our division to reach Gen. Early[14] as soon as possible. I well remember his appearances as he rode on with us, some time ahead of us, mounted on his little sorrel, leaping fences, fording streams and jumping ditches. Gen. McLaws,[15] our division commander, fearful that our rapid marching would break the men down before we reached the field of action, ordered us to march at quick time instead of at a double-quick, and so slackened our gait a little. I presumed by leave of Gen. Jackson. But Gen Jackson soon had us on the trot again.

13. Thomas J. "Stonewall" Jackson, one of the most famous Confederate generals, rose from colonel of Virginia militia to major general in just seven months in 1861. Promoted to lieutenant general in October 1862, he was given command of the Second Corps of the Army of Northern Virginia. He was mortally wounded at the Battle of Chancellorsville.

14. Jubal Early entered Confederate service as a colonel in 1861, and rose quickly to brigadier general, then major general. He led commands in the major engagements in the East, including Gettysburg and the Wilderness. Promoted to lieutenant general in 1864, he was given command of Jackson's old corps, the 2nd, and ordered to drive the Union forces out of the Shenandoah Valley. He did that, but eventually was pushed back out of the Valley by General Sheridan. In 1865, he left the country rather than surrender, and when he eventually returned to the United States, he practiced law and became the first president of the Southern Historical Society. He died in Lynchburg, Virginia, in 1894.

15. Lafayette McLaws, a Georgian, graduated from West Point in 1838. Early in the war he commanded the 10th Georgia Volunteer Infantry. By October 1861, he had risen to brigade command, and by May of the next year, he attained the rank of major general. He led his division at Antietam, Fredericksburg, Chancellorsville, and Gettysburg. In the fall of 1863, he participated in the Knoxville Campaign under General James Longstreet. In 1864, he commanded the District of Georgia and oversaw a futile attempt to impede Sherman's march across that state. In 1865, he led a division at Averasboro, North Carolina. After the war, he worked as a tax collector in Savannah, where he died on July 24, 1897.

We soon reached the field of battle. Barksdale's[16] brigade of our division went in front forming a line of battle to our right and moving forward before our brigade formed its line of battle. It was a magnificent sight — this brigade charging across the field in its front to the woods beyond, facing as they advanced a storm of shot and shell, together with a hot infantry fire. The line faltered not at all, but pressed steadily forward.

When we reached the stone-wall at the edge of the field from which Barksdale's brigade began its charge, Col. Montague, of our regiment, which was then marching by the flank, intended to form the regiment into a line of battle by first throwing the men by columns of fours into columns by companies and from columns by companies into regimental line of battle, but the enemy's missiles, shot, shell, and minies, were flying about us so thickly that the boys thought there was no time for battalion drill, and so when the first command "by companies into line" was given, they came in to line of battle by one direct movement as nicely as if no enemy had been in sight, formed into line of battle, and getting in line with the other regiments of our brigade, we immediately moved forward, about a hundred yards in rear, but to the left, of Barksdale's brigade, the two brigades moving in echelon. The fire was now very hot. Col. Montague ordered the company officers to take their positions in rear of their companies. Capt. Coke of my company, then the left color-company, said he would guide on the right of his company, which placed him immediately on my left. As we moved across the field he said to me, "John, this looks right tough! If I should be killed, tell them at home about it." I made a like request of him. We had hardly gotten half across the field, when I felt the wind of a minie ball passing in close proximity to me, and immediately heard it strike Capt. Coke. He threw his hand to his head and fell to the ground. I stopped and found he had been struck just above the knee but was not seriously wounded. I called for the ambulance corps to take him from the field and then hastened on to my position at the left of the colors.

When I reached the colors, I found that so many of the regiment had been killed or wounded that the left companies of the regiment had became detached from the colors and there was considerable space between right of

16. William Barksdale, a lawyer, politician, and avid secessionist, entered Confederate service in 1861 as the colonel of the 13th Mississippi Infantry Regiment, which fought at the Battle of Bull Run. Soon promoted to brigadier general, he led his brigade of Mississippi regiments at Antietam, Fredericksburg, and Chancellorsville. His brigade at Antietam consisted of the 13th, 17th, 18th, and 21st Mississippi regiments. He received a mortal wound during the Confederate attack against the Union left at Gettysburg on July 2, 1863.

these companies and the left of the right companies of the regiment. I at once shouted to these men on the left to rally on the colors and close on to the right, which they did in good order. By this time we had reached in a forward movement—the men had been firing as they advanced—a small rocky knoll. Here the line halted and kept up their fire upon the enemy. Our line, how-ever, was quite thin, and the men a little scattered, those in the rear rank being eight or ten paces in rear of them in the front line. I said to Bob Forrest, our color-bearer, that our men on the front line were in great danger from those in the rear line. I could feel the wind of the balls from the guns of these men in the rear line. The fire from the enemy was now very severe, several men killed right at my side. The flag-staff was cut into by a bullet, and the colors were pierced by many minies. We counted seventeen holes in the flag after the battle. One poor fellow, a member of company I, was shot in the head, and his brains were splattered over the sleeve of my jacket. Another was killed and fell on my ankle as I knelt near him. Altogether it was the warmest place I was ever in. Gen. Semmes, our brigade-commander, [I] noticed standing near me about this time, he having dismounted and walked up to our colors. He was standing near the color-bearer, watching the enemy. Capt. R. L. Hen-ley,[17] our regiment commissary, whose hope was to go into action with his reg-iment, was about this time wounded in both arms. Gen. Semmes, seeing him in this condition, said to him, "Capt. Henley, go off the field. You are disabled and can do no good here." Capt. Henley seemed unwilling to leave, remark-ing that he thought he might be of some service. Gen. Semmes then told him to go down to our left and try to rally a new regiment which had never been under us before and was not behaving so well. Capt. Henley started to go on this mission, but as he did so he was struck about the neck by a spent ball and knocked down, after which he took Gen. Semmes' advice and left the field.

Gen. Semmes now located the enemy behind a stone-wall not over sev-enty five yards in our front, from which they were pouring a deadly fire upon us. "They will kill the last one of us!" he remarked. "We must dislodge them." I well remember seeing their heads above the stone wall as they would fire at us. I fired several times at them with my Austrian rifle, so often indeed that it became foul and hot. After saying that we must dislodge this line of the enemy behind the stonewall, Gen. Semmes, rising from the ground to his full

17. Prewar lawyer Richardson Leonard Henley enlisted as a sergeant in Company C of the 32nd Virginia in April 1861. He was commissioned captain and assistant com-missary of subsistence in October 1861. Wounded at the Battle of Antietam, he was later assigned to conscript duty in 1863, and did not return to the 32nd Virginia. He resumed the practice of law after the war.

height—he had been stooping or kneeling since I first noticed him—with his long white hair and beard flowing, looking every inch a hero, shouted, "Charge! Charge them, my brave Virginians!" Color-bearer Forrest and his guard were now a few feet in front of our line, and the men were hard to move. Henry Sinclair,[18] a lieutenant in company I, shouted, "Bob Forrest, why in the devil don't you go forward with the colors? If you won't, give them to someone else!" As Sinclair said this, he was excitedly walking up to the flag. Forrest with some indignation in his manner replied, "You go to thunder! You shall not have them. I will carry them as far as any other man. You bring your men up to the line and then we will all go together!" The men were then all brought to the line of the colors, and the whole command then charged forward in good shape. As we moved towards them, we could see the enemy dropping back from the wall one at a time. As we reached the wall the whole line of the enemy broke and ran up the hill in rear of the wall to the cover of their artillery posted at the crest of the hill. Reaching the wall, we now had an excellent breastwork from which we fired upon the retreating federals. We continued to hold this position during the remainder of the day, with no more fighting on our part of the line beyond a little sharpshooting. Indeed we remained at this point all of the night of the 17th and all of the 18th.

On the 18th details were made for the burial of the dead, which was indeed sad work. When the detail from my regiment was going over the field in the performance of this duty, a member of the party of Company H, was shocked to find among the dead his brother, a member of Company A, whom he did not know was hurt until he came upon his body, stark and cold, with a bullet hole through his head. All the bereaved brother could do was to wrap him in his blanket and bury him on Maryland's soil.

Early on the morning of the 19th our army fell back across the Potomac, tired, hungry, ragged, footsore and in bad plight generally, but feeling that we had nothing to regret . . .[19]

18. Henry Stuart Sinclair enlisted as a private in Company I of the 32nd Virginia in May 1861. Elected to 2nd lieutenant in May 1862, Sinclair was wounded at Antietam. He was promoted to 1st lieutenant in October 1862. He resigned from the 32nd Virginia in February 1865 to join Company B of the 3rd Virginia Cavalry.

19. The manuscript ends abruptly here.

4

The Gettysburg Campaign and Afterward

THE WOUND BERNARD received at Crampton's Gap during the Maryland Campaign took him away from Lee's army for the rest of 1862. During his absence, the Confederates drove back Ambrose Burnside's attacks at Fredericksburg in December. The 12th Virginia was only lightly engaged that day. Bernard rejoined his unit in the spring of 1863, returning to the Petersburg Riflemen as a private. In May, a new Union commander, Joseph Hooker, launched yet another offensive against Lee. Hooker's promising plan to outflank the rebel defenses worked well at first but stalled near Chancellorsville in the forests west of Fredericksburg. Lee seized the initiative. Splitting his force, he sent a strong attacking column under Stonewall Jackson around Hooker's right flank. Jackson's assault smashed into the Federal army and eventually forced Hooker to withdraw his men from the field. Lee's resounding success was tempered by the wounding of Jackson, who died shortly afterward.

Mahone's brigade along with other units in Anderson's division served as a Confederate trip wire south of the Rapidan River at the beginning of the Chancellorsville Campaign. After the battle was joined, a fraction of Lee's army, including Mahone's brigade, demonstrated vigorously in front of Union forces as Jackson's men marched by the flank. In *War Talks of Confederate Veterans,* William E. Cameron, the Readjuster governor of Virginia during the 1880s, recounted the experiences of the 12th Virginia during this campaign. To that article, Bernard appended accounts from his diary covering this period. Cameron's article has not been reproduced here.

After the Chancellorsville Campaign, the Army of Northern Virginia slipped out of its positions along the Rappahannock in early June and headed north. After several weeks of marching, the Southerners crossed into Pennsylvania and stumbled into the Union army at Gettysburg. The gravity of those events in July was not lost on the Petersburg soldiers. On a Friday evening in November 1893, Bernard delivered an address to the A. P. Hill Camp recounting his experiences during the campaign. In 1894, his story appeared in the *Petersburg Enterprise,* an obscure local weekly.[1] Few copies of this newspaper survive and the complete issue containing Bernard's account has not been found. However, Bernard glued a clipping of the article into his notebook. The article has been reprinted here. This chapter also includes an account of the campaign prepared for Bernard by William E. Cameron, the former governor. In the spring of 1894, Bernard read Cameron's account before the A. P. Hill Camp, and later arranged for its publication in the *Petersburg Daily Index-Appeal.*

Mahone's brigade was one of the few units in Lee's army to avoid heavy combat during the three days of the battle. As suggested by the following accounts, this fact yielded some mixed emotions on the part of Bernard and his comrades. In their reminiscences, Bernard and Cameron did not dwell on a controversy that arose from the inaction of Mahone's brigade during the campaign, particularly on the second day of fighting at Gettysburg. During the Confederate assault on the Union right flank that afternoon, Anderson's division, which included Mahone's command, deployed opposite the Union line at Cemetery Hill. Anderson received orders to advance, and pushed his brigades forward in support of Longstreet's assault against the Union left. While much of Anderson's division ventured ahead, Mahone's regiments did not budge. At one point, a courier arrived with orders for Mahone to join the advance. Mahone still did not move. His inaction raised questions over the years, and even led to suspicions of cowardice and insubordination. However, letters published in the *Richmond Enquirer* in August 1863 soon after the battle confirmed that Anderson had given Mahone direct instructions to remain in place on July 2. Those letters appear to put

---

1. *Petersburg Enterprise,* March 3, 1894–April 7, 1894 (Bernard's account). The article's headline also states, "To appear in Vol. II, of 'War Talks of Confederate Veterans,' by Geo. S. Bernard." This article ("The Gettysburg Campaign") appears in Bernard's Notebook in the form of a newspaper clipping on page 109, twelve pages after the cursive portion of Bernard's Notebook, which begins on page 1 with April 19, 1861, and ends on page 97 with the entry for May 4, 1863. Bernard also incorporated portions of his War Diary No. 3 into this talk (George S. Bernard Notebook, Duke University). Cameron's account appeared in the *Petersburg Daily Index-Appeal* on May 6, 1894.

to rest concerns about Mahone's performance on the second day at Gettysburg.[2]

After the Gettysburg Campaign, the armies returned to Virginia and eventually faced each other across the Rapidan River. There followed several months of relative inactivity until Lee moved past Meade's force and into northern Virginia in October. On October 14, elements of both armies met in a short, sharp clash at Bristoe Station. Early in November, Meade forced Lee to withdraw to the Rapidan River by capturing the Confederate bridgehead at Rappahannock Station on November 7. Later that month, Meade launched another offensive, which ended in a frigid stalemate at Mine Run. The armies returned to their winter camps and remained there until the commencement of the brutal Overland Campaign of 1864.

Bernard captured some of his experiences during the fall and winter of 1863–64 in a document he prepared titled "War Narrative." This chapter includes portions of this document, along with some miscellaneous correspondence from other veterans to Bernard.

>─0─<►┤<┄┄┄►┤◄►─0─<

"The Gettysburg Campaign: The Narrative of a Private Soldier in the Confederate Army, Taken from His Diary and Note Book,"
by George S. Bernard

An Address Delivered by Geo. S. Bernard Before R. E. Lee Camp No. 1, of Confederate Veterans, of Richmond, Va., on the Evening of Friday, Nov. 3, 1893.

FROM FREDERICKSBURG TO THE VALLEY OF VIRGINIA

Comrades: Having been honored with an invitation to address your camp, I have selected as my subject the Gettysburg Campaign, in which it was my fortune to participate as a private soldier, being a member of the Petersburg Riflemen, Co. E, 12th Va. Regiment of the infantry, Mahone's brigade. It is not to be expected that a man in the ranks should give from his own knowl-

2. *Richmond Enquirer,* August 5–6, 1863. For a general discussion of the controversy, see Bradley Gottfried, "Mahone's Brigade: Insubordination or Miscommunication?" *Gettysburg Magazine,* January 1998, 67–76.

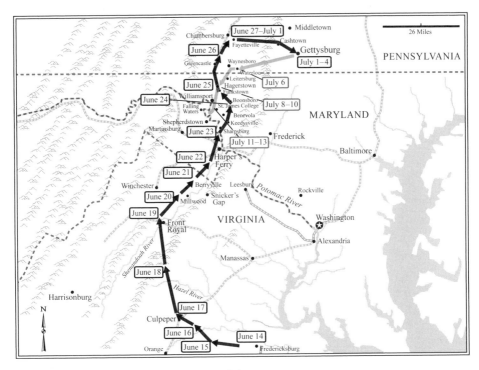

GETTYSBURG CAMPAIGN, JUNE–JULY 1863

edge any comprehensive account of the more important movements of the troops, Confederate and Federal, that marched and fought, and made the great battle that took place about the quiet old Pennsylvania town one of the most famous in the history of the world, and I shall make no attempt to do so.

The narrative I shall give you will simply embrace the personal impressions of one of the many thousands of men in the ranks of the Confederate infantry that followed Gen. R. E. Lee in Pennsylvania as these impressions were briefly recorded at the time in a diary, and later were more fully written out in a note book at the request of a comrade whilst we were doing duty on the lines around Petersburg; and what will be read this evening, it is hoped, will serve to recall to the minds of many of the old soldiers whom I have the honor of addressing many personal recollections of individual experiences on this famous expedition.

To begin, I will state that, as soon as the fighting around Chancellorsville was over, Mahone's brigade went into camp about two miles south of Salem Church, and there remained from about the 7th of May to the 2nd of June, 1863, but on the last mentioned day was marched to Fredericksburg to relieve Barksdale's brigade, which had been on duty at that place for several months.

After doing duty there for nearly two weeks, on Sunday, the 14th of June, our command evacuated the place and began its march up the Orange plank road—going whither we knew not. Let the story of the march be now told from the diary and note book, taken from the latter, in the way of notes to the former, such paragraphs, or parts of paragraphs, as will serve to complete the narrative, and commencing with the following entry made whilst at a picket post in Fredericksburg near the river a few minutes before the last of the Confederates occupying the town evacuated it:

3 o'clock, P.M. Sunday, June 14th.

Last evening about 6 o'clock, half a dozen or so shots were exchanged between our batteries and the Yankee battery on Bray's Hill. The rain that came up probably put a stop to the firing, as I heard yesterday evening it was our intention to open upon the enemy. All last night there was a considerable stir with the enemy across the river, and down about the pontoon bridge—trains moving all night, wagons loading and unloading, hammering as if boxing or unboxing something, and the whole sky illuminated by large fires, one of which seemed to us on post to be about the depot. This morning the fact was learned that the enemy on this side of the river had left leaving a few of their rear guard which were all captured. Evidently they are moving from this position. A few moments ago those of us at the picket pits received orders to pack up and leave for the regiment at Marye's Hill, one at a time, and three of those at this stand have now left leaving only myself who will be called for by Lt. Keiley[3] and Hartwell Harrison.[4] What is our destination I do not know, but if it be true that those of us who bring up the rear are to proceed up the Plank Road until we overtake the regiment, I rather think we are going to join the main body of our army somewhere on the Upper Rappahannock.

[At a May strategy meeting in Richmond with President Jefferson Davis, Lee had proposed an invasion of Pennsylvania. The operation would provide supplies to Lee's army and move the enemy forces out of Virginia. It would also reap political benefits by emboldening Northern war opponents and boosting the possibility foreign powers would recognize the Confederacy. As Bernard's account indicates, Lee began this operation in mid-June, pulling his forces out of their positions near Fredericksburg and marching west and then north into the Shenandoah Valley.]

3. Anthony Keiley is discussed in note 16, chapter 1.
4. Hartwell B. Harrison enlisted in Company E of the 12th Virginia in April 1861. He was promoted to corporal in 1862 and sergeant in 1863. He was paroled at Appomattox.

The entries during the four succeeding weeks commencing on Monday, June 15, and ending on Sunday, July 21, were as follows:

On Orange Turnpike 2 miles of Chancellorsville,
Monday morning, June 15, '63.

About 3 o'clock I was notified to leave my post and going up the street towards the C.H. fell in with Thad Pagand[5] and Dick Davis[6] and went towards Marye's Hill where we found others of the Riflemen and many of Captain Wilson's[7] company. There was some misunderstanding as to where we were to assemble, most of the men understanding that we were to meet at Marye's Hill. Lt. Keiley and Hartwell Harrison not coming up, at Captain Wilson's suggestion we started up the Plank Road and overtook the regiment with Lt. Keiley and several members of our company about 3 miles from town. The whole brigade soon getting together, we took up our line of march up the Plank Road until we struck the turnpike, up which we proceeded to this point, halting about sunset having marched about 8 miles. We are now within two hundred yards where we supported a battery the evening of Saturday, May 2nd, and were under such a severe shelling. It is said our destination is Culpeper C.H. The strength of our regiment is now about 435 men, including staff officers, detailed men, musicians, teamsters, &c.[8]

5. Thaddeus Pagand, a cashier at a dry goods store in Petersburg, enlisted as a private in Company E of the 12th Virginia in April 1861. He was promoted to corporal in 1862 and sergeant in 1863. Wounded and captured at Gettysburg, he spent time in hospitals in Gettysburg and Baltimore before his exchange in September 1863. When he returned to military service he transferred to the 3rd Company, Richmond Howitzers.

6. Richard Beale Davis, a college student when the war began, enlisted in Company E of the 12th Virginia as a private in April 1862. He was wounded at Seven Pines and the Crater, surviving both wounds to serve until the surrender of the 12th Virginia at Appomattox. After the war, he practiced law, ran a business, and held political office in Virginia.

7. Charles Wesley Wilson enlisted as a private in Company A of the 6th Virginia Infantry Regiment in April 1861. He was promoted to 1st lieutenant in May 1862, and to captain in November 1862. Captured at Cold Harbor, he was sent to Fort Delaware Prison. He took the oath of allegiance in June 1865 and returned to Virginia.

8. GSB: The following is the account in the note book of our first day's march:

"Sunday, June 14—To-day our brigade (Mahone's) left its position at the foot of Marye's Hill, Fredericksburg, where it had been in line of battle for a week previous, during which time our company, (Co. E, 12th Va. regiment) and Capt. Wilson's of the 6th Va. regiment had been doing picket duty in the city along the river banks. The night before the enemy, who had been in some force down about the Bernard house on the south side of the river, evacuated their position there and probably commenced moving towards Northern Virginia. About midday Sunday those of us on picket received orders to get ready to march, and, when notified to leave, to do so one by one, and to

Near Culpeper Plank Road, 4 miles beyond
Germanna Ford, Tuesday, June 16th, 1863.

Started yesterday soon after sunrise and halted about an hour by sun, after marching about 17 miles. The day being very warm, the marching was very severe. I have heard that several of the brigade died from sunstroke, some say 5 or 6, some say 10 or 15. Our line of march was up the turnpike to Chancellorsville, thence along same to the Wilderness, thence by the Culpeper Plank Road to Germanna Ford, where we crossed the Rapidan upon a roughly constructed foot-bridge, and thence to this point about 4 miles beyond. The numerous graves of men and horses from Chancellorsville to the Wilderness speak plainly of the recent hard fighting in that vicinity. The horses are still offensive. There is difference of opinion as to the distance marched yesterday, some even thinking we marched 20 miles.[9]

Camp near Culpeper C.H., Wednesday, June 17, 1863.

Started yesterday morning about 7 o'clock and made quite an easy march to this point a mile NW of Culpeper C.H., reaching here about 2 o'clock and having marched about 13 miles, passing through the villages of Stevensburg and Culpeper C.H. After reaching here, Lt. Manson, Jim Nash, and myself went to the C.H. to visit relatives there. Yesterday we heard very good news

---

go by different streets as quietly as possible to Marye's Hill, where we would assemble. Accordingly, about 3 o'clock P.M., we received orders to move, and soon various stragglers were to be seen making their way towards the place of rendezvous, the whole of the two companies arriving at which we were marched on to Orange C.H. plank road until we overtook the brigade which had been resting about 2 miles from town. About sunset we halted within 2 miles of Chancellorsville going upon the old turnpike road and having marched about 8 miles. The march of this evening was not without interest as our route was over two battle-fields on which our regiment had been engaged, that of Salem Church and that of Zoar Church or Chancellorsville."

9. GSB: The march on Monday is thus narrated in the note book:

"Monday, June 15.—This morning the troops were in motion by a little after sunrise, much refreshed by their previous night's rest. For several miles now, that is, until we reached the Wilderness run, was our route interesting, passing as we did over the hard-fought battle-fields of Chancellorsville and the Wilderness, where Jackson routed the celebrated Dutch Corps. At the Wilderness run, 5 miles beyond Chancellorsville, we struck the branch plank road leading to Culpeper C.H., which road we now took, crossing the Rapidan at Germanna upon a foot bridge temporarily constructed, and halting a little before sunset about 10 miles from Culpeper C.H., having marched altogether about 17 miles. The weather being very warm, there was much straggling, and our brigade being the lead brigade of the division many of the stragglers from the other brigades claimed to belong to Mahone's brigade, thus playing quite a trick on us and causing Gen. Anderson to inquire why it was there was so much straggling from Mahone's brigade. The roll being called before we were dismissed, the trick was discovered."

from Ewell in the Valley. He has whipped the enemy at Winchester, and, it is said, captured 10,000 prisoners, all the enemy's artillery and commissary wagons, having stormed their works. This rumor appears to be reliable, coming from Lee's headquarters. It is said we are to move to-day to Gaines' Cross Roads, 22 miles distant and somewhere in the direction of Winchester. We move to-day with 10 day's rations ahead, the men carrying 3 days' rations in their haversacks, the regimental wagons 3 days', and the wagons of the division commissary trains 4 days' rations. Yesterday's papers brought information that the enemy had all left Falmouth.

> Rappahannock Co.
> June 18, 1863.

Left camp near Culpeper C.H. yesterday morning about 9 o'clock and halted about a mile west of Hazel River, which we forded, having marched about 11 miles. The march was one of the severest the brigade ever took, the heat being excessive. There never was more straggling during the march to Maryland last year. To-day the weather has been equally hot, but we have been halting oftener. We have marched this morning about 8 miles and we are now halted, it is said, to rest three hours and a half when we will resume our march for Gaines' Cross Roads, three miles distant.[10]

> Near Foot of Blue Ridge, and 8 miles of
> Front Royal, Friday June 19, 1863.

After rest of 3 1/2 hours, we started yesterday afternoon, and about sunset halted about half a mile west of Flint Hill, a little village 5 miles west of Gaines' X Roads, after marching in all yesterday about 16 miles. From Gaines' X Roads to the point at which we halted we had quite a thunderstorm, but we did not get very wet, being generally supplied with oil cloths. This morning we started soon after sunrise, and as the day bids fair to be cloudy we will probably be marched beyond Front Royal. Last evening we had good news from

---

10. GSB: The account in the note book of our march on June 17th, our fourth day's march, is as follows:

"Wednesday, June 17.—Started this morning about 10 o'clock and marched the first three or four miles very rapidly. The weather to-day excessively hot and straggling commenced very early. The roadsides were soon lined with stragglers, many of whom were completely exhausted by the heat, many suffering from and some dying, it was said, with sunstroke. When the brigade made its first halt to rest, it was a mere skeleton of what it was when it started, so many were behind. About sunset the division went into camp, that is, bivouacked on the north side of the Hazel river, just 11 miles from Culpeper C.H., after one of the most fatiguing marches I ever took. To add to the trials of this celebrated march of the 17th day of June, the place where our brigade bivouacked was a most disagreeable one, on the side of a steep hill, and at night the heat was so great it was difficult to sleep."

the West, (which however I fear is untrue), viz: that Grant had attempted to cut his way out from Vicksburg but had been repulsed by Johnston, who, in some way, cut him off. We had other rumors also of an extravagant character, to the effect that Harper's Ferry was being invested by Ewell.

DOWN THE VALLEY AND ACROSS THE POTOMAC INTO MARYLAND

One Mile N.W. of North Fork of Shenandoah
River, Saturday Morning, June 20 '63.

Yesterday about 1–1/2 o'clock P.M., we reached the heights near Front Royal, where we remained about 3 hours, and then moved on to the village, through which we passed, taking the Winchester Turnpike and fording the South and North branches of the Shenandoah, halting at this point about 10–1/2 o'clock, having marched in all yesterday about 14 miles, and part of the way in a drenching rain. We found the country on this side of the Blue Ridge apparently in a more cultivated condition than that immediately on the other side. The little town of Front Royal rather disappointed my expectations in its general appearance. As someone expressed it, it is a "sorry" looking little place. But the ladies appeared to be rejoiced at the sight of our troops, judging from their demonstrations, to which we responded with many a cheer. Last night was very bad on the men in consequence of the heavy rain.[11]

The disagreeable experiences of this night the lapse of thirty years has not effaced from my memory. Just as my messmate (Jim Nash[12]) and myself had

11. GSB: The incidents of the march on Friday, June 19th, are told in the note book as follows:

"Friday, June 19.—Started about sunrise and halted about midday on a high hill within a mile of and overlooking the village of Front Royal in Page [Warren] county, having crossed the Blue Ridge at Thornton Gap. The scenery along the route was exceedingly beautiful—in some places very wild. We were struck with the luxuriant richness of the country on both sides of the mountains. How it contrasted with the worn out and devastated country to which we had been so long accustomed! About 4 o'clock P.M. our march is resumed. We pass through the town of Front Royal, our bands playing and the men cheering as the ladies wave their handkerchiefs to us. About sunset we forded the South fork of the Shenandoah and afterwards forded the North fork a half a mile further on. Night finds us still moving and so does a drenching rain. We move along very slowly and get soaking wet. About 11 o'clock we filed off on one side of the road and halted for the night. We spread our oil cloths and blankets on the wet ground, but very little sleep do we get this night."

12. James E. Nash, a "gentleman farmer" living in Petersburg at the start of the war, enlisted as a private in Company A of the 12th Virginia in February 1862. He trans-

about fallen asleep the water from the soft and wet ground where our bed was made soaked through our underlying oil cloth and blanket, and through the thick sleeves of my woolen shirt and coat, and reaching my skin thus reminded me of the uncanny condition of things. We at once got up and found it raining a little, but some of the men had already begun to make fires from the rails of a neighboring fence. To one of these fires we repaired and spent the remainder of the night alternatively drying and warming one side of our clothes and bodies whilst the other side was getting a fresh wetting from the falling rain—an experience that all old soldiers can well appreciate.

Nor have I forgotten another incident of the march from the South to the North Fork of the Shenandoah, too good to be lost. Many of the men took off their pants and drawers, as well as their shoes and socks, to ford the former, and when they reached its north bank were proceeding to put on these articles of clothing, when, being informed that there was another fork of the river only a few hundred yards ahead of them, they concluded to defer so doing until the latter stream should be reached and crossed. So, falling into line in this condition, shoes and socks, pants and drawers in hand, they were soon marching along with the column on its way to the North Fork. On the roadside between the two streams was a private residence at which were assembled a number of ladies to see and greet the troops with their patriotic cheers as they passed. Soon the head of the column hove in sight, and eyes were strained to catch the first view of the boys in gray, but only an instant sufficed to make it appear that there was a large sprinkling of them who in the distance seemed to be wearing something like *white* pants. The situation was quickly taken in by the sharp wits and keen eyes of the Valley girls, and this done, the explosion of a shell in their midst would not have produced a more sudden scampering from their place of observation.[13]

Let us again draw from the diary:

> Sunday Morning, June 21, near turnpike,
> and 8 miles of Berryville.

Left position of yesterday about 2 o'clock and halted about sundown, having marched about 8 miles down the turnpike towards Winchester, where we struck the Berryville turnpike and marched about 3 miles to this point, pass-

---

ferred to Company E in June 1862, and was one of three men left in that company after the Battle of Antietam. He was captured at Chancellorsville, soon paroled, and then wounded at Brandy Station. In July 1864, he transferred to the 10th Virginia Cavalry, where he held the rank of sergeant major. He survived the war.

13. Bernard crossed out the preceding paragraph in the clipping of "The Gettysburg Campaign" preserved in his Notebook (see George S. Bernard Notebook, Duke University).

ing about one mile from here through the little village of White Post. We are now in the county of Clarke. Many pretty residences along the road. Marched several miles yesterday through a severe rain. This morning one day's rations of *corn bread* issued to us. The country through which we are now marching very beautiful. The lands very fine. The roads are generally macadamized roads, made with limestone, which abounds in this region. Most of the fencing—certainly that along the public roads—is of stone, the same material, limestone.

Berryville (Clarke C.H.)
Monday, June 22, 1863.

Started about 8–1/2 o'clock yesterday morning and marched about 8 miles to our present camp just outside of Berryville, reaching here about 1 o'clock P.M., passing within 2 miles of Millwood, which we left to our right. We leave today, it is said, for Shepherdstown. Longstreet's Corps, which we passed yesterday about Millwood, it is said, will go to Harper's Ferry. Yesterday we heard a plenty of good news, which, of course, we received with many grains of allowance. We heard first that Gen. Lee had received a dispatch stating that Johnston had fallen upon Grant and had killed, wounded and captured 25,000 of his men and had Grant "just where he wanted him."[14] Next we heard that Stuart had captured an Indiana regiment of cavalry, and Ewell is at Sharpsburg fortifying, and Rhodes [Rodes] is in Pennsylvania. On the other hand, however, we heard yesterday that Stuart had been driven back in a skirmish at or near Snicker's Gap.

Jefferson Co. 1 mile of Shepherdstown
June 23.

Left our camp near Berryville about 12–1/2 P.M., yesterday, passed through Berryville and halted about sunset about 3 miles from Charlestown, marching 9 miles. Started again this morning soon after daylight, marched through Charlestown and halted a few minutes ago, 11 A.M., at this place, having marched about 12 miles. Berryville is an ugly little place, but Charlestown on the other hand is quite pretty. The ladies of the latter place turned out in large numbers to see us. I scarcely ever before heard such cheering as the boys gave this morning. Our company was detached from the regiment just before we entered the town, and marched through in advance of it, and continued in advance until we halted. When about half a mile from this place we thought we would soon encounter the enemy. One of Gen.

---

14. This story of Johnston's success against Grant was yet another false report from the West.

Anderson's[15] staff rode hastily back and told Lt. Keiley to keep a lookout for the enemy, and asked him how far was our command. But it soon turned out that there was no enemy about. For several days we have been passing through as fine a country as any in Virginia, and how we all wish we could be free that we might enjoy the luxuries which we know must abound! Our army horses keep in splendid condition. Whole distance marched since leaving Fredericksburg 119 miles.

On Picket near Shepherdstown
Wednesday, June 24.

Last evening about sunset our regiment was ordered on picket, and is now on duty about 3/4 of a mile east of the point we left, and in the direction of Harper's Ferry. Everything quiet last night. The rest of the brigade and division passed us this morning moving towards the river. Yesterday our boys did some successful "scouting" as we were in the advance. Many got butter, milk and vegetables. We heard yesterday that Gen. Lee has issued very stringent orders to secure respect for private property when we get into the enemy's country. We are all still utterly ignorant of Gen. Lee's design in making this move, but the army was never in better spirits or more confident of success. The loss by straggling is nothing like so great as it was in the famous campaign of last year. The commissary sergeant told me on Monday that when we started from Fredericksburg he issued rations to 403 men and 31 officers, and that the day before, one week thereafter he issued to 365 men and 31 officers, showing a loss of only 38 men.

On Turnpike 1 mile north of Boonesboro [Boonsboro], Md.
Thursday, June 25, 1863.

The brigade has just halted to rest and I take the opportunity to write. Yesterday morning about 9 o'clock our regiment moved from its position on picket, and, having marched about one mile in the direction of the Potomac, halted near the river for 3 or 4 hours to let the wagons of the different bri-

15. Major General Richard Heron Anderson commanded the division that contained Mahone's brigade. Anderson was a graduate of West Point's famed class of 1842 and served in the Army through the Mexican War and up until he resigned his commission in March 1861. He entered service as a major and was promoted to brigadier general in July 1861. In 1862, he was assigned a brigade in the Army of Northern Virginia, and stayed with that army until the end of war. He was promoted to major general in 1863 and lieutenant general in 1864 (temporary appointment). His performance as a commander was solid until the end of the war, when his troops were dispersed at Sailor's Creek. Without soldiers to lead, he was relieved of command the day before the surrender at Appomattox.

gades of our division cross the river, which they did at the ford below Shepherdstown, the wagons crossing in one train. Our regiment and the 12th Miss. of Posey's[16] brigade acting as wagon guard. The river at the ford was about 150 yards wide and took us up to our waists. Having crossed, we marched on through Sharpsburg, through the battle-field of Sharpsburg, through the little village of Ketysville [Keedysville], and halted after sundown within a mile of Boonesboro, having marched in all yesterday about 9 miles. In the villages through which we passed there were but few demonstrations of Southern sentiment, but almost all who appeared to sympathize with us seemed to belong to the first class of people. It is almost needless to say that we gave hearty cheers to every handkerchief that waved and flag displayed. It was amusing to see the long faces of the Union people. They looked as though a funeral procession were passing. One lady I have heard of made faces at us. Yesterday a party of 10 cavalry from Harper's Ferry made a dash upon the little village of Ketysville and captured a small squad of our men, among them Gen. Wright's son, his ordinance officer, who was riding some distance ahead of his father's brigade. Young Wright has but one leg, having lost one at the last battle of Manassas. He rides with two crutches hung to his saddle. This morning about 6 o'clock we were again in motion and passed through the town of Boonsboro, quite a pretty place, containing a few secessionists bold enough to wave their handkerchiefs to us. Yesterday morning, unfortunately, 11 soldiers were drowned at the ferry above Shepherdstown, by the swamping of one of the ferry boats.

On turnpike 1 mile south of Hagerstown, Md.
Thursday, June 25, 1863.

Moving on we passed through the little Union hole of Benevola and about a mile below here the village of Funkstown, where the secession demonstration was greater than in any other place we had passed. The demonstrations here, however, as elsewhere, were confined to the ladies. About 1 o'clock we halted at this point, having marched in all today about ten miles. This evening some of our boys have been into Hagerstown "scouting" and have succeeded in getting a few things to eat. The country through which we have been marching to-day is in the highest state of cultivation, and on every side are to be seen beautiful fields of wheat. Having collected some beeves while

16. Carnot Posey, a Mississippian who studied law at the University of Virginia, commanded a brigade at Gettysburg consisting of the 12th, 16th, 19th, and 48th Mississippi regiments. In October, he received a slight leg wound at Bristoe Station, which became infected and led to his death a month later in Charlottesville. His grave is on the grounds of the University of Virginia.

near Berryville, our brigade commissary offered to us this evening for the first time a ration of beef, which we have enjoyed no little.

IN PENNSYLVANIA

Franklin Co., Penn., 8 miles of Chambersburg
Friday, June 26, 1863.

Starting this morning about 6 o'clock, a most disagreeable and tiresome march through rain and mud brought us about 1 o'clock to our present camp, in the state of Pennsylvania, and within 8 miles of Chambersburg. The march was 13 miles and we halted only twice, each time for about 15 minutes only, and as a matter of course we were well-nigh broken down when we stopped. In Hagerstown we found a few sympathizers among the ladies, whom we cheered vociferously. This is quite a pretty place, and about the size of Fredericksburg, probably a little larger. Five miles from Hagerstown and immediately on the Pennsylvania line, we passed an ugly little village called Middletown, where one or two of the women, apparently of the humbler class, very timidly waved a small Confederate flag. One of our halts was in this village, where we were told by a citizen that the place was greatly "Copperhead,"[17] but we had our own opinions as to the truth of this statement. Five miles further on we passed through the town of Greencastle, not so pretty a place as Hagerstown or quite so large. Here we saw not one sign of sympathy. *Perhaps the weather too bad.* The portion of this state through which we passed to-day seems not so good as the country we saw in Maryland, but there is the same abundance of *wheat.* I noticed as I passed them to-day the "Dutch ovens," near dwelling houses, which I mistook at first for distilleries. Our army is showing much respect for private property. Our brigade mail courier brought us mail this afternoon with Richmond papers to the 22nd inst. The whole North is in a state of excitement about our invasion.

Three miles of Chambersburg
Sunday, June 28, '63.

Started about 6 o'clock yesterday morning and halted at this place about 2 o'clock, having made about 12 miles, and passing through the village of Marion and the town of Chambersburg. The people everywhere wear the same sad, disconsolate look. In spite of efforts on the part of our officers, our soldiers have committed many depredations, but a recent stringent order of Gen. Lee's will put a stop to this in a great measure. The people about here are almost frightened to death. Our men have purchased vast numbers of chickens,

17. "Copperhead" was the name attributed to Northern Democrats who opposed Lincoln's policies and generally sought an end to the war.

ducks, pigs, and lots of butter, milk and honey, at Yankee prices, paying for them [with] Confederate money.

The account of our march on Saturday, June 27th, given in the note book, after stating that at Middletown "we talk with some citizens who unanimously announced themselves in favor of peace," proceeds as follows:

Pushing further on 5 miles from this place we entered the town of Greencastle, where the people all look scared almost to death, or as melancholy as if a funeral procession were passing through the streets. Three or four miles beyond this place we go into camp about midday, very much exhausted by the day's march. In obedience to orders *fence rails* were not touched, but *havoc* is played with property of other kinds. The Dutch farmers around the places where we camp think themselves utterly ruined, as indeed many of them were. What the men don't take they buy at old prices and pay for in Confederate money—and what delicious milk and butter they get. Pitching our tents in consequence of the rain, we make the hay and straw stacks contribute abundantly to our comfort in the way of beds.

There is one incident of this day that I cannot forget. Soon after our command halted to bivouack, my mess-mate and friend, Jim Nash, of the Riflemen, and myself started out in search of some milk, and within a short distance of our bivouack came to a small farm-house, where dwelt a young farmer and his wife, both being at home and near the front door of the house as we entered the front gate, some fifty feet distant from them. Seeing us coming in, the poor woman manifested, by her horror-stricken countenance, a degree of alarm that was painful to witness, seeing which both of us bade her not be alarmed as we only desired to purchase some milk. The courteous manner of my friend, who a few years later won the heart and hand of the widow of a distinguished governor of one of our Southern states, was particularly reassuring, as he, who, I think, was the first to speak, called to the frightened lady and said:

"Madam, do not be alarmed! No harm is intended!"

From a state of great fear there was an instantaneous transition to one of confidence, and our canteens were soon filled with delicious milk, for which we paid in Confederate money—all we had. The helpless fright depicted on that poor woman's face as we entered the gate has often recurred to me as an unpleasant memory.

There being no entry in the diary during the three days intervening between the entry on the 28th of June and that on the 1st of July, I insert here the following from the note book descriptive of our three days' stay in camp near Fayetteville some three miles east of Chambersburg:

Here, as at Greencastle, the people all look sullen and melancholy. Having passed through the town, we take the Baltimore pike to the right. We are somewhat surprised at this, having supposed our march would continue northward at least until we reach Harrisburg. Three miles beyond Chambersburg we reach the village of Fayetteville, on the outskirts of which our division goes into camp, the whole division massed in a body of woods of a few acres. The men now *scout* about the neighborhood no little, scouring the country for good things to eat, and a walk through the camp of any of the brigades would have satisfied anyone that the *scouting* was not unsuccessful. The boys certainly lived *high* now. To say nothing of *substantials,* delicacies such as milk and butter, honey, molasses, delicious loaves of bread, vegetables, etc., were to be seen on all sides. To have heard the squealing of pigs, the cackling of chickens, and the quacking of ducks, the luckless victims of the Confederate appetites, one for the instant might have supposed himself on some market square.

Whilst encamped in this grove our boys keep in the best spirits. Every night the woods are made to ring with their enthusiastic cheers.

It was at this place that I recall having an interview with a young Pennsylvania girl, with auburn hair and comely looks, who refused to give me a single onion from a patch full of these vegetables, so much prized by all soldiers, upon which I was casting longing eyes through the garden palings that separated the fair young lady and myself as she stood in her garden near the coveted vegetables. Not wishing to offer her Confederate money (or not having any to offer), I tendered a Confederate stamp, thinking her desire to get one of these as a curiosity might tempt her, but the offer only brought a contemptuous curl of the lip and the declaration that she would not have one of my "Jeff Davis" stamps. It is needless to say that I left the garden fence not with pleasing impressions of the Pennsylvania beauty.[18]

Let us now resume the narrative as it is found in the diary:

18. GSB: The experiences of two comrades, Jno. E. Crow and Wm. A. Douglas, members of the Petersburg Riflemen, as narrated in a letter written by Mr. Crow December 15, 1893, from Wilmington, N.C., his place of residence, were more pleasant than mine, and may properly be given here:

"Our supply of rations was meager," says Mr. Crow. "The people would give us nothing, and with rare exceptions, we had no money that would pass current and were in a scrape. Billy Douglas, of our company, came to me and proposed a foraging expedi-

THE BATTLE OF GETTYSBURG

Near Battlefield of Gettysburg

Wednesday, July 1.

Remained quiet at camp near Fayetteville from Saturday until this morning, when we moved off in this direction, starting at 4-1/2 A.M. Passed through the town of Fayetteville and over the South Mountains, and halted at this place about an hour ago (5-1/2 P.M.), marching in all to-day about 17 miles. Heard artillery early this morning in this direction, and after cross-

----

tion. Knowing that I was without money, thinking that Billy was in the same fix, and remembering Gen. Lee's order for the protection of private property, I said: 'Billy, what's the use? We can neither buy nor take anything.'

"'Come on,' said he, 'I have one dollar and a quarter in silver, and I think we can get something to eat with that.'

"So we started out, and selecting as a place at which something good to eat might probably be had one of the best looking residences we saw, with a barn near it—you will remember that the barns in Pennsylvania were a revelation to us, far excelling in appearance the dwelling houses of their owners—we went forth, and, when near the front entrance to the grounds, we perceived a sentinel walking up and down before the door—a safety guard. We spoke to the guard and asked who lived there. He replied that he did not know the name of the owner, but that he was in the back yard, and that several soldiers were trying to get something to eat, and we could go around and try our hand.

"We walked around to the back yard and saw the proprietor of the premises, an old man—we looked upon him then as an old man, although he was only about fifty, to judge from his appearance—sitting in a chair and leaning back against a tree. A short distance off was a large brick oven, which they called a 'Dutch oven,' in which, I was told, a week's supply of bread was baked at one baking. Two young women—comely looking girls they were—whom we took for housemaids were busy baking bread, which they did by placing a large pone on a long handled paddle with a very wide blade and shoving it far back into the oven, to be followed by another and another till the entire baking was placed in the oven, when the door was shut and the result awaited.

"Billy and I lounged around, saying very little till the baking was done, hoping the other fellows would get tired and move off and give us a better chance. As the old gentleman had refused in the bitterest language to give 'a rebel' anything, we felt sure that with our silver, used as a purchasing medium, we could certainly supply our wants. Finally the smell of the freshly baked bread which the girls were carrying back into the house gave my tongue rein, and I boldly asked the old man if he would sell me some of that nice bread.

"'No! No!' he said, 'I will not sell nor will I give you any bread! You are a vile set of rebels, bent on mischief!'

"I turned to Billy and mildly remarked: 'We asked for bread and he gave us a stone!'

"The old fellow quickly arose to a standing position and said: 'What! You quoting the Bible? I looked upon you as not better than heathen.' Then he stopped, and somewhat in a soliloquizing way said: 'Yes, there's your Stonewall Jackson, as you call him.

ing the mountains learned that Heth's and Pender's[19] Divisions of our corps (Hill's) have been engaging the enemy nearly all day—two corps of the enemy said to have been engaged. At this time the fight has ceased and the enemy are retiring. We drove them into and through the town of Gettysburg, it is said. Several hundred of our men have been wounded I should think from what I

He fought against the Union. I have entertained him as a guest in my house in Philadelphia. Who would have believed it!'

"I broke in on him and again asked him to sell us some of that nice bread.

"'No sir! No, sir!' he said, 'you will get nothing here, neither for love nor money. My son-in-law,' I think he said, 'is an officer in the Union army, and lost his leg under Grant.'

"For many years I remembered both the name of the old gentleman and of his son-in-law, and the latter's rank, which was also mentioned, but cannot now recall either.

"During the conversation which took place, Billy Douglas had gone off somewhere. I was conscious of his absence, but did not turn around to look for him, I was so much occupied with the old man. When I did look around, Billy was beckoning to me from the corner of the house next to the front. I sidled off and joined him, when he said: 'You're the most everlasting talker I ever heard. I have been making signs to you for five minutes. Come along with me and let's get away from here before that old man goes into the house.'

"'What do you mean?' I asked.

"'Come along!' said Billy, 'and be quick about it, and I'll show you what I mean.'

"He then pulled me around to the front of the house, out of sight of the old man, and took me to a window which looked into a basement dining room about two feet below the window, which was on a level with the ground. Here we got on our knees, when two pairs of hands were given us, one pair to each, with hearty squeezes, and the girl to whom I have already referred said: 'We are as good rebels as yourselves, but it would not do to let the old gentleman know it.'

"Then each gave us a hearty shake, handed us a big Yankee haversack filled with that elegant bread just baked, butter scotch, butter and preserves, and, wishing good luck to us, hurried us away before the old man could catch us, kissing their hands to us and telling us we must come again; but, unfortunately, as you know, we could not do so, having to make our return trip by another route. These girls were not house-maids as we had taken them to be from the fact that they were engaged in cooking at the house of evidently a man of position in his community, but were young ladies of education, as their conversation indicated, and they were, as they informed us, relatives of the old gentleman.

"You, of course, well remember Billy Douglas, with his clean, smooth face, deep blue eyes, and poetic appearance. He was a handsome little fellow, and to his good looks our mess was indebted for the sumptuous repast we took to camp that evening."

19. William Dorsey Pender, West Point graduate and Army regular until 1861, rose from colonel to major general in two years of service. Fighting in the major battles in the East, he led his division into Gettysburg, where he was wounded in the second day of fighting. He died a few weeks later; Henry Heth, another West Point graduate and

have seen. We met on the road, also, perhaps a hundred prisoners, many of whom were wounded.

Friday, July 3, '63.

To-day I fear has been a disastrous day to our army, in this that we have done very hard fighting, lost a large number of men, and as yet have failed to accomplish anything material. Yesterday our army took position, Longstreet on right, A. P. Hill centre, and Ewell left, Longstreet and Ewell to drive in the flanks of the enemy and Hill to keep them from breaking through from the front. At four o'clock P.M. the action began. Longstreet, we learn, drove them. From Ewell I have heard nothing reliable. On the centre there was only artillery fighting and skirmishing, except along a portion of Hill's right, where a portion of our division, Anderson's—Perry's, Wright's and Wilcox's brigades—took some pieces of artillery from the enemy, but had to give them up. The shelling to which our particular brigade (Mahone's) was exposed was very severe. We lost in our reg't 1 killed and 4 or 5 wounded. This morning, about sunrise, our artillery opened again and the enemy immediately replied. This was kept up at intervals until about 3 o'clock P.M.,[20] when it appeared that all our artillery opened at once, and for half an hour the firing was terrific, surpassing anything I had ever heard and unequalled, it is said by men who were present, by that at the first battle of Fredericksburg. As soon as this

---

Army regular until 1861, began the war as colonel of the 45th Virginia Infantry and ended the war as a major general. He precipitated the Battle of Gettysburg by leading his division east along the Chambersburg Pike on the morning of July 1, 1863. Wounded at Gettysburg, he returned to divisional command, which he held until the end of the war. After the war, he sold insurance.

20. GSB: I was in error as to the hour at which the severe artillery fire of this day began, and also as to its duration.

"At length about 1 P. M.," say Gen. W. N. Pendleton, chief of artillery of the Army of Northern Virginia, in his official report, "on the concerted signal, our guns in position, nearly one hundred and fifty, opened fire along the entire line from right to left, salvos by battery being much practiced, as directed, to secure greater deliberation and power. The enemy replied with full force."

Gen. Henry J. Hunt, chief of artillery of the Army of the Potomac, giving the same artillery fire, in his official report, referring to the guns of the Confederates which he places at about one hundred and fifteen, in number, says: "To oppose these we could not, from our restricted position, bring more than eighty guns to reply effectively."

"Pegram's battalion of artillery stationed along the crest of the hill immediately to the right and front of our regiment," says Col. E. M. Feild, who commanded the 12th Va., "opened with a simultaneous fire of all of its guns. Col. Pegram, who was standing near us in position to watch the effect of his fire, remarked that he had exploded one of the enemy's caissons, and, raising his hat, gave a cheer. A few moments later a shot, or shell, from one of the enemy's guns exploded one of his (Col. Pegram's) caissons."

was over, Heth's division, which rested immediately behind ours, advanced to charge the enemy's position, but were repulsed with great loss, advancing 3/4ths of a mile across an open field within 50 yards of the enemy's line posted behind a stone fence and raked as they advanced by the enemy's batteries posted upon a commanding hill. As soon as the straggling remnant of these men got back again to our line, the order came for us to advance, and oh! how trying it was! We moved forward for about 50 yards, when fortunately a courier strained up with an order countermanding the charge. We got back then to our breastworks, where we have been ever since. This evening everything has been more quiet, except the skirmishing along the lines, which has been incessant.

The foregoing entry in the diary, made on the battlefield during the afternoon of Friday, July the 3rd, the day of the great battle, omits a move, made about dark on the preceding evening, which no man in Mahone's brigade who took part in it can ever forget. After the heavy fighting on the right, in which a portion of our division as mentioned was engaged, it was, as we understood, proposed to make a night attack, and for that purpose our brigade was taken from its position in a body of woods, or grove, on the slope of the hill where it had been since the forenoon, and marched some two hundred or more yards to our right and there taken to the crest of the hill, preparatory, as we all thought, to beginning a charge. It was, indeed, a serious and trying time, as we stood on the crest in readiness to move, the open fields to our right and front being then traversed by occasional shells whose blazing fuses made their pathway plainly visible, every man feeling that the order to go forward would soon come. Fortunately, however, for our particular command the order that came — and it came after a suspense of only a few minutes — took us, not forward to make an attack, but back to our former position, Gen. Lee having determined not to make the proposed assault. That we retraced our steps with a feeling of relief, it is hardly necessary to state. This incident of the evening of the 2nd of July, when writing in my diary on the afternoon of the 3rd, I overlooked, or deemed not worthy of mention in connection with the other over-shadowing events of those two days that were briefly recorded.

In this entry there is no mention of Pickett's famous charge, for the reason that at the time I only knew that an unsuccessful charge had been made, but was under the belief that it was made by Heth's division, the division which lay immediately behind ours.

As soon as the shelling was over, the brigade of this division which lay in line of battle some fifteen or twenty paces behind our brigade was ordered forward, and, forward it went — stepping over us as we lay in the low breastworks we had erected to protect us from the artillery fire—up the slope of the hill in our immediate front and (as I supposed) down the other slope of this hill towards the enemy. In a few minutes these same men came running back, broken all to pieces, color-bearers leading the men in their precipitous retreat. It was, indeed, disheartening. Just then we were called to attention, and ordered forward. In all the days of life I never felt so scared. It had then been my lot to be present in several other battles, and it was afterwards my fortune to be present in many more, but on no other occasion did I feel so much as if I were going forward to almost certain death. Before the shelling began I had walked forward to the crest of this gently sloping hill in our immediate front, which hill was Seminary Ridge, had looked across an open field, some three quarters of a mile or more in width, that intervened between the ridge of the hill behind which we were posted and Cemetery Ridge where the enemy stood, and accordingly knew just what we were expected to do, and in my mind's eye I saw our brigade and division descending the slope of the hill, then crossing the field, raked by artillery as we moved forward, and finally ascending the slope of Cemetery Ridge to assault the enemy in their breast-works, to be decimated by their infantry as we neared them. All of this at those portentous words "Attention!" "Forward!" came vividly before me—and indeed what I, in fancy, saw our division going forward to do was only just what a few moments before had in point of fact been done by Pickett's division in the splendid charge in which that command of Virginians achieved immortal fame, and I accordingly thought my earthly career was about to end. Seeing Lieut. Anthony Keil[e]y, who commanded our company, step forward with a quiet coolness of manner out of harmony with *my* inward feelings—I know not how I *looked*—I was struck with his apparent freedom from fear just at that time. A few years ago, meeting this gallant gentleman, now a distinguished member of the International Court at Cairo, Egypt, I told him how scared *I felt,* and how cool *he looked,* on that famous day. Said he, "I do not know how *I looked,* but *I was as scared as you were.*"

Among the many-word pictures of this historic artillery duel and the magnificent charge of the Confederates which immediately followed it, no one of them tells these more graphically than the contemporaneous telegraphic messages sent from Gettysburg by Northern correspondents during the four hours commencing at 12 1/2 P.M. and ending at 4 1/2 P. M. covering the period of this artillery firing and subsequent charge of the assaulting column.

[The aforementioned telegrams have not been reproduced here.]

When the great artillery duel was over the open field on the immediate right of our brigade upon which stood Col. Wm. J. Pegram's battalion of artillery, his guns along the crest, his caissons some fifty yards in rear of the guns, presented a sad spectacle of war's destructive work, the shot and shell of the enemy having killed and wounded several men and horses and considerably damaged the pieces of artillery. I remember being greatly impressed with the dilapidation, the havoc, visible from our brigade line in the woods when I cast a glance over this open ground and saw the results of the pitiless and withering storm of iron missiles that had howled from the enemy's guns.[21]

[Here, Bernard included several excerpts from battle reports in the *Official Records*. These have been excluded.]

Let us now resume our narrative as told in diary and note book, beginning with the following from the diary.

THE RETREAT

On Picket in Franklin Co., Penn.,
16 miles S.W. of Gettysburg, Sunday, July 5.

Everything quiet yesterday along our lines, excepting a little skirmishing and a few artillery shots fired yesterday morning. Our losses in the late engagement very heavy, estimated at 15,000. Our reg't lost 2 killed and about 25 w'd in the shelling of Thursday and Friday and the skirmishing done by one or two companies. Prisoners state that the enemy's loss was greater than in any previous engagement. Gen. Reynolds was killed and Gen. Sickles lost a leg. On our side I have heard of only Gen. Garnett as killed and Gen. Armistead

21. GSB: Mr. Jno. E. Crow, in his letter of December 15, 1893, describing the shelling during the great cannonading on the 3rd of July, says: "The air was alive with bursting shells. Fragments of shells and limbs of trees were falling in every direction. Men were being constantly wounded. We (Mahone's brigade) expected to make the charge in the front line, but Davis' brigade, which lay just behind ours, was ordered to the front and we were ordered to support it. I will state that during the terrific shelling, or during some previous shelling on this or the previous day, I saw Col. G. M. Sorrel, of Longstreet's staff, bearing an order and in doing so he presented one of the most magnificent spectacles of a warrior on horseback I ever saw. Young and handsome, to me, on the occasion referred to, he had the appearance of a demigod. His horsemanship was superb, his eyes were flashing and his valor spoke in every action. Let me here say that the heroes of my boyish admiration were Col. Sorrel and Col. Willie Pegram. Sorrel on horseback led us in the charge at the Wilderness and Pegram charged, with his guns at a full run, with us at Bristoe Station and at Cold Harbor, right up in our line."

as mortally wounded. We captured 6,000 prisoners, all of whom refused to be paroled.[22] Yesterday both armies began to move, and at dark our brigade left its position in the front line and came in this direction, marching all last night and the greater part of to-day, taking the road to Hagerstown and passing through the town of Fairfield and over the South Mountains, at the foot of which we are now on picket. On account of the deep mud and the rain, the march of last night and to-day was terrible and the straggling very great. The enemy captured _____[23] of our wagons yesterday (rather last night) not far from here. They contained mostly wounded men. Our army, I fear, is greatly dispirited at the result of the late battles.[24]

From present appearances I think we are making a retreat. It is said we are to meet Beauregard with large reinforcements at Hagerstown. We heard cheering news from Vicksburg yesterday—another fight, Grant killed and his army badly cut to pieces.[25]

Memo: Estimating distance marched Thursday morning to take our position in line of battle at 3 miles and distance marched last night and to-day

22. GSB: In the article, "Battle of Gettysburg," in Appleton's Encyclopaedea, giving the losses of the 3rd of July, the compiler of the article says: "The Confederate loss on this day was about 16,000 in killed, wounded and prisoners; the Union loss was about 3,000."

Giving the losses in the four days that the two armies confronted each other he says: "The Union loss at Gettysburg was 23,190, of whom 2,834 were killed, 13,713 wounded, and 6,643 missing. The Confederate loss has never been officially stated; but by the best estimates it was about 36,000, of whom about 5,000 were killed, 23,000 wounded, and 8,000 unwounded prisoners. The entire number of prisoners, wounded and unwounded, were about 14,000."

Col. Taylor in his "Four Years with Gen. Lee," making an estimate of the relative strength of the two armies at Gettysburg from the most reliable official data, says, 'I put the Army of the Potomac at one hundred and five thousand, and the Army of Northern Virginia at sixty-two thousand of all arms—fifty thousand infantry, eight thousand cavalry, and five thousand artillery—and _____ these figures very nearly correct."

[According to modern estimates, Union casualties for the three-day battle tallied 22,813, and Confederate casualties numbered 22,874. Confederate losses on the last day totaled approximately 10,000 (see Stephen W. Sears, *Gettysburg* [New York: Houghton Mifflin, 2003], 468, 496; and Andre Trudeau, *Gettysburg: A Testing of Courage* [New York: HarperCollins, 2003], 529).]

23. Bernard left this figure blank.

24. Major General John F. Reynolds died when a bullet entered the back of his neck at McPherson's Ridge on the first day of battle. On the second day, Major General Daniel Sickles lost his leg after a round mangled his right knee near the Trostle Farm.

25. The text here refers to more false rumors from the West. Grant won at Vicksburg.

at 18 miles, we have marched in all 203 miles since leaving Fredericksburg, 3 weeks ago to-day. Yesterday morning our reg't numbered in line 202 muskets and 22 officers.

The following from the note book tells of the march—one of great severity—on the night of the retreat from Gettysburg:

Saturday, July 4. Everything pretty quiet excepting the uninterrupted sharpshooting and occasional artillery duels. In the afternoon we have a drenching rain. At dark we begin to move back to the rear, under orders to do so as quietly as possible, leaving our fires along the lines burning brightly. We feel mortified at our failure, but rather pleased at the idea of once more going toward Dixie. We march all night through a drenching rain and over a terrible road, which the rain had made almost a continued sheet of water.[26] At day-break we find ourselves ascending the South Mountain, having taken a different route from that by which we went to Gettysburg. We are moving now southward. We halt for an hour or two half way up the mountain when our cooks overtake us with rations, which we enjoy, for we are very hungry. Plodding along up the mountain and finally getting to the other side, we find ourselves still in Pennsylvania—we had hoped we were in Maryland. Homesick and dejected as we were, even Maryland would seem home to us. Our brigade marches eastward again and takes position on picket at a commanding position a mile beyond Magnolia Springs. Here we fix ourselves to spend a comfortable night, if possible. At sunset we had pitched our tents and made ourselves good straw beds, but as soon as night came on we were ordered to march. We did not like giving up thus the prospect of a good night's rest, but on the other hand liked the idea of marching homeward once more. Marching but slowly behind a wagon and artillery train, we make but little headway and halt before day light to bivouack in the ugly little village of Waterloo.

26. GSB: In his letter from which extracts have already been taken describing the hard march on the night of the 4th of July, Mr. Crow says:

"Heavy rains had swollen all the streams, the mud was ankle deep and the night dark. We forded several streams and were wet to the skin. On the occasion of a halt on the road side, we thought for the purpose of allowing the men to rest and sleep awhile, Billy Douglas and I spread our oil-clothes, and worn out as we were—for it was a terribly hard march—we went immediately to sleep. When light came we threw off our blankets steaming with dampness and the warmth of our bodies and looked around, and to our amazement saw none of our regiment, but tracks near us, cut deep in the mud, we saw that the wheels of the artillery had run within three feet of our heads! We had slept so soundly as to be undisturbed by their passage."

....

The next entries in the diary are as follows:

> Village of Waterloo, Penn., 14 miles
> from Hagerstown, Monday, July 6, 1863.

Brigade left its position last night about dark, marching behind artillery. Jim Nash and I fell out of line and "camped" about a mile from this place and were very glad to find our brigade so near this morning. We heard firing ahead of us yesterday afternoon in the direction of Hagerstown. I hear this morning it was Stuart fighting the enemy. We are doubtless making our way back to Virginia, and probably will cross the Potomac at Williamsport. Some estimate our loss at 20,000 men. We go home with our feathers drooping.

> Camp 2 mile N.E. of, Hagerstown,
> Wednesday, July 8.

Brigade left Waterloo Monday afternoon about 5–1/2 P.M. and after a tiresome march alongside of the wagon train, reached its present camp yesterday morning about 7 o'clock, having passed through the town of Waynesborough in Pennsylvania, to the village of Leitersburg, in this state. Having marched about 8 miles, my wounded leg failing me, I dropped out of line about 4 miles from this place in company with Tom Branch[27] and Billy Scott,[28] of our company. We spent quite a comfortable night in somebody's horse stable, sleeping on corn-stalks, and by an early march overtook the regiment next morning.

From accounts the late fight at Gettysburg was not so unfavorable in its results after all. It appears that the enemy retreated at the same time, or even before we did, and it is said that their papers admit the enormous loss of 30,000. We have fallen back merely to obtain more artillery ammunition and from what I learned this morning will make a stand at this place. Day before yesterday our cavalry fought the enemy at Hagerstown, chasing them through the streets, and, it is said, captured the whole party—cavalry. We drew a ration of whiskey this morning.

Let us again draw from the note book its account of some experiences on the night of Monday, July 6th, and on the following morning:

Monday, July 6.—Get in motion about 3 o'clock this afternoon, moving towards Hagerstown, Md. About 3 miles from Waterloo we pass through the town of Waynesboro a respectable looking place. We feel cheered up as we near

27. Thomas C. Branch is discussed in note 69, chapter 2.

28. William Scott, a clerk in a merchants' firm before the war, enlisted as a private in Company E of the 12th Virginia in April 1861. Wounded at Hatcher's Run in 1865, Scott was recuperating from arm surgery at the Confederate States Hospital in Petersburg when he became a prisoner.

the soil of Dixie, though we are not yet out of Pennsylvania. It was this night that three of us of Company E—names not mentioned—feeling very tired, indeed used up, drop out of ranks and endeavor to find rest on our own hooks on the roadside. Stopping at the first house we came to we went into the back-yard and looked into the dining room to see what chance there might be for supper. A half a dozen or more rough Confederates sitting down at the table, and as many more in the room and at the door waiting for their *turn,* made the prospect rather gloomy. So we abandoned the idea of getting supper and addressed ourselves to the matter of finding a good place to sleep, which after much groping around in the darkness we thought we had discovered under an old shed attached to what seemed to be a stable. Here we spread our beds and laid ourselves down for a nap, but we had scarcely lain down before a Confederate soldier came stalking up to us and asked, "Mister can you tell us *whar* we can find some water?" to which we told him "we could not." But no sooner had he disappeared than another stumbled up and asked if there was "*ary* pump about there?" This fellow in search of the pump was no sooner gone than still another came looking for the "spring," and another in search of water, until finally, as if to clap the climax, a party of them began to catch chickens roosting somewhere in the house adjoining us, which made such a noise that we concluded we would leave the premises and seek quiet elsewhere.

So we rolled up our blankets and started on, hoping to find some quiet place of woods on the roadside in which we might bivouack for the rest of the night, but we were disappointed. After marching on about a mile and a half we found ourselves in a little village. Here we hoped we might find a nice place to sleep in somebody's front porch, but in this also we were disappointed—there were no front porches to be seen. Coming finally to an alley leading off from the main street, we determined to try that, hoping it might lead to some hospitable place. Going down it about 200 yards we were brought to a dead halt by a fence across it. Here were two houses, one on either side of the alley. Should we try these? One we found locked—the other was not. Into the latter we go, knowing nothing of the character of the place, for it was pitch dark. But we had almost gotten desperate, so wearied out were we. Satisfying ourselves by feeling with our hands that we could make a comfortable sleeping place there, we determined to try it at all hazards. So we threw ourselves down on the *corn-stalks,* for the floor was covered with these, and we were soon soundly sleeping, not waking until sunrise in the morning, when the owner of the *stable,* for such was the character of the houses, opened the door and expressed his surprise at finding three Confederates sleeping in such quarters. This gentleman, however, very kindly told us to sleep there as long as we wished, that he only wished us to shut the door when we left. But we got up very soon and started on to overtake the brigade now some distance ahead of us.

Our next adventure this morning was at a *whiskey still,* at which dozens of Confederate soldiers were filling themselves, their canteens, tin cups and everything else which would hold whiskey. The scene at this still was very ludicrous, made so by the eagerness of each man to get some of the precious article and be off. Having filled our canteens, we started with pleasant anticipations of the joy our arrival would occasion among the boys when they learned the contents of our canteens. But unfortunately for our expectations a guard whom we encountered on the road a short distance from the still very cooly took possession of each man's canteen as he would come up and would drain it of his whiskey. After a march of four or five miles we came up with the brigade encamped within a mile of Hagerstown. The village in which we passed the night was Leitersburg, in Maryland.

The three members of the Petersburg Riflemen (Co. E) referred to in the foregoing entry were Thos C. Branch, of Brunswick county (Va.), Wm. H. Scott, of Petersburg, Va., mentioned as "Tom Branch" and "Billy Scott" in the entry made in my diary on the 8th of July, and myself. I do not, however, recall Tom as present at the whiskey still, or as figuring in our experiences in connection with it, but hold in vivid recollection Billy and myself trudging along the highway after leaving the village in which we had spent the night, when, just ahead of us, near a stone bridge we were approaching, we saw several men leaving the road and running to a house a hundred yards up the creek, at which appeared to be some object of more than ordinary attraction. Curiosity, if nothing else, compelled Billy and myself to follow the crowd—the road was full of stragglers—to see what meant this rush to the house in question. We had not reached the place before the fumes of whiskey, and the reports of the men we met coming away with tin cups and canteens filled with liquor, gave us the desired information, the receipt whereof did not stop either Bill or myself in our progress to the centre of attraction—a large whiskey still, around which was surging and jostling a crowd of men in eager haste helping themselves to its contents; one tall fellow, I well remember, standing over the still, straddling it, one foot planted on one side of the rim, the other foot on the opposite side, and with his long arms reaching down with a large tin cup and dipping up the precious liquid and thus kindly filling his comrades' canteens as they were held up to him for the purpose, mine and Billy Scott's among the number.

The guard who relieved us of our whiskey was considerate enough to comply with a request to leave just "a *few drops*" in the bottom of our canteens, and to give such a strict construction to his orders as to call upon only those who, keeping the turnpike, came directly upon him to give up their canteens, and to take no notice of others behind us, who, seeing what was being done ahead of them, left the road before reaching the point at which stood the guard and so passed along unmolested a few feet away in the fields skirting the road.

And just here I should mention that this guard was one of a small detachment of men who were guarding a large body—many hundred—of Federal prisoners taken at Gettysburg, all of whom, a very few excepted, as we passed them, were lying asleep along the road, presenting a sight novel to our eyes.

The next entry in the diary is as follows:

> Camp near Hagerstown, Md.,
> Friday, July 10, 1863.

Everything quiet yesterday and today thus far, except a cavalry fight at Boonesboro and some fighting in that direction this morning. In the fight at Boonesboro it is said we whipped the enemy. Two or three days ago quite a novel affair occurred at Williamsport, in which *teamsters* and stragglers were pressed into service to assist our troops in repelling an attack from the enemy. The enemy were driven off and three pieces of their artillery captured. We continue, of course, to hear rumors from the outside world, the last of which is that New Orleans has been recaptured by our troops. This morning there are some signs of a movement. The enemy are said to be advancing from Waynesboro, where there were two corps of them last night.

The entry in the notebook covering our march on the afternoon of the 10th of July, made after making the foregoing entry in the diary, is as follows:

Friday, July 10.—Having remained quietly in the position we reached Tuesday morning until to-day, we leave this afternoon and move in the direction of Hagerstown. We indulge the hope that our next halt will be in old Virginia. We march through the town of Hagerstown, feeling rather crest-fallen. We had not accomplished so much as we had anticipated when we marched so proudly through the same place less than two weeks before. We take the turnpike to Williamsport, which we leave, however, when about 3 miles from Hagerstown, taking a road to our left, but going but a short distance before bivouacking. We hear the enemy are at or near Funkstown, two miles from us, which information makes us fear more fighting is at hand.

From the diary we take the following, its next two entries:

> Position 2 miles S.W. of Hagerstown
> Saturday, July 11.

In bad spirits this morning—feel quite sick. Division shifted position from other side of Hagerstown yesterday afternoon, marching about 5 miles.

We are camped here, it is said, to take a position of defence selected by Gen. Lee. The enemy are said to be about two miles distant on or near the Hagerstown and Boonesborough [Boonsboro] Pike, though not in large force. Two of the ordnance wagons of our brigade, those of the 6th and 16th regiments, were ordered across the river this morning. Three members of our company wounded in the Maryland campaign of last summer rejoined us yesterday, Lt. John R. Patterson, and Private Ned Spotswood[29] and John Turner.[30]

On Picket 3–1/2 miles s.w.
of Hagerstown, Sunday, July 12.

Left position of night before last yesterday morning and took our present position in line of battle, immediately erecting breastworks. Everything rather quiet yesterday, except a little skirmishing along our lines and also profound quiet today until late this afternoon when the skirmishing along different portions of the line has been pretty brisk. Our company is now in front of the regiment as skirmishers, but not on the front line, there being here a reserve line of skirmishers. The enemy are very near, I heard the drums in their camp a few minutes ago.

The foregoing entry made on the 12th of July, 1863, is the last made to the diary. The last blank page in the book had been reached, and there was no new book for further entries.

Let us here, however, draw from the note book the following, its closing entry:

Saturday, July 11.—This morning, about 8 o'clock, having remained quiet last night where we halted, we got in motion, when through the suspicious circumstance of our moving through the woods and across the fields it became evident that we were not continuing our march toward the Potomac, but were moving to take position in line of battle. Very soon we were at work

---

29. Joseph Edwin Spottswood, a clerk for a lumber dealer in prewar Petersburg, enlisted as a private in Company B of the 12th Virginia in April 1861. He transferred to Company E in April 1862 and was wounded in action at Antietam. He was detailed to enroll conscripts for seven months, at which time he returned to his unit and received a promotion to sergeant and regimental quartermaster. He was paroled at Appomattox.

30. John R. Turner, a clerk in a Petersburg dry goods firm, enlisted as a private in Company C of the 12th Virginia in April 1861. He transferred to Company E in April 1862. Wounded at Second Bull Run, he spent four months recuperating in a military hospital. Like Spottswood, he was then detailed to enroll conscripts for seven months. He returned to his unit in July 1863. Promoted to corporal in 1864, he was wounded at Burgess Mill in the same year. He was paroled at Appomattox.

building breastworks, five minutes of which work caused the fences near us to disappear like frost before the sun. It is unnecessary to speak of the details of this day and the two which succeeded it. It is sufficient to say that our army here held a good position in line of battle and offered the enemy battle for three successive days, which he did not accept. During these three days there was a great deal of rain, causing the Potomac in our rear to rise considerably which made our position very perilous. On Monday night at dark we commenced our retreat. We crossed the Potomac on a pontoon bridge at Falling Waters. By midday Tuesday the rear guard was safely across. How rejoiced we were at the idea of being once more on Confederate soil.

[Lee found himself in a precarious position at Falling Waters and Williamsport. Heavy rains hampered bridge building over the Potomac River at Falling Waters. For several days his army occupied newly dug lines, which, though strong, pinned the Confederates against the left bank of the Potomac. Eventually, Lee managed to get his tattered command across by July 14, 1863.[31]]

In the foregoing accounts of these last days north of the Potomac, no mention is made of much which is still held fast in memory's grip. I well remember that occupying, as we did, a strong position, and feeling sore from the failure at Gettysburg, the rank and file were rather hopeful that the enemy would attack us when we offered them battle, and there was a feeling of disappointment at their not doing so.

Among the incidents that cannot be forgotten is the following:

Whilst we stood on the skirmish line on the afternoon of Monday, July 13th, we suffered very much from hunger. In a field of grass that lay between our line of skirmishers and our line of battle—the latter a couple of hundred yards or more in our rear—there peacefully grazed a flock of sheep, in blissful ignorance of the presence of several thousand armed men, who, standing near them, might at any moment have fallen to shooting each other and in this bloody work would have endangered the lives of these harmless animals. Seeing this state of things to exist and feeling the sharp pangs of hunger, some of our regiment on the skirmish line proposed to kill and eat some of the sheep;

---

31. See Kent Masterson Brown, *Retreat From Gettysburg: Lee, Logistics, and the Pennsylvania Campaign* (Chapel Hill: University of North Carolina Press, 1988); and Eric Wittenberg, J. David Petruzzi, and Michael Nugent, *One Continuous Fight: The Retreat from Gettysburg and the Pursuit of Lee's Army of Northern Virginia, July 4–14, 1863* (El Dorado Hills, Calif.: Savas Beatie, 2008).

to do so, it was urged, could not be wrong under the circumstances and, the proposition being favorably received, at least one sheep,[32] to my knowledge, was forthwith caught, quickly slaughtered, and parceled out to the men on the skirmish line.

But now came a difficulty. We had no salt to season this fresh meat, and, being on the skirmish line, although this line was a rear line of skirmishers, we were not allowed to build fires with which to cook the meat. At night-fall, however, as mentioned in the note book, we retreated from the position we held, but each man who got a piece of the fresh meat, the only food of any kind we had, being even without bread, when he moved off, held fast to it, believing he would soon have an opportunity to cook and eat it. I do not remember what I did with my piece of meat that night, but have a painfully clear recollection of the terrible march we took.

Getting soon into the public highway, we found it ankle-deep with mud and water of about the consistency of batter. Through this, wearied, sleepy, hungry, we trudged mile after mile in the darkness—clouds obscuring the starlight, with I think some drizzling rain. After going along with my command a few miles, I found my lame leg giving way, as it had done on previous occasions since we left Gettysburg. So I concluded to drop out of line and make my way along the best I could by myself. Reaching an open field on the road-side, I left the road with the view of finding some place where I could refresh myself with at least a nap, and, with this purpose, came to a gap in a rail fence, some fifty yards distant from the road, and selected as my bed two fence-rails at this gap that slanted towards the ground. The ground was soaking wet and the upper side of these two rails was the only place at which I could recline without getting wet—an extremely unfavorable place in which to sleep, but the only place I could find—and a short nap was all I needed to enable me to continue on my way.

Placing myself on these rails in a recumbent position, I was soon dozing away, when some fellow riding a horse—who or what he was I know not— whilst going through the gap in the fence rode along in such close proximity to my feet—I am not sure he did not actually ride *over* my feet—that I was awakened by the heavy tread of the horse's hoofs, and concluded that, if I continued my nap at that place, I stood in great danger of having the next mounted man that came along ride or jump his horse over my head or some other part of my body. So I abandoned my effort to sleep in that place, got up and trudged ahead with the great mass of men, organized and disorganized—

---

32. GSB: Col. Field [*sic*] informs me that the *whole flock* shared the fate of the one sheep here referred to.

for the hard march had caused much straggling—that were making their way towards the pontoon bridge, and, as well as I now remember, overtook my command in time to cross the bridge with it.

My experience during this night so used me up that during the greater part of the march from the Potomac to Culpeper C.H., unable to keep my place in line, I was forced to limp along with the bare-footed and other disabled men; at one time falling into the hands of our rear-guard for a few minutes, and at another, whilst trying to get out of the way of the rear-guard, coming very near falling into the hands of the enemy.

I have now, Comrades, concluded my story of the famous Gettysburg campaign as its experiences were recorded in diary or note book, or impressed themselves upon my memory. If the recital of the story has entertained you, the purpose of the address has been accomplished.

The End.

"The Gettysburg Campaign,"
by William E. Cameron

A Letter from Ex-Gov. Cameron. Read by Mr. George S. Bernard before A. P. Hill Camp of Confederate Veterans—Interesting Incidents Vividly Narrated in Cameron's Best Style. [33]

Chicago, March 26th, 1894.

Geo. S. Bernard, Esq. Petersburg, Va.:

Dear Comrade:—You have sent a copy of your address entitled "The Gettysburg Campaign," delivered on the 3rd of November last before R. E. Lee camp, No. 4, of Confederate Veterans, of Richmond, Va., and have requested me to write out my own recollections of the campaign for publication in your forthcoming second volume of "War Talks of Confederate Veterans," in the way of notes, or as an addendum to your address; and I take pleasure in complying with this request, giving you permission, if you think proper so to do to read my letter before the A. P. Hill camp, of Petersburg, Va., on some evening when no other programme is provided.

Your address furnishes so full an account of the march from Fredericksburg to Pennsylvania that I shall mention one or two incidents only of this

---

33. This article appeared in the *Petersburg Daily Index-Appeal* on May 6, 1894.

William E. Cameron
(University of Virginia, Albert
and Shirley Small Special Collections Library)

portion of the movement. Lieut. Col. Everard M. Field[34] (Col. D. A. Weisiger, the colonel of the Twelfth Virginia regiment, being still absent on account of his wound received in the battle of second Manassas) was in command of the regiment, and I was again at my post as its adjutant, after having been de-tached for several months as brigade-inspector of Mahone's brigade. I remem-ber the fatigues and hear of the toilsome progress with painful distinctness, as I was on foot throughout the campaign; my horse (a present from Z. W. Pickrell, Billy Wilson and other Petersburg friends) having been stolen from our camp near Salem church not long before we started on the tramp to the northward.

A VERY HOT DAY

The march of June 17th from Culpeper across to Hazel river was an experience never to be forgotten. The heat of the sun was overpowering and hundreds of men fell by the wayside. A. P. Hill[35] had lately been made lieutenant-general

34. The correct spelling is "Feild." Feild, a Greensville County planter, commanded the Petersburg City Guard during the 1850s. He led the 12th Virginia during most of the engagements in 1863 and into 1864, until he suffered a severe thigh wound at Spot-sylvania. After the war, he held a variety of jobs, including deputy tax collector for the Internal Revenue Service.

35. A. P. Hill was a West Point graduate and army regular who resigned his com-mission in 1861 and entered Confederate service as colonel of the 13th Virginia Infan-

and our division (Anderson's) had been transferred to him from Longstreet, and I recall the pleasant impression made on me that day by seeing our new commander dismount from his horse and use his flask in the effort to revive a poor fellow, a private, who lay fainting in the edge of the wood through which we were passing. At mid-day we halted on a spur of the mountains for rest; but the undergrowth of the heavy forests excluded every breath of air, and we were glad when again ordered to the open road. The regiment that night stacked less than one hundred muskets on reaching the spot selected for bivouac. I recall but one experience more severe—that of the march from Charlestown to Shepherdstown on June 23rd, where we brought into camp only forty-seven out of 400 men. Of course, in both cases, the ranks were full again before morning. The straggling was not voluntary, the men, after six months in winter quarters, were simply unable to keep up with their heavy burdens in the enervating heat and under a broiling sun.

AN UNDRESS PARADE

Lever, in one of the chapters of "Charles O'Malley,"[36] tells of the sensation created at Lisbon by the landing of the first detachment of Highlanders going to Wellington's army. They wore "the kilt" of course, and their bare knees shone in the sun as they stepped proudly through the streets to the screeching of the bagpipes. The Portuguese spectators scattered in all directions, frightened by the strange appearance of these, so they called them, "devils without breeches." No less was the stampede caused among the fair population of Warren county by the appearance of our brigade as it marched across the narrow ridge dividing the South and North Forks of the Shenandoah river. Crossing the former the men had been ordered to remove their nether garments, raise their cartridge boxes above their heads and to take the water in a state (from the waist downward) of nature. The ford was pretty deep, striking the tall men to near the hips, and it was said that but for the assistance of the right file of the company next following, "Frog" Jackson,[37] who was

---

try. Promoted to brigadier general, then major general in 1862, he commanded the re-nowned "Light Division" under General Jackson. Promoted to lieutenant general in 1863, he took command of the Third Corps. Although he led his corps through the major battles of July 1863 through April 1865, his reputation as a corps commander suffered compared to his name as divisional commander. He was killed at Petersburg on April 2, 1865.

36. Cameron's reference is to *Charles O'Malley: The Irish Dragoon,* a novel in two volumes published by the Irish author Charles Lever in 1841.

37. Cameron is probably referring to Henry M. Jackson, a co-manager of a tobacco factory before the war who enlisted as a private in Company A in February 1862. Except

the last man in the rear rank of Company A, short and stumpy, would have been drowned. After the crossing had been effected, so short was the distance across to the next ford it was thought unnecessary for the men to rearrange their costumes. So up the hill, through a deep cut between the high banks, the column swung; the boys refreshed by their contact with the cool mountain stream, stepping out briskly and in high good humor. On the eminence back of the defile stood a handsome brick residence in spacious grounds, and here at the "big gate" had collected numbers of the patriotic women of the neighborhood, impatient to welcome their own southern lads—for this section had been occupied and harried by the enemy ever since the retirement of General Lee from Maryland a year ago. There they stood, the dear creatures, with eager eyes and ready handkerchiefs; but scarcely had the head of the column debouched from the defile, when as though smitten with panic, the bevy of beauties broke into flight, not even, like Lot's wife, venturing one timid glance behind them. It may have been that the martial aspect of Col. Field, who, fully clothed in all the panoply of Confederate gray and mounted on a steed of flea-bitten gray, rode in the advance, disconcerted them: certainly there was nothing in the spindle-shanks of _____, who as orderly-sergeant of Co. __, was the first undressed man in the column, to frighten the most timid. Be that as it may, we filed by without the smiles and cheers which had lain in wait for us; and we doubtless live in the memory of some stately matrons of the vicinage to this day, only as "those soldiers without breeches."

A WET NIGHT

Crossing the North Fork late in the afternoon, we halted the night of June the 19th, some time after nightfall, on a hillside corrugated with the furrows of a corn field, a thoroughly unfit place of a camp or even a bivouac, and amid a heavy downpour of rain. The ground was already soaked and the water rushed down the incline in rivulets. Dr. Jim Claiborne, our brigade surgeon, may have forgotten it, but he and I bunked together that night, and a lively time we had. Lucky we thought ourselves to find a large log lying transversely on the slope, and on the downside of this we spread, first his oil cloth, then his blanket, then ourselves, and then my blanket, and over all my oil cloth. Now the ends of the log turned off the current, the water could not trickle under, because the log was embedded in the soil; so for a time we did pretty well and dropped off to sleep. But after a while a perfect deluge descended from the

---

for periods of illness, Jackson served with his unit until captured in Petersburg in April 1865.

heavens and now our bulwark acted as a dam. The water accumulated behind it with such rapidity as finally to rise above its level, and then swept down upon our devoted heads in a torrent which nothing could resist. The rest of the night was spent hovering over sickly fires of fence rails, with the oil clothes thrown Indian fashion over our heads.

A SNAKE STORY

On the night of June 23rd having in the meantime passed through Clarke and Jefferson counties, we stacked arms on a high, rocky peak, the sterile surface overgrown with stunted and crooked oaks, a short distance from the ford at Shepherdstown on the Potomac. Here Anthony Keiley, who as lieutenant commanded the Petersburg Rifleman (Co. E) and I, made our couch in a grassy oasis between the outcropping boulders of granite, and without waiting for supper went to bed. Utterly worn out, we had not long to woo the drowsy god, though my slumbers were uneasy as every few moments the stragglers coming up would fumble about and ask questions relative to their commands. However, I lost consciousness, for a time at least. Presently there was a stir about us among the men who had built fires and were cooking their rations and then I heard excited voices: "What is it?" "A snake!" "Where is he?" "Kill him!" "There's another!" And then was heard the clatter of sticks and stones as the reptiles were hunted out and killed. I got up. Keiley lay still. After the fray was over and nearly a dozen of the reptiles had been slain, I sought again my bed and bedfellow; but sleep was effectually murdered for me. Every inequality in the bed-clothing I felt to be a writhing, slimy monster and every crackling twig announced to my excited fancy the sinuous approach of a venomous "rattler." I hate a snake, anyhow, and fear one unseen, as I do the devil; so I would start up and nudge Keiley, who would reply drowsily, "Oh, you are worse than the snakes!" At last I mounted into the tripodial fork of a scrub-oak hard by, having a vague idea that serpents did not climb trees, which I have since found to be a very erroneous one, and there snatched some sort of uneasy rest until the fife and drums of reveille sounded. Nor was this the only occasion during the Pennsylvania campaign when my slumber was haunted by serpents. On the night before going into position at St. James' college we bivouacked in a field of luxuriant clover. During the night I was disturbed by what I thought was a stick, or an uncomfortable inequality of the ground, under the oil cloth and blanket which formed our bed; but on the morning, on taking up the clothing of this luxurious couch, we found a huge black snake curled up beneath. He was dead when discovered; but whether we had killed him or not is an open question.

ACROSS THE RUBICON

June the 24th we forded the Potomac, the current deep and strong. This time I can testify that "Frog" Jackson asked for and obtained the loan of a stirrup-leather in crossing. The division set foot upon the opposite shore in fine plight, the morning report showing nearly 11,000 muskets for duty, and the men full of ardor and hope. We are told here that Ewell is pressing forward almost unopposed towards Harrisburg, that Longstreet is well up on the right, that the government at Washington is demoralized, that Hooker is at open issue with the Secretary of War, that Stuart has played havoc with the Federal trains and is about to take Washington in flank; in all of which rumors there was a grain of truth sufficient to form the foundation of sanguine hopes. For several days our route lay through a section of Maryland where sympathizers abounded. The men, as a rule, were reserved, but the women enthusiastic in their demonstrations of welcome and encouragement. At Benevola, the village characterized in your contemporaneous diary as a "little Union hole," I stopped at a gate to ask for a drink of water. The house was a humble affair of one story with a passage-way running entirely through from front to back. A girl of about ten years brought the drink and said, after I had drunk and thanked her, "Look at grandma!" And there was the old lady, away back in the hallway, waving an old-fashioned sunbonnet and performing a very dance of jubilee in the privacy of her own dwelling, knowing full well that, did she indulge in public rejoicing, the vengeance of neighbors otherwise affected would be visited upon her after we had passed by.

At Hagerstown, on June 25th, we found the secession sentiment largely prevalent, but it had become painfully apparent already that the idea of recruiting our ranks in Maryland was not to be realized. We had undoubtedly the latent and passive sympathy of a majority of the people, but they had passed the mood for resistance before having the opportunity to organize, and their quasi friendliness was in reality a source of great embarrassment to General Lee during this campaign. He could neither draw upon the resources of the country as that of an enemy, nor obtain any substantial support from the inhabitants as allies. As it was, he treated the people and their possessions with a consideration not shown to our own people in Virginia; and we left behind us for the use and benefit of the Federal forces stores, supplies, cattle and horses which would have supplied our army for a year. On this evening I joined Keiley and Hartwell Harrison in a reconnaissance to Funkstown, a friendly hamlet about three-quarters of a mile from our camping ground. We were cordially received and bountifully fed by a gentleman also rejoicing in the name of "Funk"—his daughters cultivated and musical, and sweet as roses despite the cruel fate which ruled the family nomenclature.

SPOILING THE EGYPTIANS

Later, having a permit to that effect, I went in to Hagerstown, to procure some much needed articles of wearing apparel. Chance directed me to a shop wherein were kept a miscellaneous stock—groceries, hardware, clothing, notions, and what not. So there was little difficulty in filling my requisition, particularly as the proprietor, a gentleman of Semitic descent, was assiduous in serving a customer who higgled not at all over prices. When the list had been made up, some shirts, a black slouch hat, a pair of boots, etc., I asked for a receipted bill. This was handed me (for $45) with profuse thanks for the patronage. I pulled this sum out of a fat roll of treasury notes not bearing the image and superscription of Uncle Sam, and handed them over to the Israelite, in whom, up to this moment, there had seemed, indeed, to be no guile. His expression changed, first to one of disappointment, then to one of obstinate despair. "I cannot take this money," said he. "It is the only sort I have," said I. Meantime I had handed the bundle of goods to my courier and he was safely on the road to camp with it. "I will not take the Confederate scrip," repeated the storekeeper, and he placed it on the counter between us. "Very well," said I; "that is for you to decide." I took up the despised blue-backs and started to the door. The struggle, on that man's mind, patent on his face, between his judgment and his avarice was severe but brief. I had nearly reached the street when the ruling instinct conquered. "Vell, I takes it," he said. He got it and so the interview ended. The boots were the best I ever had except a pair made for me at Captain Robinett's "brigade shoe shop" while we were holding the lines confronting the enemy at Bermuda Hundred in 1865. I think these boots worthy a place in history besides that pair which bore so conspicuous a part in your account of the first Maryland campaign and which Sydney Jones declared "belonged to the regiment."[38]

IN PENNSYLVANIA

The itinerary of our brigade being furnished in your diary, I need not mention the successive stages by which we now approached the field which was the scene of the most stubbornly contested and perhaps the most decisive

---

38. During the Maryland Campaign, a pair of extremely uncomfortable boots made its way around many members of the regiment (see Bernard, *War Talks of Confederate Veterans*, 20–24).

battle of the war. We passed by easy marches and without encountering any hostile force, into Pennsylvania. Midday of July 1st found us after a hard march begun at daylight, within easy striking distance of Gettysburg, and within plain hearing of the guns which announced that Hill's advance had struck the enemy. The first encounter was with a force of Federal cavalry under General Buford.[39] My recollection is that these sounds of conflict did not hurry our later movements very much. Hill had the divisions of Heth and Pender at the front, and doubtless felt this force adequate to deal with anything he was likely to encounter. The detour made by Stuart to the neighborhood of Washington City had left General Lee in ignorance of the rapid advance and concentration of Hooker's army, now commanded by General Meade.[40]

As we moved leisurely forward upon the Cashtown road, the firing ahead of us grew momentarily heavier until by 3 o'clock it was evident that large bodies of troops were engaged and that a severe conflict was raging. It was perhaps nearly two hours later that Anderson's division deployed into a line, formed of brigades in close columns of regimental front, upon a lofty eminence to the right of the main road. This point was perhaps two miles from the scene where Heth and Pender were now in deadly grapple with the Union corps of Reynolds and Sedgwick. It is manifest now that there was full time to have thrown our division into action. The troops were fresh, had not fired a gun since Chancellorsville, and numbered over ten thousand muskets. Such a force coming in at the close of the day on the heels of Hill's advantage would beyond a doubt have swept the already defeated remnants of Meade's advance from the field; and there would have been no battle at Gettysburg. But my purpose is not to indulge in military criticism and speculation, but merely to record and preserve some of the tragic and humorous incidents. That the Twelfth Virginia regiment and the brigade to which it belonged took small part in this series of battles is a fact for which neither they nor their immedi-

39. General John Buford led a cavalry division at Gettysburg. His efforts to delay the advance of Confederate infantry on the first day of Gettysburg allowed Union forces to establish defensive positions along Cemetery Hill southeast of the town.

40. Historians continue to argue about Stuart's operations during the Gettysburg Campaign. The conventional view, consistent with this passage in Cameron's article, is that Stuart conducted needless operations in the rear of the Federal army at the expense of intelligence gathering and vital communications to Lee. One recent study, however, argues that Stuart received more than his fair share of the blame for Confederate difficulties during the campaign (see Eric Wittenberg and David Petruzzi, *Plenty of Blame to Go Around: Jeb Stuart's Controversial Ride to Gettysburg* [El Dorado Hills, Calif.: Savas Beatie, 2006]).

ate commanders are responsible. Those of us yet living may perhaps congratulate ourselves that we were not ordered in at one or the other critical moments of the three days' context. At any rate we were there and ready to go. General Lee was present on the hill I have referred to. We spent the night there.

THE BATTLE

During the night of the 1st of the July, under advice of General Hancock, the Federal army was moved up to Gettysburg and occupied the line of Seminary and Cemetery Heights [Ridge], from which Hill had after winning them, retired. Meantime Ewell had come down from Carlisle Barracks and formed on the left of Hill, who occupied the town of Gettysburg. Longstreet was arriving and filling up the line to the right, confronting and reaching around the hill known as "Round Top," and so threatening the Baltimore road. Such was the condition of affairs of the morning of the 2nd of July, when we were ordered forward to take position, which after some shifting was finally established, at almost the exact of center of the Confederate army. While going into position through the woods the troops on our immediate right (Posey's brigade, I think), encountered a body of Federals and for a few moments the musketry was rapid and balls whistled about us in lively fashion; but we had no casualties, and very soon the enemy gave way and we reached our destination without further interruption. The line which we eventually formed was at the base of a hill on the crest of which a large number of batteries were massed, in our immediate front being the battalion of Maj. Willie Pegram, the friend of my early boyhood. During the hottest of the fire—and it was at times the severest artillery fire since Leipsic [Leipzig]—his figure was visible, mounted on a spirited black horse, moving hither and thither among the smoke and bursting shells, his face alight with the splendid agony of battle, bearing himself as one born to rule the storm. (The first time I ever saw our comrade and commander Gordon McCabe,[41] was on Sept. 30th, 1864, at the Davis house on the Weldon road. Pegram had his guns in the yard; my bri-

41. William Gordon McCabe was the son of a minister and attended the University of Virginia in 1860. He began the war as a member of Richmond Howitzers but served in a variety of posts thereafter, including other artillery units and in the Adjutant General's Department. After the war, he lived in Petersburg, where he established a school ("McCabe's University"). He later moved his school to Richmond. He was also active in the United Confederate Veterans, serving as Commander of the A. P. Hill Camp. He frequently delivered speeches on the war, including a lengthy address outlining the Petersburg Campaign which later appeared in the *Southern Historical Society Papers*. He served as president of the Virginia Historical Society and edited the papers of the Southern Historical Society for a time (see *Confederate Veteran* 28 [1920]: 325).

gade, Davis Mississippians, was formed in front ready to charge the enemy, and I was standing with my hand on the neck of Pegram's horse when McCabe, then I think, his adjutant, rode up. A moment later the guns opened, and we charged through the cornfield and gobbled up some hundred of Warren's men. I never met Pegram afterward.)

The right of our brigade line rested on an open field, but extended to the left through heavy, open timber, giant oaks and hickories, which neither obstructed the view nor impeded the movements of troops. Portions of the troops which had been engaged under Heth, and Pender the previous day were in reserve on the same line. Longstreet and Ewell attacked right and left, shortly after we took position, and for hours the thunder of cannon and crash of musketry rent the air. No movement was made in our immediate front. During the day I was ordered to detail a company for skirmish duty and detailed Captain Scott's[42] company (F). This company, with details from other regiments of the brigade, was posted in a wheat field at the bottom of the slope towards the enemy. Scott good humoredly complained when I announced this tour of duty, and said that he had become to believe that the old complaint of Jno. Patterson and Macon Martin[43] was well founded, that I kept no roster, but just selected officers by caprice. Long after the battle was over he told me that I had done him a great favor; as the line of sharpshooters was not in contact with the enemy, was out of range of the musketry in their main line, and the artillery fire direction at our batteries on the crest went hundreds of feet over their heads.

From the low rock-wall which bounded the woods at the crest of the hill, a fine view of the enemy's line and of the intervening valley could be had; but during the second day's operations the fighting was mostly on the extreme wings of the army and there the forest broke the line of vision. During this day the shelling in our front was heavy, indeed the heaviest that we had up to

42. Edward Pegram Scott Jr., son of a prominent Virginia planter, enlisted as 2nd lieutenant of Company F of the 12th Virginia in June 1861. Promoted to captain in September 1863, he was wounded and captured at the Battle of Burgess Mill in October 1864. After recuperating at several Union hospitals, he was released on parole to the house of his great-uncle, General Winfield Scott. He survived the war and moved to Texas.

43. Prewar grocer and commission merchant Nathan Macon Martin enlisted as a private in Company E of the 12th Virginia in May 1861. Elected 1st lieutenant in May 1862, Martin was wounded at Chancellorsville and spent eight months in the hospital. He had not been back with his unit for long when he contracted typhoid fever, which kept him sick for six months. When he returned to active duty, he was made commander of Company E.

that time experienced, and the ordeal of being subjected for hours to this fire from an unseen foe, without any prospect of suppressing or returning it, was trying; but the casualties were not numerous. The shot and shell had so great elevation that most of those which did not strike in front of our batteries went hurling into the country far in our rear, and our line only suffered from the few explosive missiles that burst in front of, or immediately over Pegram's guns. We were in a dip of the ground which rose again to another ridge in the rear and on the rear acclivity Meade Bernard was stationed that morning with his ordnance wagon. He was just in the right place to catch the fire and said afterwards that he thought we had forgotten him "while every cannon in the Yankee army was shooting at his wagon." Fortunately he was moved to a somewhat less dangerous place before receiving any damage.

Darkness fell at last, and with it a refreshing relief from the horrid din which had ruled the day. I saw about dusk one of General Anderson's staff officers, who told me that Longstreet had gained some advantages of position, but had not succeeded in occupying Round Top, the key to Meade's line; that Ewell had made a decided impression on the enemy's right; that an advance by Hill's right on the left centre of the Federals had failed of effect; and that our losses had been heavy, but the attack would be renewed in the morning.

A NOCTURNAL SALLY

About 3 o'clock in the evening [morning], perhaps a little later, we were ordered out of the woods and conducted to the front by a route inclining to our right, through the wheat field occupied by our skirmishers, to a position between our main line and that of the enemy, confronting, but somewhat obliquely, Cemetery Hill. The movement was made in perfect silence, without a word in explanation of its object, and I expect the heart of every man in the column was in his mouth—I know mine was—as we stole silently and swiftly through the starlit, but dark night, to what was conjectured to be some perilous enterprise. Having penetrated the field towards the Federal stronghold to the distance of some six hundred yards, maybe more, possibly not so far—I am giving my impressions—we halted in line behind a tall worm-fence. Then, through the utter stillness, I could hear the muffled tread of other marchers, and through the mist in the valley see indistinctly other bodies of men to the right and left. The suspense was unbearable, especially as, after awhile, some talk of instructing the men to fasten white bandages of some sort to the left arms began to be whispered about—the suggestion coming, as such things do, from nowhere and everywhere. This smacked of a night assault, and recalled what I had read about forlorn hopes. I determined to find out something, and crept along the fence until I saw a group of horsemen, among whom were Generals Longstreet and Anderson. Their talk soon enlightened me that an attack in the dark was contemplated, though I could not hear all that was said. The discussion lasted some minutes, during which there seemed to be some difference of opinion between the two officers. At last, General Longstreet said in distinct tones — the reasons for caution having presumably ceased with the decision — "It would be best not to make the attempt. Let the troops return." In less than five minutes we are on our way back and soon regained our former station. Just on arriving there, before the ranks had been broken, one solitary shell from the enemy whistled through the blackness and burst, it seemed to me, immediately among the men. Then all was still again. No one was hurt, and the remaining hours to daylight were unbroken by any sound save on occasional shot on the distant picket posts. I have never heard, nor do any of the reports contain, any illusion to this abandoned project.

THE DECISIVE DAY

It was understood that at an early hour of the morning of July 3rd, General Longstreet was to throw all his force except Pickett's division, upon the enemy's left and rear, and to follow this operation immediately by hurling Pickett with supporting brigades of Hill's corps against the Union center. The morrow, however, dawned in quiet. There were, however, a few exchanges of shots between the artillery about sunrise, and subsequently in the forenoon. With this exception, the hours until noon passed with a lack of disturbance which was ominous of mischief brewing somewhere. The men had scraped out a little trench, throwing the earth into the form of a light breastwork, scarcely constituting any protection against the smallest fragments of a shell. In this ditch, or behind it, they were lying quiet, their faces and very tones betraying expectancy of something eclipsing their past experiences of war. They expected to be called on for some work involving mighty issues and they looked resolute to do it when the time arrived. I went up to the stone wall among the artillerymen. The tremendous panorama of war spread out on either hand and to the front was innocent of activity as though a truce prevailed. But the guns were shotted, the ammunition was up and at hand, and the gunners were grimly waiting orders, as they said, "to commence."

The hour came soon enough. It was about one o'clock according to the reports that more than one hundred Confederate guns opened upon that portion of the Federal line which had been selected for assault. On the instant the reply came from an even greater number of Union pieces. The earth literally trembled with the concussion. The reverberations of the explosions merged into one continuous roar. The air above our position was filled with deadly missiles of all sorts, sizes and shapes, some howling, some shrieking, some whistling, some moaning, and some immense projectiles coming with rhythmic rush and rustle of a railroad train. Round shot and shell struck the ground in front, or passed over, with every instant of time, and fragments of explosive ammunition rained through the limbs of the trees almost as regularly as the pattering of hailstones.

Under this terrific bombardment our men were steady and composed, though after it had continued for half an hour there were few of them who would not have welcomed an order to charge upon, and have the chance of silencing, those murderous guns. A line of Heth's men, among them Davis' brigade, lay in our rear, and more exposed than was our own line. Among these men many of the shot which passed over the batteries fell with fearful effect, and the calls for the ambulance corps were frequent. Many soldiers were hurt by the falling of limbs from the trees. One shell fell among a group of these men, exploded under their feet and blew several of them into the air in such a mass of blood that some one cried out that a flag had been carried away. How long did this tempest of hell keep up? Two hours, say the official accounts. They seemed an eternity. No soldier who was on our line the third day at Gettysburg will ever doubt that during the slaughter of the Ammorites by Joshua's men the sun stood still.

Of incidents during these perilous and trying hours there was more than enough to fill a volume. One little fellow in the 12th, who had been court-martialed for misbehavior on a previous occasion, sentenced to death and then pardoned, went into this action determined to stick it out. So he did; but in spite of a physical terror to which ninety-nine out of a hundred would have succumbed. A shell would strike, or explode on his right; he would jump up as if possessed with a demon of unrest and rush to the left. Another would come in the last mentioned direction, and he would make frantic leaps in some other. And so throughout the crucial period he passed from trench to tree, from pillar to post. And was actually consoled, no doubt with the idea that he was dodging death.

Tom Pollard,[44] first lieutenant of the Petersburg Grays (Co. B), was lying somewhat up the hill in front of the trench; Ned Branch,[45] captain of the Richmond Grays (Co. G), to his right and rear. A solid shot, nearly spent,

44. Thomas Pollard is discussed in note 37, chapter 2.

45. Edwin W. Branch, scion of a Petersburg tobacco manufacturing family, enlisted as first sergeant of Company A of the 12th Virginia in April 1861. Elected 1st lieutenant in September 1861, he was promoted to captain in August 1862. He was killed in action at the battle of Brandy Station in August 1863.

came rolling down the hill, struck the root of the tree near Pollard, started in a direct line for Branch and was deflected by a projecting boulder rock; then, perceptibly losing speed, it lazily crawled over the breastwork I have before alluded to. Seemed barely to touch the back of a conscript who was down on his stomach in the ditch, left him dead with no abrasion of the skin, and stopped less than five feet from the corpse it had made. As I was passing down the line on some mission while the cannonade was at its height, Pat Drinkard,[46] of the Petersburg Grays, hailed me from the shelter of an immense oak behind which he had ensconced himself. Joining him for a while, I cautioned him against placing his head close to the trunk, saying, that, should a solid shot strike the three, the concussion would be fatal to any one in contact with it. He said he had already seen one Carolinian killed that way. He also told me that, when some of Heth's men returned from a brief adventure to the front, one of them, a Georgian, ran in to share his tree. As the fire became faster and more furious, his visitor was not content to lie at Drinkard's side, but, fearing that his flank was thus exposed, drew closer and closer until he fairly mounted the back of his involuntary host. There he remained until a lull in the tempest gave the opportunity for escape, when Pat discovered that his self-invited guest in the midst of his terror, had retained presence of mind enough to slip his hand into his comrade's knapsack and steal a pone of bread which constituted his reserve rations.

I lay most of the time near the right of the line with Anthony Keiley. He will doubtless recall the conversation we had amid the hurly-burly, discussing the problems of a future life, and impressing on each other matter to be attended to in case accident should befall either. I remember we talked of presentiments, neither of us attaching any importance to them; he saying that we only heard of ten which were fulfilled, and never of the ten thousand which passed without accomplishment. We saw a poor devil of a file closer who, unable to get better protection, was hugging with desperate earnestness a sapling which would not have resisted the passage of a minie-ball. Keiley pointed to him, saying, "He would find comfort in Locksley's 'willow-wand, no thicker than a man's thumb.'"[47] To our immediate right, in seemingly the most exposed location in the vicinity, the horses of the general and the regimental field and staff were tied. It seemed a miracle to us then, it seems so to me

46. Henry H. ("Pat") Drinkard enlisted as a corporal in Company B of the 12th Virginia in April 1861. Promoted to sergeant in September 1861, he was reduced to private the next June. He regained his reputation by August, when he was promoted to sergeant. He was paroled with his unit at Appomattox.

47. Cameron's "willow-wand" reference here is to Robin Hood, who, legend has it, hit a thin willow branch with an arrow during an archery contest.

now, but I do not think one of these animals was killed or seriously hurt. But enough of this; I must pass on to a conclusion.

ALMOST IN

Meantime, about 3 o'clock, there was a temporary lull in the fire of the enemy. Shortly after that we heard from the right the cheer of thousands of men. Pickett was in motion. Then again the cannon volleyed and thundered, though, most of the guns being trained on the charging column (which was not a column, unfortunately, but only a line of brigades in imperfect echelon), we were not subjected to quite the storm of shot as before. Still there was sufficient lead and iron hurtling about to make the situation far from comfortable. Presently the musketry began, first in belching volleys, and then with a continual roar and roll of angry and vicious snaps. But no need to tell that story of desperate valor over again. The assault failed. Wilcox went in and was repulsed.

Then was the time when General Mahone, coming forward from his post immediately on the right our line, sent orders down the line to form in battle order. There was a moment's hesitation before the troops responded. Doug Chappell,[48] lieutenant of Company K, was the first man in the line to leap up and throw off his rolled blanket and oilcloth. In a second every man in our regiment was over the trench and standing to his post, all but three out of over two hundred. Of those who hung back, I have the names, but to what good end expose them now?

The other regiments came up on our left and dressed on the colors. I heard a voice behind me saying to the men, as if in answer to some question: "Make up your minds to go until a bullet stops you, and we will take the works!" I turned to see who the speaker of such brave words might be, plain in phrase but worthy in sentiment in any hero. It was a private in Company D, whose name, alas! I have forgotten.

Almost at once now was heard the command to go forward. The line moved up the hill in perfect order. The wall at the crest was perhaps one hundred yards distant. Once beyond that we should be in full sight of the enemy and receive the direct fire of his batteries. A few steps further and the next step would have been irrevocable, when, lo! to the right, across an open field, a rider spurs his grey horse into desperate speed and waves his hat excitedly.

48. George Douglas Chappell, a Petersburg bar keeper, enlisted as a corporal in Company K of the 12th Virginia in May 1861. He was steadily promoted, reaching the rank of 1st lieutenant by January 1863. In September of that year he took command of Company K for eight months. Absent because of illness for a time, he returned to his unit and surrendered at Appomattox.

He reached General Mahone just in time to save our useless sacrifice; for all along the front of battle our troops have retired and it would have been only a dash of part of Anderson's division against the whole Federal army.

The messenger is Josh Miller,[49] of Company G, of our regiment, one of Anderson's couriers, mad with eagerness to save his old comrades from vain slaughter, and his horse is covered with foam when he gives Mahone Anderson's orders to stay the advance. As the troops retraced their steps, General Lee was riding among the shattered remnants of the assaulting column, praising their valor, taking all blame or failure upon himself, and showing himself greater in the hour of disaster than any man of our time has been in the moment of supreme triumph. The lines were reformed with sadly reduced ranks, ready to repel a counter attack should the enemy venture one. But Meade was satisfied with negative victory. He had won by a hair's breadth and would not put his winning to another such venture as moving upon Lee's army in position. The shadows to twilight fell upon the longest and saddest day my life has even known, and the battle of Gettysburg was over.

BACK TO VIRGINIA

I do not like to dwell upon the days which followed, for they brought among other crushing troubles tidings of the fall of Vicksburg. The night we left Gettysburg was the darkest in fact as well as [in] feeling I ever experienced. One literally could not see his hand before him. For some distance our way led by an indistinct neighborhood road through a heavily timbered country, and it was with the greatest difficulty that we kept the column closed. Often I was only guided by Col. Feild's white horse, and I have an impression that more than once I took hold of his tail. This experience lasted for some hours, and during their passage occurred a strong exemplification of the evanescence of impressions upon the mind.

During the severest shelling of the third day of the battle, my attention was called to the abject terror of a man in the ranks of our regiment. He was pallid with fright, cowering in the trench and giving utterance to audible and frantic prayers for protection, begging pardon for his past sins, and making promises of a better life, if spared. This conduct attracted all the more notice because at home and in camp he was known as a notorious bully and bruiser, reckless in personal encounters, and greatly dreaded on account of

49. Charles E. ("Josh") Miller, was a Petersburg barkeeper who enlisted as a private in Company G of the 12th Virginia in April 1861. From January 1863 to November 1864 he was detailed as a mounted courier. In November 1864 he transferred to Company C, 3rd Virginia Cavalry.

his strength and brutality. But while we were groping through the impenetrable blackness of the first night's retreat (out of reach now of the enemy's bullets) I heard the voice of this man pour forth a stream of excited profanity blasphemous enough to make the blood run cold. He had collided with a tree and hurt himself, and his good impression took wing the first moment of safety.

Either the first or second morning of the retreat we halted about sunrise in a rocky gorge at the northern base of the mountains, while the cavalry went forward to drive out a small force of the enemy which was holding the gap. The road in which we stopped was a solid mass of stone, and down this ran a considerable stream of pure water. Fitz Lee,[50] coming up, had discovered a distillery full of whiskey hard by the roadside, and fearing that the men would get hold of it, had the barrels stove and their contents emptied upon the ground. The consequence was that the very result he sought to guard against was brought about; for the whiskey mingling with the icy brook made grog just of a palatable strength, and there was more than enough to fill the canteen of every soldier convenient to the spot. Our wagons were parked in a neighboring field, and I remember that one of the regimental teamsters, Back Andrews[51] (not Bill, as one of your correspondents has called him), came along with a horse-bucket of the perilous stuff, and distributed it with lavish hand to his friends in the column.

The retrograde march was in sad contrast to that proud procession which scarcely a week previous had swept through the country strong in numbers, strong in courage, resolute to succeed and confident of success. The Army of Northern Virginia was not schooled to defeat, and accepted it with sullen grace. When at St. James college General Lee halted his columns, turned upon his pursuers and defiantly threw down the gage of battle by General Meade, the wish and hunger of our men was to have the opportunity to retain their prestige. It was not to be offered them. Leisurely we retired, showing our teeth at every cross-road, taking with us safely all our baggage, artillery, and some spoil. Ere many days we crossed the Potomac at Falling Waters, and behind the frowning gun which had been mounted to defend the pontoon

50. Major General Fitzhugh Lee, nephew of Robert E. Lee, was a West Point graduate and army regular who resigned in 1861 to join the Confederacy. Lee rose from lieutenant to major general, spending almost the entire war serving as a cavalry commander.

51. Zachariah A. ("Back") Andrews of Chesterfield County enlisted as a private in Company B of the 12th Virginia in April 1861. Detailed as a teamster for the brigade ordnance train in April 1862, Andrews continued in service until captured near Jetersville in April 1865.

bridge, I ate with Hartwell Harrison, and I think also LeRoy Edwards,[52] a dinner of fried chicken, and felt equal afterwards to whipping all the Yankees that might dare to meet us on the sacred soil.

One other episode of the invasion and I have done. Mad and footsore during the retreat through Pennsylvania, I determined to have something to show for all I had suffered in that strange land. Calling into service my acting courier, Walter Pannill,[53] I sallied forth one night to the house of a farmer near the road upon which we were marching, and in violation of all orders impressed a fine horse, jersey wagon, and set of harness. I believed in demonstrating to the Bucktails the laws of war as laid down by their own generals in the southern territory. But the way of the transgressor is hard. When we left Hagerstown on our homeward journey, Keiley suggested to me to relieve the line officers of their portable baggage by loading it up in my wagon and having my boy, Henry Smith, haul it to our stopping place over the river. No sooner said than done. A number of other captains and lieutenants turned over their blankets, etc., to Henry, and marched that day with light shoulders, if not light hearts. But while we were ordered to cross at Falling Waters, all wagons were required to use the ford at Williamsport. The river was high, the ford crowded. Henry drove too far from the middle of the watery road, and the prizes of my bow and spear, together with all the impediments of my friends, rolled down towards Washington on the tawny current of the Potomac. Mr. Smith's report of his campaign was brief, but comprehensive. He said: "I got turned over the water, Marse Willie, and the teamsters cussed at me for a d_____d awkward nigger; and the hoss and wagon was drownd-ded, and I come might near never getting back myself."

Yours Fraternally,
William E. Cameron

52. Leroy Summerfield Edwards enlisted as a private in Company E of the 12th Virginia in April 1861. Wounded at Crampton's Gap, he returned to his unit by January 1863. Promoted to corporal, then sergeant in 1863, Edwards was captured at Spotsylvania and imprisoned in Elmira for seven months. He was paroled and exchanged in 1865.

53. Walter Pannill deserves an entire article about him. Son of a wealthy Petersburg commission merchant, Pannill enlisted as a private in Company B of the 12th Virginia in April 1861. He later deserted his regiment, voluntarily rejoined it, was court-martialed, and served a partial sentence of hard labor. When he was released, he returned to his unit, only to be captured at Falling Waters (near the end of Cameron's story time). Exchanged in April 1864, he was captured again at Burgess Mill in October 1864. By 1865, he was part of the Confederate Secret Service operating in Washington, where he was arrested and sentenced to death. President Lincoln commuted his sentence. Henderson suggests he might have been a double agent (see *12th Virginia Infantry,* 146).

George S. Bernard War Narrative: July 1863–February 1864[54]

General Lee's army had come down into Culpeper county after its return from Gettysburg, and General William Mahone's brigade of infantry, of which the writer was a member, was encamped just outside of the town of Culpeper Court House enjoying rest from the fatigue of the recent campaign into Pennsylvania.

On the evening of the 31st day of [July], 1863, a few officers and men of the 12th Virginia regiment, as was their wont, were singing songs and were happily engaged in this pleasant mode of employing their time. Several having sung, some one proposed that the song known as "A soldier's life is always gay" be sung. To this an objection was raised. "Do not sing that song," said one or more of the party, "If you do, tomorrow we will have a fight. This has been our experience." These and other words of warning to this effect were uttered, but were not heeded. The song was sung by the happy young men who constituted the party, and the next day witnessed the sequence—a battle in which the 12th regiment took part.

This battle, the battle of Brandy Station[55] fought Saturday afternoon, August 1, 1863, the second fought on the same field, is one that I have often recalled with special interest. Mahone's brigade as has been stated, on this day was quartered on the outskirts of the town of Culpeper Court House, west of the corporate limits, quietly recruiting from the campaign to Gettysburg. That the Federal forces were any where in [the] vicinity was not known to the subordinate officers and men in the line.

About three or four o'clock in the afternoon the report of guns in the direction of Brandy Station—north of the town—were heard, and soon thereafter information reached us that our cavalry were being driven in and that we must prepare at once for action.

In a few minutes our men were in line and marching in the direction of the firing, and within a short distance, hardly a half a mile, were within reach of the enemy's rifles, and were thrown into line of battle and were thus advanc-

---

54. Fragments of Bernard's "War Narrative," covering events from July 31, 1863, to February 1864, are located in the George S. Bernard Papers at the Southern Historical Collection, University of North Carolina at Chapel Hill. They consist of about 80 sheets of typescript and manuscript by George S. Bernard and various correspondents. The papers were found in an abandoned house in North Carolina by Roy Jefferson in 1970 and donated by Mr. Jefferson to the Southern Historical Collection.

55. The "battle of Brandy Station" mentioned here by Bernard was a skirmish between Federal cavalry under John Buford and Confederate infantry, and not the large cavalry engagement of the same name fought on June 9, 1863.

ing. We were in a body of woods,[56] but soon reached the broad open territory which skirts the railroad between Culpeper Court House and Brandy Station, and stretched across the fields, in open ranks as skirmishers, is the enemy's line of battle, those in our immediate front being dismounted, whilst those on our left were mounted, a beautiful sight. We open fire at once, and they return it, we advancing, they retreating firing as they retire. On our right is a piece of artillery which fires upon us, but soon, as our advancing line nears it, we see the artillerists limber up and with their gun gallop away to a position near their retiring line. Our men are all in the finest spirits as they push forward, deployed as skirmishers. No one seems to apprehend danger from the enemy's missiles, although we see them strike the ground near us, making the dust rise as they bury themselves in the earth.

I have said that a long line of Federal cavalry, a part mounted and a part dismounted, presented a beautiful sight as they confronted us. No less was our own brigade, as we saw it, (our own regiment excepted) in line of battle standing a few hundred yards behind us and somewhat to our left, fringing the body of woods through which we first passed. Standing there, with colors flying, looking solid and firing, they seemed to say to us: "Drive them, boys, we are at your backs, and will support you if necessary."

Near the part of the line where I happened to be was General J. E. B. Stuart,[57] so near that at one time I was within a few feet of him, being the next man, or about the next man, to him on his left. He was sitting on his horse, humming or whistling, as was his custom, some air, and encouraging the men to continue to drive the enemy as we were then doing. About sunset we came to a branch. The enemy had of course already crossed this stream as they fell back towards Brandy Station. "Let's go across, boys" said Stuart, and across we went, but we found ourselves in a large field of corn, and, night soon coming on, we went but little further before we were ordered to fall back, which was done in good order. The loss in our company was very slight, Capt. Ed. Branch of the Richmond Greys (Co. G) being killed, and a few being wounded, among them Jas. E. Nash and Jas. R. Cowles[58] of the Petersburg Riflemen (Co. E).

56. Bernard's original text here reads, "We were not in a body of wood," but, based on the context of these words, the sentence should probably begin, "We were in a body of woods . . ."

57. Major General James Ewell Brown Stuart was one of the most famous Confederate generals. He led cavalry units in the Army of Northern Virginia from the start of the war until his death at the Battle of Yellow Tavern in 1864.

58. James R. Cowles, another son of Methodist minister H. R. Cowles and student at Randolph-Macon College, enlisted as a private in Company E of the 12th Virginia

Among the incidents of the war that I have often recalled in connection with this fight was a little battle-field episode between Lt. Doug Chappell, of Co. K, 12th Va. reg't, and Ben Hayes, a member of this company. Chappell used to say the company contained representatives of almost all classes of men, "from a Methodist preacher down to a horse thief." Ben Hayes[59] was up to this time a fellow who thought it sinful to kill an enemy in battle, and had refrained on many fields from firing his gun when in action. Seeing him on this occasion withholding from firing his gun, Lt. Chappell, who swore fearfully, with an oath ordered Hayes to fire his gun.

"Lieutenant," replied Hayes, "If you will stop cursing, I will begin firing."

A day or two after the battle of Brandy Station, the army took up its line of march for the county of Orange, and in a couple of days we were in the vicinity of Orange Court House. Believing that the lameness from a wound received in the battle of Crampton's Gap, Md., on the 14th of September, 1862, which had given me much trouble on the march from Gettysburg, would be likely to give me more if I remained in the field, I sought and obtained a detail under the post-commissary at Orange Court House, who was at that time engaged in furnishing supplies to many thousand men, the bulk of Lee's army at that time being quartered in the county of Orange. Here I was engaged for several weeks, and, being within five miles of my father's place of residence often went there—indeed whenever I was not on duty—enjoying this privilege no little.

Some time in October, the army having moved from Orange back to Culpeper, finding myself again fit for duty in the field, the lameness having passed away, I asked for and obtained a transfer back to my command, which on my return I found encamped in the vicinity of Brandy Station, the men in fine trim and as happy a set of fellows as were anywhere to be met. At the date of my transfer I had not drawn all of the rations to which I was entitled during my service in the commissary department, and, this fact coming to the knowledge of my messmates, it was quickly decided that these rations should now be drawn, to the last pound, which was done, two or more of my messmates going over to the station to bring them back.

The appearance of the party as they neared the camp on their return from

---

in July 1861. Wounded at the Battle of Brandy Station, Cowles spent the next thirteen months in a hospital. When he returned to duty he was given a job in the quartermaster department. He surrendered at Appomattox. After the war, he moved to Texas, where he became a judge. See note 63, chapter 2 for information on his brother Henry.

59. Benjamin H. Hays, an apprentice carpenter in Petersburg, enlisted as a private in Company K of the 12th Virginia in May 1861. He was promoted to corporal in 1863, and sergeant in 1864. He surrendered at Appomattox.

the station, the figure they cut, two of them carrying a long stick over their shoulders with a large piece of bacon, a middling, or the greater part of one, suspended from the pole, is one of the memories of this camp. Put Stith[60] and Joe Pollard[61] I think, were the two who brought back the meat.

Another of these memories is the way our mess enjoyed for several days the rations which I had thus been about to contribute to its larder. During the several days that these supplies lasted us Joe Pollard was our mess cook—I think he was self appointed—and I have often recalled him standing over an oven in which he was cooking biscuits, with arms outstretched and words of protest against any interference on the part of any mess mate until the biscuits were done. I never look at the picture entitled "The Cook's Prerogatives Invaded" at page 57 of Carlton McCarthy's book, "Soldiers life in the army of Northern Virginia,"[62] without having Joe brought to mind as he stood at our camp fire about his oven on those October mornings fending off his impatient comrades as they came near in their eagerness to be tasting some of its savory contents.

Another of the memories of this camp and a very pleasant one it is, is a review by Gen. R. E. Lee of a large body of his cavalry, probably three fourths of all belonging to the army of Northern Virginia, on the broad plain along the Orange & Alexandria railroad, between Culpeper Court House and Brandy Station one beautiful day in the early part of November.

The presence of these veteran horsemen, several thousand in number, on this historic battle field, with all of the distinguished officers of the cavalry in command, with Gen. Lee surrounded by his staff and several of his division and corps commanders occupying a little knoll from which he reviewed the troops, with hundreds of the infantry and artillery of the army of Northern Virginia present as spectators, the long line of cavalry extending more than a mile in length, men and horses all in splendid trim, made this a note-worthy occasion, one impressive in the extreme and never to be forgotten.

The reviewing exercises begun, the long line of cavalry, which had been

60. Putnam Stith Jr. came from a distinguished Virginia family. He enlisted as a private in Company E of the 12th Virginia in April 1861. He was wounded at Seven Pines, Chancellorsville, and the Crater. Captured twice, the second time he was captured he was sent to Point Lookout Prison. Released in June 1865, he returned to Virginia.

61. Joseph Pollard, a clerk for a grocery firm in prewar Petersburg, enlisted as a private in Company E of the 12th Virginia in April 1861. He spent much of the war in and out of hospitals, until he deserted in the Bermuda Hundred area in April 1865.

62. Bernard refers to Carlton McCarthy, *Detailed Minutiae of Soldier Life in the Army of Northern Virginia* (Richmond: C. McCarthy and Co., 1882).

standing fronting the reviewing officer, commenced to move by the right flank in columns of four, when the leading regiment after moving a few paces, wheeled into line of battle, to be followed at the same point by a like movement of the next regiment, which, in the meantime had moved up to the point at which the first regiment had wheeled into line, which movement was repeated by regiment after regiment as it reached the point at which the first regiment wheeled, and thus took its position in line of battle.

The first and each succeeding regiment thus taking its position in line of battle, one behind the other at intervals of about 300 feet, advanced in this formation in a walking gait, towards, up to and past Gen. Lee, the reviewing officer, and the group of officers surrounding him, Gen. Lee saluting each passing regiment, and being in turn saluted by its officers as it got opposite the knoll upon which he stood and those with him. Near by was a mounted cavalry band, which discoursed as each regiment passed in review beautiful music, the soft and liquid notes of which floated dreamily away in the balmy atmosphere, delighting all who heard it.

The whole cavalry force, of which there must have been over five thousand men in line, having thus passed in review was again within one or two hundred yards of the stand, advancing in line of battle as before, this and the regiment following it having, after passing the stand, again taken their places in the original line and this returning again neared the place of review.

Now came the most dramatic part of the exercises. At a word of command this leading regiment, advancing in a line of battle, with drawn sabers, brandished overhead and glittering in the sunshine, dashed forward with the "rebel yell," passing the reviewing officers at a sweeping gallop. It was a magnificent sight, stirring and electrifying all who witnessed it. This intensely exciting maneuver of the first regiment over, the next repeated it, and so did each regiment of the whole command, until the entire force had thus a second time passed the reviewing stand. No parade, no military pageant of any kind I ever saw impressed me, and so pleasantly, as did what I witnessed of this occasion. A few years ago I described to a young gentleman, too young to have been in the war, this review about as I have here narrated it. Having listened attentively he said with such earnestness, "I would have gone along to have witnessed that review."

This review was on Thursday, Nov. 5th 1863 . . .[63]

63. Bernard here proceeds to cite part of the otherwise lost diary of his fellow Petersburg Rifleman, Private Robert Emmet Butts, in support of the date given for the review (see R. Emmet Butts Diary, November 5, 1863, George S. Bernard Papers, Southern Historical Collection). Butts is discussed in note 44, chapter 1.

....

I recall nothing more of special interest whilst we were at this camp except the exuberant spirits in which the troops in our encampment and those near us—the infantry I mean—seemed to be, under the influence of a healthful locality, good rations and the fine and bracing October weather. The woods in which we were would often resound with the merry shouts and laughter of the men. One amusement in which they would indulge was to guy persons coming to, or passing by, about in this fashion: Some fellow quartered or happening to be about the outskirts of the camp sees a hundred or two yards down the road leading to it a man approaching, mounted or on foot. Immediately, with a voice audible all over the camp, the stranger's approach is announced by the cry, "He is coming" "He is coming" "He is coming" which being heard, is taken up and repeated by voices all over the camp grounds hundred[s] of times, until the subject of this clamor reaches a point along his route where it becomes evident what his purpose is, whether to stop or to proceed beyond the camp. If the latter appears to be his purpose, his ears are again greeted with the same multitude of voices now crying "No He is going" "No He is going" "No He is going" until he is well beyond the camp limits and has perhaps encountered another encampment of noisy, boyish fellows, disposed to give him a like reception.

Within a few days after the cavalry review, one afternoon orders came for us to get in readiness to march, and as the sun set we were down in the vicinity of the Rappahannock river, shivering in the frosty air. Something important was on hand. About dark, a few hundred yards down the river there was some fighting, as we could see by the flashes of the rifles, looking like fire flies, as we viewed the scene of the action from our position on the hill slope.[64] We are taken nearer the river bank, in a piece of bottom land, where there are tall weeds, and we are further chilled by the damp atmosphere of this place. Fortunately we do not remain here long—I think less than an hour—before we are ordered back to the high ground, arrived at which we take a line of march in the direction of Brandy Station and then Southwardly which means that we are falling back.

Are we running away from the enemy? Arrived at a point between Brandy Station and Culpeper Court House, we halt, and take position in line of battle. Other commands do likewise. Morning finds us waiting for the enemy, but he does not come. At nightfall fires are built all along our line, and we begin to fall back, passing through Culpeper Court House. Where are we going? We are falling back to line of the Rapidan to go into winter quarters

64. Bernard refers here to the Battle of Rappahannock Station, November 7, 1863.

in the county of Orange. Cold weather is not far off and the men are not displeased at the idea of going into winter quarters.

We march al[l] this night and next morning cross the Rapidan and set foot in Old Orange. Before noon we are halted on Bell's farm, within four or five miles of the river, on the bleak, north slope of the hill, where we were to be quartered during the following six or eight weeks. Of the night's march there is one incident that often comes back to me. Marching on the roadbed of the Orange and Alexander railroad, between midnight and daybreak we reached a branch, or creek, over which was a high trestle work, bridge of fifty or a hundred feet in length. I had on a pair of new shoes, the soles of which were of unusually stiff and unyielding leather. When I reached the bridge I became satisfied that it was unsafe for me to attempt to walk across it. To do so at night under any circumstances would have [been] hazardous, but to do so [w]earing such shoes was especially dangerous. So I quickly made up my mind to descend to the stream below and wade across it, as chilly as the night was, rather than take the risks of falling from the bridge, and announcing my purpose to do this, I left the line to go down the embankment about the abutment of the bridge. Two or three of my comrades protested against this, and one of them, a strong, athletic fellow, grasped me by the arm and bade me to walk across by his side. Having faith in his ability to take me across safely, I agreed to attempt the crossing with him, which was done quickly and with safety, my kind friend holding me firmly by the arm as I walked at his side, his steady step and iron grasp serving to dissipate all apprehensions of danger.[65]

Arriving at the place of encampment, our first work was to pitch our tents, and, cold weather now being upon us, to build chimneys, these chimneys being rude affairs, constituted of logs and mud, topped with flour barrels to improve their draft. My tent mates were all intelligent men, but as lazy a set as you could pick up in a day's march. Rarely did any member of the mess do anything for the benefit of the mess unless it was his turn to do it. All duties, such as going for wood, cutting it up when brought, going to the spring for water, going to the cooks for rations, were done by turns, and many were the learned arguments that we had in disputing a[s] to whose turn it was to do the one or the other of these and other like duties, each striving to prove that it was not his turn to do the particular thing admittedly necessary to be done. One day whilst we lay in our tent thus engaged, a passer by notified us that the barrel on our chimney was on fire. Instead of a rush to the door to knock

---

65. Bernard crossed out all but the first two sentences of this paragraph in his typescript (see George S. Bernard Papers, Southern Historical Collection, University of North Carolina).

down the burning barrel, and to remove the danger to our house of canvas, there was a momentary hesitation as to whose turn it was to discharge a duty in which all were interested.

But one night our laziness brought upon us adequate and well deserved punishment. We all knew that a small ditch around our tent ought to be dug, but, one or more of the [members] of the mess would dig it. Laziness inspiring the thought, we reasoned that we might probably move our camp before the next rain, in which event the labor constructing a ditch would be saved. So no one under took this simple work. On the night referred to however, we had all retired, mother earth, the floor of our tent, covered with a layer of oil-clothes and blankets, being our bed, all of us sleeping side by side, when a severe rain-storm began, the rain pouring in torrents and running down the slope of the hill into our tent and into our bed, from [which] we quickly bounced up, almost in the plight of drowned rats. It is quite needless to state that the ditch was dug the next day, and that no more such accidents occurred.

Whilst we were at this camp there was a military execution—that of a young man named [Joseph Adams],[66] a member of one of the companies of our regiment, shot for cowardice. The brigade being drawn up so as to form three sides of a square, leaving the fourth side open, the men facing inwards, the open grave of the condemned man was about the middle of the fourth side. The brigade being thus stationed, the whole command, including cooks, teamsters and other detailed men were present under orders to witness the execution. Every thing being now ready, the officers in charge of the prisoner, with the squad detailed to shoot him, four men bearing an empty coffin, preceded by the band [o]f the 12th regiment, commencing on the left of the formation, marched slowly along the line of men, the band playing a funeral air, whilst the prisoner, accompanied by a chaplain, walking at his side, marched immediately behind his coffin. As this solemn procession moved along in front of our company, I glanced at the poor prisoner and more abject fear and wretchedness I never saw depicted on a human countenance. His very gait, shambling as he moved unsteadily along, was that of a man thoroughly undone by fright.

[After an indeterminate number of missing pages, the typescript of this portion of Bernard's War Narrative resumes with a quote from a fragment of the

66. Private Joseph Adams of Company K of the 12th Virginia was shot for desertion on November 10, 1863 (see Leroy Summerfield Edwards to father, November 10, 1863, in Leroy Summerfield Edwards Letters, Hargett Rare Books Library, University of Georgia, Athens; and Henderson, *12th Virginia Infantry*, 106). A fisherman before the war, Adams had enlisted in Company K of the 12th Virginia in May 1861.

diary of Private John R. Turner of the Petersburg Riflemen—a missing diary except for such of it as appears in Bernard's War Narrative. In this fragment, Private Turner describes Mahone's brigade moving its camp from Bell's farm on Clark's Mountain to Madison Run Station on January 4, 1864, and the double execution of two deserters from the 16th Virginia Infantry regiment of the brigade on January 11, 1864.]

The cold and hard march from Bell's farm to the new camp that snowy day is well remembered. As soon as we reached camp Put Stith and myself, [having] obtained permission to do so, walked over to my father's about three miles distant and there spent a comfortable night. The military execution the following Sunday afternoon described by Mr. Turner, like that at Bell's farm, impressed itself deeply in my memory as one of the saddest recollections of the war. Often, in after years, when at the Madison Run Station, upon looking over at the field at which it took place—immediately north-east of the station—have I recalled its melancholy details: the two condemned men at Gen. Mahone's headquarters as we marched along from our camp to the field, the one standing up to and close behind the other, as soldiers stand when in single ranks, their appearance at the place of execution, the long waiting with the hope that an order for their respite would come to save them, and the final tragedy at sunset. The men in the line suffered very much as they stood for nearly an hour on the snow covered ground, but would have gladly stood longer and suffered more to have given the poor condemned men another chance for their lives. It has always been my impression that it was the man condemned to be shot for cowardice who met his death with such courage.

[After further brief excerpts from the diary of Private John R. Turner, Bernard's War Narrative resumes:]

From the entry last above mentioned it appears that the men of the brigade had erected a house of worship, and the fact attests the deeply religious feeling that prevailed in camp. My father used to come over on Sundays to attend services and I remember his often saying that he never saw more attentive and well behaved congregations. Many of the men made professions of religion at this time or later in the winter. All of our surroundings at the camp seemed to inspire the men to lead new lives and to prepare themselves for another world. To all it was apparent that the approaching spring would inaugurate a life and death struggle between the two great armies then watching each other, and that the men in the field, those who were to take part in the coming conflict of arms, should take a serious view of the situation, and, realizing that a larger number of them would soon be called upon to yield up their lives, were more ready to enroll themselves as followers of our Saviour, is not surprising. I well remember that whilst we were at this camp with a comrade, Leroy Edwards, I began a systematic study of the Bible, and became deeply interested in it. What we read over together and talked over in our strolls in the woods in the neighborhood of our camp became fastened in my memory.

[The remainder of this typed fragment of Bernard's War Narrative breaks off in the midst of further excerpts from the diary of Private Turner.][67]

67. The very last words of this typed fragment may be Bernard's: "The first day of spring finds us far from being pleasantly or comfortably situated. It still rains incessantly. We are al—" (George S. Bernard Papers, Southern Historical Collection).

5

Life in the Army

CONFEDERATE GENERAL James A. Walker prepared at least two accounts for George Bernard for inclusion in "War Talks, Volume II." The following letter, which includes a variety of war recollections from Walker, appeared in a Richmond newspaper in 1894 and, according to notes in Bernard's papers, was slated for publication in "War Talks, Volume II."[1]

Walker was born in Augusta County, Virginia, in 1832 and attended the Virginia Military Institute. After a stint as a civil engineer and work on the Covington and Ohio Railroad, he studied law at the University of Virginia. In 1855, he began his practice in Pulaski, Virginia, and was elected Commonwealth's attorney for Pulaski County in 1860.

At the beginning of the war, he served as captain of Company C of the 4th Virginia Infantry, one of the several regiments of Thomas "Stonewall" Jackson's Virginia brigade. He fought with Jackson during the Shenandoah Valley Campaign in 1862, where he ascended to brigade command. In May 1863, he became a brigadier general and was assigned to lead the "Stonewall Brigade." Walker commanded the famous unit throughout the campaigns of 1863 and into the Virginia campaign in the spring of 1864. On May 12, 1864, however, his brigade was virtually destroyed at Spotsylvania during the Federal attack at the "Muleshoe." During the action, Walker received a severe wound to his elbow.

Walker returned to service in July and commanded the defenses along

1. The article appeared in the *Richmond Dispatch,* May 27, 1894. The Bernard Collection at the Historical Society of Western Virginia contains a partial version of this article in a typewritten form.

the South Side Railroad until January 1865, when he assumed command of Jubal Early's old division, a post he held until the end of the war. After the war, Walker resumed his legal practice and entered politics, serving in the Virginia House of Delegates and becoming lieutenant governor in 1877. In 1894, he was elected as a Republican to the U.S. House of Representatives for Virginia's Ninth Congressional District. Walker died in 1901 and is buried in Wytheville, Virginia.

>—0—<+—1—<····▷—1—▷—0—<

"Life in the Army—The Private Soldier's Spirit," by James A. Walker

Readable Letters from Gen. Walker, Giving War Reminiscences—The Private Soldier's Spirit—The Independence and Individuality Could Not Be Obliterated—Saw Better than Leaders—Instances in Which the Rank and File Seemed to Know More of Their Surroundings than Their Commanders

Of all the letters from Confederate generals that the *Dispatch* has had the pleasure of publishing within the last two weeks—and all of them contained interesting reminiscences, fraternal greetings, or some pleasant recollections of Richmond—non[e] have given so accurate a description of the Confederate soldier as the following from the pen of General James A. Walker, who commanded the Stonewall Brigade, and received a wound that very nearly deprived him of the use of one of his arms:

Wytheville, Va.: May 25, 1894

To the Editor of the *Dispatch:*

The Spirit which animated the private soldier of the Confederate army can at this day hardly be appreciated by any but those who fought and marched by his side. His leading characteristics were independence and individuality, which could never be sunk or obliterated by the drill and discipline of the most exacting martinet. Much active service and many hardships and privations made him a veteran, but nothing could make him a regular soldier, a mere fighting machine.

He obeyed orders, he marched, fought, advanced and retreated, as ordered. He learned to take care of himself, and to endure hardships and privations, such as few troops ever endured, but through it all he was an individual, who thought and reasoned. He held his own opinions on all subjects, even on the merits and demerits of his own officers. The short-blunders and mistakes were freely discussed and unsparingly censured—around the camp-fire and on the march.

NO HEART WITHOUT CONFIDENCE

A want of confidence in the capacity and courage of their commanders was sometimes most seriously felt, for on two occasions I knew a gallant and dashing brigade to refuse to fight because they believed that the officer in temporary command was a coward. But when an officer from another brigade and another State, whom they knew, offered to lead them, they went forward with alacrity, and fought with their usual gallantry. Another characteristic of the private soldier was his cheerfulness, and even gaiety under the most trying circumstances, and while undergoing the greatest hardships and privations. On the dreariest of forced night marching, when wet, cold, hungry, exhausted, and miserable, and the utmost limit of human endurance seemed to have been reached, some voice in a spirit of irony would start the Sunday school refrain, "Yes, I'm Glad I'm in This Army," which would be taken up by the whole command, and thundered out in true camp meeting style. Sometime the song would be "Stonewall Jackson's Way," or "We'll Hang Abe Lincoln on a Sour Apple Tree."

THEIR OWN PET NAMES

They called themselves "Lee's Miserables," "Mars Bob's boys," "Jackson's Foot Cavalry." They nicknamed their officers and themselves until nearly every man in the company had his sobriquet, which illustrated some moral, mental, or physical peculiarity. General Lee was always spoken of as "Mars Bob," Stonewall Jackson as "Old Jack," Longstreet was "Old Pete," Ewell as "Dick," Early, "Old Jube." A distinguished major-general was called "Club Foot,"[2] because he had been wounded in the foot and walked with a cane and a decided limp.

The average Confederate soldier was intelligent and kept his eyes and ears open, and generally knew more of the actual situation of affairs than his regimental or even brigade commanders.

I can in no way so graphically describe these traits of the private soldier as by reciting a few incidents which came under my own observation.

---

2. "Club Foot" must have been Major General Edward "Allegheny," or "Alleghany" Johnson, who used a heavy cane or club to walk because of an ankle wound suffered at the Battle of McDowell, May 8, 1862 (see Edward S. Clemmer, *Old Alleghany: The Life and Wars of General Ed Johnson* [Darnestown, Md.: Hearthside Publishing, 2004]).

In October 1863,[3] the Federal army, under Meade, made a forward movement, crossing the Rappahannock river above Fredericksburg. General Lee's army moved from around Orange Courthouse to give him battle. Johnson's division, to which my brigade (Stonewall) was attached, marched along the turnpike leading from Orange to Fredericksburg. It was a fine, bracing day, the men were fresh and in the best possible conditions and spirits, and had no reason to believe there was a Federal command within ten miles of them. The troops were marching at route step, jesting, laughing, and singing by turns, each brigade followed by its ordnance and medical wagons, while noncombatants, chaplains, surgeons, quartermasters, commissaries, and servants rode or marched on foot in the rear of their respective regiments and brigades.

AN UNEXPECTED SHOT

Suddenly and without the slightest warning an irregular skirmish fire was opened on us from the thick forest on our left flank, several of the balls taking effect, one of them wounding a horse ridden by one of my couriers. The conduct of the men in this emergency was most admirable. Without the least confusion or excitement, and without orders, they promptly halted, faced to the left, so as to present a front to the foe, and, moving out of the road, to leave it free for the movements of trains and artillery, quietly adjusted their accoutrements, loaded their muskets, and stood in line, but not a shot was fired in return for the straggling fusillade which was kept up by the enemy.

Their experience and self-reliance taught them to face the foe and prepare for action, but their discipline and respect for authority told them it would be un-soldierly to offer to advance, or open fire without orders.

The time from which the first bullet whistled by them until they were in line ready to make or receive a charge [did] not exceed five minutes, and all the while the men were talking and expressing their views on the situation, and their conversation ran in this way "How did the Yankees slip on us in this way without anybody knowing it? Where is our cavalry, that they leave our flank exposed in this way? What is the matter with Mars Bob? If old Jack was here this wouldn't have happened," and so on. At first I was under the impression that a scouting party of our own cavalry had mistaken us for enemies and fired upon us, and hesitated to return the fire. Being on horseback, I could not see under the brush, but I was soon set right by the men who assured me they could plainly see the blue uniforms.

Colonel Colston, of the Second Virginia Regiment, was ordered to de-

---

3. This date should be "November," not "October," for the Mine Run Campaign, described by Walker in this passage, occurred in late November 1863.

ploy his command as skirmishers and advance. The enemy retired before his skirmishers until our line was out of range of their fire, but they then made a determined stand, and a heavy fight between our skirmishers and their troops took place in which the gallant Colonel Raleigh T. Colston[4] was mortally wounded, and many men and officers of his regiment were killed and disabled. The brigade had been in line about an hour waiting for orders, when our division commander, General Edward ("Alleghany") Johnson, came from the front, accompanied by his staff, and riding up to me, and in a voice loud enough to be heard by all who were near commanded me to "take your command and drive away the Yankee cavalry."

KNEW IT WAS INFANTRY

As he turned and rode away, I noticed a private soldier standing very near leaning on his musket, who as soon as General Johnson was out of hearing, said to me: "General, he said that was Yankee cavalry, didn't he?"

I answered: "Yes, that is what he said."

He looked at me rather doubtfully, as if not certain whether he should say more, but seeing that I was waiting for him to speak, he ventured to give his opinion in opposition to that of the division commander, in this fashion, "He can call it 'cavalry' if he wants to but that is infantry and there is a big lot of it too." "Don't let him fool you and go out there thinking we will only have a little brush with cavalry for we will have the biggest kind of fight-with infantry."

I asked him how he knew it was infantry, and he replied "I went out to the skirmish line to see what was going on, and crept up close to them, to get a good shot, and those Yankees have knapsacks on their backs; and nobody ever heard of cavalry bearing knapsacks."

The reasoning of the private solider was unanswerable, and I moved the brigade forward with caution, satisfied that General Johnson was mistaken, and that we were about to stir up a hornets nest of Federal infantry.

It turned out that this private soldier's reconnaissance on his own hook had been more reliable than the major-general's, for we were soon engaged with the whole of French's corps. The entire division had to be brought to

4. Raleigh T. Colston served as captain of Company E, 2nd Virginia Infantry Regiment during the 1862 Valley Campaign and the Peninsula campaigns, and rose to command the regiment after the Second Battle of Bull Run. Colston died on December 23, 1863, and is buried in the University of Virginia cemetery. Captain Colston ("Raleigh T. Colston") should not be confused with Raleigh E. Colston, the brigadier general who helped defend Petersburg against a Federal cavalry attack on June 9, 1864, and corresponded with Bernard after the war.

our support, and the battle was long and obstinate, terminating only with the coming of night, and with heavy loss on both sides.

This combat is known as the battle of Payne's Farm, and was brought on unexpectedly to both General Lee and General Meade, by reason of French's corps[5] having taken the wrong road, and, coming out on the road on which Johnson's division was marching four or five miles further to the right than it was intended it should.

DROVE THE ENEMY BACK

At the second battle of Manassas, on the afternoon of the 29th of August, Early's brigade was ordered to support A. P. Hill, whose gallant men had borne that heat and burden of the day on the left of Jackson's Corps, who had repulsed attack after attack, and when their ammunition was exhausted had held their ground and fought with stones; but at last were forced back from their position along the abandoned railroad. Early's men moved forward at a double-quick, and without a moment's pause, retook the railroad cut and embankment, from which Hill had withdrawn, driving the enemy back "pell-mell." At the point where my regiment (the Thirteenth Virginia) struck the cut it was perhaps twenty feet deep, and as I reached the top on our side the enemy was disappearing on the other, and our boys dashed after them. Just as I was starting to follow down in to the cut General Early rode up, hat in hand, and shouted above the din of the rebel yell: "Colonel, stop the men in the cut; don't let them go further." Running across the cut as far as I could, I seized my color-bearer as he reached the top of the bank on the enemy's side, and ordered him to stand where he was and rallied quite a squad of my men around him. Then turning from them to halt others, I found that nearly the whole brigade had disappeared in the woods in the direction the enemy had fled, and that my own color-bearer and the squad I had rallied around him had also disappeared, and General Early and myself were alone with the dead and wounded.

COULD NOT STOP THEM

I shouted across the cut to General Early: "I can't stop them." He stormed back, "Let them go, then; damn them; let them go." This conclusion seemed eminently wise and proper under the circumstances since they had already gone clear out of sight in the woods.

5. French's Corps refers to the Third Corps of the Army of the Potomac. Walker's force fought at the Battle of Payne's Farm on November 27, 1863.

I followed on, and a quarter of a mile in front I found them in line along the far edge of the wood; while in their front in open ground and in full view was massed a whole field full of the enemy's reserves. After enjoying this warlike display for a short while I moved the brigade back to the cut, where they lay on their arms all night and slept before the big fight of the next day, when Longstreet on the right and Jackson on the left doubled up the wings of Pope's army like the legs of a pair of dividers.

THE FREDERICKSBURG FIGHT

At Fredericksburg in December, 1862, I was in command of Early's brigade, and A. P. Hill was again in our front. Gregg's[6] brigade of Hill's division was posted along the railroad with its left flank resting on a swamp supposed to be impassable for troops, but the enemy found a path through it, attacked Gregg in flank, killing him, and routing his command. Early's brigade was ordered forward, met the victorious enemy advancing, drove him back, and reestablished the front line along the railroad at the edge of the wood. In front of the brigade and for two or three miles up and down, extending back to the Rappahannock river, was spread out a great plain, on which was mustered the whole of Burnside's army, and a grand sight it was.

"Twere worth ten years of peaceful life To look on their array!"

WERE EAGER TO FIGHT

But this warlike array seemed to possess no terrors for the little handful of soldiers composing Early's brigade, for it was with difficulty they could be induced to stop the pursuit at the railroad, and privates joined with officers in appealing to me to let them march out into the plain and attack the enemy. It would have been madness to do so, but the brigade up to that time never suffered defeat, and the men believed they were invincible. They were as near invincible as mortal men could be, and they would have confidently marched into that open plain into the very jaws of death if they had been permitted to do so. A year later they were as brave as ever, but they had learned from experience, and were less rash. They would have still marched out into that plain and attacked Burnside's whole army if they had been commanded to do so, but they would have known when the order was given that "some one had blundered."

6. Walker refers here to Brigadier General Maxcy Gregg, who commanded a brigade in A. P. Hill's division during the Seven Days battles, the Second Battle of Bull Run, and at Antietam, where he was wounded. He was mortally wounded at Fredericksburg.

CAUGHT BY HIGH WATER

I could fill a book with such reminiscences, but space will allow but one more. In August, 1861,[7] when Stonewall Jackson began his famous march to the rear of Pope's army, he marched up the Rappahannock river, and on Friday afternoon reached a point opposite Warrenton Springs. As the enemy had no troops on the opposite bank, it was decided to cross, and Early's brigade being in advance, waded the shallow stream a mile or two below the springs, and bivouacked on the north bank of the stream. During the night it rained in torrents, and by daylight the little river was a raging, angry stream, impassable for men or horses. The enemy received information that Jackson had thrown a portion of his force across the river, and early Saturday morning commenced moving troops up the river to confront his adversary. This single Confederate brigade thus cut off from all hope of retreat or reinforcements, seemed doomed to be captured. But a small creek which united its waters with the river just below Early's position, and between his troops and the advancing column of the enemy was also swollen by the rains, and rendered impassable for infantry, and this delayed the advance all the forenoon.

PRESENTED A BOLD FRONT

In the afternoon they crossed the creek, and advanced in heavy force. Fortunately, General Pope believed that the whole of Jackson's corps was across the river and immediately in his front, and the Confederate troops, by presenting a bold front and showing themselves at as many points as possible kept up the deception, and the afternoon of Saturday was wasted by the Federal commander in bringing up reinforcements and preparing for an advance in heavy force on Sunday morning. All day Saturday and Saturday night the Confederate engineers were straining every nerve to throw a temporary bridge over the river and by daylight Sunday morning it was completed. Just as this rising sun began to gild the hilltops, the imperiled brigade recrossed the river to join the rest of the corps, which occupied the hills on the south side of the river. It had not a moment to spare, for the enemy followed close on its rear, lining the hills which commanded the stream and the low-grounds of the southern side with infantry and artillery.

SUNG EVEN THEN

As the little brigade marched across the low-lands in full view of both armies their friends rent the air with cheers, and the enemy's artillery opened fire

7. This reference should be 1862, not 1861.

upon them. To this the Confederate artillery replied from the opposing heights. The enemy's shot and shell ricocheted around them, and the Confederate missiles went screeching over their heads, but the bra[v]e boys, glad to get back safe to Dixie and relieved from the fear of northern prisons, forgot their exhaustion and their perils, and, as they marched, sang in chorus.

> Let 'em bum! Let 'em bum!
> The way is always clear:
> For while they are a-bumming
> We'll take 'em in the rear!

When they reached the wooden hills out of range of the enemy's guns, as was supposed, they stacked arms, and spreading their wet blankets on the wet ground, lay down to take a sound sleep after the severe strain of the last thirty-six hours.

A SLEEPY CONGREGATION

At this time, the Rev. J. William Jones,[8] a faithful and devoted Christian, now well know[n] by reputation to all southern people, was chaplain of the Thirteenth Virginia Infantry, Early's brigade. Always at the post of duty, always ready later to the sick and dying in hospital and on the battlefield, on this Sabbath he was with us soon as the hour for morning service arrived, he stepped into the midst of his sleeping flock, as they lay scattered about on the ground, and without a word drew forth his Bible and hymn-book, and began by lining out a hymn and raising the tune.[9] A few of his congregation awoke at the sound and joined lazily in the song of praise. The hymn sung, he offered a fervent prayer, and then took his text and proceeded to preach his sermon, but before he had reached his "Secondly," a shot from the enemy's guns on the other side of the river went whizzing high over the heads of the worshippers.

At the familiar sound some of the recumbent figures raised on their elbows, and listened, but not a word was spoken, and the preacher continued his discourse. But soon a second, a third and a fourth shot followed rapidly in the path of the first, each passing lower, and lower, as the gunners began

8. Rev. J. William Jones wrote "The Stories of the 13th," which appear in volume 12 of Clement A. Evans, ed., *Confederate Military History* (Atlanta: Confederate Publishing Company, 1899), and *Personal Reminiscences of General Robert E. Lee* (New York: D. Appleton and Co., 1874).

9. This sentence is garbled in the article from the *Richmond Dispatch*. The sentence appearing in the text here is from the typewritten version found in the Bernard Collection at the Historical Society of Western Virginia. "Lining out" a hymn is a form of a cappella hymn-singing in which a leader gives each line of a hymn tune as it is to be sung.

to get the range. Still the preacher stuck to his text, while the whole regiment awoke to the situation. Presently a shell better aimed fell in the very midst of the congregation, but fortunately nobody was hurt. Then the voice of the preacher was drowned by the voice of the colonel, commanding, "Attention"; and the remainder of the services were indefinitely postponed. The men, sleepily and quietly, but without the least excitement or confusion, although the shells were falling all around, folded their blankets, formed ranks, and were marched back out of reach of artillery fire, where they again stacked arms, and lay down to rest; and to the lullaby of furious artillery drill, slept as soundly and as peacefully as babes.

James A. Walker

6

The Overland
Campaign

By THE SPRING OF 1864, the war was headed into its fourth year. Abraham Lincoln, facing an election in the fall, promoted General Ulysses S. Grant to the rank of Lieutenant General. The president hoped that this man, with control of all U.S. forces, would bring the war to a close. A superior strategist, Grant developed a multipronged plan which simultaneously threatened the Deep South, the vital rebel gateway of Atlanta, the Shenandoah Valley, and the Confederate capital at Richmond.

General George Meade, commanding the 110,000-man Army of the Potomac, moved directly against Lee's army entrenched along the Rapidan River, west of Fredericksburg. In the first days of May, Meade's forces swung around Lee's right flank seeking to flush the rebels from their defensive line and into open ground. On May 4, Lee rushed to meet the Federal column and the armies crashed together in an area known as the "Wilderness," south of the Rapidan. After several days of brutal combat, Grant ordered Meade and his army to keep moving south. Over the following weeks, the forces hammered each other in a series of ferocious engagements at Spotsylvania, the North Anna River, and Cold Harbor.

George Bernard participated in and survived this ordeal—a period of nearly continuous combat which came to be known as the Overland Campaign. In *War Talks of Confederate Veterans,* John R. Turner chronicled the experiences of the 12th Virginia at the Wilderness. That article included a letter from Bernard recounting his experiences at that battle. This chapter reproduces those portions of Bernard's largely unpublished war diary covering the campaign, including some of Bernard's writings contained in Turner's article.

This chapter also has an address by Benjamin Boisseau ("B.B.") Vaughan Jr.,[1] a member of the 1st Virginia Cavalry regiment, describing his experiences under J. E. B. Stuart's command during May of 1864, including his recollections of Stuart's mortal wounding at Yellow Tavern.

>–○–‹•–I–‹•···•›–I–•›–○–‹

"A Trooper's Reminiscences: Wilderness To Yellow Tavern," by B. B. Vaughan

An Address Delivered Before A. P. Hill Camp of Confederate Veterans of Petersburg[2]

Comrades!—During the latter part of April, 1864, the 1st Virginia regiment cavalry, Wickham's brigade, Fitzhugh Lee's division, of which I was a member, was camped in a body of old field pines, near and to the east of Hamilton's crossing.[3] The showy dogwood blossoms were brightening the woods, and all nature was proclaiming the advent of spring, a presage to the old soldier that the time for breaking camp and for action was at hand. This had proven a pleasant camp for us. We were faring unusually well since the fish season had come in. Pretty good corn meal and fat meat, with a plenty of fresh fish from the Rappahannock, were our rations, with now and then such coffee as the culinary art of the men could improvise. Jeff Davis was furnishing a splendid bill of fare, as some of the wags would facetiously remark. There was very little to do just then except light camp duties, caring for the horses, and getting as much sport out of camp life as possible.

I remember an incident which happened here that illustrates the merry

1. After attending the Virginia Military Institute in 1862, Benjamin Boisseau Vaughan Jr. enlisted as a private in Company G of the 1st Virginia Cavalry in September 1863. Wounded at Mt. Jackson, he returned to his unit only to be captured at Sailor's Creek. Imprisoned at Point Lookout, he was released in June 1865. He returned to Petersburg, where he became a tobacco dealer and member of a number of boards.

2. A transcript of Vaughan's talk appeared in the *Petersburg Daily Index-Appeal* on May 27, 1894. Bernard planned to include the address in "War Talks, Volume II." The Bernard papers at the Historical Society of Western Virginia contain a clipping of the Vaughan speech along with a cover note from Bernard.

3. Hamilton's Crossing was a few miles south of Fredericksburg near the Rappahannock River. The 1st Virginia's position there in the spring of 1864 covered approaches to the Army of Northern Virginia's right flank and rear.

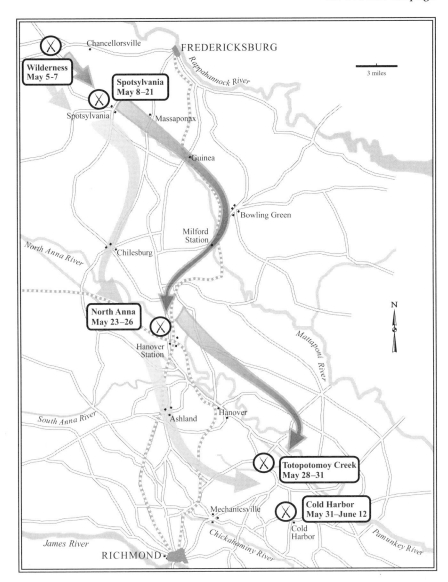

OVERLAND CAMPAIGN, MAY–JUNE 1864

humor and pranks of our boys, for many of us were scarcely more. A young fellow named Wingo[4] not quite sixteen had just come to us from Amelia county and was of course rather green. In a spirit of fun some of the boys thought they would try his mettle. A difficulty between him and a much

4. Elmore E. Wingo, a student in Amelia County, enlisted as a private in Company G of the 1st Virginia Cavalry in May 1, 1864 (at the age of sixteen). His baptism of fire

larger and older man named Godsey,[5] was easily provoked. Wingo's friends advised him to challenge Godsey, which he promptly did. The latter, being in the secret, as promptly accepted, and carbines were chosen as the weapons. I was one of the party who went to the dueling grounds, a road just on the skirt of the pines. All being ready, seconds, etc., in place the principals were handed carbines loaded with blank cartridges. Wingo on getting his deliberately opened it, and taking there from the blank cartridge replaced it with one from his own box, saying to his second, "I prefer loading my own gun." This terminated the duel, and Godsey by the advice of friends and his second made ample apologies. Wingo's nerve and pluck thus exhibited stood by him during the trying ordeal through which we were soon to pass, and not long after this he got a bullet through his thigh and he and Godsey were captured at the same time.

Wingo has told me since the war that after his capture he was taken before Gen. Sheridan,[6] who asked him to what command he belonged. "To Gen. Lee's army," was his reply. "How many troops have you?" "A whole heap of them, sir." Gen. Sheridan in rather a good humored disgust then asked, "What made you come to the army?" "To fight, sir," Where upon Gen. Sheridan said, "You had better be home tied to your mother's apron strings. Orderly take him away."

These days ran speedily by. Soon reports came of Grant's crossing the Rapidan on the 4th day of May, and orders to us to saddle up. Our company (G) then numbered about forty men present for duty. Alas! How many of them now are on the other side! We were soon on the march towards the Wilderness, and here I will quote from Major McClellan's "Campaigns of Stuart's Cavalry," that you may better know of our destination and the locality of those severe fights we had on the right flank of our army.[7]

"On the morning of the 5th," says this author, "Stuart in person conducted the advance of A. P. Hill's corps on the plank road until the enemy's lines were

---

was swift: on May 12 he was wounded and captured at Spotsylvania Court House. Sent to Elmira prison camp, he was exchanged in October 1864. He returned to his unit, and surrendered at Appomattox. After the war, he resided in Amelia County.

5. William Archer Godsey, a carpenter in Amelia County, enlisted as a private in Company G of the 1st Virginia Cavalry in May 1861. Wounded and captured at Spotsylvania Court House, Godsey was imprisoned at Point Lookout. Exchanged in February 1865, Godsey returned to his county and occupation after the war.

6. Major General Philip H. Sheridan, the commander of Grant's cavalry.

7. See H. B. McClellan, *The Campaigns of Stuart's Cavalry* (1885; reprint, Edison, N.J.: Blue and Gray Press, 1993).

reached and the battle was joined. On this day Rosser [cavalry brigade] had a severe and successful encounter with Wilson's division of cavalry on the right beyond Todd's Tavern."

"On the 6th," continues Major McClellan, "the battle was renewed in the Wilderness, and was continued throughout the day with great intensity. On the 6th and 7th the cavalry of both armies were engaged in severe conflicts on the confederate right. On the night of the 7th Gen. Grant commenced to move his army by the left flank, in the endeavor to interpose it between Gen. Lee and Richmond. The movement was discovered in time and Fitz Lee's division was thrown in front of the federal column to delay it until Longstreet's corps under Anderson,[8] could reach Spotsylvania Courthouse. This was accomplished although it entailed on Fitz Lee's division one of the severest conflicts in which it was ever engaged. Torbert's cavalry commanded by Merritt[9] and backed by the 5th corps, attacked before daylight. Fitz Lee[10] employed his whole command dismounted and presented so solid a front that the federal cavalry found it difficult to move him; and having forced him slowly back beyond the forks of the road west of Alsop's[11] they were at Merritt's suggestion relieved by a line of battle from the 5th corps."

Major John Esten Cooke, in his life [of] Gen. Lee says: "A race now began for the coveted position of Spotsylvania Courthouse and Stuart with his dismounted sharp shooters behind improvised breastworks harassed and impeded the Federal advance, at every step, . . ." and it is said this together with the extreme rapidity of the march of Anderson's corps enabled Gen. Lee to succeed.[12]

I think it was the evening of the 6th when getting in the vicinity of Todd's Tavern[13] our regiment, after having been dismounted and deployed several times met the enemy in a thick body of woods and underbrush, where one could scarcely see twenty yards in front of him. A very severe fight ensued in which our company lost several killed and more wounded. I remember one orderly sergeant, Sidney Burton,[14] as gallant a soldier as fired a carbine, was

8. "Anderson" was Major General Richard Heron "Fighting Dick" Anderson.

9. "Merritt" refers to Brigadier General Wesley Merritt.

10. "Fitz Lee" means Major General Fitzhugh Lee.

11. Alsop's Farm was about two miles north of Spotsylvania Court House.

12. See John Esten Cooke, *A Life of Gen. Robert E. Lee* (New York, 1871).

13. Todd's Tavern was about four miles northwest of Alsop's Farm.

14. William Sidney Burton, a farmer before the war, enlisted as a private in Company G of the 1st Virginia Cavalry in May 1861. Promoted to second sergeant in 1864, he was killed in action at Todd's Tavern (1864).

killed. Also William Jackson,[15] whom we called "Stonewall." John Southall[16] had a narrow escape while loading his carbine. The bullet striking the stock and going through struck the "U.S." metal buckle of his cartridge box belt and flattened it against his stomach, bruising him very badly. Frank Vaughan,[17] my bed fellow, had a small piece of his under lip taken off which caused him to bleed profusely. The front of his jacket was soon covered with blood, notwithstanding it was a slight wound, which took him from duty for about a day.

Now my comrades, I trust you will pardon this digression, and will not think me indelicate when I pay a feeble tribute to the memory of my friend and relative just referred to, Robert Frank Vaughan, to whom I was bound by the tenderest ties of affection. We were dear friends from early boyhood, and left the Virginia Military Institute where we were studying the art of war, to enter upon its grim realities. On the 19th of September, 1864, in the last battle fought at Winchester, he was shot through the head and instantly killed whilst fighting in Fort Stonewall Jackson. His was a brave spirit. "His life was gentle and the elements so mixed in him that nature might stand up and say to all the world this was a man." He lies buried in the Stonewall cemetery near Winchester. When life was in its spring, the spoiler came, and all that promised fair has sought the grave to sleep forever there.

The night after the fight on the evening of the 6th of May, our command bivouacked in a body of woods not far from where we had been fighting. The horses had to be watered and fed, besides getting food for ourselves. As we were close to the enemy, the bridles and saddles were not removed, but the merciful master would always loosen the girth and rearrange the saddle-blanket, so as to give as much comfort as possible to the poor tired and half-fed friend who was relied upon to carry him when again called to duty. I have known men to go several miles after a hard day's service in order to get some

15. William H. Jackson, an Amelia County farmer, enlisted as a private in Company G of the 1st Virginia Cavalry in June 1862. Wounded at Todd's Tavern, he died from his wound in July 1864.

16. John Turner Southall, a student from Amelia County, enlisted in Company A of the 14th Virginia Infantry in 1861. He transferred to Company G, 1st Virginia Cavalry, in February 1862. Twice wounded at Spotsylvania Court House, he was captured at Old Tavern in May 1864. Imprisoned at Point Lookout, he was exchanged in October 1864. He surrendered at Appomattox. After the war, he returned to Amelia County, where he served as Justice of the Peace.

17. Robert Francis ("Frank") Vaughan had attended Virginia Military Institute with B. B. Vaughan in 1862. Frank Vaughan enlisted as a private in Company G of the 1st Virginia Cavalry in January 1864. Wounded at Todd's Tavern, he recovered and returned to his unit, only to be killed in action at Winchester.

feed for their horses, and when stealing it from a corn field to be shot at by the safety guard put there to protect the owner.

The duty of looking after our horses and getting something for ourselves to eat over on the night last referred to, we were soon in profound sleep. From which the reveille at the dawn of day awoke us, and soon the line of skirmishers were off in the woods again. Fighting was going on all day (Saturday, May 7th) but I do not now recall any specially noteworthy incident. The night of that day was a repetition of its predecessor, only the location of our bivouack was changed. The next morning before day (Sunday, May 8th) we were moving into the woods again. My recollections are very vivid of that day's action. Fighting commenced pretty early and soon the rattle of the carbines became incessant. Our regiment was first carried in behind and in support of the 4th Virginia cavalry, where we hugged mother earth very close to avoid the bullets coming through the underbrush. It was a damp, marshy place where we were. The 4th, not far in front of us, was making a glorious fight, and stuck to their lines like heroes. We could see their dead and wounded being brought back. Amongst the wounded I remember seeing Major J. F. Strother[18] who had a ghastly wound through his cheek which laid it open as if cut with a knife; and also Walter Spears,[19] an old schoolmate, who was being borne back mortally wounded. Presently a courier came and ordered our regiment to the right, the men to be withdrawn, a few at a time, to the rear. This order obeyed, forming in the rear, we marched to the right; were deployed and ordered forward. We had gone but a short distance through the thicket, when one of [the] enemy was seen to jump from behind some bushes, immediately in front of our company. Almost immediately a number of carbines were fired at him. The last I saw of him he was tumbling over behind the bushes whether struck or not I will never know for just then our fire drew a volley from the enemy, whose line we had struck, which made us seek mother earth as speedily as possible. The intention of our commanding officer seemed to be to have us find the enemy and stop, for no forward movement was ordered. This suited me admirably, as good fortune had put a tree of just the right size in the right place for me. The opposing lines were not far apart, but, owing to the thick undergrowth, little could be seen. Whenever a glimpse of one of the enemy could be had, we would blaze away at him. Thus a constant skirmish fire was kept up. I saw a member of the

18. "Major J. F. Strother" may be Major Mordecau W. Strother, who had enlisted on April 24, 1861, as a sergeant.

19. Sergeant John Walter Spears, who had enlisted on May 27, 1862, died of his wounds May 29, 1864.

company to our right jumping from one place to another, trying to get a shot at the enemy. This daring confederate was about ten feet in front of his line. When exposing himself in his movements, he was shot down, and two men who ran to his assistance, I think, were also shot. This struck me as very foolhardy, not only uselessly risking one's life, but depriving the command of the services of a bold and fearless soldier.

[The fight ("Laurel Hill") described by Vaughan in the following paragraphs proved to be one of the pivotal points in the Overland Campaign. On the night of May 7, Federal forces left the battlefield in the Wilderness and marched south toward the critical road junction at Spotsylvania Court House. Lee, in turn, pushed his units to head off the Federal column. Union control of the road junction at the Court House would interpose Grant's men between Lee and the most direct route to Richmond. On the morning of May 8, the vanguard of the Union army (the Fifth Corps) encountered stiff resistance from dismounted rebel cavalry at Laurel Hill, a small rise several miles northwest of Spotsylvania Court House. The Southerners had won the initial race to Spotsylvania, but it was unclear whether the horsemen could hold their ground until the arrival of Lee's infantry. Vaughan recounts his experience that day at Laurel Hill without naming the engagement.[20]]

Very shortly after this [these] orders came for us to fall back, very quietly and slowly, and as soon as our line had gotten from the immediate front of the enemy, the regiment was formed in columns of fours, and taking a small road, went towards the large one on which we had entered the woods. Getting in sight of this large road, we saw General Fitz Lee sitting on his horse in the angle made by the intersection of the two roads. The 4th regiment was coming out on the other road and the men, as they came marching past him, cheered lustily, while General Lee, waving his hat, said, "You have made one of the bravest fights of the war." As a leader of troops, General Fitz Lee had great personal magnetism, and was as dashing and dauntless a soldier as ever marched to battle. Our regiment was especially fond of him. He was at one time its colonel, and by his genial manners and his superior fighting qualities had won the love and admiration of the men.

20. For modern studies of these events, see Gordon Rhea, *The Battles for Spotsylvania Court House and the Road to Yellow Tavern, May 7–12, 1864* (Baton Rouge: Louisiana State University Press, 1997), 45–88; and William D. Matter, *If It Takes All Summer: The Battle of Spotsylvania* (Chapel Hill: University of North Carolina Press, 1988), 44–95.

Going a short distance from this place, we came to the edge of the woods, and as I looked across a narrow field there met my vision a sight which gladdened my heart. You may talk about the sight of an oasis in the desert to the weary traveler, of a Yankee haversack to a hungry confederate, but none of these could have brought more joy than did the sight of that column of infantry, "with tattered uniforms and bright muskets," who were going into line of battle on the other side of that field. As I saw them they were taking off the rolls of blankets, and some were already at work throwing up dirt against fence rails, which were soon converted into very good breastworks. In marching across this field we were being taken back to the led horses, while Mason,[21] an old school mate, rode up, and we had a very pleasant, though short, meeting. He was then courier for General E. P. Alexander,[22] of the artillery, and I did not fail to express to him my joy at seeing the big guns and strong force of infantry to back them.

On getting to the led horses, we were ordered to feed, after doing which and getting something for myself, impelled by curiosity, some of us went to see the infantry fight. The enemy, after forming, had come out of the woods in beautiful order and as thick as black birds. One of the infantrymen told me after the fight that he heard of the officers shouting "Forward up men, there is nothing in front of you but a thin line of cavalry skirmishers." The men came marching confidently across the field; our men holding their fire until the enemy were in close range, and then opening on them. The enemy were sent stunned and staggering back to the woods, leaving a great many dead and wounded on the field. I went amongst them and talked with one of the wounded men. I find in the diary of the 1st army corps, at this time commanded by General Anderson, the following: "We find Fitz Lee hotly engaged on the Todd's Tavern and Spotsylvania C.H. road. Kershaw's and Humphrey's brigades turned off rapidly to the left of the road, and occupying some cover left by our cavalry, repulsed the enemy with great slaughter, dur-

21. Mason, the courier, is probably William Taylor Mason, a former student at the Virginia Military Institute who joined Breathed's Battery in March 1863. He was appointed lieutenant aide-de-camp to his brother-in-law General Alexander in March 1864. He died of yellow fever in 1867 (see Robert E. L. Krick, *Staff Officers in Gray: A Biographical Register of the Staff Officers in the Army of Northern Virginia* [Chapel Hill: University of North Carolina Press, 2003], 217).

22. A West Point graduate, Brigadier General Edward Porter Alexander was one of three officers promoted to the rank of brigadier general of the artillery in the Army of Northern Virginia. He fought in the major battles of the Eastern theater, and with Longstreet at Chickamauga and Knoxville. After the war, he was at various times a professor, railroad president, and, later, an author.

ing the fight, Haskell's battalion is sharply engaged and does good work. The enemy's forces compose the 5th corps (Warren's)."[23]

During this day, as the infantry were passing some of us frequently saw friends and acquaintances. Frank Vaughan, I remember, came in and told me that he had just seen his brother, Floyd,[24] who was ten or twelve years older than himself, a member of the 44th Virginia. He also had received a slight wound in the face the day before, and several days after this was killed on the skirmish line of his brigade. Thus in this campaign was their aged father bereft of his only sons. On the night of this day (May 8th) we went into bivouac. I think this was on the road of the Spotsylvania C.H. road, in a body of thin woods, excepting the underbrush and small saplings. Just about, or a day or two before this time there had come to our company a man named Parrott,[25] apparently between thirty five and forty years of age, and of rather large build. He impressed me by his gentlemanly appearance and deportment. He was very nicely dressed and all of his equipments were in harmony with his pretty new uniform, the contrast between himself and the other men in this particular being quite striking. Saw him sitting off to himself looking very lonely and out of harmony with his surroundings, and although scarcely knowing him, ventured to approach him, trying to make him feel at home with us. We had a very pleasant conversation; and I felt as though, notwithstanding the difference in our ages; we might be good friends. Although we had been for several days under fire, the spirit of fun and deviltry had not been completely knocked out of the boys, for they commenced guying Parrott at once, his nice appearance attracting attention, and his name becoming known, "Pretty Pol" was at once suggested, and as he would ride along the line on the march, you could hear all along from company to company "Pretty Poll." "Polly want a cracker?" He stood this with stoical forbearance.

If I remember rightly, the next day, Monday the 9th, we had some brisk skirmishing in the vicinity of Spotsylvania C.H., in which our regiment got into one of the hottest places I ever was in. Having been dismounted, we were sent forward across an old field grown up in broom straw and scattering pines. A skirmish line of infantry was to our left. Soon we were in range of the enemy's sharp-shooters, posted behind a fence and from others firing from our left. As we were going forward through the broom straw at a rapid walk,

23. The Diary of the First Army Corps, Army of Northern Virginia, appears intermittently in the *Official Records.*

24. Private Albert Floyd Vaughan of Amelia Court House had enlisted on September 1, 1862, and died Sept. 15, 1864. Frank Vaughan is discussed in note 17, this chapter.

25. James T. Parrot enlisted as a private in Company G of the 1st Virginia Cavalry in February 1864. He was killed in action at Spotsylvania Court House.

the bullets singing over our heads or striking around us, General Stuart rode up from the left and rear to my side, sitting as straight as an arrow and looking to be a very god of war. Pointing to some stragglers from the left, who were going through our line to the rear, he shouted out to me, "Stop those men, and turn them back to their command!" Whilst he was riding along by my side, several men bearing orders rode up to him. I noticed that they ducked their heads down on their horses' necks until getting up to Stuart, when they would rise and deliver their messages. His presence began to make it a little hotter on the skirmish line in my vicinity, and I was glad when he moved off to another point.

[The engagement Vaughan discusses here occurred on May 9 near the Beverly house, about a mile northeast of Spotsylvania Court House. Following the successful stand at Laurel Hill on May 8, Lee's army began to etch out a line of fortifications stretching to the Court House. On the morning of May 9, Willcox's division of the Union Ninth Corps moved along the Fredericksburg road probing the rebel defenses. This avenue of advance struck deep into the right flank of Lee's position at Spotsylvania. At the Beverly house (not far from the Ni River), Confederate infantry from Gordon's division and Wickham's cavalry brigade (which included the 1st Virginia) blocked this Union reconnaissance. Vaughan describes the fighting that resulted.[26]]

Before our advancing skirmish line moved much farther, the order was given to charge, and we rushed forward with a yell along the whole line, getting pretty close to the enemy, who ran back across a ploughed field, and we took the fence. Stopping a moment, I saw several blue spots about on the grey soil, and other blue objects making two-forty speed down the hill. It was only a moment, for our men, elated by the sight, mounted the fence, rushing over the ploughed ground, and came into broom straw and small pines again. When running across the ploughed ground I saw a member of another company, a large man with a big moustache, throw up both hands and fall backwards. I think he was killed, but going forward heard no more of him. On getting down into the broom straw we received a stunning volley from the left and front. We had struck an infantry line of battle. Standing it for a moment, we had to run out or be shot to pieces, or captured. When I turned my back to go up and over that ploughed field, seeing the dust knocked up by the bullets crossing each other, I don't think I ever felt more demoralized in my life. If the question had been asked then, "What is the distance across that field?"

26. For more on this battle, see also Rhea, *Battles for Spotsylvania*, 105–6.

I should most certainly have said, "At least a mile." Now in these piping times of peace, I should say the distance was about one hundred and fifty yards.

Starting and not deliberating about the start, I was soon lying out of breath on the right side of the fence we had left. Every step, however, across that field, I expected to be shot in the leg. Strangely I did not think of being struck in any other part of the body. Frank Vaughan was soon up and told me that John Sanderson[27] was shot through the temple and instantly killed by his side. Hill Carter,[28] running out with Norvell Harris,[29] saw Parrot lying dead, and called Norvell's attention to him. Scruggs[30] was thought to have been killed, but was badly wounded, losing a leg and falling into the enemy's hands. These were the only three I remember who were permanently lost from the company. Poor Parrott! His career as a soldier was short and glorious. He fell on the field of battle bravely discharging his duty.

When we got back to the led horses I there witnessed what was indeed a pathetic scene. George Sanderson,[31] who was one of the horse soldiers at that time was told of his brother John's death. He broke down completely, and

27. John B. Sanderson, an Amelia County laborer, enlisted as a private in Company G of the 1st Virginia Cavalry in June 1863. He was killed in action at Spotsylvania Court House.

28. Hill Carter enlisted as a private in Company G of the 1st Virginia Cavalry in April 1864. Wounded in action in May 1864, Carter returned to duty, only to be captured in March 1865. Released in June 1865, he returned to Virginia, where he became a lawyer.

29. Norvell W. Harris was living in Colorado when the war broke out. He returned to his home in Virginia and enlisted in Company G of the 1st Virginia Cavalry in September 1861 as a substitute for his younger brother Charles. He served with the 1st Virginia Cavalry until the end of the war, when he was captured and later paroled at Beaver Dam. In the late 1890s he moved to Texas and took up farming. Ironically, his cross-country trek did not deter his brother Charles from reenlisting in the 1st Virginia Cavalry in November 1861. Charles was wounded and captured during the war, but survived.

30. Joseph A. Scruggs, an overseer in Amelia County, had enlisted as a private in Company G of the 1st Virginia Cavalry in May 1861. Wounded and captured at Spotsylvania Court House, he was imprisoned at Elmira. Released in June 1865, he returned to Virginia. Years after the war, he received a state pension for his war injury (his leg had been amputated).

31. George L. Sanderson, an Amelia County farmer and older brother of John Sanderson, enlisted as a private in Company B of the 23rd Virginia Infantry in May 1861. Captured at Kernstown, he was sent to Fort Delaware prison camp, and exchanged in August 1862. He deserted in January 1863, only to enlist in Company G, 1st Virginia Cavalry, in March 1863. He served with this unit through surrender at Appomattox. He returned to farming after the war.

seemed in an agony of grief. Comrades I could not stand it. Taking my horse, I moved off.

To my old comrade, Hill Carter, who was then a slender, blue-eyed boy, just entering into manhood, bright, intelligent, and of the bravest of the brave, now an able and respected lawyer of Richmond, Va., I am indebted for the confirmation of some of the incidents mentioned and still to be mentioned, and as these facts are drawn almost entirely from memory, I have endeavored to have them verified by such of my old comrades as I could meet.

About this time, when the two armies were facing each other at Spotsylvania C.H., General Sheridan massed his cavalry, one of the best armed and equipped body of horsemen the world has ever seen, in the rear of the federal army preparatory to a raid around General Lee's right flank, in order to break his communications with Richmond, and, if practicable, in conjunction with General Butler,[32] to capture the city. The seven-shooter with which this body of cavalry had been armed was the best adapted and most effective weapon ever used in cavalry service up to that time. Besides these they had the best army pistols and sabers. The cavalry service had been a special object of attention from both Gens. Grant and Sheridan. As an illustration of this, I quote from a telegram from Gen. Grant to Gen. Halleck[33] in which he says: "Send all new cavalry equipped as infantry and mount veterans on their horses."

With three divisions numbering about 10,000 to 12,000 cavalry, and a large force of artillery, Gen. Sheridan moved to Hamilton's crossing[34] and thence to the Telegraph road on to Richmond. Gen. Stuart sent a brigade of cavalry under Gen. Gordon[35] of North Carolina to follow his rear, and Gen. Fitz Lee with Wickham's and Lomax's brigades by a near route to interpose between Sheridan and Richmond, which was done at Yellow Tavern, six miles from the city. The fight at that point was between Fitz Lee's two brigades and Gen. Sheridan's forces.

Soon after the last fight of which I have spoken, our command moved off to the right, and coming into a large road turned down it toward Richmond. An officer coming back to our company, which was on that day the rear company of the regiment, told Captain F. W. Southall,[36] our gallant company commander and to me a very kind and warm personal friend, that a small

32. Major General Benjamin F. Butler was at the time commander of the Army of the James.

33. Major General Henry W. Halleck was then the Federal chief of staff.

34. Hamilton's Crossing was just south of Fredericksburg.

35. The text refers to Brigadier General James B. Gordon.

36. Francis Winston "Frank" Southall, a Hampden-Sydney student and Amelia County farmer before the war, enlisted as second sergeant in Company G of the 1st

body of the enemy were coming down the road behind him with a view to joining their command, which had gone on before, and as our command had gotten into the road behind those who had gone on already, it was thought that by leaving Captain Southall with his company concealed in the woods until those coming on behind him had passed him, he could close in on them and drive them on the brigade in our advance, or capture them before doing so. All of us knew the object. After waiting in the woods for some time we saw a cloud of dust from the direction of the expected enemy, and very soon about twenty-five of their cavalry came in sight. It was a moment of exciting expectancy. They stopped about three or four hundred yards from the woods in which we were concealed, and when watering their horses seemed all at once in a panic, and went scampering back in the direction from which they came. Captain Southall followed them to a church about a mile from where we were, and captured one who had fallen from his horse. Hill Carter, who was one of his captors, asked him what made him fall from his horse, "Mine horse about-faced too fast for me," was the reply; which indicated the foreign birth and infantry drill of the captive horseman. Ascertaining that the party of the enemy had entered their lines, Captain Southall and his command started on the march to rejoin the brigade. This little episode, perhaps, kept us out of something more severe, as we heard on getting up that some brisk fighting had been going on during our absence. The third and fourth regiments had had some warm work with the rear guard of the enemy. I have heard Lt. Col. W. M. Field[37] of the Third, a member of our camp, whom you all know and whose gallantry on the field of battle was ever conspicuous, speak of an incident which I now relate in the words of Major McClellan. "The 6th Ohio," says the author, "was now re-enforced by the 1st New Jersey cavalry, and the rear guard thus strengthened made a determined stand. Wickham[38]

<hr>

Virginia Cavalry in May 1861. A popular soldier, he rose steadily through the ranks by election, achieving the rank of captain by July 1863. Wounded in action at the Battle of Rude's Hill (November 1864), he survived the war and returned to farming.

37. William Meade Field, a Dinwiddie County farmer, enlisted as a 2nd lieutenant in Company I of the 3rd Virginia Cavalry in May 1861. Twice wounded, he rose through the ranks to lieutenant colonel by February 1865. Paroled at Richmond in May 1865, he returned to farming in his native county.

38. Williams Carter Wickham, Virginia planter and politician, led his militia company into Confederate service in April 1861. Commissioned lieutenant colonel of the 4th Virginia Cavalry in September 1861, he served in all the major cavalry operations in the East through 1864, when he resigned his commission to take his seat in the Confederate Congress. He left the service as a brigadier general. After the war, he was president of two railroad companies and served in the state senate.

attacked promptly, but made no impression. One of two of his regiments had recoiled from the charge when he called for Matthew's[39] squadron of the 3rd Virginia with the remark, 'I know he will go through.' Matthews led his column of fours down the narrow lane and pierced the enemy's lines, but he did not return. The heavy force of the enemy closed upon the head of the column, killed five, wounded three, and captured ten men of his company. Matthews' horse was killed. While fighting on foot with his sabre, he was shot from behind and mortally wounded. His gallantry excited the admiration of his enemies, who carefully carried him to a neighboring farmhouse, leaving with him one of his company who had been captured in the charge. He died that night."

There was almost constant skirmishing with picketing and guarding intersecting road, during the hard march to Yellow Tavern, the commands marching at night as well as day. Our company lost three or perhaps more men during the march. I think it was about this time that Wingo and God-sey were captured. On the 11th day of May we reached Yellow Tavern and here occurred on this day the historic cavalry fight which took from the cavalry corps of the Army of Northern Virginia its great and glorious leader. As I remember, it was afternoon when the fight commenced. Gen. Stuart had overtaken Fitz Lee, and was now with him, having Wickham's and Lomax's brigades on the field, with some of Breathed's[40] artillery; and I do not think there was any artillery in the army of Northern Virginia which could do better fighting, or could boast of a more daring or fearless commander than Major Breathed.

The whole command was dismounted except part of the 1st Virginia regiment, which was retained as a mounted reserve. We were held in reserve some time.

In a thin skirt of woods, just in our front, the rattle of carbines was incessant, and our men seemed to be having it pretty hot. We were moved a little nearer to the woods, where coming within range of the enemy's bullets, I saw one of the men in the front squadron taken from his horse wounded. I think

---

39. George H. Matthews Jr. enlisted as a private in Company G of the 3rd Virginia Cavalry in May 1861. He received three promotions in 1862, rising to the rank of captain. He was mortally wounded at the Battle of Mitchell's Shop in May 1864.

40. James W. Breathed, a prewar physician, enlisted as a private in Company B of the 1st Virginia Cavalry in April 1861. In November 1861 he transferred to the Stuart Horse Artillery, where he was steadily promoted through the ranks to major. He fought in all the major battles in the East. Breathed is the subject of a recent biography by David P. Bridges, *Fighting with Jeb Stuart: Major James Breathed and the Confederate Horse Artillery* (Arlington, Va.: Breathed Bridges Best, 2006).

he was shot in the breast. This caused Col. Morgan,[41] the commander of our regiment, to move us under the brow of the hill, and, as he ordered us to dismount, I thought we were to be taken in on foot. Not so, however. We were ordered to stand to our horses. Pretty soon a courier came rushing up to us. In great haste we were ordered to mount, our commander leading the way rapidly to our left across the field to a road. I think it was the Telegraph road. The regiment stopped a moment to close up. Just then a message was brought from the front telling Captain Southall to dismount his squadron and send them to the front as quickly as possible. While we were obeying his command and running out to the right of the road an officer was there shouting, "Run to the front," which we did in squads, not waiting to form. The mounted portion of our regiment, moving up, soon met the enemy's charge with a ringing yell. Some of our dismounted men ran on before me. When I got to the front the charge had just been made and our mounted men seemed to be pressed very hard and somewhat in confusion. Captain Hammond,[42] of Company B, who with his company, led the mounted charge, was killed.

It was here our dismounted men got in their work. The mounted enemy were all about us, and we shooting at them as rapidly as possible. I had left my jacket strapped on my saddle, and, with shirt sleeves rolled up, went into the fight. It was a very hot sultry day. After having shot my carbine, I do not know how many times, I discovered that my left arm just above the wrist, was black and burned from the powder blowing back from my old carbine, which, from some cause, did not close up tightly. And here let me say that our carbines would bear about the same comparison to the seven-shooters of the enemy as an old flint lock musket would to an Enfield rifle. I tied my Bandanna handkerchief around my arm and kept on shooting. We were in the edge of a thin skirt of woods. On the right side of the road from our position, and scattered along for some distance, were the enemy charging on our mounted men and we were trying to stop them.

41. William Augustine Morgan, a prewar farmer, enlisted as a private in Company F of the 1st Virginia Cavalry in April 1861. Elected captain in July 1861, he was subsequently promoted through the ranks to colonel (December 1864). Wounded at Gettysburg, he returned to duty and commanded first a regiment, then a brigade. At Appomattox, he chose escape to surrender, though he later disbanded his regiment (Payne's) at Lynchburg. He was paroled at Winchester. He returned to farming and served as deputy sheriff of Jefferson County, West Virginia, for twenty-seven years.

42. George Newkirk Hammond, a graduate of the Virginia Military Institute and prewar farmer, enlisted as a 1st lieutenant of Company B of the 1st Virginia Cavalry in April 1861. Elected captain in August 1861, he retained that rank for the next three years. Wounded at Yellow Tavern, he died in a Richmond hospital five days later.

During the fighting I saw a federal officer fall from his horse. He was gallantly leading his men and using his sabre vigorously on our mounted men. A braver man never fell in battle. Immediately Norvell Harris, a member of our company, a man of great strength and with nerves of steel, who was not far from me, ran to the fallen federal officer and got a silver watch and a pistol from his person. Hill Carter has recently told me that he witnessed this incident, and that Norvell gave him the pistol. I do not know who the officer was, but, from the following extract from the report of Gen. Custer on this battle, I am led to believe that he was Major Granger,[43] of the 7th Michigan cavalry. "The 7th Michigan commanded by Major Granger," says Gen. Custer, "was ordered forward at a trot and when near the enemy's position was ordered to charge with drawn sabers. Major Granger, like a true solider, placed himself at the head of his men and led them bravely up to the very muzzles of the enemy's guns, but notwithstanding the heroic efforts of this gallant officer the enemy held their position, and the 7th Michigan was compelled to retire, but not until the chivalric Granger had fallen pierced through the head and heart by the bullets of the enemy. He fell, as the warrior loves to fall, with his face to the foe."

And just here let me narrate another incident: One of the enemy, pistol in hand, riding up to Jim Blanton,[44] who was looking and fighting in another direction, got the drop on him, and Jim was about to surrender. Briggs,[45] seeing Jim's dilemma, came to his rescue. This turned the tables. The poor federal's attention being diverted from Jim, whilst trying to save himself he was brought down from his saddle by a well-directed shot from one of the carbines of his confederate assailants, both of whom were amongst the best and coolest fighters of our company.

Ad. Fowlkes,[46] whom we called "Bullet," has often talked with me of this fight. Fowlkes was apparently without fear, and seemed to revel in danger. I

43. Henry W. Granger enlisted as a 1st lieutenant in the 7th Michigan Cavalry in August 1861. Steadily promoted to the rank of major, he was killed in action at Yellow Tavern.

44. James Anderson Blanton, an Amelia County farmer, enlisted as a private in Company G of the 1st Virginia Cavalry in May 1861. Promoted to corporal in 1864, he was paroled at Burkesville Junction in April 1865. He returned to farming.

45. George R. Briggs, a student at the University of Virginia and prewar teacher, enlisted as a private in Company G of the 1st Virginia Cavalry in May 1861. Wounded at Shepherdstown, he returned to duty and was promoted to fourth corporal in May 1864. He was paroled at Burkesville Junction in April 1865. After the war, he taught school, and later practiced law in Georgia.

46. Adrian "Bullett" Fowlkes, former Hampden-Sydney student and prewar farmer, enlisted as a private in Company G of the 1st Virginia Cavalry in May 1861. Detached as

have often thought if there were men in the world who could sit under a galling fire and say it was delightful excitement as Stonewall Jackson said to Gen. Dick Taylor[47] at Port Republic,[48] Ad. Fowlkes was one of them. Once, when sitting by a camp fire, no one else being present, I said to him, "Bullet, don't you ever feel scared in a fight?" "I would be a d_____d fool if I didn't," was his laconic reply. In this fight, he, with some ten or twelve others, being in a position some little distance from me, had ranged themselves along the embankment of a deep cut in the road, and as the enemy were coming through kept up a merciless fire on them a few feet away, down in the bed of the road. Recently, speaking of this, Bullet said, "We shot them at so close range that we could see the bullets hit them. As the enemy passed this point, other of us, being ranged along and further up the road, had our turn at them, firing at them as they charged by, we being on the edge of a body of woods skirting the road and like the party on the embankment only a few feet distant from the road on which the enemy's mounted men were charging. Gen. Stuart was in person directing the fight, and being in the very midst of them, would say to the men, 'Shoot this one! Shoot that one,' as he pointed them out. It was near this place that he received his mortal wound. As he was being carried off on his horse, a soldier supporting him on either side, Gen. Fitz Lee galloped up, but had to go away in a few moments to the front to command the troops. As he left Gen. Stuart shouted out, in a strong, ringing voice, 'Go ahead, Fitz, old fellow, I know you will do what is right.'"[49] It was J. E. B. Stuart's last command on a battle field. Captain Dorsey[50] of our regiment, in writing of this to Major McClellan, says: "Immediately on the Telegraph road, about eighty men had collected and among these the general threw himself and by his personal example held them steady while the enemy charged entirely past their

---

a courier for General Stuart in September 1861, he served with the 1st Virginia Cavalry through the end of the war, receiving promotion to corporal during that time. Paroled at Farmville in April 1865, he returned to farming after the war.

47. Jackson spoke to then Brigadier General Richard Taylor.

48. The Battle of Port Republic was fought in the Shenandoah Valley on June 9, 1862, at the culmination of Jackson's famous Valley Campaign.

49. The text of Vaughan's article contains no quotation marks denoting the end of Fowlkes's quote. This point in the text appears to be a reasonable location.

50. Gustavus Warfield "Gus" Dorsey enlisted as a private in Company K of the 1st Virginia Cavalry in May 1861. Wounded five times in five separate battles, Dorsey also rose steadily through the ranks, achieving the rank of major in June 1864. He transferred to the 1st Maryland Cavalry in August 1864, where he was promoted to lieutenant colonel in February 1865. He disbanded the 1st Maryland Cavalry at Salem, Virginia, in April 1865. He returned to his town of Brookville, Maryland, where he farmed after the war.

position. With these men he fired into their flank and rear as they passed him, in advancing and retiring, for they were met by a mounted charge of the 1st Virginia cavalry and driven back some distance, as they retired one man who had been dismounted in the charge and was running out on foot, turned as he passed the general and discharging his pistol inflicted the fatal wound."

In a recent letter describing the wounding of Stuart, Hill Carter says: "I remember distinctly that just before Gen. Stuart was wounded (which would result in his death) at the battle of Yellow Tavern, he was on horseback in the fight, shooting his pistol at the enemy and calling to his men to shoot different ones of the opposing forces, pointing to them and saying to us, 'Shoot that man. Shoot this fellow.' This will give you an idea of how close together and mixed up the opposing forces then were. I did not see Gen. Stuart at the instant he was shot, but hearing Norvell Harris who was standing near me (we were on foot) exclaim, 'Gen. Stuart is shot,' I looked to my left, in which direction Gen. Stuart was, and saw him wheeling his horse around and start towards the rear. He sat so straight and so firmly on his horse that I doubted whether he had been shot, though I saw him only a moment. A short while afterwards, after the charge of the enemy had been repulsed, I asked Harris what made him think Gen. Stuart had been shot. He replied that he 'saw the dust or lint fly from his coat where the bullet struck him.' This made an impression on me, because I was not then familiar with the fact (not having been long in the army) that such an appearance of dust, or lint, often accompanied a bullet wound, though I afterwards noticed it frequently.

"I also remember that Harris got a silver watch and pistol from an officer of the enemy who was killed in this fight, and that he gave the pistol to me, I having lost my pistol by it escaping from the holster, which was unbuttoned."[51]

Late in the afternoon of the fight Captain Southall took us dismounted men back from the scene of action in good order, deployed as skirmishers, and then to the led horses. It was getting very dark on account of a black cloud overhanging, which soon burst in a deluge of rain, accompanied by lurid lightning and deafening peals of thunder, which seemed to be making sport of earth's artillery. This thunder storm, perhaps, saved our command from the enemy's artillery. As we were crossing the Chickahominy flats going to the bridge over that river, and but for the storm they would have probably given us the benefit of shot and shell as we retired.

About this time I was sent off on some duty and in going soon lost my

---

51. Again, the text does not provide quotation marks identifying the end of Hill Carter's letter. This appears to be the correct location.

way. I had put my gum cloth over my shoulders, thanks be to our friends, the enemy, for my having it. The darkness was getting intense, there being no light to see anything save the frequent and vivid flashes in lightning. In this dilemma I rode along the road hoping to come up with some of our command. Getting into another road, I heard the rumbling of artillery wheels and by the flashes of lightning could see a battery of several guns in motion ahead of me. Getting closer and riding up to an along side of the guns, I could see by the lighting that the appearance of everything was that of that enemy, and the accent of the drivers as they urged their horses on was not pleasant to my ears. I thought Point Lookout[52] would soon have me. No one, however, noticed me, and the first good opportunity that presented itself I turned off in the woods and let the artillery pass, without making any inquiries concerning their destination. Whether or not I had been with friends or foes I do not know to this day, for as soon as I thought it safe, I took another direction, and wandering about, I knew not whither, late in the night came in sight of camp fires. Thinking these were camp fires of the enemy's cavalry, I hesitated about going forward, but not knowing what else to do, made the venture, and soon found that they were those of Wickham's brigade. I was soon with my company, and the next morning when the command came out of that bivouack it was as wearied and worn out a set of men and horses as were ever beheld. Much work was still before us, for even on this day (May 12th) we had a skirmish with the enemy in which Col. Randolph,[53] of the 4th Virginia, was killed, and little Fitz, as his command was wont to call him, was not the leader to give much rest, as the subsequent history of this campaign will show.

Our cavalry had lost many valuable men in these battles and some of its most gallant officers had fallen; Col. H. Clay Pate,[54] of the 5th Virginia, at Yellow Tavern; Col. Randolph, of the 4th Virginia,; Gen. Gordon,[55] of the

52. Point Lookout was a prison camp in Maryland.

53. Law student Robert Lee Randolph enlisted as a 1st lieutenant and rose to the rank of lieutenant colonel before his death.

54. Henry Clay Pate, lawyer and newspaper publisher, enlisted at Petersburg in June 1861 as the head of a cavalry regiment nicknamed Pate's Rangers. Elected lieutenant colonel of the 5th Virginia Cavalry in June 1862, he was promoted to colonel in February 1864. He fought in a number of battles in the East, and was killed in action at Yellow Tavern.

55. "General Gordon" refers to James Byron Gordon, a North Carolina farmer, merchant, and politician before the war. Enlisting as a private in 1861, he rose quickly to colonel, then general, in 1863. He commanded the North Carolina brigade which fought under General Stuart. He was mortally wounded in the fight at Meadow Bridge (which occurred the day after the Battle of Yellow Tavern).

North Carolina brigade, and others of less rank. When the announcement of Stuart's death was made, great gloom immediately overshadowed the whole command, as if some great personal sorrow had come to each man. In the eloquent words of Major John Esten Cooke,[56] in his life of Gen. R. E. Lee, I will tell you of the esteem in which Gen. Stuart was held by our great commander, the ideal man whose birthday we have so recently celebrated. Major Cooke says: "Near Yellow Tavern, in a stubborn engagement, in which Stuart strove to supply his want of troops by the fury of his attack, the great chief of cavalry was mortally wounded and expired soon afterward. His fall was a grievous blow to Gen. Lee's heart as well as the southern cause.

"Endowed by nature with courage which shrank from nothing, active and immense physical stamina, which enabled him to endure any amount of fatigue, devoted heart and soul to the cause in which he fought, and looking up to the commander of the army with child-like love and admiration, Stuart could be ill spared at this critical moment, and Gen. Lee was plunged into the deepest melancholy at the intelligence of his death. When it reached him he retired from those around him, and remained for some time communing with his own heart and memory. When one of his staff entered and spoke of Stuart, Gen. Lee said in a low voice, 'I can scarcely think of him without weeping.'"[57]

A few words more comrades, and I am done. Not long since I heard one of my old comrades say that he could not bear to think of the war, and wished he could blot out from his mind all memory of it. I felt sorry, for he was a good soldier, and a man of education and intelligence, and bears on his body a scar received in battle. Perhaps others, being bruised and stung by the slings and arrows of outrageous fortune, may indulge like feelings. Comrades, let us keep our camp fires burning brightly to cheer and comfort these. The proudest recollection of my quiet and uneventful life, that to which memory clings with the greatest tenacity, is of the part I took, humble and unconspicuous as it was, in that incomparable army, the Army of Northern Virginia, whose glorious achievements won the admirations of the world.

56. John Esten Cooke, a lawyer, enlisted as a sergeant in the Richmond Howitzers in April 1861. He joined General Stuart's staff in 1862 and served with him until his death. After the war, he wrote biographies of Stuart, Jackson, and Lee.

57. Once again, the text does not provide quotation marks identifying the end of Major Cooke's remark. This is the correct location.

"Confederate Cavalry at Spotsylvania,"
by George J. Hundley

[George Jefferson Hundley was born in Amelia County, Virginia, in 1838. Before the Civil War, he attended Hampden-Sydney College and studied law under Judge John W. Brockenbrough in Lexington. After serving in the cavalry during the war years, he resumed his law practice, eventually becoming a partner and political ally of James A. Walker. Hundley prepared several war accounts for Bernard for inclusion in "War Talks, Volume II." The following letter describes Hundley's experiences with the cavalry at Spotsylvania. Bernard intended to attach it as an addendum to B. B. Vaughan's account.[58]]

Amelia C.H., Va.,
April 29, 1895

Geo. S. Bernard Esq., Petersburg, Va.
My Dear Sir:

In compliance with your request I here add some of my recollections of the great fight of our cavalry against Federal Infantry at Todd's Tavern, or Spotsylvania C.H. in May 1864, to those which have been so well told by our friend B. B. Vaughan.

For three days in that vicinity Fitzhugh Lee's Cavalry division stubbornly resisted the efforts of Grant to seize that important position and thus turn Genl. Lee's right and take him in rear, as the latter's army advanced from the Rapidan to dispute with him the road to Richmond. To say that our ranks were decimated would not half express the truth. More than half our numbers were placed *hors de combat* in those three terrible days. Our small division, armed with carbines and partially with pistols, dismounted, contested every inch of ground with Warren's corps of infantry, splendidly armed and equipped, and no one at a distance listening to the steady roll of musketry would have known but that a heavy infantry engagement was in progress. In fact, on Sunday our advancing infantry hearing the rolling fire refused to be-

---

58. Hundley's article is in the Bernard Collection at the Historical Society of Western Virginia. Hundley prepared an extended account of his experiences at First Bull Run and during the Appomattox Campaign which appeared in a Richmond newspaper (see the *Richmond Times* for January 26 and February 2, 1896) and in the *SHSP* (33:294). Given its wide availability, it has not been included in this book. Hundley's biographical information is based on word portraits in the Bernard Collection, Historical Society of Western Virginia, and the Bernard Papers, Southern Historical Collection, University of North Carolina.

lieve that it was cavalry fighting infantry, and were not convinced until we had the honor of introducing them to the enemy as they deployed right and left behind our line of battle, and gave us a breathing spell.

The late Capt Wm. A. Moss[59] of the Buckingham troop, 4th Cavalry, gave me the following amusing illustration of the incredulity of the infantry.

> Our wagon trains and disabled men and horses were back at an old church, a couple of miles in rear on the road by which our army was advancing and Rev. William Meredith, an Episcopal minister and chaplain of the 4th Cavalry was there with them. As the head of the infantry column passed, one of the men, addressing Mr. Meredith[60] said, "Who is that fighting in front of us?" "It is Fitzhugh Lee's Cavalry," replied Mr. Meredith. "Oh, that ain't so, you don't know what you are talking about, young fellow." But said Mr. Meredith, "I belong to the cavalry myself and I do know what I am talking about. I tell you that is Fitzhugh Lee's Cavalry fighting Yankee infantry and they have been fighting them for three days that way." "Now, I know you are lying," said the infantryman — "no cavalry ever fought that way;" and having discomfited the modest preacher completely, away went the infantryman with a ringing laugh, which ran all down the line.

That Sunday morning, with scarcely any breakfast, our tired boys left their bivouac by break of day to renew the obstinate fight. Wickham took the lead and our small brigade (Payne's) was drawn up mounted, as a support just behind him. Wickham's men were dismounted and formed line along a fence on the edge of the woods, pulling down the fence and piling the rails in front for protection, there then lay down and maintained for hours one of the hottest contests of the war. Not one inch did they give, but steadily kept to their work, the only moving figures to be seen through the smoke being the ambulance corps bearing off to the rear the dead and wounded. We ourselves had been in the hottest of it the two previous days, and that morning as we sat there prepared to charge on the enemy and help our friends to get to their horses, if they were too hard pressed, when the inevitable time came to fall back, our line was not half as long as when two days before we first camped in the "Wilderness" and sunk to sleep by the lullaby of the whippoorwill's song (there seemed to be thousands of these birds in those sombre woods).

About mid-day, Wickham began deliberately to withdraw his men, for the

---

59. Captain William A. Moss had enlisted as a private on March 10, 1862.

60. The Reverend William Meredith had enlisted as a private on April 27, 1862, and was promoted to chaplain on August 14, 1862.

enemy were closing in on our flanks. We waited for Wickham to pass and regain his horses, and just as the enemy threw forward a heavy line of skirmishers in our front, we filed to the left under a rattling fire and followed Wickham. Fitz Lee came hurriedly along and ordered us to move more quickly. So
we all moved off at a slow trot to Spotsylvania C.H. and we well know that
when Fitz Lee moved to the rear at a trot things were getting desperate. Gallant old Fitz had done all that a mortal could do. He had fought his command
to a frazzle, but he had saved our army the mortification and danger of having
Grant launch his mighty army in its rear and between it and Richmond. He
had fought and worried and puzzled Grant and kept him entangled in that
wilderness until his illustrious uncle could bring his infantry to bear and say
"check" to Grant in his first move. And now the situation was becoming desperate for us. I think they had almost surrounded us, but we trotted out and
dismounted again in the village, and were just preparing for a last desperate
struggle, when help came, just in the nick of time. If it had been planned for
the purpose it could not have turned out more opportunely. We had about
done all that men could do, and then were preparing "to set our teeth and
die hard," I do not think we could have maintained ourselves an hour longer. We should have been swallowed up, for Grant's whole army were coming upon us. Being near the broad Gordonsville road, I heard a sort of stifled
shout which rose and suddenly subsided. Looking with anxious eyes in that
direction, my heart almost leaped out of my breast. It was the gladdest sight
that ever met my gaze. There was Stuart riding slowly along, his heavy black
plume floating back in the breeze. The hand was raised in deprecation of that
rising cheer and with the other he pointed back behind him. These poor
tired, hungry veterans of his understood the silent pantomime and stifled the
shout. They had heard that Stuart had gone back to hurry up the infantry
and, sure enough, there they were tramping behind him. Everything then
become silent as the grave. Nothing could be heard save that steady tramp,
tramp of Longstreet's legions as they came up and defiled right and left into
line of battle behind us. I noticed on their faces, that grim, stern, expression,
mingled with awe inspired by approaching battle, which always marked the
appearance of veterans going into action. They seemed inspired with a new
feeling of admiration for the cavalry and we exchanged mutual promises to
stand by each other as they passed us, we remaining for a while in line behind
them. It was not long now before that hitherto silent infantry spoke with ten
thousand tongues of fire to the confident, advancing enemy and then the long
pent up joy of the cavalry boys found vent in one long continued cheer. Will
any of Fitzhugh Lee's division ever forget those three days of dreadful fighting
and that welcome reinforcement? If it had not been for that pitting of cavalry

against infantry, though, Yellow Tavern would have told a different story a few days later and perhaps our great chieftain, Stuart would have lived. Well now I have fulfilled my promise and I hope these random recollections will not bore your readers.

Your Friend

Geo Hundley

George S. Bernard War Diary: March 24, 1864–June 13, 1864[61]

On Picket Rapidan RR Bridge

Thursday March 24, 1864

I will no longer postpone commencing this little diary. If I have been wait-ing for something unusual to occur I am now without such an excuse. Ac-cording to all accounts our regiment is doing the most trying tour of picket duty as ever fallen to its lot, an account of which would not be out of place here. On Monday morning at 7 o'clock precisely we left our camp near Madi-son Run Station[62] and without halting one minute marched to this place a distance of 11 miles arriving here at 11 o'clock, a march which was very fatigu-ing although our band accompanied us as far as Orange CH & considerably refreshed us by its enlivening music as we passed different places & [*illegible*] ing at the bridge, our company was one of those sent forward as the outposts and as good luck had it the half of the company in which I happened to be was assigned a very good position, just at the ford, & was charged with the duty of preventing persons from [*five illegible words*]. My "partner" Char-ley Mead,[63] being one of the ambulance corps, being separated from me, I accepted Jim Nash's[64] offer to share his Yankee tent with me which I imme-diately pitched thinking now we would have a comparatively nice time. But not so as it turned out, the weather becoming very cold. That night (Monday night) I managed to sleep some little but not comfortably, and I think the

61. Bernard's entries here are taken from war "Diary No. 4" in the Bernard Papers, UVA.

62. Madison Run Station was a spot along the Orange & Alexandria Railroad about five miles south of Orange, Virginia (see *Atlas to Accompany the Official Records of the Union and Confederate Armies* [Washington, D.C.: Government Printing Office, 1891–95], Plate XLV, 1).

63. Though several Meades served in Bernard's regiment, it is unclear who "Charley Meade" was.

64. Jim Nash is discussed in note 12, chapter 4.

most pleasant part of it was when Emmet Butts[65] & myself were on post from 12 o'clock till 2 o'clock, when seated around a blazing fire we chatted away the two hours most pleasantly.

Tuesday March 29th I was interrupted by an order to get ready to march, the relief unit 16th Va. Reg't, having arrived to take the place of our regiment. At first I supposed the sudden rolling up of blankets, putting on accoutrements &c meant something less pleasant. Ben Hatcher[66] of our company moving up stairs into the room in which many of the company were quartered and saying "Boys, there is fighting across the river—Don't you hear the firing? Musketry?" But I must return to the point at which I left off. Tuesday about midday it set in to snowing, and at dark four inches of snow on the ground, and the snow still rapidly falling made the prospect of the night anything but agreeable. At this time few were around our fire, the rest being snugly sleeping under piles of blankets & under the protection of our miserable little shanties or have gone off to neighboring houses to seek shelter. The prospect of leaving the fire to go any-where through the snow being very disagreeable & knowing that I would have to be up sometimes at least during the night, I concluded to "stick it out" where I was, at least for the time being, and if I could not do better when I got very sleepy to trying the experiment of sleeping under a covering of snow. After I had experienced a trying time of it around our badly built fire, my eyes suffering no little from the smoke, some of the boys made their appearances from the houses. It was now between 10 & 11 o'clock. I concluded now to try the experiment of sleeping in the snow in preference to going to the places from which the boys just arrived had come. So, taking two wide planks, I laid them down on the snow, into which they sank pretty quickly & laying down an oil cloth & my overcast, I got one of the boys to spread three blankets above me. Suffice it to say I did not leave my novel couch until daybreak & got through the night better than anticipated. Had I not been a little unwell & my feet wet, I believe I would have slept elegantly. It did not snow much after I got to bed and the sun shone brightly the next morning. Before 10 o'clock this morning our company was relieved by Co. F and we were all glad to get back to even the dirty houses in which we found the reserves quartered. The room into which most of our company went almost beggars description. It is the garret room of an old

65. Robert Emmet Butts is discussed in note 44, chapter 1.

66. In referring to "Ben Hatcher," Bernard most likely means Robert "Bones" Hatcher (because Benjamin Hatcher had been killed at Crampton's Gap), who had enlisted as a private in Company E of the 12th Virginia in March 1862.

country store. In it there was no fireplace but there was what went for a stove, as it no doubt was in former days. This [*illegible word*] was entirely open on top and without the important appendage of a stove pipe. The room at times was often filled with a dense & almost suffocating smoke. The floor of this room was less in [*illegible word*] than the atmosphere—as filthy a place as one ever looked at. Leaving my things here I sought comfort elsewhere, but as it turned out, everything considered, I concluded I better avail myself of an offer of a member of my company to share with me two heavy U. S. blankets, which with mine, my overcoat & oil cloth I know must contribute much to making me have a comfortable night. So making up my mind to the smoke and to chances of the building catching fire from the sparks that continually fell among the exposed rafters above (which I confess I very much feared) and determining to brave another danger, "The Confederates,"[67] I retired quite early, not however until after being much entertained by an account of his escaping, wandering, & on the evening of & day succeeding the battle of Crampton's Gap given me by one of my old comrades in Co. I, Sandy Harrison.[68] As good luck had it the smoke was not so bad as I had anticipated, the men in the house soon got quiet and I slept the night out as well as I ever did in my life.

Getting in motion Thursday morning between 12 & 1 o'clock, we were back in our old quarters before sunset & I for one at least very much fatigued.

Camp near Mad. Run Station

Friday Apr. 27

Our old company, originally the "Petersburg Riflemen," now known as Co. E, 12th Va. Reg't entered upon its fourth year of active service on Wednesday the 20th inst. Of the 65 men who reached Norfolk on the memorable night of Saturday April 20, 1861 but ten are now present with the company. These men are 1st Lt. John R. Patterson,[69] Serg't William W. Tayleur,[70] Leroy S. Edwards,[71] Serg't Marcellus W. Harrison,[72] Privates G. S. Bernard, Thaddeus

---

67. By "the Confederates," Bernard means lice.

68. Alexander W. "Sandy" Harrison enlisted as a private in Company I in February 1862 and was a member of the 12th Virginia Infantry's color guard. Wounded in action in 1864, he survived the war.

69. John R. Patterson is discussed in note 7, chapter 1.

70. William W. Tayleur is discussed in note 9, chapter 3.

71. Leroy Summerfield Edwards is discussed in note 52, chapter 4.

72. Marcellus W. Harrison, a clerk for a Petersburg clothier, enlisted in Company E as a private in April 1861. Captured at Chancellorsville, he was paroled and then promoted to sergeant. He was killed at the Crater.

Branch,[73] Jas. T. Keen,[74] Jos. B. Pollard,[75] Putnam Stith,[76] & R. H. May.[77] The following table will show at a glance what has become of the remaining fifty-five.

Killed in battle	6
Died by disease	2
Discharged acct of health	5
Put in Substitutes	6
Deserted	3
Now hold Commissions in C.S. Army	10
" " offices of a civil character	4
Now in other branches of service (Cav, Art, Navy)	4
Discharged on acct of health & now a conscript	1
Discharged as foreignors	3
brt forward	44
Detailed in departments	8
Absent wounded	2
" sick	1
Present with company	10
Went to Norfolk with company Apr. 20, 1861	65

Of these sixty-five besides the six killed as shown in the above table, there have been over 12 wounded & five prisoners. From Apr. 20, 1861 to the present time there have been one hundred and seventy-three members of the company of whom there are now present with the company only thirty-eight including two who are absent on furloughs of indulgence. Of these 173, seven (7) have been killed in battle, twenty six (26) have been wounded, and fifteen (15) have been prisoners. Up to the present time the company has been in

73. Thaddeus Branch, a schoolteacher in Petersburg, enlisted as a private in Company E in April 1861. Wounded at Second Manassas, he spent seven months in hospitals before returning to his unit. Promoted to corporal in 1864, he was paroled at Appomattox.

74. James T. Keen, a clerk to a clothing retailer, enlisted as a private in Company E in April 1861. Wounded at Seven Pines, he returned to his unit only to be jailed for a month in 1864 (charges unspecified). Sick for seven months in 1864, he returned to duty in time to be captured at Burgess Mill. He took the oath of loyalty at Point Lookout Prison in February 1865, and reportedly "moved north."

75. Joseph B. Pollard is discussed in note 61, chapter 4.

76. Putnam Stith Jr. is discussed in note 60, chapter 4.

77. Richard Henry May, son of a Petersburg physician, enlisted as a private in Company E in April 1861. He served in the 12th Virginia until paroled at Appomattox. After the war, he entered the field of education, where he eventually became superintendent of Lunenburg County schools.

thirteen different engagements in which the regiment participated and in one in which the regiment did not participate.

> Picket Post near Rapidan
> R.R. Bridge Sunday May 1 '64

Reg't now on picket & will be relieved tomorrow. Everything in this section profoundly quiet. Nothing to be seen of the Yankees except at night when a camp fire or two may be seen upon a mountain side about two miles distant. Yesterday's papers bring us some good news from the Yankees. Gold had again gone up to *184*.

Read today books of Ruth, Daniel & Jonah & looked over Joshua & Judges.

> Wednesday morning
> On the road near
> Gen. Mahone's Headquarters
> Wednesday May 4, '64

Brigade received orders last night to prepare to move by 7–1/2 o'clock this morning. Line formed at this time but we have not yet started. Expecting however to move every minute. I hear our orders are to report to Gen. Anderson whose headquarters are about two miles beyond Orange CH. No doubt we are merely moving to the front that we may be more conveniently put in position when the enemy advance. On Monday we had rumors that Burnside[78] had crossed the Rappahannock at Kelly's Ford. News yesterday of fall of Washington, N.C.[79]

> Bivouack near [Percell's] house
> May 5, 1864

Got in motion yesterday morning about 9 o'clock & marching slowly & resting often we reached this place about 5–1/2 o'clock in the afternoon— distance marched about 10 miles—heard at the CH that the enemy had crossed the Rapidan at Germanna Ford. Papers of yesterday bring good news from Yankeedom. Pennsylvania troops refuse to be held in service beyond their time—Grant endeavors to have Fremont[80] & McClellan[81] reinstated for moral effect on his army & the government at Washington refuse his ap-

78. Major General Ambrose Burnside, commander of the Federal Ninth Corps.

79. On April 30, 1864, Confederate forces under Major General Robert F. Hoke captured Washington, North Carolina, only hours after Union troops fled the town.

80. Major General John C. Frémont was on active duty at the time, resigned his commission June 4, 1864, and was for a short time a candidate for president in 1864 (see Warner, *Generals in Blue*, 161).

81. Major General George B. McClellan ran for president as the candidate of the Democratic Party in 1864.

plication.[82] Everything quiet this morning but we would not be surprised to receive orders to move at any moment. Received letters from my sister & Miss Sue Haskins[83] last evening.

Battlefield near Wilderness

Saturday afternoon May 7, 64[84]

Have at last summoned resolution to enter a few items. Reached the battlefield about half past eight o'clock yesterday morning & went immediately into line of battle, our division being turned over to Gen. Longstreet. About 10–1/2 o'clock our brigade went into action on the enemy's left flank and Lt. Patterson was told by Dr. Pryor this morning that Gen. Longstreet told him that the brigade behaved very well & the 12th Reg't most gallantly. We drove the enemy beautifully for a half a mile or more through the woods killing & wounding many of them.

[On the morning of May 6, Lee and Longstreet scraped together an assault force of four brigades, led by Lt. Col. Moxley Sorrel of Longstreet's staff. Part of this column moved undetected along the bed of an unfinished railroad and reached the exposed flank of the Union Second Corps. The attack that followed smashed the Union line and sent the Second Corps reeling back to the Brock Road.[85]]

The casualties in the 12th were five killed Wm. F. Pucci,[86] Co. A, D. McCracken[87] Co. B, Jno. Mingea[88] Co. B, W. A. Jelks[89] Co. B, and R. B.

82. The rumor Bernard notes about the reinstatement of Frémont and McClellan was unfounded.

83. "Miss Sue Haskins" may refer to Susan E. Haskins of Brunswick County, who would have been around twenty-six at the time.

84. Bernard published this entry in the *Petersburg Daily Index-Appeal* of August 20, 1881 (see clipping in the Bernard Papers, Duke University).

85. In an article titled "The Battle of the Wilderness," in Bernard's *War Talks of Confederate Veterans,* John R. Turner detailed the role played by the 12th Virginia in this fight.

86. William F. Pucci, son of a master cabinetmaker in Petersburg, enlisted as a private in Company A in April 1861.

87. David McCracken, a Petersburg baker, enlisted in Company B in April 1861. Though AWOL for a month in 1863, he returned to his unit, only to be killed in action at the Wilderness.

88. John F. Mingea of Petersburg enlisted as a private in Company B in May 1861. Promoted to corporal in 1862, he was reduced to private in 1863. He was killed in action at the Wilderness.

89. William A. Jelks enlisted as a private in Company B in April 1861. Hospitalized in Charlottesville for most of 1862, he returned to his unit and was promoted to corporal in November 1863. He was killed in action at the Wilderness.

Barnes[90] Co. F and forty seven wounded, two of whom are thought mortally wounded, Ben White[91] Co. C & Wm. Delbridge,[92] Co I. Among the wounded are Capt. Stephen White,[93] Co. C, Serg't Geo Morrison[94] Co. A, and private Jno. Lee[95] of Co E. There were unfortunately three cases of accidental wounding in the reg't. What were the casualties in the other reg'ts of the brigade I have not heard. Among those in the brigade however I hear of Capt. R. Taylor[96] of Gen. Mahone's staff & one of the General's couriers Bernard[97] being wounded & also Lt. Col. Minetree[98] of the 41st. A most

90. Robert B. Barnes enlisted as a private in Company F in June 1861. He was killed at the Wilderness.

91. Benjamin B. White, a clerk in Petersburg before the war, enlisted as a corporal in Company C in April 1861. Sick for half of 1862, he returned to his unit in 1863, and was promoted to 1st sergeant in August 1863. He died from wounds received at the Wilderness.

92. William A. Delbridge enlisted as a private in Company I in February 1862. Sick for four months with rheumatism, he returned to his unit in 1863. He was killed at the Wilderness.

93. Steven Gill White, a Virginia Military Institute graduate and clerk for a wholesale grocer in Petersburg, enlisted as a 2nd lieutenant in Company C in April 1861. He rose steadily through the ranks to captain and began commanding Company C in July 1863. He survived his wounding at the Wilderness, returning to his unit after five months at Poplar Lawn hospital. Paroled at Appomattox, he lived well into the twentieth century, residing in Dinwiddie County.

94. George J. Morrison, a dry goods clerk, enlisted as a private in Company A in June 1861. Promoted to sergeant in May 1862, he survived his wounding at the Wilderness. After three months in a hospital, he returned to Weisiger's brigade and was put on light duty in the Quartermaster's Department. Paroled at Appomattox, he re-entered the dry goods business, eventually owning his own company, which employed another 12th Virginia veteran, James E. Whitehorne.

95. John H. Lee, a Petersburg bookkeeper, enlisted as a private in Company E in March 1862. He died from the wounds he received at the Wilderness.

96. Richard C. Taylor, prewar teacher and railroad auditor, enlisted as a captain in Company H of the 6th Virginia in April 1861. He subsequently served in the artillery, on Mahone's staff, as a judge advocate, and as commander of the post at Chaffin's Bluff. Twice wounded, he survived the war and returned to teaching. He was one of four brothers who served as staff officers during the war.

97. The Bernard referred to here was courier Thomas S. Bernard, who had enlisted as a third corporal in the 16th Virginia in April 1861.

98. Joseph Powhatan Minetree, a Virginia Military Institute graduate, was commissioned as a 1st lieutenant in July 1861 and made adjutant of the 41st Virginia. He rose quickly through the ranks, reaching the rank of lieutenant colonel within a year. Wounded at Malvern Hill and the Wilderness, he recovered enough each time to return to his unit. He assumed command of the 41st Virginia in February 1865, and surrendered at Appomattox. After the war, he was a purchasing agent for the Southern Railway.

unfortunate affair occurred just as the 12th was returning from the advanced position to which they had charged the enemy. They were fired into by the 41st & I hear also a part of the 61st Reg't who took us to be the enemy. This fire wounded & perhaps killed some of our men, but what is more unfortunate, it wounded also Gen. Longstreet & killed Gen. Jenkins[99] who were riding along the plank road just at this time. Our division & Heth's are now in line of battle in reserve. From what I can gather we gained not much by the fight of Thursday except 4 pieces of artillery & I hear 3000 prisoners. We lost heavily in wounded judging from the large number we met on the road yesterday morning. In the fight of yesterday we had greatly the advantage, driving the enemy perhaps a half mile & killing large numbers of them. Yesterday afternoon they went to building breastworks. This morning they made two or three attempts to dislodge the line of battle just in our immediate front (Wilcox's old brigade) but failed. They may attempt the same thing this afternoon. Now whilst I write the skirmishers are at work though not exactly in the same place. We hear that Ewell has been doing good work on our left, captured with one brigade (Gordon's) last night 2 Brigadier Generals & 500 men, and repulsed yesterday an attack on one part of his line by five separate lines of battle, moving one behind the other, in which attack it is said he killed a large number. It is now reported that he has possession of the road heading to Germanna Ford. Many thought Grant would recross the river last night, and it was remarked this morning by a member of Gen. Hill's staff that anybody else but Grant would have done so. There has been but little artillery used in the fight thus far on account of the nature of ground, a densely wooded field, much of which is swampy. Among the incidents of the fight I must mention the conspicuous gallantry of a member of our company, Jim Farley,[100] now of the sharpshooters, who received two wounds, one in the shoulder & the other in the face but continued to charge on with the reg't, going with them to the most advanced position. The gal-

99. Micah Jenkins, a colonel from South Carolina at the start of the war, was promoted to brigadier general in July 1862. He served with the First Corps through the Tennessee Campaign and into the Battle of the Wilderness, where he was mortally wounded by the friendly fire that also wounded his commanding officer, James Longstreet.

100. There were two James Farleys in the 12th Virginia. Bernard most likely refers to James M. Farley, who enlisted as a sergeant in Company D in April 1861. Though temporarily reduced to private in December 1861, he was reappointed sergeant in December 1862. Promoted to 1st sergeant in February 1862, he was serving as one of Mahone's sharpshooters when wounded at the Wilderness. He survived the wounds and was on the final roll of the regiment.

lantry of Lt. Col. Sorrel[101] of Longstreet's staff was also very conspicuous. He led us into action on horseback, waving his hat & crying out "Come on Virginians." Gen. Wadsworth[102] of the Yankee army was found wounded—it is believed mortally—in that portion of the field over which the left of our brigade charged & is therefore supposed to have been wounded by our brigade. The brigades in the breastworks immediately in front of us have it is said several loaded guns to each man which they have picked up around them & captured today when they were charged upon by the enemy. These they keep at their sides. One of our company asked one of these men if they did not wish to be relieved. "Relieved h____l!" he replied "The fun is as good as at a camp meeting!"

The bodies of the five men of our reg't killed yesterday were this morning brought up to where we now are & buried. The Rev. J. C. Granberry[103] read the burial service over two of them, Wm. F Pucci & Jno Mingea. Why not over the other three I have not understood.

[More than twenty years after the war, Bernard had the fortune to meet with Longstreet while the Georgian visited William Mahone in Petersburg. The following is taken from Bernard's diary from the 1880s, located at the University of Virginia.]

Wednesday night
Jan'y 30, 1885

Gen. James Longstreet being in town, the guest of Gen. Mahone, a great many old Confederate soldiers have called to see him. Tonight Jno. T. Parham,[104] Dick Davis[105] & myself called. The old veteran has aged considerably since I last saw him, which I think was in June or July, 1863, during the Gettysburg campaign. He was then apparently in the full vigor of man hood, under

101. Lieutenant Colonel Gilbert Moxley Sorrel of Georgia served on Longstreet's staff and launched Mahone's brigade on the charge of May 6, 1864, during Longstreet's flank attack.

102. Brigadier General James Wadsworth did die from the wound he sustained at the Wilderness.

103. The Reverend John Cowper Granberry, a graduate of Randolph-Macon College, had enlisted in the 11th Virginia Infantry on July 4, 1861.

104. On John T. Parham, see chapter 3.

105. Richard Beale Davis, a student at Randolph-Macon College and the son of a teacher, enlisted as a private in Company E in April 1862. Wounded at Seven Pines and the Crater, Davis recovered enough to rejoin his unit. Paroled at Appomattox, he became a lawyer in Petersburg, and later a member of the Virginia House of Delegates.

forty five years of age. His big red beard I well remember. Now he is a feeble old man, verging upon three score and ten, with beard & hair white, and quite deaf.[106] I talked with him about the occasion of his being wounded in the Wilderness on the 6th of May, 1863 [1864]. The same party of Confederates who wounded him & killed Gen. Jenkins fired into the 12th Va. regiment as we were skirmishing from our advanced position across the plank road, that is in the north side of it, to the south side of it from which we had charged, we being supposed to be Federals as we came from this direction in which the enemy had just fled.

I understand that Gen. Longstreet has been very much gratified at the attention he has received from our old soldiers, all of whom, I believe, have been very much pleased at having an opportunity to show this attention. I sincerely hope that the new administration will provide for the old gentleman.

[Bernard's war diary continues here.]

Extreme right of line of battle
Sunday Morning May 8, '64

Last evening we had it reported that prisoners said that the enemy would carry our works today at all hazards. At dark our brigade & probably the whole division moved towards the right and passing along the line of battle saw large numbers of the enemy dead. Reaching what was then I suppose the extreme right after much annoyance in the way of being apparently unnecessarily called to attention & moving about along the line we finally got to sleep. I slept until after sunrise when we were marched still further to right to our present position which is at right angles to our general line of battle & is intended to meet a flanking movement of the enemy on this side. We at once set to work at throwing up breastworks which we have now (about 8 o'clock A.M.) completed. Everything apparently quiet along the lines.

3–1/2 o'clock P.M.

Sharpshooters of our brigade wounded & captured this morning a man who was evidentially a spy—his conduct very curious—remarked when captured that he "was innocent of any charge that might be brought against him," when no charge had been made. Said "he was looking for his chaplain"—had on a Yankee overcoat, Yankee cavalry jacket & grey pants & red sash. Yankee loss thus far supposed to be 30,000[107]—Gen. Ewell has buried 2000 killed

---

106. Longstreet may have looked feeble, but he lived on until January 2, 1904.

107. According to modern estimates, Union casualties at the Wilderness were approximately 18,000 (see Gordon C. Rhea, *The Battle of the Wilderness: May 5–6, 1864* [Baton Rouge: Louisiana State University Press, 1994]).

on the left. Gen. Early[108] now in command of Hill's Corps, Gen. Hill having fainted today. A yankee reg't started into our lines yesterday afternoon apparently for the purpose of surrendering & were fired into both by our men & the enemy & were nearly completely annihilated. A yankee started into our lines & being fired upon & wounded deliberately took out his knife & cut his throat—probably he thought we were fighting under the black flag. Since this morning the enemy have left our front & swung around to their right. Our army has made a corresponding move. Longstreet's corps (under Anderson) being on the extreme right at Spotsylvania C.H. it is said—Ewell on the centre & our corps under Early on the left. Our brigade was occupying, it is said, the extreme left.[109]

Monday Morning battle field of Bradshaw House[110]

Yesterday afternoon about 3–1/4 o'clock we were put in motion & moved through the woods by the right flank approximately in a South Easterly direction, Co. E being sent out in front deployed on both sides of the road to feel for the enemy. After moving about 3/4th of a mile we came upon a line of mounted skirmishers facing towards us but whom we soon ascertained to be our own men. Going now a quarter mile farther we were halted & rejoining the reg't we went now in another direction about East & had not gone a half a mile before we came to an open field. When our company & others of the reg't were deployed as skirmishers & getting into the field soon discovered a line of skirmishers on an opposite hill about 350 yds distant. These some recognized at once as the enemy but I was not sure they were as I could not see distinctly their uniforms and as we had before met with our own men confronting us in the same way. Another reason also which made me rather think they were our own men was our not firing upon them & their not firing upon us. As it was we advanced towards them going down the slope of the hill so fully in view that they might easily have shot us all down. But they leisurely put on their knapsacks &c & waited until we had crossed a little branch at the foot of the hill & ascended, possibly fifty yards, the slope upon which they were when they opened on us. Those of us on that portion of line could not fire at all as we could not see them without running the greatest risk with scarcely any chance of success as things then were. So we lay there under

108. Bernard refers to Major General Jubal Early.

109. In addition to the personnel changes described by Bernard, General Mahone was promoted to division command on May 7, and Colonel Weisiger was placed in charge of Mahone's Virginia brigade, which included the 12th Virginia (see *O.R.* 36: pt. 1, 967).

110. The Bradshaw house was about a mile west of Todd's Tavern.

a severe fire from them for several minutes. Three of our boys on our left, however, getting the shelter of some houses & giving them a very brisk fire. Just here I must mention the conspicuous gallantry of Oscar Mull[111] (Right General Guide) who was with those of us this night. The enemy now opened a sort of a flank fire on our left when we were ordered to retreat and oh! what a terrible time of it was now at hand! which I had been fearing for some time. The enemy's skirmishers came rushing after us, giving us a galling fire as we retreated as best we could up the hill. There were two houses (perhaps a stable & a crib) between the branch & the line of battle, for which most of us made, to get their protection as we retreated beyond them. As it happened, we reached them singly & how the balls did whiz through those old buildings! This retreat I can never forget. I thought every instant I would be shot down & in addition to this I was so exhausted I could scarcely move out of a walk. When I got near the top of the hill, at which was our line of battle, that is that of all the brigade except our reg't which appears to have been out as skirmishers. I fell in here just behind Co. G, 41st Va. Reg't and found two or three friends with them. I loaded my gun once or twice for Capt. Hunter[112] of this Reg't who was standing near me.

The Yankee line of battle advancing immediately after our skirmishers were driven in were fired into by our brigade & being broken by the fire was driven back. We could see them picking up their wounded afterwards.

We lost only two missing from Co. E, Serg't Leroy Edwards & pvt. Ello K. Daniel,[113] who I believe was last seen by myself at the ditch from which we retreated. It is most probable that they were wounded & captured. The loss

111. Oscar Oglesby Mull enlisted as a private in Company G in April 1861. Though declared AWOL in April 1862, no charges were preferred, because he had left to attend to the burial of his wife and child. Promoted to corporal and assigned to the color guard in May 1862, he then was hospitalized for almost a year with bronchitis. Reduced in rank to private, he returned to his unit only to be wounded at the Battle of Petersburg. He was captured in the unit's retreat to Appomattox. He resided in Richmond after the war. He kept a diary during the war, which is at the Virginia Historical Society.

112. William H. Hunter had enlisted as a private in the 16th Virginia Infantry in May 1861. He transferred to the 41st Virginia in August 1862, when he also received a commission as a 2nd lieutenant. Twice wounded, he was promoted to captain in July 1864. He was killed in action at Cumberland Church in April 1865.

113. Ello K. Daniel, a native of South Carolina, enlisted as a private in Company E in September 1862, transferring from Company F, 13th Virginia Cavalry. Captured at Bradshaw's Farm (Spotsylvania) in May 1864, he was imprisoned at Point Lookout and Elmira. Exchanged in October 1864, he returned to his unit and was paroled at Appomattox. Leroy Edwards is discussed in note 52, chapter 4.

in our reg't was 3 killed, Lt. Williams[114] Co. K, Serg't Mitchell[115] Co. K, and private Ned Hall[116] Co. C, 18 wounded & 2 missing.

[The combat at Bradshaw's farm described by Bernard in his "Monday Morning" (May 9) diary entry occurred as the armies lurched south out of the Wilderness toward the new battleground at Spotsylvania. At the behest of General Jubal Early, Mahone's division performed a reconnaissance in force on May 8 to determine if the Federals had occupied Todd's Tavern near the intersection of the Brock and Catharpin roads. As Mahone advanced, cavalry units under Wade Hampton discovered Union troops from Miles's brigade of the Second Corps planted in Mahone's path west of Todd's Tavern. As evening approached, Hampton and Mahone attacked the brigade. After some fierce fighting, the Union forces withdrew to Todd's Tavern.[117]

Long after the war, Sergeant Edwards's account of this battle elicited the following comments from Bernard,[118] which included a diagram with the noted positions marked by letters; for ease of reference, this information has been incorporated into the map of Bradshaw's Farm.]

Leroy says that five of the Petersburg Riflemen, advanced beyond the branch up the hill to and over the fence F.F. he recalls three of these five besides himself—Cha. M. Walsh,[119] Ello K. Daniel and Frank Robbins.[120] The fifth man

114. Joseph H. Williams of Petersburg enlisted as a private in Company K in May 1861. He rose through promotion, then election, to the rank of 2nd lieutenant by May 1863. Wounded at Spotsylvania, he spent five months in military hospitals before returning to his unit. He was at home convalescing when the war ended. After the war, he worked for a railroad.

115. Robert Garrett Mitchell, a Petersburg baker, enlisted as a private in Company K in May 1861. Promoted to corporal, then sergeant (November 1862), Mitchell was killed at Spotsylvania.

116. Edward W. Hall, a clerk in Petersburg, enlisted as a private in Company C in August 1861. Promoted to corporal in August 1863, he was killed at Bradshaw's Farm.

117. See Rhea, *Battles for Spotsylvania,* 78–80.

118. The following comments are from a note of April 3, 1891, contained in a letter from Leroy Summerfield Edwards to Bernard, dated March 25, 1891, in the George S. Bernard Papers, Southern Historical Collection.

119. Charles M. Walsh, a Petersburg stone cutter, enlisted as a private in Company E in April 1861. Promoted to corporal in October 1864, he was paroled at Appomattox. After the war, he returned to Petersburg, and served in the Virginia House of Delegates from 1877 to 1881.

120. Frank M. Robbins enlisted as a private in Company E in July 1861. Though sick for part of 1863, he returned to his unit and fought at the Battle of Weldon Railroad, where he was wounded. He survived the wound, and was paroled at Appomattox.

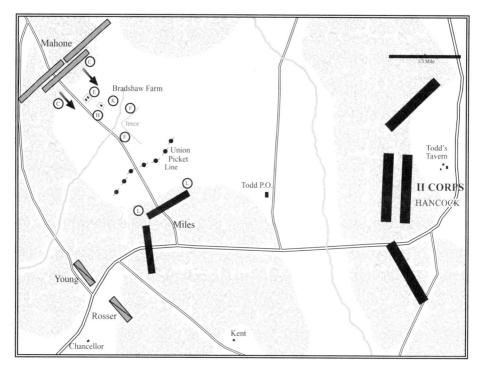

BRADSHAW'S FARM (SPOTSYLVANIA CAMPAIGN), MAY 8, 1864

he does not recall. I was at the fence F–F but did not go over it, but up the hill along-side of it, keeping in line with those who got over the fence, the fence at this point I think making an angle about as shown in the following diagram [see the map of Bradshaw's Farm].

Of those about the fence F–F *four* of us (certainly Daniel, Walsh, Edwards & myself) fell back to the branch. Whilst there (I was about the point H) I remember seeing men stationed about and behind the Bradshaw house, or guns holding around the house, firing at the enemy. In a few minutes it became apparent that the crisis with our little party had arrived. I saw that the enemy had gotten around towards K. Some one about those buildings orders a retreat. What route should we take? Each man determined the question for himself. I concluded that I would take my chance by running up the hill and accordingly struck out, making for the two buildings at E, some seventy five yards distant. Almost completely exhausted from the fatiguing duties of the previous three days, when I attempted to run, loaded down as I was, with gun, baggage & accoutrements, I found I could not move faster than in a slow trot. I could hear, or fancied I heard, the jeers of the enemy's skirmishers. About their bullets there was no question. Not only did I hear them whistling past me, but I could see them striking the ground near me and every instant I expected one to strike me in the back. I will remember how, when I reached the enclosure around the buildings at E and passed through a set of draw bars, these missiles angrily struck against fence rails or buildings.

When I got through the stable yard and put its buildings and fence between me and the enemy, I lessened my speed to a walk, and made my way towards the line of battle then at the fence C–C where the brigade stood, rather were kneeling, with their guns in readiness to fire, awaiting the return of the incoming skirmishers.

As soon as we got in, the men in the line of battle opened upon the Federal line of battle which had begun its advance across the plateau beyond the branch.

[Bernard's war diary continues here.]

> Line of battle near Spotsylvania
> Monday afternoon May 9.

Moved this morning from battlefield of yesterday afternoon to this position of extreme right of line of battle. March here most fatiguing—8 or 9 miles in length & very hot. Our army has, it appears, the advantage of position & a position in which artillery can be used. We have thrown up breastworks. The enemy may attack us tomorrow.

> Behind part of McIntosh's batt. Art. as support
> [Tuesday] about 4 P.M. May 10

Our brigade & Heth's division about 1 o'clock last night moved around to extreme left, it seems, to protect our wagons from attack. Our reg't detached from the brigade which with Heth's division crossed the River Po. About 12 o'clock we were ordered around to support the artillery, 2 pieces from McIntosh's battery, which fortunately perhaps for us [*illegible word*] yesterday & the day before. Last night's rest however has considerably refreshed us. Every thing seems profoundly quiet this morning. We have not heard yet that the [*illegible word*] has retreated. Thus far our army has gained a most brilliant victory. But Grant seems the most obstinate of men but he cannot confront us much longer. I hear that Gen. Lee says he has been attempting the most hazardous thing he ever heard of—i.e. any attempt to outflank a victorious army.

> Right of line battle around
> Spotsylvania CH May 14, '64

Have written none in this journal since Wednesday thinking it was lost—was rejoiced to find it a few minutes ago. Have been through perhaps the most terrible battle of the war since then, but must go back & relate things in their proper order. Wednesday morning soon after I finished my last entry, we fell back from our then position to better position in the woods & immediately went to throwing up breastworks. In the afternoon the enemy shelled these woods a little & there was some skirmishing to our front & we thought the enemy were advancing. Soon the skirmishers of the enemy were driven back & every thing was quiet for the remainder of the evening, during which however we had a rumor to the effect that Grant had laid down his pontoons at Falmouth & had crossed some cavalry & his wounded stragglers. We also heard of the capture of an order of Grant's published to his troops that Butler had fought a successful battle near Petersburg & was marching upon Richmond with but little resistance and that Sherman had whipped Johnston in the West.[121] Thursday morning at about 2 o'clock we were moved up (we had pitched our little tents on count of the rain) and ordered to be in readiness to march but everything was perfectly quiet until light when about the centre of the line we heard sharp musketry & artillery & immediately afterward we were ordered to march in that direction, when we started & double quicked most of the way to the centre of the line where we halted for a few minutes some two hundred yards in rear of the breastworks. Whilst here Gen. Lee rode up and was joined by Gen. Early, Gen. Mahone & Col. Weisiger who with their staff of officers & couriers formed a group of perhaps 20 or more men, when the enemy commenced shelling & one of their shells struck among the party, exploded & disabled the horses of two couriers. Soon the shelling ceased just here & our brigade was marched around to the extreme right of the lines where it remained for perhaps two & a half hours during most of which time it was raining, notwithstanding which the battle raged on the left & centre the whole time. About ten & a half o'clock (perhaps) we got orders to move & now marched back to very near the position we were in when the shell exploded so near Gen. Lee. We were here but a few moments before shelling at this point began. Gen. Lee again rode near us unattended save by one officer or courier & rode with a little piece of pines just in front in which seemed the focus of the fire from two different batteries of the enemy's. Very soon we were marched through these same pines & under this severe shelling & took position beyond them under shelter of some hills. A few minutes more & we were marched back to near the first position at which we were shelled and were now marched outside of the breastworks and forming with Lane's brigade a line of battle outside at right angles to the

121. Butler was advancing at the time, as was Major General William Tecumseh Sherman, the Federal commander in Georgia, against his Southern counterpart, General Joseph Eggleston Johnston.

breastworks marched down upon the flank of a line of battle. When attacking the breastworks the left of our line came within a few feet of the Yankee lines and there was actually hand to hand fighting. Those of us on the right of our reg't were not so near. Just as we got to the edge of the woods where the enemy were I caught a glimpse of hundreds of them skiddadling through the pines. The fire upon us here was very heavy, particularly from a battery apparently not more than 200 yds. distant. Our loss was very heavy. In our company we lost Dr. Disoway[122] killed, one of the best of men and a splendid soldier and Johnny Armistead[123] & Dick Harrison[124] wd, the latter losing his left arm & leg. The loss in the reg't was very heavy, 12 killed, 42 wd & 3 missing. Our color bearer, a most gallant soldier, Ben May[125] was wounded mortally it is believed. He was within ten feet of the man who shot him & was using his pistol. This flanking movement resulted in the capture of 1 stand of colors by our reg't,[126] 2 by the 41st reg't,[127] and at least 400 prisoners most of whom were taken by these two reg'ts.[128] It also resulted in relieving the centre of the line which was very much pressed at that time by the enemy. Retiring from this position our brigade was reformed near the CH and sent with Cook's brigade again in front of the breastworks to reconnoiter, during which we were until dark at times very near the enemy's lines of battle which retired before us, leaving their breastworks & were under a sharp fire from artillery & sharpshooters, during which we had Col. Feild[129] of our reg't wd

122. Israel F. Disoway, a Petersburg dentist, enlisted as a private in Company E in April 1862. Promoted to corporal in March 1864, he was killed in action at Spotsylvania.

123. John R. Armistead enlisted as a private in Company G in April 1861. He was sick for much of the war, in and out of Confederate and Union hospitals in 1862–63. Wounded at Spotsylvania, he returned to his unit in October 1864, where he was detailed to quartermaster duty in Mahone's division.

124. Richard S. Harrison had a brief military career. Conscripted as a private in Company E in March 1864, he died from his wounds in the summer of 1864.

125. Benjamin Harrison May is discussed in note 55, chapter 2.

126. A soldier of Bernard's regiment indisputably captured one of the flags (see *O.R.* 36: pt. 3, 802).

127. Col. William H. Stewart of the 61st Virginia was sure that his regiment had captured one of the flags (see William H. Stewart, *A Pair of Blankets: War-Time History in Letters to the Young People of the South* [New York: Broadway Publishing, 1914], 130).

128. First Lieutenant Charles R. Denoon of the 41st Virginia claimed three hundred of the prisoners for his regiment (Charles E. Denoon to Father and Mother, May 15, 1864, in Richard T. Couture, ed., *Charlie's Letters—The Civil War Correspondence of Charles E. Denoon,* 2nd ed. [Collingswood, N.J.: C. W. Historicals, 1989], 96).

129. Colonel Feild is discussed in note 34, chapter 4.

& Lt. Col. [Niemeyer][130] of the 61st killed. At dark we retired from this advanced position & marched around the extreme right of the line very much fatigued by the day's operations. At dark all fighting along the lines ceased. Yesterday we remained in quiet in our present position. The enemy seemingly indisposed to renew the attack. By Gen. Lee's orders bands came to the front & played along the lines.

[Early on the morning on May 12, a devastating Union assault overran a large bend in Lee's line known as the "Mule Shoe" and nearly split the Confederate army in two. Scraping together scattered units, Lee successfully halted the advance, but only after many hours of brutal fighting at a section of the line dubbed the "Bloody Angle." Sensing weaknesses elsewhere in Lee's defenses, on the afternoon of May 12, Grant ordered the Union Ninth Corps to hurl itself against the earthworks on the rebel right flank near Spotsylvania Court House at a spot known to the Confederates as "Heth's salient." To meet this threat, Lee ordered two brigades under Lane and Weisiger (which included the 12th Virginia) out of the defenses and into the flank of the attacking column. Bernard's diary entry recounts his role in this partially successful attack. Afterward, a controversy ensued about whether Weisiger's Virginians could rightfully take credit for the capture of prisoners and colors mentioned by Bernard in his diary entry. In Lane's view, Weisiger's men not only failed to support the attack but also mistakenly fired into his North Carolinians during the fight. The dispute pitted the irascible Mahone against Lane and Early, and continued to simmer well after the war.[131]]

Sunday morning May 15 '64

Everything pretty quiet yesterday excepting a little fighting in front of us done by Chambliss's cavalry yesterday morning & Wright's brigade yesterday afternoon. Wright's brigade was sent out to reconnoiter. The enemy have moved around towards our right. We today changed our lines on the right a little, running a new line at about right angles to the old one & in front of it. Our brigade has on its right Perry's brigade. We are well entrenched this morning. We were up at three to be in readiness to meet an attack. Our loss in prisoners on Thursday was very heavy being 2,500 from Johnson's division including Gen.'s Johnson & Steuart.[132] We also lost 15 pieces of artillery. The

---

130. Bernard misspelled Niemeyer as "Nehemiah."

131. See Rhea, *Battles for Spotsylvania,* 294–301; Matter, *If It Takes All Summer,* 233–43.

132. Major General Edward "Allegheny" Johnson and Brigadier General George H. "Maryland" Steuart.

enemy broke through our lines at the point held by this division & captured there 15 pieces of artillery before they could be put in position. All day Friday they were commanded by our sharpshooter guns & could not be carried off but on Friday night they were gotten off by the enemy.

Line of battle near Spotsylvania CH

Tuesday morning May 17, '64

Everything pretty quiet since last Sunday, except an occasional stray picket fire or a little artillery firing now & then on our left. Our army & that of the enemy occupy pretty much the same positions except the enemy seems to be moving around to their left & a portion of our troops it is said have made a similar move. Yesterday our brigade & those immediately on its right ran another line of breastworks between those we built Sunday and the original line, pulling down the former.

Sunday afternoon we had read to us an order from Gen. Lee announcing several victories by our troops, Smith's over Banks, Price's capture of Steele & 9000 men, Imboden's capture of Seigel's wagon train in the Valley of Virginia, Wm. E. Jones' defeat of Averill's cavalry, the failure of the Cavalry expeditions against Richmond, & their returning to the Peninsula and lastly on congratulating this army upon its successfully repelling the recent assaults of the enemy.[133]

We still keep on the lookout for another attack from the enemy, are waked up every morning before light. We heard yesterday good news from the Valley of Va. Breckenridge[134] had sever[e]ly whipped Siegel's command which was then forced to retreat across the Shenandoah, burning bridges after it. We heard last night that the enemy, 40,000 strong, were between Richmond & Petersburg, confronted by Beauregard[135] who was to have attacked them a day or two ago.

Poor Ben May, our ensign, who was mortally wounded on Thursday morning last, died yesterday. A more gallant soldier never lived.

133. Bernard refers to Lieutenant General Edmund Kirby Smith's defeat of Major General Nathaniel P. Banks in Louisiana; exaggerates Major General Sterling Price's repulse of Major General Frederick Steele in Arkansas; alludes to an episode in the 1864 Shenandoah Campaign between the Confederate forces of Brigadier General John D. Imboden and the Union forces of Major General Franz Sigel; and mentions an action between the Southern cavalry of Brigadier General William "Grumble" Jones and the Northern cavalry of Brigadier General William W. Averell.

134. Confederate Major General John C. Breckinridge, a former vice president of the United States, defeated Sigel at the Battle of New Market, May 15, 1864.

135. General P. G. T. Beauregard was the Confederate commander at Petersburg in the early fighting there.

Line of battle near Spotsylvania C.H.
Wednesday afternoon May 18 '64

At sunrise this morning our artillery & the enemy's commenced work & continued for several hours, at times the firing being very heavy. At one time the enemy attempted to charge a portion of our works with their lines of battle but their men could not be gotten to come boldly up & were easily repulsed. This was somewhere on the left of our lines & was at that point occupied by Gordon's & Thomas's brigades. The heavy cannonading ceased perhaps about 11 o'clock but since that time to the present (5 P.M.) there have been occasional guns fired.

We had read to us today an order from Gen. Lee announcing that Gen. Beauregard had defeated Butler's forces, storming his works & driving him to the shelter of his gunboats.

[Beauregard defeated Butler at Drewry's Bluff on May 16, 1864, and bottled up his army between the James and Appomattox Rivers.]

Bivouack near Hewlett's Station[136]
Central R.R. Monday morn May 23

Left position at breastworks near Spotsylvania CH Saturday night & after a most fatiguing march reached this place last night about 10 o'clock. From appearances we are on our way to Richmond. When we started we thought we were going to Bowling Green. The enemy are no doubt shifting to the Peninsula. Thursday afternoon at Spotsylvania CH Ewell got around the enemy's right flank & drove them but afterwards fell back. According to report there was an unsuccessful little affair at Guinea Station.

Lines of battle 4 mile N of Hanover
Junction Tuesday May 24

After a march of six or eight miles yesterday morning reached this place & went into camp about 10 o'clock—and this afforded a great relief to us, but it was only an hour or two before the firing of pickets a half a mile or so on our right informed us that the enemy were near. Soon after this the artillery on our right began to operate & until almost four in the afternoon a constant firing was kept up. At this time the enemy threw a shell or two quite near our resting place & immediately put us all in motion. At sunset we formed ourselves in line of battle in front of some artillery which did some very noteable firing. I make no mention of various marches & counter marches. We were at

136. Hewlett's Station lay on the Virginia Central Railroad about eight miles west of Hanover Junction.

dark put in a new position and our company with others of the reg't sent out on picket.

After being hauled about almost incessantly and taking various positions as skirmishers until after midnight we were carried back to the lines of battle which were soon thereafter moved a distance of perhaps 2 miles to this point when, almost completely exhausted, we stacked arms & slept till after sunrise when we formed a line of battle at this point & commenced entrenching. Incessant artillery firing on our right up to this time 5 P.M. Skirmishing on right pretty heavy at this time. Ben George[137] of Co. D, sharpshooter was killed this afternoon, also Tom Weaver[138] Co. I.[139]

Line of battle

Thursday afternoon May 26, 1864

Commencement of heavy skirmishing in our front & on the right together with some shelling from the enemy, some of which enfiladed our part of the line brought my last entry abruptly to a close. Some of the skirmishers on our right were in full view. I hear that on that afternoon the enemy made an assault on our extreme right but were repulsed. Yesterday & most of today at the present time (2 P M) the skirmishing in our front has been almost incessant & at times quite heavy. Many of the enemy's balls have passed over our works & today one came within a few inches of the head of one of our company whilst standing in the trenches. Yesterday the enemy startled us a little by opening upon our lines with a piece or two of artillery posted about half mile distant on the edge of the woods in our front. One of their shots struck the breastworks near us & threw dirt upon several of our company. They have

---

137. Benjamin B. George enlisted as a private in Company D in April 1861. Absent for a month in 1862, he returned to the 12th Virginia until October 1862, when he was detailed to the Quartermaster Department as a teamster. He was killed in action at North Anna River.

138. Thomas C. Weaver enlisted as a private in Company I in February 1862. He was killed in action at North Anna River.

139. The events on May 24 provided Lee with a rare opportunity to strike back at Grant's column. Using the terrain south of the North Anna River, Lee and his engineers devised a clever defense line in the shape of an inverted "V." The apex of this line rested on the North Anna and the flanks tapered away from the river. When Grant advanced over the river, Lee's defensive line isolated portions of the Union troops on the river's south bank. The Army of Northern Virginia, concentrated in its oddly shaped line, was poised to attack the hapless Federal units isolated below the river. But it was not to be. Lee, plagued by dysentery, was confined to his tent and too weak to coordinate the operations of his army. According to one of his staff, Charles Venable, Lee exclaimed helplessly: "We must never let them pass us again. We must strike them a blow" (see Charles Venable, "The Campaign from the Wilderness to Petersburg," *SHSP*, 14:535).

fired a little today from their battery with only the effect however of causing a stampede to the trenches of the boys collected in the stables & granary post in our rear in which they have for the past two days sought shelter from both the rain & the heat of the sun.

We have rumors that Grant is again swinging around to our right.

In the skirmish of yesterday the sharpshooters lost another very good soldier, Bradley Paine[140] of Co. A, a northerner by birth. Capt. Taylor[141] of Co. D commanding the detachment from the 12th was wounded. The sharpshooters were relieved yesterday morning by the 41st reg't who lost two men killed, one of them Capt. Brinkley[142] of Portsmouth, a most gallant man.

Line of battle
about 8–1/2 A.M. Friday May 27, 1864

It was ascertained this morning that the enemy have left our front— whither gone I have not heard. A few moments ago we got orders to pack up & be ready to move. The artillery around us also in readiness to move. A few straggling prisoners were brought in from the front this morning. A little artillery firing now going on our right.

Last night we drew an unusual quantity of rations for such times as these. Besides the usual quantity of bread we drew 1/2 lb of pork instead of a 1/4 lb bacon as heretofore and a small ration of sugar, coffee & molasses! We have had it rumored for a day or two that we would have this increase in rations & that Gen. Lee has said that his boys should have a plenty to eat whilst they are having so much fighting to do. The first ration of tobacco was issued last night. We are given 1 lb of plugs for one month.

On the road to Atlee's Station Central R.R.
five miles of that place
May 28, '64

Started yesterday about 12 o'clock and after many delays & [*illegible word*] halts, continued along behind a wagon train, made about 6 miles in the direction by 10–1/2 o'clock last night, at which time we went into camp. On the march yesterday we crossed the "Little River" and the South Anna and two other smaller streams & passed by the celebrated Hanover Academy. At sunrise this morning we were again in motion & had a tiresome march of perhaps

---

140. Conscripted in April 1862, Private Bradley Payne of Company A was captured at Chancellorsville and paroled within ten days. He was killed in action at North Anna River.

141. Bernard refers here to Captain James E. Taylor, who had enlisted as a private in Company G on April 19, 1861. In 1864, he commanded a sharpshooter battalion. He ended his service at Appomattox.

142. Robert B. Brinkley is discussed in note 30, chapter 2.

six miles to this point when we were marched out in an open field & have rested for the past two hours (12–1/2 o'clock). Atlee's Station six miles from Richmond seems to be our destination today. We have rumor afloat today that Grant is very sick & has gone to Washington. We heard today of the death of John Lee of our company wounded in the arm at the Wilderness May 6. He was a most excellent young man & would have made a good soldier. The battle in which he received his wound was his first battle. He had but a few days returned to his company, having been detailed in the Q.M. Dept. for more than two years.

The line of battle near Atlee Station
Sunday afternoon May 29th '64

Yesterday afternoon marched to Atlee Station & about 1–1/2 miles in a southeasterly direction & about sunset bivouacked in a piece of woods adjoining the road remaining in perfect quiet until about 7 o'clock this morning. Last night for the first time since leaving our bivouack near [Percell's] house in Orange (May 5th), we had an unbroken night's rest and it is almost needless to say we enjoyed it this morning. Our division was marched to this point about 1 mile NE of Atlee's Station & out in line of battle. The balance of the corps I understand is back where it stopped last night. Saw Gen. Breckenridge this morning. He looks very much hardened to the service. His division may be here with ours & I heard this morning we were going to support him.

There was a cavalry fight yesterday four or five miles from this point, in which it appears that our forces were driven back.

[Bernard refers here to the battle of "Haw's Shop," one of the largest cavalry engagements of the war. Confederate units screening Lee's army and under the command of Wade Hampton clashed with Sheridan's troopers in a day-long vicious engagement at Haw's Shop and Enon Church north of Totopotomoy Creek.[143]]

In trenches near Atlee's Station
Tuesday afternoon May 31, '64

Sunday afternoon moved our position a little forward & entrenched. Monday morning it was determined to change the line of battle to the present line changing our portion of this brigade about 100 yds to the rear. This

143. For a detailed account of this battle, see Gordon Rhea, *Cold Harbor: Grant and Lee, May 26–June 3, 1864* (Baton Rouge: Louisiana State University Press, 2002), 61–91.

done in order to give Breckenridge & Innes a better position. By dark we had run a new line of entrenchments & destroyed our old lines. Some little artillery firing along the line. Papers of yesterday brought news of a success with Johnston's army on the 28th. This morning skirmishers in Breckenridge's first division ordered in and the enemy have advanced their artillery & infantry to within approximately 200 or 300 yds of his lines. A good deal of artillery fighting has been going on just to our right, but none of the shot or shell have passed immediately over us. A minnie ball or two from the skirmishers have passed over us. I hear there is no skirmish line between Breckenridge's line of battle just on our right & the enemy. At any rate the enemy were fired upon from the breastworks today.

[For several days at the end of May, Lee's army dug in behind the Totopotomoy Creek, a swampy, slow-running stream less than twenty miles northeast of Richmond. Grant's commanders probed and pushed against this new rebel line but found no opening for attack. Bernard's unit manned the earthworks on the left of this line, facing troops from the Union Sixth Corps.[144]]

Wednesday afternoon
June 1, '64

Skirmishing continued until dark last evening and a battery a little to our left threw a few shells near us. Our reg't was on picket last night. The rifle pits & the position at the place we were on duty excellent. Normally we are kept awake all night, I dozed a good deal however. Was amused by a dream from which I was aroused by a stray shot or two on my right, thought the line was falling back & bounced up in great alarm, seizing my companion's gun & hurriedly putting on my luggage.

The Yankee line was about 200 yds in our front and I see them at times walking about with lights in their hands. We were relieved at daylight. Newspapers of this morning report a fight on our right yesterday afternoon in which Early drove the enemy into their works. There has been fighting this morning on the right & cannonading is still in process. The enemy are believed to be moving to our right & it is also believed that Butler is reinforcing Grant.

[Bernard's June 1 entry refers to the Battle of Bethesda Church, which occurred May 30. Jubal Early, newly in command of the Confederate Second Corps, successfully attacked several divisions of Warren's Fifth Corps that

---

144. Ibid., 92–113.

were isolated in the vicinity of Bethesda Church south of the Totopotomoy Creek.]

Cold Harbor
Friday afternoon June 3

A great battle has been fought today. It appears that the enemy have assaulted our whole line & been repulsed signally everywhere except in a part of Breckenridge's line which they broke through but the position of which was recovered by Finnegan's brigade of our division. Our division is in reserve & we occupy excellent breastworks.[145] The battle began about sunrise this morning & raged furiously for at least 3 hours this morning. Since that time artillery firing & skirmishing have been incessant. The enemy's works & ours are, it is said, just in our immediate front only 200 yds apart & the skirmishing is done between these lines of battle. The enemy loss seems to have been very heavy—ours almost insignificant. I have not yet seen a wounded man today. There was fighting along the lines yesterday afternoon. We thought our division would get into it. The minnies pass over us pretty freely.

Night before last Grant shifted his lines from the position about Atlee's Station to this point. It is thought the disaster of today will make him move tonight. We hear that Ewell holds Malvern Hill.

Saturday June 4, 1864

Skirmishing & occasional artillery firing continued until dark when we were all startled by the most terrible musketry about 900 yds on our right. We learned this morning that it was a fight between a detachment of Finnegan's, Echols & Wharton's brigades & a force of the Yankees about to make a charge. The detachment were advancing to recover rifle pits lost in the morning's fight. These rifle pits were recovered & the enemy driven from their breastworks. Soon after this our division began to move to the right, when getting in the woods nearby we were subjected to a very heavy artillery fire, the enemy now making a heavy charge along the line opposite to us. Getting around to this point about a half a mile to the right, our brigade relieved Wharton's brigade of Breckenridge's division. This morning we have been much annoyed by sharpshooters. The enemy's line of entrenchment is in full view & the Yankee flag floats defiantly from it. The Purcell battery of Pegram's battalion one of whose lines are within a few feet of our company, has been shelling this line today. The enemy are shelling a little at this time. This morning they threw several shells at us evidently from a mortar.

145. Mahone's position lay behind the main Confederate line south of the Cold Harbor road in the vicinity of New Cold Harbor (ibid., 321, 363).

Monday June 6, 1864

Nothing of much interest to note for Saturday afternoon & yesterday except that Saturday about dark & last night about the same time there was some sharp fighting on our immediate left, that is about Finnegan's brigade. Until this morning the sharpshooters of the enemy have been very annoying to our men at the entrenchments. Several have been wd & one other killed by them. I should mention that a shot from the Purcell battery on Saturday afternoon cut down the yankee flag in our front. Yesterday they decided it no doubt imprudent to replace it. Last night a breastwork was run in front of Harris's position & quite near the enemy's line & our sharpshooters have from this kept the enemy rather quiet today. Last night I was detailed as one of a fatigue party made up from our division to pull down the earthworks in front of Finnegan, these lost by Breckenridge Friday, recaptured by Finnegan, & abandoned Friday night.[146] We found it not such dangerous work as anticipated. We were at work until day break. Many dead yankees were to be seen lying about them & I saw one wounded whom I helped get out of a ditch. Rumor says the enemy have left Ewell's front. Ewell is on our left. We have sent out reinforcements to our skirmishers who it is said are to charge the enemy for the purpose of ascertaining their strength in front of our positions.

Tuesday afternoon
June 7, 1864

Our skirmishers charged the enemy yesterday. Went nearly to the breastworks & found them still in force. The detail of ten from our reg't lost thus: David May[147] & Serg't Raferty[148] Co. A and Gunn[149] Co. G who were doubtless captured. By agreement between Gen. Lee & Grant there was a sus-

146. Bernard's repeated references to "Finnegan" are for the Florida regiments in a brigade under the command of General Joseph Finegan (commonly misspelled "Finnegan"). The brigade had been transferred from Florida to Virginia in May 1864.

147. Davis Fitzhugh May, older brother of Benjamin H. May, had enlisted as a private in Company A in August 1861. Wounded at Chancellorsville, he recovered after five months in a hospital. Returned to his unit, he was indeed captured at Cold Harbor. Imprisoned at Point Lookout, he was exchanged in February 1865. Paroled at Appomattox, he died within five years of the war's end.

148. Patrick Raferty, a native of County Galway, Ireland, worked for a commission merchant in Petersburg before the war. He enlisted in Company A as a private in April 1862. Promoted to corporal, then sergeant, he was wounded at Crampton's Gap, and captured at Cold Harbor. Initially imprisoned at Point Lookout, he was moved to Elmira in July 1864, where he was not released until May 1865. After the war, he became a businessman in Petersburg.

149. Eugene K. Gunn enlisted as a private in Company G in June 1861. Discharged to join Otey's Battery in 1862, he returned to the 12th Virginia in 1864, only to be cap-

pension of hostilities from 8 to 10 o'clock P.M., it was said for the purpose of burying the dead. Grant having made, it was said, three different applications. Probably by someone's mistake there was some little firing between the pickets during these two hours, but never on our immediate front. There was a great deal of picket firing during the night. Everything pretty quiet today until a few minutes ago (4 P.M.) when artillery fighting began on our left being in progress now. The customary skirmishing however has been uninterrupted.[150]

Friday June 10 '64

Things have been for the last three days pretty much in *status quo*. There being not sufficient time Monday evening for the transmission of the proper orders. There was not as I had anticipated, a regular suspension of hostilities from 8 to 10 o'clock. The pickets in front of our line were withdrawn but the yankee officer in command of those of the enemy confronting ours said he had received no orders about the truce. However there was a mutual removing of the dead between the lines at this point. The next evening however (Tuesday) there was a general suspension of hostilities from 6 to 8 o'clock, during which time there was profound quiet which continued with but little interruption during the night & until 8 or 10 o'clock next morning. The men on either side showing themselves pretty freely on the breastworks. Our company was on picket Tuesday night. A mortar from our side has been throwing shells at the enemy today. Some of which seem to have been very well thrown. Sharpshooters on our left continue to annoy us. Three men in our reg't have been wd & Col. Weisiger commanding the brigade was struck yesterday but only bruised a little.

Monday June 13, 1864

Enemy left our front last night. Scouts & skirmishers sent forward a mile or more have returned & reported none within that distance. Col. Weisiger has just received orders to form his brigade to go forward to reconnoiter. Abe Lincoln & Andy Johnson have been nominated by the Baltimore Convention. From all accounts the Petersburg Militia distinguished themselves in the affair of last Thursday, fighting very desperately.[151]

---

tured at Cold Harbor. Imprisoned at Point Lookout until exchanged in February 1865, he was paroled at Appomattox.

150. For a vivid description of this action, see the account of Lt. James Eldred Phillips of the 12th Virginia Infantry's Company G, the Richmond Grays, in James Eldred Phillips's Memoir, in the James Eldred Phillips Papers, Virginia Historical Society.

151. One of the leaders of the militia was Col. Fletcher H. Archer, formerly an officer of Bernard's regiment, and his account of the "affair of last Thursday" is set forth in his article, "The Defense of Petersburg," in *War Talks of Confederate Veterans*.

7

The Petersburg Campaign

INITIAL BATTLES

AS BERNARD AND THE Army of Northern Virginia struggled against Grant during May and early June 1864, Union forces under General Benjamin Butler sailed up the James River and gained a lodgment at Bermuda Hundred south of Richmond. Butler made several unsuccessful attempts to move on Richmond and Petersburg. One of these was an attack against Petersburg on June 9. On that day, Union infantry under Major General Quincy Gilmore and cavalry led by Brigadier General August Kautz appeared outside Petersburg's fortifications, the so-called Dimmock Line. A small force of citizens and militia along with a few regular units repelled the raid, a feat celebrated in Petersburg long after the war. In *War Talks of Confederate Veterans,* Bernard afforded substantial attention to the June 9 fight.

This chapter includes two letters related to the June 9 battle. The first, written by Professor William Carr, contains his eyewitness description of events at the front that day. Carr's account, which appeared in the *Petersburg Daily Index-Appeal* in 1898, also includes a letter from General Kautz commenting about the battle. The second letter, which appeared in the "People's Column" of the *Petersburg Daily Index-Appeal* in 1903, describes W. H. Hood's participation in the initial stages of the Petersburg Campaign. Hood commanded a battalion of Petersburg's militia in 1864. He prepared the letter after attending a banquet conducted by the A. P. Hill Camp in 1903.[1]

---

1. Bernard planned to include additional accounts of the June 9 battle in "War Talks, Volume II." One piece was prepared in 1895 by Raleigh Colston, a key player in the battle. Colston's letter to Bernard eventually appeared in the *Petersburg Daily Index-Appeal,* on June 7, 1903, under the heading "From MSS. of Geo. S. Bernard's War

While Butler threatened Petersburg, Bernard and his comrades sat in the Cold Harbor trenches east of Richmond. In mid-June, however, the Army of the Potomac slipped away from Cold Harbor and headed south. Fearing a direct strike on Richmond, Lee shuttled the bulk of his forces into the works east of the capital. Grant, however, had no intention of taking the direct route. Instead, his men passed Richmond altogether and crossed the James. By June 15, several Union corps stood at the gates of a lightly defended Petersburg. With Grant's decisive move over the James, a swift assault would bring Petersburg's fall, and severely jeopardize Richmond. But P. G. T. Beauregard, the Confederate commander at Petersburg, scraped together all available units, shuffled men here and there, and successfully held the city until the arrival of Lee's veterans. The Creole general had saved Petersburg. Despite this momentary encouragement, the future was bleak for Lee and his army. Indeed, Grant's strategic vision had yielded a secure base for the Union forces at City Point on the James as well as a position outside Petersburg within striking distance of Lee's supply lines. Absent an extraordinary turn of events, Petersburg and Richmond's fate had been sealed. But the Confederates still had plenty of men and plenty of fight left. After the initial assaults failed, Grant settled down for what came to be known as the Petersburg Campaign, a series of large-scale Union offensives both at Petersburg and Richmond.

During the campaign's opening phase, the 12th Virginia Infantry participated in the repulse of the initial Union assaults in mid-June, the successful Confederate attack against the Union Second Corps on the Jerusalem Plank Road on June 22, and the storied Crater battle on July 30, where a creative Union plan to mine under and obliterate the Confederate line ended in di-

---

Talks of Confederate Veterans, Vol. II." Colston's 1895 letter was almost identical to an account he had prepared for *Century Magazine* in the 1880s. That article was published in the four-volume set, *Battles and Leaders of the Civil War* (New York: Century Company, 1884–87), 4:535–37. By 1895, Colston was suffering from a terminal illness which would shortly claim his life. His personal correspondence with Bernard at the time contains additional details about Colton's views on the battle. In particular, an October 7, 1895, letter to Bernard reveals Colston's bitterness at the failure of the people of Petersburg to recognize his contribution to the city's defense on June 9. He wrote to Bernard on October 7, 1895: "I confess that I have felt hurt that in the commemoration of the fight of June 9, 1864, which have taken place in Petersburgh [*sic*] year after year, no mention whatever has been made of my name in the City papers or the addresses delivered, so that it might be imagined that I was not there at all" (Bernard Papers, Southern Historical Collection, University of North Carolina). Bernard also planned to include an address by John F. Glenn about the June 9 battle. Glenn's speech appeared in volume 35 (1907) of the *Southern Historical Society Papers*. Given their availability elsewhere, both Colston and Glenn's accounts have been omitted from this chapter.

saster for the attackers. The Battle of the Crater had a special significance for Petersburg veterans because many of them, as part of the 12th Virginia and other regiments, participated in the crucial counterattack organized by William Mahone that day. The efforts of Mahone's men helped to seal off the Union advance at the Crater itself.

This chapter contains George Bernard's diary entries from the summer of 1864 as well as the transcript of a memorial address he delivered at Blandford Church in 1911.[2] During the last few decades of his life, Bernard paid special attention to the memory of the Crater battle. In *War Talks of Confederate Veterans,* he published an extended account of his brigade's role in the Crater fight. That chapter, arguably the centerpiece of *War Talks,* includes an address Bernard delivered in 1890, along with dozens of letters from fellow veterans meticulously describing the event's details. The Crater chapter in *War Talks* also includes Bernard's eyewitness account of the horrific treatment African American soldiers received at the hands of their rebel captors.

><>-0-<>-|-<-....->-|-<>-0-<

"Battle Of The 9th Of June,"
by Prof. Wm. N. Carr

An Interesting Account of the Fight by a Participant — Letter from Gen. Kautz Disavowing Responsibility for Blunders[3]

Thursday, June 9, 1864, was to me a memorable day, on account of events that occurred in Petersburg and on its suburbs. I had barely arisen before a class of young ladies in the Petersburg Female college on Sycamore street, of which the venerable Dr. Blackwell was the president, and was in the act of distributing to my class the several problems of recitation in Algebra or Geometry, when Prof. Staubly, of the modern language department, opened my door to make to me the rather startling announcement that the Yankees were

2. Bernard also wrote a long letter on the Crater to the *Richmond Times* in 1899. Believing the *Times* had unfairly characterized Mahone's role in the battle, Bernard firmly responded with detailed accounts of Mahone's actions from fellow veterans. Bernard's letter demonstrated not only his vast knowledge of the battle itself, but also his continued loyalty to the politically unpopular Mahone even four years after the general's death (see George Bernard, "Great Battle of the Crater," *SHSP,* 38:204–21).

3. This letter appeared in the *Petersburg Daily Index-Appeal,* December 18, 1898.

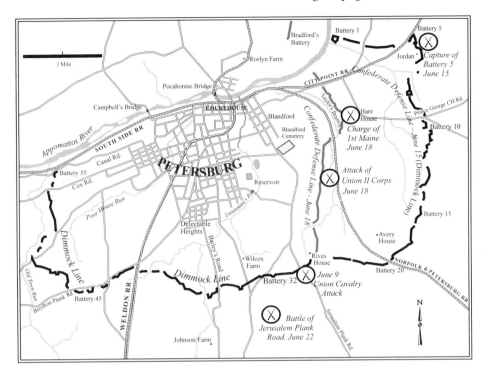

PETERSBURG, JUNE 1864

coming and that he and I were expected at camp. Colonel F. H. Archer[4] was in command of the two companies of our little battalion, that of Captain Rogers[5] and that of Captain Wolff.[6]

We had been called out for local defense on the 5th of May, and had gone to Mr. Charles Friend's farm, strengthened the fortifications there, moved along our line gradually, had reached the neighborhood of the Rives farm, and had become tolerably familiar with the necessary drill, when the teachers in the battalion and perhaps some other of the command were formally allowed, instead of remaining idle in camp, to ply our vocation in our respective schools, with the understanding, however, that the moment occasion re-

---

4. Lieutenant Colonel Fletcher H. Archer, who had formerly led Company K of Bernard's regiment, on this day led the 2nd Virginia Militia Infantry. For more on Archer, see note 151, chapter 6.

5. "Captain Rogers" may actually refer to Captain Owen H. Hobson, who led Company A of the 2nd Virginia Militia.

6. Captain James E. Wolff led Company B of the 2nd Virginia Militia.

quired our services, we should obey the summons and hurry to our respective posts of duty.

On our way to join our comrades, we discussed the possibilities of false alarms or of facing the invading foe, and yet reached our camp and equipped ourselves in ample time to see that foe advance and spread out his lines some half mile from us. We learned later that we had before us General Kautz's cavalry, numbering from 1,300 to 1,500 men, and perhaps a considerably larger force. Our 122 men must have made a very meager show in their eyes, but to make our little band present as formidable an appearance as possible, we were ordered to stand (I think) six feet apart. Our enemy, in addition to being mounted, were, at the most moderate figures, more than ten times our number.

While we were standing in line and awaiting an attack with no little anxiety but, so far as I could see, without any appearance of alarm or perturbation, a messenger, Mr. John Jefferson, passed along the western end of our line and announced his message in these words, "Colonel Archer wants three reliable men to stand upon the breastworks as 'lookouts' and give him information as to the movements of the enemy. Mr. Davis, you take positions about the center of the line; Mr. Davidson, you go to the extreme left, and Mr. Carr, you go to the extreme right." These three lookouts must have appeared to the foe quite conspicuous objects tall as they were and standing erect upon the little breastworks, and I have often since wondered that we were not picked off by sharpshooters.

My own position in the line was peculiar; immediately on my left was a Napoleon gun, ably and faithfully loaded and fired, during the entire action that followed, by General Raleigh Colston, of Richmond, almost, if not quite alone and unaided; just in rear of him and myself, and reaching far to our rear and to our right, was a large body of heavy timber. Partly by the Napoleon, and perhaps still more by the large dense forest trees, I was, when I took my place in the trenches, almost isolated from my comrades. When I stood upon the breastworks, I could see far down our line on my left but my attention was not attracted so much in that direction as toward the enemy in front, whose movements it was my duty and pleasure to watch.

After halting in front of our line, and being, I suppose, a half-mile from us, they threw themselves in three divisions: one to flank us on our right, another to flank us on our left, and a third to attack our line in front. That flank movement to the west startled me, for I remembered that they would not have far to march in that direction before they would reach the road that led straight into Halifax street and into the heart of Petersburg. Could I arrest that westward movement? I would try. I had not yet taken my position in the trenches, but was still acting the lookout upon the breastwork; so, rising to my tiptoes and swinging my slouch hat up westward toward our empty lines, I tried by an inviting gesture, vigorously and persistently kept up, to make myself understood as beckoning to some large force away up our westward line, and earnestly inviting and urging them to come where they were more needed, as not being at all needed where they were. I will not say that my stratagem was successful; I can only say that that flank movement, which I so much dreaded and confidently believed then and still believe was commenced, was after a time suspended and it is well known that we were attacked in front, and that our left was quite surrounded.

It is possible that this ruse made the attack more severe on Archer's little battalion; but it is almost certain that it served to put off the evil day for Petersburg for a period of some nine months.

It is scarcely necessary to add that our little band of defenders was more than decimated, but that, crippled as it was, it kept the enemy at bay until Dearing's cavalry came to its aid in time to give them an effectual repulse. Well nigh 31 years afterwards, I addressed to General Kautz[7] the following of inquiry:

Hamilton, Va., March 6, 1895.

General A. V. Kautz:

Dear Sir.—Though a total stranger, I take the liberty of asking your attention for only a brief space. I happened to be one of that small battalion of local defenders whom you encountered on what I presume was your first visit to the suburbs of Petersburg, on the 9th of June, 1864. I am now an old man of 75 years, living much in the past, and the scenes of that to me memorable day often return to me with an interest that I can not repress. I can still in fancy see your 1,300 mounted men falling into line some half-mile (I suppose) from our line of defense, spreading out in our view, a formidable force, and preparing, as I thought to come upon us in three columns, one to attack our left, a second to attack us in front, and a third, your left wing, marching out westward, parallel to our line of breast works, and then, as if changing tactics, and facing about, returning to join one of the other attacking parties. And here, General, is the point at which I beg to ask information: Why did that left wing, after first moving westward a short distance toward the railroad, change front and aid the attack either in front or on your right? I ask

7. August Valentine Kautz, a German American, commanded a cavalry division in Benjamin Butler's Army of the James in 1864. He suffered more than his share of setbacks during the Richmond-Petersburg Campaign, but on April 3, 1865, he entered Richmond at the head of a division of African American troops from the Twenty-fifth Corps. After the war, he held various posts in the army. He died in Seattle, Washington, in 1895, and is buried in Arlington Cemetery.

this for reasons entirely personal to myself, and without intending, I do assure you, any thought of criticism upon any order or movement of yours, I have so long deferred my query only because I have all along these 30 years and more been hoping at some time or other to see you in person and raise my question face to face.

Hoping that you will honor me with an early reply, I remain, my dear sir.

Very respectfully and truly yours.

Wm. B. Carr.

To my inquiry General Kautz promptly submitted the following reply, in which he virtually admits that he was not on the field, when his men were deploying, when the first attack was made on our line, and when other "stupid" movements were executed by his subordinates. But I herewith enclose the general's letter, in which he shall speak for himself:

Annapolis, Md.,
March 14th, 1895

Wm. B. Carr, Esq., Hamilton Va:

Dear Sir,—Yours of the 8th was forwarded to me here. In reply to your inquiry I am obliged to state that I have no recollection of the movement you mention and it was perhaps some stupid movement of which there were others on that occasion, the worst of which was the squadron that was sent in mounted by Colonel Spear,[8] and which met the fate of his stupidity. Fortunately I reached the head of the column in time to prevent a second squadron from being sent in to a similar fate. There was nothing contemplated in my orders when I came upon the scene except to form line out of range, dismount and move on the works. There were many blunders perpetrated in that eventful year in and around Petersburg, that will require a wise historian to set right and to account for. In the hope that I have fully answered your inquiry, I remain.

Yours respectfully.

August V. Kautz

8. Samuel Perkins Spear was commissioned as Lieutenant Colonel of the 11th Pennsylvania Cavalry on September 25, 1862, at the age of fifty. Promoted to colonel in 1864, he was wounded at Five Forks, Virginia, on April 1, 1865. He died in New York City in 1875.

"The Defense of Petersburg,"
by W. H. Hood[9]

[Account of Battles in May–June 1864]

Petersburg, Va.,
January 18, 1903

A. P. Hill Camp Confederate Veterans and Heroes gave a most enjoyable banquet this afternoon in commemoration of the birth day of our beloved R. E. Lee, quite a large number being present. Captain John R. Patterson, chairman, called the meeting to order. Addresses by distinguished speakers were made. Rev. Dr. Pilcher, Rev. Dr. Battle and others, after which, we were marched to the banquet hall, where a most sumptuous supper was spread, enough to say, in keeping with Petersburg's generous hospitality. After which Captain Whittle, for navy; General Battle, army; Professor McNeal, southern chivalry and our beloved chief; Dr. J. Herbert Claiborne, the army, private soldier and our beloved, heroic, self-sacrificing women. Oh! What a hallowed memory. What an inspiration. References were made to the defense of Petersburg, to which I may be permitted to allude.

The defense of Petersburg. On the 5th of May, 1864. The city bells tolled, signalizing that the vandal hordes of Ben Butler's army were marching on our beloved town. The young men fitted for active service, had long since gone to the front, in Lee's army. The citizen soldiery, old men, boys, merchants, lawyers, physicians, mechanics and artisans, rallied as one man to the defense. We soon had every available man in line, and in the breast works. That day the enemy only made a feint, attacking our picket lines, which they kept up until

---

9. William H. Hood's letter was published in the "People's Column" of the February 1, 1903, issue of the *Petersburg Daily Index-Appeal.* Hood commanded "Hood's Battalion," a militia unit in the Virginia Reserves which was made up of iron workers, railroad employees, and mill workers from Petersburg. Because activation of this unit closed many of the city's vital industries, it was mobilized only in the "most grave emergencies" (see William D. Henderson, *Petersburg in the Civil War: War at the Door* [Lynchburg, Va.: H. E. Howard, 1998], 109). William H. Hood began the war as a captain in the 3rd Virginia Infantry regiment, but left the unit after its reorganization in 1862. He then took command of the reserve battalion bearing his name. He was captured in June 1864, held at Morris Island, South Carolina, and exchanged in December of the same year. He died in 1908 in Henderson, North Carolina. Bernard's papers contain no mention of Hood's letter. However, given the letter's connection to the A. P. Hill Camp and its relevance to the June 9 battle, it has been included in this chapter.

the early morning of June 9th, when General Gilmore vauntingly boasted, that if General Butler would furnish him with 5 regiments cavalry (Kautz's), 1 regiment colored and four regiments white troops, he would take Petersburg. So about day break on 9th he advanced. His cavalry, 5 regiments, made an attack on battery No. 24 on Plank road. Colonel F. H. Archer with about seven companies of citizen soldiery most gallantly defended that battery, until about 3 o'clock after losing nine of the best men of Petersburg. Blanks, Banister, Scott and others fell, all homage to their memory. Dearing's battery of artillery opened fire and put to ignominious route, with the aid of Archer's seven hundred men, Kautz's five regiments of cavalry. On the Appomattox river batteries No. 1, 4, 5 and 7 held in check supported by seven companies of infantry numbering about seven hundred men, Gilmore's five regiments of picked troops. Gilmore at sunrise drove in our pickets and advanced to the Beasley homestead with his staff, placing a picket on top of the mansion, his line on the ditch at the front gate about 300 yards from dwelling. Captain Thomas Bond's[10] company of about one hundred men held him in check. At about 2 o'clock a young, beardless man came riding up to me, and offered his services. As our troops were holding batteries No. 1, 4, 5, 7 more than a mile from the extreme points, he came at a most opportune time. I put a sergeant and 5 or 6 men, under this courier and directed he move towards Gilmore's right flank which was near the Appomattox river. It was in what was known as Rowlett's rye field, the rye concealed their movements, so that as they moved along and fired, it gave some appearance of a solid line. Soon I saw a cloud of dust in Beasley's front, and Gilmore and staff went to the rear, and soon firing ceased and the whole five regiments disappeared, leaving their dead near Beasley's gate. Thus Petersburg was saved from pillage, plunder and rapine, from a most infamous horde and vandals. Everything was comparably quiet until on 15th June our lines had been strengthened, Colonel Bembo, of S.C., and Wise's brigade, commanded by Colonel Page, being added. Our position was still on the left, but about daybreak we were ordered to battery No. 24 on Plank road, we held that position until about 12 o'clock. General R. E. Colston came out in a carriage, being on sick list. Captain Louis Marks,[11] who had not recovered from his wounds came. My alert beardless courier reported the enemy advancing on No. 14. I immediately communicated with Colonel

10. Thomas H. Bond is discussed in note 39, chapter 1.

11. Louis Leoferick Marks, an 1858 graduate of the Virginia Military Academy and a lumber mill owner, had also led a company in Bernard's regiment, until he was wounded at Second Manassas.

Page,[12] commanding Wise's brigade, and asked permission to go to No. 14, to which he readily agreed. Went to No. 14, I saw they were in front of Peeble's barn, opposite to No. 7 and 5. Met Colonel Page near No. 7. No guns in this battery. Told Colonel Page I would go to No. 7. He extended his hand, told me good bye, saying if you choose you can go. I never saw the gallant Page again. Found the enemy in column ready to advance on No. 5 and No. 4. Captain Hero,[13] of Louisiana, commanded at No. 4, Major Sturdivant[14] at No. 5. Captain Wheary's company was in trenches supporting No. 5. The firing on each side was terrific for two of three hours, finally at about 7 o'clock when ammunition was getting scarce, had dispatched several for it, but none returned. I sent my beardless courier, who I knew would return. Fifteen minutes past seven o'clock the 157 N.Y. regiment with many others, about 8,000 charged and captured Major Southerland,[15] Major Batte,[16] Colonel Council,[17] who was on a visit to Major Southerland, myself, Captain Wheary[18] and his 100 men.

The rest of my command escaped as their line was not immediately occupied, also my beardless courier in discharge of his hazardous duties was cut off, and could not get aback to me. We were prisoners. This attack was made by General Baldy Smith's corps of 20,000 men—infantry and artillery. We were carried to Ben Butler's headquarters, near Bermuda Hundreds. Next morning he sent for some of our men to talk to him. Major Anthony Keiley[19] was selected, we knew he was well equipped to parry with the wiley Butler, and well did he do it. We went to Bermuda Hundreds. Colonel Fuller, Gilmore's adjutant-general had charge of us. He was courteous and polite: He said when General Gilmore returned on 9th June, failed to take Petersburg, General Butler took from him his sword. We were held in transports at the

12. Colonel Powhatan Robertson Page, a veteran of the Mexican War, had enlisted in May 1861 as a captain in the 26th Virginia Infantry. He was killed on June 17, 1864, in the fighting at Petersburg.

13. Captain Andrew Hero Jr. belonged to the Washington Artillery.

14. Nathaniel A. Sturdivant is discussed in note 5, chapter 10.

15. "Major Southerland" may refer to Captain S. F. Sutherland.

16. "Major Batte" may refer to Major Peter Batte, who had enlisted in the 12th Virginia in April 1861 and transferred to Branch's Battery the next year.

17. Colonel James Calvin Councill, a graduate of the Virginia Military Institute, had enlisted as a captain in the 26th Virginia Infantry in June 1861.

18. Captain William H. Wheary led at least part of Hood's Reserves Battalion that day.

19. Major Anthony Keiley's last name is misspelled "Kelley."

pontoon bridge. Saw Grant's baggage wagons and beef cattle cross, then sent
to Point Lookout. When the guards and our men told of the escape of a prisoner in the river and that he had to swim four or five miles, this was my beardless courier, Simon Seward,[20] of Petersburg.

W. H. Hood

George S. Bernard War Diary: June 14, 1864–August 16, 1864[21]

Line of battle Frayser's Farm
Tuesday afternoon June 14 1864

Our brigade did not go forward to reconnoiter yesterday morning but
about 9 o'clock we got in motion for that place, crossing the Chickahominy at the McClellan bridge, passing across to the Chas City road & coming
down that road until we got near the Darbytown road into which we turned
at the same point at which we entered it on our march to Malvern Hill in '62.
Places along our route after reaching Chas. City road very familiar. Just as we
reached the point at which we turned off to get on to the Darbytown road
we got within range of the enemy's bullets & Corp. Faison[22] of Co. D was
wounded, also Capt. McAlpine[23] of the sharpshooters. There was sharp skirmishing then going on. We soon formed a line of battle & went to entrenching. All afternoon there was heavy skirmishing in front of us & the enemy
were driven some distance and as I learn this morning Scale's brigade came
very near capturing some artillery. About sunset our brigade moved its position a quarter of a mile farther to the front and after much delay got its proper
position & again went to fortifying. About midnight a portion of our reg't
including Co. E was sent on picket. Everything very quiet today. No enemy

20. Seward's account of his escape from Point Lookout appears in Bernard, *War
Talks of Confederate Veterans,* 74. Another detailed account of his escape, and a description of Seward's postwar return to Point Lookout, appeared in the *Washington Star* (see
a reprint of that article in the *Petersburg Daily Index-Appeal* for July 30, 1899).

21. The entries for June 14 through June 24 appear in "War Diary No. 4" in the
Bernard Papers, UVA.

22. William P. Faison, a Petersburg cotton mill worker, had enlisted as a private in
Company D of the 12th Virginia in April 1861. Promoted to corporal in February 1864,
he was wounded at Cold Harbor, then detailed to light duty at Jackson Hospital in
Richmond.

23. Captain Charles R. McAlpine had enlisted in the 41st Virginia in June 1861. He
later transferred to the 61st Virginia.

seem to be very near. We hope Grant has at last concluded to retreat. We are now on the battle field of Frayser's Farm fought June 30, '62. Our reg't is within 50 yds of the Frayser house. I saw, yesterday evening the skull & other bones of a soldier who was doubtless killed in the battle of Frayser's farm.[24]

[The skirmishing mentioned here in the diary most likely refers to the combat between Union infantry (Crawford's division of Warren's Fifth Corps) and Confederate forces at Riddell's Shop on the Charles City Road. The Union troops demonstrated vigorously in Lee's front east of Richmond to cover their army's move across the James to Petersburg.[25]]

Bivouack Frayser's farm
Wednesday afternoon June 15, 1864

Last evening about 6–1/2 o'clock we left our position at the breastworks & marched to this point about 400 yds distant on a hill of woods where we bivouacked for the night. How delightful was the information that we were to bivouack! None but those who have been through what we have for the last six weeks could appreciate our feelings. Last night the second time only since leaving our bivouack near Percell's house May 4th did we enjoy the privilege & luxury of unrolling our blankets & going regularly to bed. But alas, before retiring we received orders to be ready to march at 9 this morning & accordingly at this hour we were aroused from our sweet slumber. Just as we were about to fall in the orders to march were countermanded & we have not yet moved (6 P.M.). The occasion of this was the reported advance of the enemy. I hear this evening that the enemy are several miles below this point apparently lying idle. Our destination seems to have been the South side.

Entrenchment of Wilcox's farm[26]
1 mile south of Petersburg
Sunday June 19, '64

Yesterday afternoon about 5 o'clock we reached this place after a most severe march of 26 or 27 miles coming from within 3 miles of Malvern Hill. We crossed the James at Chaffin's Bluff on a pontoon bridge. Struck the turnpike

---

24. The Battle of Frayser's Farm on June 30, 1862, was also called the Battle of Glendale.

25. See Noah Andre Trudeau, *The Last Citadel: Petersburg, Virginia, June 1864–April 1865* (New York: Little, Brown, 1991).

26. The Wilcox farm was located about one mile south of Petersburg, several hundred yards from the main defense line in the vicinity of Battery 32. As Bernard's diary indicates, the 12th Virginia spent much of the Petersburg Campaign posted there (see *Atlas to Accompany the Official Records of the Union and Confederate Armies*, Plate XL, 1).

near the Halfway house on R & P R.R. & marched through Petersburg. As we marched up Sycamore it was difficult to realize that we were within range of the enemy's shells & that we were marching to take positions in line of battle. The great number of ladies that greeted us along the streets made us feel more as though we were going to participate in some festivity. Reaching a body of woods near this point we bivouacked until about 2 o'clock this morning when we took position in the breastworks. Last night the City of Petersburg sent us out some refreshments; a huge barrel of coffee & a large quantity of crackers. Our ration of late has been so good & abundant I rather think we live quite as well as the citizens. Everything pretty quiet this morning. A little shelling has been going on this morning on our left. Yesterday afternoon the enemy threw several shells into the city.

Entrenchments Wilcox's farm
Friday afternoon
June 24, 1864

For several days past I have neglected to write in this little book rather from want of inclination than absence of any worthy of interest. From Sunday afternoon until Wednesday morning everything was pretty quiet. We remained quietly in the trenches & were visited by many of our citizen friends who brought out with many little good things to eat & drink. Many of our boys, as might have been expected, ran the blockade into town and on Tuesday evening 50 men from the brigade were granted regular permits by order of Gen. Mahone and by division to visit Petersburg allowing them to go in at 6 P.M. & return at 8 o'clock next morning. The men pledging themselves to return to their command immediately in the event of an attack from the enemy. I was fortunate to be one of those fifty and went into town spending however more pleasant a time than I anticipated, in consequence of the absence of friends & relatives whom I was very anxious to see. Wednesday our brigade, Wright's & Saunders (Wilcox's old brigade) were moved outside of our breastworks & put in position in a line perpendicular to the line of the breastworks & along the edge of the woods just in front of our position. Here we encountered the enemy who seemed to have moved there that morning or the night before. The fire to which our brigade was exposed was very severe as we moved by the right flank to get into position on the right of Wright's brigade. One man of our reg't (Hall[27] Co. C) was severely wd here. Getting

27. James Ellis Hall had enlisted as a private in Company C of the 12th Virginia in May 1861. Wounded during the June 1864 fighting in Petersburg, he spent the next six months in the hospital. He returned to service but was captured near High Bridge during the Battle of Sailor's Creek in April 1865.

into position Wright & perhaps Saunders [Sanders][28] also moved forward with a yell, our brigade moving at the same time but rather I think behind Wright. The enemy were soon put on the run & continued to give way until they were driven fully 3/4 of a mile back to their breastworks & then out of them, which we occupied & from which we repulsed attempts to assault us firing upon the enemy heavy volleys, almost every man having two or three guns. Suffice it now to say that this repulse is considered a most brilliant one that resulted in the capture of 1742 prisoners, 4 pieces of artillery & 5 stands of colors (5 of latter by our brigade), with a loss of perhaps only 300 or 400 on our part. We killed a great many of the enemy. The loss in our reg't was only 2 wd and very slight in the other reg'ts of our brigade. About midnight we fell back to our old positions leaving the skirmishers at the yankee works until day, thus enabling our men to collect 1500 or 2000 stand of arms & bring off many hundreds of the wd, yankee & confederate.

[After the failure of the initial assaults on Petersburg (June 15–18), Grant immediately moved to cut off the main roads and rail lines into the city. By June 22, troops from the Second and Sixth Corps had seized the Jerusalem Plank Road to the southeast and were advancing to the Weldon Railroad. Unfortunately for these men, William Mahone commanded many of the Confederates in this sector. Chief engineer of the Norfolk and Petersburg Railroad before the war, he knew the ground south of Petersburg as well as anyone in Lee's army. On the afternoon of June 22, he moved three brigades down a hidden ravine and then attacked the Federal position. Awkwardly arranged west of the Jerusalem Plank Road and generally unprepared, the Union Second Corps broke as Mahone's men swarmed into its flank and rear. The numbers provided by Bernard here are generally accurate. The elite Union Second Corps, which had seen more than its fair share of combat during the Overland Campaign, paid dearly for the negligence of Union commanders that day.[29]]

Next day (Thursday) our division went along march down the Weldon R.R. and entrenching, the enemy skirmished with them & captured about

28. The Confederate generals referred to by Bernard are Ambrose Wright and John Calhoun Sanders (often misspelled by Bernard and others as "Saunders"). Wright led a brigade of Georgians for much of the war and served as Georgia state senator while he commanded troops in the field. Sanders commanded an Alabama brigade until his death at the age of twenty-four during fighting along the Weldon Railroad on August 21, 1864.

29. See John Horn, *The Petersburg Campaign: June 1864–April 1865* (Conshohocken, Pa.: Combined Publishing, 1993), 77–83.

500 prisoners.[30] Our reg't was engaged in the skirmish. I myself was fortunate enough to miss this tramp going to Petersburg on surgeon's certification to have a tooth extracted. Today we have been under marching orders since early this morning, but everything is quiet now. We heard heavy cannonading with some musketry down about this morning. We have heard there was an unsuccessful attempt on part of Gen. Hagood with 400 men to capture an important position of our old entrenchments.

[On June 24, 1864, Field's division and Hoke's division, each from a different corps of the Army of Northern Virginia, were supposed to attack together along the southern bank of the Appomattox to unhinge the Federal line, but failed to coordinate; only Hagood's brigade of Hoke's division attacked, and it met with repulse, losing about 200 men.[31]]

WAR DIARY NO. 5[32]

Entrenchment nearby Wilcox
Near Petersburg, July 2, '64

Wednesday, June 30[33] our brigade was on duty on the Petersburg and Richmond RR near "six mile" house,[34] protecting some wagons [*two illegible words*]. Returning to our old position in the breastworks that night have only [*two illegible words*] by the day's duty, the first news that greeted us was that we were to return next morning & to move at 2 o'clock. As ordered we were up before light & in motion as also the remainder of our division, Wilcox's &

30. On June 23, Mahone's men once again ventured out of the Confederate defenses. Discovering Union troops isolated near the Weldon Railroad, the Confederates virtually wiped out the Vermont Brigade of the Sixth Corps (see Horn, *The Petersburg Campaign*, 85; see also David S. Cross, *A Melancholy Affair on the Weldon Railroad: The Vermont Brigade, June 23, 1864* [Shippensburg, Pa.: White Mane Publishing, 2004]).

31. See Horn, *The Petersburg Campaign,* 88.

32. Notes Bernard on the cover of this diary: "All of the entries in this diary as appears in close inspection prior to that of May 22, 1865 were made originally in pencil and within the last ten days I have retraced in ink all of the pages that had not been previously so retraced. Those retraced recently are the first and all of the subsequent pages some 8 or 10 excepted (in which the ink appears pale). George S. Bernard, Dec 7, 1891" (Bernard Papers, UVA).

33. The diary says "Wednesday June 30" (Bernard Papers, UVA). But Wednesday of that week was June 29. June 30 was a Thursday, and the activities described took place on that day.

34. "Six Mile House" was also known as "Yellow Tavern" (not to be confused with another "Yellow Tavern" north of Richmond where Jeb Stuart was mortally wounded), and as "Globe Tavern."

Kershaw's Divisions with artillery & cavalry. We were soon satisfied that our destination was Reem's[35] Station where we had learned the night before that a large force of the enemy were entrenching. Arriving within 2 miles of Reams, the Cavalry who had gone forward to reconnoiter reported to us that the enemy had left the place so we were ordered back to the entrenchments.[36] The march back was exceedingly wearing on account of heat & dust and no little was the straggling. On my return to the breastworks I got a permit to meet my sister in Petersburg. I went in as soon as I could get off. I found many of my friends [*illegible word*] [*illegible*]ing since everybody seemed to be leaving that can possibly get away. The citizens fear that Grant will shell the city on Monday (the 4th), his lucky day. For the past fortnight he has been throwing shells at intervals into the city, huge 32 pounders. Many private residences have been disabled by them, some of which exploded within the lines.

Friday Afternoon July 8

Our reg't ordered to the rear today to allow men to do washing &c. It appears that it was intended we should go to the river but by mistake we only went to a neighboring branch. A few minutes ago we got orders to return to the breastworks. It was said to be ready to march at 4–1/2 o'clock. Col. Weisiger, who has just ridden up has evidently relieved us by telling us we were only under orders to be ready to repel any attack that might be made as at 4–1/2 o'clock our batteries are to open upon the enemy's batteries which have been shelling the city. Weather continues hot & dry. Some prospects of rain this evening.

Sunday afternoon July 10

Friday afternoon about 4 o'clock from several batteries along the lines there were first 2 or 3 rounds, then cheering, a little skirmishing & everything was quiet. I have just heard that the orders were that after 3 rounds from the batteries the men were to mount the breastworks & cheer as if about to charge. This appears to have been done up the lines as far as Saunders (Ala.) brigade on our left. Last night there was much commotion among the enemy on the left & a little after daybreak there was sharp skirmishing in that section leading us to think we were about to have a fight. The enemy opened a battery from their position nearly opposite to our brigade yesterday afternoon & threw a few shells near us causing our quartermaster a half a mile to our rear to strike his tent & move further back. No rain as yet.

35. The correct spelling is "Reams."

36. Union cavalry under Kautz and Brigadier General James H. Wilson fought at Reams Station on the way back from an ill-fated raid on the railroads southwest of Petersburg (see Greg Eanes, *Destroy the Junction: The Wilson-Kautz Raid and the Battle for the Staunton River Bridge* [Lynchburg, Va.: H. E. Howard, 1999]).

Monday July 18 1864

The long looked for rain has come at last. This is a regular "rainy day." Everything quiet along the lines. Our company goes on picket tonight.

I learned yesterday from our adjutant that the casualties in our reg't during the present campaign foot up thus far are as follows:

23 Killed on field of battle

17 died of wounds

97 Wounded

<u>12</u> Missing

149 Total loss in battle & skirmishes

Monday July 25, 1864

On picket last night—a most disagreeable tour of duty—a cold driving rain falling all night. I returned to the entrenchment in very bad plight. Our camp visited by the Yankee shells today one of which passed but a few feet from my tent.

Sunday July 31 '64

Yesterday witnessed a bloody drama around Petersburg,[37] perhaps as bloody as any affair of the war, Fort Pillow[38] not excepted. At this point about 1/2 mile southeast of the old Blandford Church,[39] the enemy exploded a mine under a fort in our works, blowing up 4 pieces of Pegram's Artillery[40] with 2 Lieutenants, Lt. Hamlin[41] & Chandler[42] and 22 men together with 5 companies of the 18th SC Reg't of Elliot's Brigade, whereupon they immediately rushed upon & captured that portion of our works and about 200 yds of the

37. Bernard is describing the famous Battle of the Crater. Much of his first book, *War Talks of Confederate Veterans,* contains reminiscences of this battle. Several excellent books on the Crater have recently been published; see Earl J. Hess, *Into the Crater: The Mine Attack at Petersburg* (Columbia: University of South Carolina Press, 2010); and Richard Slotkin, *No Quarter: The Battle of the Crater, 1864* (New York: Random House, 2009).

38. The reference to Fort Pillow concerns the massacre of African American troops by Confederates under Major General Nathan Bedford Forrest at Fort Pillow near Memphis on April 12, 1864. A good recent study is by Andrew Ward (*River Run Red! The Fort Pillow Massacre in the American Civil War* [New York: Viking, 2005]).

39. Built around 1735, Blandford Church fell into ruin after the American Revolution, but after the Civil War it was restored as a memorial to the Confederate war dead.

40. Before the reorganization of the Confederate army in April 1862, Pegram's Artillery had been an infantry company in Bernard's regiment.

41. "Lt. Hamlin" probably refers to 1st Lieutenant William B. Hamilton, who had enlisted in May 1861 and was commissioned into Branch's (later Pegram's) Artillery.

42. Second Lieutenant Christopher F. Chandler enlisted at Richmond in April 1861, and joined Branch's Light Artillery afterward.

works to the left of the exploded portion. This occurred soon after sunrise, soon after which our brigade & Wright's, which occupied the extreme right of our line, were put in motion for this point approaching it cautiously by the military roads recently constructed. We were not long in learning that our brigade would be assigned the task of capturing the works, supported by Wright's. Arriving at the works, fortunately just at the moment we were about to charge the enemy were also about to charge, when seizing our advantage & rising with a yell we rushed forward & got into the works, about 100 yds distant, receiving but little fire from the enemy, who turned out to be negroes! The scene now baffles description. But little quarter was shown them. My heart sickened at deeds I saw done. Our brigade not driving the enemy from the inner portions of the exploded mine, Saunders & Wright's brigades finished the work. I have never seen such slaughter in any battlefield. Our reg't lost 27 Kd & Wd, the majority of whom were killed & among them Emmet Butts,[43] of our company. Put Stith,[44] of our company, was wounded. Col. Weisiger,[45] commanding the brigade, was wounded. From what I have seen the enemy's loss could not have less than 5 to 700 killed, to say nothing of those wounded and between 500 & 1000 prisoners. Ours probably did not exceed 400 killed, wounded or missing.[46] Negotiations under a flag of truce are now pending. Probably Grant wants to bury the dead between the lines. Permission was granted today to water his wounded. I observed several citizens from the enemy's lines take part in this act of humanity. They were probably members of the sanitary committee. I also saw a woman standing in the Yankee breastworks. We indulge a hope that our brigade will be relieved tonight & return to its quiet position on the right.

Tuesday Aug. 2, 1864

Back at Wilcox's farm. Our brigade & Saunders relieved last night. Truce for 4 hours yesterday morning for burying of the dead between the lines. Express of this morning states that only about 12 of our men were found between the lines & about 700 of the enemy. There could not have been as many as 700. We made the negro prisoners carry out their dead comrades to the Yankee line, where the Yankees made their negroes bury them. Loss in our reg't 18 kd & 24 wd. The 6th reg't lost 70 kd & wd out of 80 carried in

43. Robert Emmet Butts is discussed in note 44, chapter 1.

44. Put Stith is discussed in note 60, chapter 4.

45. David Weisiger is discussed in note 6, chapter 1.

46. One recent study estimates that Union casualties at the Crater were 504 killed, 1,881 wounded, and 1,413 missing (or captured), and Confederate casualties were 358 killed, 731 wounded, and 403 missing (see John F. Schmutz, *The Battle of the Crater: A Complete History* [Jefferson, N.C.: McFarland, 2009], 355–56).

the fight. The remainder of the reg't was on picket. Co. C, of sharpshooters, a detachment from the 12th, lost out of 15 5 kd & 8 wounded. The enemy admit a loss of over 4000. Col. Thomas,[47] commanding one of the negro brigades, told Capt. Jones (of our reg't) yesterday during the truce that he carried in 2200 men & brought out only 800. It is said we captured 20 flags from the enemy & that the prisoners captured represented 2 corps, 9th (Burnside's) & 6th[48] (Hancock's).

Thursday Aug. 5

Yankee accounts of the affair put their loss in kd, wd, & prisoners at 5000. They say the plan was to spring a mine at 3 o'clock Saturday morning, but that the fuse failed to ignite the powder twice—that they had six tons of powder in the mine. The 9th & 18th corps made the charge and the 5th was in reserve. Our losses foot up 1200, of which 300 are no doubt prisoners, the enemy claiming to have taken that number.

Saturday August 6th

Yesterday afternoon we sprung a mine in front of Gracie's Brigade Johnson's Division but for some reason I have not yet learned, we made no charge. There was considerable commotion about this time. Our troops & the enemy have been throwing hand grenades at each other, so near is the opposite lines at some points. The loss of our brigade in the fight of Saturday was 270 kd, wd, & missing of whom 88 were killed on the field, just one-half of the whole number (176) that had been killed from the battle of the Wilderness to the present time.[49]

47. The "Colonel Thomas" referenced here was Henry Goddard Thomas, who began the war as a private, and later a captain, in the 5th Maine, and fought at the Battle of First Manassas. Later in the war, he was involved in the recruitment and organization of African American troops. He resumed field command in 1864, and led a brigade of United States Colored Troops (USCTs) at the Battle of the Crater. After the war, he remained in the army until retirement in 1897.

48. Bernard noted that the "2nd was intended rather than 6th" Corps, but neither was in fact involved. As Bernard's next diary entry makes clear, the Ninth Corps was supported by the Eighteenth.

49. The *Official Records* corroborate Bernard's account, though the mine apparently was not intended to presage an attack. An August 6 dispatch from P. G. T. Beauregard to General S. Cooper, adjutant and inspector general, reads: "An experimental mine was fired successfully last night in front of Gracie's line. Enemy appeared much alarmed. All quiet today." On the Union side, E. S. Parker, assistant adjutant general, reported to Grant that "Rebels exploded a small mine this evening about forty yards in front of Ord's left. No damage done to our works" (see *O.R.* 42: pt. 2, 52, 1163).

Monday August 8th, 1864

Gen. Mahone in a congratulatory order to Mahone's, Saunder's [Sander's] & Wright's brigades for their conduct in the affair of Saturday, July 30, says that with an effective force of less than 3000 men & with a casualty list of 598, they killed 700 of the enemy's people, wounded, by his own account, over 3000 & captured 1101 prisoners, embracing 87 officers, 17 stands of colors, 2 guerdons & 1916 stand of small arms, deeds which entitle their banners to the inscription, "The Crater, Petersburg, July 30, 1864." He says the enemy had massed against us three of his corps & 2 divisions of another.

[Forty-seven years after the Battle of the Crater, citizens of Petersburg crowded Blandford Church to witness the unveiling of a tablet to the memory of the Confederate soldiers who died during the battle. The tablet was the gift of the Crater Legion, a group composed of the battle's survivors, and was given to the Ladies' Memorial Association. The attendees included Governor William Hodges Mann, a former member of the 12th Virginia Infantry. At the ceremony, George Bernard delivered an address on behalf of the legion. A transcript of his address is reprinted below.[50]]

"Tablet to the Heroes of the Crater," Memorial Address (1911) by George Bernard

We are assembled in this historic church this afternoon to pay tribute to the memory of the one hundred and nineteen men of Mahone's Virginia brigade who lost their lives in the Battle of the Crater, when the brigade under the gallant lead of General David A. Weisiger and the skillful direction of Gen. Wm. Mahone made its famous charge on the 30th of July, 1864.

It is indeed fitting that this day, the forty-seventh anniversary of the battle, should have been selected to do honor to those who yielded their lives on that memorable field. Upon the beautiful tablet which adorns the walls of this old building of sacred memories are inscribed the names of these men, the rank of each, his company and regiment, the careful and loving work of one of the gallant field-officers of the brigade who led his regiment, the 61st Virginia, in the charge—Lieutenant Colonel Wm. H. Stewart.

50. A transcript of Bernard's talk appeared in the *Petersburg Daily Index-Appeal* on August 1, 1911.

WHY DID THEY DIE?

Why did these men die? Why were they and their comrades taken from their position in the breastworks on the Wilcox farm, marched under the shelter of the hills skirting Lieutenant Run to the old Hannon pond, thence across the Jerusalem Plank Road by covered ways and ravines to the low ground in rear of the Confederate breastworks running northwardly from the Crater, and there on the slope of the hill placed in battle array a couple of hundred paces from these works then swarming with the enemy's troops? Was this a mere maneuver in a harmless game of war intended for the instruction of young soldiers or the amusement of onlookers? It was not. On the contrary, a terrible tragedy was about to be enacted, the work of grim, red-handed war, in which blood was to flow freely and many men on both sides were to surrender their lives. The men of the brigade, veterans who had participated in nearly a score of battles, veterans who had heard the hiss of hostile bullets and the violent, angry, rush of shot and shell on many famous fields, well knew what was about to take place. The breastworks in their front teem with men in blue preparing to charge. Their standards, in numbers indicating the presence of a very large force, are defiantly floating above them. This was the situation when the hundred and nineteen men whose memory we are here to honor and their comrades, prepared to do their duty at whatever cost, at the cost even of life itself, rested on the hill-slope ready to begin the deadly work, each man feeling that within the next few minutes he might be in another world.

General Mahone calls the regimental commanders before him and delivers a striking address in which he tells that the men then in line are the only barrier to the enemy's occupying the city of Petersburg.

HEROIC WORDS

Returning to his regiment from this meeting of officers Captain Richard W. Jones,[51] who commanded the 12th Virginia regiment, stepped in front of the regiment and with great coolness of manner spoke these impressive words:

---

51. Richard W. Jones, son of a wealthy landowner and graduate of Randolph-Macon College and the University of Virginia (M.A., 1861), enlisted as captain of Company I of the 12th Virginia in February 1862. He commanded the regiment for two weeks in September 1862, and was promoted to major in July 1864. He was in command of the regiment when it surrendered at Appomattox. After the war, he had a productive career as a college professor and eventually college president.

Men, you are called upon to charge and recapture our works, now in the hands of the enemy. They are only one hundred yards distant. The enemy can fire but one volley before the works are reached. At the command "forward" every many is expected to rise and move forward at a double-quick and with a yell. Every man is expected to do his duty.

It is said that when Lord Nelson's ships were bearing down on the French and Spanish fleets off Cape Trafalgar he hoisted the signal "England expects every man was to do his duty" and that this [the men] received with tremendous cheering by the whole fleet. The men of Mahone's brigade did not cheer when they received a like admonition. The death grapple of these men with the enemy was closer at hand than was that of the English sailors with their foe. It was not the time to cheer. It was the time for action.

Within a few minutes the charge is ordered. The Virginia brigade and a small part of Wright's Georgia brigade, in all less than a thousand men, spring forward, move across the intervening field in a beautiful line of battle, with great rapidity, apparently as if in a race to reach the goal, the breastworks, the regimental colors of the five regiments of the brigade held aloft and conspicuously floating in the breeze as they are borne by their gallant color bearers, many men falling killed or wounded before the works are reached.

RECAPTURE THE WORKS

The works are reached and recaptured from the Crater [n]orthwardly but not until there has been much hand-to-hand fighting in which bayonet and clubbed muskets were freely used and great bravery displayed on the part of men on both sides.

It is not proposed to give the details of this unique engagement nor to tell how the men of Wise's brigade under Col. J. Thomas Goode,[52] of Elliott's brigade under Col. F. W. McMaster[53] and of Ransom's brigade under Col. Lee M. McAfee[54] on the flanks, or how the artillery helped the Virginia brigade in its work. Suffice it to say that a few hours later the Alabama brigade of Mahone's division, led by General Jno. C. Saunders, completed the work of the day by capturing the Crater and thus restoring the broken Confederate lines.

52. Colonel J. Thomas Goode of Mecklenburg County, Virginia, served in the 34th Virginia Infantry.

53. Colonel F. W. McMaster led the 17th South Carolina Infantry.

54. Colonel LeRoy Mangum McAffee, of Cleveland County, North Carolina, had been commissioned a major on April 12, 1862, and reached the rank of colonel on November 1, 1862.

I have asked, why did these men whose memory we are honoring die? Why was all of that carnage on that July day on the field of the Crater and on hundreds of other days and other fields during the four years from April, 1861, to April, 1865, in which the Confederate States enrolled in their armies six hundred thousand and the United States in theirs over two million, seven hundred thousand, and in which nearly a half million of men lost their lives?

Our dead comrades fought and died in defence of their rights, their homes and their firesides.

A SETTLED QUESTION

Some contend that this stupendous struggle might have been avoided. It might have been postponed, but not avoided. In 1820 and again in 1850 premonitions of the gathering storm appeared in the debates in halls of Congress and in the utterances of the press. In 1861 the great Ruler of the Universe, in the plentitude of His power, for His own purposes, allowed the storm to burst in all of its terrific fury and permitted the great war, then begun, to be fought through four years to a finish. The results have been many and far reaching, but none more striking than the growing conviction among thoughtful minds of the world, those of the North included, that the people of the South, however unwise or inexpedient may have been their act of secession, were, under the circumstances that surrounded them, justified in resorting to arms to maintain the right of their States to withdraw from the Union, if they saw fit, as they did to exercise this right. But it is proper to add here that the same omnipotent power, in His infinite wisdom has allowed future events so to shape themselves that all now regard the question of secession as finally settled against the right as claimed by the seceding States and no people of our re-united country are more loyal to it or would go further to defend it than the people of the South and especially the Confederate veterans. Had those brave men who fell at the Crater lived to be with us today, it is fair to presume that patriotic as they were, they would have shared this view.

Ladies of the Memorial Association of Petersburg, by direction of Col. Stewart,[55] Chief of the Crater Legion, I now commit to your keeping the tablet on which are the names of the gallant dead of Mahone's brigade who fell on the Battle of the Crater, satisfied from your splendid record of forty odd years of good works that you will carefully preserve it along with other mementos of the cause for which they died.

---

55. Colonel Stewart, the author of *A Pair of Blankets,* had been commissioned July 11, 1861, as a captain. See note 127 in Chapter 6.

8

The Battles for the Weldon Railroad

IN AUGUST 1864 THE ARMIES continued to man the lines around Petersburg and Richmond. Tethered to its supply base at City Point, the Union army partially enveloped Petersburg, cutting off all approaches to the city from the southeast. The Confederates continued to draw supply from the Weldon Railroad, the Boydton Plank Road, and the South Side Railroad. On August 14, Grant began another offensive, striking with the Union Second and Tenth Corps at Deep Bottom, north of the James River. When that thrust stalled, the Federals attacked south of Petersburg with the Fifth Corps, under Major General Gouverneur K. Warren, advancing west from the Jerusalem Plank Road to gain a lodgment on the Weldon Railroad. The Confederates immediately counterattacked, and several days of combat followed.

In 1896, Bernard received an invitation from the Calcotte-Wrenn Camp of Confederate Veterans to deliver a "war talk" of his choosing. On August 19, the thirty-second anniversary of the Weldon Railroad battles, Bernard traveled to Isle of Wight Courthouse and gave a lengthy address on Warren's offensive against the rail line. Bernard's talk focused on the 12th Virginia's role in the fighting on August 19, 1864. A transcript of his talk, reproduced in this chapter, appeared in the *Petersburg Daily Index-Appeal* in 1898, in four parts. Bernard's articles contain numerous excerpts from the *Official Records,* which have been excluded here and replaced with brief descriptions of the excerpted material.

>—◦—◅◆┃◁····▷┃◆▷—◦—◅

"The Weldon Railroad Fight: Gen. Mahone's Brilliant Move," by George S. Bernard[1]

In the Federal Rear—Graphic and Thrilling Account of the Battles of Aug. 18–21, 1864, Including the Engagement of Aug. 19, About Aiken's Farm—Gen. Mahone's Account.

An address delivered by George S. Bernard on the 19th of August, 1896, before Calcotte-Wrenn Camp of Confederate Veterans on the occasion of its annual reunion at Isle of Wight, C.H., Va.:

Comrades: Honored by an invitation from Calcotte-Wrenn Camp of Confederate Veterans to give its members a "War Talk" on this 19th day of August, 1896, after casting about for an appropriate subject, I have selected the movement of the Federal forces under General G. K. Warren on the Weldon railroad during the four days from August 18th to August 21st, 1864, embracing the engagement about Aiken's farm on the 19th of August, 1864, in which it was the fortune of many citizens of this county, some of whom are present here today, to participate as members of Weisiger's brigade, of Mahone's division.

This day marks the lapse of thirty-two long years since that memorable afternoon in which General Wm. Mahone, with a comparatively small force, consisting of three depleted brigades, his old brigade commanded by General David A. Weisiger among the number, pierced the Federal lines and moving down on the right flank and in the rear of the line of battle of Warren's corps, then stretched across the Weldon railroad and facing northwardly, captured probably more prisoners than the three brigades had men, and only retired when two divisions of Parke's corps came to the relief of Warren, attacked and nearly surrounded these Confederates.

To recount some of the features and incidents of these moves on the military chess board of the day and particularly of General Mahone's dashing exploit on the 19th of August, 1864, one of the most striking in the history of the siege of Petersburg, as they have been gathered from the official records and from the statements of participants, and as they are vividly remembered by one who was present as a member of one of the Petersburg companies belonging to the 12th Virginia regiment of Weisiger's brigade, it is believed will

---

1. Bernard's account of "The Weldon Railroad Fight" appeared in the *Petersburg Daily Index-Appeal* in four installments: January 1, 9, 16, and 23, 1898. The heading for the first installment states: "The following will appear in "'War Talks of Confederate Veterans,' Vol. II."

not fail to interest the grisly veterans here assembled and the young men to whom the eventful four years of our great struggle are but a tradition.

For the better understanding of the situation it should be stated that after the Federal disaster at the Crater on the 30th of July, 1864, there were several days of comparative quiet along the lines of both armies about Petersburg. On the night of the 12th of August, however, General Grant began what is historically known as "the movement to Deep Bottom," in which General Hancock with his own corps (the Second) and the Tenth corps (now under General D. B. Birney) made a move on the north side of James river, resulting in some severe fighting and in drawing, of course, to that side of the James some of the forces General Lee had about Petersburg.

There was fighting about Deep Bottom on the 14th and on the Charles City road on the 16th, with some skirmishing on the 15th. It will be recalled that on one of the two last mentioned days, the 16th, the Confederates lost two gallant brigadier-generals, General John R. Chambliss of the cavalry, and General Victor J. B. Girardey, of the infantry, who, promoted from a captaincy, had held only a for a few days the commission of a brigadier-general given him for gallant conduct at the battle of the Crater and on other fields whilst acting as a staff officer of General Mahone. . . .

[The article includes several excerpts from the *Official Records* that are not included here.]

This move to the north of the James was unsuccessful. But General Grant saw that it gave an opportunity to make a move on his left toward the Weldon railroad.

[Drawing heavily on the *Official Records,* Bernard describes the situation his regiment faced on August 19, 1864. The Union Fifth Corps and its attached cavalry reached the Weldon Railroad, fended off a Confederate attack, and began to dig in. The Federals attempted to picket the heavily wooded gap between Warren's force and the left of the Northern Army, which rested three miles away on the Jerusalem Plank Road. The Union high command dispatched reinforcements from Parke's Ninth Corps to reinforce Warren.]

We have now the situation of affairs on the night of the 18th, pretty clearly disclosed by the contemporaneous correspondence of the leading actors.

Warren is upon the Weldon railroad with a line of battle stretching a half mile westwardly toward Poplar Grove church and eastwardly probably over a mile in the direction of the Jerusalem plank road. There has been heavy fight-

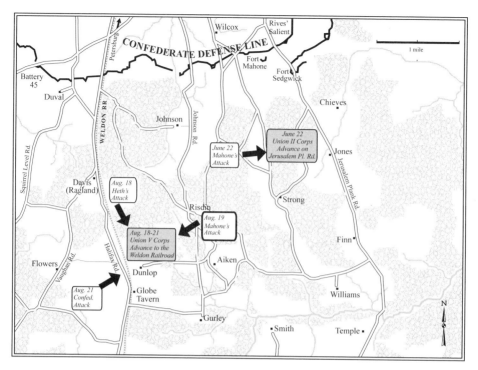

BATTLES FOR THE WELDON RAILROAD, JUNE–AUGUST 1864

ing during the day. Grant thinks that Lee means to attack in force the next day and orders Parke[2] to take some 6,000 of his troops to the support of Warren. Accordingly arrangements are made to take all of Parke's white troops. There is an interval of from a half to one mile, held only by a picket line of Federal cavalry between the right of Warren and the left of Parke's corps. This thinly guarded interval, with its line of cavalry pickets is to prove an important factor in the events of the day.

Let us see what has been transpiring on the Confederate side of the lines. I regret that I can not furnish you more than what appears in the diary of a member of the Virginia brigade (Weisiger's) of Mahone's division who carried a musket. It is, however, given for what it is worth.

On the 17th and 18th I made the following entries in this diary:

2. Major General John G. Parke, Burnside's former chief of staff, took command of the Union Ninth Corps after Burnside was relieved following the Crater battle. Parke, a native Pennsylvanian, remained in the army after the war and eventually served as superintendent of the U.S. Military Academy. He died in 1900.

Wednesday Aug. 17 '64

Last Friday night whilst our company was on picket, our brigade moved from its position at the breastworks to quarter of a mile to the rear with instructions to remain there until further orders. Various were the surmises to the meaning of this move, the most popular of which was that we were to go out to Hicksford or Stoney Creek on the Weldon railroad to repel a cavalry attack. Sunday night we were moved back to our old position, Saunders [Sanders] and Wright having left in the afternoon, going somewhere across the river. Last evening, Harris moved off to Chaffin's Bluff it is said, and we were moved to the left and now occupy the positions recently held by both Saunders [Sanders] and Harris, being strung out in one rank.

On Picket Thursday Aug. 18

Yesterday afternoon got a permit and went out to Mr. Peter Cogbill's, 2–1/2 miles in Dinwiddie, returning to the breastworks by 11.00 o'clock last night & then coming out here to the picket line. My visit a very pleasant one—such a treat to get away from camp even for a short time. This morning about 2 o'clock there was very heavy artillery firing along the lines. I hear we were shelling the enemy who were massing troops on our left. The enemy replied very feebly—the pyrotechnic display of the blazing shells very pretty. A cavalry fight this afternoon about the Weldon RR apparently near Ragland's house[3] 5 miles from town. Report says we drove back the enemy's cavalry—at any rate the fighting has ceased. We are to be relieved this evening. A great mass meeting of the Peace democrats of New York to be held today in Syracuse, N.Y.

The picket line upon which the last entry was made, the line, along which the pickets from Weisiger's brigade did duty at this time, as they had done for several weeks, previously, ran along the northern edge of the heavy body of woods then standing south of the Wilcox and east to the Johnson house. The axe of the woodman has felled nearly all of the large trees in this historic body of timber, in which General Mahone on the 22nd of June 1864, made a brilliant swoop upon Barlow's division of Hancock's corps, capturing about 1,600 prisoners, 4 pieces of artillery and 8 stand of colors. The Johnson house, burned in 1870, has been replaced by a modern structure.

The Ragland house . . . still stands, within and near the forks of the Hali-

---

3. As Bernard explains later, Federal military maps refer to Ragland house as the "Davis" house (see *Atlas to Accompany the Official Records of the Union and Confederate Armies* [Washington, D.C.: Government Printing Office, 1891–95], Plate LXXVII).

fax and Vaughan roads, distant from the corporation line, not five, as I supposed when referring to it in the diary, but only about one and a half miles.

It is interesting to note that the official reports show that the heavy shelling referred to in the last entry originated with the Confederates in a purpose to shell the Negro troops.

[On the morning of August 19, General Beauregard, the Confederate commander at Petersburg, scraped together a force to drive Warren's Federals from the Weldon Railroad. Warren's soldiers continued to improve their position.]

Back in the breastworks of the Wilcox farm on the 19th, some time before the hour of 1 p.m., I made the following entry in my diary:

Breastworks
Friday August 19

The fight of yesterday turns out to have been more serious than a mere cavalry fight. The 5th Corps (Warren's) drove in our Cavalry as far as Davis's house 1 mile from town when Walker's and Davis' brigades drove them back 3/4 of a mile, when the enemy by its superior force succeeded in flanking *us* and forcing our troops to retire a short distance. It is said the enemy have torn up 2–1/2 miles of the railroad commencing at the Yellow Tavern [also known as Globe Tavern] & coming this way. Our loss is said to be about 400 or 500 and the enemy's very heavy. We captured about 200 prisoners and lost about 30.[4] A few minutes ago our brigade was formed, it was reported, to march against the enemy at this point, but we were ordered back to our quarters to await orders. Our batteries opened on the enemy again this morning, about 2 o'clock, the enemy replying very feebly. The *New York Herald* of the 16th boldly urges peace, calls for great mass meetings of citizens; New York City to appoint 500 commissioners to wait upon Lincoln to urge him to send peace commissioners to Richmond to make overtures of an armistice and a convention of the states to agree upon a peace mutually satisfactory.

I feel uneasy about safety of my Brother Meade[5] who was to have left Greensville yesterday for this place coming on horseback. I fear he has fallen into the hands of the enemy as this line of battle straddles across the road he was to travel.

4. The Federals lost more than 900 men, including almost 200 prisoners. Confederate casualties totaled about 350, at least 50 of whom were prisoners (see John Horn, *The Destruction of the Weldon Railroad: Deep Bottom, Globe Tavern, and Reams Station, August 14–25, 1864* [Lynchburg, Va.: H. E. Howard, 1991], 68, 222n157, 222n158).

5. David Meade Bernard Jr., George S. Bernard's half-brother, is discussed in note 20, chapter 1.

....

I will now reproduce a full, clear and graphic statement written in July, 1895, by the late General Mahone a few weeks before his death, narrating the part taken by the three brigades placed under his command in the move to strike the enemy a blow. . . .

STATEMENT OF WILLIAM MAHONE

Responding to your request for a brief account of the attack made by the troops under my command on the 19th day of August, 1864, I give you the facts as follows:

My division at this time was occupying the trenches from the Rives salient, just east of the Jerusalem plank road, to the Branch house, the right of the right brigade resting about the bluff overlooking the dam of the new reservoir recently constructed by the city of Petersburg. On the 18th of August the enemy had made his appearance on the Weldon railroad at Yellow Tavern.

General Dearing[6] was there with his small command of cavalry and had saluted his coming with two cannon shots, fired in quick succession.

Seated at my headquarters in the yard of the Branch house, I heard these cannon shots and soon thereafter a member of General Hill's staff came up. I asked their meaning. He informed me that the enemy had made their appearance on the railroad at the place mentioned, and that General Hill had sent General Heth with two brigades of his division to the point of attack. Of General Hill's three divisions two—Heth's and Wilcox's—were not in the trenches.

In my conversation with this staff officer I called attention to the fact that, the left of the enemy's main line then terminating about Fort Sedgwick on the Jerusalem plank road, there was probably an intervening space of fully a mile between this line and his position at the Yellow Tavern, and also that there was nothing between the small force sent out under General Heth and the city, should he need help either for purpose of attack or defense, and I further expressed the opinion that the proper thing to be done was to move a column of attack up the deep ravine west of the Branch house (the ravine in which the reservoir above mentioned is located) in the direction of the Johnson house, and keeping the column out of the enemy's sight by the ravine and the intervening woods skirting the field east of the house and reaching his vidette

---

6. Brigadier General James Dearing, a former West Point cadet who had resigned in 1861 to serve in the Confederate army, commanded a brigade of cavalry during the Petersburg Campaign. He entered Confederate service as a lieutenant and attained the rank of general, leading cavalry in the last two years of the war. On April 6, 1865, he was mortally wounded at the age of twenty-four during fighting at High Bridge.

line, which I supposed would be found in the woods south of the field above mentioned, on the right of the force of the enemy at Yellow Tavern, to plunge through this line to the right flank and rear of his now probably extended position about the railroad. It was not reasonable to anticipate that he had so quickly covered the space intervening between this and the plank road, but it was reasonable to suppose he would rely upon the heavy growth of the woodland to save him from any surprise from this quarter. This view of the situation was subsequently ascertained to be precisely correct.

After my interview with General Hill's staff officer, who was Capt. R. H. Adams,[7] of Lynchburg, Va., I rode out in the afternoon to General Heth's line and found him in line of battle across the railroad, facing south and confronting the enemy.

The next morning—the morning of the 19th—I received a message from General Hill saying that General Beauregard desired that I would attack the enemy at Yellow Tavern according the plan I had explained to his (General Hill's) staff-officer, that General Beauregard would send me two brigades from Hoke's division and that I should take one of my own brigades to make up the attacking force.

In response to this message I suggested that as troops always fought better under their own commander than under a stranger, and both commander and troops generally did their best when accustomed to each other, it would be best for General Hoke[8] to take charge of the attacking force. The suggestion, however, was not acted upon and soon two brigades of General Hoke's division, Colquitt's and Clingman's were at my headquarters at the Branch house the Virginia brigade (Weisiger's) of my division having been in the mean time quickly withdrawn from the trenches.

It was now after midday. The column, being formed, moved to the ravine and up it in the direction of the Johnson house, Colquitt leading, Clingman following and Weisiger bringing up the rear. We reached the field in front of the Johnson house and crossed to the body of woods southeast of the house,

---

7. Captain Richard Henry Toler Adams had enlisted as a private in the 11th Virginia Infantry in April 1861. He served as acting assistant adjutant and inspector general beginning in August 1864. He worked as a banker and businessman in Lynchburg after the war.

8. Major General Robert Hoke of North Carolina, who attended the Kentucky Military Institute, began the war as a 2nd lieutenant. In 1863, he was promoted to brigadier general in command of several North Carolina regiments. In 1864, he attained the rank of major general and commanded a division during the Petersburg Campaign and later during fighting at Wilmington. After the war, he returned to manage his family's iron business, and died in Raleigh, North Carolina, in 1912.

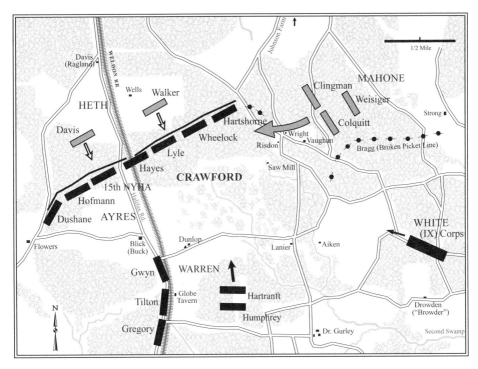

WELDON RAILROAD: MAHONE'S ATTACK, AUGUST 19, 1864

and went briskly on 'till we pierced the enemy's vidette line in these woods. Some shots were fired at our column but were not returned. I had located in my mind quite accurately the position of the enemy at Yellow Tavern and when I got, as I believed, fully behind his line of battle that faced General Heth and in the right relation to his works, I formed line of battle, Colquitt on the left, Clingman on the right and Weisiger in column of regiments behind Colquitt's left, it being on the left that I apprehended might come an attack from any reinforcements the enemy might send over from the plank road.

The line of battle being thus formed, I called up the brigadiers commanding the front brigades and explained to them the position of the Yellow Tavern, and that a steady advance would bring the attacking force in rear of the enemy's line facing General Heth and upon General Warren's headquarters. General Clingman[9] desired to know what was to become of our rear—what was to protect the attacking force from an advance of the enemy on the plank road. My reply was: "that is my look-out, general, your duty is in the front." I

9. Brigadier General Thomas L. Clingman of North Carolina, a politician before the war, had begun the conflict as a colonel and was appointed brigadier general in

then cautioned the brigadiers to pay no attention to the fire of any vidette or picket line we were likely to encounter, but to hold their fire till the works and main body of the enemy was reached.

Magnificently and with steady step the three brigades moved off and shortly we flushed the enemy's vidette line, which drew the fire of our front line, but onward the attacking force proceeded, reaching an old saw mill and a small open field, where I met litter-bearers carrying off General Clingman who had been wounded in the leg. His brigade, however, could not be seen. I rode to General Colquitt,[10] whom I saw on the fringe of this open space, and enquired where his brigade was. Pointing to a small body of men, possibly not more than one hundred and fifty, he replied, "These are all I have left."

We were now at the point where the work of attack had to be done. The enemy had drawn back his artillery and was firing indiscriminately into the woods in which the main portion of my attacking force was moving and had veered off to the right. Meanwhile the enemy's line of battle to Gen. Heth's left had thrown down their guns and been captured and taken off to my right by Clingman's and a good part of Colquitt's brigades. At this moment I sent off Maj. R. P. Duncan, of the division staff, to go by a short road to the right of General Heth (where I knew General Hill had gone) to request General Hill to have General Heth extend his front. In a few minutes I saw Major Duncan[11] in my rear a prisoner in the hands of a number of Federals, who, themselves, retreating, had met and captured the major. I rushed upon the squad of Federals and ordered that they be gone in the direction I indicated or they would be fired upon. They obeyed with alacrity and Major Duncan was free again. Meanwhile I dispatched my courier, [Robert] R. Henry, now Major R. R. Henry,[12] of Tazewell C.H., Va., to take General Hill the message I had given Major Duncan. At this juncture I ordered General Weisiger

---

May 1862. He fought with his brigade at Cold Harbor, Drewry's Bluff, Petersburg, and Weldon Railroad (where he was severely wounded). After the war, he worked as a lawyer and also explored and measured the Allegheny mountains.

10. Brigadier General Alfred H. Colquitt, a Princeton graduate, was a native of Georgia. He fought in most of the major engagements in the Eastern Theater. In 1864, he commanded Confederate forces at the Battle of Olustee, Florida. He led his brigade during the Petersburg Campaign. After the war, he served as governor of Georgia and in the U.S. Senate. He died in 1894.

11. R. P. Duncan, an attorney who studied at the University of Virginia, served on the staffs of both Generals Richard Anderson and William Mahone. He died in 1905.

12. Major Robert R. Henry began his war service at the age of sixteen with the 12th Virginia. He was wounded at Burgess Mill on October 27, 1864. Henry's version of this incident, mentioned in the text here, is in the George S. Bernard Papers at the Southern

to form line and move upon the enemy's works. In a few moments Courier Henry returned with two Federal soldiers—Colonel William R. Hartshorne[13] and his courier. He had met them on a by-road on his way to General Hill and demanded their surrender, himself without weapon of any kind, not even a pocket-knife. I gave him the sword and pistol of Colonel Hartshorne and directed that he take the prisoners to my headquarters.

I now set out to find General Hill myself, and found him, but no help could be given. So I hastened back to withdraw the now isolated Virginia brigade, but met it retiring in good order after it had been engaged with the enemy as narrated by Colonel Stewart and yourself. It had been confronted and out-flanked by reinforcements from the plank road.

There were captured in this attack over 2,600 prisoners, including a staff officer of General Warren. It was a good day's work, and if I had two more brigades, we would doubtless have captured Warren's position and his corps.[14]

[With Hancock still at Deep Bottom, the Federals had run out of reinforcements for Warren. The Confederates, however, failed to mount another counterattack on August 20th. After reviewing the material in the *Official Records* and registering his differences with the Northern accounts (excluded here), Bernard resumes his narrative.]

Mahone's and Heth's forces together are less than 6,000 men. Meade estimates them at 12,000 and tells Grant that Warren after his losses ought to have nearly 20,000!

. . . Warren informs us which of the troops of Parke's corps are those that came to his rescue, and their number, and we thus learn that Weisiger's brigade, isolated, as General Mahone says it was, with but a few of the other two brigades, was attacked by two divisions numbering 2,200 men! General Warren's statement that the Confederate troops, "in great confusion fell back" to their intrenchments, is not in accordance with the statement of General

---

Historical Collection. There Henry related drawing a revolver captured at the Crater but not in working order. See also Horn, *The Destruction of the Weldon Railroad*, 84, 225n111.

13. Colonel William R. Hartshorne of Pennsylvania had begun the war as a 1st lieutenant. He was wounded and captured at Mechanicsville, Virginia, on June 26, 1862, and exchanged several months later. He was promoted to colonel in the 190th Pennsylvania. He died in Philadelphia in 1905.

14. The Union lost about 3,000 men, including about 2,700 prisoners, while the Confederates lost about 600, 300 of them prisoners (see Horn, *The Destruction of the Weldon Railroad*, 88, 226nn138–139).

Mahone nor of any other surviving member of his command with whom I have had an opportunity to confer, and it is to be sincerely hoped that there is a like mistake as to the instance of brutality on the part of a Confederate officer which Warren mentions. Here is what he says . . .

OFFICIAL REPORT OF GEN. GOUVERNEUR K. WARREN

[The Federal divisions of Willcox, White, Crawford, and Ayres counteratacked,] engaged Colquitt's brigade of the enemy, and drove it back, capturing about 40 prisoners. The enemy in great confusion rapidly fell back to his intrenchments, carrying with them the disorganized parts of the command, which had become so by the attack from the rear in the woods, and also a large portion of those on picket. An instance of brutality occurred on the part of a rebel officer which deserves execration. Finding he was too closely pressed to carry off Captain Newbury,[15] Twelfth U. S. Infantry, a prisoner, he deliberately put a pistol to his breast and shot him. This is the testimony of the dying man himself. Before this flank attack began, signal officers reported troops moving against my front on the railroad, and General Ayres[16] reported their arrival on his front. These made repeated attempts to force him back after he regained his line but failed.

The enemy's loss must have been heavy in killed and wounded.

Let us draw again from the diary:

Saturday August 20, '64

Got orders to move yesterday about 1 o'clock. I saw Captain Taylor of Hill's staff just before we started who informed me that our destination was down the RR & that 5 brigades were going out to drive away the enemy. The five were Davis and Walker's of Heth's Division, Clingman's & Colquitt's of Hoke's and ours. The three last moved on the left flank, the two first in the front. I will not further describe the action than to mention that our brigade was in the warmest place we were ever in being subjected to a fire from the front, right flank, and rear all at the same time. The flanking brigades drove the enemy into the brigades moving upon the front. The result being the capture of 3,000 of them. The brigades in front carried two lines of breastworks but did not attempt the third. The loss in our brigade was 187 killed,

15. Captain Samuel Sergeant Newbury, a native of Indiana, had enlisted in May 1861 as a 1st lieutenant.

16. Brigadier General Romeyn B. Ayres, a West Point graduate and Mexican War veteran, served as artillery officer early in the war and later as infantry division commander. He remained in the army following the conflict and died in New York in 1888.

wounded and missing out of over 600 muskets carried in, and our regiment [lost] 6 killed, 29 wounded and 2 missing out of 90 and odd officers & arms bearing men carried in. The loss included 2 men in the ambulance corps. The killed were Lieutenant Leath,[17] company D, and Beale,[18] company H, privates Alley[19] and Robert Fenn,[20] company A. Walker,[21] company H, David Ridout,[22] company F., and among the wounded were Captain Jones, commander regiment, Sergeant-Major Maclin,[23] and privates Robins [Robbins],[24] R. A. Machen,[25] company E, the latter probably mortally. Most of our badly wounded fell into the hands of the enemy when we were withdrawn at sunset.

My brother [Meade] reached Petersburg in safety yesterday afternoon about 3 o'clock.

17. William C. Leath, one of three brothers who served in the 12th Virginia Infantry, enlisted as a 1st sergeant in Company D in April 1861. Promoted to 1st lieutenant in February 1863, he was acting company commander for the next eighteen months. He was wounded and captured at the Battle of Weldon Railroad in August 1864, not killed as Bernard states.

18. Charles T. Beale, a brick mason, enlisted as a sergeant in Company H of the 12th Virginia in April 1861. Reduced to private in October 1861, he was later restored to sergeant (January 1862) and then elected to 2nd lieutenant in April 1862. Captured at Chancellorsville, he was exchanged in May 1863. He returned to his unit only to be killed in action at the Battle of Weldon Railroad in August 1864.

19. Francis P. Alley enlisted as a private in Company A of the 12th Virginia in May 1862. He was twice wounded (Malvern Hill and Spotsylvania) and twice hospitalized. He was killed in action at the Weldon Railroad.

20. Private Robert H. Fenn, a Petersburg student, enlisted as a private in Company A in May 1862. He was killed in action at Weldon Railroad.

21. William H. Walker, a carpenter, enlisted as a private in April 1861. Captured at Chancellorsville, he was later exchanged. He was not killed at the Weldon Railroad, but captured and eventually released from Point Lookout prison in May 1865.

22. David C. Ridout enlisted as a private in Company H in March 1862. He was wounded and captured at Weldon Railroad (not killed as Bernard states).

23. Joseph J. Maclin, a clerk for Petersburg commission merchants, enlisted as a private in Company B in the 12th Virginia in May 1861. Wounded at Crampton's Gap, he recovered and later rejoined his unit, receiving promotion to sergeant major in February 1864. Wounded in four places during the Petersburg fighting, he survived the war and lived into the twentieth century.

24. Frank Robbins enlisted as a private in Company E of the 12th Virginia in July 1861. Wounded at Weldon Railroad, he returned to his unit and surrendered at Appomattox.

25. Richard Avery Machen, a contractor and architect, enlisted as a private in Company E of the 12th Virginia in April 1862. Sick for almost a year, he was detailed as a ward master at Virginia Hospital for eleven months. He returned to his unit only to be mortally wounded at the Battle of Weldon Railroad.

Heavy cannonading along the lines on the right last night—too sleepy to get up to see what was "to pay" although the battery not 50 yards from our tent was lumbering away pretty freely.

About 3 o'clock this afternoon orders reached us to have cartridge boxes filled and 1 day's rations prepared by 7 o'clock. Conjecture immediately interpreted this as meaning a night march through Dinwiddie to get in the rear of the enemy who still hold the Weldon railroad. A few minutes ago (6:30 p.m.) we received orders to form at the breastworks with guns & accoutrements at 7 o'clock. What does this mean? Perhaps our guns are to open on the enemy.

This account of a memorable engagement is meager. I trusted to memory to hold its principle details. After the lapse of thirty-odd years I find the impressions made are still retained with great vividness, almost as if the events were those of yesterday.

The march up the ravine west of the Branch house; our going by the same route we took on the afternoon of June 22, 1864 when General Mahone took us out to fight Hancock's men in the woods in front of the Johnson house; our march across the field in front of Johnson's house to the southeast corner of this field; our entering the woods there, wheeling into line of battle and rapidly advancing westwardly towards the railroad; the bursting up in the air near the advancing column of one or more of the Federal shells fired from a battery in the neighborhood of the railroad; these and other incidents hereinafter to be mentioned are fresh in mind.

Gen. Weisiger's Great Skill In Handling His Brigade Under Difficult and Perilous Conditions—Statement by Gen. Weisiger, Col. Stewart, Col. Groner and Other Participants[26]

The appearance of at least one of the picket posts so hastily deserted by the Pennsylvanians attracted my attention and is well remembered, the savory dinner smoking by the little fire at which it was being cooked plainly disclosing the fact that its owners had left in a hurry. Our brigade had just faced to the west and was double-quicking, or rapidly marching, in line of battle towards the railroad, the enemy's shells bursting about us as the line pushed forward. This picket post was in the yard of a small settlement.

[The shelling caused at least as much damage among the Federals as among the Confederates. The Union infantry in the front line had been instructed

26. This installment of Bernard's article appeared in the *Petersburg Index-Appeal,* January 9, 1898.

to withdraw by the flank if driven from their position. Seeing Confederates appear behind the Northern trenches, the Federal gunners assumed their infantry had evacuated the trenches and the artillerists opened fire. They drove the Confederates back into the woods, but blasted the bluecoats of Crawford's division as well.]

Shelled as we advanced, within a few minutes we had reached a small branch running southwardly in a ditch, the stream considerably swollen by rain water. Along this ditch we moved a short distance, perhaps a hundred or two yards, southwardly, to a point at which we had a body of second growth pines in our rear about a hundred yards distant and slightly raising ground in our front on the west side of the branch. Arriving at this position we saw a line of battle to our right and front facing northwardly, we then facing westwardly and being of course to their rear. This was a Federal line of battle confronting Heth's men, and some of the men in our line were in favor of charging this body of the enemy, not more than 150 yards from us. I well remember seeing Sergt. Emmet Richardson,[27] of Co. K of our regiment (12th Va.) leap to the west of the ditch and start up the hill, attempting to lead a charge, saying as he did this, "Come on boys! They are Yankees! Let's charge 'em."

Just at this juncture I recall Clingman's or Colquitt's brigade, certainly, a few men of one or the other of these two brigades, as passing along by us, going (I think) down the course of the ditch towards our left. Before we had been ten minutes in this position—a critical one indeed—a part of our brigade, certainly the 12th regiment, and from what I have recently learned perhaps also a part of the 41st regiment, the next on our left, ordered to about face and moved back to the edge of the pines already mentioned, taking a position in the edge of the pines about one hundred yards east of the branch. But we had hardly taken this position before a body of Federal troops appeared in these pines about 150 yards to the east of us and immediately opened fired upon us, which we promptly and vigorously returned, our men lying down and firing in this position. It was a rainy, dismal, evening, and it was, or seemed to be, nearly sunset. So, we could see nothing in front, in the dense pines, but the flashing of the enemy's rifles, and occasionally the figure of a man. Whilst we were thus engaged, we were the recipients not only of the fire from our front, but also of a fire from our right and rear, the latter doubtless coming from some of Warren's men we had seen when at the branch, an experience to which troops are seldom subjected.

27. First Sergeant Thomas E. Richardson, an iron molder, had enlisted as a private in May 1861.

There occurred just at this time an incident which I have often recalled. To my immediate left, some five or six feet away, was Richard A. Machen, of the Petersburg Rifleman, Co E, 12th Va. Regt., whose groans attracted my attention and strongly appealed to me to help him. Leaving my position, where I had been lying down, loading and firing, I went to him, and finding him badly wounded, could only endeavor to cheer him by telling him that I thought the battle would soon be over and that then the ambulance corps would take him from the field. I returned to my position, and, as I had told Machen would happen, without any reason for expressing this opinion beyond a desire to encourage the poor fellow, the firing slackened and the battle soon ceased. Our men were ordered to fall back a few paces and within fifteen minutes of the time I had spoken to my wounded comrade we were marching in good order in four ranks northwardly, withdrawing from the position in which we were nearly surrounded by Warren's men to the west of us and by the men of Parke's corps who had attacked us on the east in the pines and also from the south, this movement, executed without excitement, attesting the splendid discipline of our command.

Poor Machen was left on the field, as were other of our dead and wounded, and was never afterwards heard from.

From a recent examination of the ground, and after correspondence with some and personal interviews with other surviving comrades who participated in this battle, I am able to make the following explanation of it:

The ditch with its branch (the latter appearing on the military map of the territory around Petersburg) at the point at which our brigade engaged the enemy, which I would locate as about three hundred yards north of a straight line drawn from the Dunlop to the Lanier house, runs southwardly, makes a short bend of elbow eastwardly and then runs southwardly.

When the brigade reached the ditch the 12th regiment being on the extreme right of the brigade, was highest up the ditch and faced westwardly towards the Weldon railroad.

The 41st was on its left and stood along the ditch, also facing westwardly, except the part of the 41st about the bend or elbow. At the bend, or elbow, on the left of the 41st, was the right company of the 61st. This company and the part of the 41st in the elbow faced southwardly. The remaining companies of the 61st were bent around, together with the 16th and the 6th regiments, so as to face eastwardly: the brigade being placed by General Weisiger in this horse-shoe shape to prevent the large force of the enemy he saw confronting his small command, which could not have numbered more than 600 muskets, if so many, from overlapping and surrounding the brigade. Seeing that the overlapping was greatest on the left, or east, flank where the 6th, 16th, and

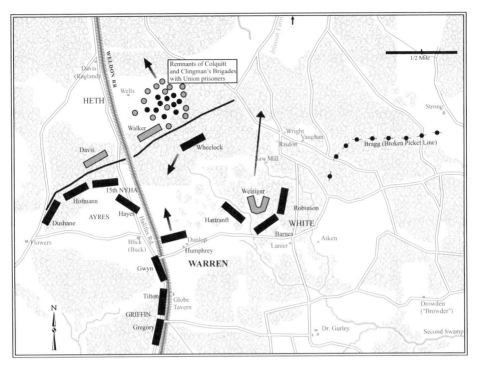

WELDON RAILROAD: UNION COUNTERATTACK, AUGUST 19, 1864

a part of the 61st were placed, fronting in that direction, he withdrew the 12th and (he thinks) probably also a part of the 41st, from their position on the right along the ditch and placed them on the extreme left in the edge of the pines to the left of the 6th, the left regiment of the brigade. This was done a few minutes before the enemy opened upon us in these pines as already narrated.

On this occasion General Weisiger handled his brigade with great skill in its exceptionally critical position, surrounded as it was by Warren's corps on its west, and by Parke's two divisions on its south and east. General Weisiger's account of the fight is very clear....

STATEMENT OF DAVID WEISIGER

General Mahone's orders to me were to keep the Virginia brigade in the rear of the other two brigades in supporting distance, as the three brigades moved forward in line of battle, so as to support either flank that might require assistance. We had advanced but a short distance in this order, when one of the enemy's batteries opened fire on us, the shots coming from our front and left as we moved forward, wounded two or three men of my brigade. Mahone, who was near by, then ordered me to charge this battery. This order was promptly obeyed. So, changing direction toward our left, I moved the brigade towards the battery, but upon reaching a branch, which was in a deep ditch, discovered that in our front, and on our left, was a heavy force of infantry, at least a division, which I then thought and now know were reinforcements sent to support Warren. This body of the enemy, as well as I could judge, were moving in line of battle on my command, and was so large that my brigade, which had been very much depleted in the recent battle of the Crater, was overlapped on both flanks, the overlapping being more on my left than on my right. So, I forwarded the center and drew back both flanks, thus forming the brigade in a semi-circle, or horse-shoe, and as the greatest overlapping was on the left, I moved the 12th, and probably also a part of the 41st, from their position in and about the ditch (the 12th being on the right of the brigade and the 41st next to the 12th) across to the extreme left of the horse-shoe, so as to prevent, if possible, the enemy getting in my rear on this (my left) flank.

We soon became heavily engaged with this large force of the enemy, which, from General Warren's official report, appears to have been two divisions of the 9th corps, and the position of things was so serious that there was fear that the enemy would charge and capture the whole command, which was now completely, or practically isolated, only a few of Colquitt's men being about the ditch (as hereinafter mentioned) and was having a very unequal contest with the enemy's large force. Such was the apprehension of capture, the gallant color-bearer of the 12th regiment, Wm. C. Smith,[28] tore the colors from the flag-staff and concealed them about his person.

About sunset, the enemy's heavy fire, having first slackened for a short while, entirely ceased. I then confidently expected the enemy would charge, and believed they would capture the whole brigade, as we were nearly surrounded and had no chance of support from any source. To my surprise no movement was made by the enemy, and as night was coming on, I quietly withdrew my command, forming on the edge of the body of pines east of us in which were the force of the enemy on our left all of which was done in good order. We had, however, to leave upon the field our badly wounded,

28. William Crawford Smith, who had two brothers in the 12th Virginia, enlisted as a private in Company B in May 1861. Wounded and captured at Crampton's Gap, he was later exchanged. Promoted to sergeant in August 1863, he received a wound in the Wilderness. He recovered and returned to the regiment, surrendering at Appomattox. He resumed his professional life in Nashville, Tennessee. A contractor and architect, he designed several buildings at Vanderbilt University and was involved with the 1896 Tennessee State Expedition. He led a regiment of Tennessee Volunteers in the Philippine War of 1899, dying in his saddle from heat stroke during the campaign.

much to my regret. After forming we marched to the rear about 200 yards and here formed another line of battle and awaited the advance of the enemy. No advance being made, after a short time we withdrew and marched toward our lines. We then met General Mahone, with Colquitt's and Clingman's brigades and their prisoners, a confused mass of men, Confederates and Federals, in much disorder, all moving in the same direction that is, towards our lines. The organization of the Virginia brigade, however, was intact.

Before my brigade became engaged a small number of Colquitt's brigade took position in the ditch on my right. I never knew what became of them. I think, however, that when I withdrew my command they and a few of the forty-first regiment of my brigade remained in the ditch and were captured.[29]

If the Virginia brigade had not checked and finally halted the advance of the Federal forces that attacked it the damage would have been very serious to all of us, as Colquitt's and Clingman's brigades were disorganized and overburdened by having in charge the twenty odd hundred prisoners they had taken from Warren's forces during the afternoon.

In justice to my command I must say that they displayed the highest degree of courage and coolness during the whole of this engagement. When they marched to the rear to the place where we formed our new line of battle as above mentioned, they moved as calmly as on an ordinary march, although there was reason to believe the enemy would follow us as we withdrew.

Other interesting details of the engagement are given in the following statements of participants:

STATEMENT OF HUGH R. SMITH

Mr. Hugh R. Smith,[30] of Petersburg, Va., adjutant of the 12th Virginia regiment, who was acting as a staff-officer of General Weisiger in this fight, says:

When we reached the ditch in which ran a branch, we saw on the hill in our front and on our right some Federal forces, some of whom seemed to be breaking from the attack in their front. Our brigade was immediately formed in a curve, or horse-shoe shaped, with the opening on the north side. I was

29. GSB: It is probable that the presence of these few men of Colquitt's brigade among the 40 prisoners which Gen. Warren says were captured led him into the error of supposing that it was Colquitt's brigade that White's division encountered.

30. Hugh Ritchie Smith, younger brother of William C. Smith, enlisted as a private in Company C of the 12th Virginia in April 1861. He rose steadily through the ranks, to captain and regimental adjutant in November 1863. He surrendered at Appomattox and returned to his home at Petersburg, where he was a businessman, civic leader, and House of Delegates member.

with General Weisiger about the left of the curve. General Weisiger sent me back to see General Mahone and tell him that we were nearly surrounded. I rode out on General Weisiger's horse, and met, as I went out, Bob Henry, Mahone's courier, on horseback, bringing a message from Mahone to Weisiger to withdraw the brigade. I received the message, took it to General Weisiger and by his order passed the order down the lines to the commandants of the regiments to quickly withdraw their men. As I returned I met Sergeant-Major Joe Maclin of the 12th coming out wounded. When I got back to the place where I left Weisiger I found Walsh[31] of the Richmond Grays, whom I had left not ten minutes before standing by the general, lying dead.

We retired from the place in good order. It was one of the closest places we were in during the war.

STATEMENT OF WILLIAM C. SMITH

Captain Wm. C. Smith, of Nashville, Tenn., who bore the colors of the 12th Virginia regiment in this action, says:

I take great pleasure in complying with your request to put on record my recollections of the battle of August 19, 1864, in which the speedy capture of the whole of Mahone's old brigade never seemed so apparent to the rank and file of the command. The three brigades under General Mahone's command were moving in column of brigades in echelon. As soon as the brigades in front, or one of them, struck the enemy, our brigade made somewhat of a turn or wheel towards the left, and in doing so not only soon became engaged with the enemy, but also found itself in a dangerous pocket, if I may so term our surroundings. Our situation was indeed a serious one as we were receiving a fire from the enemy on our front, left flank and rear. To resist this it was necessary to extend our lines until the brigade was a mere skeleton line, in a horseshoe shape, with a distances of less than seventy-four yards from one side to the other. The men in a part of this line stood in a ditch up to their knees in water. At this juncture the writer, then acting ensign of the 12th Virginia regiment, deeming the danger of our capture imminent, removed the flag from its staff and concealed it in his haversack, to prevent its falling into the enemy's hands if we ourselves should be captured.

It was in this engagement that the gallant Thomas S. Walsh, of the Richmond Grays (Co. G of the 12th Va.), to whose hand-to hand contest with Federal officer at the battle of the Crater I referred in my letter relating to

31. Thomas C. Walsh enlisted as a private in Company G of the 12th Virginia in April 1861. Wounded at Spotsylvania, he returned to his unit only to be killed in action at Weldon Railroad.

that battle, was killed while standing by the side of General Weisiger and the writer. He had just directed attention to a sword which some one had placed against a tree within three or four feet of us and enquired if either of us knew to whom it belonged, when a shot from the enemy struck him in the face and instantly killed him. I have seen other men on this and other occasions, in the heat of battle, shot down, killed or mortally wounded, but the fall of none so impressed me as did the death of this cool and brave young soldier.

STATEMENT OF WILLIAM H. STEWART

Colonel Wm. H. Stewart, of Portsmouth, Va., lieutenant-colonel of the 61st Va. Regiment, of Weisiger's brigade, says:

You have sent me a copy of General Mahone's letter to you written in July 1895, giving an account of the engagement of the 19th of August, 1864, near or on the Aiken farm south of Petersburg, in which about 2,700 prisoners were captured and Mahone's brigade got into a very close place:

General Mahone's account is so full I have but little to add. I well remember how disagreeable it was to the troops as they made their way through the thick undergrowth in the woods southeast of the Johnson house, but they pressed on, as they did so, hastily gathering whortleberries that abounded. Soon we came to the Federal vedette line and captured their dinner of pork and beans, as it was being cooked. We passed on without returning fire, and the column was placed in battle-array, Clingman and Colquitt in front and our Virginia brigade in the reserve.

In this form we moved steadily forward towards the Yellow Tavern, Warren's headquarters, and being in the rear and on the flank of Warren's line of battle, his people soon falling in the hands of Clingman's and Colquitt's brigade until in fact they were, with the exception of a small part of Colquitt's brigade, overwhelmed with prisoners.

The Virginia brigade was wheeled off towards the left, and reached a ditch in a ravine. A part of the 61st regiment advanced a little beyond the ditch, but was soon withdrawn, so that the right company occupied the ditch, whilst the balance of the regiment was formed through a pine thicket, recently burnt over, and there remained during the terrible fire to which it was soon subjected.

Just before the firing began I advanced in front on the line into the field in our front, ascending a slight hill on the opposite side of the ditch, and from my point of observation I saw on the left the head of the column of troops marching by the flank and emerging from a body of woods into an open field. At the head of the column were several mounted officers. From my knowledge of the battle acquired by reading the official reports and particularly the article in the January number, 1895 of the *Blue and Gray Magazine,* written by Dr. W. V. White, of New York, who was serving on the medical staff of General Julius White,[32] who commanded the first division of Parke's corps in this engagement, I am satisfied that it was the head of this division coming into action and the general and his staff that I saw. They were doubtless then moving by the left flank to form connection with the right of the third division of Parke's corps then commanded by General Willcox,[33] preparatory to an advance on our brigade as narrated by General White in his report of August 23, 1864.

I returned at once to our line and reported what I saw and quickly our men opened fire, which was promptly returned by the troops I saw, who had now placed themselves in line of battle, and had begun their attack upon our brigade, which continued until about sunset, when there was a cessation of the heavy firing that had been going on for about a half hour.

Upon the cessation of this heavy firing, the 61st, which I think occupied about the most southerly position in the brigade line, fell back perhaps a distance of seventy-five or a hundred yards across a muddy field to the point at which the other regiments of the brigade were reforming, your regiment (the 12th Va.) having been, as described [by] you, engaged in the pines of the enemy. As we retreated to this point, the enemy kept up a hot fire on us, and I remember that the muddy condition of the ground under foot and the slope of the hill-side as we left the position where we had been engaging the enemy made this short retreat dangerous and uncomfortable work. Arrived on the level ground, we found the other regiments of the brigade taking position in line with a view to their retiring, which the brigade did in good order, marching by the flank.

It was probably at this point that you, as described in our recent conversation, saw Colonel V. D. Groner,[34] who commanded the 61st regiment, on his crutches assisting in placing the men in line, and I also think it probable that,

32. Brigadier General Julius White entered Federal service as colonel of the 37th Illinois Infantry. After the Crater battle, White took command of the First Division of the Ninth Corps. After the war, he was involved in the Military Order of the Loyal Legion. He died in Illinois in 1890.

33. Brigadier General Orlando B. Willcox, a Mexican War veteran and lawyer, had entered Federal service as colonel of the 1st Michigan Infantry. Wounded at Manassas, he rose to division command, a position he held to the war's end. He died in 1907 in Ontario, Canada.

34. Virginius Despeaux Groner enlisted in October 1862 as colonel of the 61st Virginia. He had previously served as a courier bearing the order to fire on Fort Sumter. Wounded at Chancellorsville and then again in May 1864, he returned to service and surrendered at Appomattox. He died in Norfolk in 1903 after a career as a shipping agent.

when the enemy saw the 61st making its short and hasty retreat as above described to join the other regiments of the brigade then being formed in line, they assumed that our whole force was retreating in confusion and accordingly so stated in their official reports, when the fact is that there was only this hasty falling back of our regiment to join the remainder of the brigade and march out under the order of its commanding officer. General Mahone having sent his order to General Weisiger to withdraw the brigade and General Weisiger not executing it.

The badly wounded were left on the field.

In the January No. 1895, of the *Blue and Gray Magazine* already mentioned, in an article describing this battle, I stated that "out of less than two hundred rank and file, seventy-seven were killed, wounded and missing."

From this article I take the following, its concluding paragraphs:

> Captain William Curtis Wallace, of company A, an efficient young officer and a noble man, received his death wounds. He was carried, after our retreat, by the enemy to their field hospital, and there died on the 22nd of August. Dr. Whitman V. White,[35] surgeon in charge, wrote in a memorandum book, found in his pocket, the following;
>
> "Captain Wallace was wounded August 19th in both legs,—left limb in knee, right limb much shattered. When brought to the hospital was much prostrated by shock. After administering stimulants, limb was amputated on the 20th. He commenced sinking about twelve hours afterwards, and died on the 22nd. In him I found elements of true manhood, and regretted his fate. I will forward his pocket book and their effects which may be valued as souvenirs by his friends."
>
> (Signed) W. W. White
>
> Surgeon [1]st. division 9th Army Corps.

Dr. White's kindness of heart, as expressed here, cannot fail to draw tears of gratitude from every friend of the noble young hero, whose memory is still enshrined in many bleeding hearts. True, indeed, in Wallace were all the elements of true manhood—brave, yet gentle and affectionate in disposition as a woman, and as pure in heart as [a] Christian martyr:

> And such is human life, so gliding on, it glimmers like a meteor, and is gone.

But a life so spotless and pure as his leaves a living light to guide eternal ages. He was born in Glencoe, in the county of Norfolk, on the 23rd of

---

35. Dr. Whitman V. White served as surgeon, first of the 47th New York Infantry and later of the 57th Massachussetts Infantry. He died in 1905.

March, 1842, and consequently was only a few months over twenty-two years of age when he fell. He graduated at Hampden-Sydney college with distinction at the age of nineteen years, receiving the degree of M.A. He was also awarded a gold medal as the best debator, and was during the last session one of the editors of the college magazine. While serving a gun in the masked battery on Sewell's Point, near Norfolk, during the engagement between the ironclad *Virginia* or *Merrimac* and the United States frigate *Congress* he received a slight wound in his foot from a shell that burst on the gun. Though engaged in nearly every battle of his regiment, he escaped with this exception until the fatal 19th of August, when he, one of the noblest men that ever filled a soldier's grave, fell bleeding at two mortal wounds. Here, too, Lieutenant J. Thompson Baird, a soldier as brave as a lion, lost his limb while worthily commanding the old company of [the] 6th Virginia regiment, once so proudly lead by the chivalrous Barrand,[36] who fell in its front at Bristoe Station. After the war, Lieutenant Baird returned to his home at Portsmouth, Virginia, where his upright manhood bound him close to the hearts of the people who eight times elected him to the chief magistracy of this city, and for sixteen years he served them with [fidelity] as true and high as his valorous conduct on the battle field, which he had sealed with his blood.

This grand, though incomplete triumph over overwhelming odds secured by Mahone's matchless management of his troops showed that he was possessed of a mind with each and every qualification of a dashing and successful leader. With the force of a division at his command no doubt he would [have] captured Warren and all his twenty-thousand troops and repossessed the Weldon railroad. Such an event at that time would have greatly weakened the northern forces, and might have resulted in the recognition of the Confederate states.

STATEMENT OF V. D. GRONER

General V. D. Groner, of Norfolk, Virginia, the colonel of the 61st Va. Regiment, who particularly arrested my attention as he hobbled about his crutches about sunset, busily engaged in adding in the work of getting our men in line preparatory to our retiring as narrated by Colonel Stewart—he was the only man [I] ever saw on crutches on a battle-field—in a recent letter says:

I am glad to hear of your contemplated address on the subject of the engagement of the Confederate forces under General Mahone on the 19th of

36. Thomas Lawson Barrand, a lawyer and merchant, had enlisted as a 2nd lieutenant in Portsmouth the same day as Baird. Barrand, too, is listed in the Confederate Roll of Honor.

August 1864. This was one of the most brilliant movements which a small force of Confederates against four or five times their number of Federals ever made during the war, and Mahone should be given the credit for its success.

As you say, I was in the fight on crutches, having been wounded at Spotsylvania C.H., in the battle on May 12, 1864. I was able to ride when assisted to mount, but was unable to use my leg. So, when the 61st fell back, from its advanced position at the close of the fight, I found myself in a very uncomfortable condition and either had to surrender or to make an effort to go with my men to join the brigade, then about a hundred yards in my rear in the act of reforming. The ground being soft, I used my crutch, turning the side which was used under my arm to the ground, and, as the boys say, with a hop, skip and jump, moving under a severe fire, kept up with my men and reached the remainder of the brigade and assisted in the work of reforming them. Finding my horse at this point, and, assisted to mount, I rode along out in command of my regiment, the whole brigade being under the command of General Weisiger and moving in good order from this position by the most direct route to the Johnson house and thence to the breastworks on Wilcox's farm.

STATEMENT OF W. A. S. TAYLOR

Captain W. A. S. Taylor, of Norfolk, Va., adjutant of the 61st regiment says:

I remember the incident of the mortal wounding of Captain Wallace, and the good time we all had to make in leaving our advanced position when the order to fall back came. Poor Wallace was a noble fellow, a brave soldier, a Christian gentleman, who practiced the religion of love. I was standing by his side when he exclaimed, "Adjutant, I am shot!" I said, "Go to the rear." Lying down on the ground with his company he attempted to rise, when he said, "I am shot again."

At this juncture the order to fall back came, and Wallace was left to his fate. Thinking he was then dead, the next day we endeavored to recover his body under flag of truce.

Colonel Groner, who as he did on this, had on many other battle-fields illustrated his high courage, had on the day of the battle returned from a furlough given on account of a shell-wound received from a shell at Spotsylvania. He rode in the fight with his crutch hanging from the pummel of his saddle, and when he dismounted used the crutch to assist his locomotion. Of course he was the cynosure of all eyes. When the rapidity of the enemy's fire as we retired from our advanced position made rapidity in our retreat necessary, I felt it my duty to offer my colonel assistance, but found my help unnecessary, as with his crutch he made as good time as I did with my unaided legs to the place at which General Weisiger was forming the brigade in line for the purpose of withdrawing it.

STATEMENT OF GRIFFIN F. EDWARDS

Mr. Griffin F. Edwards,[37] of Portsmouth, Va., sergeant-major of the 61st, says:

The 61st, in its most advanced position was in low grounds in the edge of a thicket and among some burnt pines. The right company, "A," was in the ditch, facing southwardly. The other companies of the regiment faced eastwardly. The 41st regiment was on our immediate right. Those of our men who were killed or wounded were shot from the right flank, those in company A excepted, who were in the ditch as above stated and received the bullets from their front.

STATEMENT OF THOMAS P. POLLARD

Captain Thomas P. Pollard,[38] of Richmond, Va., captain of company B, 12th Va. Regiment, says:

One of the incidents of the fight was the gallant conduct of Alexander M. McCann,[39] who received his death wound in my presence. He was on that day acting as courier for General Weisiger. When the general gave the order for the regimental commanders to withdraw their men from the advanced position on the right, McCann took the order. As he was going to deliver it, he was wounded in the calf of the leg by a Minnie ball, but did not stop until the order was delivered and the men withdrawn. When the line was reformed and the brigade began to retire, finding he could not go further without help, he placed his arm around the neck of young Robert Fenn, a member of the ambulance corps, who came to his assistance, and thus assisted was in the act of hobbling off, when a cannon ball from one of the enemy's guns came howling through the ranks, and cut off both of Fenn's legs and one of McCann's below the knee. Fenn died in a few minutes, McCann bled profusely. I partially stopped the flow of blood with my handkerchief and assisted in bearing him on a stretcher and its burden on the ground. Just then Mac said to me, "Tom, let me see how badly I am wounded." Taking

37. Griffin Fauntleroy Edwards enlisted as a private in the 61st Virginia in February 1862. Wounded at Salem Church in 1863 and Cumberland Church in 1865, he survived the war. He worked as a lawyer in Portsmouth, Virginia, until his death in 1905.

38. Thomas Pollard is discussed in note 37, chapter 2.

39. Private Alexander M. McCann, a Petersburg bricklayer, enlisted as a private in Company B of the 12th Virginia in April 1861. He served as a militia drill master for over a year, then was detailed to be a courier for Colonel Weisiger in March 1864. As noted, he died from wounds he received at the Weldon Railroad.

hold of the sides of the stretcher, he raised himself in a sitting posture and took a look at his leg. When he saw it, he remarked, "It is all over with me." I told him not to give up. With his usual manly bearing, he replied: "No, Tom, you know me too well for that. I do not give up, but I think this is the last of me." We placed him the ambulance and when we had done so he called me to his side and sent a message to his mother and to a young lady to whom he was engaged, which I delivered that night. I gave directions to the ambulance driver to take him to the Poplar Lawn Hospital, the nearest, with a request to the surgeons to operate at once on him. Instead of taking him there, the driver took him to the Fair Grounds, in a distant quarter of the city. The long trip so exhausted him that he could not stand the operation and he died the next morning. There was not braver soldier in our or any army than Aleck McCann.

STATEMENT OF SYLVESTER J. ROBERTS

Mr. Sylvester J. Roberts,[40] of Isle of Wight county, Va., in a recent statement says:

I was present in the fight on the 19th of August, 1864, as a member of the Isle of Wight Grays, Company D, of the 16th Va. Regiment, and well remember our being about the ditch and seeing the enemy's line of battle on the hill to our right, with their backs to us. I could see the men through the bushes. Shots fired by these men in our immediate front killed four of our company,[41] James Morris,[42] Corporal Jonas Edmunds[43] of the color guard, Graves Neslett[44] and Adolphus Outland.[45] I remember distinctly the enemy coming up in the small pines east of the ditch. We marched out by the flank with our organization complete.

40. Sylvester James Roberts enlisted as a 3rd corporal in April 1861. He was captured at Germanna Ford in 1863. He survived the war and died in 1915.

41. All of the men mentioned by Sylvester Roberts served in the 16th Virginia.

42. Private James J. Morriss (Roberts wrote "Morris"), a farmer, enlisted as a private with Sylvester J. Roberts.

43. The Corporal Jonas Edmunds referred to by Roberts here was probably James J. Edwards, also a farmer who had also enlisted as a private with Sylvester Roberts. Edwards was wounded and then captured in the August 1864 fighting at Petersburg; he died of his wounds soon thereafter.

44. Roberts probably refers here to Graves Niblett, who enlisted as a private in March 1862.

45. Roberts probably refers here to John G. Outland, who enlisted as a private at the same time as Niblett. Outland was wounded at the Battle of Second Manassas and at the Weldon Railroad. Private Adolphus Outland (mentioned in Roberts's statement) was wounded at Malvern Hill in 1862 and died of disease in May 1863.

....

Mr. Roberts is one of seven sons of a widowed mother, Mrs. Mary Ann Roberts, of Isle of Wight county, Va., who enlisted in April, 1861, to fight for the cause of the Southern Confederacy. Mills W., Stephen W., John W., Sylvester J., Benjamin C., Francis C., and Nathaniel C. Roberts, all of whom were members of the Isle of Wight Grays, except Stephen W. Roberts, who enlisted in the 15th N.C. infantry and became an officer; all of whom were wounded in battle except Sylvester J., who was present in all of the great battles in which Mahone's brigade participated, Gettysburg and Chancellorsville excepted. Five of these sons were wounded. One of them John W., lost an arm at Spotsylvania C.H. Mr. Sylvester J. Roberts states that on his return from the surrender to Appomattox C.H., he met at Burkeville a wounded Federal soldier who told him that he was the last survivor of seven sons whom his parents had sent to fight for the cause of the Union.

The parents who sent these fourteen sons to do battle for their respective causes were worthy to be classed with any of whom history makes mention. The Spartan mothers when they sent their sons to battle bade them return "with or upon" their shields. Mrs. Roberts, I am informed, bade her seven sons not to disgrace her. Her injunction was obeyed. She said she believed they would return in safety. Her prediction was fulfilled. We know not the history of the seven brothers who fought for the union. Let us believe they were counterparts to the seven Roberts brothers, and that their respective parents were imbued with patriotism equally to that of Mrs. Roberts.

STATEMENT DR. W. V. WHITE

Any account of the incidents of this memorable afternoon would be incomplete, without the following paragraphs from the *Blue and Gray Magazine* article of that kind-hearted and genial gentleman, Dr. W. V. White, of New York, mentioned by Col. Stewart.

At three 3 a.m. I was awakened by the long roll. An aide from corps headquarters brought an order for the division to move immediately to the Weldon railroad, about eight miles distant, to the support of a division of the 5th corps that had been attacked the day before and repulsed. Instead of going back to the hospital, I sent my orderly to order the ambulance train and medical staff to follow on. As the skeleton of my regiment passed the place where General White and I were standing, a young private said to me, "Doctor I have no musket; may I go to the rear," I said to him, "Go with us, my boy, we will take care of you." On the march I saw him trudging along. . . .

We followed an aide from the 5th corps, and an occasional shot in the distance told us that we were nearing the Confederate lines. I was riding with

General White and his staff as we entered a cornfield, not one of us suspecting that we were near the line of action, when from a piece of woods which skirted the field we received a volley of musketry on our right flank. The worn out little private who had asked me to go to the rear when we started lay dead with a bullet through his forehead. When I saw his lifeless form as he lay between the rows of corn, I reproached myself for not allowing him to go to the rear.

The house and yard where I had established the temporary field-hospital, was soon filled with wounded from the 5th corps, our division, and some Confederates, among who was Captain William C. Wallace, of the 61st Virginia. The moment I saw him I was attracted toward him. He was fatally wounded through the body, and all recognized the result, which he accepted with great calmness. The thoughts which seemed uppermost in his mind were, Had he done his duty? And that he fell in a battle for the right. He was very appreciative of all we tried to do for him, was wholly uncomplaining, and perfectly resigned. As occasion permitted, I sat beside him from time to time during that night and day. He spoke very affectionately of his family, and took from his pocket the Bible that his mother had given him, and gave it to me with his personal effects, asking me to send them to his relatives within our lines. As he did so he gave me such a look of grateful confidence and assurance that I would do it, that I could not have violated my promise to him even if in keeping it I had lost my right arm.

I have always felt the effect for good of this occasion. Such an object lesson of devotion to one's conviction of what is right, even to giving up one's life without a murmur of regret, is patriotism of the highest order that can be conceived. No blood richer in all that makes a man noble ever mingled with the soil of Virginia than that of Captain William Curtis Wallace.

I made no distinction among the wounded so far as personal comfort was concerned, but attended to operations for our own men first, if there was not immediate necessity for doing otherwise. Among the Confederate wounded was an Irishman, with a bread brogue. His right limb was shattered below the knee; he had a wound through the thigh, and a flesh wound in the abdominal wall. This Irishman, I think, was from a Louisiana regiment. He was made comfortable while he waited for me to amputate his leg. As he lay on an improvised bed I went to him and said, "Pat, I didn't expect to find you fighting against the old green flag." His reply was, "Shore, they made me think it was, for the old green flag that I was fighting. I have been in the south for eleven year." I told him that we were going to do for him just as we did for our own, and his leg must come off. He said he knew it and wanted the job done. In a playful way I said to him, "You will not be able to march with a wooden leg, but you can ride a horse, so if I get you well you can join the cavalry." His reply was, "A [*two illegible words*] step will I go." I asked him if the Confederates did not owe him pay. He said, "Yes, eleven months." "You'll go back for that?" I questioned. "Not much," was the reply, "it would take a month's pay to get a good dinner in Richmond; you might as well have the leaves off the bushes."

[Bernard resumes:]

Within the last thirty days, for the first time since the afternoon of the 19th of August, 1864, I have revisited the battle-field. This was done to make the examination already referred to. The ditch, with the little branch running therein, the low grounds along the ditch and the sloping hills adjoining, are just as when the battle raged on that eventful day. But the pines upon the plateau east of the ditch—those where the 12th lay, with their russet carpeting of pine-tags, photographed in memory as if I saw them yesterday, and those where the 61st was in line, burnt over as mentioned by Colonel Stewart and Sergeant-Major Edwards, and remembered by them with equal vividness—have all disappeared, as have in great part the heavy woods in which stood the line of battle of Crawford's and Ayres' divisions when Colquitt's and Clingman's brigade swept down on their right flank and rear. In the place of the pines are cultivated fields; in the place of the heavy woods in some places are only a few straggling trees, with thick undergrowth, whilst in others are fields entirely clear of trees. The Aiken and Gurley houses still stand, but with another set of owners and occupants, as is true also of the Ragland or Davis house, in the forks of the Halifax and Vaughan roads. The Old Globe or Yellow Tavern no longer stands. It was dismantled by Federal soldiers during the siege. Its bricks and timbers, it is said, were used by the troops in the construction of their winter quarters. Years ago, since the war, stones from its foundation walls were used for a like purpose in a neighboring building. The present generation of strangers that own, live and move about these historic fields and places know but little of the deeds done upon them in the vicinity, the memory which as the actors are passing away is being rapidly lost.[46]

46. GSB: With a view to obtaining further information about localities, on the afternoon of September 9th, 1896, I rode with Mr. Wm. T. Lawrence, of Petersburg, over the battlefield of August 19th, and learned much from him. Mr. Lawrence has known this section of the counties of Prince George and Dinwiddie well for many years. The day before the battle of August 18th, 1864, as a member of the 5th Va. Cavalry, he did service about the Gurley house. Soon after the war he married a daughter of Mr. Richard Aiken, the owner of the Aiken house. Subsequently the owner of the place and lived there.

The information obtained from Mr. Lawrence may be summed up as follows:

The 20th of August was a day of quiet. There was no actual collision between the opposing forces. But they were not idle. Preparations were being made on one side for attack on the other for defense. . . .

The morning of the 21st witnesses the attack expected by Warren. It is a failure. . . .

[Bernard's brigade did not participate in this attack. In his article, he quotes at length from material published elsewhere, the *Official Records,* the memoirs of Brigadier General Johnson Hagood, and an article by T. J. Mackey in the August 1894 edition of *McClure's Magazine,* on the disastrous Confederate assault, focusing on the near-annihilation of Hagood's brigade, which lost 449 of the 740 men it took into action. This portion of Bernard's article has been excluded here. The fate of Weisiger's brigade on August 19th might well

---

About one hundred and fifty yards south of the site of Fort Howard in August, 1864 stood a small settlement owned by Richard Vaughan. Within the site of the fort at the same time stood another small settlement, owned by John Wright. Neither now stands; but within a few feet of the site of the former stands the small settlement of John Riter, a Bohemian settler. From its location, from the lay of the ground, and from other circumstances I am satisfied that it was in the yard of the Vaughan settlement I saw the deserted picket-post with the savory dinner of its late occupants.

Some 250 or 300 yards west of the site of Fort Howard, along the line of the Federal earthworks, no longer standing at this point, Mr. Lawrence pointed out the site of Risden's saw mill, referred to in General Mahone's statement.

The locality pointed out to Mr. Lawrence as the place at which Weisiger's brigade was formed in a horse-shoe shape to defend itself against the attack of Parke's men, he says, was not on the Aiken farm, but west of it. The Lanier house, he says, stood in August, 1864, in an open field within 200 yards and a little northwest of the site of the house now owned and occupied by Fred. G. Yaxley, a new settlement. With a copy of serial 88 of the official reports before us on the battlefield, I read from General Julius White's report of the battle made August 23d, 1864, [how White's division formed line west of the Aiken house, advanced, and encountered the Confederates in line of battle a short distance "within the edge of the woods," and after half an hour drove them in disorder from the field, where their dead, wounded, and small arms remained].

The "open field" referred to by General White, Mr. Lawrence and myself were both satisfied, was the open field then about the Lanier house, now about the Yaxley house, and "the woods," a short distance within the edge of which General White says he encountered the enemy, were a small body of second growth pines then skirting this field, and lying between the Lanier house and the branch west of the house—the pines so well remembered by the survivors of Weisiger's brigade who participated in this action. The land on which Weisiger's brigade fought was then owned by Mr. Matthew Weddell, of Tarboro, N.C.

have been the same as that of Hagood's brigade on August 21st.[47] Bernard provides his diary entry for that day as follows:]

Let me here draw from my diary its entry made during the afternoon of this day. It records the adverse tidings from the battle-field as they reached the men in the trenches down about the Jerusalem plank road. Here is the entry:

Entrenchments near Jerusalem Plank Road
Sunday Aug. 21, '64

At seven o'clock last night we fell in as ordered and our arms were inspected. At dark we began to move down the breastworks to the left in one rank. This move pleased us much, signifying that we were not to take part in the move against the enemy on the Weldon railroad. By 1 o'clock we had taken the position occupied by Finnegan's [Finegan's] Brigade whose brigade occupied the position immediately to our left. About 3 o'clock this morning our batteries opened very heavily upon the enemy along the lines and the cannonading was kept up with but little interruption until almost 1 o'clock this afternoon. About 9 o'clock this morning we heard the guns of the contending parties on the railroad and for about two hours the cannonading was very heavy, since which time there has been little or none heard from that quarter. The rumors from the battle-field are very contradictory and altogether rather unfavorable. We have sent a large force out there as evidenced by the fact that we have in the trenches now almost every man it has been possible temporarily to place there, the Petersburg Militia, City battalion, men of all sorts and all stragglers that could be caught up. I have been today on a detail to gather up recruits of the latter class and had quite a worrying time to it. We are to move further to the left tonight.

One of the brigades of Mott's division, of Hancock's corps, made a[n ineffectual] demonstration on the part of the lines occupied by these troops. . . .

[Bernard draws on the *Official Records* to describe the demonstration, which did not involve his brigade. This portion of his article has been excluded.]

With the following entry from my diary I close the record of these four eventful days:

47. See Johnson Hagood, *Memoirs of the War of Secession* (Columbia, S.C.: The State Company, 1909), 290–99; T. J. Mackey, "The Bravest Deed of the War," *McClure's Magazine* (August 1894), 272; and Horn, *The Destruction of the Weldon Railroad,* 97–98, 103–7.

Wilcox's Farm, Wednesday afternoon
Aug. 24, '64

At dark Sunday night we moved about 100 yards to the left and after the others moving first to the right and then to the left, on yesterday morning upon coming in from the picket line we found ourselves stopped at our old position at this point on Wilcox's Farm where we have been most of our time since reaching Petersburg. Harris's and Saunders' [Sanders'] brigades occupy their same old positions on our left, the militia, city battalion and other commands being relieved or sent back to their proper places. The affair of Sunday proved a failure due it was said to the giving way at a critical time of Finnegan's Brigade. Our loss put down as 1000 killed, wounded, & missing. The railroad is still in the possession of the enemy who are very strongly established in their position at the point they hold. From appearances the road has been abandoned to them. Our brigade is under orders to move at a moment's warning. Rumor says we are going with a wagon train to Stoney Creek.[48]

I have now, comrades, given you the history of four important days in the historic siege of Petersburg. The period of nearly a generation has come and gone since the gallant men on both sides who yielded their lives on these days and on other occasions in the cause of patriotism thus sealed their devotion to duty. Were these lives given in vain? Did your countrymen, Lieutenant Walter Wrenn,[49] at Second Manassas, and Colonel Alexander Callcote,[50] at Gettysburg, die without good results? Did Wallace, Walsh, Machen, Fenn, Beale, McCann, Morris, Edwards, Leath, Alley, Walker, Ridout, Neslett, Outland

48. The Confederates lost about 1,300 men, the Federals fewer than 500. During struggle for the Weldon Railroad from August 18 to August 21, 1864, the Confederates lost approximately 2,300 soldiers, including around 800 prisoners, while the Northerners lost nearly 4,300, including more than 3,000 prisoners (see Horn, *Destruction of the Weldon Railroad,* 230–31n137). On August 25, 1864, Weisiger's brigade proceeded to Reams Station, where on August 25, 1864, it participated in the climax of the August fighting around Richmond, the Second Battle of Reams Station, where the Federals lost about 2,600 soldiers and nine guns, and the Confederates lost about 720 men (ibid., 171).

49. Walter Wrenn attended the University of Virginia and schools in France and Germany. He served as a captain in the 3rd Virginia early in the war. He was killed at Second Manassas on August 30, 1862, and was buried near the Stone House on that field.

50. Alexander Callcote, from Smithfield, Virginia, was a captain in the 3rd Virginia. He was killed at Gettysburg on July 3, 1863.

and others of Mahone's men die in vain? Did the young private of whose pathetic death Dr. White tells us, or the valorous Dailey whose intrepid conduct brought him death at the hands of the gallant Hagood as necessary to prevent the surrender of Hagood's brigade,[51] shed their blood for naught? No. It was the hand of the great Ruler of the universe that so shaped and guided the clashing political opinions of the people of the two great sections of this grand country of ours that we should cease wrangling and settle by arms the questions then at issue; and it was He who in His infinite wisdom allowed the greatest of modern wars to be fought to the finish, in order that, as a result, we should enjoy the blessings of a reunited country, with a large addition to its galaxy of illustrious military heroes, who have high niches in the temple of fame; this addition to embrace hundreds of thousands of men unknown to fame composing the rank and file of both armies, whose splendid records as soldiers, well known to their surviving comrades, are unsurpassed, either in deeds of valor or in patriotic devotion to duty, by those of the warriors of any country, in any age, ancient or modern. These are the heritage of the bloody years from 1861 to 1865 to be transmitted to posterity.

ADDENDUM: STATEMENT OF MAJOR RO. R. HENRY

Major Ro. R. Henry, of Tazewell county, Va., one of General Mahone's couriers in a letter dated August 29, 1896, referring to the assault on the Federal lines on the morning August 21st, says:

As to the fight on the Weldon railroad on the morning of August 21st, my recollection is, that we left our lines early that morning and went down one of the public roads which ran west of the railroad and southward in the direction of Reams' Station. When we got opposite to the point held by the enemy, which was on our left, we halted and deployed in front of it and parallel with the railroad. Three of the five brigades of our division were present taking part in this movement—the Alabama brigade, commanded by General Saunders [Sanders], the Florida brigade, commanded by Col. Brevard,[52] and the

51. Dailey did not die of his wounds. On August 21, 1864, Captain Dennis B. Dailey, a staff officer of Crawford's division, had ridden out from Federal lines to demand the surrender of Hagood's brigade. An altercation followed between Dailey and Hagood, who finally shot Dailey and led the remnant of the South Carolina brigade back to Confederate lines. Later, when Hagood was governor of South Carolina, he helped Dailey obtain a Federal pension for his wound. This story is told at length in the previously omitted material from Hagood, *Memoirs of the War of Secession*, 290–99.

52. Colonel Theodore Washington Brevard Jr. had enlisted as a captain in July 1861 in Tallahassee, Florida. He was captured at Sailor's Creek. He died in Tallahassee in 1882.

Mississippi brigade, by whom commanded I do not now recollect. Hagood's brigade of South Carolinians was on our right.

The Florida brigade was about the center of the line. This brigade, which had before but three regiments, and which had won a deservedly high reputation in the Army of Northern Virginia, participating in most of its hard-fought battles until it was sadly depleted, was reinforced in the spring of 1864 by several numerically strong regiments, which came to Virginia under General Finegan,[53] a genial and fearless son of Erin, who had recently distinguished himself in the battle of Ocean Pond in Florida.

The advance, made by our whole force upon the enemy's position along the railroad, which was protected by strong earthworks defended by heavy masses and bristling with artillery, was splendidly made under a heavy fire, across old fields dotted with scrubby pines and other small growth; at least such was the character in our immediate front. I think the Florida brigade was the first to reach the enemy's works. The other brigades were, however, well up, when the new Florida regiments broke under the assault of a reserve column of Federals and retreated in much confusion. Our whole line was then forced to fall back. The officers of Florida regiments, with General Mahone and his staff, made every effort to rally and reform their broken ranks, but the men, or many of them, were panic stricken and could not be held. In aiding in this service my horse was disabled by a vicious shot from the enemy's lines. We afterwards renewed the attack, but without success. The brave commander of the Alabama brigade, Gen. J. C. C. Saunders [Sanders], fell in this engagement.

53. Joseph Finegan (often misspelled "Finnegan" by Bernard and many others), a Florida planter, mill operator, and politician, first entered Confederate military service as a brigadier general in 1862. He spent most of the war in Florida, with his greatest military success coming at the Battle of Olustee, on February 20, 1864. Sent north to lead the Florida brigade under General Lee, he participated in Cold Harbor and some of the fights around Petersburg. After the war, he returned to Florida and was elected a state legislator.

9

The Petersburg Campaign

AUGUST 27, 1864–MARCH 21, 1865, INCLUDING THE BATTLE OF BURGESS MILL

FROM THE OUTSET OF THE Petersburg Campaign, Grant sought to strangle Lee's army by severing the roads and rail lines that led to the city. After blocking the Weldon Railroad in August, Union forces gained more ground during an offensive in late September. By October, only Boydton Plank Road and the South Side Railroad linked Petersburg to the balance of the South. Just weeks before the presidential election, Grant launched simultaneous attacks against Richmond and Petersburg, seeking to block the South Side Railroad. The operation, if successful, would doom Petersburg and, most likely, the Confederate capital. On October 27, Mahone's men again marched out and repulsed the spearhead of the Federal advance, which was led by the Federal Second Corps under Winfield Hancock.

In the vicinity of Burgess Mill southwest of Petersburg, Bernard and his comrades in the 12th Virginia joined a small force under Mahone's direct command and attacked Hancock. In 1896, Bernard prepared an article about the battle using portions of his diary, letters from other veterans, and Mahone's own account of the affair. After the battle, Bernard's unit experienced no further significant combat until the fighting at Hatcher's Run in February 1865. The intervening months were some of the war's most grueling in the trenches around Petersburg.

>–○–‹•›–◁····▷–•›–○–‹

George S. Bernard War Diary: August 27, 1864–October 10, 1864[1]

Entrenchment Wilcox's Farm

Aug. 27, '64

Today is my 27th birthday. I must not let it pass without writing something in my diary. I scarcely realize I am so old. And to think of it more than these 4 years wasted, it seems, in this army, necessitating a beginning anew of life should I be spared & to see the end of this war. Thanks to God there are prospects now of its early termination. A great revolution of feeble sentiment is in rapid development in the North, looking to a suspension of hostilities. God grant the movement may result in peace. All eyes are turned to the great Democratic Convention to assemble on Monday next at Chicago.

On Thursday morning last we got in motion a few moments after I finished writing. Passing by an old Mill Dam which I suppose was once the dam of "Armstrong's Mill Pond" & which was only 200 yds from where our brigade camped we moved slowly along, halting frequently & resting, leaning in our route towards the left until we got within a mile of the Railroad just above Ream's Station. Here our brigade & Saunders' [Sanders'] somewhat in the rear of the line of battle to prevent against any attack from the left flank. Without mentioning details, suffice it to say that in our position in the rear we were subjected to a little shelling until the works were carried by the attacking columns when one of Hill's staff officers rode rapidly up to us shouting "the works have been carried & thousands of prisoners captured." In a few moments we were put in line of battle & advanced towards the captured works bearing toward the right. When we got within 200 yds. of the works we see in the ditch on our side of the railroad hundreds of Yankees, most of whom however were coming in as prisoners whilst the remainder were moving up the ditch & getting away. These Yankees were, it was said, forming here to sweep around on the right flank of the men who had captured the breastworks & no doubt would have done so but for our timely arrival. They did not fire a gun at us as well as I could see as we charged upon them. Saunders' [Sanders'] brigade moved down to the extreme left & immediately upon our getting to the works, Hampton's Cavalry bore down upon the enemy's left flank, sweeping everything before them. Upon reaching the works some of our infantry turned the captured guns upon the enemy & did perhaps some of the wildest shooting of the war, causing some of the cavalry as they neared them to reign up their horses and ask "What in the world was to pay." The first shot fired cut off the top of a pine tree near the gun. The artillery soon

---

1. From "War Diary No. 5," George S. Bernard Papers, UVA.

came up however & served the pieces. The result of the fight, as far as I have yet learned, was 2000 prisoners, 9 pieces of artillery, & a large number of small arms captured to say nothing of the killed & wounded of the enemy with but slight loss on our part. In our reg't there were but 2 casualties, one killed Joe Bell[2] Co. "C" & Pvt. Marsh[3] Co. I, wounded, which I believe were all the casualties of the brigade. About midnight the infantry were withdrawn from the field & were marched about 5 miles in the direction of Dinwiddie CH. About 9 o'clock next morning we started back to this place & after a long *detour* in taking a road a [few] miles nearer the CH than that by which we marched when going to Reams' Station, we straggled into Petersburg that afternoon, very much broken down by the travel.

[After Union forces occupied the Weldon Railroad near Globe Tavern, Grant sought to destroy more sections of the railway further south. On August 23, portions of Hancock's Second Corps began tearing up track in the vicinity of Reams Station, a stop on the Weldon Road about ten miles south of Petersburg. Despite Warren's success at Globe Tavern days earlier, the Weldon link was still capable of serving Lee's army. Confederates could offload supplies at stations safely out of reach of Union lines and haul material to Petersburg along roads to the west.

Lee would not allow destruction of large sections of the line without a fight. He ordered Hampton's cavalry and two of A. P. Hill's infantry divisions to drive Hancock from the tracks. As Bernard describes in the preceding diary entry, on August 25, the Confederates attacked, and aided by defects in the Union defenses, overran the hapless Second Corps in the late afternoon. The fight at Reams Station marked a rare occasion during the war where an attacking force successfully overwhelmed an entrenched position.[4]]

Thursday Sept. 1 '64

Brigade moved 200 yds to the right, night before last. Present position more pleasant than our last. Enemy have begun to shell the city again. Last Monday night they shelled very vigorously. I spent last Sunday night in town at Cousin Eliza Bragg's—had a very pleasant time. Visited Mr. [J.] Brandis near here yesterday afternoon—spent an hour so very pleasantly—was on

2. Joseph R. Bell, a clerk, had enlisted as a private in Company C of the 12th Virginia in July 1861. He was promoted to sergeant in 1862.

3. Private James W. Marsh had been conscripted into Company H of the 12th Virginia in January 1864. He surrendered at Appomattox Court House in 1865.

4. See Horn, *The Destruction of the Weldon Railroad,* 154–76.

picket last night, not having gone on with my company the night before. The nights are getting rather *chilly.*

Tuesday Sept. 6, 1864

Past week has been eventful. Chicago Convention nominated McClellan for President & Pendleton of Ohio for Vice President. The platform favors cessation of hostilities with a view to negotiation for peace on basis of a restored nation. Atlanta has been given up. Hood's Army,[5] at last accounts, confronts the enemy at LoveJoy Station on the Macon RR 29 miles south of Atlanta.

Saturday Sept. 10 '64

Last night enemy made a raid on picket line in front of Finnegan's & Harris's brigades & proceeded in capturing it with how many prisoners I have not heard.[6] In the affair some way or other we captured 75 prisoners. Our pickets hold at these points lines a little behind their old lines. Perhaps Gen. Mahone may oust the Yankees from this position tonight. Grant has built a railroad connecting with either the City Point or Norfolk & P Road and running in rear of his works around to his left. For the last two or three days we have heard his trains on this road. Lincoln has postponed indefinitely the draft which was to have been made in this month last Monday the 5th. He expected military enthusiasm to supply a sufficiency of volunteers. Grant says he wants only 100,000 more men to enable them to capture Richmond.

Sunday Sept. 18, 1864

A ten days armistice commencing last Monday prevails between the Armies of Hood & Sherman. The object of this is to send away the citizens of Atlanta, in which town Sherman doubled his forces to establish his winter quarters. . . .

McClellan has written a letter accepting the Chicago nomination in which letter he virtually repudiated the peace platform. It is thought the peace men will make another nomination. The whole North is jubilant over their recent military successes and there is much despondence in the South. We heard yesterday of a successful raid of Gen. Hampton's,[7] in which he vis-

5. Bernard is referring to General John Bell Hood's Army of Tennessee.

6. The *Official Records* refer to the fight on September 9 as the "Assault on the Confederate Works at the Chimneys." Union troops from the Third Division of the Second Corps attempted to capture a new Confederate picket-line works along the Jerusalem Plank Road not far from Fort Mahone (also referred to as "Fort Damnation"). After initial success, a Confederate counterattack regained portions of the line (see *O.R.* 42: pt. 1, 342–43 [Report of General G. Mott], and 1245 [Confederate correspondence]).

7. Wade Hampton, a wealthy South Carolinian planter and politician before the war, took command of Robert E. Lee's cavalry following J. E. B. Stuart's death in May

ited the rear of Grant's Army & returned with 2500 head of cattle & 300 prisoners.

Thursday Sept 22, '64

Our last tour of picket duty was at the new line about 400 yds in advance of the old line at that point where our reg't did duty. We saw lying about in the woods, the unburied bodies of Yankee soldiers killed in the action of Wednesday June 22nd. These bodies were nothing but skin & bones & were not offensive. They were clad in uniforms just as they fell. Today's papers bring us bad news from Early. He has been whipped near [Winchester][8] & has fallen back to Strasburg. Our prospects look gloomy.

In trenches Rives' Farm
Friday Sept. 30 '64

Our brigade relieved Davis's last night. Our right is about the site of Rives' house to the left of Plank Road. We have to keep low to avoid the minnies from the sharpshooters, who are constantly popping away. Important movements are on the [*illegible word*] at this time (about 5–1/2 PM) I hear fighting on the extreme right. There was fighting there yesterday afternoon & this morning. We have a rumor that we have captured two brigades of Yankee cavalry. We hear also that there has been fighting on our left—across James River—in which we were successful, though one result was the capture of Fort Harrison, a Fort of which I never before heard. The papers of today have cheering news from other quarters.

[In late September, Grant launched his fifth offensive of the Petersburg campaign against the rebel defenses outside Petersburg and Richmond. Over several days of fighting at New Market Heights and Fort Harrison north of the James, and at Peebles' Farm south of Petersburg, the Union forces captured significant sections of the Confederate lines but failed to achieve a decisive breakthrough.[9]]

1864. Though lacking formal military training, Hampton proved a superb tactician, ably leading Confederate horsemen during much of the Petersburg Campaign. After the war, he served as South Carolina governor and in the U.S. Senate. He died in 1902. Hampton's escapade came to be known as the "Beefsteak Raid" (see Edward Boykin, *Beefsteak Raid* [New York: Funk and Wagnalls, 1960]; and Richard W. Lykes, "The Great Civil War Beef Raid," *Civil War Times Illustrated* 5, no. 10 [1967]).

8. Bernard left a blank here. The correct location is Winchester. Sheridan defeated Early at the Third Battle of Winchester on September 19, 1864.

9. See Richard J. Sommers, *Richmond Redeemed: The Siege at Petersburg* (New York: Doubleday, 1981).

Sunday afternoon Oct. 2 '64

Went in to Petersburg yesterday & there heard the sad news of my Brother Dick's death.[10] He was killed whilst on picket near Mt. Jackson in the Valley on Friday Sept. 23. The fatal bullet struck him upon his neck, producing instant death. Poor fellow, he had passed through many hard fought battles and at last has filled a soldier's grave. I can scarcely realize that he is now among the dead. His comrades performed the last sad offices to his remains, giving them a hasty burial before the enemy got possession of the field. His memory will ever be fondly cherished by relatives & friends, beloved by all who knew him. During the past 48 hours there has been heavy fighting on our right upon the farms of Messrs. Peebles, R. H. Jones & Pegram. One result certainly was the capture of about 1400 prisoners up to yesterday midday. The rumors are rather conflicting, but in the main they are favorable. I hear nothing reliable from the extreme left, except that attempts to dislodge the enemy from the captured salient (Fort Harrison) have failed, but on the other hand, attempts of the enemy to carry other points have also been equally repulsed. Our reg't furnished the 100 men for picket last night, our company contributing a part of the 100. The rifle pits were, most of them, filled with water, which with the rain & the constant sharp-shooting of the enemy made the tour of duty a most disagreeable one. Banging away at the enemy served very well to keep our eyes open. All night long, notwithstanding the constant firing, our men & the enemy were exchanging words. At day light we had a short truce to relieve the pickets. There has been but little picket firing today, both parties being disposed to keep up the truce.

Camp Mahone's brigade Wilcox Farm

Thursday Oct. 6th

Sunday evening at dark our brigade stretched further to the right so as to occupy one half of the front of Saunders' [Sanders'] brigade which also moved further to the right. This movement threw our company into a better position. At about midnight a very heavy picket firing all along our whole front aroused us but the affair was soon over. About daylight Wise's brigade came up to relieve us and about 10 o'clock we left the trenches & halted at this point in the pines just in rear of our old position, the one so often occupied by us. We are now regularly in camp, and would enjoy the quiet very much but for the great uncertainty we feel as to our remaining here. We enjoy an entire exemption from duty of all kinds, even to picket duty.

The fighting on our right mentioned in my last entry did not result quite so favorably as I then supposed. Though we succeeded in driving back the enemy

10. Richard F. Bernard had enlisted as a private in the 13th Virginia in April 1861.

to our captured works, punishing them with a loss of about 4000 to them with less than 400 to us, yet we did not succeed in capturing Fort MacRae, a part of their works & finally had to fall back to another position, thus allowing the enemy to gain a mile & a half in his advance towards the S. Side Road.

But accounts from other quarters of the Confederacy are very cheering. The latest news from Missouri (Oct. 2) is that Price is within 50 miles of St. Louis with an army of from 20 000 to 25 000 veterans & 5000 recruits. From Georgia we have quite authentic information that Hood's Army is well in the rear of Sherman's & Forrest is ruining the railroads bridges &c further north. From the Valley news is good. Sheridan is at a stand still, successfully checked in his "On to Lynchburg" by old Early. And in Southwestern Virginia near Saltville Burbridge's[11] command of 6000 have met a bloody repulse at the hands of the local forces (Militia, detailed men &c).

Saturday Oct. 8, 1864

Our forces under Gen. Anderson gained a decided victory yesterday on the Darbytown Road driving the enemy out of his lines of breastworks and capturing several hundred prisoners & 10 pieces of artillery. Among the killed was Gen. Gregg of the Texas brigade. Last night there was a sudden change in the weather and today is like December. For some days past the weather has been very warm. During the last week our company has sustained a loss in the death of a most excellent soldier, Richard Wilkes.[12]

[Seeking to regain ground lost during Grant's September attacks outside Richmond, Lee ordered an attack against the Federal right flank north of Fort Harrison. Early on the morning of October 7, two rebel infantry divisions and a brigade of cavalry routed Union horsemen posted at Dr. Johnson's farm on the Darbytown Road. The Confederate attack then veered south toward the Union infantry's right flank and rear, threatening to cut off a substantial portion of Federal army. Delays in the advance, however, allowed the Union Tenth Corps to realign itself along the New Market Road and repulse further attacks that afternoon. Despite the initial gains, Lee's men withdrew to their lines without a significant victory.[13]]

11. Bernard is referring to Major General Stephen G. Burbridge, who led a Federal raid into southwest Virginia.

12. Private William Richard Wilkes enlisted in the 13th Virginia Cavalry in March 1862. He transferred to the 12th Virginia Infantry in January 1864. He died of disease in September 1864.

13. See Horn, *The Petersburg Campaign,* 167–69. During the fighting, Brigadier General John Gregg, commander of the Texas brigade, died during an attack against the Union lines along the New Market Road.

Wilcox's Farm

Monday Afternoon Oct. 10

Saturday morning there was a little affair with the pickets in Scale's front on our right and before sunset our brigade was in motion for the scene of action but everything was quiet when we reached "Fort Lee" on the Plank Road (Boydton), at which point we filed off into the woods & went into bivouack. Oh, how cold it was! The cutting wind, it seemed, would almost freeze us. At one o'clock this morning we were lined up & put in motion. Some supposed we would ere this have been on the North side of [the] James River, as we had heard the enemy were moving his troops from our right perhaps to make another attempt on our left. But we soon learned that our destination was somewhere on this part of the line. At one time from certain movements we thought we were going to relieve some brigade in the trenches but about 3 o'clock we stacked arms at this point near Wilcox's Spring, where we have been ever since. We are now in line to return it is said to our late camp in the *pines*.[14] We accepted the change with great pleasure. This is a bleak, cold place. Mr. Hobbs[15] of our company died suddenly at our bivouack at the Plank Road. He was an excellent old man & a fine soldier.

"Fort Harrison: The Most Destructive Single Shot, September 29, 1864," by Cornelius Tacitus Allen[16]

[The following account was found in the form of a handwritten note in the Bernard Collection at the Historical Society of Western Virginia in Roanoke. As part of Grant's fifth offensive at the Richmond-Petersburg front, Union

14. In the wake of Lee's attack along the Darbytown Road on October 7, Grant ordered Meade to push forward the Petersburg sector. Several Ninth Corps and Fifth Corps divisions ventured toward the rebel earthworks south of Petersburg, sparking inconclusive combat along the lines on October 8 (see Richard J. Sommers, "The Battle That No One Wanted," *Civil War Times Illustrated,* August 1975).

15. Private Albert W. Hobbs had enlisted in March 1863 as a substitute and died of disease in October 1864.

16. Cornelius Tacitus Allen, a graduate of Richmond College, enlisted as a 2nd lieutenant in the 20th Virginia in May 1861. In 1862, he joined the Lunenburg "Rebel" Light Artillery. He lost a finger from his right hand as a result of the fighting at Fort Harrison. He returned to service and was captured at Sailor's Creek.

forces under General Benjamin Butler stormed Fort Harrison, a key position on the Confederate line protecting Richmond. Captain Allen manned one of the defending batteries near Fort Harrison that day, September 29, 1864. The following is an anecdote that Allen wrote about that battle.[17]]

In September, 1864, Grant was pressing Lee around Petersburg, and there were, comparatively, but few troops around Richmond. I was in charge of the Iron Battery on James River at Chaffin's Bluff, ten miles below Richmond and one mile below Drewry's Bluff. On the morning of September 29th, about 2 or 3 o'clock, the troops at Chaffin's Bluff, three or four companies, were aroused and hurried out to the intrenchments. News had come that a large force of Federal troops had crossed over from the South side of James River and were preparing to attack Fort Harrison, about one mile from Chaffin's Bluff. Our men were strung out along the line of intrenchments running from the River eastward to Ft. Harrison. Ft. Harrison mounted some 25 or 30 big guns, and we had there only about 30 or 40 men. My men were armed with rifles, and also had [illegible word] of a few pieces of light artillery. I took some 8 or 10 men and two six-pounders and took position at a redoubt about 200 yards from Ft. Harrison and west thereof. In front of Ft. Harrison, look-ing east, south southwest, was an open field. At daylight, we heard the pickets firing. Soon they came in and reported a heavy force coming. We prepared for action, well knowing that we had no [showing], owing to our small force.

Soon after sunrise the Federal forces appeared in sight, coming along the public road leading from the direction of Dutch Gap canal to Ft. Harrison. They did not seem to be in a hurry at all. They formed for a charge at Ft. Har-rison and seemed to be forming by brigades. Some of the big guns in Ft. Har-rison—for there were not enough men to work all—opened on the Federals as soon as they came in sight, and continued the fire until the fort fell.

My little six-pound battery had a fair broadside fire upon the enemy as they advanced upon Ft. Harrison. They did not fire a single shot that I now remember—they kept advancing without the least faltering. The distance from the edge of the timber, where they first came in sight, to Ft. Harrison was some three or four hundred yards.

As soon as they came within 300 yards of my battery, I opened on them, and did some execution. I fired one shell at a cluster of horsemen, believing

17. For a detailed account of the attack on Fort Harrison on September 30, 1864, see Sommers, *Richmond Redeemed*. Allen wrote another account of the Fort Harrison fight (see Captain C. T. Allen, "Fight at Chaffin's Farm, or Fort Harrison," *Confederate Veteran* 13 [1905]: 418).

from the uniforms sabres, feathers in the hats &c. &c. that it was the Commanding General with his staff. I missed them by a scratch but they noticed that I had my guns on them and scattered. I was afterwards told by a prisoner that it was Gen'l B. F. Butler and his staff. In a few minutes after they started on the charge, the Federal columns were at Ft. Harrison, and they crowded upon the broad parapet of the Fort and shot down our men at the guns and on the inside of the fort. I heard their exclamations of pain as they were shot, and I felt revengeful. I ordered the gunner to put in a double charge of "grape." He suggested that it would burst the gun, but he put it in. Just as that time, the Federals on the parapet gave the shout of victory. I aimed the gun at that crowd and pulled the lanyard! The shot cut a swath through the crowd that was appalling. The gun "reared up" and fell backwards. I stooped beneath the smoke, saw the terrible effect of the shot, and then ran for dear life down the line of intrenchment to Fort Maury—where the line crossed the turnpike going to Richmond.

A year or two after the war, I met with a Federal officer—a Capt. Fessenden—a Freedman's Bureau officer—at my father's house in Lunenburg County, Va. We were talking of our experiences during the war, and he referred to the charge on Ft. Harrison on September the 29, 1864, as a small affair owing to the small Confederate force, but said it was the occasion of the *most destructive single shot of the war.* That statement, although merely his opinion, interested me. In answer to questions from me he said he was in the charge and gave an accurate description of its incidents, told how the men crowded on the parapet of the fort, and how destructive was the last shot from the neighboring battery. I then told him that I had charge of that battery and fired that last shot. He then said "Then, sir, you fired, in my opinion, the *most destructive single shot of the war. It killed and wounded [32] men on the parapet.*"

"War Recollections: A Celebrated Engagement," by George S. Bernard[18]

The Battle of Burgess Mill October 27, 1864 — Interesting Narratives of Participants

We produce below some extracts from chapter xxii of Mr. George S. Bernard's forthcoming second volume of "War Talks of Confederate Veterans,"

18. This article appeared in the *Petersburg Daily Index-Appeal,* June 14, 1896.

in which the story of the battle of Burgess Mill October 27, 1864, one of the series of the important actions fought in the great effort of the Federal army to capture Petersburg is fully and vividly told.[19] Between the extracts from contemporaneous official reports, General Mahone's narrative and what Mr. Bernard furnishes from his diary and from his own personal recollection and those of other participants, the reader gets a clear and comprehensive idea of the clash of arms on that rainy October afternoon.

[With the presidential election just weeks away, Grant launched another operation in late October seeking to break the thin rebel lines now stretched for miles in front of Richmond and Petersburg. Federal commanders assembled a 40,000-man strike force to sever Petersburg's last remaining supply lines, the Boydton Plank Road and the South Side Railroad. The plan called for a coordinated assault by three army corps. The Fifth and Ninth Corps, under Warren and Parke, respectively, were to punch through newly constructed rebel works extending southwest from Petersburg along the Plank Road, while the Second Corps under Hancock was to march well south around the Confederate defenses, pass over the Boydton Road, and occupy the South Side Railroad. To aid Meade's columns south of the James, Butler was to conduct a significant demonstration against the lines east of Richmond.[20]]

The account of this engagement, beginning with the entry in respect to it made in the author's diary, is as follows:

THE BATTLE OF BURGESS MILL

On Picket near W. W. Davis's house on Squirrel Level Road, Monday, Oct. 31.

After a rest of more than two weeks which we spent in the pine grove near Mr. Ex. Branch's house last Thursday morning we were put in motion and before sunset our brigade found itself charging the enemy near the Burgess house on the Boydton plank road. Our brigade lost in this action 410 killed, wounded and missing, most of the latter of whom are no doubt prisoners—our regiment 43 killed, wounded and missing—2 killed, John E. Burwell,[21]

19. In various accounts, the location of the October 27, 1864, battle is spelled "Burgess Mill," "Burgess' Mill," and "Burgess's Mill." Bernard used different spellings even within this single account. For consistency, we have inserted "Burgess Mill" throughout the text.

20. See Horn, *The Petersburg Campaign,* 175–88; and Trudeau, *The Last Citadel,* 218–54.

21. John Eaton Burwell enlisted as a private in Company E of the 12th Virginia in June 1861.

Company E, and King,[22] Company D, 12 wounded and 30 missing. Our company lost killed, as mentioned above, 1 wounded, John Turner,[23] and 4 missing, Privates Wm. S. Clapton [Clopton],[24] Craig Riddle,[25] Henry Ellington[26] and James Keen.[27] Three stands of colors were captured by our brigade,[28] 2 of which were captured by members of our regiment.[29] Six pieces of artillery were also captured, but could not be brought off. The enemy's line was completely cut in two, but we had not force enough to follow up our advantage. The enemy must have suffered heavily, as they withdrew with their troops for the Plank Road Thursday night. The heavy loss of prisoners on our part was due to the men losing their way in the dense woods. There were many instances of men being captured two or three times and finally getting away. The recruits distinguished themselves by the valor with which they fought.

Next morning we returned to our old camp in the pine grove, but at dark moved up to the breastworks near battery No. 45.

In passing along the old Boydton and Petersburg plank road, on the occasion of trips from Petersburg to Dinwiddie C.H., hundreds of which I have

22. Charles B. King enlisted as a private in Company G of the 12th Virginia in July 1861 and transferred to Company I in 1863.

23. John Turner is discussed in note 30, chapter 4.

24. William S. Clopton enlisted in the 12th Virginia in October 1861. After the Battle of Burgess Mill, he remained confined at Point Lookout, Maryland, until exchanged in February 1865.

25. James Craig Riddle, a tobacconist, had been conscripted as a private in the 12th Virginia in October 1864. Also held at Point Lookout, he returned to his unit and surrendered at Appomattox. His letters are at the Virginia Historical Society.

26. William Henry Ellington enlisted as a private of the 12th Virginia in April 1862. He was wounded during the Antietam Campaign.

27. James Keen, a clerk, enlisted as a private in the 12th Virginia in April 1861. Keen took the oath of allegiance at Point Lookout, Maryland, in February 1865.

28. Bernard describes the capture of two sets of colors, but the third stand of Federal colors may also have been captured by his regiment, by Major J. Richard Lewellen, who led the regiment that day, and Private John James Campbell of Company C (see Statement of Robert George Thompson, Notes of St. George Tucker Coalter Bryan, Grinnan Family Papers, Virginia Historical Society).

29. Bernard's regiment lost 3 killed, 13 wounded, 89 missing—numbers more consistent with the 410 he says his five-regiment brigade lost (see Rolls 514–34, Compiled Service Records of Confederate Soldiers Who Served in Organizations from the State of Virginia, Record Group 109, M324, National Archives, Washington, D.C.; Confederate Service Records of Virginia Soldiers, 1861–1865, Confederate Rosters, vol. 2, Virginia State Library, Richmond, Virginia; and Henderson, *12th Virginia Infantry*, 106–67).

made since the close of the war, I have rarely ridden over that part of the road within a mile of Hatcher's Run bridge, on either side, without recalling the battle of Burgess Mill. When Mahone's brigade, marching up the plank road, had reached the top of the hill west of Picture Branch, we were filed off to the left in a southwesterly direction—passing two or more pieces of artillery in position immediately to the left of the plank road—marched to a point on Hatcher's Run, perhaps a quarter of a mile below the bridge at Burgess mill, and crossed the stream at what was known as General Hampton's dam, and pushed our way in a southwesterly direction for a distance of possibly a third of a mile, having moved quietly along. Reaching a body of oak woods with thick undergrowth, we were halted, and, facing to the front, formed a line of battle, and were informed that the enemy were in the woods immediately in front of us in close proximity.

In a minute or two we were ordered forward, and came immediately upon the enemy's line of skirmishers, who were in the woods not a hundred feet in front of us. Some of our men began to fire at these skirmishers as they rapidly retreated, myself among the number. I saw a Blue Coat not fifty feet in front of me and fired at him, but must have missed him. Looking on the ground at the place where he would have been, if he had fallen, killed or wounded, I saw nothing to indicate that my shot had taken effect. My examination, however, was hastily made as I passed along with the command charging through the woods. The men were yelling, loading and firing, as they moved forward. A hundred yards through the oak woods and undergrowth brought us to the edge of the woods, with an open field between the woods and the plank road immediately west of the little branch to the west of the Burgess house. In this field were numbers of the enemy in full retreat, at whom we gave parting shots.

Our brigade was now out in the open field, in fine feather. I did not look to our right, but did to our left, and at a distance of less than two hundred yards I saw a line of battle of the enemy, standing behind a fence, which ran obliquely to the plank road on the southeast side of it, this line of battle extending nearly to the plank road. Some of the men in this line were stooping, or crouching under shelter of the fence, and I noticed a mounted officer with his sword motioning to his men, as if giving them instructions of some kind. During all this time the men of our brigade, standing out in the open field, in fine spirits, were banging away at this line of battle, and at the other bodies of the enemy visible beyond this line in the direction and neighborhood of the Rainey house, which stood about the point at which the Quaker road comes into the plank road. From the diagram published at page 233 of serial 87 of the official records of the war along with General Hancock's report of the November 10, 1864, this line of battle appears to have been that formed by General De Trobriand's brigade, Mott's division.[30] From this report and diagram it further appears that the troops we encountered at the edge of the woods were Pierce's brigade of the same division. The troops on the hill in line of battle about the Burgess house, facing towards Petersburg, were Egan's division of Hancock's corps. The artillery that fell temporarily into the hands of our brigade were a section of Beck's artillery. As appears from the diagram, McAllister's brigade, of Mott's division, was posted about this artillery west of the intersection of the White Oak road and the plank road.

It will be proper here to give some extracts from official reports:

General Hancock, in his report above mentioned, after detailing the movements of his troops, including the occupation of "the crest of ridge near Burgess' Tavern" by Egan's division, and mentioning that "very soon after the order to halt" at the plank road "was received, General Meade came on the field, accompanied by Lieutenant-General Grant," and that General Meade informed him that "Crawford's division of the Fifth Corps, was feeling its way along up the south bank of the run," and that General Meade desired him (Hancock) "to assist in making the connection by extending to the right" says that "about 4 p.m. a volley of musketry" immediately on his right, "which was followed by a continuous fire, left no doubt that the enemy were advancing."[31]

Continuing, General Hancock says:

"The small force of Pierce's brigade in the woods were over-run by weight of numbers and the enemy broke out of the woods just where Metcalf's section was placed. Metcalf changed front, and fired a few rounds and the part of Pierce's brigade in support endeavored to change front, but were unable to do so successfully, and most of the brigade were driven back in confusion, rallying at the plank road, this section falling into the hands of the enemy. At the first sound of this attack I sent Major Mitchell, my senior aide, to General Egan, with orders for Egan to desist from the attack on the bridge and to face his command to the rear and attack the enemy with his whole command. When Major Mitchell reached General Egan he found that the general, with the instinct of the true soldier, was already in motion to attack the force in the

---

30. Bernard is referring to reports and a diagram in *O.R.* 42: pt. 1, 230–39.

31. Meade's orders to his subordinates for this operation suggested that the Confederate works were incomplete along the Boydton Plank Road. To the contrary, the rebel works were complete and manned from Battery 45 in the Petersburg main defense line (the "Dimmock Line") down to Hatcher's Run just east of the Burgess's farm and mill pond. Warren and Parke were unable to find any weak spots in their front. The Federal attack quickly ground to a halt as Hancock's Second Corps proceeded unsupported around the rebel flank (see *O.R.* 42: pt. 3, 340).

rear. I do not think the enemy comprehended the situation precisely. They pushed rapidly across the Boydton road, and facing south, commenced firing. De Trobriand's brigade was quietly formed in front of the Dabney's Mill road, with Kerwin's brigade of dismounted cavalry on its left. Roder's and Beck's batteries were opened on the enemy."[32]

LOST IN THE WOODS

One of the striking features of this move was the fact that in the densely wooded country in which it was made there was much confusion as to directions—it was cloudy all day—and many lost their bearing entirely.

"So thick were the woods and so tangled the undergrowth, that it was almost impossible to proceed, and it was only practicable by using the compass," says General Crawford in his report (Official Records, serial 87, pp. 495–496.)

"Crawford's march up the west bank of Hatcher's Run," says Swinton in his "Campaigns of the Army of the Potomac," "proved to be one of great difficulty the country being densely wooded and nearly impracticable. Great numbers of the men became lost—in fact whole regiments losing all idea of where to find the rest of the division."[33]

"Crawford did not reach the plank road by nearly a mile," and says Swinton "was full three fourths of a mile from Hancock's right." It was in this interval between Crawford and Hancock that General Mahone took our brigade and the Alabama brigade being massed by regiment immediately behind ours.

When our men fell back into the woods from which they made their assault, many lost their way in the thick undergrowth, some being captured, others narrowly escaping capture.

STATEMENT OF JOHN R. TURNER[34]

Mr. John R. Turner, of Petersburg, Va., mentioned in my diary as wounded, in a recent letter says:

Having been wounded in the knee soon after emerging from the woods I made my way back to the woods as best I could. Adjutant Hugh R. Smith[35]

32. At this point, the article states "[Here follows extracts from the official reports for Confederate as well as Federal officials.]" Bernard did not include the referenced extracts in the newspaper article.

33. Bernard refers to William Swinton's *Campaigns of the Army of the Potomac: A Critical History of Operations in Virginia, Maryland, and Pennsylvania, from the Commencement to the Close of the War, 1861–5* (New York: Charles B. Richardson, 1866).

34. John R. Turner is discussed in note 30, chapter 4.

35. Hugh R. Smith is discussed in note 30, chapter 8.

having kindly loaned me his horse, a member of the ambulance force (who, I think, was Dick May,[36] of Company E, of the 12th Virginia regiment) mounted the animal and took me behind him, and we thus undertook to get out of the woods by the same route by which we had entered, but missing our way in the undergrowth, with nothing to guide us that cloudy evening, we had gone but a few hundred yards before we came to the edge of the woods and, to our surprise, saw in an open field within forty or fifty yards of the woods, a Federal battle line.

A Federal Line of Battle

We immediately turned back, not being observed, or, if seen, not being recognized, but had not retraced our steps far before we halted, doubtful in what direction we could now safely go, the enemy seeming to be on all sides of us. Whilst we were standing still it being now about sun-set, a mounted man, staff-officer or courier, came riding along from the direction in which we had just seen the Federal line of battle, and enquired of us where General Crawford was. In reply my comrade of the ambulance corps politely requested him to dismount, informing him that he was our prisoner. At this the Federal seemed astonished, and, observing that we were not armed, hesitated to comply. Just at this time, however, a party of five or six straggling Confederates, who had been filling their canteens at a branch near by, came up, and, seeing that they had their guns, the mounted man dismounted and my comrade, taking possession of his horse and accoutrements, turned the owner over to the custody of the stragglers. I have for some time thought it probable that our prisoner was Maj. Bingham, of Hancock's staff.[37]

Captured and Recaptured

The party of Confederates to whom Mr. Turner refers may have been some of those referred to by Major Roebling, of Warren's staff, who, in his statement appended to General Warren's report say:

> Rejoined General Crawford about 4:45; little firing going on; was astonished to see rebel stragglers coming in on our left and rear. They reported Wilcox's division in the woods a short distance

36. GSB: Dick May was my mess mate at the time and I well remember that after our return to the east side of Hatcher's Run and going into bivouac on the night of October 27th, Dick turned up with a neat and new looking hand-satchel which he stated he had captured from a member of Hancock's staff and narrated some of his experiences in escaping after being captured. [Richard Henry May is discussed in note 77, chapter 6.]

37. Major Henry Harrison Bingham of Hancock's staff, who had enlisted in August 1862 as a 1st lieutenant in the 140th Pennsylvania, was indeed detained during the fight.

behind us. General Crawford had just changed the front of one brigade (Hoffman's) to look out for this contingency. I delivered my order to him, but we both concluded it would not be advisable to make the attack under the circumstances, 5:15 growing dark rapidly; started back. Some of these rebel prisoners had some of the Second Corps prisoners. They reported that Hancock had been flanked by them and had broken and run. This was the first intimation that General Crawford had that things had been going wrong with the Second Corps. When I got near the Crow house voices shouted out of the pines, "Stop That Man on Horseback."

They turned out to be eight rebels under charge of two of our men who had lost their way. I brought them in. These men of ours had been taken prisoner by the rebels in the first place, but not one of the whole party knew where they were, so they had made up their minds to follow the first man who knew where anywhere was. At 5:45 reach our headquarters; pitch dark and raining. Captain Cope came in shortly afterwards with eight rebels.[38]

General Warren in his report says:

The attack on General Hancock must have occurred while I was near General Crawford and yet in the woods—the sound of the musketry did not reach us. There was beside no road known to us leading directly to General Hancock, and that same woods for two or three miles was certain to prevent him arriving for any contemplated emergency. What would have added still greater delay to communicating with General Crawford supervened by the rebels getting in on the road by which we communicated between him and myself. The enemy became so bewildered in these woods that upward of 200 of them strayed into General Crawford's line and were captured. These men before being taken captured three of our ambulances a mile in rear of General Crawford. Six of them captured Captain Cope, of my staff; but finding themselves in our lines gave up to him and he brought them in. Major Bingham, of General Hancock's staff, on his way to General Crawford, was captured by them, but made his escape, and three officers of my staff, in attempting to avoid the road thus infested by the enemy, became lost in coming from General Crawford to me and had to stay out all night in the woods.[39]

38. GSB: *O.R.* 42: pt. 1, 440, 442.
39. GSB: *O.R.* 42: pt. 1, 438.

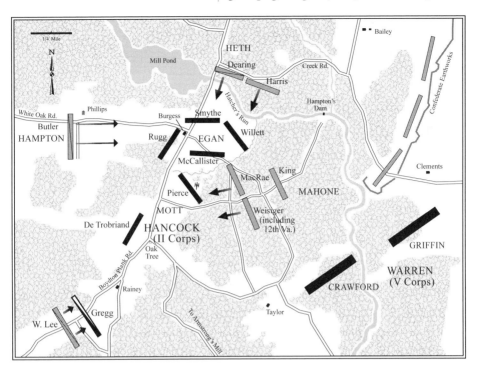

BURGESS MILL, OCTOBER 27, 1864

Referring to General Hancock's determination to withdraw his forces on the night of the 27th, the historian Swinton says:

> This appears to have been a fortunate decision, for during the night the Confederates massed at the position where the fighting ceased fifteen thousand infantry and Hampton's cavalry, with which they intended to await Hancock at daylight on the 28th.

In a foot note to this paragraph Mr. Swinton says:

> The Confederate General Heth stated to me that they remained all night in the position they held when the fighting ceased on the evening of the 27th, and during the night massed fifteen thousand infantry and Hampton's cavalry, with which they intended to have advanced upon us at daylight of the 28th.[40]

40. The quote is part of a letter written by General Heth to General Hancock after the war (see Swinton, *Campaigns of the Army of the Potomac*, 547).

STATEMENT OF WILLIAM MAHONE

General Mahone gives his recollections of the battle in the following letter:

Petersburg, Va.,
August 16, 1895.

Geo. S. Bernard, Esq, Petersburg, Va.

Dear Sir: Responding to your request for my recollections of the battle of Burgess Mill, October 27th, 1864, I will state that on the morning of that day my division was occupying its old position in the trenches from the Rives Salient to about the Branch house, the division of Gen. Wilcox being on the right of mine and that of Gen. Heth's next on the right of Wilcox's, with his (Heth's) right resting on Hampton's dam across Hatcher's Run a short distance below Burgess Mill, Gen. Dearing's cavalry formed a vidette line from the dam for some distance westwardly in the direction of Dinwiddie Court-House.

The cavalry under Gen. Hampton had the day before been transferred south to the neighborhood of Stony Creek, where the forage was better and fresh. The right of my division was some eight or more miles away from Burgess Mill. Gen. Lee was in or below Richmond and Gen. A. P. Hill was in command of the forces about Petersburg. This was the condition of affairs on the morning of the 27th of October.

On the forenoon of this day I received a message from Gen. Hill to send a brigade to the point on the Boydton plank road between Butterworth's bridge and Battery 45 at which the Squirrel Level road leads from the plank road southwardly to Heth's front. The object was to locate a brigade in supporting a distance of Heth's front. I ordered two of my brigades out and to the point designated, and proceeded myself to the designated point to see really what was up. Arriving there I met Captain Ham Chamberlayne[41] right from Heth's front and ascertained from him that nothing was going on there, but that at Burgess Mill the enemy had made his appearance. So Capt. Chamberlayne said he had heard.

I had complied with the order of Gen. Hill. Leaving a courier to hurry on my two brigades (which were the Virginia brigade under Gen. Weisiger

---

41. John Hampden Chamberlayne, a native of Richmond, served in various artillery units throughout the war, rising to the rank of captain in August 1864. After the war, he eventually founded the *State* newspaper in Richmond. He died in 1882 (see John Hampden Chamberlayne and Churchill Gibson Chamberlayne, eds., *Ham Chamberlayne—Virginian: Letters and Papers of an Artillery Officer in the War for Southern Independence, 1861–1865* [Richmond: Press of the Dietz Printing Co., 1932]).

and the Mississippi brigade under Gen. Harris[42]) when they should reach the point to which they had been ordered, I rode rapidly toward Burgess Mill, meeting on the way the cooking train of Dearing's cavalry and learning from those in charge that the enemy had in fact appeared at the mill.

Some mile or two before reaching the mill I rode up on General Heth and staff sitting on the road side. I reined up my mare and enquired what was up and the response was, "Dismount. Let's talk over the matter," I replied, "No, we will ride and talk."

General Heth mounted and on we hastened, to find that General Dearing had retired to the east, or Petersburg side of Hatcher's Run and that the enemy was in the act of placing artillery in position on the opposite high ground near the bridge, as if intending to cover a crossing. I did not know General Dearing; it was General Heth's front, and I had no business there. This was really the condition of things. But I thought I realized that the situation was perilous and called for prompt and decisive measures. So, after some talk between Generals Dearing and Heth, I interposed and asked General Dearing what was in his front—behind that battery which the enemy had now placed in a threatening position. He replied that there was nothing but cavalry, as far as he had been able to discover. I then asked him if there was any way to cross the mill-pond which lay immediately to our right, towards the South Side railroad, only three miles away. His answer was that there was no way within two miles. I then desired to know if there was any way to cross the mill-race, which had been dammed up, and quickly came the reply from both General Heth and himself that we could cross it on Hampton's dam against which General Heth's right abutted. I then said, "General Dearing, we will cross on General Hampton's dam and get shortly behind whatever force there is in your front, and as soon as you hear our guns, press the enemy in your front and force a crossing."

At this moment the head of MacRae's (N.C.) brigade of Heth's division appeared, coming up the plank road, and the Virginia and Alabama brigades of my division were immediately behind. The column was diverted through the pines southeastwardly for Hampton's Dam.

After crossing the dam, which would admit only about two men going

---

42. Brigadier General Nathaniel H. Harris entered the Confederate army in April 1861 as a captain in the 19th Mississippi. During the Petersburg Campaign, he commanded a brigade of Mississippi units. After the war, he worked as a lawyer in Vicksburg, Mississippi, and engaged in business in California. He died on a business trip in Malvern, England, in 1900.

abreast, and getting a short way in the woods beyond, and when I thought we should have out a skirmish line. I halted, and asked General Heth who was to command there—he or I? His reply was, "I turn the command over to you." I then asked that he direct his brigade-commander (General MacRae[43]) to report to me, and, remarking that there was no need to have two of us there, I requested him to go back to Dearing and see that a crossing was effected as soon as I opened, stating to General Heth at the same time that Harris' Mississippi brigade of my division, which, after my interview with Captain Chamberlayne, I had instructed to follow the other two brigades, would be up by the time I opened.

General MacRae reported as ordered and I directed the formation of a skirmish line, which was promptly done, and I caused the officer in charge of it to instruct each man of the line under no circumstances to fire a gun, but upon coming upon the enemy to engage him in conservation and gave [give] me, right behind at the head of the column (which would continue to move forward by the flank in the wood-path it then was in,) the agreed signal. Thus the attacking force moved forward, inclining to the right. Shortly the skirmish line halted and I was given the signal that the enemy had been reached. At this moment Major Duncan, of the division staff, whom I had sent back to the trenches to withdraw Harris' brigade, rode up and informed me that the brigade had joined Dearing at the mill-race. I directed him to return to General Harris and direct him to force a crossing on hearing the guns of the attacking force. But for the woods we were in, and possibly the crest of an intervening hill, the attacking force and Harris brigade were in sight of each other.

Three Brigades Formed for Attack

Being now advised that we had reached the enemy, I immediately formed my attacking line (under cover behind the skirmish line), MacRae's brigade on the right, the Virginia brigade on the left and the Alabama brigade massed in column of regiments behind the center, and a skirmish line on the left perpendicular to the line of attack, to avoid any surprise on the left flank. I reasonably supposed the enemy had come by a country road not far from my left and that, if he was present with any force, that road would be occupied by some of his troops.

43. William MacRae, a civil engineer, had enlisted as a private but became a brigadier general by 1864. MacRae commanded a brigade of North Carolina regiments during the Petersburg Campaign. He worked in the railroad business after the war. He died in 1882.

The line being now formed and required to fix bayonets and dress on the colors, I passed down it, giving words of cheer to the troops and urging that they reserve their fire and rely on the bayonet. I then gave the command to forward, and off the line moved, going forward with an impetuous step, and quickly encountered a fusillade from the enemy's repeating rifles. The left of the Virginia brigade became at once involved with the forces on its left, while the right of the brigade swept over the field in its front and reached the plank road as least a quarter of a mile west of the bridge across Hatcher's Run, and finding itself unsupported returned to the woods, whence it started, bringing along several artillery officers captured. At this moment, General MacRae, whose brigade had faltered under the heavy fire, reported to me that his brigade was flanked on the right, and quickly the Alabama brigade was deployed to that flank. An immediate investigation, however, assured me that General MacRae made a mistake. There was no enemy on his flank.

The Enemy Change Front — Grant, Meade and Hancock on the Field

Meanwhile the enemy had reversed the four guns on the high ground near the bridge confronting Dearing and Harris and was firing into the woods occupied by the attacking forces. One of these shots wounding my horse, I exchanged horses with Courier Blakemore[44] who was always at my side, and rode to the edge of the field into which the Virginia brigade had in this attack emerged from the woods and from this point viewed the open ground along the plank road to my right, front and left, to find that there was a considerable force of the enemy in view, a part in the field about the Burgess house on our right and part in the fields between us and the Rainey house on our left, with a complement of artillery ordnance wagons and ambulances the wagons and ambulances being about the Rainey house, and the force, as I subsequently learned, being two divisions of infantry under the immediate command of General Hancock, with some cavalry and artillery. The pieces of artillery facing Dearing to which I have referred were supported by one or more brigades under the command of Brigadier-General Egan,[45] which, as if fearing an attack far from the woods from the western point of which my force had made their attack immediately change front, presenting his flank to Dearing and Harris, whilst the four pieces of artillery limbered up and galloped away

44. Hamilton Blakemore enlisted as a private in the 12th Virginia in April 1862. He served on General Mahone's staff in 1864. After the war, he lived in New York.

45. Brigadier General Thomas W. Egan commanded a division in the Union Second Corps in October 1864. He joined the 40th New York Infantry at the beginning of the war and was appointed Lieutenant Colonel. A tax collector after the war, he died in 1887.

westward up the plank road towards the main body of the enemy near and in the direction of the Rainey house, passing as they did so in my sight and within hardly more than a hundred yards of the place where I sat on my horse near the edge of the woods. The whole Federal force, save Egan's troops on my right, were in great disorder and utter confusion. General Hampton had reached the ground with his cavalry and closed in on the northwest side of the plank road and also had some force up the plank road in the enemy's rear beyond the Rainey house, and was so near us that bullets from his troopers fell at my feet whilst I was making the observation here mentioned. At this very time, as I subsequently ascertain, Generals Grant, Meade, and Hancock sat on their horses under an oak tree to my left near the plank road and within two hundred yards of the spot from which I quietly surveyed the situation.[46]

Why The Attack Failed

I had made my attack, but was powerless to do more, I had, however, immediately after the assault and Egan's change of front, made an effort to get at his somewhat detached force and attack it on the flank, but was prevented by an intervening impassable quag-mire, along the bed of the little branch that runs between the high ground on which Egan's troops were and the field in which my troops had emerged from the woods and made the attack. It now began to rain and darkness came on. So, I headed my command and took them out and into our lines by the route by which we had come. If the force at the mill race consisting of Dearing's cavalry and Harris and Scales brigades of infantry had forced a crossing as they might have done—Captain John D. Young,[47] with his sharp-shooters, of Scales' brigade, I have been informed, did in fact effect a crossing—and as was understood would be done, nothing could have saved the Federal army from a great disaster, for not only the large body of troops massed on the field about the plank road would have been captured, but Grant, Meade

46. GSB: The tree to which General Mahone here refers to many years was standing, but has now (1895) disappeared, whether by the hand of the axeman or under the blast of some severe wind-storm I do not know. It stood not two hundred yards west of the fence behind which I saw De Trobriand's brigade. Oftentimes during the first twenty years after the war did I recall the historic incident mentioned by General Mahone as I rode past this oak on my way to and from Dinwiddie Court-House. Here it may be mentioned that the open [area] here, the corn-field, of 1864, between the plank road and the woods from which Mahone's brigade emerged is well covered with stout second-growth pines, which extend all along the plank road to the Quaker road. Within the last five years the Rainey house has been burned.

47. Captain John D. Young was the author of "A Campaign with Sharpshooters," which appeared in *The Annals of the War Written by Leading Participants North and South* (Philadelphia: The Times Publishing Co., 1879).

and Hancock would most likely have fallen into our hands.[48] As it was, the effort of the Federals in force to reach and effect a permanent lodgment upon the South Side railroad, the only highway between Petersburg and the interior now remaining open, was foiled and defeated, and by that result the ability of the Confederates to prolong the struggle to Appomattox made possible.

After getting back into our lines my troops bivouacked.[49] I sent for Major Duncan and enquired whether he had delivered General Harris my order to force a crossing when I should attack. Being informed by Major Duncan[50] that he had, I sent for General Harris, himself a gallant officer, and enquired of him why he had not executed my order, and was informed by him that he had not done so because General Heth had directed him to hold the position at all hazards! It is needless to state that in plain words I told General Harris of his error in not obeying the command which came directly from me, his superior officer, who had planned and made the attack.

To Renew the Attack Next Morning

About midnight General Hill, who was in Petersburg, sent me a message that he desired to renew the attack the next morning where I had made it that afternoon. In response I requested him to send me three fresh brigades, which I suggested might be taken from the divisions of Generals Heth and Wilcox, and further stated that with these I would attack the enemy the next morning, but according to my judgment. I was upon the ground and thought I knew best the thing to do. The fresh brigades came in time to able me to make an early start—as I did—to the head of the mill-pond, and to get in between the enemy and the railroad and to form a junction with Hampton. I had hardly passed the head of the pond when I came upon General Hampton, who, after learning my program, promptly mounted his horse and off we moved to join forces and attack the enemy.

48. According to several Federal sources, Grant and Meade were present at the oak tree on the Boydton Plank Road that afternoon but left around three o'clock to return to the Union lines. Mahone's attacking column hit Hancock's corps about 4:15 p.m. An account from one of Grant's staff officers suggests that the commanding general and his entourage almost stumbled into the teeth of Mahone's attacking column during their return trip (see Horace Porter, *Campaigning with Grant* [1897; reprint, New York: Konecky and Konecky, 1992], 311; Gregory A. Coco, ed., *Through Blood and Fire: The Civil War Letters of Maj. Charles J. Mills, 1862–1865* [Gettysburg, Pa.: G.A. Coco], 212–13; and *O.R.* 42: pt. 1, 36–37).

49. GSB: We bivouacked on the slope of the hill immediately east of and very near Picture Branch.

50. The "Major Duncan" mentioned here was most likely Robert Perry Duncan, described in note 11, chapter 8.

The Enemy Retreat

Gen. Hampton and I had gone but a short distance before we met Gen. P. M. B. Young,[51] of the cavalry, who informed us that the enemy had retreated. I advised that he be headed off by projecting the column of troops now on the road directly out from Gen. Heth's line of works, but this was not done. I spent a good portion of the day in going over the ground on which the battle of the day before was fought as well for instruction as to care for the dead and wounded and to gather up firearms.

This briefly is the story of Burgess Mill, where the enemy had concentrated a large force under the command of one of his favorite generals, not for the purpose of making his way into Petersburg but of striking a more effective blow by seizing the South Side railroad not then more than 3 miles away and thus compelling, if not the surrender of General Lee's army, a disastrous withdrawal of it from the works covering Petersburg and the capital of the Confederacy.

Yours truly,

Mahone

[The Battle at Burgess Mill (or Hatcher's Run) would mark General Hancock's last battlefield command. The Second Corps, humiliated earlier in the year by Mahone's men at Jerusalem Plank Road and Reams Station, held together well against the coordinated assaults from Mahone's infantry and Hampton's dismounted cavalry. Despite the face-saving performance of Hancock's troops, Grant's overall operation (his sixth offensive) failed to gain any of its objectives. Afterward, Union commanders attempted to paint the operation as a demonstration or a "reconnaissance in force." However, the plan had greater designs: it was no less than a concerted effort to bring the war in the east to a rapid end.[52]]

DEEDS OF VALOR

This chapter should not be closed without mention of some of the deeds of individual valor done on this memorable evening.

Gen. Pierce,[53] in his report dated October 30, 1864, at p. 369 of serial 87 of the official reports, says:

51. Pierce Manning Butler Young, a native of South Carolina, commanded cavalry units for most of the war, serving in Virginia in 1864 and then in the Carolinas in 1865.

52. See *O.R.* 42: pt. 1, 32, 42; pt. 3, 317–18.

53. Byron Root Pierce, a native of New York State, began the war as a captain in the 3rd Michigan and eventually rose to brigade command. During much of the Petersburg Campaign, he led a brigade (and sometimes a division) in the Second Army Corps. He died in 1924.

"Captain Peck, commanding First U. S. Sharpshooters, mentions a case of personal bravery which I consider worthy of mentioning and should be honorably rewarded. He says:

> I wish to call your attention to the bravery displayed by Sergt. Alonzo Woodruff[54] and Corpl. John M. Howard.[55] They were posted on the extreme left of the line as the enemy passed our left flank. After discharging their rifles and being unable to reload Corporal Howard ran and caught one of the enemy who seemed to be leading that part of the line. He being overpowered and receiving a severe wound through both legs, Sergeant Woodruff went to his assistance. Clubbing his rifle, had a desperate hand-to-hand encounter, but succeeded in getting Corporal Howard away, and both succeeded in making their escape.

"I saw the above encounter," says General Pierce, "being a few rods from it." Further in his report he states that the 105th Pennsylvania Volunteers "lost three stands of colors with the color bearers and color guards taken prisoners. Had the commanding officer lived the result might have been different," he says.

STATEMENT OF THOS. EMMET RICHARDSON

One of these flags was captured by Orderly Sergeant Thos. Emmet Richardson[56] of Company K, of the 12th Virginia Infantry, a man of stalwart frame and one of the most valorous men of the brigade, the other by Corporal Robert (Bones) Hatcher,[57] of the Petersburg Riflemen, who, though as fragile as Richardson was strong, was no less brave. In recent letter Sergeant Richardson, says: "The 105th Pennsylvania regiment was in our front. They had a beautiful stand of state colors borne by as brave a man as ever was. He was in the front of his regiment. I only fired one shot before we were together. I made for the stand of colors and got hold of them, but this color bearer tried to keep me from taking him or his colors either. They had been presented to his regiment by the ladies of the town in which it was organized. Whilst I was wrestling with the man for his flag a big red-headed fellow aimed his gun to shoot me. A comrade, I think Bob Atkinson[58] of your company, came to

54. Sergeant Alonzo Woodruff enlisted as a private in March 1862 and was awarded the Medal of Honor for his heroism at Burgess Mill.

55. Corporal John W. Howard had enlisted as a private in August 1862.

56. Thomas Emmet Richardson is discussed in note 27, chapter 8.

57. Robert Hatcher is discussed in note 66, chapter 6.

58. Robert Atkinson, a clerk, enlisted as a private in the 12th Virginia in July 1861. He deserted in March 1865 and took the Oath of Allegiance at City Point, Virginia.

my rescue, knocked this fellow down and saved my life. I have met several of the members of the Pennsylvania regiment within the last few years and have been invited to attend several re-unions of the regiment which takes place on the 18th of October of every year."

How Corporal Hatcher captured the colors taken by him is not recalled. He passed over the river many years ago.

STATEMENT OF THOMAS P. POLLARD

Captain Thomas P. Pollard, of Company B, of the 12th Virginia, who was temporarily serving on the staff of General Weisiger commanding Mahone's brigade in a recent letter says:

By the time we reached the fence at the edge of the woods the enemy's line was broken, and they were retreating across the field towards the plank road, followed by our troops. I was about the center of the brigade (General Weisiger allowed me to remain there, so that I might supervise my company, which was without other officers), and was within 25 or 30 yards of Sergeant Richardson when he captured a stand of colors. To my right Sergeant H. H. Drinkard,[59] of my company, came upon a Federal soldier and ordered him to throw down his arms and go to the rear. Instead of doing so, he undertook to bayonet Drinkard, and to prevent this Drinkard seized the bayonet, and in his effort to keep the Federal soldier from using it upon his body got his hand cut, the bayonet being a sabre-bayonet. Fortunately one of the regiment came to Drinkard's rescue and captured, or killed, the Federal soldier.

A Narrow Escape

Quickly after this I had a narrow escape. When the brigade emerged from the woods into the open field, it split into two parts, a part wheeling towards our left, a part continuing towards the plank road, and obliquing towards our right. I found myself in the opening between the two wings, and, coming upon a Federal soldier with a gun in his hand, ordered him to throw it down. I had on a captured blue cap and blue pants and he at first took me to be a Federal officer, but soon discovering his mistake, he undertook to bayonet me. Catching his gun between the first and second tail bands, I shoved him off, drew my pistol (all of the barrels of which, save one, had been discharged) placed it at his temple, and pulled trigger. There was only an explosion of the cap. The determined fellow still held to the gun, not releasing his hold until I caught the small of the stock and jerking it across my knees forced the gun

---

59. Sergeant Henry H. Drinkard had enlisted as a corporal in the 12th Virginia in April 1861. He surrendered at Appomattox.

from him. He then moved toward the fence muttering something in a foreign language.

Whilst I was engaged with this Federal soldier, another some ten yards away stood loading his gun, with his eyes directly on me. I thought to myself, "Will no one shoot that man?" Just then, as he adjusted the cap on his gun, some one about the fences to my rear shot him dead. I heard the thud of the ball as it entered his body. Throwing away the gun I had taken from the Federal soldier, I hurried on with the portion of the brigade moving towards the plank road, arrived at which a part was halted, whilst many followed the retreating enemy across the road into small undergrowth striking the road just beyond the little bridge. I remember a piece of artillery, without limber or caisson, standing in the field to our right as we charged through the field, with some eight or ten of the enemy still around it.

Reaching the plank road as above stated, I soon discovered that the enemy on our right on the hill in the neighborhood of the Burgess house were moving by the right flank towards our rear, and also that the line up the road towards the Rainey house was moving by the right flank to make a union with those on the hill, about the Burgess house, which move, if successful, would have cut us off and necessarily resulted in our capture. I called General Weisiger's attention to this and he instructed me to go back and inform General Mahone. I had gone but fifty yards in the field on my way to General Mahone when General Weisiger called me back and ordered me to form the brigade, the men being in much confusion, hardly a half dozen of a company together. With this order, I stepped up on the embankment alongside of the plank road, called on the men to follow me and into the field in fours regardless of companies. This was done and when we got into the field a line of battle was formed, and in this way, by General Weisiger's order, we charged back over the field to the woods, reaching them before the two bodies of the enemy made their intended union.

George S. Bernard War Diary: November 9, 1864– March 21, 1865

On Picket near W. W. Davis's house
on Squirrel Level Road Nov. 9 '64

After much falsification the enemy finally admitted a loss of more than 1000 men in affair of the 27th Ult. on the Burgess Farm. From all accounts it was only 2 pieces of artillery we captured that afternoon which could not be brought off. Nearly all of the sharpshooters of our brigade were captured, so that the organization has been broken up.

Camp of Weisiger's Brigade
Near Boydton Plank Road
Sunday Nov. 20 '64

We are now in winter quarters. Our whole division marched out from the trenches on Friday the 11th inst. Our Brigade (Weisiger's) is encamped about 3 miles from Town. Going into winter quarters was very unexpected to us. Our division still does picket duty on that part of the line next to the Weldon RR. Another fight is expected soon. Confidence is felt in the result. During the past week my father has been in Petersburg. My little brother Willie & he left for Orange yesterday morning. I spent a pleasant time in Petersburg with them.

Monday Dec. 5 '64

During past week or so our division has twice been under marching orders. On Friday last we moved out from camp at daylight, but went only a mile up the Plank Road before we were halted & kept until 2 or 3 o'clock in the afternoon awaiting orders, when we were ordered back to camp. The occasion was the movement of Yankee raiders upon Stoney Creek. Weather for past two weeks has been remarkably warm for the season.

Bivouack on Road from Dinwiddie CH to Wyatt's Mill,
Thursday Dec. 8 '64

On a farm whither we know not. Our division left camp last evening about an hour by sun encamped at Burgess Mill last night. We started at about 8-1/2 o'clock this morning & halted about 4 this afternoon at this place 3-1/2 miles from Dinwiddie CH. Rumor says the enemy are near Belfield with II corps of infantry & 1 division of cavalry. We are under orders to move tomorrow morning at 5-1/2 o'clock.

[In early December, Grant sent the Fifth Corps and a division of the Second Corps on a raid against the Weldon Railroad far south of Petersburg. In response, Lee ordered A. P. Hill's infantry and Hampton's cavalry in pursuit. This expedition, which resulted in the demolition of track along portions of the railroad between the Nottoway and Meherrin Rivers, came to be known as the "Hicksford Raid," or "Apple Jack Raid."[60]]

60. See Horn, *The Petersburg Campaign,* 189–97; and Trudeau, *The Last Citadel,* 262–85.

On picket near W. W. Davis house
Sunday Dec. 18, 1864

Friday morning, Dec. 9, we moved at sunrise—weather very cold—had changed during night. After a very tedious march of about 22 miles we bivouacked about dark within 7 miles of Belfield, having crossed the Nottoway at Wyatt Mill when near which point we heard artillery ahead of us. During the afternoon we had a slight fall of snow. After we had gotten into camp, Billy Wilson[61] & myself were ordered to report to Gen. Mahone. We found we had been sent for especially as part of a safe guard for Mr. Land's house, in which Gen. Heth & Gen. Mahone had their headquarters. Here we learned it was our intention to attack the enemy next morning & that our whole corps was along. Next morning we were not relieved as was expected. So we had a nice time of it, not leaving until next morning (Sunday). Sunday night our safe guard partly overtook the brigade in bivouack about 2 miles this side of Wyatt's Mill. The next night Joe Pollard[62] & myself stopped with Judge Mann (?) at Col. Hayman's near Dinwiddie CH, the brigade bivouacking near the CH. By 1 o'clock next day we were at our old camp. The enemy left the Weldon Road Friday night, but not until they had done no little damage. A salute was fired by the enemy at sunrise this morning somewhere on our left. No drums have been heard on the Yankee's lines this morning.

[A January 20, 1895, article in the *Petersburg Daily Index-Appeal* states that Bernard delivered a "war talk" during a meeting the previous night, in which he "told of how he got in and out of Castle Thunder, one day in Christmas week, 1864." The article provides no details and Bernard's diary does not mention this.]

Sunday Jan. 1, 1865

New Year's Day & very cold. John Jolly[63] & myself dined today with Willie Meade at Capt. Thomas's Com's. On Friday last I got back to camp after 5 days furlough during which I visited Orange. Our prospects look very gloomy. More so than ever before.

61. Private William Daniel Willson, like Bernard, had joined the 12th Virginia Infantry twice. Willson enlisted on April 19, 1861, at Petersburg, and was discharged May 17, 1862. He appears to have rejoined the regiment in 1864.

62. Private Joseph B. Pollard is discussed in note 61, chapter 4.

63. Private John R. Jolly was conscripted into the 12th Virginia in February 1864. He surrendered at Appomattox.

Bivouack on the Battlefield of Burgess Mills
Wednesday, Jan. 25th 1865

Our division received marching orders last night & marched out from camp this morning, about 4 o'clock & halted at this place at dark. Rumor says our destination is Halifax, N.C. We are now bivouacked in the woods through which our brigade charged the enemy on the 27th of last October. Weather cold & clear.

Bivouac at Junction of Boydton & Lawrenceville Plank Roads
Thursday Jan. 26.

Marched out from our bivouac a little after daylight & halted here a little before sundown. Roads very ragged being hard frozen. Our immediate destination is Weldon near Hicksford or Belfield. Gen. Finnegan commands our division but Gen. Mahone is to meet us at Weldon. Weather still very cold.

Bivouack on Lawrenceville
Stage Road 5 miles of
Belfield Greensville Co
Jan. 27

Left bivouac a little after daybreak this morning & halted at this place about sunset after a severe march of 21 miles. This morning, judging from rumors, it was Gen. Finnegan's intention to take us to Belfield tonight to take the train to Weldon immediately after our arrival there, but from the circumstances of our halting here & from other rumors we may tomorrow turn our faces towards Petersburg.

Ben Hatcher & myself stopped this afternoon at Lt. Manson's[64] (about 3 mile back) & got dinner. We had a pleasant time. Cousin Charlotte kindly filled our haversacks & canteens. Weather much moderated.

Powell's Hotel near Nottoway Bridge Dinwiddie Co.
Monday Jan. 30 1865

Charles Friend,[65] David Meade[66] & myself are on guard at this place. The troops bivouacked last night on Lawrenceville Plank Road about 4 miles from this place, having marched to that point yesterday from the camping ground near Belfield. Saturday evening Benj. Hatcher & myself were sent on

64. Joseph Richard Manson is discussed in note 53, chapter 1. Manson had carried the wounded Bernard off the battlefield at Crampton's Gap (see Bernard's article, "The Maryland Campaign of 1862," in *War Talks of Confederate Veterans*).

65. Charles J. Friend had enlisted as a sergeant in April 1861, and later transferred to Bernard's company as a private.

66. David B. Meade enlisted as a private in Company E of the 12th Virginia in March 1862. He transferred to Company K in June 1862. Later that year he was dis-

guard to Lt. Manson's where we remained until after the troops & most of the stragglers had passed yesterday morning. Many rumors afloat about recognition, an armistice, peace, & c. [Certain it is?] gold has fallen very much in the Confederacy. Weather clear & cold. Troops are expected along very soon as it is after sunrise now — nearly 8 o'clock.

Camp near Petersburg
Wednesday Feb. 1 '65

Division got into camp yesterday about 12 o'clock having marched from its bivouack 1 mile this side of Dinwiddie CH. Charley Friend & myself did not leave Mr. Powell's until about 12 o'clock the day before. Charley stopped with a friend at the CH. I continued my journey & came up with the brigade well after dark.

Last evening I walked in to Mr. Branch's & returned about 11–1/2 o'clock, not very tired. Peace rumors are very rife. These commissioners, Judge Campbell, Vice-President Stephens & Senator R. M. T. Hunter passed through the lines yesterday afternoon at Rive's house on their way to Washington. Mr. Blair has returned to Washington after a third visit to Richmond. Rumor says the Yankees have proposed their terms; a recognition of our independence, a restoration of all our territory, reimbursment for damages done, with an alliance offensive & defensive to enforce the Monroe Doctrine. I hope such news may be true.[67]

Thursday Feb. 9 '65

Back at camp again after a very severe five days campaign beginning Sunday afternoon, ending yesterday afternoon. Monday evening our division led by Gen. Finnegan charged the enemy & drove them beautifully for more than a mile. The engagement took place in a body of woods on the right of Hatcher's Run & about 3–1/2 miles below Burgess Mill. The enemy had first attacked Pegram's division, turning it back, and had been in turn driven by Evans's division, which they then drove back & were driven just as we were put in line of battle. We lost in our reg't 23 kd & wd. The kd were Billy Willson of our company, a good fellow & a fine soldier, Geo. Spence[68] of Co. H,

---

charged, and furnished a substitute. Conscripted in October 1864, he returned to his original unit, Company E. Captured at Petersburg in April 1865, he was released from prison in June 1865. He returned to Petersburg and became a merchant.

67. On February 3, the Confederate delegation referred to in Bernard's diary met with President Lincoln and William Seward aboard a vessel off Fort Monroe, Virginia, to discuss a negotiated end to the conflict. The conference yielded no results.

68. Private George A. Spence was conscripted and assigned to Company H of the 12th Virginia in September 1863. He was the brother of Private E. Leslie Spence.

a good soldier, Pattaway[69] of Co. K and Baughn[70] of Co. G. Among the wd were "Billy" Scott[71] & Hamilton Martin[72] of our company, both excellent soldiers. Lt. Ben Grasswit[73] & Doncey Dunlop[74] of Co. C, Bob Eckles[75] & Jackson Bishop[76] of Co. A, I myself received a slight scratch on the cheek, the position of my head only saving me from a dreadful wound or perhaps death. In company E several others were struck—David Meade, Thad Branch,[77] Ben Peebles[78] & Ello Daniel.[79] I hope to return to my friends as safe guard today.

[In early February, Grant sought to destroy wagons and supplies traveling along the roads between Lee's army and the Weldon Railroad. The Second Corps, now under the command of Major General Andrew A. Humphreys, and Warren's Fifth Corps moved to the vicinity of Hatcher's Run to support Gregg's cavalry, which had moved further south and west to attack the roads supplying Lee. As had been the case throughout the Petersburg Campaign, the Confederates counterattacked the Union movement. On February 6, Mahone's division, under temporary command of General Joseph Finegan, pushed the Federal line back. The next day, Union troops regained ground, but eventually withdrew from the field. This offensive, usually referred to as the Second Battle of Hatcher's Run (or sometimes simply "Hatcher's Run"),

69. Richard H. Pettaway, an apprentice carpenter, enlisted in Company K of the 12th Virginia as a private in May 1861.

70. Stephen D. Baughn was conscripted and assigned to Company G of the 12th Virginia in October 1864.

71. William H. Scott is discussed in note 28, chapter 4.

72. Hamilton Martin enlisted as a private in Company E of the 12th Virginia in September 1864.

73. Benjamin W. Grasswit, a clerk, enlisted as a corporal in Company C of the 12th Virginia in April 1861. Later promoted to 1st lieutenant, he was mortally wounded at Hatcher's Run.

74. Donald McKenzie Dunlop, known as "Doncie," enlisted as a private in Company C of the 12th Virginia in April 1861. Later promoted to sergeant, he survived the war and lived well into the twentieth century.

75. Robert Stith Eckles, a clerk, enlisted as a private in Company A of the 12th Virginia in April 1861. He surrendered at Appomattox and lived until 1930.

76. Jackson C. Bishop enlisted as a private in Company A of the 12th Virginia in June 1861.

77. Thaddeus Branch is discussed in note 73, chapter 6.

78. Private Benjamin John Peebles had transferred to Bernard's regiment from the 53rd Virginia in October 1864.

79. Ello K. Daniel is discussed in note 113, chapter 6.

allowed the Federals to stretch their lines further to the west below the Confederate right.[80]]

Camp near Petersburg
Saturday Mar. 4

A rainy, dismal day & under marching orders I learned last evening & further amended at midnight last night by an order to be in readiness to march at daylight this morning but daylight came & we did not move. Of course there is much speculation as to our destination. Some think Petersburg and Richmond are about to be evacuated. What a trial this would be! But I will not then despair. I have a firm faith that a great God will not suffer the enemy to conquer us, however much he may chastise us. But there are thousands both in & out of the army who really do not [*illegible word*] the liberty for which the Southern Army was struggling, but the worst a vile enemy can do. It is enough almost to make one's heart sicken to hear of the numerous desertions to the enemy that are now & have been for four or five months past a daily occurrence.

Chesterfield Lines Near [Church?]
Tuesday Mar. 7 1865

Saturday night about 7 o'clock we moved out from old camp. Some supposed our destination was the S. Side R.R. to embark for the High Bridge or Lynchburg. But it soon appeared our destination was the lines on this side of the Appomattox to relieve Pickett's division. By daylight what was left of our brigade took positions in the trenches about a half mile to the left of Mrs. Davis's house & about 1 mile from the Appomattox River. Only about ten privates of our company were present when the reg't took position. Tom Branch[81] & myself halted for the night near the Railroad near the Swift Creek Bridge. The march in the woods was *terrible*. Last evening our reg't was shifted farther to the left & are now within range of the gunboats in James River. The enemy are very near at this point—the picket lines of the two armies only 60 yds apart & the main lines about 400 yds apart. Our works are exceedingly strong. Four desertions from our reg't last night. Bob Atkinson[82] of our company, a desertion which surprises very much and Henry Stevens,[83] [*three illegible words*] of Co. K.

---

80. See Horn, *The Petersburg Campaign,* 199–207.

81. Thomas C. Branch is discussed in note 69, chapter 2.

82. Robert Atkinson is discussed in note 58, this chapter.

83. Henry Stevens enlisted as a sergeant in Company K in May 1861. Later demoted to private, he was wounded at Spotsylvania Court House, and deserted in March 1865.

On Picket Sunday March 12, 1865

Have been interested most of today in the trading which has been going on between the "Johnny Rebs" & "Jimmie Yanks," "Johnny" furnishing tobacco; "Jimmy" trades sugar & coffee, chocolate, soap, newspapers & orders for "Rebel Deserters" & occasionally throws in a treat "hardtack." The tradesmen exchange their commodities by throwing them across to each other or by advancing to a log which lies about midway between the lines & then depositing them. Various business notes have passed between the parties engaged. "White Coat" (Confederate) writes to "Black Hat" (Yankee) to get him a knife or some chocolate. "Black Hat" replies that he will accommodate him as soon as he can send back to the sutlers. B. H. adds in his note that if W. C. knows any pretty Northern "gal" whom he wants to inform of his whereabouts, he, B. H., will take pleasure in giving the necessary information. "White Coat" being a married man & having no such message to send & added a PS to his note requesting B. H. to inform my friend Mr. Clopton, prisoner at Pt. Lookout, that I was well &c, &c. Several officers shamed themselves on this picket line.

In The Trenches Howlett's Farm
Saturday Mar. 18

Thad Branch & myself walked into town yesterday. Our permits (12 hours) expiring in the night time, we made our return trip this morning, leaving the police office, where we napped for 2 hours before starting, about 1 o'clock & reaching camp about 3 o'clock, our walk being by moonlight & quite pleasant, though between six & seven miles in length. My visit to town was quite pleasant.

Monday Night March 20 '65

On picket yesterday & last night; had quite a dull time; all intercourse with the enemy prohibited. Heard during night shots fired at deserters—the first early in the night & the last between 1 & 3 o'clock. This firing at deserters, a thing of nightly occurrence. A few minutes ago I heard as many as eight or ten shots fired, apparently on our brigade picket line. Night before last, it is said, one deserting "Gopher" (Floridian) was killed & another captured by an officer who stationed himself outside of the picket lines & laid in wait for them. This is the first instance of killing or capturing deserters going from the picket line of which I have heard for several months. Heard musketry & a little artillery on the lines across the James this morning about 10–1/2 o'clock. Heard much artillery firing for about 2 hours this afternoon apparently at Petersburg. Rumor says Johnston has whipped Sherman near Raleigh N.C.[84]

84. During the last months of the war, desertion rates increased in the Army of the Northern Virginia. In his study, *General Lee's Army: From Victory to Collapse* (New

I expect a 15 day furlough tomorrow.

Thursday Mar. 21 '65

Operations of Mahone's Division during campaign of 1864 as shown by official reports. The command has captured:

Prisoners 6,704

Pieces of Artillery 15

Stands of Colors 42

Small Arms 4,367

Horses 235

Wagons & ambulances 49

Slaves 537

According to enemy's own statements, the losses in killed & wounded in their commands which at different times have fought Mahone's Division foot up 11,000 from which it appears that the division during the campaign inflicted a loss of 17,704 men upon the enemy. The loss of the division during the campaign foots up 5,240 Killed, wounded & missing.

York: Free Press, 2008), Joseph T. Glatthaar devotes an entire chapter to this subject (chap. 32, "Desertion," 408–20). Those with the lowest desertion rates were the men Bernard felt closest to—the men who had joined the Confederate army with him in 1861 and 1862.

10

The Petersburg Campaign

MISCELLANEOUS ACCOUNTS

T HE PETERSBURG CAMPAIGN HELD a special significance for Bernard and many other natives of the Cockade City. These men were defending their homes, literally. And, after the war, many spent the rest of their lives in the midst of this former battleground. After publication of *War Talks of Confederate Veterans* in 1892, Bernard solicited several articles and letters from fellow veterans related to the Petersburg Campaign. Many of these recollections subsequently appeared in the *Petersburg Daily Index-Appeal*. This chapter includes the recollections of P. C. Hoy and James Jackson, members of Bradford's Battery; the story of a scouting mission, by former Virginia governor William E. Cameron; an incident on the Petersburg lines, by Joseph Eggleston, a member of Lamkin's Battery; and an account of life in Dinwiddie County during the campaign, by Jno. C. Griffin.

➤━०━◇━▷━◁┄┄▷━▷━०━◇

"Of the Siege of Petersburg: Some Interesting Recollections of an Officer of Bradford's Battery,"
by Lieut. P. C. Hoy[1]

This letter was read before A. P. Hill Camp of Confederate Veterans of Petersburg, Va., at its meeting on the evening of Thursday, August 1, 1895.

Petersburg, Va.
May 31st, 1895

George S. Bernard, Esq., Petersburg, Va.,

Dear Sir: As requested, I will give you an account of personal experience during the siege of Petersburg.

Capt. Wm. D. Bradford's (Mississippi) battery, of which I was junior first lieutenant, came to Petersburg about the first of May, 1864, from North Carolina with Gen. Hoke's command, and was stationed first, at Battery 42, near Butterworth's Bridge, and then at the famous Battery 5 on the Jordan farm within two or three hundred yards of the City Point railroad. At the last mentioned place we remained for ten days, until we were transferred to the Howlett's house on the Chesterfield line a day or two after the battle of Drewry's Bluff on the 16th of May.

[In May, Major General Benjamin Butler and his Army of the James landed at Bermuda Hundred, a wide spit of land on the James River south of Richmond. Between May 12 and 16, a large portion of Butler's force clashed with troops under command of General P. G. T. Beauregard at rebel fortifications in the vicinity of Drewry's Bluff. After the fighting, Butler's force withdrew to its strong fortifications at Bermuda Hundred.[2]]

On the evening of the 14th of June I obtained a twelve hour's leave of absence, to begin at 5 o'clock the next morning to visit my wife at her father's in the city of Petersburg. I left camp on the morning of the 15th, and was in Petersburg after an hour's ride. Upon reaching Pocahontas bridge, I was halted

---

1. This article appeared in the *Petersburg Daily Index-Appeal* on May 3 and 10, 1903. The article states, "From MSS. of Geo. S. Bernard's 'War Talks of Confederate Veterans,' Vol. II." Hoy also wrote a similar account in "A Brief History of Bradford's Battery, Confederate Guards Artillery," a pamphlet released in the summer of 1903.

2. See William G. Robertson, *Back Door to Richmond: The Bermuda Hundred Campaign, April–June 1864* (Baton Rouge: Louisiana State University Press, 1987); and Herbert M. Schiller, *The Bermuda Hundred Campaign* (Dayton, Ohio: Morningside House, 1988).

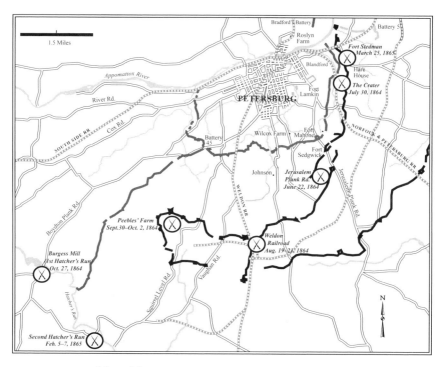

PETERSBURG, 1864–1865

by a sentinel, who stated that he had instructions to arrest all soldiers and send them to the office of the provost-marshal. I asked the occasion of this and was informed that the enemy were investing the city. The sentinel wanted to take me in charge, I demurred, as I was an officer on leave of absence, insisted on his sending for the officer of the guard, and was by that officer allowed to pass the bridge. I went at once to the residence of my father-in-law (Mr. R. F. Jackson), found the family at breakfast, took a hasty meal and then went to the custom house, the headquarters of Gen. R. E. Colston, and there learned the true state of affairs, namely, that the city was in fact being invested. I offered my services for the day, which were accepted by Gen. Colston's adjutant (Capt. Bagwell), who expressed himself as very glad that I had done so, as he wished to send a message at once to Maj. Francis J. Bogg's who commanded the artillery on the lines at that time.

[In the early morning hours of June 13, Grant began to withdraw the Army of the Potomac from the Cold Harbor lines. As the massive force slid south toward the James, Lee raced to protect the most direct routes to Richmond, anticipating more fighting on the ground that had been contested during the

Seven Days' Battles in 1862. Grant, however, did not turn toward the capital, but continued south. By June 14, Union troops began moving on Petersburg, some crossing the James over a remarkable 2,100-foot pontoon bridge. The next day, the Federal vanguard, men from Major General William "Baldy" Smith's Eighteenth Corps, assaulted the Dimmock Line in the countryside just east of Petersburg. For the next three days, exhausted Federal troops hurled themselves against the Petersburg defenses in a series of uncoordinated assaults.[3]]

Receiving the message to Maj. Boggs, I took it at once to him, finding him with some pieces of artillery about the Rives house near the Jerusalem Plank Road, at the point at which the battalion of reserves under Col. Archer had a few days before, on the 9th of June, distinguished themselves in the fight with the Federal cavalry. It was expected both by the officials at the custom house and by Maj. Boggs that another assault would on that day be made at this point, as it was believed that, as the breastworks and forts were stronger on the left of the lines in the direction of the river, it was not so likely that an assault would be made at any point to the left, or north, of the plank road. When I delivered the message to Maj. Boggs he was all anxiety, expecting at that very time the appearance of the enemy in his front. We could then hear a few musketry shots down about Battery 5.[4] This firing, I remember, Maj. Boggs thought was only the result of a feint, and that the main assault would be made about Jerusalem road, where he had his artillery.

After a few minutes' interview with Maj. Boggs, he gave me a dispatch to take to Capt. Nat Sturdivant,[5] who with his battery occupied Battery 5. This I took by the most direct route to Battery 5. As I rode from the Jerusalem road along the military road towards Battery 5, the firing about this point consid-

---

3. See Thomas J. Howe, *The Petersburg Campaign: Wasted Valor, June 15–18, 1864* (Lynchburg, Va.: H. E. Howard, 1988).

4. Battery 5, a large redoubt in Petersburg's Dimmock Line, formed a strong salient well in advance of other positions. The fortification featured a six-foot-deep ditch immediately in front, along with slashing, abatis and rifle pits in its fields of fire (see Howe, *Wasted Valor,* 27).

5. Captain Nathaniel Sturdivant commanded a battery named after him from 1862 until his capture in 1864. His single howitzer held off a large Union cavalry force under General Kautz on June 9, 1864, during the famous "Battle of Old Men and Young Boys" (the defense of Petersburg at the Battle of Rive's Farm). Captured on June 15, 1864, Sturdivant was exchanged in time to rejoin his old unit in the last months of the war. He was promoted to major in March 1865 (see W. Cullen Sherwood and Richard L. Nicholas, *Amherst Artillery, Albemarle Artillery, and Sturdivant's Battery* [Lynchburg, Va.: H. E. Howard, 1996]).

erably increased, so much so that I deemed it best not ride directly into the fort (Battery 5), as I intended, but to dismount at the foot of the hill near the City Point railroad crossing, tie my horse there and proceed on foot to Battery 5 on the crest of the hill.

Having tied my horse, I started up the road towards the battery, but had gone but a few paces before, very much to my surprise, a line of Federal sharp-shooters in the open field to my left between the railroad and the public road leading to City Point, opened fire upon me. It is needless to state that I made good time in running up the hill, anxious as I was, to bear my message to Capt. Sturdivant and to inform him of the presence of this body of Federals then working around towards his rear. It was about forty yards before I reached shelter and the enemy's bullets made this part of my journey anything but pleasant. I will state here that between this point and Battery 1, which was immediately upon the Appomattox river, there was only a very thin line of troops manning our works.

Getting under shelter after running the gauntlet of the fire from sharp shooters in the field as above mentioned, I was quickly within the fort, finding as I entered it from the rear that Capt. Sturdivant, having discovered the presence of the body of Federals, whose fire at me had disclosed their position, was hastily getting in readiness for action two guns on the side of the fort fronting towards the river and bearing on this field. I promptly delivered the message I bore him from Maj. Boggs. Capt. Sturdivant expressed delight at seeing me and asked if Bradford's battery or any other re-enforcements were coming to his support, I told him I knew of no re-enforcements coming, and explained how I happened to be present, telling him of my having come to Petersburg that morning on a twelve hours' leave and having tendered my services as already narrated. Capt. Sturdivant seemed anxious about the situation, which from the spirited energy with which he was directing the movements of his men and the firing of his guns—he had been firing to his front and was now getting ready to fire upon the enemy on his left and rear—I saw he was serious.

Learning how I came to be present, Capt. Sturdivant asked me to give him my spare time and to take charge of the two guns he had placed in position for use on his left and rear, these guns being manned by convalescents from the hospitals in Petersburg, who, I soon learned, knew little or nothing of the artillery manual. These convalescents just from sick beds in the hospitals deserve more than passing notice. They were from all parts of the South, and from every branch of the service, strangers to each other and to the officers in charge of them, yet they were willing, obedient soldiers and deeply interested in the success of the engagement. I especially remember the passionate ardor of an intelligent infantry sergeant, from Vicksburg, who served as one of the gunners. Fortunately only a desultory fire was needed from these guns to scatter the small bodies of the enemy that showed themselves occasionally in the field above referred to. But throughout all that day the enemy, whilst making no assaults upon the eastern front of the fort, kept up a constant musketry fire upon it, with occasional shots from artillery, this fire seeming to increase as the day advanced.

Capt. Sturdivant, in his shirt sleeves, the embodiment of energy and gallantry, was personally superintending and directing the fire of the guns in his eastern front. In the fort were some infantry, who were of the Petersburg city battalion of boys under command of Maj. Peter V. Batte and a part of Wise's brigade. About and on the east side of the deep ravine in front of the fort were our pickets, visible from the fort. The fire from the front at these pickets and at the fort made it very dangerous for a man to show his head above the breastworks, and during the day several were wounded.

About four in the afternoon, my leave of absence then drawing to a close, I deemed it proper that I should make my way back to my command, although Capt. Sturdivant was very anxious that I should continue with him longer. So returning to my horse, which had been tied at the foot of the hill all of the several hours I had been in the fort, I mounted her and rode hastily back to the Rives house (my mare being a very fleet animal and considerably excited by the firing), bearing a verbal message from Capt. Sturdivant to Major Boggs that he anticipated an early assault and was in urgent need of re-enforcements. I well remember how Maj. Boggs seemed to realize and appreciate the critical conditions of things—his manifest sympathy for our comrades in this struggling fort, whom he was powerless to assist. From the rattle of musketry, we both, however, felt that it was infantry more than artillery that Capt. Sturdivant needed.

After spending a short time with Maj. Boggs, I bade him good-bye, rode into the city, saw my wife, explained to her the serious situation out on the lines, made my apology to her for not giving her my twelve hours leave, which was justly her due, took leave of her and rode hastily to my battery at the Howlett's house.

As I crossed Pocahontas bridge, about sunset, I heard, in the still summer atmosphere, three distinct Federal cheers—ominous they were to me—in the direction of Battery 5, and I felt sure that the fort had been assaulted and captured, and upon my arrival at the Howlett house, reported this circumstance to my captain. The information I took was the first the officers and men of the battery had of the serious condition of things about the Petersburg lines that day.

The cheers I heard were in fact, as I subsequently learned, those of the Federal forces who carried Battery 5.[6] I will mention here that immediately after the war, in the summer of 1865, in a conversation I had with Col. Strawbridge, of the 2nd Penn. Heavy Artillery, stationed in Petersburg about that time, he gave as a reason for the Federal forces not pushing forward that evening beyond Battery 5 after their capture of it, the fact that they saw in Friend's field a line of earth works (those that were first erected for the defense of Petersburg, and were subsequently abandoned for the outer line, of which Battery 5 formed a part), and, thinking that these must be manned by a reserve body of Confederate troops, concluded that it was safest, in view of the very heavy losses the Federal army had sustained in its campaign from the Wilderness to Petersburg to run no risks, as it was believed that the people at the North would brook no more disasters.

About midnight of the 15th, while near the Howlett house, Capt. Bradford received orders to proceed with his battery to Petersburg and await orders at Pocahontas bridge. Obeying this order, we were in Petersburg at the bridge at sunrise, where we found a courier awaiting our arrival with instructions to take us through Roslyn across Old Town Creek to Archer's house on the north bank of the Appomattox about opposite Battery 5. Arrived at this place (Archer's), we went at once into battery on the bluff upon which the mansion house stands, a few yards southwest of the buildings and opened fire upon Battery 5. Our first shots, owing to defective ammunition, fell short, but, Capt. Bradford sending to Petersburg for a supply of finer and stronger powder, when this arrived, we were able to put both shot and shell into the fort. The enemy, we knew, were getting guns into position, and our fire was rather desultory, intended only to annoy and delay their work.

During this, or the next day, the 17th, the infantry pickets who were stationed at the foot of the bluff about the river bank informed us that a party of mounted men were assembling in or about Puddledock (Mrs. Martha E. Beasley's residence), which was between the river and the City Point public road. Capt. Bradford, rightly assuming that this was a Federal general with his staff and couriers, directed two shots to be fired at the house, which was done. A short time afterwards some of our battery learned from a member of Mrs. Beasley's family who had come through the lines to Petersburg, that the second shot fired passed through the dining room and spoiled a dinner which

6. Sturdivant's Battery was one of a number of Confederate units that surrendered to General W. F. Smith's swift attack on the evening of June 15, 1864. They included three companies of the 26th Virginia and portions of Hood's and Batte's Reserve battalions (see Sherwood and Nicholas, *Amherst Artillery,* 202–5).

was in readiness for the general and his staff, but did no further damage to them.

We remained at Archer's from the morning of Thursday, the 16th, to the afternoon of Saturday, the 18th, firing occasional shots at Battery 5, and at the fields along the river on the Prince George side, wherever we would see bodies of troops. About four o'clock on the afternoon of the 18th a courier rode up in a gallop with a message to Capt. Bradford to take his battery as quickly as possible to the house of Mr. Crump, near Old Town Creek, now the residence of Mr. Wm. H. Cole, at which point he would be directed to a position. We limbered up at once, and with all possible speed made our way to the Crump house. Here we were met by Capt. R. Freeman Graves, who was acting on the staff of Col. Wm. Butler of South Carolina, and were conducted by him in a gallop to a point in the Roslyn field immediately opposite the Jno. Hare house on the south bank of the river. Here we were ordered to unlimber and immediately open fire upon the enemy's infantry, who were then in heavy force assaulting our lines on the south bank of the river, all the way it seemed, from the river southwesterly towards O. P. Hare's residence on the hill upon which Fort Stedman was subsequently built, and perhaps further around towards the Jerusalem plank road. Although there was not, as now, intervening undergrowth along the river to obstruct the view, we could not distinctly see the men in the assaulting [column] except within a hundred to two yards of the river bank, as they were cut off from view by the dense volume of smoke, but, from the smoke and the heavy musketry, we could hear, we knew that a hard fight was in progress.

Our position was excellent, about eight hundred yards from the right flank of the Federal attacking column, and our guns were quickly enfilading the right flank of the line with shells, and two or three rounds from this battery thus delivered served to materially slacken the fire of the enemy, and within a short time the fire on the bluff almost entirely ceased making it clear that the timely arrival of our battery at this critical stage of the assault probably saved Petersburg from capture on the afternoon of the 18th.

I have often thought of this exciting incident of the siege and recalled the telling flank fire with which our guns, put into battery at a gallop, made themselves felt by the assaulting columns of the enemy on the fields between the river and the City Point railroad, and possibly also by the attacking forces on the race-course field on Mr. O. P. Hare's farm between Prince George county road and Hare's hill (the site of the future Fort Stedman). In September last, as you remember, when several members of the A. P. Hill Camp, you and I among the number, were present at the dedication of the monument erected on this field by the survivors of the First Maine Heavy Artillery, to commemorate the bravery and valor of the 632 members of this regiment killed and wounded on the afternoon of June 13th,[7] in the charge of this regiment about this place where the monument stands (some 200 yds northwest of the site of Fort Stedman), we met and talked with several of the regiment who took part in the charge, and from what they said I am satisfied that they were engaged with our infantry on the part of our lines about this point just about the time our battery opened fire as I have narrated.[8]

The position selected for our battery on this occasion, for the credit of which Col. Butler is entitled, was so commanding it was determined to erect a fort there, and this was at once done, and our battery was kept in this fort during the whole of the siege. Many were the artillery duels we had with Battery 1 and Fort McGilvery, and sometimes the heavy guns from Battery 5 would give us a plunging shot. From the river to Fort Stedman the Federal lines were more or less enfiladed by our shot. Within a few weeks after the close of the war I visited the Federal lines within the range of our guns and was struck with the heavy traverse works, both on the picket line and the main line, that were manifestly erected to protect against our enfilading fire from the Chesterfield side. I may mention here that on the occasion of this visit, which was between the 1st and the 15th of May, 1865, I noticed the unburied bodies of several Federal sol[diers] — [*missing text*][9] 18th of June, 1864, lying between the opposing picket lines on the Jno. Hare farm between the City Point railroad and the river.

---

7. Hoy is in error here. The actual date of the assault was June 18th.

8. GSB: The First Maine Heavy Artillery, of Mott's brigade, of Birney's division, of Hancock's corps in this famous charge, made about half past four in the afternoon of the 18th of June, sustained a loss unequaled by that of any other Federal regiment in any engagement of the war. In a recent letter, Maj. Fred. C. Lowe, of Gloucester, Mass. who commanded company B of the regiment after this action until April 6, 1865, says: "Our regiment went into the charge with 900 men (some of our officers think we had only 850 men in line). We charged in three lines of battle, four companies of each, the regiment being commanded by Major (afterwards Bvt. Brig. Gen.) Russell B. Shepherd. In five minutes 632 men and officers were killed and wounded, of whom 210 (whose names I read at the dedication of the monument) were killed and died of their wounds. The casualties in the regiment were in excess of those officially reported. The records show no heavier loss in any other Federal regiment in any one engagement of the war — indeed, no loss so heavy on any regiment on either side." [Bernard also included a lengthy excerpt, excluded here, from an article about the First Maine Heavy Artillery written by Charles J. House and published in the *Maine Bugle* (Campaign II, Call 2, April 1895, 87).]

9. The printer appears to have omitted a line in the article here. Presumably, the missing words refer to Federal soldiers killed during the failed assault on the 18th of June.

During our occupancy of the position taken on the afternoon of the 18th of June, as already mentioned, and held until the night of April 2nd, 1865, we had many artillery duels with the enemy's batteries.

On the morning of the 30th of July the Federal batteries in our front, together with Battery Five, were unusually active in shelling our lines, and also directing a few into the city. Capt. Bradford quickly joined in the engagement which lasted with severity until about midday. I will state that it was late in the morning before we knew definitively of the explosion and of the terrible fight at the Crater, and that Pegram's men and guns had been blown to destruction. Pegram's battery was one of the batteries of our battalion.

On the night of the 25th of August, 1864, the day of the fight at Reams' station, the Chesterfield line about Roslyn farm was strengthened by the addition of thirty eight rifle cannon which, with the two guns of Cumming's battery and three guns of our battery, made forty-three pieces of artillery, and according to previous orders at two o'clock in the morning of the 26th, all of these guns opened fire upon the enemy's main line and fields in rear of this line along the valley of Harrison Creek from the river to the rear of Fort Stedman. The purpose of this fire was not known to us, but it was supposed to have been intended for such bodies of the enemy as might have been massed in this valley or about the lines with a view to an assault. After the firing ceased and quiet was restored the Federal pickets along the line of the river in our immediate front called over to our pickets on the north bank of the river and wanted to know what was the matter, saying at the same time that they "had done nothing to provoke such a shelling."

Some time in January, or February, of 1865, the watchman of our battery called to Capt. Bradford and informed him that the Federal works were covered with men and ours too. Capt. Bradford, after viewing the situation and remarking that he had not been notified of a truce or any other cessation of hostilities, said to one of the gunners: "Give them a shot at high range." The gunner did as directed and it is almost unnecessary to state that the breastworks were instantly cleared. For a little while there was no reply to this shot, but when the reply did come, it came with vengeance, Batteries 1 and 5, and Fort McGilvery concentrating their fire upon us for a full half-hour, giving us the heaviest shelling we had during the siege. We learned through the Petersburg Express of the next morning that there had been a truce about the City Point railroad at the time we saw the troops on both sides crowding the breastworks. The Federal batteries reserved their response to Capt. Bradford's shot until this was at an end, and then opened with terrific fury. Several nights work was required to repair our embrasures and other portions of our works after this severe shelling.

From this time on to the 24th of March, very little firing was done by either side. We strengthened our works, and we could plainly see through the naked boughs of the trees of intervening woods and undergrowth that the Federal were strengthening theirs. On the 24th of March, Capt. Bradford received orders to have on hand a full supply of ammunition, and early in the night of this day he received orders to open fire the next morning at a certain hour (which I think was 4 o'clock) and to fire some of the guns at high range upon the body of woods in the rear of Fort Stedman, the fire to be continued for a certain time, an hour I think.

On the morning of the 25th, in obedience to these orders the guns of our battery opened and kept up their fire as directed, and then ceased firing. About the time we ceased, we heard some musketry about Fort Stedman and an occasional cannon, but the reports sounded peculiarly, seeming to be muffled, some of the men remarking that the firing sounded "as if in the ground," the dense fog enveloping everything at daylight that morning doubtless producing this effect. As, however, the fog lifted, the reports of musketry and artillery reached us with distinctness, and we became satisfied that a fearful battle was going on in the vicinity of Fort Stedman. As an evidence of this, as the fog lifted, we noticed that the guns of Fort McGilvery were being fired at Fort Stedman, which fact satisfied us that our troops then held that fort. We then gave McGilvery the direct fire of our guns and mortars but received only an occasional shot in reply. Fort McGilvery was about half way between us and Fort Stedman.

About seven o'clock the artillery fire about and beyond Fort Stedman was very severe. The Federals had some siege guns on their rear line (our original line) which they were now firing—guns that, I am satisfied, were never in action before or afterwards during the siege. From the fact that these siege guns as well as some of the guns in Fort McGilvery were directing their fire upon Fort Stedman, we knew that our troops were in possession of the fort. It was several hours later (between 11 and 12 o'clock) before we learned the result of the desperate battle of this morning and that it had been so disastrous to our side.[10]

From this time on to the 2nd of April, the firing was almost incessant. Our battery was constantly engaged, with but brief intermissions. On the morning of this day, April 2nd, at early dawn, from the batteries in our immediate front, from Forts Stedman and Haskell and from other points around the city

---

10. Here Hoy describes the Battle of Fort Stedman on March 25, 1865. For a recent summary of this failed Confederate assault, see A. Wilson Greene, *The Final Battles of the Petersburg Campaign: Breaking the Backbone of the Rebellion* (Knoxville: University of Tennessee Press, 2008).

came the reports of booming cannon, accompanied at some points with the same rattle of musketry. With daylight enabling them to see their way, the Federals assaulted and captured our picket lines between the City Point railroad and the south bank of the Appomattox, and, encouraged by this success, moved vigorously upon our main line about this point, but were repulsed by the Confederates in the trenches here and retreated under a rapid and destructive fire from our men.

As the day wore on, towering columns of black smoke ascending from certain localities in the city told us plainly that the government stores were being burned to prevent their falling into the hands of the enemy, and that our fears of an evacuation were about to be realized. Sure enough, as the shades of evening lengthened, the looked for courier came with orders for us to abandon our works. Our orders were after dark to get every thing in readiness with the utmost stillness and at 11 o'clock to pull our guns, by hand, to a convenient place for getting the horses hitched in readiness for our marching.[11]

At this hour our guns were taken out of the fort to a point a few yards distance, and there the horses were hitched, for the first time since the 18th of June, and we proceeded to the Richmond and Petersburg turnpike, and reaching this road, went a short distance down it towards Petersburg to the point at which the Woodpecker road begins and there awaited orders. Here we found the other batteries of our (Coit's) battalion, which were Wright's, Pegram's and Coit's old battery, which had arrived from Petersburg, and between daylight and sunrise the whole command turned into the Woodpecker road and took upon the line of march westward—for what point bound we knew not.

When we thus turned our backs on Petersburg, it was, indeed, a sad and trying ordeal. At four different times during its service had our battery been stationed about or near the city. The members of the command had made many friends among her citizens, had often been entertained socially at their houses, and several of us had found wives among her fair daughters. With hearts full of hope, with never a fear of defeat, all had been brightness and sunshine. To turn away now and leave all that was dear to us in the hands of the enemy was almost more that we could stand, and as our column marched along, it was with the solemnity of a funeral procession.

We had proceeded on our march some three or four miles with nothing to disturb us save our own gloomy thoughts when an incident occurred that I have often recalled: I had been placed at the head of the marching column of

11. The burning of stores and the rampant fear in the city are ably described by A. Wilson Greene is his book, *Civil War Petersburg: Confederate City in the Crucible of War* (Charlottesville: University of Virginia Press, 2006).

our battalion, when all at once on my left came a body of infantry marching on the high ground on the road-side, and quickening their pace, and so passing ahead, the leading files of this command marched right down into the a road-way just at the head of the front team of the battalion, and a moment later came the colonel in command with orders to his men to "halt the artillery." He did not address his command to me, but to his men. Being in charge of the head of the column with special orders to keep moving, I spurred my horse forward, and touching my cap to the colonel told him I was in charge of the column and could not halt as my orders were to keep moving. His reply was, "Damn it, halt! My orders are to keep moving, too." Not being in a pleasant frame of mind, I thought it best not have any words with this officer, but took care not to halt, whereupon he came at me with another order to halt, to which I gave no heed, but called his attention to the open woods along the road, in which he might march his men and easily get ahead of us. At the point we then were the road was in a cut, and being narrow, there was not room for infantry or artillery to march side by side. Not heeding my suggestion, with an oath he said: "I'll stop you!" He then called to the officer in command of the leading company of his regiment and said: "Make your men about face, fix bayonets and halt that damned artillery!" This order was promptly obeyed. A file of men, with fixed bayonets, planted themselves, directly across the road in front of the leading team, the men standing in the position of "charge bayonets." It is needless to say that the artillery was halted and long enough for the colonel's command to pass forward to the front. My blood was pretty hot, and so I think, was the colonel's. I never learned his name, nor what was his regiment, except that they were Georgians. Time has healed all of my hard feelings towards him, and I hope his towards me. I would like to meet him now and shake his hand.

Your Comrade,

P. C. Hoy

ADDENDUM: STATEMENT OF JAS. P. JACKSON

The following letter from Mr. Jas. P. Jackson,[12] of Petersburg, Va., a member of Bradford's Battery, adds to Lt. Hoy's narrative many details of interest:

Petersburg, Va.,

June 13th, 1895

George S. Bernard, Esq., Petersburg, Va.,

Dear Sir: At your request I give you some recollections of service as a member of Bradford's Battery of artillery, which I joined when it was sta-

---

12. James P. Jackson was Lieutenant Hoy's brother-in-law and joined the battery in the trenches at Petersburg, according to Hoy's history of Bradford's Battery.

tioned on the Roslyn farm in Chesterfield county during the siege of Petersburg, I being then a boy of sixteen.

The battery consisted of two twelve-pounders, three twenty pound Parrott guns and two eight-inch mortars. A detachment of this battery, with the twelve-pounders, was stationed at Belfield, Va., guarding the railroad at that point. The remainder of the command were at the Roslyn farm where I joined it, just across the Appomattox from the Federal fort known as Fort McGilvery (this fort being on the farm then owned by my uncle, J. Alex Pace, and now owned by Mr. Richard A. Young), and was stationed in this position for the purpose of enfilading the Federal lines from the river to Fort Stedman (on Hare's hill) and also for the purpose of drawing fire from the Federal forts whenever they would shell the city. It was seldom that we were not doing some firing, and of course receiving some in return, as may be inferred from the fact that members of the battery picked up at and around our fort more than 100,000 pounds of shot, shells and fragments of shells and sold the same to the Confederate government.

On the morning of March 25th, 1865, when the assault was made upon Fort Stedman our fire was directed upon the body of woods in the rear of the fort as we were ordered, but our troops got into these woods ahead of the time they were expected to do according to the arranged programme, and received some of our fire before we ceased firing upon their front. We had been ordered to fire at these woods a given length of time and then cease. We then turned our attention to Fort McGilvery and the neighboring Federal earthworks.

On the morning of the 2nd of April we witnessed the assault of the Federal infantry upon the portion of the Confederate lines between the City Point railroad and the river. Our picket line was carried, but the attacking column was driven back when they assaulted our main works at this point. A few minutes after this we saw a courier rapidly riding up from our rear. Asking for the officer in command, who was Lt. P. C. Hoy, now of our city, he delivered to him instructions to immediately open fire with our mortars upon our main line of works on the south bank of the river, stating as he did so, that these works were then in possession of the enemy. Lt. Hoy, upon hearing this statement, informed the courier that our main line of works had not been captured, but were still held by our troops, and stated that he would not fire as ordered, as he knew there was a mistake and that the fire at such close range would prove very destructive. The courier in reply to Lt. Hoy said, "I leave this matter with you," and then rode away, but in a short time returned with great haste, his horse reeking with perspiration, and asking again for the officer in command, stated to him that General Gordon sent him his compliments for his close observation of the fight and for not firing on our men.

About dark that night we received orders to evacuate our position, but did not leave until several hours later. We carried off all of our guns mounted on wheels, but having spiked the mortars left them behind. Going directly [onto] the Richmond and Petersburg turnpike, we there halted until between daybreak and sunrise, awaiting the arrival of the remainder of our battalion (Coit's) which had been doing duty on the south side of the river. I need not detail the march of our command during this and the next five days, as we had no collision with the enemy, or other experience of special interest until the afternoon of Saturday, the 8th of April, when we were quietly parked within a half mile of Appomattox Station and were unexpectedly attacked by a body of Federal cavalry.

On this afternoon several batteries besides our own had halted and like ours had parked in an open field on the left of the public road leading from the Lynchburg road to Appomattox Station, the men and animals enjoying the much needed rest. The gun to which I was attached was on the extreme right of the line of parked guns. Between our line of guns and the station was a thin skirt of woods. Whilst we were enjoying this quiet, I walked across the road leading to the station and bade Lt. Hoy good bye, as, being quite ill, he was about to be taken in an ambulance to the station to be thence transported with other sick and disabled soldiers to Lynchburg in a train then standing at the station in readiness to start. Returning to my gun, I lay down in front of it to rest. In a very little while, hardly three quarters of an hour, Sergeant Leak Milam, of our battery who had accompanied Lt. Hoy to the station and put him on board of the train, rode rapidly up to our battery and surprised us with the startling information that a body of Federal cavalry, then forming along the railroad at the station, were about to charge us. Looking in this direction we could see them through the thin skirt of woods above referred to, in considerable numbers.

The men at once sprang to their guns, and unlimbering them opened fire upon the enemy, some of whom were dismounted. This was done with remarkable quickness, considering the fact that no one suspected the presence of the enemy and the men were scattered about through the encampment, and many were asleep.[13]

13. GSB: Mr. Hoy in a recent statement says: "I was in the rear coach (about the rear door) of this train, a very long one, filled with sick and wounded men, and the train was moving very slowly about four miles from Appomattox Station, when an engine and tender filled with men overtook our train with the information that a few minutes after our train pulled out from the station the Federal cavalry charged the place, took possession of it and burned the freight cars then standing there. The occupants of this engine

When we fired our first shot, which was a charge of canister, the Federal line of dismounted men immediately in front of the guns of our battery were only 300 yards distant. Several charges were made but we repulsed them. After we had kept them back for half an hour or more, the mounted men on the right and to our left began to flank us, and we were then forced to abandon our guns nearly all of the batteries to our left and rear having by this time withdrawn their guns. Some of the men of our battery, having received sabre cuts from the charging Federal cavalrymen before we were driven from our pieces.

[Jackson here describes the Battle of Appomattox Station, where Union cavalry under Brigadier General George A. Custer attacked Brigadier General R. Lindsey Walker's artillery train on April 8. After several hours of fighting, a final charge by Custer's troopers broke Walker's line and succeeded in capturing 25 field pieces. Walker's fleeing men managed to take 75 guns from the field, but the unit's effectiveness as a fighting force was doubtful and, within 24 hours, irrelevant.[14]]

There was a little ravine just in our rear into which all of our battery who could get away retreated. Getting into this ravine we followed it until we reached the Lynchburg road which we had passed over a few hours before, and which we now found crowded with abandoned wagons, ambulances and pieces of artillery. Going down this road towards Appomattox C.H. a few hundred yards I met our late townsman, Chas. A. Jackson, then a member of Martin's Battery and in charge of some ambulance wagons. He said, as I saw was the case, that his wagon train was blockaded by obstructions in the road ahead of him, and asked me what was the matter. I told him that the enemy were near us, and that if he would wait a little while he would find this out for himself. It was then growing dark.

Bidding Charlie Jackson good-bye, I leaped a fence skirting the wood, accompanied by a member of our battery. Going a few hundred yards into the woods north of the road, we concluded that it was best to stop where we were for the night, which we did, resting in the branches of a large fallen pine tree. At daylight next morning we crept out from our novel resting place

---

and tenders had barely time to cut them loose from the cars to which they were coupled and make their escape."

14. See Chris M. Calkins, *The Battles of Appomattox Station and Appomattox Court House, April 8–9, 1865* (Lynchburg, Va.: H. E. Howard, 1987), 28–44.

to discover that we were by no means alone. A number of other Confederate soldiers had occupied like positions during the night in the branches of neighboring fallen pine trees.

Starting off, we moved back towards Appomattox, C.H., but, before reaching it, took another road leading in a northerly direction west of the C.H. Soon hearing that Gen. Lee was about to surrender his army, we then determined, if possible, to get to Johnston's army. Following the road we had taken we reached a church or school house, where we found a large number of wagons, some with and some without mules. Seeing a very nice team, my companion and myself took steps to provide ourselves with mounts. The first animal I mounted threw me over her head. Not discouraged, I tried another, but this time the saddle mule, minus the saddle.

After a short ride, we reached a ferry on the James river. Here we found Sergeant Leak Milam of our battery. At this ferry we found also probably as many as an hundred Confederates all waiting to get across. The ferry boat having been destroyed, our only chance to get across was to swim over. An officer (a colonel, I think) among those at the ferry endeavored to impress upon us that if we attempted to guide our horses, or mules, whilst swimming we would endanger our lives as well as those of the animals. We heeded this advice and safely swam across. On the opposite bank I luckily found a saddle.

The river crossed, with some little difficulty we crossed the canal, which runs parallel to the river bank, and it was about three o'clock in the afternoon.

Taking the first public road we struck, we followed it in a westerly direction until after dark, when we discovered ahead of us an encampment of some kind. Upon reaching it, much to our surprise, our party, now numbering five (including a North Carolinian and a captain from Pittsylvania) were arrested as deserters. The encampment was that of a foraging train escorted by a small body of cavalry. We protested against the arrest, stating that we were from Lee's army, that Lee had surrendered that day at Appomattox C.H. and that we were on our way to Johnston's army, then about Greensboro, N.C. Our story was not credited and we were detained under arrest of two hours or more, until the guard having brought in another party of Confederates eight or ten in number, among them one or more others with whom the officer in command of the wagon train was acquainted, and he corroborated our statement of Lee's surrender.

The following day (Monday) we crossed the James River ten or fifteen miles above Lynchburg, and struck for Greensboro by as straight a course as practicable, being directed by our comrade, the captain from Pittsylvania, under whose command we placed ourselves; and whose name I regret I can not recall. This gentleman took us by his house in that county, a magnificent establishment, where we were most hospitably entertained by his father and mother. The old gentleman finding that I was from Petersburg, insisted that I should, after remaining with him several days, return home. Having no intention of leaving my comrades, I declined his invitation, and, after spending one night at his delightful place, went along with them towards our place of destination.

Reaching Leaksville, N. C., we found Capt. Bradford (of our battery) and also Capt. Cumming who commanded a battery on the Chesterfield line near ours. After making inquiries of Capt. Bradford about other members of our battery, we proceeded on our journey, and, reaching Greensboro about noon one day, we found Johnston's army occupying a considerable portion of the town and quite a commotion on the streets. Enquiring the cause of the stir, we found that some of Wheeler's cavalry had charged upon the buildings of the commissary department to get whiskey, and that Beauregard had ordered his men to fire into them, which had been done, resulting in the killing of several of the cavalry. One of these cavalrymen fell near the gate of my aunt, who resided in the town, and I assisted in taking him into the house, where he died a few days later. This affair occurred during the armistice between Johnston and Sherman.

Besides myself and my comrades above mentioned there were in Greensboro several other soldiers from Lee's army. One day we called upon Gen. Beauregard to ask what we should do, and were told by him that we had better make our way back to Virginia and surrender as members of Lee's army, it not being then known upon what terms Johnston's army would be surrendered. So we turned our faces homeward, and walked the whole distance from Greensboro to Nottoway C.H. getting our paroles at Danville. At Nottoway C.H., we found a freight train loaded with supplies and coming this way, and like tramps stole a ride to Petersburg.

Arriving in Petersburg about two o'clock in the morning, and, going directly home. I knocked at the door. My father raised a window and wanted to know who could it be at that hour of the morning. I told him who I was. My father was no less surprised than pleased to see me. Having heard from various sources that I had been killed in the engagement at Appomattox Station, he had given me up as dead. Another James Jackson had not been killed, but severely wounded, and this had originated the reports that had reached my family.

Your Comrade,

James P. Jackson

"The Confederate Scout, The Bold Expedition Recalled," by William E. Cameron[15]

Ex-Gov. Cameron Relates His Experiences in Connection with a Scouting Party which Went into the Federal Lines in Search of Information

[While his army manned the trenches at Cold Harbor in early June 1864, Lee detached the much-depleted Second Corps under Lieutenant General Jubal A. Early to expel U.S. Major General David Hunter from the Shenandoah Valley. In a matter of weeks, Early's expedition evolved into a full-scale raid which threatened Washington and Baltimore. Early's progress raised the alarm north of the Potomac and yielded desperate pleas for reinforcements from the armies investing Richmond and Petersburg. Concerned about Grant's reaction to Early's threat, Lee sought to discover details about federal troop movements.[16] The following account by William Cameron describes a little known part of this intelligence-gathering effort.]

A. P. Hill Camp Hall was packed to overflowing last night with the members of the camp and others, including a large number of ladies to hear an address by ex-Governor William E. Cameron, whose subject was "The Confederate Scout." Seated on the platform besides the speaker were Captain W. Gordon McCabe, commander of the camp, and General Battle, of North Carolina, father of Rev. H. W. Battle, D.D., pastor of the First Baptist church in this city. Commander McCabe introduced the ex-governor, and at the conclusion of the latter's address thanked him on behalf of the camp. The ex-governor spoke in part as follows:

It was on the 6th of July, 1864, that I received notice of General Lee's anxiety to obtain intelligence on this point. The brigade (Davis', of Heth's division) to which I was then attached as inspector-general was situated in the trenches east of Petersburg, and the monotony and discomfort of life in the lines, the dust and heat and the petty annoyance of the enemy's pickets was so irksome that I welcomed the opportunity to gain temporary release from it for a few days. Besides, there was the certainty of exciting adventure and the possibility of rendering important service. The idea was no sooner conceived than acted on. In five minutes I had applied for and received the requested permission from General Davis and was mounted and on my way to obtain the sanction of General Heth. Arriving at the headquarters of the latter, I

---

15. This article appeared in the *Petersburg Daily Index-Appeal* on March 27, 1895.
16. See *O.R.* 37: pt. 2, 594–95 (Robert E. Lee to Jefferson Davis).

obtained a cordial approval of my project and authority to take with me four of the most noted of the corps of division scouts—Hooker, Arnold, Ritchie, and Nunez, all but the latter hardy Mississippians, and he a Spaniard with a cross of Indian blood. Nunez was the hero of more desperate adventures than any man I met during the war. His daring was reckless, but equaled by his skill and good fortune as a scout. He literally lived within the enemy's lines and knew the organization of their army more intimately than I did that of our own.[17]

This digression as to my companions has occupied as much time as was required to make our simple preparation for a start. At my instance[18] we were all in Confederate uniform (which was not the habit of the scouts when bound on such expeditions), but wore light blue cavalry cloaks which might be deceptive at close quarters. Our baggage consisted of a blanket and rubber. I carried two heavy navy revolvers and the rest of the party, had, in addition, each a Colt's repeating rifle. We were well mounted and unless forced or surprised into a fight, expected to make more use of our horses during the trip than of our weapons. So about two o'clock in the afternoon, with light hearts and after hearing all manner of cheerful prophecies from the members of the staff, who envied our good fortunes, we galloped off to the Halifax road, intending to force the federal picket line somewhere above the head of the Blackwater swamp, and then take the Jerusalem plank road down the country. Ascertaining from our cavalry outpost the position of the enemy's videttes, we found no difficulty in passing between below Lee's mill and traveling by neighborhood roads until we reached the house of Mr. Proctor. We there passed out into the highway and only drew reign at Hawkinsville, spending the night in the thicket back of Major Belcher's farm. All of these places are as familiar as household words to the old soldiers of both armies. The next morning, bright and early, we struck out for Waverly, then a mere station of the Norfolk railroad, now a thriving Virginia town, meeting no interference but stopping by the way at the house of a Mrs. Mason to obtain an excellent breakfast. At Waverly we were joined by a bright, handsome lad of fourteen or fifteen whose name, I think, was Sidney Clary, of whom I have heard that he still lives near the borders of Prince George and Surry counties, but have never seen him since. Learning our mission, the brave boy saddled his pony and undertook to guide us in our journey towards the river. In the meantime he gave us many valuable points, and reported that the country below was full of stragglers from Wilson's cavalry, who, having been cut off at Ream's

---

17. "* * *" appears here in the article.

18. The article here reads "instance." It probably should read "insistence" instead.

station the week before, were now seeking to regain their lines, of this more hereafter.[19]

Late in the day, Clary in the meantime having left us, we arrived at Surry Courthouse and found it deserted save by the old gentleman who gave us dinner and by a superannuated negro or two. Here two expeditions were planned. Arnold and Nunez were to strike for the river at the nearest point in search of information, while the rest of us were to spend the night on the line of the military telegraph, hoping to make a prisoner from the patrol and to gain from him the desired intelligence. The telegraph line ran from Fort Powhatan to Swan's [Swann's] Point.[20] It had been so frequently interrupted, particularly by the members of the Prince George and Surry troops of cavalry who knew the country well and who were thus able to elude observation, that a special guard of negro soldiers was kept moving up and down the route to protect the line; and General Butler had become so exasperated at the futility of his efforts to keep the communications open that he had issued a proclamation of outlawry against all scouts apprehended in that territory, and especially against the men of the commands above mentioned. So, knowing that, if caught, our shrift was likely to be short, we proceeded with great caution on to a point in the woods where we could lay in ambush near to the line. About midnight the tramp of hoofs and sounds of voices admonished us of the approach of the patrol of about forty negro cavalrymen jogging leisurely along and talking in loud angry tones. It seemed that the lines had been tampered with the night before and they had been drawn over the coals for lack of vigilance and they were swearing vengeance against any d——d rebel who might come into their hands. Waiting until they had passed we quietly fell into the rear of their movement up the river and found a malicious pleasure in cutting the line at short intervals over an extent of three miles. We followed in their track nearly to Cabin Point, but made not prisoners, as they evidently stood in wholesome fear of bushwhackers and kept well together. However, we came upon their rear just before abandoning the pursuit and fired a volley as a parting salute. At daybreak we reached the appointed place of rendezvous with the other party, and, finding that they had procured satisfactory

19. Cameron refers here to the ill-fated Wilson-Kautz raid in late June 1864. Several thousand Federal cavalrymen were nearly cut off and captured at Ream's Station during their return from the operation (see Greg Eanes, *Destroy the Junction: The Wilson-Kautz Raid and the Battle for Staunton River Bridge, June 21, 1864 to July 1, 1864* [Lynchburg, Va.: H. E. Howard, 1997]).

20. Fort Powhatan lay on the south bank of the James River approximately 15 miles east of Petersburg. Swann's Point is about 10 miles east and downstream from Fort Powhatan and directly across the James from historic Jamestown.

evidence that Rickett's division had been ordered north, Hooker and Arnold were sent back to Petersburg with the intelligence while the rest of us determined to push on towards Nansemond river.

Moving rapidly eastward we encountered no enemy until late in the afternoon when a cloud of dust announcing the approach of troops, we betook ourselves into a field of luxuriant corn and waited developments. A small column of cavalry passed westward at first, well closed up but then came scattered groups of five and six and then parties of two or three straggling at long intervals. I held the horses while Ritchie and Nunez crept near the road. They watched their chances and would slip out suddenly with drawn pistols and bring in two and more prisoners at a time, until they had accumulated thirty-two. This was thought to be as many as we could manage, so no attempt was made to interfere with belated laggards who were still passing by. We lay there for more than an hour when the last of the procession was well gone, compelling those we had corralled to keep silence on pain of death. But they needed no coercion, said they were tired of fighting and asked nothing better than to be paroled. Accordingly, (after some discussion in which Nunez expressed the opinion that they had better be treated as we would be if caught), it was determined to take their paroles to report at Franklin station, on the Seaboard road, the nearest Confederate post, and I made out their papers and started them on their journey, rejoicing. That night after a hard ride I slept in a house in the lower end of Southampton county. The owner reported that a squad of Federals had been there that day searching for Confederate scouts suspected to be in the neighborhood, and warned us that there would be danger in remaining over night. We concluded, however, that having found nothing suspicious they would hardly be apt to return, and we had ridden hard and constantly and both horses and men were in need of rest. As a matter of precaution, the two scouts picketed the horses in the rear of the dwelling and spread their blankets beside them. I, on the contrary, had already had symptoms of malaria and determined to share the chamber of a lad who was visiting the family. We retired directly after supper, and it required no rocking and little time to send me into a dreamless sleep aided, no doubt, by a monster dose of apple brandy and quinine which our hostess administered as the sovereign remedy against "Ague-n-fever." Some hours passed in quiet. When I awakened it was to hear shouts, oaths, trampling of hoofs, heavy blows upon the outside doors of the house and to realize that my outlook for escape was of the slimmest. However, what better to do than to be still did not occur to me, so I gathered my clothes under the bedding, hid my pistols under the pillow and waited in fear and trembling for what should come next. A few moments, which seemed a month, went by, and then heavy feet upon the stairway seemed to give notice that the crisis was at hand. I thought a great deal in a very short time. They would surely hang me, if detected, so I had as well make a fight for it. I slipped one hand under the holster, grabbed a cocked revolver and tried with indifferent success to swallow my heart. The steps grew nearer, the door flew open and Ritchie burst in with a mighty oath. "No time for bed, captain! Hustle on your clothes. We killed two of them and took to the house as your only chance. If they have gone we must break out now and try for the horses."

Here was a relief. But the salutation was bad enough still. I got up, dressed in a jiffy, went out into the hall where the good lady was wringing her hands in despair, and the good man was handling his double barreled gun and saying grimly, 'As well be shot for an old sheep as a lamb.' Nunez now crept out of the kitchen window to reconnoiter. He soon cried out that the enemy had disappeared, and we found out from the negroes in the outhouse that there had only been four of them, one of whom had been badly hurt and another dismounted by a wound to his horse. They had decamped without looking for our horses. But it was certain that they would return with reinforcements, so with short delay we saddled up and journeyed onward. Before daylight, however, we halted, and spent the day snugly concealed in the forest. At night we ventured to a house for supper, took to the woods afterwards and were not disturbed.

The next day, early in the afternoon, found us cantering boldly through the little village of Chuckatuck, the very name of which overwhelms me with a flood of pleasant memories. Our destination was the mansion of Squire Riddick,[21] famed for his patriotism and for his hospitality, a princely gentleman of the old school. Here we were welcomed with open arms to most luxuriant entertainment. How my eyes feasted upon the adornment of a well appointed home. How sweet the long unfamiliar peace which brooded over the whole establishment. How tempting the cool white beds. How delicious, the French brandy juleps fragrant with tender mint and sweetened with old fashioned loaf sugar, brimming with crystal ice and all compounded by the deft hands of a fair Virginia maiden. Verily I had found an oasis in the desert of war.

Of course, within these portals, refreshments to the guests was the first duty to be disposed of. That done, a grave consultation followed as to the means of most speedily accomplishing the main object of our visit. Mr. Riddick was a warm adherent of the Confederate cause and had already rendered valuable service in reporting the designs and movements of the Federals. He

21. Cameron is probably referring to Nathaniel Riddick, owner of the grandest house in the area at the time, nicknamed Riddick's Folly by townspeople. Built by his father, Mills, the house had twenty-one rooms and sixteen fireplaces. Today the house is a museum.

was ready with suggestions of sending a messenger over the river to obtain the latest and most accurate information, and the plans soon arranged were successfully carried into effect the same night. By the following morning we were in possession of full and reliable knowledge as to the reinforcements sent against Early, and nothing remained but to convey it to General Lee as speedily as possible. A start that night was decided on. But in the meanwhile my sickness had developed into a regular case of bilious fever. I was unable to travel. There was nothing to be done but that my companions should hasten on the return to Petersburg leaving me to be nursed into health and to find my way back as best I could. Let me say here that Ritchie and Nunez reached the army in safety, and the news they bore was exactly in accordance with the facts; but their report had been anticipated by earlier advices from another source, so we gained no renown by our exploit.[22]

Governor Cameron next narrated in a charming manner the hospitalities of which he was the recipient at the hands of Mr. Riddick and the members of his family, telling how he was beautifully entertained whilst he was recovering from his sickness, and how he made his way back to the Confederate lines.

"Artillery Experiences at Petersburg and Elsewhere," by Joseph W. Eggleston

An Address Delivered before A. P. Hill Camp of Confederate Veterans, of Petersburg Va., by Dr. Jos. W. Eggleston on the Evening of Thursday, January 3rd, 1895

[On the night of January 3, 1895, Dr. Joseph W. Eggleston rose before the A. P. Hill Camp and delivered the following address about his war experi-

22. Lee's surviving dispatches indicate that he gleaned information about Grant's troop movements "from deserters, prisoners, scouts, and citizens." Lee shared his findings with President Davis and Early. In a July 11, 1864, dispatch to Early, he wrote: "I ascertained some days ago that on the 6th instant General Grant sent off a portion of his troops, and, as far as I am able to judge, they consisted of Ricketts' division, of the Sixth Corps, and their destination was Washington City. . . . I learn this morning from our scouts on James River that about the same number of troops, judging from the transports, descended the river yesterday, and I presume they are bound for Washington City" (*O.R.* 37: pt. 2, 594–96). These additional troops mentioned by Lee were most likely two divisions of Wright's Sixth Corps sent to Washington by Grant to reinforce Ricketts (see Horn, *The Petersburg Campaign*, 101).

ences. Eggleston was born in Indiana in 1844 but came from an old Virginia family. After his mother died in 1857, he left the Hoosier State and moved to his family's home. When the war came in 1861, he joined the Amelia Minutemen, a unit which later became Company H of the 44th Virginia Infantry. After suffering health problems during the Rich Mountain Campaign in western Virginia, Eggleston transferred to the Nelson Light Artillery, also known as Captain James N. Lamkin's Battery. Lamkin's men served along the South Carolina coast and fought at the Battle of Pocotaligo, where Eggleston received a leg wound. Later the unit transferred to Virginia, arriving without its horses and guns. During the Overland Campaign, the battery members carried Enfield rifles and supported the artillery pieces of Haskell's battalion. At Petersburg, the unit served in the trenches as a mortar battery. During that campaign, Eggleston managed to find time to court Miss Lucy A. Jefferson of Amelia County. The two married in November of 1864 and eventually had thirteen children. After the war, Eggleston tried his hand at farming, then journalism (in New York), and then dentistry in Fishkill, New York, on the Hudson River. His older brother, the noted writer George Cary Eggleston, also resided in New York during this time. Suffering from ill health, Joseph Eggleston moved back to Virginia in the 1890s and settled in Amelia County. In 1903, he published a historical novel, *Tuckahoe: An Old-Fashioned Story of an Old-Fashioned People* (New York: Neale Publishing). He died in Richmond in 1922.[23]]

Comrades:

The present generation, our children, are too tired of our war talks and not far enough removed from the events of 1861–5 to take sufficient interest in the history we made in those four years. They are neglecting to secure and preserve many things that would be of inestimable value to future generations. But after them will come our grandchildren who will ransack garret and closet for old books and papers bearing on those heroic days. They will appreciate the work done by the Geo. S. Bernard's of the South in saving some of the material for future history.

My purpose in preparing this paper has been to contribute my mite, and it seems to me that, as I was only a man in the ranks, the best I can do is to give some personal recollections of service in the artillery, and particularly of

---

23. Sources for Eggleston's biographical information include a handwritten sketch in the Bernard Collection of the Historical Society of Western Virginia. A different version of the sketch is in the Bernard Papers, Southern Historical Collection, University of North Carolina.

mortar service in the siege of Petersburg, I shall not attempt to go into details, but shall tell, in the main, what transpired under my own eye, or practically within my own knowledge, and in doing so shall endeavor not to be the hero of my own story, except the first installment, and this I am sure you will credit more to mischievousness than vanity.

Some years ago I found myself in a store in one of our Virginia villages and a perfect stranger to the half-dozen or so loafers around the stove. Many and marvelous were their tales of the war and of their own feats of valor and heroism. One told how he fired the shot that turned the tide of battle at a critical moment on some famous field; another how he had given valuable advice to Stuart or Fitz Lee; another how some distinguished general had confided his plans to him and asked his advice; and another recounted his wonderful feats of coolness and daring.

To all this I listened with thorough disgust, casting about for some means of letting them all see how small a value I placed upon their stories. After each one had, to his satisfaction, demonstrated what a stupendous mistake it was that he had not been entrusted with high command, I found an opportunity and began as follow:

"Not withstanding all you gentlemen have said, I claim to be the greatest hero produced by the war on either side, and can prove it by my record. I began the war in the famous Rich Mountain campaign as a private in the 44th Va. Infantry, in which campaign we retreated for four days and three nights with scarcely a halt. I closed my glorious military career as a participant in Lee's famous retreat of April, 1865, in which we left the works below Richmond on Sunday night and reached Appomattox Station on the following Saturday night, during which week I belonged to two different batteries of artillery, both of which were captured, but I made my escape both times." Here I stopped. There was no comment, but in a few minutes pressing business engagements called the last man away from around that stove. I shall endeavor tonight not to violate good taste as they did. But, I must begin my story: The battery of Capt. J. N. Lamkin,[24] to which I had been transferred

24. James M. Lamkin of Lynchburg enlisted in 1861 as a 1st lieutenant of the newly formed artillery unit organized by Captain Woodville G. Latham of Lynchburg. When Lamkin was elected captain in 1862, Latham left the unit, later supervising the Confederate Ordnance Laboratory. The battery took Lamkin's name, and he commanded the unit until the end of the war. Described by General E. P. Alexander as a "big, handsome fellow," Lamkin, at six-feet-four, towered over his men. He was known for his energy and his stamina, as well as his height. For more on Lamkin's battery, see W. Cullen Sherwood, *The Nelson Artillery: Lamkin and Rives Batteries* (Lynchburg, Va.: H. E. Howard, 1991).

in April, 1862, had seen two years' service on the coast of South Carolina as an unattached battery, as stated by Comrade Myers of our battalion, now of Petersburg, in his statement giving an account of the Battle of the Crater, which appears in the chapter of "War Talks of Confederate Veterans" and had been assigned to Haskell's battalion of Longstreet's corps on its return to Virginia in November, 1863.

When the battery arrived at Orange C.H. it found its outfit of guns and horses left by the German Artillery of Charleston, with which it had by mutual consent exchanged, turned over to the Washington Artillery to supply losses. Other guns were furnished, but the horses were never supplied. For this reason when the following campaign began in the Wilderness, Capt. Lamkin volunteered to have his men armed with muskets and do service as supports between the guns of the other batteries of the battalion until better arrangements could be made.

The battalion was commanded by the heroic boy major, and later Lieutenant Colonel John C. Haskell, of South Carolina, who had lost his right arm charging breastworks in one of the Seven Days' battles around Richmond, he being at the time an assistant-commissary with the rank of captain. The four batteries composing the battalion were one of them from South Carolina, two from North Carolina and ours from Virginia. They were commanded respectively by Captain Hugh R. Garden, Capt. Ramey, Capt. Potts (who was mortally wounded at Spotsylvania C.H. and succeeded by Capt. Henry G. Flanner) and Capt. James N. Lamkin.

As I stated, our battery served with Enfield rifles from the Wilderness to Petersburg, losing men on every field. When we reached Petersburg, the need of Coehorn mortars was sorely felt, but as the Confederate Government had no bronze of which to make them, Capt. Lamkin volunteered to try iron ones in the face of the fact that all authorities had argued up to that time that only bronze would stand the tremendous strain. They were cast at first for our battery, in Richmond, eight Coehorn or 24 pounders, one eight-inch, or sixty-four pounder, and two little 12 pounders which were carried about from place to place and used at such short ranges as to be practically a link between Coehorn mortars and hand-grenades. Besides these Capt. Lamkin had made as an experiment one mortar of wood, banded with iron, which proved to be the only failure of them all. Capt. Lamkin was a civil engineer by profession, and was not only brave and cool, but very fertile in expedients and a man of unusually good judgment. I still remember the simple plan he devised by which we were able to drop our shells, night or day, on any point the range of which we had ever obtained without the necessity of seeing the object at all. The accuracy with which we did this caused the frequent remark among the infantry that we "could drop a shell in a horse-track the darkest night that ever came."

Besides the eleven mortars of our battery there were two I remember under Lieut. Langhorne of Capt. D. N. Walker's battery,[25] located some distance to the right of our position. Six of ours were placed in the Jerusalem plank road at intervals from the Gee house to the point at which the covered way crosses the road near the present Jewish Cemetery.

Just here I wish to explain that the redoubts just east of the road at this point and only a few yards from it were at the time of the battle of the Crater unfinished and unoccupied except for a short time that morning by part of Elliot's brigade.

The road here was then, as it is now, in a slight cut, the eastern bank of which served as our parapet, our mortars, being placed in the road. The eight-inch mortar under Sergt. J. P. Wilkinson[26] was placed in the pines, then standing, north of the covered way and in rear of Capt. S. Taylor Wright's battery.

In a little depression just east of Blandford Cemetery, near Ransom's headquarters, was a small earth-work of two pits which we called "Fort Lamkin." Its site is now just visible. It was under the command of my brother, Serg't Major George Cary Eggleston,[27] who was acting lieutenant. I was the sergeant in command of the two mortars with my detachment, a very pleasant arrangement for both of us.

Sergeants are not often left, even temporarily, in command of forts, but on the evening of the 29th of July the captain needed my brother's services elsewhere for the time and detached him, but for fear of an accident to me, and accidents were not uncommon about that time, he sent another sergeant, John Coffey, down, to temporarily share my responsibility, with of course no idea that a great battle was impending.

On the morning of the 30th of July the explosion failed to awaken us, as we had been firing nearly all night, but the sentinel on duty called us. I was

25. GSB: D. N. Walker, Richmond, VA, Capt. of the Otey Battery. [David Norvell Walker enlisted as a 1st lieutenant into the Virginia 13th Battalion Light Artillery in March 1862. He was promoted to captain of Otey's Battery upon the death of Otey in October 1862. He served as commander of the battery until surrender in 1865.]

26. GSB: John P. Wilkinson, Nelson Co., VA.

27. GSB: Geo. Cary Eggleston, Editor, *New York World*. [George Cary Eggleston of Indiana and Virginia enlisted as a private in Company G in the 1st Virginia Cavalry in May 1861. He transferred to Lamkin's Battery in December 1861, rising to the rank of sergeant major. In the last year of the war, he served with the sharpshooters in Petersburg. He had an illustrious postwar career, writing a number of books on the Civil War and serving as editor of the *New York World*.]

asleep in my usual place on the powder chests in the magazine, just in rear of the traverse between the two pits.

Aroused, we were soon convinced that one or more mines had been exploded over towards the salient occupied by Pegram's Petersburg battery and Elliott's South Carolina brigade. We soon found that the close fighting was inside of our lines at that point. After brief consultation as to the best use we could make of our mortars under the circumstances, we concluded that, as they are useless when fired at a moving object, and as we had the range of various points, some of them opposite the salient, arranged so that we could at any time drop our shells accurately upon them without the necessity of seeing them, we would be able to do most damage by using our ammunition this way. We, therefore, opened fire and immediately drew upon ourselves a most terrific cannonade. We kept up our fire for some hours until our supply of shells was exhausted, and then sent what powder and fuses remained up to the main battery.

Having nothing to do and being obliged to remain in our place unless we received orders to go else where, we had a fine opportunity to observe the battle. We thought the bottom had dropped out, as part of our lines were, and had been for hours, in the enemy's possession, and we knew of no reserves who could be called on to drive them out. From what we saw and heard the fighting was desperate and little progress has been on our part, when we at least heard that Mahone's brigade was marching in through the covered way, which gave us our first gleam of hope.

And just here let me say that the cannonade was so furious that at times no single report, or even the bursting of shells near by could be distinguished. The sound was all merged into one continuous roar, producing an atmospheric concussion so great that the very ground seemed to vibrate.

It seemed a long time to us before the first charge occurred and I as well as others have since been mistaken in stating the time at which it was made, but this is a very natural thing, for time passed very slowly that day to most of us. As an illustration of how slowly it does sometime seem to pass, I clearly recall that once when we had been told to hold a brigade in South Carolina and stay there till reinforced, although we had been well whipped by a superior force for hours, the sun, as I have often since expressed it, seemed to get hung, when half way down the western sky, and the hours seemed days in length.

How on the morning of July 30th, the Virginians did charge at the critical time, and in spite of fearful losses, did carry the works almost up to the Crater itself, and how Wright's Georgians, and Saunder's [Sander's] Alabamians, made the other charges, is well known history. An astonishing thing to me, however, has always been that Mahone's men themselves do not seem even now to realize the grandeur of their conduct on that immortal field. Talk to one of them of the charge at the Crater and he will at once wander off to Second Manassas, Crampton's Gap, Gettysburg or more likely still the Wilderness. I know that their flags deserved to be inscribed with the names of these and other fields, but they seem unconscious of the fact that at the Crater they went in not only under fire, which is a difficult and trying [thing] even for veterans, but that they formed their line and charged under the heaviest cannonade mortal man has ever heard on land, Gettysburg alone excepted, and in addition, to that they charged for two hundred yards at a ten foot ditch packed with infantry and carried it. Why they were not exterminated can only be accounted for by the fact that the enemy in our works, had, from our artillery and mortars, been having a hard row to hoe for hours, and were somewhat demoralized. Even allowing for all this, Mahone's charge is unsurpassed, if equaled in daring, and certainly in results, for no sensible man can doubt that the enemy ought to have taken Petersburg and hastened the end on that day, and but for this charge would have done so. There is abundant evidence that they were ordered to advance and were even leaping over the edge of the Crater and out of the ditch to the north of it when they saw the advancing line.

We of the artillery had been wondering all the morning why the enemy did not advance earlier. Some years ago I met Judge Drury A. Hinton, who had been a staff officer in Mahone's brigade, at Amelia C.H., and asked him if he knew why the enemy did not advance that day. He said that one of the prisoners, an officer, told him in answer to that same question, that the troops that were in our works were only expected to carry our front line and hold it, and that others were to have been sent forward to carry that other line (pointing as he said this to the covered way which he evidently thought constituted our second line). They doubtless reasoned that as they, the Federals, would never have attempted to hold Petersburg with a single line, so Gen. Lee would not dare to do it; just as Pope and Hooker doubtless reasoned at Second Manassas and Chancellorsville, that as they would never dare to divide their forces in the presence of a foe superior in numbers, so Lee and Jackson would not dare to do so bold a thing; and like Pope and Hooker they lost a game they might have won, had they been able to measure Lee's matchless daring.

Capt. Lamkin opened fire from the six mortars in the Jerusalem road as soon as we did and rained a pitiless fire into the Crater, and the enemy's works beyond, all day. Generals Lee and Beauregard came up and had their headquarters in the brick basement of the Gee house. Gen. Lee in person ordered Capt. Lamkin to man two field pieces which had been left in the road in front of the Gee house without men to work them, for some reason, which (if I ever knew) I have forgotten. In less time than it takes to tell it Sergeant James Coffey (we had in the battery fourteen men of this name, scarce as the article was in the Army) called out two detachments, selecting each man for his well known skill at the special post to which he was assigned, and in a few minutes was trimming the crest of the Crater with canister, and raking the adjoining works with shrapnel. These two and Flanner's six, together with Wright's four from the left and Davidson's one under Capt. D. N. Walker from the right were the guns alluded to by the Federal officers who were in the Crater as preventing their men even looking over towards our lines.

After the first charge by Mahone's old brigade under the gallant Col. Weisiger our two twelve pounder mortars were carried, by our men, up the ditch which Mahone's men had just recaptured, and fired from among the infantry into the Crater less than 100 yards away, using scarcely a thimbleful of powder. The shells from them could be plainly seen, so slow was their flight, and must have done much to add to the demoralization of the enemy.

I always understood that Capt. Lamkin's special services that day attracted Gen. Lee's notice and was the cause of his adding large numbers of men from disbanded batteries and conscripts from Camp Lee to the battery to increase it to a battalion of mortars. I do know that when the retreat occurred we had 210 men and the captain had sent in his appointments for officers for two batteries.

Pardon a soldier's pride in his command, but I cannot refrain from mentioning that on the South Carolina coast in Oct. 1862 Gen. Beauregard sent our battery a battle-flag parade, with a complimentary speech, on account of the services rendered at the battle of Pocotaligo, on which field we lost in killed and wounded exactly half the officers and men and exactly half the horses carried in. This, so far as I know, was the only instance in which a single battery received a flag from the commanding general.[28]

Of the other troops who conducted themselves so handsomely at the Crater I think it right that I should testify. I may overlook some commands unintentionally, not because they did not do enough, but because their work did not come under my own personal observation.

The gallant Elliott,[29] I knew him well, in South Carolina in 1862–3 when he was captain of the Beaufort Artillery. He was a son of Bishop Elliott of the

28. See Sherwood, *The Nelson Artillery*, 1–45, for more information on the battle actions described by Eggleston.

29. Stephen Elliott Jr. organized and equipped a light battery, the Beaufort Artillery, in 1861. Commissioned as a captain, Elliott would rise to the rank of brigadier general, distinguishing himself in battles and raids throughout South Carolina between 1861 and 1863. Part of his brigade was destroyed in the Crater explosion of 1864, and he himself was wounded during the subsequent counterattack. He recovered enough to

P. E. Church. For his gallantry as senior captain and acting chief of artillery in one battle and the burning of the gunboat Geo. Washington in Coosaw river with his battery and ours, he was made major, and afterwards put in command of Fort Sumter after it was declared untenable, and held it heroically for nearly or quite a year, and on Christmas morning, 1863, after 200 days of silence under bombardment when the fleet and forts, some in our hands and some in the enemy's, fired in rotation, the Christmas salute, as had been customary before the war, he fired in his turn and the Federal fleet dipped their flags in his honor. His brigade, a part of it blown away by the explosion, broke as any troops in the world would have done, for all of us thought there were three mines being dug, and they naturally expected other explosions to follow. He at once began the work of rallying them; but was soon shot through the lung and borne from the field. Col. McMaster did rally them and reoccupy as much of their works as he could and also formed a partial line in the unfinished redoubts just in front of the Jerusalem road. The men in this latter line, I have always understood, though I cannot certify to it, joined with Mahone's men and reentered the works with them.

Next on the left in our infantry line came Ransom[30] and his men closed to the right all they could and helped McMaster gain ground up the trenches, thus preventing the enemy from holding so wide a front as would have made Mahone's success impossible.

Wright's and Martin's batteries to the left, ours and Flanner's immediately west, and Davidson's and Walker's on the right of the Crater, together with Wise's splendid brigade, did all that men could do before the arrival of Mahone. The fighting of the Confederates on that day was as a whole such as, to quote Senator Daniel, in a heroic age would have inspired the poet and minstrel.

At Cold Harbor our battery was acting as supports between the guns of Capt. Garden's, occupying ditches cut from gun to gun. One day when there

---

hold command again of a brigade in North Carolina in 1865, where he surrendered with General Johnston.

30. GSB: Matt. W. Ransom, U.S. Senator & Minister to Mexico. [Matt W. Ransom was commissioned lieutenant colonel of the 1st North Carolina Infantry in June 1861. He was promoted to colonel commanding the 35th North Carolina Infantry in April 1862. He fought with the Army of Northern Virginia in 1862, then was transferred to North Carolina, where he commanded units in 1863 and 1864. Promoted to brigadier general in 1864, he fought in all the major battles around Petersburg until surrender with General Lee at Appomattox. He returned to his home state of North Carolina after the war, where he would be elected to the United States Senate in 1872, holding that seat for twenty-two years.]

was nothing going on but the usual sharp-shooting, I walked down to the left along our lines some three hundred yards to see a friend in the 22nd South Carolina regiment. Just to the right of the position of this command was a swampy place which made a break in our works, and when I reached this place the men in the trenches called out to me to trot across as the enemy's sharp shooters could see any one passing there. I cheerfully complied, and on arriving among the South Carolinians, they asked me who was the artillery officer in a black overcoat, who had just come down the hill ahead of me. I told them it was Capt. Garden. They expressed admiration for his coolness and told me that when he reached the swampy place referred to they told him to trot over it, but that he coolly walked along and they saw the dust fly from his sleeve, but as he did not even quicken his pace they concluded that he was unhurt, but that when he got again behind the works he called them and told them he was hit, and they found he had received a painful wound. On being questioned he explained that he had made no sign in order to prevent "that rascal" as he called the Federal marksman, from finding out that he had the range and thus being able to hit some one else. Capt. Garden[31] probably does not know to this day that any of his battalion ever learned of his heroism on this occasion.

The day before this, during an artillery duel, one of his gunners was shot through the body with a ball from a shrapnel and desperately wounded of course. When the litter-bearers started to the rear with him the shells were flying, and one burst very near them, causing one of the men to squat and nearly spill the wounded man on the ground. Capt. Garden saw it and yelled out to him, "If you do that any more, I will come there and slap your jaws." This caused a great laugh of course, the idea of the man being more afraid of his delicate hand than the enemy's shells.

At Spotsylvania C.H. we were just to the right of Pott's (afterwards Flanner's) battery, in our front the enemy had driven in our skirmishers and they had to fire from the main works. Our position and that of the battery spoken of, occupied a reentering angle, some 300 yards in front of which was an old fashioned chimney of immense size and in the same grove an old out-house. For a day [or] two, sharp shooters from this picking off our men, could not be accurately located. At last a sergeant of Flanner's battery, who commanded a 24 pounder howitzer, (I wish I knew his name) exposed himself to be shot at

31. GSB: I have since seen Capt. Garden in his office in N.Y. and he expressed great surprise that any one knew the circumstances of his being wounded on this occasion. [Hugh R. Garden enlisted as Captain of Company C in the South Carolina Palmetto Light Artillery in 1861.]

until he succeeded in locating them as lying on the ground behind the chimney. He then went back to the gun, and after determining to his satisfaction the exact distance, cut his own fuse, and was a long time aiming the gun carefully. At last he stepped back and said, "I am going to cut off about four feet of the top of that chimney and burst the shell at the same time." He then gave the command, "Ready" — "Fire," and the result was exactly what he promised. This was one of the best shots, all things considered, I ever saw, and of course evoked a cheer. We were troubled no more from that point, and on the next day, the 14th, of May, when we drove away the enemy's skirmish line (which by the way was the only time I was ever engaged in skirmishing), my position in the line brought me right by the chimney and I saw four dead men under the bricks.

I have often been asked what was the bravest act, I ever witnessed — a very hard question to answer in view of the many heroic to be rather the rule than the exception in our army. And yet it has always seemed to me that the conduct of Lieut. James M. [Muldrow][32] of Garden's battery rather transcended any other exhibition of cool but modest bravery [I] ever saw. His battery had gotten into a duel with a Federal battalion some nine hundred yards away. Garden's guns were mounted enbarbette, that is, each piece stood on the solid ground with a semicircular ditch cut around in front of it, the dirt from which was thrown forward for a parapet, which was nearly as high as the muzzle of the gun, but the gun was free to fire in any direction over the top. The cannoners standing in the ditch were comparatively safe, but, the Lieut. in command was fully exposed. The other guns on our side had been ordered to cease firing leaving one to continue the duel, and of course the enemy were firing on it alone.

The Lieut. was anxious that it should be fired exactly as the enemy's shell burst for two reasons; first in order that the enemy might not from the puff of smoke be able to determine exactly when it did fire, and secondly to show them that his men were not intimidated. Human nature is but human nature, however, and the number four would crouch down a second until the enemy's shell burst and would then pull the lanyard. This did not at all satisfy the Lieut. and after one or two trials he told his men plainly that, when he saw the puff of the enemy's gun he would say: "ready," and when their shell burst, he would say "fire," and unless the gun was fired exactly at that instant, he would move gun and men out in front of the works and fight it out without protection for them. He stood out to the side of the gun, the only man fully

32. GSB: James M. Muldrow, Maysville, S.C. [James R. Muldrow enlisted as a 2nd lieutenant in the same unit as Garden in 1861.]

exposed, well knowing that the shell would come straight at the gun not five feet away. My position at the right at his feet, but being down in a ditch, I and my men were in almost perfect security. I could look right up in his face, and I watched him closely. Presently seeing the puff of smoke, he commanded "ready," and stood calmly waiting till the shell passed within a foot or two of his head, and burst so close as to set fire to his long yellow hair. "Fire" said he, as he brushed the fire from his hair, and that gun did fire. Our men cheered him, but he in a low tone, blushingly said, "I believe I would have said fire if my head had been blown off."

Lieut. Fletcher T. Massie[33] of our battery, now living near Lowesville, Amherst Co., Va., was as brave as Napoleon's McDonald, and like McDonald, only at his best when in the midst of much smoke. In the winter of 1864–5 he happened to be in command of the battery, which was in front of Fort Harrison on the north side of the James, we having left Petersburg on the 29th of Sept., to take part in the assault on the 30th. The battery had been, as I have stated, recruited up to 210 men and was I believe, the largest company in the army, as it was being organized into a mortar battalion. We were then manning 26 mortars. There was at this point usually no sharp shooting or shelling going on, and our life was rather monotonous. Massie, the best and kindest of men, had allowed all who asked him, on any sort of pretext, leave to be absent, some for a day or two, and some only for a few hours. When the enemy, as we afterwards learned, received news one day of the capture of Savannah by Sherman, they opened on us a shotted salute. When Massie called to the men to stand to their guns there were only enough of us to man three mortars. He opened fire however, and fought like one possessed, with his own hand helping work first one gun and then another. As last we silenced the enemy fort as we could always manage to do. Massie was in a furious rage with himself for having been too yielding with his men and having let so many go, and said in my hearing: "I'm going to resign an office I am too weak to hold and go back to the ranks where I belong." I told him he should do no such thing, and jokingly said that he ought to be kept, by those in authority, in a pit covered with rails, and well fed, and wherever the enemy opened fire it would only be necessary to pull off the rails and hand him his sword. He saw the point and said: "If that is true I am satisfied. If I am of any account in a fight that is all I care about, for that is what I came here for." To show what manner of man he was in a fight, let me take you back two years to the battle of Pocotaligo, South Carolina.

33. Fletcher T. Massie enlisted as a corporal in Latham's Battery in September 1861. He was promoted to 2nd lieutenant in 1862. He served with the battery until the end of the war, surrendering at Appomattox.

We fought that morning, Oct. 22nd, 1862, at Yemassee Creek till flanked on both sides when we fell back a mile and a half to Old Pocotaligo, where we pulled up to the bridge and took position just 225 yards from the enemy, without works of any kind. Our force was only 250 men (on morning report), composed of two batteries of artillery, two companies of dismounted cavalry and part of a company of infantry. The enemy had six regiments of infantry, two of cavalry and twelve pieces of artillery. In this second fight, on account of heavy losses on the first, we could only man four guns in the two batteries, but were obliged to hold this, the last bridge, till reinforced by the railroad, which ran past our rear only a few miles away. If this road was gained by the enemy Charleston and Savannah would be lost.

Long before night, we were a badly broken and well whipped command, but late in the afternoon I noticed Massie, who was then in command of our two guns and the few men left, with the sponge staff in his hand, sponging, ramming the gun himself. [In a] very few minutes I could hear him, like "Bozzaris, cheer his band,"[34] calling out in his clarion voice, "Boys, remember the state you came from and the girls you left behind you!" As we were at that time the only Virginia company in South Carolina, you can imagine the effect. He would now and then go to the trail and aim the gun at one of the enemy's pieces and, being a fine shot, more than once he dismounted their guns and was cheered for it.

Late in the afternoon Capt. Elliot, as chief of artillery, ordered him to go the rear as wounded, but he loudly protested because, he only had a flesh wound in the arm and a trench cut by a minie ball across the side of his head. This latter had somewhat dazed him, however, and doubtless Elliot was wise in ordering him to the rear.

When in the trenches at Petersburg our commissioned officers and sergeants took turns at standing in the infantry works and observing the drop of our shells, and sending back orders to alter the charges of powder and length of fuses, thus getting ranges for future use. All the rest of us, except Massie and one other, used the sand bag loop-holes; I know I always did, but they would look over the top of the works. Of course, this was not so dangerous when the shell was going over, but Massie would occasionally peep over between times, in spite of constant warning from the infantry. One day he did this once too often and a ball struck him in the forehead and plowed its way over the scalp, and of course knocked him senseless. The bystanders thought he was killed. He afterwards told me that the first thing he was conscious of was hearing this

34. Eggleston refers to the well-known poem by Fitz-Green Halleck, "Marco Bozzaris." Bozzaris had died fighting for Greek freedom from Turkey in 1821. Halleck was sometimes called "America's Byron."

pitying remark of one of the infantrymen: "Well, that d——d fool has got his soap gourd broke at last. I've been looking for it all summer."

In my detachment were three brothers, Sam, Gus, and Oscar Bowles, tip top soldiers. One day we were all sitting around under our brush shelter at Fort Lamkin, when a bullet whacked through the crowd causing my brother to exclaim: "Who is hit?" "It's me!" said Gus, "No. It's me!" said Oscar, who was sitting on the other side of the semicircle. The ball had passed through Gus' hand, shattered it, and, crossing over, had hit Oscar in the leg. Before we could get them off to the rear Gus was insisting on Oscar's saving his bullet for him when it was cut out, claiming it on the grounds that it struck him first; while Oscar vehemently disputed the claim because he had stopped it, and they were still quarrelling over the bullet when we saw them last as they were carried to the rear.

I knew one instance of a man in Ramsey's battery of our battalion—I think he was a sergeant—whom we consoled for a severe wound by reminding him that he could always truthfully say that his eye was shot out by a 12 pound solid shot. It was near the South Anna river and we were in the works supporting this battery, when a solid shot struck on top of the parapet and dislodged a gravel with so much force, that it carried away his eye.

While at this same point some of us were using individual fly-tents, and one of our men, Geo. Campbell, was lying under his asleep, and the captain was lying with his head not far from Campbell's feet, but he was not under a tent and was awake. We heard a ball strike his canteen as we thought, which was lying near his head, but in a moment Campbell came crawling out, feet first, with stormy words against the man, whoever he was, that "hit him with that rock?" so sure was he that some one had struck him on the foot. His foot, however, was so shattered by the ball as to make amputation necessary.

The Otey battery, commanded by Capt. (afterwards Major) D. N. Walker, of Richmond, Va., was a splendid body of men. I used often to go to their position to visit my cousin, Eugene C. Jefferson, who was always called "Juanita," because that was the only tune he knew. One day just as I got within about one hundred yards of his battery, I saw a mortar shell burst high in air, a piece of which struck Charles A. Spence of the battery, in the face. I saw the poor fellow carried to the rear, killed as everybody thought, but he still lives, a citizen of Richmond, although one side of his face was carried away.

Another fine battery which did service near us at Petersburg was that of Captain—now Rev. Dr. S. Taylor Martin,[35] of the Union Theological

35. S. Taylor Martin enlisted as a captain of Company B, Virginia 12th Battalion Light Artillery in 1862.

Seminary, Hampden-Sydney, Va. It was commanded at Petersburg by First-Lieutenant S. H. Pulliam,[36] now of Richmond. Its position was near Fort Lamkin, on a hill just in rear of Captain S. Taylor Wright's battery, and its view was extensive. At first we did not know what battery it was, but such was its belligerent habit that is seemed to use that every time things got comparatively quiet, and we began mending our clothes or writing letters, this battery would open and stir up a fuss that involved us all. Finally this became such a nuisance, that my brother determined to go and see if he could not arrange some sort of concert of action, so that the little rest we might get in the daytime would be less disturbed, as we of the mortar battery had to fire all of the time at night to keep the enemy's attention devoted to us, and thereby somewhat relieve the infantry, whose service on the works was continuous. Our men were never relieved, as were the enemy's troops every day or two.

When my brother reached the battery he was greatly surprised to find it commanded by his old college-mate, Sam Pulliam. He asked Pulliam why he was so unreasonably belligerent, and was informed (by the latter) that he had been told to make requisitions for a supply of ammunition on General Bushrod Johnson's ordnance department, and that after he had done so General R. H. Anderson's ordnance officer notified him that he was the man to call on (for such supplies). So he made a second requisition as directed. But the next day, before any ammunition had arrived, General E. P. Alexander, chief of artillery of Longstreet's Corps, came around and told him that both orders were errors, and that his battery was still in the First Corps. He therefore made a third requisition, and it happened that all three requisitions were filled the same day.

You all remember how very accommodating the Confederate was in supplying ammunition, and even it did as to clothes and rations. One of his guns being knocked into junk soon after this, Pulliam became uneasy, fearing that his over supply of ammunition would be exploded by a shell from the enemy's guns; and he asked General Alexander what he must do. He received his characteristic reply: "Shoot at every thing you see an inch high, a foot long, or a year old." And he was simply doing it.

And now I will relate an incident which is so unusual that I fear that some of you will call it a romance of the Munchausen order. I can only hope that those who know me will not think so, if not from confidence in my veracity, at least because they will be sure I could not invent the story, from lack of ability. As evidence to you that I could have no motive in inventing it, even if capable, bear in mind that the heroes were then, as now, entire strangers to me.

36. Samuel H. Pulliam enlisted as 1st lieutenant of the same unit in 1862.

One night at Fort Lamkin, about half-past eleven, while we were firing slowly, trying to attract the attention of the enemy—and occasionally doing it—as our orders required, two gentleman, in white duck suits, of jackets and pants, stepped up to us from the little ravine in our immediate rear (just back of the Blandford grounds), which was then filled with bushes and small trees. One of them spoke to my brother, and stated that they were cavalry officers, and, not having seen any mortar practice since they left West Point, were interested in our work, and had come out from camp to look on. My brother gave them his name, but neither stranger gave his. One of them spoke of the other as "the Colonel, a member of my staff," so we took this officer for a general. To show his appreciation of the compliment paid our arm of the service by warming the activity of the engagement, my brother said to me: "Joe, try the railroad iron battery," a very unwelcome order, for this battery was a veritable hornets' nest, which had our range to a T with its mortars, and, in addition, always opened on us with a six-gun rifle battery alongside. We called the Federal battery "the railroad iron battery," because, seen with a glass, it appeared to have a protection of railroad iron over its guns. I was talking to "the Colonel" when this order was given me, and turned only one mortar on the battery mentioned, and as soon as that began to draw I quietly changed to another point, as I had not been ordered to stir up the hornets all night. The strangers exposed themselves with the utmost apparent unconcern, which I noticed all the more because it necessitated my doing more of that same thing I would otherwise have considered at all necessary. I used judgment in directing the gun, and after a while got things more comfortable. "The General," as we supposed the office of superior rank to be, expressed great satisfaction at our work, and after a while asked who was on the front on the infantry line. We told him that Ransom's brigade occupied that part of the line. He then asked it if would be possible to go to the skirmish line and have a look around. We told him there would be no difficulty whatever, and directed him how to find the path through the works. Both officers then thanked us for our kindness and for the beautiful pyrotechnic display we had given them, and walked in the direction of the infantry works, and we saw them no more.[37]

My brother had been a cavalryman the first summer of the war, and curious as both of us were to find out who our visitors were, made every inquiry he could among officers and me of this branch of the service, as opportunity

37. Bernard published Eggleston's account about the incident at Fort Lamkin in a letter to the *Maine Bugle* (Campaign II, Call 3, July 1895, 218–21). The text draws both from that published account and from the typewritten Eggleston narrative found in the Bernard Collection at the Historical Society of Western Virginia.

offered, to trace them, but the war closed without our getting a clue to their identity. In 1871 I met my brother for the first time since we parted in 1865. He asked me if I remembered the incident I have narrated, and told me he had the sequel.

He then informed me that some time about 1866 or 1867 he boarded a steamer at Cairo, Illinois, one night, on his way to Memphis. After a few words to the clerk, not feeling sleepy, he took up a newspaper and sat down to read, when a gentleman stepped up, and politely apologizing for the intrusion, asked if his name was not Eggleston. "It is," said my brother. "Did you not command a small fort near the cemetery at Petersburg, containing two mortars?" inquired the stranger. "I did," replied my brother. The gentleman then asked my brother if he remembered the incident of two cavalry officers, dressed in white duck, visiting his fort one night during the siege of Petersburg, and was informed that the incident was well remembered. "I am one of those two officers," said the stranger.

"Well," said my brother, "who are you? I have always wanted to know."

The gentleman gave his name—which I regret I have forgotten—and stated that he was a brigadier-general of cavalry from Maine. He then explained that he and his companion were neither spies nor scouts, and but for their not being dressed in uniform would have surrendered to us. Of course dressed as they were, in citizens' dress, they would have been promptly hung as spies. He further explained that they had gone from their camp to their own works for the very purpose stated to us—to witness the mortar firing— and from there had gone out to their skirmish line, some half a mile south of our position, and were walking along from [pit to] pit, talking to the men, and at last, to their surprise, found from the accent of the men near them that they were within our lines. Discovering this, and casting about as to how they could escape, they concluded that they would be less likely to be questioned by men busy at the front, than those whom they might encounter not so engaged; so, after making a circuit to the rear, they came up to our little fort because they saw we were engaged, and succeeding in their plan, made their way to our skirmish line, and thence across to their own, finding it easy in the darkness to slip over to their own men.

The gap in our works through which they wandered to our side of the lines, I suppose, was the one that existed for a while between Wise's and Elliot's brigades, due to the wet spongy ground, near the position of the Davidson battery, on the Baxter Road, and they probably lost their bearings from watching the fuses of the mortar shells crossing the sky. The general said he recognized my brother's voice when he was talking with the clerk, as everything connected with that night was burned into his memory.

One Sunday afternoon, to our surprise, two beautiful girls dressed in white, [were] walking along with arms around each other, on the Jerusalem road, among the men of our battery, opposite the Crater. They looked to us like angels from another and better world. Every hundred yards or so they would stop and sing that inspiring poem, Bayard Taylor's "Song of the Camp,"[38] the closing verse is—

> As, soldiers, to your honored rest[39]
> Your truth and valor bearing;
> The bravest are the tenderest,
> The loving are the daring.

The impression was magical and, to quote again—

> Yet as the song grew louder,
> Something upon the soldiers' cheek
> Washed off the stains of powder.

These lovely young ladies were risking their lives for the sole purpose of cheering the men, and it is easy to understand why "all the world wondered" at the valor of the men of the South when the very girls were cast in so heroic a mould.

The last battle it fell to my lot to take part in was exceptional and so far as I know unique, it being a battle on a considerable scale between artillery alone on one side and cavalry alone on the other. On Saturday, April 8th, 1865, Gen. R. Lindsey Walker, chief artillery officer of A. P. Hill's corps, was ordered to push ahead of the army towards Lynchburg with one hundred and fifty guns belonging, I believe to all three corps, for the apparent purpose of saving them for use with Johnston, but about midday, as he afterwards told me, he received orders to turn to the left and go into camp near Appomattox Station, why he never knew.

I must here explain how I came to be in this command. My wife, a bride of a few months, was, when the retreat occurred, at our home in Amelia County and I got permission to turn aside from the line of march to see her and bid her good by, conditioned on my not remaining longer than an hour. I got a horse at home and just as I mounted to return to the command I heard the firing of the raid which captured Ramsey's battery of new Blakeley rifle guns, before they could fire a shot, and also our men and mortars immediately in his rear, besides a wagon train of some miles in length. My brother had been

---

38. Bayard Taylor was a poet, novelist, translator, journalist, and diplomat. The "Song of the Camp" was one of many of his popular poems.

39. The correct line is "Sleep, soldiers! Still in honored rest" (see George E. Teter, *One Hundred Narrative Poems* [Chicago: Scott, Foresman, 1918], 187).

sent by our captain to Amelia C.H. to ask permission to bring our mortars into the great battle we thought would be fought there. He also thus escaped capture. The next morning he and I with three other members of the battery, all mounted, offered ourselves to the 1st Company of Richmond Howitzers and were accepted although it must be said to their credit they did not need us having come out of Richmond almost to a man.

When we went into park on the afternoon of April 8th, between the Lynchburg road and the railroad west of Appomattox C.H. I lay down on my saddle blanket and was soon asleep. How long I slept I do not know, but I was awakened by being rolled down the hill with the exclamation "Get up Joe! The Yankees are charging us!" It was a beautiful spring afternoon, the sky clean as crystal, with a peculiar softness in the atmosphere not in keeping with the cruel work of war. The charging was at first over to our right, but we soon saw a long line of cavalry forming in the woods in our front, which front faced south, or towards the railroad. At once the guns near us opened with shell and kept up their fire till the enemy seemed about to charge, when they were loaded with canister.

An officer I have always fancied was Gen. Custer rode up and down the line and when about the center, in a loud voice, plainly audible to us, gave the command to charge, and led the men forward in the most gallant style. Nearing the guns they received the fire of canister and recoiled. They charged again and again, sometimes passing in among the front guns and being driven out by those more to the rear. The artillerymen tied prolongs from wheel to wheel and those cavalrymen would charge up and actually hack at those ropes with their sabres. The fighting lasted from sunset until well after night-fall. The moon shone down on the contest. The scene was impressive. The long line of cavalry forming under a heavy fire and charging gallantly time after time; the riderless horses galloping over the field with stirrups flying; the cool work of the men at the guns, without support of any kind, obeying the artilleryman's instinct to stand his guns to the last; and the line of Federal infantry we could see in the distance formed across the fields between us and our main army *with their backs towards us;* all of this formed a picture I can never forget.[40]

Our men were only fighting for a chance to spike and leave the guns they could never hope to move again, and this they finally succeeded in doing as

---

40. Eggleston describes some of the fighting between General Walker's artillery and General Custer's cavalry at Appomattox toward the end of the day and into the night of April 8, 1865 (see William Marvel, *Lee's Last Retreat: The Flight to Appomattox* [Chapel Hill: University of North Carolina Press, 2002], 146–52).

to most of them. Gen. Walker afterwards told me that he got away with about 40 guns [*ten illegible words*]. I heard soon afterwards that Capt. S. Taylor Martin's battery had filled a road-cut full of dead horses and men in their front, and long years afterward I asked the Captain about it and he told me that what I had heard was literally true.

All of us of the artillery, so far as I know, escaped, but as individuals only, all organization being lost.[41] Three of us made our way to a small mountain towards James River and slept on top of it. I was awakened next morning, the morning of the memorable 9th of April, by a man in a blue Yankee cap bending over and shaking me. I thought I was a prisoner sure, but soon found he was a North Carolina infantryman seeking information and food, neither of which we had to give him. I was thankful that he had not made off with my horse.

Being now awake, we made our way down to the foot of the mountain and came to a large plantation where we found the owner in charge with negroes, who were shelling corn to hide from the enemy. We could get little information here, and nothing to eat but corn, of which I carried off a good half bushel for myself and horse. Concluding that we had flanked the enemy, we made for Appomattox C.H., where we were told the army probably was. When near the village we met some thirty or more cavalry men riding away, in a gallop. I inquired what was the news, but got no reply. From the expression on the faces of these men, however, I saw that something was up, and turning my horse galloped along beside a lieutenant who was in the lead and pressed him as to what was the matter. His reply was: "Gen. Lee has surrendered the army." I did not believe him, but he went on to state that Gen. Wm. H. F. Lee had announced to his men the fact, and advised that as many as could do so to get away and carry off all the horses they could. I afterwards heard that Gen. Robert E. Lee censured him for this, but do not know that it was so. I do know, however, that the idea flashed across my mind that I, then had left to me in the world, as surely mine, no earthly possessions save the horse I rode and the clothes I had on (except the little wife at home) and was sure that my only chance to save the horse would be to cross James River. I therefore, "joined the cavalry," not to "have a good time," but to save my horse. We rode straight for Bent Creek bridge, but found on our arrival nothing but the piece standing, Sheridan having burnt the superstructure a short time

---

41. Eggleston himself prepared this footnote: When the fighting began all horses were ordered out of the park of guns by Col. Cabell and we at once began forming a line to look like cavalry supports to the left of the guns. Being well known, I was detailed to get all the _____ men together into this line and was [manuscript is torn at this point].

before, and as the only boat we could hear of was on the opposite side, we were in a fix indeed. After talking with some of the residents of the neighborhood we learned that there was, some three miles above, an old ford that had been used before the bridge was built, and which could be safely crossed when the river was low, but which was probably not fordable in its then somewhat swollen condition. A plucky lad volunteered to be our guide and we mounted him on one of the extra horses. When we arrived at what he said was the ford, we had to take his word for it, for there was no indication that man or beast had ever crossed there before. We plunged in, however, and what a time we had. The horses were sometimes swimming and sometimes fording. There were immense rocks under water to climb over and slip off of. I took the precaution to give my bag of corn away before I rode in, and it was well I did, or I might not have reached . . ."[42]

"Near the Enemy's Lines: Life in Dinwiddie Co. in the Vicinity of the Opposing Armies during the Last Years of the War," by Capt. Jno. C. Griffin[43]

[While the armies occupied the lines around Petersburg, civilians in the city and surrounding counties struggled to endure life in the war zone. In gathering stories for "War Talks, Volume II," Bernard obtained the following detailed account of some events in Dinwiddie County during the last years of the war, as told by John C. Griffin. Dinwiddie County, and its seat Dinwiddie Court House, lay southwest of Petersburg on the right flank of Lee's line.

Griffin's stories recounted here are full of examples of that integral figure in the Lost Cause, the loyal slave. David Blight, Gaines Foster, Leon Litwack, and many other historians have analyzed this phenomenon, probing

---

42. The manuscript ends with several illegible sentence fragments.

43. The Bernard Collection at the Historical Society of Western Virginia contains this account and a biography of Griffin. The outside of the document containing Griffin's account reads: "Near the Enemy's Lines: Life in Dinwiddie Co. in the vicinity of the opposing armies during the last years of the war. By Capt. Jno. C. Griffin. This is my copy of Capt. Griffin's letter, which will constitute Ch. 15 of Vol. 2 of War Talks of Confederate Veterans. In the type written original all errors are carefully corrected. To it is an addendum by Mr. G. A. Boisseau, 'The little small boy' referred to on the last page. G.S.B. Nov. 9/95." Another biography of Griffin appears in the form of a letter written to Bernard on April 16, 1895 (in the Bernard Papers, Southern Historical Collection, University of North Carolina).

not only its factual basis (or lack thereof), but its very purpose as part of the Lost Cause. As with most of the stories in this volume, the reader only learns one side of a story, that of the speaker. Moreover, the loyalty that the speakers highlight over and over could have a much simpler rationale in many instances: self-interest. Not knowing how the war would end, or what would happen if the Confederacy lost, slaves often had to confront three stark choices: help their masters, refuse to help their masters and face punishment, or flee. While historians estimate that several hundred thousand chose to flee, the majority stayed in place, and had to make life-or-death decisions even as Union armies roamed through their counties. Of course, some slaves did act out of loyalty and concern for their masters; but without written explanations of their actions, from them, we can never be sure what motivated them.

Griffin was born in Charlotte County, Virginia, in 1832. After attending Hampden-Sydney College, he purchased a farm in Dinwiddie County, six miles south of the Court House there. At the beginning of the war, he joined Company C, of the 3rd Virginia Infantry regiment but was forced to return to his home in Dinwiddie due to health reasons. After the war, he opened an office in Petersburg, known as the Virginia Land Agency.]

Chesterfield County, near Petersburg, Va.
May 23, 1894

Geo. S. Bernard, Esq.
Petersburg, Va.
Dear Comrade:

Complying with your request to give you some account of life in the county of Dinwiddie during the last months of the war I will jot down a few reminiscences.

The county of Dinwiddie was for a period of over nine months the theatre of military operations. Within its limits were fought several bloody battles and upon its territory large bodies of the opposing armies constantly confronted each other in the trenches or upon the field of battle. Having in the early parts of the war resigned the captaincy of the Dinwiddie (Co. of Va. Infy.) _____.[44] In consequence of ill health, I returned to my home in Dinwiddie and there resided during the remainder of the war, and holding the position of justice of the county, which officers, as you know, under the then constitution of Virginia constituted the county court and as such had the management and control of the county government, I had exceptional oppor-

44. Griffin most likely refers here to the Dinwiddie Grays, Co. C, 3rd Va. Regiment.

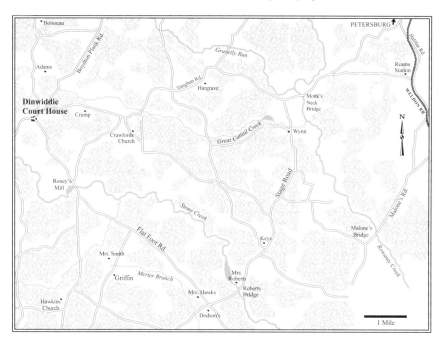

DINWIDDIE COURT HOUSE AND VICINITY, 1864–1865

tunities to witness the stirring events from June of 1864 to April of 1865 as the same occurred in our county where we constantly heard the harsh sounds of war as they reached our ears from the lines about Petersburg and everything was in an abnormal state of unrest and excitement.

Let me first say that the loyalty of the slave population during this trying period is a striking fact and the splendid conduct of the negro received only justice at the hands of the lamented Henry W. Grady[45] in his famous Boston address delivered in 1889 a short time before his death. During the last two years of the war there was not a day that concerted action of the negroes in a move against their masters would not have been disastrous. A conspiracy between them could not have been early thwarted, as in large portions of the rural districts the farm on which there was a white man was the exception not the rule, whilst the number of male negroes was lessened but little by those sent to the army to do service in building fortifications, or to serve as team-

45. Griffin refers to the famous speech by New South spokesman Henry Grady, entitled "The Race Problem in the South." For alternate views of the actions and motivations of slaves during the war, see chapter 1, "The Faithful Slave," in Leon Litwack, *Been in the Storm So Long: The Aftermath of Slavery* (New York: Random House, 1979); and chapter 3, "Many Thousands Gone," in Ervin L. Jordan Jr., *Black Confederates and Afro-Yankees in Civil War Virginia* (Charlottesville: University of Virginia Press, 1995).

sters or in other capacities, and they constantly had opportunities to lay waste our homesteads and destroy our families.

It has been suggested by some inconsiderate writers that this might have been prevented by martial law, but it should be remembered that no soldiers could have been spared from the front to execute such law. The truth, however, is that the wonderful loyalty of the negroes to their masters, constantly proven by their conduct, gave no occasion for even the thought of resorting to any such remedy.

In my neighborhood, six miles south of Dinwiddie C.H. although within eight or ten miles, sometimes a less distance, of the Federal lines, when all could have easily escaped at any time, but few did so, and many even when forcibly taken by Federal raiding parties made their escape from capture and returned to their homes and remained to the end of the war. After the close of hostilities and the freedom of the negro became established many remained in the service of their old masters as his employees, such were the kindly feelings that existed. Indeed at this time, nearly thirty years since the close of the war, there are, to my personal knowledge some negroes living on the same farms on which they were born as slaves. This, however, has in the main its explanation in the strong local attachment often found in the negro.[46]

During the raid made by the Federal cavalry in the summer of 1864 known as the "Wilson raid" several of my negro men whilst chopping wood near Ford's depot on the South Side Railroad, some twenty miles from my farm, were captured by this party of raiders.[47] The first night after being taken six of them escaped and reached home the next day. The seventh by some accident was killed. One of the men, Chamberlain Nelson, who had been a house servant and was quite intelligent, in reporting his experiences at the time of the capture told me that the Yankees came upon them (the negroes) very unexpectedly, but upon seeing them (the Yankees) he concluded to make them think he was glad to see them, and when they came up he so expressed himself and they, pleased at this, gave him a mule to ride whilst they forced the other negroes to walk. When the head of the column reached Ford's Depot, the command was halted and the depot buildings burned. During this halt Chamberlain asked permission to ride the mule back (he was in the extreme rear of the column) and water the animal at a branch they had just passed, and getting permission to do so, rode back, his purpose being to ride into the

46. Two generations of historical literature on Reconstruction and the New South question this assertion by Griffin; the list of books to consult is too exhaustive to list here.

47. See note 19, this chapter, on the Wilson-Kautz raid.

bushes to escape with the mule as soon as the column began to move. When, however, the bugle sounded for the forward movement, the mule could not be prevented from keeping the road and going forward to the command a short distance ahead. Thinking, he said, that I would prefer losing a mule (which he intended bring to me) to losing a negro (himself), he dismounted from the mule, turned it loose and slipped into the bushes and so escaped from his captors. This was his account of the adventure.

Having no use for these negroes on my farm just at this time, upon their return to me I sent them to work on the dam of my mill on the Nottaway river, the old Spencer Mill in Greensville county, at which place they remained until again captured by the same Federal cavalry who passed the mill on their way back to the lines after their raid through the counties west and southwest of Dinwiddie.

Among the party here captured was another negro, Charles Cross, who had been sent from my farm to the mill, and I would do gross injustice to the memory of a most loyal and devoted servant if I omitted here to make particular mention of this excellent and faithful black man. Charles was quickly released from capture and immediately came home to let me know what had occurred, arriving about midnight. He gave me a very graphic and amusing account of his capture and release. "The Yankees," said he, "dropped down like they came out of the clouds—thousands of them, and called for fire or matches with which to burn the mill." Charles stated to them, he told me, that my crops had been taken by the Confederates and that the mill was the only reliance for bread for my negroes and that I was "an old Union man"— these were his words. He said they had about concluded to spare the mill when he gave the last mentioned reason for their not burning it, but hearing that I was, to use Charles' language "an old Union Man" they said I must be a d——d hypocrite and they would burn anyway, but listening further to Charles' appeals, they spared the property. He said that he told them a lie to save the mill and was surprised to find that what he said about me appeared to have the contrary effect.

Having narrated his experiences at the mill he implored me to go into the woods and secrete myself until the enemy could pass my house and go into their lines, as he felt sure I would be captured and would die in prison as my health was delicate. I was, however, too unwell to act upon his suggestions. I thought also that it was not likely that this body of cavalry would leave the Stage Road, from which my house was distant about a mile as they were near their own lines and were likely to be pressed by the Confederate cavalry hanging in their rear. But, for fear they might leave the road I directed Charles to post negroes at day-break on the different approaches to the house, so that I could be informed in time to secrete myself. About day-break Charles, who left very soon after the mid-night interview knocked at my door and being admitted informed me that the Federal Cavalry were passing along the Stage Road "by thousands." There was, however, no indication of any of their leaving the road to come to my house until about ten o'clock in the morning, about which hour Charles notified me that here were some horsemen in sight entering the grove and approaching the house and that they looked "very blue."

Believing that my premises were about to invaded by a party from the Federal column, I told Charles that I would arm myself and go into the garden, and that, if the men we saw were Yankees, I wished him to see that all doors and other places were unlocked and that these men could take what they pleased without excuse for breaking, and that, if they confined themselves to robbery, he was to make no resistance, but, if they insulted my wife, to notify me at once and I would attack them without regard to consequences. I was armed with two navy six-shooters, a Sharp's repeating rifle and a double barrel shot-gun loaded with buck-shot. Having given these instructions, I went into the garden, but soon was notified by Charles that the party we had taken for Federal soldiers were five Confederates and that they were enquiring for me. These men were cavalrymen who had been at home on furlough and being on their way to rejoin their commands had come up to my house to get something to eat.

Having refreshed these cavalrymen with mint juleps and the first meal they had (according to their statement) eaten in twenty-four hours, I proposed that we go down towards the fighting then going on about Monk's Neck Bridge, to render such assistance as we could. This suggestion being acted upon, we accordingly started for the Stage Road, and, arriving within a few hundred yards of it, we dismounted, tied our horses and advanced, deployed as skirmishers in the direction of the road, going, as we advanced through the scattering young pines near the road. When within about eighty yards of the road we discovered a group of soldiers, dismounted, and lying in the grass in an old orchard along side of the road, at the sight of whom our little party immediately raised their carbines and were about to fire when I ordered them not to do so, and called their attention to the fact that one of the party we saw had on a straw hat, and I remarked that I believed that the men in the orchard were Confederates. Their clothing was so covered with dust that we could not discover the character of their uniforms. Hearing, or seeing us, these men hastily mounted their horses and were off rapidly in the direction of the firing which was quite brisk and approaching us, being at that time about Robert's bridge over Stony Creek about two miles distant.

We then moved up to the road, and, looking in the direction they had gone, as soon as the dust stirred up their hasty ride settled a little we discovered the same man with the straw hat now lying on the ground in the road. His horse had fallen and caught his leg and thus held him and he was trying to extricate himself. A few paces from him stood a soldier mounted, carbine in hand, guarding the fallen horseman. Being now within about eighty yards of these two men, several of our party raised their carbines to shoot the mounted men, but I prevailed upon them not to do so, as this might imperil the fallen man, who, I now felt sure, was a Confederate soldier and a prisoner. The mounted man seeing the guns raised to shoot him, spurred his horse and, moving but a few feet, was out of sight behind some bushes, and the Confederate, extricating himself from his horse, got up from the ground, remounted and rode off.

This occurred at Old Richieville, the former home of Dr. Thos. Scott, of Dinwiddie, who recently lived and died in Petersburg. We discussed what we had seen and tried to unravel it, but none could offer a reasonable explanation. I then suggested that, down in the direction of the firing, there was a large field about a half mile distant which bordered the road and gave to one upon the edge of or in this field, a full view of the road for some distance, and I proposed that we should go to this field, the firing then rapidly approaching that part of the field. To this my companion objected, not being willing to leave their horses so far. So, I started to go to the field alone and had gone about half way to it, when, making my way through the bushes along the bank of Merter Branch, I came in sight of about twenty Federal soldiers, who, seeing me and doubtless, supposing there were others along with me concealed in the bushes, deflected to the right, which enabled me to pursue the course I had taken.

The sight of these Federals explained the situation of affairs. These men, I was satisfied, were dismounted cavalrymen who had been routed in the fighting then going on ahead of us and were attempting to escape capture. I therefore concluded that I would go up the branch to the point at which it crosses the Stage Road, which point was about a half mile east of where I left my companions, and this I did. But just as I neared the road (being still in the branch), a Federal cavalryman rode rapidly down the hill from the direction of the firing, then to over a quarter of a mile distance, and just as he got opposite to me, only a fence and about thirty feet intervening between us, his horse fell. Slipping off, he deliberately walked around to his horse's head, and with his pistol fired a ball through the animal's head, killing the horse instantly. Cutting the girth, he then took off the saddle, threw it over the fence within twenty feet of me, jumped the fence himself a few yards further down and disappeared in the bushes, not having shown in all of these acts the slightest excitement or haste although the bullets from the Confederate forces on the top of the hill and now near by were flying near him and me in such uncomfortable number that I deemed it best to straighten out myself flat on the ground and as straight as an arrow behind a cedar tree, a volley which was fired soon after he left bringing down on my back several bows from this cedar.

In a little while the firing was over and our cavalry continued to pursue the enemy westwardly up the Stage Road. Leaving my position I made my way back to the place at which I had left my cavalry friends and thence on home. Around at my house, I found that they had captured several prisoners. These we kept under ground in a camp near the house during the night and the next morning increased their number by other captures.

As my cavalry friends were occupied in guarding these prisoners I concluded to go down to the Stage Road and try my hand alone at capturing other straggling Federals who might be passing along or near this road.

I had gotten about half way to the road when hearing the clank of sabres and carbines, and looking, I saw three Federals on horseback approaching me on the road leading up to Mrs. Ann Ragsdale's house, and seeing an old barn on the side of the road between me and these horsemen, I ran down to the barn, keeping it, as I ran, between me and them so as to escape observation, and when I found that they were about the building I stepped from behind it, leveled my rifle and demanded their surrender, to which command they promptly acceded crying out, "We surrender."

I ordered these men to dismount and stack arms, which they promptly did, asking me not to shoot them. This, of course, I told them I would not do. One of them was white, the other two were very black negroes mounted on mules, who, although in full uniform and armed and equipped as regular soldiers, claimed to be only servants who waited on officers. I marched them up to the residence of Mrs. Ragsdale, a few hundred yards distant, and sent for their arms. After allowing the white soldier to wash his face, I marched the three on to my house and, putting the negroes under the charge of Charles Cross, I sent them to the camp at which we had the other prisoners under guard. On my way home I took quite a fancy to the white prisoner. He was quite young, only about eighteen, very intelligent and evidently a gentleman. I took him to my house, gave him a drink and something to eat, for which he was very thankful. He told me his name was Evans, that he belonged to the 8th New York Cavalry and that his residence was New York City, where his father, I think he said, was a merchant.[48]

After the young man had eaten, my wife engaged him in conversation, and asked him what he thought of Genls. Lee and Jackson. He replied that he never heard their names without feeling like throwing up his hat and hurrahing for them. My wife then remarked that his entertaining such sentiments was not consistent with the fact that he was arrayed against us and being engaged in a raid. Seeing that the conversation was drifting to dangerous ground, I stopped it. The young soldier having lost his hat, I gave him another and took him to the prisoners' camp on my place down in the woods. Before starting, however, having observed that he had a nice hand satchel, I remarked to him, that if he had any papers or letters he did not wish read he had better give them to my wife to keep for him until the war was over, or better still, burn them. The latter course he pursued.

The next morning when I had all of the prisoners in readiness to start for the Court House for delivery to the proper authorities at that place, this young man appreciating the treatment he had received, asked to be allowed to bid my wife good bye, which he did with many thanks; being allowed by me to leave the guard one hundred and fifty yards down in the grove and go alone to the house for the purpose. One of the guards suggested that he would attempt to escape. I said I did not believe he would; as the fact that he desired to thus show his appreciation of the treatment he had received demonstrated to me that he was an honorable man and could be trusted. My cavalry friends took the prisoners in charge, and, as I subsequently learned, safely delivered them at Dinwiddie Court House. I never saw them (the cavalrymen) again.

When the Wilson raiders started out they left at Dinwiddie C.H. at a little shanty near the intersection of the Boydton Plank Road and the road leading from the Plank Road to Vaughan's Road several of their wounded, and several others were left by them at Mrs. Crump's, about a mile below the Court House on the same road leading to Vaughan's Road. Having been told about those at the shanty, I went there to look after them and found that their wounds had not been dressed, and, indeed, that no one was in charge of them save a resident of the village and his little son, who were keeping off the flies, giving the wounded men water, & c. A physician of the county who had been

48. The young cavalryman from the 8th New York Cavalry Regiment may have been Nelson E. Evans, who had been captured once before, at Harper's Ferry during the Antietam Campaign of 1862.

attending my family, riding up and dismounting, approached the door of the shanty where I was standing, and, as he did so, I remarked to him that I was glad to see him as he could dress the wounds of these soldiers. He replied, with considerable temper, that if we were to dress their wounds, which he declared he did not intend to do, they would not live twenty minutes. Surprised and indignant at this statement, I replied that he should never administer another dose of medicine to any member of my family or to any servant under my control and that I would find a doctor that had more humanity, and furthermore that I did not wish to have anything further to do with him. I at once determined to go and ask the assistance of Dr. Jas B. Boisseau, another physician of the county, who lived about three miles distant, and was about starting, when the boy above referred to stated that there was a Confederate surgeon down at Mrs. Crump's looking after the wounded there. I at once rode to Mrs. Crump's to secure the services of the surgeon, and when I arrived in sight of the house I saw a group of men near the grove in front of the house who seemed to be placing wounded men in a wagon. I at once approached this group and found among their number the surgeon I was in pursuit of. I spoke to him at once and notified him of the presence of the wounded Federal soldiers at the Court House and requested his attention to them. He replied, with some brusqueness of manner that he would look after them after dinner. I then informed him that these Federal soldiers had been wounded nearly twenty-four hours and that their wounds had not been dressed and that I felt satisfied that under the circumstances he would not delay several hours before he went to see them, and that he had time to look after them and return before dinner hour. He walked off in the direction of the house in high dudgeon and did not say what he would do. All this occurred in the presence of several gentlemen, one of whom remarked, "Captain, you can't get him to leave the ladies, even on a mission of humanity." Tying my horse and dismounting—I was on my horse when I addressed the surgeon as above mentioned—I replied, "I will start him in ten minutes, or I will ride down and report him to Gen. R. E. Lee within the next two hours." Mr. David G. Carr of Dinwiddie, who was standing by and heard all that had been said, offered me his hand and said with some feeling, "Captain, I will never forget this." I did not at the time attach any importance to Mr. Carr's remark, but I had cause to appreciate it several months later when the Federal forces reached Dinwiddie C.H. in March 1865, as this gentleman mentioned what came within his observation on this day to a Federal officer in command at the Court House, who had my household goods and other personal property well guarded, and when the war was over returned to me intact.

I must return to the surgeon. He went at once from the place of our interview, above referred to the front porch of Mrs. Crump's house and there engaged in conversation with a young lady—one of the handsomest in the county. He was a young man of twenty years of age and good looking and was dressed out in a new uniform liberally adorned with gold braid. Seeing him seated in the porch, I went there, walked in and spoke to the young lady referred to and who introduced me to the surgeon. I merely bowed, not wishing to touch the hand of the man who had so little humanity, and walking into the hall, requested to speak privately with the young lady. She came at once into the hall and I explained to her the situation, remarking that I knew that she would not entertain the surgeon when wounded men were suffering for his attention. She ordered his horse at once, and whilst I was talking to her mother, I saw the little fellow start on his horse, a wiser, if not a better, man.

Let me now return to Mr. Carr.

[Two pages appear to missing from the manuscript at this point.]

During the fall of 1864 it became so unsafe on my farm, by reason of the vicinity of the enemy and our liability to being overcome at any time by a raiding party, I determined to move my family to Dinwiddie C.H. and accordingly rented the buildings in the grove immediately on the Boydton Plank Road then and still known as the _____ Hotel property. At that time the old Courthouse hotel buildings standing immediately on the public road (Boydton Plank Road) in front of the courthouse building, and which were destroyed by fire about the year 1867, were occupied by Mr. Jno. W. Butterworth, who kept the hotel. At my place, however, in the grove, Confederate soldiers, from officers of the rank of Major General down to privates, were welcome to come and get a meal, free of charge, whenever they pleased, and, as you can well understand, I soon closed up the hotel of my friend Butterworth, for which I think he was grateful, as five dollars in Confederate money, the price of a meal did not, as he indeed told me, pay expenses.

Early in 1865, however, before Mr. Butterworth closed the hotel, a force of Federal Cavalry, under General Gregg started on a raid from their lines around Petersburg to reach the South Side railroad, but came only as far as Dinwiddie C.H. and then returned. I was notified of the approach of this force by friends Capt. Wm. A. Adams (then clerk of the county court of Dinwiddie) and Capt. Robert E. Bland and his brother Wm. Bland of the Prince George Cavalry, the last two mentioned gentlemen being charged by Gen. W. H. F. Lee with the duty of keeping in front of this raiding party and advising him (Gen. Lee) by couriers of their progress and probable destination.

When I was notified of their approach, the enemy were within a mile of my house coming up the road leading from Vaughan Road to the Boydton Plank Road. A soldier was sent to the point of the intersection of the plank road with the road up which the enemy were advancing to give us information of their reaching the Plank Road, and I posted a servant in the portico of the Boisseau hotel (where my family were) with instructions to notify me when he saw this soldier begin to retreat. I had my riding horse—a very fleet mare—saddled and tied in the grove near the front porch, and made other arrangements for flight. I called up Charles Cross and directed him to have some apple brandy (several barrels of it) rolled down to the branch a few yards in rear of the house and to knock the heads out of the barrels and let the brandy run into the branch. Charles was greatly shocked at the idea of such waste, as I indeed was when I contemplated the necessity of it; but as he had never failed to obey an order I fully calculated that he would carry out my instructions. My wife at the same time delivered to him her jewelry, watch and silver ware and directed him to put them in a bag and bury them.

Soon the sentinel posted in the portico announced that the vidette stationed on the plank road at the intersection of the road leading from Vaughan's Road was flying, hearing which I immediately mounted and rode down the plank road to await the arrival of the vidette, who was soon at my side hallowing, "They are coming!" "They are coming!" We rode at once up the road to the Butterworth hotel, arrived in front of which I called lustily to my friends Adams and the Messrs. Blands already referred to, who at the time were testing some of friend Butterworth's best Southampton apple brandy, and who abandoned this pleasant pastime with such reluctance that the Philistines were almost upon us before they could "mount and away." Soon, however, these gentlemen were in the saddle and all of us making good time up the plank road (westward) with about two hundred Federal cavalry charging after us firing at us with their navy shooters.

The shots of our pursuers all missed their mark, and no one was captured save Mr. Butterworth, who with two glass candy jars held fast in his hands, filled with Confederate notes closely wrapped in little rolls and packed in the jars like sardines in a box, was attempting to make his escape on foot, but was halted and told to "stand and deliver!" His captors enquired what he had in the jars and upon being informed that it was Confederate money they expressed astonishment at his solicitude about it and with some strong expletives as to its worthlessness, they bade him return to his house and assured him that no one should disturb him.

This party, however, relentlessly pursued my other friends Capt. Adams and the Messrs. Blands and myself and a few other persons about the C.H. at the time, who, like ourselves deemed it best to make their escape. As Capt.

Adams and myself rode side by side, I suggested to him that we would be in less danger, if we would separate—there were five of us then riding near together and go in different directions. To this he agreed, and after our party had ridden a short distance up the road, I turned off to the right in the direction of Village View, Dr. E. Harvey Smith's place of residence. My road was down hill and rough, but I kept up my Gilpin Speed and did not, like Lot's wife, look back. My mare was a thoroughbred, as fleet as a deer and as sure footed as an antelope. But a few days previously I had ridden her over this road and remembered that there was a rotten bridge just ahead of us, about fifteen feet in span. I felt satisfied that the mare had discovered its condition when we crossed it before, I therefore relied upon her leaping it when we would reach it and this she did beautifully, alighting so far on the other side of it as to nearly unseat me in my saddle. Before recovering my seat entirely, I ran into the lane leading up to Dr. Smith's house and regarding as a sort of "cul de sac," I made my mare leap the fence to my left and then a deep gully ten feet wide, and a few yards further over a second fence. Then riding rapidly—as would most men with a body of hostile cavalry riding rapidly after them—my speed accelerated, if possible, by the whiz of an occasional bullet, I soon felt that I was safe, and then stopped and looked back, to discover my pursuers just at the bridge, at which place having discovered its dangerous character and having sufficiently amused themselves with me, they halted, and hollered to me to come back. I pointed to the brush in my rear and invited them to come over, we being now about two hundred and fifty yards apart. This invitation they laughingly declined and rode back to the Court House and told my wife that I was well mounted and a fine rider and that they would capture me later.

This command of cavalry whilst at Dinwiddie C.H. behaved excellently. I had told my wife, before leaving that, as soon as they arrived, she must ask for the officer in command and request a guard to protect my property. This she did and the guard was promptly furnished and nothing was disturbed. Charles Cross, however, was captured and taken away, against his earnest remonstration and did not return until several weeks later after the general break up.

When the Federal cavalry had retired and I returned to the Court House, I learned from one of my house servants that Charles had not obeyed my instructions about the apple brandy, but had taken some empty cider barrels which I had under a back porch and had placed them in front of the barrels containing the apple brandy and by this clever ruse had saved the brandy then worth $200 a gallon. The silver jewelry and watch given him by my wife to secrete could not be found for several weeks as he was carried off by his captors before he had an opportunity to inform my wife where he had hidden them. Some of my neighbors insisted that he had turned the property over to the Yankees but, knowing his trustworthiness, I never for a moment believed this to be true. This worthy man lived for several years in the neighborhood of my old farm and there died several years ago, respected by all who knew him.

Just before the close of the war desertions from the Confederate army were very frequent and with a view of helping the military authorities in their efforts to check this serious trouble, the governor of Virginia issued an order requiring justices of the peace to have deserters arrested whenever opportunity to make such arrests offered, and I shall never forget my first and only experience in this line. One day when I was about the Court House a handsome and well dressed young man, wearing a beautiful pair of cavalry boots which had evidently just run the blockade, walked up with one of the village boys and asked me if I knew a Mr. Bryant who lived, he said, 6 miles south of the Court House. I told him I knew of but one Bryant in the county and he lived at Ream's Station, and that there was certainly no one of that name living in the locality he mentioned. The young man then remarked that Mr. Bryant certainly resided in the neighborhood he mentioned, that he was his uncle and was keeping a horse for him. He then enquired which way was south, and upon being informed started off in that direction.

After he had gotten out of sight, I remarked to some bystanders that I was satisfied that the young man was a deserter and that, if I had my pistol, I would pursue and arrest him. A gentleman present offered me a six-shooter and though it was smaller than I liked I took it, mounted my horse and soon overtook the young soldier. Some of the village boys wishing to see the arrest ran across Ettenborough's field so as to be present when I should make it. Coming up to the young man in the woods about three hundred yards in rear of the county jail, I politely halted him, and explained to him that I was a magistrate and had orders to examine the papers of all persons of military age passing through the village. Hearing this explanation of my business, he replied, with considerable temper, that he had no papers. I then told him that my duty was still more disagreeable as I was required to arrest all parties who had not satisfactory papers. Upon this statement to him, his eyes, which were large and very black, fairly blazed with passion as with an oath he said "Your whole d——d village can't arrest me." As soon as he said this I raised my pistol (which I had already drawn and was concealed from him by the [*illegible word*] of my horse), and, pointing it full in his face, told him that, if he moved hand and foot, I should shoot him. In a perfect fury he replied, "Shoot and be d——d. It is not the first time I have been shot." Holding the pistol still aimed at his face—I was within six feet of him—with my eyes fixed upon him, I told him that I would greatly dislike to shoot him, but to arrest him, was my sworn duty and I should shoot, if he moved.

At this juncture the boys I have above referred to ran up to us, and I at once told them to run over to the Court House and tell some men detailed to make shoes who were at work there to come to me with their muskets at once. The boys did as directed. The young soldier and myself neither moved nor spoke during the several minutes that the boys were executing these orders until the detailed men appeared approaching us, when he, seeing them coming, broke the silence and said, "I suppose I had as well surrender." He then asked that no indignity be done him. I assured him that none should be.

As the soldiers had arrived, I dismounted and giving over my horse to one of the boys, I had begun to walk along with the young man to the village, the detailed men following close behind us. Seeing this he requested that these men should walk sufficiently far from us not to hear what he wished to say, and this request I granted.

He then told me his name, and something of his history. He said that when the war began he was just fourteen years of age, that he lived in Texas, that when the Texas Rangers left for the front he took one of his mother's carriage horses and ran off with this command that for nearly four years he had kept himself mounted by capturing horses, either in battle or on scout until ten days before I saw him when he had a horse killed under him and had had no opportunity to secure another before an order came directing all dismounted cavalry men to be placed in the ranks of the infantry, and that feeling that he had been badly treated he had determined to leave the army and make his way home. His statement and manner impressed me very much. There was everything to indicate that he was a gentleman save of course his desertion, which he seemed to think was justified by the treatment he had received. I should have mentioned that he told me that he had been wounded in battle. Indeed I had observed that he limped. I deeply sympathized with the poor fellow, and told him that I hated indeed to commit him to jail until he could be sent to the authorities in Petersburg. He promptly said that he would make no effort to escape but remarked that he was totally unarmed, he said he was truly thankful, and he felt satisfied I was only doing my duty in arresting him, but, had he been armed, he would have died before suffering an arrest. "Yes" said he, "if I had not given my pistol away yesterday from something to eat, one of us would not be here now."

I took him to my house, introduced him to my family and entertained him until the next morning. The ladies played cards with him and treated his as a guest, none knowing, none suspecting, that he was a deserter, save my wife, who begged me to release him and shed many tears. There was but one course for me to pursue and that was to send him, as I did, under guard to Petersburg. On their way to Petersburg he told the guard that, if he had not promised me not to attempt to escape, he would, as he told them he could, take their guns from them and escape.

Having been delivered to the authorities in Petersburg he remained there in prison for about ten days, when the commandant of his company, hearing of his being there, came for him and intended taking him to camp next day. That night, however, when two men were taking him from prison under guard he broke away and ran off. Both of the guards fired but he escaped, as he had sent me word from Petersburg he intended to do. What became of the young man, I never heard, but I have often recalled his sad history in the closing days of the war.

During the last week in March, 1865, two or three days before the Federal forces made their final advance to their neighborhood of Dinwiddie Court House, Genl. Wm. H. F. Lee[49] and his staff spent the night with me. The next morning before leaving Genl. Lee remarked to me that I had been very kind to himself and to Confederate soldiers generally, and he would give me, in the strictest confidence, some information which would be of service to me. I assured him that I would hold inviolate whatever he might communicate to me. He then told me that our lines in the enemy's front were so attenuated that, as soon as they began to advance, our troops would fall back to the White Oak Road and make that our line, and that accordingly the portion of the county south of this road including Dinwiddie Court House, would be open to the advance of the enemy and would fall into their hands, and as this might occur at any hour he advised me to take my family away at once.

Having given me this information and advice, Genl. Lee and staff were about leaving, when another cavalry general, with his staff, rode up. This officer Genl. Lee directed to remain at my house until the following morning, which he did. As soon as he left, acting upon Genl. Lee's advice, I took my wife and children to "Sunnyside," the residence of her mother on the south side of Stony Creek about six miles south of Dinwiddie Court House.

Having moved my family from the Court House—I left my household effects, and house servant in the house I had thus occupied—on the morning of _____, March 1865, when the enemy began their expected advance towards this place. I rode over there from Sunnyside to learn the news and soon learned that the enemy were approaching the Court House in heavy

49. William Henry Fitzhugh Lee ("Rooney") was the second-born son of Robert E. Lee. At the time Griffin met him, he was a major general commanding a cavalry division. He and his men would soon be on the run after the devastating defeat they suffered at the Battle of Five Forks, April 1, 1865.

force. There were at this time several men in the village and these I advised to leave before the enemy arrived in sight as our presence would simply exasperate them and we could be of no possible service. I further remarked that if we waited until the enemy came up, we would have to make a hasty retreat, as we had done on a previous occasion, and I thought that for the reputation of the village we had best not let this occur again.

My advice was taken and accordingly several of us started westwardly up the Boydton Plank Road. The news of the enemy's advance had already preceded us, resulting in the stampeding of a number of teamsters of a wagon train then on the road between Stony Creek and Dinwiddie Court House on its way to Petersburg with commissary and other army supplies, the demoralized teamsters unhitching their mules and abandoning their wagons. Some of the wagons of the train, however, we succeeded in turning back, remaining with them on their way back to Stony Creek until they reached and crossed the bridge and were comparatively safe.

A short time before this a part of the records in the county clerk's office were by order of the county court removed to a place called "the cottage" beyond Stony Creek and about five miles southwest of the Court House, a place of safety. To the Cottage, I now made my way, and on my arrival there found Capt. Adams,[50] the county clerk in charge of the records and also Capt. Thos. E. Hargrave, the county surveyor, and then, as now, living on the Vaughan Road about four miles from the Court House. Late in the afternoon the sun being not more than an hour high, we were sitting in the yard, our horses tied near us, and were listening to the troops passing northwestardly along the Hawkins Church Road a half a mile to the east of us going in the direction of the Boydton Plank Road. To which army these moving troops belonged, not being able to see them, we knew not. For aught we then knew they may have been a column of Federals. Just at this time we heard in the edge of the woods near by the cracking of small trees and bushes indicating the approach of some moving body, and, looking to the place whence proceeded this noise, we saw a solitary horseman ride out of the woods, bareheaded and riding bareback, within about one hundred yards of us, and then, as he manifestly saw us, ride rapidly off in a westernly direction. He wore the blue overcoat of a Federal soldier, as also did Capt. Adams and Tom Hargrave.

As the horseman rode away, Adams remarked, "There goes a Yankee. I would capture him if my horse were not lame." I replied that I would capture him. I immediately mounted my house, pursued and overtook him after a

50. William A. Adams enlisted in May 1861 as captain of Company I, 3rd Virginia Cavalry. He left military service in April 1862, claiming fraud in the election of officers.

ride of about a half mile. Nearing him, I raised my pistol and demanded his surrender, when I recognized him as a Confederate soldier and I thought I recognized him also as an acquaintance, a son of Col. Wm. H. Sprately of Greensville County. I asked him if he was not Sprately of Greensville, and if he did not know me, at the same time giving him my name. He replied that his name was Sprately and that he was from Greensville and knew me through his brother, who, with his friend Walter Chambliss of the same county, had recently spent a night at my house on their way to their command. He seemed greatly relieved to find that he was with a friend and at my suggestion rode back with me to the cottage, arrived at which he was furnished with a cap and after considerable persuasion consented to go to Sunnyside with me. Before reaching the Cottage he gave me a history of his day's experiences, which were indeed trying enough to put the best material in the jaded plight in which I found this young gentleman.

He said that at daybreak that morning the enemy charged the picket post on Rowanty Creek where he was on duty and that he made his escape without time even to get his saddle; that, making Dinwiddie Court House his objective point, he started with a view of crossing the Stage Road, and after making his way in the direction of the Court House as best as he could he had succeeded in getting as far as this road when he was fired into by the enemy that he then turned back and going into the woods rode in a southwesterly direction parallel to the Stage Road, intending to cross Stony Creek at Roberts Bridge on Stage Road, but, just as he reached this point and rode up on the bridge, a volley was fired at him from Mrs. Roberts house—the bridge of that day being within a hundred yards of her house and several hundred yards above the spot of the present bridge—this fire, however, not preventing his getting across the bridge; that he succeeded in reaching Harding's (Roney's) mill higher up the creek by taking the Flat Foot Road and was riding on the bridge at this place and about to cross to the east side of the creek, when another volley was fired at him from this side of the stream, that he turned back and made across the country to the Hawkins Church Road intending to take this road he was charged by two cavalrymen, and said he "I took to the woods and came out near yourself and two other gentlemen who were dressed in blue. You then charged me as you know, and halted me, and having been riding ever since day-break, and bare-back at that, I am literally worn out, and, to tell the truth, pretty badly demoralized."

Sprately's consent having been, as I have already stated, obtained to go with me to Sunnyside, just before dark we left the Cottage to go there, but, as to get to our point of destination we had to cross the Hawkins Church Road along which troops were still passing, which troops Sprately insisted were those of the enemy, giving as a reason that his division of cavalry had the enemy before, to his knowledge, as he said, gone down in the direction of Stony Creek depot on the Weldon Railroad and as the troops we heard could be no other Confederates they must be Federals. So it was determined by us not to attempt to go on this road, but make our way as far as possible through the woods and fields skirting it, until we could get across it and then to make our way through the farms to "Sunnyside." As night came on it began to rain, and it being very dark, before we had gone more than a mile through the pines, we were compelled to dismount and lead our horses. Just at this juncture I lost my hat, but Sprately insisted that, as I was in delicate health, I should take his cap and let him go again bare-headed, as he would suffer less exposure, he being in good health.

Proceeding in this manner we had not gone much farther before our progress was arrested by a fence, arrived at which we peered through the gloom, we could see a short distance ahead of us, a small but steady light evidently at a house. I suggested to Sprately that he take care of the horses and that I should make my way on foot to the light, and, if possible, learn from the occupants of the house what troops were passing along the road near by in front of the house—the road being Hawkins Church Road. The darkness was intense but I managed to reach the house and hearing female voices within I knocked and this brought to the door one of the inmates, who in reply to my enquiry, said she did not know whether the troops in the rear were Federals and Confederates. A deep cut in the road and an intervening fence prevented the occupants of the house from seeing who they were. Bodies of troops had been passing, she said, since two o'clock in the afternoon but none of them had been to the house.

I then concluded to go up to the road for the purpose of satisfying myself as to the character of these passing troops, and did so, going within ten feet of the column, but no word did I hear uttered. They were cavalry moving along in perfect silence. After remaining at the fence about five minutes I returned to Sprately and notified him of the result. When I reached him, however, he complained so much of exhaustion and expressed himself as so anxious to sleep, I concluded to wait there with him and allow him to sleep. Straightening himself out on an old corn furrow depression in the second growth of pines he was soon fast asleep, and never stirred until I woke him just before day-break the next morning, although some rain had been falling all night.

Sprately being now awake we were soon mounted and on our way to the road which he insisted on crossing at once as we could then hear some cavalry coming up the road towards us from a southwesterly direction. Having crossed the road we had barely gotten into the body of woods on the opposite side, when my horse stepped into a stump hole and threw me over his head, injuring three of my ribs and stunning me for a while. I was now indeed in a pitiable condition. Having stood up all night in the rain, my throat sore and my ribs injured, I told Sprately that I should not on any account leave the road again, if my life depended upon it. Finding that he could not persuade me from this, he followed as I rode ahead along the road. I drew my six-shooter and proceeding down the road soon met the cavalry we heard, but it was too dark to discover their character. I believed them, however, to be Federal Cavalry, and thinking they might halt me I thought it best to speak first. So, as seeming an authoritative manner, I cried out to them "Close up!" "Close up!" This order they promptly obeyed and I pursued my way a little further on until I saw ahead of me on the side of the road a small group of mounted men, apparently in consultation. I concluded to pass this party in silence, if possible, determined, however, if they halted me, to fire rapidly into them and make my escape in the confusion. I had my pistol in hand ready for this, contingency, and rode as near the opposite side of the road as I could. Just as I reached a point of the road abreast with this party one of them halted me. Thinking I would try the role of officer, I answered in a tone of assumed authority. "Where is the wagon train?" One of the party in reply enquired "What wagon train?" I knew then a crisis had been reached, that there was no wagon train, and that my ruse was at an end, and I was in the very act of firing when one the party said, much to my relief, "Is not that Captain Griffin?" I replied in the affirmative and enquired who he was. He promptly replied "Bob Lee" and I at once recognized him as Lt. Robert E. Lee[51] and ascertained that he was in command of a picket post, stationed at that point. He cautioned me not to speak loud as there was a picket post of the enemy's cavalry a short distance from us on the Goodwynsville road. This gentleman was with his brother Genl. W. H. F. Lee two or three nights before that when the latter and staff spent the night at my house at Dinwiddie Court House as already narrated.

From Lt. Lee I learned that it was the troops of his brother's division of cavalry who in detachments and at intervals had been passing up Hawkins Church Road since the previous afternoon and they had been swinging around towards the White Oak Road by way of Sappony Cross Roads on the Boydton Plank Road.

51. Robert E. Lee Jr. was the youngest son of Robert E. Lee. He enlisted as a private in the Virginia Rockbridge 1st Light Artillery in March 1862. Promoted to 1st lieutenant in November 1862 upon his transfer to the cavalry, he was serving as an aide-de-camp to his older brother, General William H. F. Lee, when Griffin met him.

About this time it was beginning to be light. Seeing Sprately approaching Lt. Lee enquired who he was and being informed by me he remarked that he was one of the most gallant men in his command.

Suffering considerably from my injuries, and loss of sleep I bade Lt. Lee good bye, and made my way to Sunnyside without further adventure. Sprately remained with Lee.

Before closing this letter, already longer than I had intended to make it, I must make special mention to poor Adams, as gallant and chivalrous as soldier as ever drew a sword, as generous and high-toned a man as ever lived. During the first year of the war he was in the field as the first captain of the Dinwiddie Cavalry. Losing his commission at the election of officers at the reorganization in the spring of 1862, he was subsequently elected clerk of the county court in Dinwiddie.

A few days after the eventful night in which I had the trying experiences in making my way with my friend Sprately from the Cottage to Sunnyside I have just narrated, having spent several days in bed with my fractured ribs. I rode over to the residence of Mr. J. F. Young on Stony Creek two miles west of the Court House to get my commission as a member of the legislature to which I had been chosen as the delegate from Dinwiddie at an election held a short time before. Mr. Young, Capt. Adams and Mr. Jno. W. Butterworth (to whom I have before referred) were the commissioners of election. At Mr. Young's gate I met Adams and he told me of an encounter he on that morning had with two Federal officers in the neighborhood of the creek.

His residence was about two miles northeast of the Court House and he had attempted to get there—the County in the immediate neighborhood of the Court House was then occupied by small bodies of Federals—but was unable to make his way to his home. He then went on up to see his sister who lived in the neighborhood of Five Forks, and was returning and within a mile of Stony Creek, when two horsemen pursued him, he riding rapidly from them. Concluding to try issues with these men having seen that there were only two of them, he gradually reined his horse and allowed his pursuers to pass him on their precipitous charge to overtake him, which they did, one at a time, but in quick succession. Availing himself of the opportunity, an expert marksman, he emptied both saddles with his six-shooter and then road rapidly to the creek and crossed a short distance above the place where I met him. The first Federal who reached him fired at him as he rode past him, but without effect. Whether he killed these men, or either of them he did not know. This was the account of the encounter he gave me the morning he had it.

A little incident here occurred illustrative of the character of the man. A little boy whose mother lived near the Court House came up to us as we were talking. Adams advised him to return to the Court House, telling him that the Federal Soldiers would not disturb him, and he might be of some service to his mother. Taking from his pocket a two dollar greenback—all the money he had—he gave it to the boy and said "Take this with you, and give one half to your mother, the other half to my wife. Both may have had everything taken from them by the Yankees and they may be in need of bread." These last words were but too true so far as Mrs. Adams was concerned; some dastardly fellows wearing blue uniforms had robbed her of everything and for days the family were glad to get the waste corn that fell from the mouths of the horses of Federal cavalry quartered about the premises—corn stolen from her. But this poor Adams never lived to know. On the _____ of April at the house of Mrs. H. Jerard Heartwell who lived about fourteen miles southwest of the Court House, in an office in the yard, a deadly encounter took place wherein Adams shot and killed a young Confederate scout, Cleale, and was immediately shot and killed by another Confederate scout the comrade and friend of Cleale, the tragic affair being the result of a mistake, and thus died this brave man.

Sincerely, your friend

John. C. Griffin

ADDENDUM: STATEMENT OF G. ADOLPHUS BOISSEAU

Mr. G. Adolphus Boisseau, of Dinwiddie County, Va,. Having read the foregoing letter, under date of Sept. 21, 1894, makes the following statement:

I am the little boy referred to in the last paragraph of Capt. Griffin's letter to you and shall never forget the experiences of those days about the close of the war. I was then about twelve years of age, living with my mother and my three sisters at the Grove hotel at Dinwiddie C.H. My father, the late Robert G. Boisseau and four of his sons were about in the Confederate army.

On Thursday morning, March 30, 1865, the Federal cavalry reached Dinwiddie C.H. having come into the flank road by way of Vaughan's Road. The Jeff Davis Legion of cavalry met and fought the advance force of the enemy, falling back before them. I left the village in company with Capt. Adams and Mr. Isaac S. Kesler and a party of Confederate cavalry which had been stationed around the Court House for several months doing duty as relay couriers. Many went [rapidly] up the plank road and made for the bridge across Stony Creek and took up the planks as soon as we crossed. There was another bridge a half mile lower down the creek. The lieutenant in command of the couriers sent some of them to take up the plank on this bridge also and this was done.

Our little party, Captain Griffin and Adams excluded, spent the night in a barn on the farm of Mr. W. D. Young on the plank road, about a mile west of the bridge. The [*illegible word*] and established a picket-post on the hill immediately west of the bridge. About dark the pickets reported that the enemy were repairing the bridge. The fact was they were leaving at dawn, fearing that W. H. F. Lee's cavalry then marching across the county from the neighborhood of Stony Creek depot towards Chamberlain's Bed Run (where there was a severe fight the next day, Friday the 31st) might attack from the west side of the creek. During the night the lieutenant sent a member of his command, a mere boy, eighteen years of age, named Lawrence and from North Carolina, to Sappony Cross Roads, where Gen. Lee's command was then crossing the plank road on its way to a point in the vicinity of the scene of the engagement of the next day. Being very fond of Lawrence—he and I during his several months' service about the Court House had become great friends, although he was several years my senior—I went along with him, being myself well mounted. Just as we reached a point on the plank road about a mile east of Sappony Cross Roads (which is about _____ miles west of the bridge), the night rainy and very dark, we rode upon a fence built directly across the road, the tallest fence I ever saw. Our horses stopped on their own accord when they reached this obstruction. Just as they stopped, their heads touching the fence-rails, we heard the click of (it seemed) six or eight rifles or carbines, with voices from behind the fence demanding to know who we were. Lawrence answered "Friends!" "Don't Shoot!" Without difficulty Lawrence satisfied the party who challenged us—they were from Barringer's[52] brigade of cavalry— that we were friends and explained his business. We were then allowed to pass forward. I am satisfied the men at the fence were napping, as they would have otherwise sooner discovered us. They built the fence, they told us, to aid them in arresting the progress of any cavalry or other mounted men that might approach from the direction of the creek. Their expectation being that the Federal cavalry would cross the creek. The barrier served its purpose well, so far as Lawrence and myself were concerned. No Federal cavalry, however went over the plank road as far west of the creek as this for several days.

52. Rufus Barringer raised a company of cavalry from his home county of Cabarrus in 1861, and was chosen captain of F Company, 1st North Carolina Cavalry. He rose steadily through the ranks, reaching the rank of brigadier general in 1864, commanding several North Carolina regiments. A fighting officer, he was in 76 actions and sustained three wounds. On April 3, 1865, he was captured in Virginia by "Jesse Scouts," Union soldiers disguised as Confederates. After the war, he returned to North Carolina and became active in politics, supporting Reconstruction and the Republican Party. He died in 1895.

Arrived at the Cross Roads, Lawrence found that Gen. Lee himself had already passed. He then returned to Mr. Young's and reported this fact to the Lieutenant, I with him. We reached the barn before day break. . . .

I was at the Cottage for several days. When I returned to the Court House I found that the Federal authorities had established a hospital in the Brown hotel, that my mother and sisters had been getting plenty to eat and were faring well.

11

The Fall of Petersburg

THE END CAME FOR Confederate Petersburg in the spring of 1865. By
that time, the rebel armies, outmanned and outgeneraled, braced against
the flood of Union blue that swept over much of the South. Grasping for
secession's fading rays, Lee considered abandoning the Petersburg-Richmond
front to join Joseph Johnston's army, now pinned down by Sherman in North
Carolina. To buy time for such a withdrawal, Lee launched a desperate assault
in late March against Fort Stedman on the Union lines in front of Petersburg.
Following a plan hatched by John B. Gordon, a Lee favorite in the war's dying
days, the attack enjoyed initial success but quickly lost impetus and collapsed
in the face of ample Union reinforcements. After the failed Confederate attack on Fort Stedman, Grant launched the final operations at Petersburg,
eventually overcoming Lee's defense network and flushing the Confederates
out of the Cockade City. Days after the attack on Fort Stedman, Union forces
overran Confederate forces at Five Forks and then crashed through the thin
rebel lines around Petersburg. Lee was forced to abandon the city. Bernard,
on leave from his unit in late March, did not witness the fall of his home
town.

To add to his second volume of "War Talks," Bernard solicited several
accounts of Petersburg's demise from fellow residents. He also received a
letter from Union veteran C. W. Maynard describing his experiences during Petersburg's fall, along with a contribution from English native James C.
Kemp describing what he saw that day. More than forty years after the fight,
Bernard received a story of Fort Stedman's defense from Union veteran Milton Embick, an officer in the Ninth Corps during the war.

"A Deadly Assault: The Attack upon Fort Stedman on Friday, March 25, 1865, described by an Eye-Witness,"
by J. Campbell Kemp[1]

A Bloody Episode during the Closing Scenes of the Siege of Petersburg— Incidents of Great Dramatic Interest.

The following interesting letter has been handed to the *Dispatch* by the gentleman to whom it is addressed:

Petersburg, Va.,
May 7, 1894

George S. Bernard, Esq., Petersburg, Va.:

Dear Sir,—Responding to your request to furnish you my recollections of the assault on Fort Stedman on the morning of Friday, March 25, 1865, I will state that, being at the time a British subject, resident in Petersburg, I was not required by the Confederate authorities to enroll myself among the soldiers of the South, and this gave me an opportunity as an on-looker to witness from a civilian's point of view the varying fortunes of the war as they affected the people of Petersburg. But I feel a little reluctant to give you for publication this scribbling of a mere looker-on to take its place among the narratives of so many of the "dramatis personae" of the great war-drama, men who on many field witnessed of the falling of "The red rain that makes the harvest grow."

It was still dark on the morning of the 25th of March, 1865, when the loud and continuous sound of battle from the lines on the east of Petersburg proclaimed to the inhabitants of the beleaguered city that some event of importance was happening. I was aroused from sleep by the clamor of battle, but waited until dawn before leaving my lodging-room, on Sycamore street opposite the West-Hill warehouse near which in the mean time several stray shells from the Federal batteries had exploded.

WITH EQUANIMITY

Most of the citizens of Petersburg had left that part of the city where I resided as above described, and, on Sycamore street, its main thoroughfare, only a

---

1. Kemp's account appeared in the *Richmond Dispatch,* June 24, 1894. George Bernard compiled the following biographical sketch of Kemp: "Born in Glasgow, Scotland, in 1827. Left for Virginia in 1852 and found employment as a bookkeeper in Petersburg with N. M. Martin and Donnans, wholesale grocers and commission merchants. Worked as a bookkeeper after the war, and in 1888, became Clerk of the Mayor of Petersburg, an office he held until 1892."

few scattered groups were visible. From these I learned that an attack upon General Grant's works near Fort Stedman, under the immediate leadership of General Gordon, had been made early that morning; and I was further informed that the roads leading to the point of attack had been crowded with the soldiers of Pickett's Division, ready to take advantage of any success that might be achieved by the assaulting columns. These citizens with whom I talked and from whom I gathered this information discussed it, it seemed to me, with strange indifference to the probable issue of the battle then in progress, and it was apparent that in the presence of "the ills they had" these people had come to regard with equanimity whatever fate the future had in store for them.

The sound of battle, instead of diminishing, seemed to swell louder and louder, and excited in me a great desire to witness the fight, which I felt sure could be done from some point on the heights, which extended for some distance along the north bank of the river, and command a fine view of the city and surrounding territory. So I determined to gratify this desire. The purpose formed, I started to put it into execution. Quickly, however, as I walked along Sycamore street, near the corner of Tabb and Sycamore I encountered a horseman, galloping at full speed, "bloody with spurring, fiery-red with haste," who, halting near me, demanded in tones harsh and imperious, directions for reaching Gordon's headquarters. I surmised—and correctly as it turned out—that my imperious friend was one of the General's aides bearing to Mrs. Gordon tidings of the fight. It needed but a glance at the face of the messenger to guess their import.

Yea; this man's brow did, like a title-page, Foretell the nature of a tragic volume.

I gave the information desired, whereupon the rider put spurs to his horse and disappeared round the next street corner.

IMPRESSIVE ROAR

Having obtained the provost marshall's permission to cross the Appomattox, after a long walk I reached the desired point of observation on the north bank. The white walls of the old Roslyn mansion gleamed through the trees to the West as I wended my way towards them. In more tranquil time, in my walks, I had often paused at this point to admire the quiet beauty of the hills and fields on the South side of the river. Now, over there in Prince George, a change had come, compared with which the most startling "transformation scene" ever devised by a pantonist "paled its ineffectual fires." The green slopes, which I remembered so well were covered by a cloud of gray smoke, from out of which came an impressive roar—the sound of modern battle when many thousand muskets and scores of pieces of artillery are blending their reports. The shriek of this jagged iron from the exploding shells was the only sound that rose above the general uproar. Sometimes, as I looked across the scene of deadly conflict, the favoring wind would waft the smoke aside, and then I caught a view of the grim earthworks of besiegers and besieged stretching away from the river southward, in many a serpentine fold. Nearest to my point of observation (which I should have stated was about 150 yards to the southeast of the Roslyn House) I could distinguish the bulk of the Union redoubt of Fort McIlvery [McGilvery], looming up near the river with its "red artillery" flashing fast and furious from its embrasures. The hurley-burley was tremendous. "Villanous saltpetre" was holding high carnival.

ONLY ONE MAN

But where was the food for all this powder? Within 2,500 yards of where I stood probably not less than from 40,000 to 50,000 men, from every "coin of vantage," plied rifle, cannon, and mortar; and yet during the period of my watch—some 50 minutes in duration—I saw only one man, and to me he will always be a mystery. Through the smoke on the Federal breastworks, near the river, appeared this single man, moving along the parapets. For forty or fifty yards, as well as I could judge, he thus made his way, and then seemed to jump down behind the embankment out of my sight. Why he appeared where I saw him—why some Confederate rifle did not cut short his career of what seemed reckless daring—I have never understood.

ADVERSE RESULTS

At this stage of the fight the Confederates abandoned the offensive. They had taken Fort Stedman, but the guns of Fort Haskell—the nearest Union fort on the south—and the fort above the City-Point road—the nearest Union fort on the north—were turned upon these assailants, and from the furious fire of these they were now seeking protection, and a little after were fleeing to their own breastworks, across the narrow ridge lying between these and Fort Stedman. Had I tarried longer at my place of observation I might have seen the last assailants now in retreat, torn by the grape and canister from the Union batteries, but being satisfied that there was a failure of the assault, and now knowing how this might affect the status of things in the city, I deemed it best to turn back and did so, to find, when I got to the office of the provost marshal, that the adverse result of the move was there known.

ALWAYS BE MEMORABLE

Happening as did this assault upon Fort Stedman on that Friday morning, during the closing scenes of the siege of Petersburg, it has not attracted the attention it would have otherwise had, but this bloody episode of the civil war will always be memorable as the last offensive movement of the Army of Northern Virginia, and its details will ever attract the general reader, abounding as they do with incidents of great dramatic interest.

I will state that on the Sunday after the evacuation of the city I visited Fort Stedman, and went over the battle-field. One thing that particularly struck me was the number of grape-shot lying about on the ridge between the fort and the Confederate earthworks.

SCENE OF DEATH

I was also struck with the number of skeletons of half-buried soldiers slain on the 18th of June, 1864, about this point. After leaving the scene of death with my companions I sauntered along the line of the works as far as Fort Haskell, and was forcibly struck with the evidence furnished by the debris of the trenches and deserted bomb-proofs, that there was a vast difference in the way the Federals and their adversaries, the Confederates, fared in the way of provisions. Hundreds of empty tin cans whose contents had furnished good meals to the men in blue were to be seen in the outer ditch wherever the eye rested.

UNDISTURBED

There was one sad sight I witnessed on my stroll on this Sabbath day which impressed me very much. On the old Hare race-track, about that part of the course nearest to Fort Stedman, I saw the remains of a poor Confederate, who from his appearance manifestly fell in the action of June 18, 1864, his forehead pierced by a bullet, his rifle at his side, his overcoat enveloping his form, his hat at his head, and everything unmistakably indicating that he had lain as he fell during all the long months of the siege, undisturbed by friend or foe.

Yours very respectfully,

J. Campbell Kemp

"Battle of Fort Stedman: A Federal Soldier's Account,"
by Milton A. Embick

Of a Pathetic Incident Illustrating the Devotion of a Widowed Southern Mother to the Confederate Cause—Letter Urging Her Son to Return to His Command Found in the Dead Boy's Hand as He Lay in the Front Line of the Confederate Dead—Beautiful Tribute to the Confederate Soldier

To the Editor of the *Index-Appeal:*

Satisfied that the subjoined letter written by a Federal soldier who participated in the battle of Fort Stedman will very much interest the readers of the *Index-Appeal,* I send it to you for publication.[2] The writer, Hon. Milton A. Embick,[3] a former member of the General Assembly of the Pennsylvania, is the Secretary of the Third (Hartranft's) Division of the Ninth (Parke's) Army Corps and one of the Battlefield Commission appointed under an act of the Pennsylvania legislature and charged with the duty of erecting a monument commemorating the part taken by Hartranft's division in that famous action and in the hard-fought battle of Sunday, the 2nd of April, 1865, at and about Fort Mahone.

Yours very respectfully,

Geo. S. Bernard

Boiling Springs, Pa.,
March 5th, 1907

Mr. George S. Bernard, Petersburg, Va.

My Dear Sir:—Complying with the request you made when we met last in your city I want to give you in writing the incident of the letter I found on the battlefield of Fort Stedman on March 25th, 1865. Before doing so it may not be out of place to give you a brief history of our side of that battle, which if too long or uninteresting you may consign to the waste basket. Our six regiments of Pennsylvania troops consisting of the 200th, 205th, 207th, 208th, 209th and 211th were first placed under Butler in September, 1864. We were unfortunate enough to reach his front a day or two after General Wade Hampton's cavalry had captured in Prince George county about 2500

2. The letter appeared in the *Petersburg Daily Index-Appeal* on March 28, 1908.

3. Embick was a key player in the dedication of Pennsylvania monuments on the Petersburg battlefield in 1909, at Fort Stedman and at the site of Fort Mahone (which had been demolished by that time). He also compiled and edited *Military History of the Third Division, Ninth Corps, Army of the Potomac* (Harrisburg, Pa.: C. E. Aughinbaugh, 1913).

head of beef cattle which we understood were intended for Butler's Army of the James. In consequence we were issued codfish, which we piled outside of our breast-works, reserving the largest to place over the chimneys of our comrades who had gone to bed where they were soon smoked out. In this army, the Army of the James, we had but little to do save picket duty, but that was fierce and our average was forty hours on picket out of forty-eight. There we remained until the night of November 17th, 1864, when the Confederates made an attack on our picket line, capturing Col. T. B. Kaufmann of my regiment, the 209th, with a large number of officers and men and killing and wounding others. A few days after this we were moved across and to the south side of the Appomattox and became the Third Division of the Ninth Army Corps, with Brigadier General John F. Hartranft[4] as our commander. We now moved into substantial winter quarters, my regiment occupying a camp near and west of Meade's station on the military railroad. And here let me say that in a ravine, but a short distance north of our camp, welled forth a little spring, into an oaken barrel, as sweet a water as I ever drank and which was guarded night and day by a sentry, so that no one could fill his canteen save by a tin-cup that hung by the side of the spring. This spring supplied the entire regiment. Five years ago, as a party of us were hunting around for our old camp, we found this spring with the same oaken barrel in it, and again on my last two visits I drank from it. Mrs. Webb, who lives just south of our camp, says that she has lived there for forty-two years and gets her water from the same spring and that the barrel there now is the barrel that was there forty-two years ago (so that my regiment has one of the best landmarks of any in the Army of the Potomac).

While in camp at this place we had little to do, but drill, which we did incessantly. Save for a march to Hatcher's Run in mid-winter, where we remained for a couple of days and nearly froze, and a forced march to Stoney Creek one night to help out the Fifth Corps, we drilled all the time. My own

---

4. A prewar civil engineer turned lawyer, John F. Hartranft of Pennsylvania took a winding path to reach the rank of brigadier general in May 1864. When his militia regiment bolted at the Battle of First Bull Run, Hartranft stayed and fought. He returned to Pennsylvania to raise the 51st Pennsylvania regiment, serving as its first commander. He fought in a number of battles prior to achieving some distinction at the Battle of Spotsylvania Court House. Given the command of a division, he stopped the Confederate attack on Fort Stedman in March 1865. He was brevetted major general for his role in that battle. He served as special provost marshal for the trial of the Lincoln conspirators and then left the service to return to political posts in Pennsylvania, including two terms as governor (see Ezra J. Warner, *Generals in Blue: Lives of the Union Commanders* [Baton Rouge: Louisiana State University Press, 1964], 211–12).

regiment marched a mile and a half every afternoon to a large field in our rear and there for nearly two hours we went through battalion drill. I have often since looked at our National Guard in our division encampments, and not without disgust at their regimental formation and alignments on parade, as contrasted with our war-time drills in the old Prince George drill-ground. Our line on which we lay in camp was perfectly safe from shot and shell from yours, and it was an interesting pleasure to us to gather on our company streets every evening and night and watch the flaming shells you hurled at our devoted front line and which never touched us.

Thus time passed on. On the morning of the 25th of March, 1865, I was lying half awake or less in my upper bunk. There were five of us, two above and three below, when I heard cheering on the Confederate lines. We called it then "the rebel yell." I returned to my sleepy comrade and said, "The Johnnies must have heard good news on their picket line." Frequently we would hear cheers like that and the next day hear that the "Johnnies had whipped the Yanks" on some other field. My bunk-mate went to sleep, but I began to philosophize. I knew it must be about four o'clock, and I knew also from experience how dead sleepy pickets were at that time in the morning. So I thought they must have mighty good news to make them cheer like that at that time in the morning. The firing on the picket line as I thought became more incessant, but I did not think so much of that, for many a time I had stood on the picket line in the Army of the James and thought that the armies across the river were fighting all the time. Just across the ravine from us on a hill was a fort, on our reserve line, the Dunn House Battery.[5] A single gun from that brought me out of my bunk as quickly as if its shot had struck our tent. Just then a staff officer, Capt. Daillion, a French officer and a graduate of St. Cyr who fell mortally wounded two hours later, dashed into our camp and riding up and down our company streets shouted, "Turn out this regiment! Turn out this regiment!" In my excitement I thought he also said "and get to the rear." I said to my tent mates, "My God, boys, the Johnnies are on us, sure." I had a pair of boots taken from home and a pair of light government shoes. I grabbed for the boots, but concluding that, if we had to "get to the rear," I could run faster with the shoes, I put them on. When I reached for my cartridge box and belt I thought it felt light, but opening the flap I found it as I supposed full, forgetting that I had taken the lower twenty rounds out for march and drill and left the upper full for inspection. I went into that fight

5. The Dunn House Battery and Fort Friend were on a hill about one mile to the rear of Fort Stedman, forming an artillery-fortified interior line.

with twenty instead of forty rounds in my cartridge box and I hope that no home was made desolate on account of one that I fired.

In one-fourth the time it takes to read this we were formed in our company streets and you could plainly hear the thud, thud of the spent bullets that struck our tightly drawn tent covers. Strange that not a man that I know of in the regiment was struck at that time. Our regiment was marched rapidly to the rear and right of the Dunn House Battery and halted along a steep bank where we lay with ample protection. Just on our left was the 200th regiment on a hill, but farther in the rear than we were. This regiment was led by Gen. Hartranft himself and in the gray dawn I could see its commander, Lt. Col. W. H. H. McCall,[6] step in front of his regiment, and could plainly hear his command, "Forward, guide center, march!" They started forward as though on dress parade, firing as they went, which I thought was murder, as, until I saw their men going down by scores, I had not realized but that the front line of our army had fallen back instead of being gobbled up as some were by Gordon's men. There we lay in perfect safety, in advance of the 200th under orders not to join them until they had reached our line, their men plunging forward, staggering backward, or sinking limp as they were shot. It is accorded to but few regiments to be in battle as close as we were to them and to see it rage for half an hour almost, for they broke and rallied three times before they reached us, and we in perfect safety. Just as soon, however, as they touched our left we were ordered up and charged across the field until we came to a water drain about four feet deep that ran parallel to our line and half way across the field. Here we were halted until the four other regiments of our division were brought up from the left, the 211th, Major Brown's regiment, double-quicking for five miles. In the first charge we made before we reached the drain I had noticed two slight lines of earthworks, almost as straight as a furrow, evidently hurriedly scooped out by the Confederate line of battle as it halted for a moment or two, and their farthest line was perilously near our camp and it has always been a mystery to me as to why they did not go in. The Confederate advance was led by Gen. Henry Kyd Douglas[7] of Hagerstown, a dear friend of mine and as gallant a

6. William Henry Harrison McCall of Pennsylvania rose from private to brevet brigadier general in his four years in the Army of the Potomac. He served for three years in the 34th Pennsylvania Infantry, then joined the 200th Pennsylvania Infantry. For his actions in the battles around Petersburg in March and April 1865 he was promoted to brevet colonel, then brevet brigadier general.

7. Henry Kyd Douglas also rose through the ranks, in his case in the Army of Northern Virginia. Primarily a staff officer, he was captured at Gettysburg. Released in 1864,

soldier as ever drew sword in any cause. I had him attend our second division reunion held in York, Pa., in 1891, where he made a splendid address on the battle.

Our regiment in the meantime was vying with the 200th in its losses, among those who fell, a bullet hole through his heart, being the gallant Lieutenant Hugh Jones,[8] of Company C, whose son is Seward W. Jones, of Jones Brothers, of Boston, the large quarry owners who are to erect our monument of Fort Mahone.

The final charge was made as soon as the other regiments came up and in that charge I saw a young fair-haired boy about sixteen years old lying with his feet toward our lines and his wide staring blue eyes toward the sky. In his right hand between a bloody thumb and finger I saw a letter, without envelope, and reaching hurriedly down as I took another look into the boyish face I took the letter, thrust it in the pocket of my blouse and ran to join my comrades in the charge. Fort Stedman was taken in that charge; our lines re-established; our brigadier made a major-general by brevet before we returned to our camp and a much-needed breakfast. After breakfast I thought of the letter, and took it out of my pocket to read. It proved to be from a mother in North Carolina to this son who lay dead upon the field. The mother was uneducated, as the letter showed. It was written upon paper such as was used in the last days of the Confederacy. The ink seemed to have been made from the juice of poke berries, if such could be the case. It was written closely on every page and on every margin. From it I learned that the father of this son must have enlisted and given up his life in the Confederate army some time before that; that this boy had two sisters, at least, as the mother always spoke of them in the plural; that this boy, who had enlisted to take his father's place, with some other comrades, had deserted and was in hiding, and that this letter was written by this mother to her boy the same day she had found out where he was. The letter was one continued prayer to her boy to at once go back to his regiment, to take whatever punishment the officer might see fit to inflict upon him, but to go back; only go back. Over and over again she appeals to him to do this. She appeals to him by his father's memory and asks him what he thinks his

---

he returned to staff work until the last weeks of the war, when he was given command of a Virginia brigade. He wrote a popular account of his wartime experiences, *I Rode with Stonewall,* that made him familiar to students of the Civil War.

8. Hugh Jones enlisted into Company C of the 209th Pennsylvania Infantry in September 1864. Promoted to 2nd Lieutenant that same month, he was one of two officers in the regiment to be killed in its first year of service.

father would think if he knew of his desertion. She appeals to him to lift the disgrace from their home, saying that his sisters had not been to a neighbor's house since they heard of his desertion, and that if they were out of the house and would see any one coming along the road they would come in so as not to be seen; and that she shared that feeling. Her prayer was answered; her boy went back, and I had seen his fair curly head lying out on the field and had taken from his blood-stained fingers the last letter she wrote him. I made up my mind then and there that if I lived to get through the war I would write to that Spartan mother and tell her that her boy listened to her prayers and that I had seen his fair young face as it lay in one of the very front lines. I put the letter in the inside pocket of a citizen's vest I had for cold weather along with a little money and of couple of letters from home. On the night of the third of April I was guard on the flanks along with the others, and every halt we made I would throw myself down and go to sleep, as we were worn out from the day's fight before and the night watches for a week before that. The night was warm, and I carried my vest on the butt of my gun, and in one of my hurried wakings it slipped off and was lost. I have written this to you because I deemed it worthy of preservation as showing the wonderful patriotism of your women of a class where you might not be led to expect it.

I have spoken above of General Hy. Kyd Douglas being at a division re-union in York in 1891 by my invitation. General B. F. Fisher, of this State, fol-lowed General Douglas and paid this tribute to the veterans who followed the fortunes of that matchless leader, Gen. R. E. Lee. Speaking of the last scene in the drama, General Fisher said:

> No soldier can lose his own self-respect, no citizens of the United States can do his country a wrong, or commit an error from which posterity may draw an improper lesson, by speaking of the honor, the courage, the bravery of the foe, which enabled the soldiers of the Republic to win the renown that they have won. One of the most remarkable scenes in my judgment that the world ever saw as reflecting endurance, the devotion, and the courage and the bravery of men was that displayed by the Confederate army, as it stood waiting the shock of arms which they expected just prior to the announcement of the surrender. Picture it, if it is possible, you who were not present and saw never the scene. There stood the decimated regiments, to which reference has already been made by Colonel Douglas—ragged, hungry, many of them with empty knapsacks, and some without muskets or cartridges, but grim, determined-visaged, awaiting whatever might be the end.

Surrounding them upon every hill-top stood the soldiers of our thoroughly equipped army, with all the paraphernalia of war that wealth and abundance was able to gather in defense of the Republic, ready to open up what would have been simply an avalanche of iron and lead, if the command had been given for another battle. Before all that array of arms, with all that array of soldiery, outnumbering them from three or four to one, flushed with the victories which they had been reaping for days and days, eager and earnest to end the fray, there they stood. Well did they know that if the order had been given to advance it meant simply annihilation to them; but they never faltered; they never flinched; there they stood as they had often stood before, to meet the shock of the Army of the Potomac. I say today that such an exhibition of courage, of endurance, of faith to a cause then lost, of faith to a principle which they themselves long had doubted, of faith in their commanders, and with a determination to accept whatever might be the result, is without precedent. Wrong as you and I always felt they were, yet ill would it become you or me to question the honesty of the rank and file of that army. No men who did not honestly believe that they were right under the circumstances could possibly have presented the front which they presented. This little tribute I have felt it a proper thing to pay in the presence of one whom I knew thirty-three years ago, from which time until tonight I have never seen him. I have often heard of the position which he held in the army upon the other side, and I knew that he was actuated by the utmost confidence in the righteousness of the cause for which he battled, that he never shirked a duty, never turned his back, although it was not possible for the combined strength of the army with which he was acting to overcome what was in their front.

To this tribute of General Fisher, let me add mine; not so eloquent but equally, if not more, sincere—more sincere in that it has been my privilege and pleasure to meet in your city, after almost half a century, many who were Confederate soldiers. I beg to remain,

Yours, very sincerely,

M. A. Embick.

"Cockade City's Surrender, Delivered to the Federals," by J. P. Williamson[9]

Reminiscences of the Last Days of the Siege of Petersburg, and How the City was Turned Over to the Federals

A letter read by J. P. Williamson, Esq., before A. P. Hill Camp of Confederate Veterans of Petersburg, Va., at its meeting on the evening of June 7, 1894:

Petersburg, Va.,
May 22, 1894.

Geo. S. Bernard, Petersburg, Va.:

Dear Sir:—At your request I will give you my recollections of some of the closing incidents of the siege of Petersburg. A few weeks before the 25th of March, 1865, General John B. Gordon, by his gentlemanly deportment, had elicited the sympathy of my better half in favor of his lovely wife, who always kept as near him as the enemy and other circumstances would permit, and we had extended Mrs. Gordon and himself an invitation to make our house their home, which was accepted. His presence as inmate of my house gave me an opportunity to learn from him much that was not generally known by the other citizens during the later days of the Confederacy.

At seven o'clock on the evening of March 24th, 1865, General Gordon came in from the lines as usual and requested me to secure for him two bolts of white cloth—which I promptly purchased for him, the late Confederacy still owing me what I paid for the goods—and he and I with the assistance of our wives tore the material into strips of three inches width, which were soon in the hands of an orderly and on their way out to the men on the lines. General Gordon then explained to me that he was ordered to make an attack on Fort Stedman before daylight, and these strips of white cloth were for the sharp-shooters and others who were to go in the advance to tie around their arms in order that in the darkness they might be distinguished from the enemy.

Bidding us good-bye the general left to lead in the early morning the forlorn hope. How the charge was successfully made and the fort taken by surprise, and how the movement finally resulted in a sad disaster, is a part of the history of the last days of the siege. Feeling a deep interest in what was being

---

9. J. Pinckney Williamson, along with D'arcy Paul, and Alexander Donnan (the latter two are noted later) were elected members of the Petersburg Common Council (see Greene, *Civil War Petersburg*, 296n59). Williamson's letter appeared in the *Petersburg Daily Index-Appeal* on June 17, 1894.

done, at daylight I left my house, which was on South Market street, to learn what I could from the front. Just as I passed along Washington street in front of Jarratt's hotel (now the Albemarle) I observed a lone horseman coming slowly towards me from the direction of Sycamore street, an orderly walking and leading the horse and the rider. As the horseman and his attendant approached—we were meeting each other—the former said to the latter, "Let me dismount and lie down, I am about to faint." Hearing this I was immediately at the man's side assisting him, whom I found to be Brigadier-General Philip Cook,[10] one of Gordon's brigade-commanders. He (Gen. C.) said he was slightly wounded and was trying to get to the Georgia hospital in the clump of pines across the river just beyond the Ettrick cotton mills. I insisted on his going to my house, but he was averse to troubling a private family with his presence in his then condition. After much persuasion, however, I prevailed on him to do so. I found him to be a man of great spirit and courage, with only one leg, having lost the other in the early part of the war.

General Cook was an inveterate hater of the Blue Coats, and when alluding to them his language was not always of the most polite character, but, as the sequel will show, he became very much mollified after a more intimate acquaintance with them under their kind ministrations in his affliction. In a letter he wrote me last summer from Atlanta, Ga., where he holds the position of auditor of the state of Georgia, he informed me that he was "still kicking," although a short time previously a hackman had driven over him and dislocated several ribs. Surely this brave and gallant gentleman was not born to die by violence.

After the attack on Fort Stedman, matters were again quiet for several days, but to all reflecting minds it was manifest that the days of the Confederacy were probably numbered. Sunday, April 2nd, the last day of the occupation of Petersburg by Lee's army, was a sad one. In the early forenoon instead of the church bells and the streets thronged with worshippers on their way to the churches, we had the curling smoke and the lurid flames issuing from West Hill and Centre warehouses, in which were stored large quantities of tobacco and cotton which the military authorities deemed proper to burn. To me this was an unmistakable sign that the end of our hopes was at hand.

10. Prewar Georgia lawyer Phillip Cook rose from private to brigadier general in the Army of Northern Virginia. Beginning the war in 1861 in the 4th Georgia Infantry, he held both field and staff positions for various units within the Army of Northern Virginia, rising steadily through the ranks. He was commanding a brigade within Grimes's division when he was wounded at the Battle of Fort Stedman. He survived, and held both state and national political offices (congressional representative from Georgia for five terms) after the war.

Fortunately there was no wind blowing and consequently no spread of the flames, a circumstance that saved our city from a serious conflagration. I will here state for many months the burning of the tobacco was contemplated in the contingency of an occupation of the city by federal forces and for this purpose in each warehouse there was kept packed between the hogsheads there stored combustible material—kindling wood and resin—which needed only the application of a match to promptly start the flames. The tobacco and cotton destroyed this morning would have brought its owners several hundred thousand dollars in greenbacks could they have saved it.

With the burning came the thundering of artillery and roar of musketry from the river on the left to Fort Gregg on the right. Attention to his duties at the front kept General Gordon engaged all day, but at night when quiet had been restored, he returned to my house and soon sought a private interview with me, in which he said: "I have a secret to tell you." My reply to this was, "I anticipate you. You are going to surrender?" "Not yet," said he. "We are going to leave here tonight with the army and the city will be left in the hands of the mayor and the council to take the most peaceable and quiet surrender they can." Upon my enquiring where the Confederates were going, he said they would try and get to General Johnston, then, as you know, in North Carolina, confronting Sherman. "How and which way?" I asked. "Your only outlet is by Campbell's bridge." I mentioned this bridge across the Appomattox as I knew the lower bridge (Pocahontas) was within easy range of the enemy's batteries, and did not think it likely that this bridge would be used as I found afterwards it was for purposes of retreat. I then suggested to General Gordon, rather in a playful manner, that I predicted that the Confederate army would probably surrender about Chesterfield C.H. "No," said he, "We can do better than that." Very soon some members of his staff and other gentlemen came in and supper was prepared for all, after which the party left, all with haversacks well filled, the work of my wife's forethought. Mrs. Gordon and young "Johnny Reb" Gordon—less than a week old—were left with my wife and myself, the general requesting me to take the best care of them and of General Cook I could. As the party were leaving the clock struck twelve. Then came a stillness in our vicinity and over the city that was actually painful. Being a member of the city council, at one o'clock a.m. I walked down to the residence of the late D'Arcy Paul on Union street immediately south of St. Paul's church, at which place we had been summoned by the mayor to meet for the purpose of deliberating on the situation as to the best course to be pursued in meeting the issue, to wit, the enemy soon to take possession of the city. On my lonely walk from my house to Mr. Paul's at this hour of the morning the grave-yard stillness of everything seemed to raise the hair on my head. I could see no living being, man nor beast. No sound could I hear, not even the barking of a dog. What a contrast to the experiences of the preceding nine months, when it was rare that the booming of the artillery and the crack of the rifle along the lines was not heard both night and day! The extraordinary stillness of everything at this hour made the uncertainty of events which were to come with the approaching day extremely oppressive.

Upon reaching the house of Mr. Paul, who was one of the oldest and most prominent members of the council, I found most of the members already arrived. Very quiet arrangements were made for the meeting of the expected Federals. Not certain which of the several roads leading to the city they would come in, and indeed thinking it more than likely that they would come in by all roads leading in the city from Prince George and Dinwiddie counties—for the city was then completely encircled by their forces except on the north or Chesterfield side of the river—we deemed it prudent to divide our members in squads and so send some to meet the advancing Federals upon each avenue of approach to the city leading from the union lines. We accordingly sent squads to Bollingbrook, Lombard and Wythe to meet whatever force might come from an easterly direction, to South Sycamore and Harding streets to meet those who might advance from a southeasterly or southern direction, and to Halifax, Farmers and Washington streets those who might advance from a southwesterly or westerly direction.

To the late Alexander Donnan and myself fell the lot of going to Wythe street to meet those who might come by the avenue of approach, and just as the gray dawn of the morning was visible we were proceeding out that street and were nearing the bridge which crosses Lieutenant Run when we heard in front of us on the opposite hill in the neighborhood of Mr. Hannon's place (now Highland Terrace) the sound of voices breaking with yells the stillness of the early hour. We halted the party from whom these voices came and they demanded to know who we were: "Friends!" answered my companion, whilst I with my handkerchief improvised a white flag. Hearing our reply, they directed to us to stand still where we were till they came up. In a moment or two they had reached us. We informed them who we were and that General Lee and his army were then probably many miles away from Petersburg having evacuated the city the early part of the night. At this information they expressed great surprise and stated Grant expected to make a general attack all around the lines that morning, and that they were a squad, a sergeant and six men, from an Indiana regiment—the number of which I cannot now recall—which had been ordered to feel our picket line their immediate front at daylight, which having done, and having to their surprise found the advance Confederate works unoccupied, they had gone forward under like orders to our main line, to find the same condition of things there, and that they then came with a rush right along into the city, that they might be the first to capture Petersburg, as I have reason to believe they were.

Starting on up the hill towards Jefferson street they requested us to follow on and show them the principal streets, as they wished to capture any stragglers they might find. Doing as requested Mr. Donnan and myself proceeded with them to Sycamore and then up Oak Street to Market and thence down Market. Arriving at my house, I requested the party to wait a few moments until I could go in and inform the ladies as well as General Cook that there would be no disturbance of any kind. To this request they acceded and we then went up Washington Street as far as the Second Presbyterian church where they encountered the first Confederate, a poor fellow prostrate in the church yard and dead. We then went across to High Street and made a search in the hospital at the corner of High and Cross streets, and as they could find no Confederate there who was able to walk, no captures were made. We then requested them to turn their steps down High street and go to the courthouse, at which place, as they informed us they had been ordered to meet others of their particular command. The sun was now just rising, and as we reached Courthouse Avenue, looking up to the courthouse, we beheld the fixture of Madame Justice which surmounts the steeple enveloped in flags. Floating the stars and stripes in mute silence she appeared to have been suddenly "reconstructed." Another party of Federals had already reached this place and taken possession, and were displaying flags, big and little, from all parts of the building from foundation to steeple top. These decorations were indeed a striking and beautiful spectacle.

Introducing myself to the officer in command at the courthouse, I explained to him the situation of General Cook and Mrs. Gordon, and asked him to give me a safety guard. Complying readily with my request he gave me, and put me in charge of, the sergeant and squad of men whom Mr. Donnan and myself had been with all the morning as narrated. I was thus for the first and only time in my life in command of Federal troops. I marched them to my house and stationed them in the front yard, but it was not long before I gave them an order to charge on a good breakfast, an order which they readily obeyed, seeming to enjoy rebel rations very much.

A little while after breakfast the sergeant, hearing a noise in the direction of Halifax Street, said to his squad, "Men, fix bayonets!" In a few minutes the head of a dark column was visible up the street about Halifax, and Birney's command of Negro troops[11] came marching down Market street singing "John Brown's body lies mouldering in the ground." Things now began to assume a more serious aspect. The column halted on Market Street, a part of the troops right in front of my house. The street was full of them.

General Birney took possession of the residence of T. T. Brooks (now Mrs. Victoria Romaine's) then vacant, the family being away, doubtless intending to make it his headquarters.

Although the presence of the Negro troops created some apprehension among the citizens, still, with a few trifling exceptions, there was no disturbance or invasion of private premises. One little incident, however, came within my personal observation. Looking across the street to the front gate of my neighbor, Rev. A. J. Leavenworth, now the residence of Mr. John McGill, I observed him leading a Negro soldier by the collar from his premises and was informed by him that the intruder had invaded them under the pretext of getting a drink of water. Emboldened by Mr. Leavenworth's treatment of that trespasser, I ejected from my kitchen a little later in like manner a black fellow in uniform who was there without authority.

About half past nine o'clock we were relieved of the presence of the colored troops on Market street by the appearance of General Grant and President Lincoln on horseback riding from Washington street up Market street to the house of Mr. Thomas Wallace (now Mr. Simon Seward's) with a retinue of staff officers and couriers. Mr. Wallace invited the party into his front porch, where they sat for some time consulting their maps. The arrival of this distinguished party was soon followed by an order to General Birney to move on with his colored command, which was done by taking them westwardly up Washington Street.

These troops out of the way, they were quickly followed by white troops, who began to come in from all directions, it seemed, not only during Monday, but for several days subsequently, their fine equipments of all kinds being in striking contrast with those of the Confederates with whom our people had been so long familiar.

In a very short time peace and quiet reigned in our city, all uncertainty and apprehension as to the future disappearing.

Sutlers from the Federal army at once opened stores and it was sometimes

---

11. Williamson refers to General William Birney's Second Division, Twenty-fifth Corps, Army of the James. Son of famed antislavery advocate James G. Birney, William Birney served for four years in the Union army, the last two as commanding officer of various units of black troops. He left the army in August 1865 as a brevet major general.

amusing to witness the haste and scramble of all who could command a little ready money to purchase their first piece of cheese or package of genuine coffee. To needy families rations were liberally issued by the Federal authorities and thus much suffering was prevented.

Mrs. Gordon and "Johnny Reb" fared well with blue coats all around them until the return from the closing scene at Appomattox of their natural protector, while General Cook, receiving the medical attention of [a] Federal surgeon, and being visited in a social way by a number of Federal officers, no longer spoke of the "cussed Yankees," but, accepting the situation, soon recovered from his wounds sufficiently to return home.

Your Respectfully,

J. P. Williamson

ADDENDUM: STATEMENT OF WILLIAM E. MORRISON

[In a letter dated May 25, 1894, Mr. Wm. E. Morrison of Petersburg provided an account related to the Williamson story.[12]]

F. E. Coyle's Burial

The poor fellow dead in the yard of the Second Presbyterian Church to whom Mr. Williamson refers, was a member of the Washington Artillery, killed sometime during the previous day, whose body was left where Mr. Williamson saw it by some of his comrades whose orders to leave with the retiring forces of Gen. Lee gave them no time to bury the body of the dead soldier, but only time to place it in the church yard and to pin upon his breast a placard upon which was written in large bold characters the following—

F.E. Coyle,[13] 3rd Co. Washington Artillery. Killed at the front on Sunday. Some kind friend will please bury this man.

Stiff and stark against the wall of the church with this pathetic appeal for burial, sat this dead Confederate, his blanket rolled [*illegible word*]-fashion across his chest, his hands clasped across it, a stern and gruesome object.

12. The Bernard Collection at the Historical Society of Western Virginia contains Bernard's transcription of Morrison's original letter, prepared for publication. See also a 1902 manuscript of the recollections of Marie E. Morrison on "The Evacuation of Petersburg and the entrance of the Federal Army on April 3, 1865," housed at the University of Virginia Library. The manuscript, which is seven typed pages, contains a description of the burial of Private Frank E. Coyle.

13. Frank E. Coyle worked as a clerk in New Orleans before the war. He was wounded at Gettysburg on July 3, 1863 (Marie E. Morrison, Manuscript concerning the evacuation of Petersburg, 1902, Accession #10839, Albert and Shirley Small Special Collections Library, University of Virginia, Charlottesville, Va.).

The Rev. Churchill J. Gibson[14] at that time, as he did up to the date of his death, resided on Washington Street immediately opposite this church, and I, a refugee from my residence on Marshal Street, was temporarily occupying a house on Perry Street near Mrs. Gibson's. Having discovered the presence in the church yard of the body of the dead Confederate with its mute, but eloquent appeal for burial, Mr. Gibson came over and asked my assistance in burying him.

We then secured the further assistance of Mr. Wm. H. Lappey of Petersburg, and of a colored man, Jack Hill, the slave of Mrs. Julia E. Meade, who resided at the corner of Washington and Perry streets, and began the work of digging a grave in the church yard, Mr. Gibson assisting with his own hands.

By the time the work of digging the grave had been completed the troops of the Federal army had begun to pass the church in large numbers, going up Washington street. The grave being [in readiness], Mr. Gibson began the burial service of the Episcopal Church, and just as, in his sweet, sonorous voice, he uttered the impressive words—"For as much as it has pleased the Almighty God, in his wise providence, to take out of this world the souls of our deceased brother"—and we lifted the body wrapped in its blanket waiting for the words—

"We, therefore, commit his body to the ground." A Federal soldier, from his accent evidently a foreigner, lounged up to the fence near us and asked in drawling, contemptuous tones "Putting Johnnie in an ice house? Eh?" Taking no notice of this attempted interruption, Mr. Gibson calmly proceeded with the service, and the words "earth to earth, ashes to ashes, dust to dust," fell from his lips, a Federal officer, apparently of high rank, stepped up to the sidewalk, and probably ashamed of the heartless fellow who had just spoken, addressing our party, said, "A brave soldier, no doubt! Give him a soldier's burial, a blanket and a grave!" This was just as we lowered the body. Mr. Gibson, with a wave of his hand requested us not to proceed to fill the grave, and, taking the spade from my hands, handed it to the officer with these solemn and impressive words, "Yes! A brave soldier! Whom perhaps *you* killed! Would you not like to throw a few shovel-fulls of earth upon him?"

Tears sprang to the officer's eyes and, putting the brim of his hat down over his brows, he exclaimed, "My God! This brings war home to a man!

14. The Reverend Churchill J. Gibson founded Grace Protestant Episcopal Church in Petersburg and served as its rector for fifty years. His son, Robert, would follow his father into the ministry, and rise to the rank of bishop (see *Encyclopedia of Virginia Biography*, volume 4 [New York: Lewis Historical Publishing, 1915], 153).

Glory seems far away when the dead lie so near!" Saying no more, he moved quickly away from the fence where he had been standing.

Just at this juncture a company of Federal soldiers came marching along the street. The gallant officer in command, as did the heartless straggler and the tender-hearted officer above mentioned, also noticed what was going on at the church-yard, but in his brave breast, as in that of the officer who had been so moved by the spectacle, only chivalrous emotions were awakened by what he saw. Halting his men, he faced them to the burial party and at his command they came to a "present arms" and immediately thereafter resumed their line of march, all of this being done in silence, with no word uttered save those of the command under which this beautiful [tribute] of respect was paid by a noble officer and his men to a fallen foe. Of all the Southern soldiers who fell in defense of the Lost Cause, it is safe to say that, all the circumstances considered, none had a grander funeral or was buried by saintlier hands than F. E. Coyle of the Washington Artillery.

The body of this brave soldier lies buried, says Mrs. Jos. B. Jones, nee Miss Nancie Joynes, of Petersburg, Va. "with thirteen other members of the battalion in the Washington Artillery square in Blandford Cemetery, having been removed from its grave in the Presbyterian Church yard in the winter of 1868–9."

"A War Reminiscence,"
by C. W. Maynard[15]

In a Letter to a Citizen of Petersburg, a Federal Gives an Account of the First Troops that Came into the City in 1865.

The following letter written to Mr. J. P. Williamson, of this city will be read with much interest here.

Detroit, Mich.,
Jan. 28, 1906.

Mr. J. P. Williamson, Petersburg, Va.:

My Dear Sir,— In compliance with your request, I give you very briefly some information regarding the situation (on the Union side) during the last

---

15. Charles W. Maynard enlisted as a 1st sergeant in July 1862. Mustered into the 20th Michigan Infantry, he would serve for the duration of the war, earning promotion to 1st Lieutenant in January 1865. Maynard's letter was published in the *Petersburg Daily Index-Appeal* on February 4, 1906.

days of the Civil War, before Petersburg in 1865, and the occupation of the city by the "Yankees" after its evacuation on the night of April 2d.

During the winter of 1864–'5 the regiment of which I was a member—the Twentieth Michigan Infantry[16]—occupied "Battery 9," a small fort in the first Federal line of entrenchments around the city, which was situated close to the City Point road, midway between Fort McGilvery (near the Appomattox river) and Fort Stedman.

The regiment took an active part in the battle resulting from the skillfully planned attack on the brilliant capture of the latter fort by General Gordon on March 25th.

From that time there were frequent "alarms," and the men were almost constantly under arms. Some great impending event seemed to be "in the air." We knew not whether it was a rush to death against the formidable forts and breastworks in our front or a quick march to a bloodless victory.

Very early in the morning of April of 3d the regiments composing the Second Brigade, First Division, Ninth Army Corps, the First Michigan Infantry (my regiment), and two others formed in line, and as soon as it became light enough to see, led by Major C. A. Lounsberry (of the Twentieth Michigan), brigade staff officer, and preceded by the Second Michigan Infantry (also belonging to the brigade), deployed as skirmishers, the column marched up the City Point road into the city and halted in the courthouse yard. The Michigan regiments unfurled their colors from the cupola of the building.

The surrender of the city was made to Major Lounsberry,[17] representing the brigade commander, Colonel Ralph Ely[18] (a Michigan man), who joined his command at the courthouse later in the morning.

As soon as the excitement incident to the change in the situation had somewhat subsided, a provost guard was organized to patrol the city, pick up

16. The 20th Michigan Infantry was organized in 1862 and served with the Army of the Potomac, the Army and Department of Ohio, and the Department of the Tennessee. It served the last year of the war with the Army of the Potomac.

17. Clement A. Lounsberry enlisted in the Michigan 1st Infantry as a 1st sergeant in May 1861. Wounded and captured at the Battle of Bull Run, he was exchanged and returned to his unit. He mustered into the 20th Michigan Infantry in August 1862, and would serve mainly with that unit until the end of the war. He received steady promotions, rising to the rank of brevet colonel by March 1865.

18. Ralph Ely enlisted in August 1861 as a Captain of C Company, 8th Michigan Infantry. He rose through the ranks, reaching colonel by May 1864, and brevet brigadier general by April 1865. He commanded the Second Brigade, First Division, Ninth Corps, at the time of the occupation of Petersburg.

stragglers from both armies and to protect persons and property. No other Federal troops came into the city for several hours.

As you know, I was detailed as a safeguard at your residence during the night of April 3d, there being in the house at that time as your guest, the wife of General John B. Gordon, and the wounded Confederate General Phillip Cook, afterwards the Secretary of State of Georgia, whose son now occupies that position.

Recently learning through that distinguished lady, Mrs. Gordon, your name for the first time, the result has been the renewal of the acquaintance begun under such unpleasant circumstances and very interesting correspondence.

These lines are written on paper which I found on the desk in the courthouse the morning we entered the city, which I stamped with the seal of the "Mayor of Petersburg," and which after more than forty years is now returned to you. When the Grand Army men visited Petersburg 1892 they enjoyed the hospitality of A. P. Hill Camp of Confederates, and the writer—one of the number—who wore the blue takes this opportunity to extend greetings to the members of A. P. Hill Camp, who wore the gray.

Sincerely yours,

C. W. Maynard

Late First Lieutenant Twentieth

Regiment Michigan Infantry.

"Interesting Facts Connected with the Occupation of the City by the Federals following Evacuation in April, 1865," by G. W. Camp

Mr. G. W. Camp,[19] of Norfolk, sends in an interesting contribution to the *Index-Appeal*'s war literature as follows:

Noticing that Mr. J. P. Williamson will shortly give some recollections of the siege and surrender of Petersburg, I have thought that something from me would be of interest to your readers.

It was Saturday, March 31 [April 1], 1865, when it was whispered about

19. During the war, Camp served as Commissioner of the Revenue for Petersburg. Exempted from military service, he was a member of the Petersburg Home Guard, acting most of the time as assistant commissary. For several years after the war, he owned

that the city was to be evacuated; that the brave army of Confederate soldiers that for so many long and weary months had stood as a bulwark between the city and the federal troops, would march out of their fortifications and yield to the enemy that for which they had spent so much in blood and treasure to secure.

Sunday morning, April 1st,[20] was a day never to be forgotten. The air was balmy and the sun was bright, but the pall of death seemed to hang over the town. No church bells rang out their notes of invitation calling the worshippers to the house of prayer. The streets were filled with soldiers moving here and there. Dense columns of smoke were seen rising from tobacco warehouses and other places, whose contents were being burned by order of the Confederate government to prevent their falling into the hands of the enemy. Shells from Federal batteries were bursting in every direction. Pocahontas bridge, over which troops were passing and commissary wagons hurrying, was being heavily shelled, and in the neighborhood several persons were killed, among them a gentleman named Wilkinson, who carried on the business of a huckster.

All that day there was heavy fighting going on to the southwest of the city, the federals endeavoring to get possession of the Petersburg railroad and thus cut off all supplies from the south. As night came on, the excitement among the people increased; the streets were filled with passing troops. And citizens gathered on the corners discussing the situation and feeling that the star of the Confederacy was about to go down in the darkness of defeat, and knowing that in a few hours they would be at the mercy of the dreaded Yankees. There was no such thing as sleeping in Petersburg that night. Men, women and children waited with anxious hearts for the coming of the day, not knowing what was the lot in store for them.

FIRST FEDERALS TO ENTER

I well remember that just about daybreak on Monday [April 3] morning a company of Federal soldiers who had come into the city by the road south

---

the *Petersburg Daily Express,* the precursor to the *Daily Index-Appeal.* Camp was born in Petersburg in 1833 and lived there until 1877, when he moved to Norfolk, where he was employed as a bookkeeper and performed some newspaper work. He was a Methodist and a member of the Prohibitionist Party serving in the Common branch of the Norfolk City Council for a time. These and other details of Camp's life are found in a short letter written by Camp to Bernard on September 1, 1895 (see Bernard Papers, Southern Historical Collection, University of North Carolina). Camp's letter appeared in the *Petersburg Daily Index-Appeal* on June 10, 1894.

   20. It is likely that the author meant to refer to Sunday, April 2, here (not April 1).

of the water works, passed my house on Mars Street singing and shouting. I watched them from the window until they turned into Sycamore Street, and then followed them downtown to see what was to be done. They made for the courthouse, which had already been taken possession of by another detachment that came through the lines from a point near the river. There I found the United States flag floating from the courthouse steeple, it having been hung out through the face of the clock in which there was an opening. Soon the news was all over the town that the Yankees had come. The courthouse square was filled with them, and soldiers were at once sent out to order all the men to report at this place; as soon as they reached there they were put under arrest and told not to leave until they had further orders.

At that time I was Commissioner of Revenue and occupied the office which is now used by Mayor Collier. When I reached the building I found some Federal officers searching for a place to establish their headquarters. I handed them the key to my office and invited them to make themselves at home, which they did without much ceremony. Wishing some writing paper, I offered to go out and procure some for them, and they sent a soldier along with me to see that I was not arrested by the guards on the streets.

GAVE THE "YANK" BREAKFAST

It was then breakfast time, and not knowing when I would be released I proposed to my escort that if he would see me home I would give him a warm breakfast. To this he gladly assented and we were soon enjoying a meal of hot rolls made from flour costing seven hundred dollars per barrel, home made butter, coffee that was a mixture of the genuine article with sweet potatoes, and sorghum syrup that my wife says she paid fifty dollars a gallon for.

Hurrying back, I procured the stationery on the way and handed it over to the officers with an apology for my delay. I found them very kind and from one of them I got my first twenty-five cent greenback in exchange for a $1 Confederate note. My first investment was in a copy of the *New York Herald*, for which I paid ten cents, and I was soon seated on a curbstone eagerly reading the war news. It was about noon when the citizens were set at liberty, and when I reached home I found that my wife had been visited by some of these hated Yankees, who treated her respectfully and had left her a handful of greenbacks in exchange for corn bread and milk, of which they were very fond.

And so the much dreaded Yankees had come and were in full possession of the city, and I say to their credit that I do not think any one had cause to complain of any ill treatment at their hands. There were no acts of lawlessness. Private property was respected and from one end of the city to the other soldiers were stationed night and day and the best order was preserved. I am sure that I laid down and slept tranquilly at night when I could look out of my window and see a Federal soldier with his shouldered musket marching back and forth in front of my house.

CITIZENS GIVEN FOOD

Of course there was much destitution among our people. Confederate money was no longer of any use, and a peck of it would not buy a pound of meat. Of greenbacks there was none. But the people were not allowed to suffer. One of the first things done was the opening of a commissary, where, on application, the people, both white and black, were plentifully furnished, free of cost, with the same rations that were supplied to the United States troops. This was done for some time, just how many months I do not now remember; but it was not very long before Col. Martindale had the city council called together and the city government was turned over to the federals.

I think I was about the last man that ever paid money to the Confederate government. For about a year I had been acting as agent for the city selling government coal to the people, and at the end of each month I would settle with Major Wallack, who was the quartermaster at that time. When I saw the troops leaving the city, I hunted up the major and found him about midday on Sunday, April 1st, near the old canal basin, packing up his effects and getting ready to leave the city. I told him that I had money belonging to the government and wished him to take it. He at first refused, but at last consented, and I turned over to him $7,500—and took his receipt for the same.

CHRISTMAS DINNER, 1864

Will you allow me to give the menu for our dinner on Christmas day, 1864. We had black eyed peas and some fried strip bacon, corn bread, and milk, and for dessert my wife had gotten hold of some dried applies and with them she made some pies—and do you know we enjoyed that dinner about as much as any dinner we have had before or since then. I well remember this dinner, as the times were getting very tight, provisions were becoming very scare, and we sat down and gave thanks for what we had. I called over the bill of fare and said I wonder what it will be next Christmas. Thank God, before next Christmas the clouds of war had all rolled by and we had turkey with cranberry sauce, &c. But it was no more heartily enjoyed that was the plain fare of the Christmas before.

12

The Appomattox Campaign

O N A N A U T U M N E V E N I N G in 1897, George Bernard stood before the A. P. Hill Camp and read a letter from William Mahone describing the general's reminiscences of the Appomattox Campaign. Unlike many of the other "War Talks" slated for Bernard's second book, Mahone's letter never found its way into publication in the Petersburg papers. A version of the letter, however, was found in the collection of documents discovered in Roanoke in 2004. On the outside of this manuscript, Bernard had written the following note: "The within article, a transcript of General Mahone's original article marked 'A' hereto annexed, was carefully read over to, discussed with and signed by General Mahone. I was very much impressed by the original article which he read to me with great emphasis. Geo. S. Bernard, April 28, 1896." Mahone prepared the account in July 1895, just a few months before his death on October 8th of that same year.

In 1971, the *Civil War Times Illustrated* published a "previously unknown document" that contained Mahone's recollections of Appomattox but was undated and not addressed. William C. Davis, the editor of that article, speculated that Mahone had prepared it for James Longstreet, for use in the Georgian's memoirs. That letter, which is now housed at Auburn University, is nearly identical to the account transcribed by Bernard and read before the A. P. Hill Camp.[1]

---

1. See the *Petersburg Daily Index-Appeal* for October 8, 1897; see also William C. Davis, ed., "On the Road to Appomattox By Major General William Mahone," *Civil War Times Illustrated* 9 (January 1971): 5–47.

Mahone's recollections make for fascinating reading, but must be approached warily, especially his memory of conversations he had with General Robert E. Lee. In few of the conversations was a third party present, and one key time it was his friend and later fellow ex-Confederate pariah, James Longstreet. The most thorough recent study of the last days of the Army of Northern Virginia, William Marvel's *Lee's Last Retreat,* did not include a single one of these conversations, undoubtedly because they could not be corroborated. The conversations invariably present Mahone as strong, determined, loyal, yet realistic, reassuring Lee that the decision to surrender was right and necessary. He may have indeed conveyed such a message to Lee, but only he and Lee would know for sure. As editors of this document, we decided not to analyze each line of conversation, but rather keep with our policy of providing brief backgrounds on events and individuals noted by the speakers.

>-0-<+-I-<····>-I-+>-0-<

Bernard's Biographical Sketch of William Mahone[2]

Gen. William Mahone, born at Monroe, in Southampton County, Va., Dec'r 1, 1826, was educated at the Virginia Military Institute, from which he graduated in 1847; taught school for two years and then began the duties of his profession as a civil engineer as surveyor on the Orange and Alexandria railroad. Subsequently, he became [*illegible word*] the chief-engineer of the Fredericksburg and Orange plank road and chief-engineer of the Norfolk & Petersburg railroad. Upon the completion of the last mentioned roads he was elected president of the company, which position he held at the beginning of the war and continued to hold until 1871, when this road, the South Side railroad and the Virginia and Tennessee railroad was consolidated with the Atlanta, Mississippi & Ohio railroad.

Immediately after the secession of Virginia, the subject of this sketch was appointed by the "Virginia Council" chief-quartermaster of the Virginia forces. This position he held for about ten days, when he was appointed to lieutenant-colonel of infantry and assigned to the command of the post at Burwell's Bay, but, before he accepted this position was made colonel of the 6th Va. Infantry. A few weeks later Col. Mahone was appointed a brigadier-

2. This biographical sketch of Mahone was included as a footnote to Mahone's Appomattox letter located in the Bernard Collection at the Historical Society of Western Virginia.

general, receiving his commission from the Confederate States government, and placed in command of the troops of the Norfolk district, of the department of Norfolk, and so continued until the evacuation of the department in May, 1862.

From 1861 to 1864 Gen. Mahone continued in command of what was known as Mahone's brigade, of which the 6th, 12th, 16th, and 41st Virginia regiments were always members, and which up to some time in 1862 embraced also the 3rd Alabama regiment, and when the last mentioned regiment was transferred to another brigade had the 61st Virginia put in its place. Receiving a severe wound at the battle of 2nd Manassas, he was not with his command again until the battle of Fredericksburg.

In May, 1863, Gen. Mahone was elected a member of the state senate, but did not take his seat in this body until January, 1864, and then only for a few days. When Gen. Longstreet was wounded in the battle of the Wilderness on the 6th of May, 1864, Gen. R. H. Anderson was placed in command of his corps and Gen. Mahone in command of Anderson's division, which was composed of the five brigades of Mahone (Va.), Wright (Georgia), Harris (Miss.), Saunders' (Ala.) and Perry (Fla.). This division General Mahone continued to command until the surrender at Appomattox CH, receiving a few days after the battle of the Crater his commission as Major General dating from the engagement (July 30, 1864).

The war over, General Mahone again turned his attention to the business of railroading, was elected president of the Southern railroad, and also of the Virginia and Tennessee railroads and soon succeeded in consolidating these two railroads with the Norfolk and Petersburg railroad (of which he had been president for several years) and organizing the Atlanta, Mississippi & Ohio railroad, of which he became the president, which office he held until the road was sold in 1881.

During all of these years General Mahone was unquestionably the [*two illegible words*] man in Virginia. No one had more influence in shaping the public affairs of the commonwealth. In 1880 he was elected to a seat in the senate of the United States and served, as a member of that body from March 1881 to March 1887. In 1889 he was the Republican nominee for governor, but was defeated by Hon. Phil. W. McKinney.

William Mahone
(Prints and Photographs Division, Library of Congress)

"What I Saw and Heard during the Closing Days of the Army of Northern Virginia,"
by General Wm. Mahone

Petersburg, Va.
July 25th 1895

Geo. S. Bernard Esq.
Petersburg Va.
My Dear Sir:

In compliance with your request I will give you my recollection of what I saw and heard from the time of leaving Gen. Lee's line covering Richmond and Petersburg to the close of his army's career at Appomattox.

Mahone's division comprised of five brigades, the Alabama brigade under Brig. Gen. Wm. H. Forney, the Florida brigade under Col. David Lang, the Georgia brigade under Col. Geo. E. Tayloe, the Mississippi brigade under Brig Gen'l Nathaniel H. Harris and the Virginia brigade under Brig. Gen'l David A. Weisiger, on Sunday April 2, 1865 occupied that portion of the Confederate line between the James and the Appomattox rivers commonly called the "Chesterfield front."[3] The aggregate strength of the division at this time was something between thirty-five hundred and four thousand muskets.

3. The "Chesterfield front" strung across the portion of land between the James and Appomattox known as Bermuda Hundred.

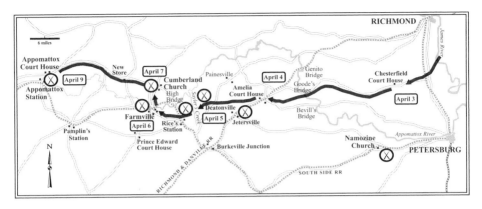

APPOMATTOX CAMPAIGN

On the night of April 1st, Gen. Lee, still holding his long line of defence, telegraphed me to know if I could spare him a brigade of my division. I immediately withdrew the Mississippi brigade from its position in my line and set it in motion to report directly to Gen'l. Lee at Petersburg about five miles away and notified him of this fact. This brigade reached Gen. Lee Sunday morning and a part of it took part in the heroic defense of Fort Gregg near the Boydton Plank road, within its walls the remainder of the brigade under the immediate command of Gen. Harris were otherwise engaged on the lines about this fort, and rejoined the division at Amelia Court House.

Sunday night I received orders direct from Gen. Lee (and from that time to the end all of my orders came direct from him) to retire at daylight the next morning for Amelia Court House, covering the rear of the troops from Richmond when I should reach the road from Richmond where it came into the county road leading from Chesterfield Court House to Goode's Bridge over the Appomattox.

The division moving under these orders reached Chesterfield Court House in the forenoon of Monday, the 3rd of April. I found the court-house grounds and the county road as I approached the court-house crowded with all manner of vehicles with men women and children who had fled from Petersburg in advance of the common foe. A brief halt was made at the place and the troops given opportunity to breakfast, whilst I busied myself in hurrying off and away such military wagons as had reached the place and also the retreating caravan of vehicles and noncombatants we had there encountered.

During the preceding night, when I had perfected the details for the retirement of the division and my telegraph operator was about to take up his instrument, an enquiry came from Commodore J. R. Tucker commanding at Drewry's Bluff to learn if I could tell him what was going on. I replied by referring him to the Secretary of the Navy. Shortly the commodore rejoined that he could not get at the secretary. I knew he could not—for I knew that the Departments at Richmond had already been abandoned, but my knowledge of the devotion of naval officers to rules of etiquette prompted me to make the suggestion I had. I then telegraphed the commodore that he had better send over to "Chaffin's" and find out what was going on there. In a little while he responded that every one at "Chaffin's" had gone, and asked that I would give him orders. I told him he was not under my command, but I would advise him to follow the movement of the troops on his right, and said to him that, if he would face his command around and march forward, he would reach Chesterfield Court House, for which point my division would quickly move. I further advised that his withdrawal be effected as quietly as possible and above all precautioned that the enemy be not advised of our withdrawal by the blowing up of his magazine or other like demonstrations. Curious enough, the head of my division had just reached Chester, about the dawn gray of morning when there came the deafening report of the terrific explosion of the magazine at Drewry's Bluff, lighting the heavens and fairly shaking the earth in all that region.

Shortly after my division reached Chesterfield Court House Commodore Tucker arrived with his naval battalion, containing about two hundred marines, well clad, armed with cutlasses and navy-revolvers, every man over six feet and the picture of perfect physical development and each frightfully loaded with a compactly filled tarpaulin.

Here one of the officers of the battalion, considerably under the influence of whiskey, seized and undertook to appropriate to his own use the riding horse of Maj. Drewry, whose battery on the 15th of May, 1862, had kept back the ironclad Galena and other vessels of the Federal fleet on their attack upon the fort at Drewry's Bluff badly disabling the Galena. At my command the lieutenant surrendered the horse.

Leaving the Court House, the division camped Monday night at Capt. Wm. G. Flournoy's[4] and the next night at Goode's Bridge immediately after crossing the Appomattox. Here I received an order from Gen. Lee, now at Amelia Court House, to communicate with General Dick Anderson and to proceed the next morning (Wednesday morning) to Amelia Court House, which was done.

In reaching Amelia Court House early Wednesday morning I reported in person to Gen. Lee, whom I found seated with Gen. Longstreet on the fringe

---

4. The transcript of Mahone's letter at Auburn University refers to a Captain "Murray" in this sentence. The letter transcribed by Bernard says "Flournoy."

of a small oat-field near the Court House. Gen. Longstreet gave me his seat and went off to attend to some business. The chat with Gen. Lee was pleasant. I noticed that he was in full uniform save the yellow sash. He was wearing his best clothes, and equipments, his gold spurs and magnificent sword and belt included. I was impressed with the idea that he anticipated some accident to himself and desired to be found in that dress.

Our beloved corps-commander, Lieut.-General A. P. Hill, had been killed on [Sunday] morning on the lines near Petersburg, and was not with us. Whilst Gen. Lee was sitting as above described the other two division commanders[5] of Hill's corps came up, and, after saluting Gen. Lee, desired to know to whom they should report. Without responding to the salutation, Gen. Lee pointing to some wagons near the Courthouse, exclaimed, "Gentleman, whose wagons are those? Send your staff wagons to the wagon-train. Depend on your haversacks as I shall do. Report to Gen. Longstreet."

In a short while the army left the Court House, Gen. Longstreet taking a by-road diverging from the public road and leading southwardly to the Richmond & Danville railroad. I passed this diverging road and had proceeded but a short distance when I came upon the wagon-train. Here I found Gen. Lee, who informed me of my mistake and suggested that I turn back and take the road Gen. Longstreet had gone. This was done and it was not long before I found that some Federal cavalry had intervened. They were quickly driven off, but not out of the way, and my division united with the rear of the column. Gen. Longstreet had men up against the Federal cavalry at Jetersville. Gen. Lee sent for me to come to him. I found him near Gen. Longstreet's line of battle on the porch of a farm-house. He got out his map and wanted to know what I thought of pressing the fight. It was near sun-down—quite sun-down in fact. I argued that it was too late in the evening to effect results and that his army was not sufficiently compact to deliver a telling blow—that we should diverge to the right, and, as soon as could be done, get the army as compactly together as it could be and then turn upon the enemy and give him a stunning blow and then hasten on our march.

To this Gen. Lee agreed and directed me to take the diverging road to the north leading by Amelia Springs. I came after a short march along this road to a stream the bridge on which had given away. A pioneer corps were engaged in repairing the bridge. This necessitated a halt of my division, which was ordered to rest, the troops to remain in their places.[6]

---

5. These two division commanders were Henry Heth and Cadmus Wilcox.

6. One or more of these meetings with Lee may have occurred, though William Marvel does not mention any of these meetings between Lee and Mahone in *Lee's Last*

After the bridge had been repaired, the leading brigadier, acting improperly under the orders of a staff officer of Gen. Lee's staff, gave the order "forward" but failed to send word back along the line and have the troops then asleep waked up. So he proceeded with only a few troops following. I was at the time a little way off the road at a farmhouse where I had gone to get something to eat and to this place, the same staff-officer came and said to me "Gen. Lee says, 'Move on,'" and after drawing upon a bottle of "pine-top" whiskey left. I then without supper—for I was too much exhausted to prefer food to sleep and had been asleep on the floor of a room in the house—proceeded to the place where I had left the head of the division, to find it gone. I followed in the direction I supposed it had moved, soon overtaking a small body of straggling troops, the brigadier-general above referred to at their head proceeding along as though he headed a well closed division. I halted the command at once and sent back details to wake up the remainder of the division and bring it forward, and censured the brigadier-general for his un-officer like conduct and warned him that, as long as I commanded the division, he must not again take orders from any other authority. For the first time during the war, I had a straggling command, and this was brought about by the unwarrantable interference of a staff-officer. During the night, Gen. Lee sent me a note in which he said he was sorry to hear my division was straggling, to which I replied that this was true for the first time, but was due entirely to the improper interference of a member of his staff and that, if that officer repeated the like, he (Gen. Lee) would be short a staff-officer.[7]

My division being again collected together and put in motion, it proceeded on its march in the usual good order, passing the wagon-train and closing up on the column which had halted at Sailor's Creek. It being now after daylight Thursday morning, I got a meager breakfast from my saddle-bags carried by a courier, dividing with Gen. Pickett.

It was not long before Gen. Lee sent for me to press the ordnance-wagons and artillery intervening and come with my division to the front where Gen. Longstreet was now, at Rice's Station, engaged with the enemy who had crossed his path. On the way, I found Gen. Lee at the junction of the [wood-

---

Retreat: The Flight to Appomattox (Chapel Hill: University of North Carolina Press, 2002), 53–63.

7. The transcript of Mahone's letter at Auburn University identifies that staff officer as Charles Marshall. Bernard's version of the letter does not refer to the officer by name. Marshall, a lawyer in Baltimore, Maryland, before and after the war, served as one of Lee's aides for much of the war (see Robert E. L. Krick, *Staff Officers in Gray: A Biographical Register of Staff Officers in the Army of Northern Virginia* [Chapel Hill: University of North Carolina Press, 2003], 254).

road we were on and a blind-road] leading towards the enemy. He asked for a brigade to be detached and sent from this [blind road]. I detached the Florida brigade and he sent it down this road, and I never saw the brigade any more. It was captured, as I afterwards learned.[8]

Sometime after reaching Rice's Station, where Gen. Longstreet was engaged with the enemy slightly, Gen. Lee, now that Gen. Longstreet was being more vigorously pressed, ordered me up to his support and as we were moving up in line of battle to reinforce Gen. Longstreet, Gen. Lee, riding along with me, complained that I should not have gotten mad at the conduct of his staff-officer and written him (Gen. Lee) as I had done. I reasserted by criticism of the staff-officer's interference with my division and my purpose not to permit it again. Just then Col. Venable of Gen. Lee's staff rode up and enquired of Gen. Lee if he had received the message he (Col. Venable) had a short while before sent him. Gen. Lee said he had not and then Col. Venable told him that the message was that the enemy had captured the Confederate wagon-train at Sailor's Creek. Gen. Lee exclaimed, "Where is Ewell? And where is Anderson? It is strange I can not hear from them." Lieut.-Gen. Ewell commanded the reserves brought up from Richmond and Lieut. Gen. (temporary-rank) Anderson perhaps commanded two divisions. These commands were in the rear of our column and with the exception of some portion of Gen. Anderson's command (which had been dispersed) had been captured at Sailor's Creek on this day (Thursday, April 6th). Gen. Lee then turned to me and said, "Gen. Mahone, I have no other troops and you will have to go to Sailor's Creek." At once the division, then in line of battle, was faced to the left and by the left flank moved in the direction of Sailor's Creek. Gen. Lee rode along with me and saw some of our fleeing troops hotly pursued by Federal cavalry on the road I had recently passed over. Reaching the high ground over looking the open ground bordering upon Sailor's Creek, a sluggish little stream flowing northwardly into the Appomattox, we had a commanding view of the situation, and the scene beggars description. Gen. Lee, surveying the field and straightening himself in the saddle, looking more of the soldier, if possible, than ever, exclaimed, as if to himself, "My God! Has this army dissolved!" Recovering self-control, for the moment lost, I replied, "No, General, Here is a division ready to do its duty." Returning to himself, Gen. Lee said "Yes, General, there are some true men left."

8. The historian William Marvel confirms that Lee gave this order to Mahone and that the Florida brigade was indeed captured, accounting for many of the "missing" officially reported by Mahone after the war (see Marvel, *Lee's Last Retreat,* 78–80, 256n27, 257n30).

From this elevated position overlooking Sailor's Creek, we could see the massive columns of the enemy's infantry deploying in good order on the opposite side of the fields as if to prepare for an attack or to guard against a resolute assault, while below and on the main road which the wagon-trains had been travelling, where it crossed this stream, could be heard a single piece of artillery firing. Gen. Lee thought, as I did, that Gen. Gordon was there resisting the advance of the Federals, but this was not so, for Gen. Gordon, with whatever force he commanded, had gone on. The force we heard engaged turned out to be Gen. Rooney Lee's cavalry.

As Gen. Robert E. Lee sat upon his horse—the finest specimen of physical manhood I ever saw—and beheld the scene before him approaching, and heard of people, not soldiers—for but few of them carried arms—fleeing from the enemy, he said to me, "Gen. Mahone, will you keep those people back?" He always spoke of the Federals as "those people." My division was quickly placed in line of battle, although it was apparent to me that the enemy did not mean, and would not be likely to, make any further advance that evening as it was too late in the evening—nearing twilight. Meanwhile the herd of fleeing people, men without guns, many without hats, all mingled with teamsters riding their mules with dangling traces, a Confederate flag here and there, had surrounded Gen. Lee and were hallowing, "Hurrah for Gen'l Lee!" I turned to him, to find him holding up a battle-flag as if to rally and encourage this herd to a sense of duty. I rode up and said, "General, give me that flag. These people here are in my way. There is no fight in them. Let them be gone to the rear." He then handed me the flag, saying, "That is true, general."

In a few minutes I saw in the tail-end of the fleeing rabble my old division commander, Gen. Dick Anderson, who had been a popular commander, enjoying the highest confidence of the authorities and who had illustrated his undoubted courage on many fields, having heard Gen. Lee say that it was strange that he could not hear from Ewell or his division, I rode down and met Gen. Anderson. I discovered at once that he had lost heart in the cause. "Gen. Lee wishes to see you, General Anderson." When we came up to Gen. Lee, I said, "General Lee, here is General Anderson." Without turning his head towards Gen. Anderson, Gen. Lee, with severe emphasis, said, "General Anderson, take command of these stragglers and go to the rear," signifying the emphasis by a violent sling of his left arm towards the rear. Gen. Anderson rode on, the herd following him.

Shortly after this Gen. Lee called me to his side and said, "General Mahone, you know the country. How are we to get away from here?" I told him I knew nothing of that region. "But," he rejoined, "did you not build the railroad?" meaning the South Side railroad. I answered that I did not and that no such blunder as the location and construction of this road attached to my record. I said, however, "General, I know where I am and already take in the geographical features of the country, so that I am quite certain as to the course of the Appomattox, but a short distance away, the location of the High Bridge and of Farmville." I further said that, if Gen. Longstreet, whom we had left at Rice's Station, would follow the road he was on, it would take him to Farmville and that I could march through the woods and strike the High Bridge. Gen. Lee then said that he would rejoin Gen. Longstreet and take him to Farmville and that I must leave the place where we then were overlooking the field at Sailor's Creek and cross the river at the High Bridge. I enquired what I should do after crossing the river. Gen. Lee's reply was, "Exercise your judgment."

As the enemy was in close pursuit, I desired to know what should be done with the High Bridge and the temporary bridge below used for wagons after I should have crossed. "Burn them," replied Gen. Lee. I suggested that the destruction of one span of the High Bridge, a prodigious structure, would as effectively delay the enemy for our purpose as burning of the bridge and asked him to call upon Col. T. M. R. Talcott[9] (who was on the high-ground a few paces from Gen. Lee) commanding a regiment of pioneers, and himself charged this officer with the work of destroying the bridge. This Gen. Lee did and his instructions were explicit to destroy the bridges at day light—one span only of the High Bridge to be destroyed. He then left for Gen. Longstreet.

I then rode down the road eastwardly to go where I supposed Gen. Gordon was and had been fronting the enemy. I quickly met Gen. Rooney Lee with his cavalry retiring. It was now a little after dark. I halted Gen. (Rooney) Lee, but he protested that we should get away as the enemy were upon us with overwhelming force. "No," said I, "General Lee, your father says we must keep these people back, and really there is no danger they will not come any further tonight." So, he halted his command, and we remained at this place several hours, meanwhile being treated to a warm meal at a hospitable farm house near by. After this supper, Gen. Lee with his cavalry took the road to Farmville, and under the guidance of a colored man I marched my division through the woods to the High Bridge. Reaching the bridge, I found the railroad and the temporary wagon bridge below firmly guarded by sentinels posted at each, with orders from Gen. Anderson to allow no one and no thing

9. Born in Philadelphia, Colonel Talcott served in a number of staff positions, including aide-de-camp for General Robert E. Lee for over a year, before receiving command of the 1st Confederate States Engineers on April 1, 1864. He died in 1920 and is buried in Hollywood Cemetery in Richmond.

to cross. I further found that the grounds in the immediate vicinity of the wagon bridge on the east side of the river were filled with a miscellaneous caravan, including some few ambulances, some pieces of artillery, some wagons, and the herd of stragglers already referred to.

My first effort was to find Gen. Anderson, and, failing, my mind was made up to take possession of the bridges, if to do so it should be necessary to shoot down the sentinels. But my effort to find Gen. Anderson was successful. I found him a little way off from the bridge in consultation with Gen. Gordon. I was asked to dismount and join them, with the statement that they were discussing the situation. I said that before I did so I wished Gen. Anderson to change his instructions to the sentinels at the bridge, so that my division might cross the river by the railroad-bridge, whilst the caravan below might cross by the wagon-bridge. Gen. Anderson replied that Gen. Lee had ordered him to collect the stragglers. "Yes," I rejoined, "but I would be as well to collect them on the opposite side of the river, as we may reasonably expect the enemy to be here at the dawn of the day." Gen. Anderson then changed his instructions to the sentinels and my division crossed, as did the caravan—the troops by the railroad bridge.

After the division started to cross, I returned to the place when I found Generals Anderson and Gordon, and the consultation was resumed. They expressed the opinion that our army had gone so fully to pieces that the time had come for a surrender and desired to know what I thought. My answer was that, as a Confederate officer, I might venture to say that I had seen what had happened at Sailor's Creek and that, whilst I should follow the flag so long as there was a man to command, our army, I felt that our cause was lost and suggested that, with their views, as Gen. Anderson was the next ranking officer to Gen. Longstreet, he, Gen. Anderson should proceed at once to see Gen. Longstreet and state the situation to him and suggest that he see Gen. Lee and ask that he, Gen. Lee, delegate the situation and its treatment to his officers. This programme was agreed to and Gen. Anderson was to start right away for Gen. Longstreet. That he ever saw Gen. Longstreet on the subject I do not know. At this conference, brought about as I have explained, I made known Gen. Lee's instructions to Col. Talcott about the burning of the bridges. What command Genl. Gordon had or where it was, I never knew. I urged and it was agreed that he, Gen. Gordon, should detail a staff-officer to see that Col. Talcott executed Gen. Lee's order as to the destruction of the bridges for I knew the enemy would be upon our heels early the next morning and that it was all important to our retreating army to impede his progress.

I left and after parking (so to speak) the division on the opposite side of the river, I spent the balance of the night in exploring the country for roads, returning to the division just as the sun could be seen, to find that the bridges had not yet been fired and that the Federal skirmishers were rushing upon them. They were fired at once and I had to send in a brigade to cover the work. I remember to have seen just at this time Gen. Gordon sitting at the rear end of his wagon shaving himself and saw him no more after this.[10]

I took the road leading to Cumberland Church, and, reaching this place, found Gen. Anderson and the caravan with many additions, among them Col. Thos. H Carter's[11] battalion of artillery which had actually parked, un-hitched and was feeding. I hurried Col. Carter forward, and, like the gallant soldier he was, he promptly moved on, taking the road leading to Lynchburg, as did the caravan under Gen. Anderson. I knew the enemy would be where we then were shortly and got my division in line of battle. The division then numbered, I suppose, some three thousand muskets and the troops had lost none of their discipline and willingness to do duty. The line was short and did not cover the ground I desired. So I had to prolong it by placing Col. W. T. Poague's battalion of artillery on my right; Col. Poague[12] was a splendid officer. I had not fairly gotten the whole line into position before Col. Taylor[13] of Gen. Lee's staff bore me a message from Gen. Lee at Farmville directing me to do precisely what I had done and Gen. Miles[14] came up and

10. Mahone goes to great lengths to exonerate himself from any responsibility for the failure to destroy High Bridge and the wagon bridge nearby. Talcott, the engineer in charge of the destruction, had a different memory of the event, and Marvel sides with his version in *Lee's Last Retreat,* 121–22 (Talcott's version had no role for Gordon; Talcott had simply waited for orders from Mahone, which came too late).

11. Thomas H. Carter joined the King William Artillery as a captain in June 1861, and never left the artillery after that. He rose to the rank of colonel, and commanded artillery battalions or divisions in the East until the end of the war.

12. GSB: Lt. Col. Wm. T. Poague. [William Thomas Poague was another highly respected artillery officer. He served for four years in the Army of Northern Virginia, rising from 2nd lieutenant to lieutenant colonel. He saw action in all the major battles fought in the East, and surrendered with his unit at Appomattox.]

13. Walter Taylor was General Lee's adjutant for four years, and proved to be an invaluable source on Lee and his command after the war, especially in his work, *Four Years with General Lee,* published in 1877.

14. Nelson Miles was that rare individual in the Union army who never attended a military academy yet rose from 1st lieutenant in the 22nd Massachusetts Volunteer Infantry to major general of volunteers. When the Regular Army was reorganized in 1866, Miles was appointed colonel of the 40th U.S. Infantry (a new unit, comprised of black troops). He would stay in the army through the Spanish American War, ultimately achieving the rank of lieutenant general. He fought in most of the major battles in the Eastern theater, including the pursuit of the Army of Northern Virginia to Appomattox.

made a direct, but feeble, attack on my front, which was easily repulsed. Subsequently, seeing that Poague was unsupported by infantry, the enemy made an attack with a strong skirmish line upon Poague's guns and for a few moments held them, but in the nick of time I caught up a body of North Carolina troops, of Grimes'[15] division I think, which just had come from Farmville and flung them in upon the enemy and quickly recaptured the captured guns. Meanwhile, Gen. Longstreet came up and took position on our right.

Later in the day, Gen. Miles turned my left, unprotected, with a brigade of Federals. I saw the movement and sent to Gen. Longstreet's for two brigades. Fortunately one reached me in time. The Federal brigade had gotten around to the rear of my left flank and were forming into the rear of my line, when with the brigade from Gen. Longstreet I cut them off and quite annihilated the command in its attempt to get back. This closed the fighting at Cumberland Church, which took place during the afternoon of Friday, the 7th.[16]

Night came on and about eleven o'clock we left our position where we had been remaining in line of battle and marched all night over a terribly muddy road. Whilst, we were at Cumberland Church, some time after night-fall, the enemy sent in a flag-of-truce. Capt. Jno R. Patterson, the provost-marshall of my division, who had been serving on my staff since the morning of April 2nd was sent out to receive the flag and brought from Gen. Miles two things— one a letter from Gen. Grant to Gen. Lee, the other my wife's miniature. The letter turned out to be Grant's first letter to Lee where in he suggested that the time had come when the latter should end the unhappy struggle by the surrender of his army. After handing me the letter, Capt. Patterson said, "I have something for you with the compliments of Gen. Miles." I replied, "Captain, hold on I have a presentiment and can tell you what it is. It is my wife's daguerreotype." Straight away he took from the breast-pocket of his coat the miniature and handed it me. I said, "Gen. Miles' command got my wagon. It was not burnt." This miniature was in my trunk, in the top of which I had two hundred and sixty five thousand dollars in the brand new Confederate notes. I returned to Gen. Miles my card of thanks for the courtesy.

We marched all of next day, Saturday, the 8th, and went into camp late in the afternoon near Appomattox Court House in the most god-forsaken

15. Bryan Grimes began the war as a major in the 4th North Carolina infantry, and ended the war as a major general. He commanded troops in most of the major battles fought in the East, and was present at the surrender at Appomattox.

16. For a more detailed description of the fighting at Cumberland Church, see Chris M. Calkins, *Thirty-Six Hours before Appomattox: The Battles of Sayler's Creek, High Bridge, Farmville, and Cumberland Church* (Farmville, Va.: Farmville Herald, 1998), 53; and Marvel, *Lee's Last Retreat*, 127–32.

neighborhood one can well conceive of. My headquarters were in a miserable log hut occupied by a family of deformed people, whom it made one shudder to behold, whose deformity and forlorn condition forcibly suggested that we were nearing the end. My wagon, which had fallen into the enemy's hands, was rich with supplies for a campaign—a store house of all that one needed for sustenance and comfort. My cow had also been captured and we had no rations. Altogether things were far from comfortable. The bed in the miserable cabin we were occupying was only about four feet long. I spread my oil-cloth upon it and sought rest.

Whilst at this place I received a copy of an order from Gen. Lee assigning "the remnant"—this was the language—of Pickett's division to Mahone's division.[17] The only man of this "remnant" I ever saw was the quarter-master of the division, who reported to me the next day whilst Gen. Lee was on his way to meet Gen. Grant to negotiate about the surrender of the army. When the quarter-master reported—a major—I directed a courier to take him down to the line and gave him a musket, as I had no use for quarter-masters. I never saw him again.

The next morning, Sunday, the 9th, we started off a little before day break and about sunrise the column was halted. Shortly afterwards a courier came from Gen. Lee summoning me to him. I found Gen. Lee with Gen. Longstreet and the former's staff, about midway the column, surrounding a fence-rail fire. The morning was chilly. To find Gen. Lee around a fence-rail fire excited my suspicion for he had always been scrupulously particular to enforce respect for private property. Gen. Lee asked his staff to retire. He then said, "General Mahone, you know that I always send for you when I am in trouble." "What is the matter now, general?" was my reply. "General Grant," said he, "has demanded surrender of the army and I want to know what you think about it." My reply was, "Let me warm, for my teeth may chatter and you may think I'm scared." The truth is I had passed that possible condition. Gen. Lee responded, "Certainly! Warm!" I did so, thoroughly, and rose. Gen. Lee then added, "You know there are but two organized bodies of troops in the army—your division and Field's and only about eight thousand muskets." I said, "I presume your object is a junction with Gen. Johnston in Weldon, North Carolina." "Yes," he replied. Then I said, "This army is entitled to the

17. Controversy has existed since 1865 concerning Lee's dismissal (or lack thereof) of three leading Confederate generals—Richard Anderson, Bushrod Johnson, and George Pickett—in the last few days of the war. Marvel unravels the history of this episode in appendix C of *Lee's Last Retreat,* 214–17. He states unequivocally that no written order has ever been found dismissing Johnson and Pickett, nor any written order transferring Pickett to Mahone's command.

most honorable terms—to be paroled here and go to their homes—officers with their side-arms and officers and men with their personal property. If such terms are proffered, then, General Lee, you are called upon to discharge the most painful and yet the highest duty that can devolve upon the commander of an army. I sympathize with you in this supreme trial as much as man can, while no man [can] measure the anguish to you of the moment. It is your duty to surrender upon such terms. It would be criminal indeed, murder to sacrifice another life in this hopeless cause. You have now the best men that ever followed a commander, save those who have fallen a glorious sacrifice to the cause. They will cut through the enemy's line of battle now across your path, but what then? Harassing pursuit will follow, and when you reach Johnston how are you to recruit your army and to supply it? No, sir, it is your duty to surrender, if the terms indicated are accorded. The Confederate government is now fleeing. Confidence in the cause had gone—hope has given place to despair. You are abandoning square miles of country, women, children, non-combatants to the incidental hardships, and severities which accompany an invading army." This in substance, if not in words, is *what* I said, as I now recall it. At this juncture, Gen. Lee handed a letter he had received from Gen. Grant.

I read the letter and thought it was not clear whether we were to be paroled to go to our homes or to prison, and I urged that Gen. Lee go to Gen. Grant and settle the matter, and suggested that, if satisfactory terms were not accorded, we would fight it out on that field. Gen. Lee now said to Gen. Longstreet—who was all the time during the interview standing by leaning one arm on a sapling and regaling on a *dry* smoke—"What do you say. General Longstreet?" "I agree with Mahone," was the laconic response of the war-worn hero. "But," said Gen. Lee, "What will the country think of me?" My response was: "The country will approve whatever you do. Go to Grant." He expressed fear that it was too late and that he would be unable to find Grant. I suggested that it was not too late to make the effort and that there was his horse, and straightaway he mounted and started to find Gen. Grant, saying, as he did so, "General Longstreet, you will take command.[18]

18. GSB: In his statement already referred to Capt. Jn. R. Patterson says:

"Early in the morning of the surrender Gen. Mahone informed me that Gen. Lee had sent for him, and I rode with him to Gen. Lee. Reaching Gen. L. we found Gen. Longstreet with him. Gen. Mahone joined them and they had quite a conference. Whilst this was going on, I was talking with some of Gen. Lee's staff, a few paces off, out of hearing of what was being said by the three generals who alone constituted the conference. No other person being present. After the conference was over, as Gen. Mahone and I rode back to our division he informed me that Gen. Grant had made a demand

There was now a truce proceeding on the front, in the direction of Appomattox Court House west of us. Gen. Longstreet, however, directed me to place my division in line of battle facing the north. Gen. Field's division covered the rear. As soon as I ordered my division to its position, I saw Gen. Field and suggested that he send out a flag as the enemy would soon be upon us and a collision should be avoided. I informed him that there was a flag of truce to our front towards Appomattox Court House. He desired to know what was up. I replied that he must draw his own inferences.

As soon as my troops were in line, they began to entrench as was the custom. They were full of spirit and eager to have a chance at Sheridan. I ordered that the entrenching be stopped. The men began to look at each other as if startled by a suspicion of what was going to happen. They seized each other and in tears and anguish gave vent to their disappointment. Officers would run the blades of their swords into the ground and break them off and men their bayonets, till the scene was too much for me and I had to ride off. Subsequently and when our army was now surrounded by "Yellow Jackets"—as we were wont to call the Federal cavalry—I rode forward to see what was going on at the front and there I found Gen. Lee on the roadside near a little stream not far from the Court House, standing by himself and some of his staff fifty or sixty feet away. Exchanging compliments with Gen. Lee, I passed on to his staff. A few minutes later there came hurriedly a Federal officer, with a courier following, from the direction of the Court House. Nearing Gen. Lee, when about one hundred feet from him, this officer dismounted and then approached still nearer and when about thirty feet from Gen. Lee halted and formally saluted the general, placing his cap under his left arm. Col. Taylor, of Gen. Lee's staff, was directed to approach the Federal officer and did so. With

---

upon Gen. Lee for a surrender, and that, Gen. Lee would accede to the demand provided the officers were allowed to retain their side arms and private property, and if this were not agreed to Gen. Lee would cut his army out with what he could. Perhaps Gen. M. said that Gen. Lee would insist that the men also should be given the privilege of retaining their personal property but this I do not recall.

"Whilst I was talking with members of Lee's staff as above mentioned one of them said 'I am going to get out of here some way. There is going to be some tall hanging here today!' As we rode along I told this to Gen. Mahone. 'Hang, hell!' he replied. 'They won't hurt the hair of a man's head.'"

In this connection I should mention that in a supplemental statement furnished by Gen. Mahone in August 1895, he states that Gen. Henry A Wise told him at Appomattox C.H. that, before the surrender had actually taken place, Gen. Lee sent for him (Gen. W.) and said that as he (Wise) was very objectionable to the Federal authorities, he (W) was at liberty to take care of himself and that his (W's) reply to Gen. Lee was that he wanted to share the fate of his men.

some note or message he returned to Gen. Lee and quickly returned to the Federal officer with a reply. The latter again saluted Gen. Lee, put on his cap, returned to his horse, re-mounted and departed in the direction where he came. A little while later the same Federal officer returned and went through the same graceful and respectful salutations when approaching Gen. Lee. The note he bore was received by the same staff-officer and the answer returned as on the first visit, upon which the Federal officer, repeating his salutation to Gen. Lee, departed as before. Gen. Lee then tore what appeared to be the note he had received into many pieces and deliberately stamped them into the ground. He now mounted his horse and with a staff-officer rode off in the direction in which the Federal officer had come and gone. I was greatly impressed by these interviews between Gen. Lee and the Federal officer in which the graceful and truly officer-like conduct of the latter were no less conspicuous than the dignified bearing of Gen. Lee.

After the completion of the details of the surrender, I went over to the headquarters of Gen. Lee to bid him goodbye. I sat with him in the front part of his tent. He was obviously full of grief, offering, however, no outward sign except the watering eye. He said that Gen. Meade had just left his head-quarters and that this Federal general was greatly surprised to learn that the effective force of the Confederate army at the time of the evacuation of the lines covering Richmond and Petersburg did not exceed thirty-six thousand men of all arms and that he, Gen. Meade, had never estimated it at less than sixty thousand. Gen. Lee then remarked that he had advised the Confederate authorities at the start that the contest on which we had entered could not be over-estimated and that our chance to win was to be found by throwing the whole military or fighting power of the Confederacy vigorously into the struggle, which, whilst not saying so, he manifestly thought had not been done.

He further said that, in the winter preceding the evacuation, he advised Mr. Davis to make terms, as it well would be impossible when the spring came and the campaign opened for him, Gen. Lee, to get away with his army. The roads being bad and transportation inferior, whilst the army confronting him was full-handed and fresh, with every means of earnest pursuit at hand.

To these arguments Mr. Davis, he said, replied "No, you must fight."

I then suggested to Gen. Lee that just there he had made a mistake, that he was in fact the Confederacy, enjoying the affectionate confidence of all, that there was of it, and he should have taken matters in his own hands, held a conference with officers and told them the situation, and that they would have commissioned him on behalf of the army to see Grant and effect a settle-ment. His reply was, "But there was the government at Richmond." I said, "Yes, and I would have taken my division over there and dispersed it."

He asked me what we should do now, my answer, prompted by the emotions natural under such circumstances, for no man could have been more ardently desirous of dissolving the nation, was, that if any uninhabited place could be found, I would wish that all of us, followers of the Confederate cause, could make it and there eke out an existence as best we might. "But," said Gen. Lee, "as this plan could not be carried out, we should all go home, respect the Government and obey the law," and I have no reason to suspect that he ever entertained any other thought. He was the most perfect specimen of manhood and the proudest man I ever saw. He had no appreciation of a joke. He was polite, but stern and matter of fact in all things. His long service in the regular army had filled him with a reverence for authority and a rigid respect for rules and regulations which were unfortunate and hurtful for one in command of an army of revolution. He should have gone to the field unfettered and his will should have been the law.[19]

Yours Truly,
Mahone

"Some Recollection of Service by One Who Claims to Have Been the Youngest Confederate Who Surrendered at Appomattox,"
by Walter N. Jones

An Address Delivered before the A. P. Hill Camp of Confederate Veterans of Petersburg Va. on the Evening of Thursday, April 5, 1894

[Walter M. Jones was born in Manchester, Virginia, on August 3, 1850. After the death of his parents, he lived with his uncle Dr. Francis T. Jones of Gloucester, then moved to Dinwiddie County. In early 1864, he took a job as a clerk in a wholesale grocer in Petersburg. After the war, he continued to work in the grocery business and, at the age of nineteen, opened his own business in Richmond as a grocer and commission merchant, under the name of Lorraine & Jones. He continued in mercantile and manufacturing enterprises in Richmond and Petersburg. Walter N. Jones married the daughter

19. The second-to-last sentence in the paragraph of Bernard's transcribed letter appears to contain the word "revolution." The letter at Auburn University has the word "volunteers." Fittingly, we used the Bernard version. Bernard included an "Addendum" to Mahone's letter containing an excerpt from Fitzhugh Lee's report from the *Official Records*. This excerpt has been omitted.

of B. B. Vaughan, whose account of the Overland Campaign is included in chapter 6.[20]]

Comrades:

The commander of our camp has requested me to give you my experiences, as a boy volunteer, in the battle of Thursday, June 16th, 1864, before Petersburg, and also from Petersburg to Appomattox, the following April. With diffidence I comply. One who was so young in years and service, hardly desires to have his military experience compared with that of the veterans of many battles. In such presence he had rather hide his diminished head; but when he reflects, that youth alone, prevented his having a larger share in the glorious achievements in the Army of Northern Virginia, led by the immortal Lee, then his breast swells with pride that he was counted worthy, in any way, to do duty in that incomparable army. I am further induced to give you these recollections, by the reflection, that if one who is certainly among the least in point of service, does not refuse to recount his brief experience, this may encourage some comrade of extended service, who has not yet favoured the camp with any account of his experiences, to give us the benefit of his recollections, and thus add much to the interest of our meetings and the truth of history.

With the advance of Butler to the south side of the Appomattox, June 15th, 1864, I, a boy of thirteen, shouldered a musket and reported for duty to the battalion of Petersburg Reserves,[21] who were then, as I remember, in the trenches on our extreme right, at or near Wilcox farm. I went to the company in which Mr. Thos. Smyth[22] was lieutenant, that gentleman being a kinsman and I being in his employ as a clerk in his grocery and commission house in Petersburg.

About day break the morning of June 16th, we were ordered to move to the left, as Butler was making a strong forward movement on our extreme left, with but few men to oppose him, these few being under Beauregard. When we reached a point near the Jerusalem Plank Road, Lieut. Smyth ordered me to fall out of ranks, to take a message home for him. Upon my demurring to

20. Jones's address, along with a short biographical sketch, is housed in the Bernard Collection at the Historical Society of Western Virginia.

21. The Petersburg Reserves were officially designated the Third Battalion of Virginia Reserves under a reorganization order issued on May 16, 1864. They were commanded by Colonel Fletcher Harris Archer (see note 151, chapter 6; see also Greene, *Civil War Petersburg*, 34, 174).

22. Thomas Smyth was a 2nd lieutenant in Company A of the Third Battalion of Virginia Reserves.

such a procedure at that time, he said, that as I had been placed in his charge by relatives and friends, he would not permit me to go into the impending battle, if he could prevent it. Feeling in duty bound to obey his orders, I went on his errand, with the determination to return again to our lines. On reaching the city, at the hill, just at the head of what is known as the New Road, near the Reservoir, I found a dozen or more people gathered, drawn thither by the rumors of the advance of the enemy. Among them was a man with musket in hand, a stranger to me, who said he was a member of the Petersburg Reserves. He was excitedly saying that his command had been removed, he knew not whither, and that he feared he would be left out of the battle. As I had just left them, I told him where he could find his command. He still hesitated. Telling him that, if he would wait about ten minutes, I would return, and that we together would go to the front. To this he agreed. I then hastened on my errand, and soon reached Mr. Smyth's house, which was only a short distance away. Without waiting for breakfast I took a biscuit or two in my hand and hastily returned to the stranger on the hill. He seemed to have some misgivings as to my ability to pilot him and when I reflect I am not surprised. I told him I would show him the Yankees, and stay as long as he did. We reached our lines somewhere near the Jerusalem Plank Road, and, with all other recruits passing that way, at the time, were stopped, as we were pressing around toward the left, soon after we reached our works to support a heavy stationary cannon, which as I recall it, was stationed there, and which, it was thought, was threatened with attack. No attack, however, was made and we were allowed to proceed to the left, where there was heavy firing. Just here I lost the comrade who came with me to the front. Crossing over the bridge, spanning the deep cut on the Norfolk and Petsbg. R.R. known as "Summit Cut," a few hundred yards southwest of the Avery House, and going forward a short distance (towards but not as far as the Baxter Road at the point where our lines crossed it), we came within range of the enemy, meeting a heavy artillery fire and considerable musketry, the enemy having an enfilading fire on us from a commanding position, north of us in the neighborhood of the public road from Petersburg to Prince George C.H.

Pushing my way around to the left, endeavoring to reach the Petersburg Reserves and being several times warned by the old soldiers in that part of the works, a heterogeneous mass of men, hastily collected from the hospitals, guard-houses, and other places in Petersburg, and called by Gen'l Wise, in that day, "The P.P.'s" (patients and penitents), and who where then hugging the best cover they could find, that, I was very dangerously exposing myself and that I had best stop where I was, I did so, and followed their example as to protection. The enemy, having captured a good portion of our lines, north of the Baxter Road, had massed there, a considerable quantity of cannon and large bodies of troops, and continued to pour a galling flank fire into our thin ranks, our men being some five or six feet apart in the trenches. Our line of breastwork was held by the Petersburg Reserves to a point a short distance north of the Baxter Road. The enemy had on the night before captured our works or batteries from No. 5 to No. 9 inclusive, and our troops, that had occupied the captured batteries, had been withdrawn to a line at right angles with our line of breastworks and extending in a westerly direction near the north of and parallel with the Baxter Road. On the evening of March 7th 1894, in company with Col. Fletcher H. Archer, who commanded the battalion of Petersburg Reserves, Comrade Andrew J. Clements, a member of Co. G. of battalion, (then a boy of 15 years, both of whom were present in this action and received wounds) and Comrade Geo. S. Bernard, I visited the scene of these occurrences, and by the ditches and mounds constituting the remains of the line of Confederate earth works, held by the reserves on that day, we easily located the position of this battalion, and of the enemy. The battalion, according to the statement of Col. Archer and Comrade Clements, was stationed with its right on the south side of the Baxter Road, and its left about battery No. 16 on the north side of this road about 400 yards north east of the Avery House. This battalion suffered severely in this engagement, having about fifteen of their men killed and wounded in about one hours time.

My position with the "Patients and Penitents" was just to the right of the Petersburg Reserves. At this point I stayed the greater part of the day with no comrade that I had ever seen before, no immediate commander or command, and under my baptism of fire. About 12 o'clock in the day Genl. Lee's reinforcements began arriving. About 2 or 3 o'clock in the afternoon I began to be pinched by hunger, such as only a boy knows after a long fast, a condition of things rather demoralizing to a youthful recruit, who had no friends or acquaintances near him.

Just then, to my relief, my comrade of the morning came by homeward bound, somewhat in a hurry. Without waiting for an invitation, I joined him, telling him, that, as I had only promised to stay as long as he did, I was now at liberty to return with him. In our retreat we had to cross a field that was being literally ploughed by shot and shell, which was very much more dangerous than remaining in the trenches. We crossed this field (which was the open ground east and southeast, of the Avery House) at a double-quick, falling forward flat on the ground, as the shells came close over us, sometimes bursting and scattering the fragments, and a plentiful supply of dirt around us. My comrade began saying to me: "I told you not to come out here!" punctuated by a long stop, whilst we dodged a shell—"Now you see what we have gotten into"—and so on. I do not, however, remember, that he gave this advice. We both got off safely, and just as we were getting from under fire I began to reproach myself for thus leaving, and tarried a few moments. Meanwhile my comrade hurried on, and I do not know that I ever saw him again. Just here I remember to have seen a mounted officer, one of Lee's veterans, who was coming from a direction southwest of the Avery house, a route somewhat more protected than the field we had crossed. I was struck with admiration at this apparently fearless demeanor, as he rode forward at a swift gallop, and realized then the power of intrepid leadership. Just as this officer came up we reached the bridge over "Summit Cut" on the Norfolk and Petsbg. Railroad. We both were on the bridge, he a little in advance. At that moment, a shell dropped immediately in front of the officer on the bridge and slided off into the cut below, where it exploded with a deafening report.

About that hour, four o'clock in the afternoon, the Petersburg Reserves were brought off and their places filled with veterans. The enemy, I think must have been entirely out of range of my old smooth bore musket. I had been saving my ammunition for closer work, but as I was leaving, I took one parting shot at the enemy, which I did from an elevated position in a tree near the bridge over the railroad, which I climbed for the purpose, so as to shoot over the heads of our men. I did no more service until about the time Genl. Lee evacuated Petersburg, April 3rd, 1865, both in the trenches before Petersburg, and with raiding parties in Dinwiddie county.

On March 29th, 1865, I came to Petersburg from my home near Dinwiddie Court House, with a pony and wagon. Returning next day upon reaching Burgess Mill, I found the enemy had advanced his line within the previous twenty four hours in our front, at this point, and also on our right at Five Forks. At both points the enemy was then being engaged by our troops. Hearing from Genl. Henry A. Wise, who was in command at Burgess Mill, that I was entirely cut off from home by the enemy, I determined to await the developments. Realizing that there was not much probability of our being able to dislodge the enemy, I immediately thought I could gratify a cherished wish, and that I would soon have the opportunity of joining the army, with a good pony to ride. With this in view, I traded with some prisoners captured by Genl. Wise, for a blanket and gum cloth, giving Confederate money in exchange. About 1 or 2 o'clock the morning of April 2nd, the wagon trains of Genl. Wise's command were ordered to move. The enemy on our right, at Five Forks, greatly out numbering us, had begun to push our forces back toward the South Side railroad, and hence the necessity for our speedy retreat from Burgess mill. The following night (the night of April 2nd) Genl. Lee evacuated Petersburg. Having a wagon on my hands, I began the retreat with Genl. Wise's trains. We took a road running in a northernly direction, leaving the White Oak Road, at a point not far from its intersection with the Boydton Plank Road, and continuing on until we intersected the River Road, which road we took, going to Amelia C.H., followed closely by the enemy. The enemy occupying the country and the roads south of the Appomattox, obliged Genl. Lee when he evacuated Petersburg the next night, to cross over the river, and to retreat by the roads north of the Appomattox.

After daylight I stopped at the house of a hospitable farmer to leave my wagon. The kind host fed my horse and gave me breakfast. He endeavored to dissuade me from joining the army on account of my youth, I being then only 14 years old, but I was not to be dissuaded and left my wagon with him. Then mounting my horse, with only a blanket for a saddle, and a pair of saddle-bags containing a change of clothing, I pushed on toward Amelia C.H. to appointed rendezvous of our army.

The next day after reaching Amelia C.H., I went over to a Mr. Rowlett's (an acquaintance), a short distance from the Courthouse to dine. Here at dinner I met, among other officers, Capt. A.L.C. Tennille,[23] commissary of Anderson's brigade, Field's division, to whom I offered my services, as a volunteer. He accepted the same and made me his courier. Leaving the dinner table with these officers, we went out of the house into the yard. From this point, looking toward a field, we saw a large body of cavalry in this field, a few hundred yards away drawn up in line. We were told it was Sheridan's cavalry. Whether it was or not, I do not know. We thought it was and hastened back to Amelia C.H., where I was given a saddle by Captain Tennille and put in charge of some wagons of our trains. Sometime thereafter we started again on our retreat to Appomattox C.H. My duty was to keep the teamsters in place (they were mostly negroes) and to keep our part of the trains closed up. This, with the attacks of the enemy, was constantly stopping us. We moved, or tried to move, almost from Amelia to Appomattox C.H. The trains were attacked frequently, the cavalry being marched, and countermarched, many times to protect some threatened point. The soldiers were apparently all in good spirits, in spite of their hardships, and rations of only three ears of parched corn daily, for each man. Many of them, as they passed and repassed, would "guy" me, on account of my size and the size of my horse.

On the morning of the 6th of April our part of the trains was attacked near Sailor's Creek, and, having no adequate defense at hand was captured, though

---

23. Alexander St. Clair Tennille was born in Washington County, Georgia, in 1838. Before the war, he attended the University of Nashville. After the war, he was a physician in Florida and then mayor of Troy, Alabama. Tennille died in 1907 in Montgomery, Alabama (see Krick, *Staff Officers in Gray,* 284).

most of the attendants escaped capture, by beating a hasty retreat, I among the number. The enemy set fire to the wagons, and burned quite a number of them, before we recaptured the train. I was sorry to find the wagons in my charge, were among those burned, especially so, since my saddle bags, with my only change of clothing, was in one of them. The saddle-bags, were, however, taken from the wagon before it was set fire to, by Capt. Chas. F. Bowers,[24] quartermaster of the 8th New Jersey Regiment. My mother's name, and her late home (Richmond, Va.) was written on them. Seeing this, Capt. Bowers, like a true soldier, as he was, after the war was over, desired to return them to their rightful owner. Through correspondence conducted by Genl. Wm. Ward[25] (formerly colonel of the 8th New Jersey) and then postmaster at Newark, N.J. and Capt. Chas. W. Williams, then commander of R. E. Lee Camp, No. I, Confederate Veterans Richmond, Va., the owner was located, and in due time, October 16th, 1883, my long lost saddle bags were returned to me through Lincoln Post, No. II Dept. of N.J. G.A.R., in a very handsome morocco case appropriately marked, as to their capture, and the manner of their return. I now preserve them in their case as a precious heirloom. You will pardon this digression, as I desired to pay tribute to the worthy gentlemen named.

Being a young campaigner in more senses than one, my impressions and recollections are necessarily crude, and perhaps somewhat disconnected.

Captain Tennille, being now without Commissary Stores or wagons, pushed on the night of April 6th toward Farmville, where he hoped to have other wagons assigned us, replenished with stores. We rode as rapidly forward as circumstance would permit, to within three or four miles of Farmville, and there we turned into the woods to rest, and feed our horses, and to get a night's rest for ourselves. We slept the sleep of the wearied, whilst our army was passing slowly by. This, I think, was the only time I lay down between Amelia and Appomattox C.H.

Early the next morning (April 7th) we went into Farmville. In the depot there were found a quantity of provisions. A number of wagons had already been loaded, but owing to the close proximity of the enemy, all were now hastening through the town without tarrying. The depot of stores was then thrown open, to the troops passing that way, and soldiers would help themselves to such provisions as they could conveniently carry. Yet there was

24. Charles F. Bowers served with the 8th New Jersey Infantry from 1861 to 1865. He enlisted as a quartermaster sergeant, was promoted to 1st lieutenant in 1862, and served as the quartermaster for his regiment for most of the war.

25. William Ward enlisted as a captain in the 8th New Jersey Infantry in 1861. He was promoted to lieutenant colonel in 1862.

perhaps two or three wagon loads of provisions left. I was ordered by Capt. Tennille to wait at the depot in Farmville, until he could arrange to have the wagons sent to me, to be loaded with bacon and flour. I waited patiently for the wagons, until seeing evidence of the complete evacuation of the town by our troops. I then strung two pieces of bacon on my horse, and mounted, hesitating, however, to leave without orders. Just then the crack of the musket and the whistle of the bullets from the enemy (who were then entering the town, firing down the road towards our retreating troops) convinced me that I had best not stand on the order of my going. So I made a rapid exit from Farmville, being perhaps the last Confederate to pass over the old country road bridge, which had already been set on fire by our rear guard, who were remaining there to hold and burn. As I rode across they greeted me with the exclamation, "You just saved your bacon." Without tarrying to talk, as the Yankees were making it rather hot around there, I hastened up the hill on the north side of the river. Beyond the crest of the hill, I came upon Capt. Tennille and some other mounted officers, who were at the extreme left of a line of battle, that had been drawn up, in this strong position to retard the rapid advance of the enemy. Here occurred what I think is called the battle of "Cumberland Church." The enemy had driven off our rear guard at one of the bridges near Farmville, over the Appomattox, before the bridge was burned, and by this bridge they crossed and pressed hard after us. An instance of kind consideration for me occurred here. Some general who was in the group of officers referred to, and who I think was in command, (I am not sure of his name) said to Capt. Tennille soon after I rode up. "Captain where is your courier? I want to send a message over yonder," pointing to an exposed position on the right of his line. Capt. Tennille pointed to me as his Courier, and called me up, but the general declined on account of my youth to send me on so perilous an errand. I was then ordered forward by Capt. Tennille to take charge of two wagons that had been assigned him after he left Farmville, and I was therefore not in the engagement at Cumberland Church, but was told that we repulsed the enemy at this point.

That evening, I think it was, our part of the trains was attacked very suddenly by Genl. Gregg's[26] cavalry. Without warning of any kind, whilst we were standing still, on account of some obstruction in front, we were startled

---

26. John Irvin Gregg served as a cavalry officer from May 1861 until the close of the war, when he remained in the regular service. He fought in most of the major battles that occurred in the East, rising from captain to brevet major general. Leading the Second Division of the Cavalry Corps to victory at Dinwiddie Court House, Five Forks, and Sailor's Creek, he suffered the ignominy of three days' captivity after a brief action at Farmville on April 7, 1865.

by the crack of carbines and the whistle of bullets. Fortunately for us a part of Field's Division, as I was informed, was just on the opposite side of the train. Rushing through the train they gave the charging Yankees a volley, which made them recoil. A piece of artillery was also at hand, which opened fire on them, and with Fitz Lee on the flank, we soon had them on the run. I was riding on behind our advancing men cheering. I had no gun or other arms with which to help them fight the battle.

Genl. Gregg was captured in this engagement, and, as he was being brought off, his guard wanted to impress my horse for Genl. Gregg to ride. My horse being private property, I declined to be dismounted and without waiting for further parley, I rode quickly back to my position with the trains. The guard afterward found a government horse for the General.

That night and the next day we retreated in comparative quietness. Genl. Grant was about to mass his forces ahead of us it seemed in the vicinity of Appomattox C.H. We reached that point the evening of the 8th of April, and were ordered to park the wagons for the first time since leaving Amelia C.H. We were soon making ourselves as comfortable as circumstances would permit, little dreaming of surrender on the morrow. We slept soundly that night and awoke next morning much refreshed. Genl. Lee's headquarters were in sight of our fly-tent, not one hundred yards distant. We did not move at day break, as had been expected, but remained quietly in park. After a while it was rumored that negotiations looking to surrender were pending. All hearts were saddened as we realized the inevitable. I for one was very much concerned fearing that we would be sent to a Northern prison, and I thought I would make some effort to get out of our lines, and by the enemy in some way. I accordingly sliced up a ham of bacon, that I had brought off from Farmville, and had in one of our wagons, stored it in my haversack, mounted my horse, and set out to see if I could get through the lines. My observations and inquiries, soon convinced me, that I had best remain and share the fate of the army. Returning, I awaited quietly for some further news. A sudden commotion around Genl. Lee's headquarters attracted my attention. Hastening thither with others, we met Genl. Lee and his staff, returning from the place of meeting with Genl. Grant. The men crowded around him, conveying to him in many ways, their love and admiration. Genl. Lee was too much moved to talk, and asked one of his staff to tell the men the terms of surrender, which he did. Col. Walter H. Taylor in his "Four Years of Lee," describes the meeting of Lee and his men on this occasion with much pathos as follows:

> The scene witnessed upon the return of Genl. Lee was one certain
> to impress itself indelibly upon memory; it can be vividly recalled
> now, after the lapse of many years, but no description can do it

justice. The men crowded around him, eager to shake him by the hand, eyes that had been so often illumined with the fire of patriotism and their courage, that had so often glared with defiance, in the heat and fury of the battle, and so often kindled with enthusiasms in the hour of success, moistened now, cheeks bronzed by exposure in many campaigns, and withal begrimed by powder and dust, now [blanched] from deep emotion and suffered the silent tear; tongues that had so often carried dismay to the hearts of the enemy in that indescribable cheer which accompanied "the charge" or that had so often made the air to resound with the paean of victory, refused utterance now; brave heart's failed that had never quailed in the presence of the enemy; but the firm and silent pressure of the hand told most eloquently of souls filled with admiration, love, and tender sympathy, for their beloved chief.

After witnessing the impressive scene just described, I returned to my quarters. Shortly afterward I bade farewell to my Georgia Comrades, and joined my kinsman, Maj. John T. Jones, Surgeon, of Forney's[27] Alabama Brigade, with whom I intended to leave Appomattox. As I was not on any muster rolls, I determined, if possible, to get away from Appomattox without a parole, so that I might be free to do that which I might think best, as to trying to get to Johnston. Thanks again to my youth and size, I succeeded in getting out of the Federal lines, with little difficulty and without a parole. I was wisely dissuaded by older heads from attempting to join Johnston.

I have always claimed, and shall continue to claim, until my claim is disproved, that I was the youngest Confederate who surrendered at Appomattox Court House.

Excerpts from George S. Bernard's Diary, 1865–1866[28]

[While Petersburg fell and Lee's army began to disintegrate, Bernard was on leave visiting his father in Orange County. In "Last Days of Lee and His Paladins," by Dr. John Herbert Claiborne, the penultimate address published in

27. Brigadier General William H. Forney commanded the brigade named after him, consisting of six Alabama regiments. The brigade was part of Mahone's division.

28. These diary entries are excerpted from Bernard's manuscript diary in the George S. Bernard Papers, UVA.

War Talks Of Confederate Veterans, Bernard shared his account of the eventful days in March and April 1865. Here we have some excerpts from his postwar diary that were not in his published address. The months after the war were very difficult for Bernard and other former veterans. The loss of so many men in the war, poor economic prospects, and the Union occupation sank the spirits of many. Bernard, like so many other veterans, began to rebuild his life piece by piece.]

Petersburg

Thursday June 15, '65

After three or four weeks of idleness, during which I have suffered no little from despondency at the gloomy prospects for making a living I have finally settled down not into the practice of law but into my office, my card having appeared in the papers of this morning. My room and office are at present one & the same, as I have taken possession of Cousin Bob Feild's room in his absence. Jim Nash for the present will room with me and we have made our arrangement to take our meals in our room.

Thursday June 22, 1865

Staid last night at Mr. Branch's—had a very pleasant horseback ride this morning with Cousin Sallie Branch, visiting Fort Gregg, observatory on Peeble's Farm & Poplar Springs Church so elegantly fixed up by the Yankees, & returning down the track of the Weldon R Road now a regular country road. This afternoon twelve months ago our brigade (Mahone's) had its first engagement around Petersburg. How we used up the Yankees that memorable afternoon!

Octagon—Brunswick Co. Va.

Aug 26: '65 (Saturday Afternoon)

After remaining in Petersburg for several weeks very despondent at having little or nothing to do in my profession & the many obstacles in the way of succeeding at anything else, on Saturday last I fell upon a new plan and determined to make a trial of it which was to get employment with the proprietors of the Petersburg Express in some capacity connected with their editorial department. On Wednesday last I succeeded in getting the position of local editor of the paper to commence operations as soon as could take a trip of a week or so to this county. The duties of this position will not conflict with my instructing a class of mathematics in the school of Miss H_____ Clarke and also attending to what little legal business I may get. I reached here on yesterday having made the trip in a road wagon—expect to spend a pleasant time.

Petersburg
Sept. 15, 1865

Back at home—trip to Brunswick very pleasant—returned as I went up, in a road wagon, reaching here Wednesday Sept. 6th. Commenced next day with the Express—am kept pretty busy collecting items & writing—am also doing a little in my profession—have my office now with Jno. Mann—gave up the room at Mrs. S. C. Clain's on Bank St. at end of my month (Sept. 5), have a very pleasant one now in Dr. Lapitus' building, 7th[?] St. Take my meals just now with Cousin Bob Feild & Dr. Jas. Claiborne at Jack McCrea's old eating house, but expect next week to commencing "Room Keeping" here with Tom Goodman, one of my neighbors on same floor—did not feel at liberty longer to accept the kind hospitality of Gen. & Mrs. Weisiger.

Xmas Night '65
Petersburg Va.

Many weeks since I last wrote in this book. Continued my connection with the Express until Wednesday the 11th inst. Have returned to the practice of my profession having an office in the exchange building. Professional business at present gloomy. Have kept "Bachelor's Hall" to the present time, my finances not justifying boarding.

Sunday night Dec. 31 1865

The eventful year of "sixty five" expires tonight. But few there are in the United States to whom the last twelve months have not brought much pleasure or much unhappiness. With myself it has been productive of much of both. Never perhaps, in the course of my whole life have my experiences been so varied. This little book would furnish abundant evidence of a chagrined fortune, but on tomorrow a new year will be commenced. At its end, if living, in how many particulars will my condition be better? Many indeed are the difficulties before me. I have resolved to face them. I commence the year with a room with Jno. Turner, an old comrade of Co "E." We will "batchelorize" for the present at least.

Feb. 8, 1866

This little book for months past seems but a record of melancholy. It would not be otherwise if a true one, myself being the subject. What is in store for me? I often ask myself. It really seems that if it is intended that life should prove a *success* with me, even in the ordinary acceptation of the term, it is time I had begun to experience some earnest of it. Thus far however nearly nine years since I left college, it seems *practically* a failure.

Wednesday July 4th 1866

We take our pen to enter the fact that today has been celebrated in this city only by the negroes and there has been no suspension of business. How changed! Who would have conjectured such five years ago? Since making my last entry Feb. 8, my prospects in life have somewhat improved. Professionally I have had some little earnest of success.

Monday, Aug. 29, 1866

I enter my thirtieth year today, perhaps too little thankful that I have been allowed to attain it.

Index

Italicized page numbers refer to maps or photos; **boldface page numbers** indicate notes identifying people or places. Military units are indexed by commander and/or number under their armies, save for regiments, which appear by number under their states. The abbreviation GSB is used for George S. Bernard.

A Nation Divided: Studies in the Civil War Era